Mathematics

Detailed Explanation to all Objective & Subjective Problems

CLASS

08

Mathematics

Detailed Explanation to all Objective & Subjective Problems

CLASS 08

Amit Rastogi • *Shivani Jain*

arihant

Arihant Prakashan (School Division Series)

arihant

Arihant Prakashan (School Division Series)

卐 Administrative & Production Offices

Regd. Office

'Ramchhaya' 4577/15, Agarwal Road, Darya Ganj, New Delhi -110002
Tele: 011- 47630600, 43518550

卐 Head Office

Kalindi, TP Nagar, Meerut (UP) - 250002
Tel: 0121-7156203, 7156204

卐 Sales & Support Offices

Agra, Ahmedabad, Bengaluru, Bareilly, Chennai, Delhi, Guwahati, Hyderabad, Jaipur, Jhansi, Kolkata, Lucknow, Nagpur & Pune.

卐 **ISBN** 978-93-27197-36-5

卐 **PRICE** ₹375.00

PO No. : TXT-59-T068268-12-25

Published by Arihant Publications (India) Ltd.

For further information about the books published by Arihant, log on to www.arihantbooks.com or e-mail at info@arihantbooks.com

Follow us on

PREFACE

The Department of Education in Science & Mathematics (DESM) & National Council of Educational Research &Training (NCERT) developed Exemplar Problems in Science and Mathematics for Upper Primary Stage, Secondary and Senior Secondary Classes with the objective to provide the students a large number of quality problems in various forms and format *viz.* Multiple Choice Questions, Short Answer Questions, Long Answer Questions etc., with varying levels of difficulty.

The problems given in Exemplar books are not meant to some merely as question bank for examination but are Primarily meant to improve the quality of teaching/learning process in schools and finally will impart the problem solving skills in students and it is a widely at acknowledged fact that in this century analytical thinking, problem solving ability, creativity and speculative ability will be key skills for success.

This book **NCERT Exemplar Problems-Solutions Mathematics VIII** contains Explanatory & Accurate Solutions to all the questions given in NCERT Exemplar Mathematics book.

For the overall benefit of the students we have made unique this book in such a way that it presents not only hints and solutions but also detailed and authentic explanations. Through these detailed explanations, students can learn the concepts which will enhance their thinking and learning abilities.

With the hope that this book will be of great help to the students, we wish great success to our readers.

Authors

CONTENTS

1

Rational Numbers

Multiple Choice Questions (MCQs)

Q. 1 A number which can be expressed as $\frac{p}{q}$, where p and q are integers and $q \neq 0$ is

(a) natural number (b) whole number
(c) integer (d) rational number

Sol. *(d)* A number which can be expressed as $\frac{p}{q}$, where p and q are integers and $q \neq 0$ is a rational number.

Q. 2 A number of the form $\frac{p}{q}$ is said to be a rational number, if

(a) p, q are integers (b) p, q are integers and $q \neq 0$
(c) p, q are integers and $p \neq 0$ (d) p, q are integers and $p \neq 0$, also $q \neq 0$

Sol. *(b)* A number of the form $\frac{p}{q}$ is said to be a rational number, if p and q are integers and $q \neq 0$.

Q. 3 The numerical expression $\frac{3}{8} + \frac{(-5)}{7} = \frac{-19}{56}$ shows that

(a) rational numbers are closed under addition
(b) rational numbers are not closed under addition
(c) rational numbers are closed under multiplication
(d) addition of rational numbers is not commutative

Sol. *(b)* We have, $\frac{3}{8} + \left(\frac{-5}{7}\right) = \frac{-19}{56}$

Show that rational numbers are closed under addition.

$\left[\because \frac{3}{8} \text{ and } \frac{-5}{7} \text{ are rational numbers and their addition is } \frac{-19}{56}, \text{ which is also a rational number}\right]$

Note *The sum of any two rational numbers is always a rational number.*

Q. 4 Which of the following is not true?

(a) rational numbers are closed under addition
(b) rational numbers are closed under subtraction
(c) rational numbers are closed under multiplication
(d) rational numbers are closed under division

Sol. ***(d)*** Rational numbers are not closed under division.

As, 1 and 0 are the rational numbers but $\frac{1}{0}$ is not defined.

Q. 5 $-\frac{3}{8}+\frac{1}{7}=\frac{1}{7}+\left(\frac{-3}{8}\right)$ is an example to show that

(a) addition of rational numbers is commutative
(b) rational numbers are closed under addition
(c) addition of rational numbers is associative
(d) rational numbers are distributive under addition

Sol. ***(a)*** Given, $\frac{-3}{8}+\frac{1}{7}=\frac{1}{7}+\left(\frac{-3}{8}\right)$

Let two rational numbers, $a=\frac{-3}{8}, b=\frac{1}{7}$

$\therefore \quad a+b=\frac{-3}{8}+\frac{1}{7}=\frac{-21+8}{56}=\frac{-13}{56}$

and $\quad b+a=\frac{1}{7}+\frac{-3}{8}=\frac{8-21}{56}=\frac{-13}{56}$

Clearly, $a+b=b+a$

So, addition is communication for rational numbers.

Q. 6 Which of the following expressions shows that rational numbers are associative under multiplication.

(a) $\frac{2}{3}\times\left(\frac{-6}{7}\times\frac{3}{5}\right)=\left(\frac{2}{3}\times\frac{-6}{7}\right)\times\frac{3}{5}$
(b) $\frac{2}{3}\times\left(\frac{-6}{7}\times\frac{3}{5}\right)=\frac{2}{3}\times\left(\frac{3}{5}\times\frac{-6}{7}\right)$
(c) $\frac{2}{3}\times\left(\frac{-6}{7}\times\frac{3}{5}\right)=\left(\frac{3}{5}\times\frac{2}{3}\right)\times\frac{-6}{7}$
(d) $\left(\frac{2}{3}\times\frac{-6}{7}\right)\times\frac{3}{5}=\left(\frac{-6}{7}\times\frac{2}{3}\right)\times\frac{3}{5}$

Sol. ***(a)*** Given, $\frac{2}{3}\times\left(-\frac{6}{7}\times\frac{3}{5}\right)=\left(\frac{2}{3}\times\frac{-6}{7}\right)\times\frac{3}{5}$ [by associative property under multiplication, $a\times(b\times c)=(a\times b)\times c$]

$\Rightarrow \quad \frac{2}{3}\times\frac{-18}{35}=\frac{-12}{21}\times\frac{3}{5}$

So, $\quad a\times(b\times c)=(a\times b)\times c$

Hence, the given expression shows that rational numbers are associative under multiplication.

Q. 7 Zero (0) is

(a) the identity for addition of rational numbers
(b) the identity for subtraction of rational numbers
(c) the identity for multiplication of rational numbers
(d) the identity for division of rational numbers

Sol. *(a)* Zero (0) is the identity for addition of rational numbers.
That means,
If a is a rational number.
Then, $a + 0 = 0 + a = a$

Note *Zero (0) is also the additive identity for integers and whole number as well.*

Q. 8 One (1) is

(a) the identity for addition of rational numbers
(b) the identity for subtraction of rational numbers
(c) the identity for multiplication of rational numbers
(d) the identity for division of rational numbers

Sol. *(c)* One (1) is the identity for multiplication of rational numbers.
That means,
If a is a rational number.
Then, $a \cdot 1 = 1 \cdot a = a$

Note *One (1) is the multiplication identity for integers and whole number also.*

Q. 9 The additive inverse of $\frac{-7}{19}$ is

(a) $\frac{-7}{19}$ (b) $\frac{7}{19}$ (c) $\frac{19}{7}$ (d) $\frac{-19}{7}$

Sol. *(b)* We know that, if a and b are the additive inverse of each other, then $a + b = 0$

Suppose, x is the additive inverse of $\frac{-7}{19}$.

Then, $x - \frac{7}{19} = 0 \Rightarrow x = \frac{7}{19}$

Hence, additive inverse of $\frac{-7}{19}$ is $\frac{7}{19}$.

Q. 10 Multiplicative inverse of a negative rational number is

(a) a positive rational number (b) a negative rational number
(c) 0 (d) 1

Sol. *(b)* We know that, the product of two rational numbers is 1, taken they are multiplication inverse of each other. e.g.
Suppose, p is negative rational number, i.e.
$\frac{1}{p}$ is the multiplicative inverse of $-p$, then, $-p \times \frac{1}{-p} = 1$
Hence, multiplicative inverse of a negative rational number is a negative rational number.

Q. 11 If $x + 0 = 0 + x = x$, which is rational number, then 0 is called

(a) identity for addition of rational numbers
(b) additive inverse of x
(c) multiplicative inverse of x
(d) reciprocal of x

Sol. *(a)* We know that, the sum of any rational number and zero (0) is the rational number itself.
Now, $x + 0 = 0 + x = x$, which is a rational number, then 0 is called identity for addition of rational numbers.

Q. 12 **To get the product 1, we should multiply $\frac{8}{21}$ by**

(a) $\frac{8}{21}$ (b) $\frac{-8}{21}$ (c) $\frac{21}{8}$ (d) $\frac{-21}{8}$

Sol. *(c)* Let we should multiply $\frac{8}{21}$ by x. Then, according to question, $x \times \frac{8}{21} = 1$

Hence, we should multiply $\frac{8}{21}$ by $\frac{21}{8}$, for getting the product 1.

Q. 13 **$-(-x)$ is same as**

(a) $-x$ (b) x (c) $\frac{1}{x}$ (d) $\frac{-1}{x}$

Sol. *(b)* $-(-x) = x$

Negative of negative rational number is equal to positive rational number.

Q. 14 **The multiplicative inverse of $-1\frac{1}{7}$ is**

(a) $\frac{8}{7}$ (b) $\frac{-8}{7}$ (c) $\frac{7}{8}$ (d) $\frac{7}{-8}$

Sol. *(d)* We know that, if the product of two rational numbers is 1, then they are multiplicative inverse of each other.

Given number is $-1\frac{1}{7}$, i.e. $\frac{-8}{7}$.

Let the multiplicative inverse of $-\frac{8}{7}$ be x.

$$\Rightarrow \quad \frac{-8}{7} \times x = 1$$

$$\Rightarrow \quad x = 1 \times \left(-\frac{7}{8}\right) \quad \text{[by cross-multiplication]}$$

$$= \frac{-7}{8} \text{ or } \frac{7}{-8}$$

Hence, $\frac{7}{-8}$ is the multiplicative inverse of $-\frac{8}{7}$.

Q. 15 **If x is any rational number, then $x + 0$ is equal to**

(a) x (b) 0 (c) $-x$ (d) Not defined

Sol. *(a)* If x is any rational number, then

$$x + 0 = x \quad [\because 0 \text{ is the additive identity}]$$

Q. 16 **The reciprocal of 1 is**

(a) 1 (b) -1 (c) 0 (d) Not defined

Sol. *(a)* The reciprocal of 1 is the number itself. $\left[\because 1 = \frac{1}{1} = 1\right]$

Q. 17 The reciprocal of -1 is

(a) 1 (b) -1 (c) 0 (d) Not defined

Sol. *(b)* The reciprocal of -1 is the number itself. $\left[\because -1 = \frac{1}{-1} = -1\right]$

Q. 18 The reciprocal of 0 is

(a) 1 (b) -1 (c) 0 (d) Not defined

Sol. *(d)* The reciprocal of 0 is not defined. $\left[\because \frac{1}{0} \text{ is not defined}\right]$

Q. 19 The reciprocal of any rational number $\frac{p}{q}$, where p and q are integers and $q \neq 0$ is

(a) $\frac{p}{q}$ (b) 1 (c) 0 (d) $\frac{q}{p}$

Sol. *(d)* The reciprocal of any rational number $\frac{p}{q}$, where p and q are integers and $q \neq 0$ is $\frac{q}{p}$.

Q. 20 If y is the reciprocal of rational number x, then the reciprocal of y will be

(a) x (b) y (c) $\frac{x}{y}$ (d) $\frac{y}{x}$

Sol. *(a)* If y be the reciprocal of rational number x, i.e. $y = \frac{1}{x}$ or $x = \frac{1}{y}$.

Hence, the reciprocal of y will be x.

Q. 21 The reciprocal of $\frac{-3}{8} \times \left(\frac{-7}{13}\right)$ is

(a) $\frac{104}{21}$ (b) $\frac{-104}{21}$ (c) $\frac{21}{104}$ (d) $\frac{-21}{104}$

Sol. *(a)* Given number is $\frac{-3}{8} \times \left(\frac{-7}{13}\right)$

The product of $-\frac{3}{8} \times \left(\frac{-7}{13}\right) = \frac{21}{104}$.

Hence, the multiplicative inverse of $\frac{21}{104}$ is $\frac{104}{21}$.

Q. 22 Which of the following is an example of distributive property of multiplication over addition for rational numbers.

(a) $-\frac{1}{4} \times \left\{\frac{2}{3} + \left(\frac{-4}{7}\right)\right\} = \left[-\frac{1}{4} \times \frac{2}{3}\right] + \left[-\frac{1}{4} \times \left(\frac{-4}{7}\right)\right]$

(b) $-\frac{1}{4} \times \left\{\frac{2}{3} + \left(\frac{-4}{7}\right)\right\} = \left[\frac{1}{4} \times \frac{2}{3}\right] - \left(\frac{-4}{7}\right)$

(c) $-\frac{1}{4} \times \left\{\frac{2}{3} + \left(\frac{-4}{7}\right)\right\} = \frac{2}{3} + \left(-\frac{1}{4}\right) \times \frac{-4}{7}$

(d) $-\frac{1}{4} \times \left\{\frac{2}{3} + \left(\frac{-4}{7}\right)\right\} = \left\{\frac{2}{3} + \left(\frac{-4}{7}\right)\right\} - \frac{1}{4}$

Sol. ***(a)*** We know that, the distributive property of multiplication over addition for rational numbers can be expressed as $a \times (b + c) = ab + ac$, where a, b and c are rational numbers.

Here, $\frac{-1}{4} \times \left\{\frac{2}{3} + \left(\frac{-4}{7}\right)\right\} = \left[\frac{-1}{4} \times \frac{2}{3}\right] + \left[\frac{-1}{4} \times \left(\frac{-4}{7}\right)\right]$

is the example of distributive property of multiplication over addition for rational numbers.

Q. 23 Between two given rational numbers, we can find

(a) one and only one rational number
(b) only two rational numbers
(c) only ten rational numbers
(d) infinitely many rational numbers

Sol. ***(d)*** We can find infinite many rational numbers between two given rational numbers.

Q. 24 $\frac{x+y}{2}$ is a rational number.

(a) Between x and y
(b) Less than x and y both
(c) Greater than x and y both
(d) Less than x but greater than y

Sol. ***(a)*** Let x and y be two numbers.

Case I If $x < y$

Then, $\frac{x+y}{2}$ lies in between x and y such that

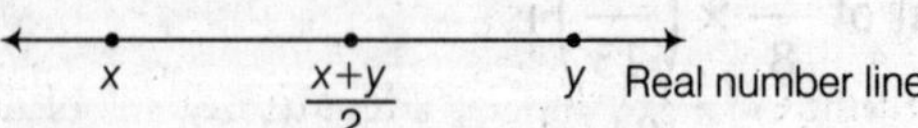

Case II If $y < x$

Then, $\frac{x+y}{2}$ lies in between x and y such that

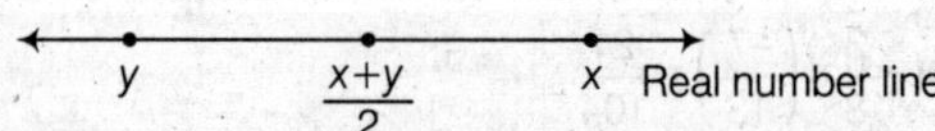

Q. 25 Which of the following statements is always true?

(a) $\frac{x-y}{2}$ is a rational number between x and y
(b) $\frac{x+y}{2}$ is a rational number between x and y
(c) $\frac{x \times y}{2}$ is a rational number between x and y
(d) $\frac{x \div y}{2}$ is a rational number between x and y

Sol. ***(b)*** Here, $\frac{x+y}{2}$ is a rational number.

Then, it always lies in between x and y either $x < y$ or $y < x$.

Fill in the Blanks

In questions 26 to 47, fill in the blanks to make the statements true.

Q. 26 The equivalent of $\frac{5}{7}$ whose numerator is 45, is_____.

Sol. $\left(\frac{45}{63}\right)$

Take $\frac{5}{7}$, $\frac{5}{7} \times \frac{9}{9}$ [on multiplying numerator and denominator by 9]

$= \frac{45}{63}$

Hence, $\frac{45}{63}$ is equivalent to $\frac{5}{7}$.

Q. 27 The equivalent rational number of $\frac{7}{9}$, whose denominator is 45 is_____.

Sol. $\left(\frac{35}{45}\right)$

Take $\frac{7}{9}$, $\frac{7}{9} \times \frac{5}{5}$ [on multiplying numerator and denominator by 5]

$= \frac{35}{45}$

Hence, $\frac{35}{45}$ is equivalent to $\frac{7}{9}$.

Q. 28 Between the numbers $\frac{15}{20}$ and $\frac{35}{40}$, the greater number is _____.

Sol. $\left(\frac{35}{40}\right)$

Given numbers are $\frac{15}{20}$ and $\frac{35}{40}$.

LCM of 20 and 40 $= 2 \times 2 \times 2 \times 5 = 40$

2	20, 40
2	10, 20
2	5, 10
5	5, 5
	1, 1

Now, $\frac{15}{20} = \frac{15}{20} \times \frac{2}{2}$ [on multiplying and dividing by 2]

$= \frac{30}{40}$

On comparing,

$$\frac{35}{40} > \frac{30}{40}$$

$$\Rightarrow \quad \frac{35}{40} > \frac{15}{20}$$

Hence, $\frac{35}{40}$ is greater.

Q. 29 The reciprocal of a positive rational number is ________ .

Sol. **positive rational number**

The positive rational number is of the form $\frac{p}{q}$, where p and q both belongs to I^+ (positive integers) or I^- (negative integers).

Hence, the reciprocal is of the form $\frac{q}{p}$, where p and q both belongs to I^+ or I^-.

Q. 30 The reciprocal of a negative rational number is ________ .

Sol. **negative rational number**

The negative rational number is of the form $\frac{p}{q}$, where $p \in I^+, q \in I^-$ or $p \in I^-, q \in I^+$

Hence, the reciprocal is of the form $\frac{q}{p}$, where $p \in I^+, q \in I^-$ or $p \in I^-, q \in I^+$

Q. 31 Zero has ________ reciprocal.

Sol. **no**

The reciprocal of 0 is $\frac{1}{0}$ and $\frac{1}{0}$ is not defined.

Q. 32 The numbers ________ and ________ are their own reciprocal.

Sol. **1, – 1**

The reciprocal of 1 and – 1 are $\frac{1}{1}$ and $\frac{1}{-1}$, i.e. 1 and – 1 respectively.

Q. 33 If y is the reciprocal of x, then the reciprocal of y^2 in terms of x will be ________ .

Sol. x^2

Given, $\frac{1}{x} = y$ ... (i)

Now, reciprocal of $y^2 = \frac{1}{y^2} = \frac{1}{\left(\frac{1}{x}\right)^2}$ [from Eq. (i)]

$= x^2$

Q. 34 The reciprocal of $\frac{2}{5} \times \left(\frac{-4}{9}\right)$ is____.

Sol. $\frac{-45}{8}$

Here, $\frac{2}{5} \times \left(\frac{-4}{9}\right) = \frac{-8}{45}$

Hence, the reciprocal of $-\frac{8}{45}$ is $\frac{-45}{8}$.

Q. 35 $(213 \times 657)^{-1} = (213)^{-1} \times$ ______.

Sol. $\frac{1}{657}$

Suppose, $(213 \times 657)^{-1} = (213)^{-1} \times x$

$$\Rightarrow \quad \frac{1}{213 \times 657} = \frac{1}{213} \times x$$

$$\Rightarrow \quad x = \frac{213}{213 \times 657} \Rightarrow x = \frac{1}{657}$$

Q. 36 The negative of 1 is __.

Sol. -1

The negative of 1 is -1.

Q. 37 For rational numbers $\frac{a}{b}, \frac{c}{d}$ and $\frac{e}{f}$, we have $\frac{a}{b} \times \left(\frac{c}{d} + \frac{e}{f}\right) =$ ___ +

Sol. $\frac{ac}{bd}, \frac{ae}{bf}$

If $\frac{a}{b} \times \left(\frac{c}{d} + \frac{e}{f}\right) = \frac{a}{b} \times \frac{c}{d} + \frac{a}{b} \times \frac{e}{f} = \frac{ac}{bd} + \frac{ae}{bf}$

Q. 38 $\frac{-5}{7}$ is______than -3.

Sol. **greater**

First, we convert the given rational number into like denominator. Now, LCM of 7 and 1 = 7.

$$-3 = \frac{-3 \times 7}{7} \qquad \text{[on multiplying and dividing by 7]}$$

$$= \frac{-21}{7}$$

As, $$\frac{-5}{7} > \frac{-21}{7}$$

i.e. $$\frac{-5}{7} > -3$$

Hence, $-\frac{5}{7}$ is greater than -3.

Q. 39 There are_____ rational numbers between any two rational numbers.

Sol. **infinite**

There are infinite rational numbers between any two rational numbers.

Q. 40 The rational numbers $\frac{1}{3}$ and $\frac{-1}{3}$ are on the_____sides of zero on the number line.

Sol. **opposite**

–1/3 0 1/3

Q. 41 The negative of a negative rational number is always a____rational number.

Sol. positive

Let x be a positive rational number.

Then, $-x$ be a negative rational number.

Now, negative of a negative rational number $= -(-x) = x$

$= \text{positive rational number}$

Q. 42 Rational numbers can be added or multiplied in any ____.

Sol. order

Rational numbers can be added or multiplied in any order and this concept is known as commutative property.

Q. 43 The reciprocal of $\frac{-5}{7}$ is ____.

Sol. $\frac{-7}{5}$

The reciprocal of $\frac{-5}{7}$ is $\frac{1}{\left(\frac{-5}{7}\right)}$, i.e. $\frac{-7}{5}$.

Q. 44 The multiplicative inverse of $\frac{4}{3}$ is___.

Sol. $\frac{3}{4}$

Let x be the multiplicative inverse of $\frac{4}{3}$.

By the definition,

i.e. $$x \times \frac{4}{3} = 1 \Rightarrow x = \frac{3}{4}$$

Hence, the multiplication inverse of $\frac{4}{3}$ is $\frac{3}{4}$.

Q. 45 The rational number 10.11 in the form $\frac{p}{q}$ is___.

Sol. $\frac{1011}{100}$

Let $x = 10.11$

$\Rightarrow 100x = 10.11 \times 100$ [multiplying both sides by 100]

$\Rightarrow 100x = 1011$

$\Rightarrow \frac{100x}{100} = \frac{1011}{100}$ [dividing both sides by 100]

$\Rightarrow x = \frac{1011}{100}$

Hence, the rational number 10.11 in the form $\frac{p}{q}$ is $\frac{1011}{100}$.

Q. 46 $\frac{1}{5}\times\left[\frac{2}{7}+\frac{3}{8}\right]=\left[\frac{1}{5}\times\frac{2}{7}\right]+$ ____.

Sol. $\frac{1}{5}\times\frac{3}{8}$

$\frac{1}{5}\times\left[\frac{2}{7}+\frac{3}{8}\right]=\frac{1}{5}\times\frac{2}{7}+\frac{1}{5}\times\frac{3}{8}$.

Q. 47 The two rational numbers lying between –2 and –5 with denominator as 1 are ____ and ____.

Sol. – 3, – 4

–5 –4 –3 –2

– 3 and – 4 are the two rational numbers lie between – 2 and – 5 with denominator 1.

True/False

In questions 48 to 99, state whether the given statements are True or False.

Q. 48 If $\frac{x}{y}$ is a rational number, then y is always a whole number.

Sol. *False*

If $\frac{x}{y}$ is a rational number.

Then, x and y are integers, where $y \neq 0$

Hence, y is always a non-zero integer.

Q. 49 If $\frac{p}{q}$ is a rational number, then p cannot be equal to zero.

Sol. *False*

If $\frac{p}{q}$ is a rational number.

Then, p can be equal to any integer.

i.e. p can be zero.

Q. 50 If $\frac{r}{s}$ is a rational number, then s cannot be equal to zero.

Sol. *True*

If $\frac{r}{s}$ is a rational number.

Then, s can be any non-zero integer.

Hence, s cannot be equal to zero.

Q. 51 $\frac{5}{6}$ lies between $\frac{2}{3}$ and 1.

Sol. ***True***

First, we convert the given rational numbers with denominator as 6, we get

$$\frac{2}{3}=\frac{2}{3}\times\frac{2}{2}=\frac{4}{6}$$

$$1=1\times\frac{6}{6}=\frac{6}{6}$$

$$\because \quad \frac{4}{6}<\frac{5}{6}<\frac{6}{6}$$

$$\therefore \quad \frac{2}{3}<\frac{5}{6}<1$$

Therefore, $\frac{5}{6}$ lies between $\frac{2}{3}$ and 1.

Note *We know that, if a and b are two rational numbers, then $\frac{a+b}{2}$ is a rational number between a and b such that $a<\frac{a+b}{2}<b$.*

Q. 52 $\frac{5}{10}$ lies between $\frac{1}{2}$ and 1.

Sol. ***False***

First, we convert the given rational numbers with denominator as 10, we get

$$\frac{1}{2}=\frac{1}{2}\times\frac{5}{5}=\frac{5}{10}$$

$$1=1\times\frac{10}{10}=\frac{10}{10}$$

$$\frac{1}{2}\text{ is equal to }\frac{5}{10}.$$

Therefore, $\frac{5}{10}$ does not lie between $\frac{1}{2}$ and 1.

Q. 53 $\frac{-7}{2}$ lies between -3 and -4.

Sol. ***True***

First, we convert the given rational numbers with denominator as 2, then we get

$$-3=-3\times\frac{2}{2}=\frac{-6}{2}$$

$$-4=-4\times\frac{2}{2}=\frac{-8}{2}$$

$$\because \quad \frac{-8}{2}<\frac{-7}{2}<\frac{-6}{2}$$

$$\therefore \quad -4<\frac{-7}{2}<-3$$

Therefore, $\frac{-7}{2}$ lies between -3 and -4.

Q. 54 $\frac{9}{6}$ lies between 1 and 2.

Sol. ***True***

First, we convert the given rational numbers with denominator as 6, we get

$$1 = 1 \times \frac{6}{6} = \frac{6}{6}$$

$$2 = 2 \times \frac{6}{6} = \frac{12}{6}$$

$$\because \quad \frac{6}{6} < \frac{9}{6} < \frac{12}{6}$$

$$\therefore \quad 1 < \frac{9}{6} < 2$$

Therefore, $\frac{9}{6}$ lies between 1 and 2.

Q. 55 If $a \neq 0$, the multiplicative inverse of $\frac{a}{b}$ is $\frac{b}{a}$.

Sol. ***True***

If $a = 0$, then multiplicative inverse of $\frac{a}{b}$ is not defined.

So, if $a \neq 0$, then multiplicative inverse of $\frac{a}{b}$ is $\frac{b}{a}$.

Q. 56 The multiplicative inverse of $\frac{-3}{5}$ is $\frac{5}{3}$.

Sol. ***False***

The multiplicative inverse of $\frac{-3}{5}$ is $\frac{1}{\left(\frac{-3}{5}\right)}$, i.e. $\frac{-5}{3}$.

Q. 57 The additive inverse of $\frac{1}{2}$ is -2.

Sol. ***False***

Let additive inverse of $\frac{1}{2}$ be x.

i.e. $$\frac{1}{2} + x = 0 \Rightarrow x = \frac{-1}{2}$$

Hence, additive inverse of $\frac{1}{2}$ is $\frac{-1}{2}$.

Q. 58 If $\frac{x}{y}$ is the additive inverse of $\frac{c}{d}$, then $\frac{x}{y} + \frac{c}{d} = 0$.

Sol. ***True***

If $\frac{x}{y}$ is the additive inverse of $\frac{c}{d}$.

i.e. $$\frac{x}{y} + \frac{c}{d} = 0$$

Q. 59 For every rational number x, $x + 1 = x$.

Sol. ***False***

For every rational number x,

$$x + 0 = x$$

Q. 60 If $\frac{x}{y}$ is the additive inverse of $\frac{c}{d}$, then $\frac{x}{y} - \frac{c}{d} = 0$

Sol. ***False***

If $\frac{x}{y}$ is the additive inverse of $\frac{c}{d}$.

i.e. $\frac{x}{y} + \frac{c}{d} = 0$

Q. 61 The reciprocal of a non-zero rational number $\frac{q}{p}$ is the rational number $\frac{q}{p}$.

Sol. ***False***

The reciprocal of a non-zero rational number $\frac{q}{p}$ is the rational number $\frac{p}{q}$.

Q. 62 If $x + y = 0$, then $-y$ is known as the negative of x, where x and y are rational numbers.

Sol. ***False***

If x and y are rational numbers and $x + y = 0$.

Then, y is known as the negative of x.

Q. 63 The negative of the negative of any rational number is the number itself.

Sol. ***True***

Let x be a positive rational number. Then, $-x$ be a negative rational number.

Now, negative of negative rational number $= -(-x) = x =$ Positive rational number

Q. 64 The negative of 0 does not exist.

Sol. ***True***

Since, zero is neither a positive integer nor a negative integer.

Q. 65 The negative of 1 is 1 itself.

Sol. ***False***

The negative of 1 is -1. $[\because 1 + (-1) = 0]$

Q. 66 For all rational numbers x and y, $x - y = y - x$

Sol. ***False***

For all rational numbers x and y,

$$x - y = -(y - x)$$

Q. 67 For all rational numbers x and y, $x \times y = y \times x$.

Sol. ***True***

For all rational numbers x and y,

$$x \times y = y \times x$$

Q. 68 For every rational number x, $x \times 0 = x$.

Sol. ***False***

For every rational number x,

$$x \times 0 = 0$$

Q. 69 For every rational numbers x, y and z, $x + (y \times z) = (x + y) \times (x + z)$

Sol. ***False***

For all rational numbers a, b and c.

$$a\,(b + c) = ab + ac$$

Q. 70 For all rational numbers a, b and c, $a\,(b + c) = ab + bc$.

Sol. ***False***

As, addition is not distributive over multiplication.

Q. 71 1 is the only number which is its own reciprocal.

Sol. ***False***

Reciprocal of 1 is 1 and reciprocal of –1 is –1.

Q. 72 –1 is not the reciprocal of any rational number.

Sol. ***False***

–1 is the reciprocal of –1.

Q. 73 For any rational number x, $x + (-1) = -x$.

Sol. ***False***

For every rational number x,

$$x \times (-1) = -x$$

Q. 74 For rational numbers x and y, if $x < y$, then $x - y$ is a positive rational number.

Sol. ***False***

For rational numbers x and y,

if $x < y$, then $x - y$ is a negative rational number.

e.g. Let $x = \frac{1}{2}$, $y = \frac{1}{3}$ are two rational numbers.

Then, according to equation,

$$x - y = \frac{1}{2} - \frac{1}{3} = \frac{3-2}{6} = \frac{1}{6}$$

Q. 75 If x and y are negative rational numbers, then so is $x + y$.

Sol. ***True***

e.g. $\left(-\frac{1}{2}\right)+\left(-\frac{1}{2}\right)=-1$, which is again a negative rational number.

Note *Sum of two negative rational numbers is equal to a negative rational number.*

Q. 76 Between any two rational numbers there are exactly ten rational numbers.

Sol. ***False***

There are infinite rational numbers between any two rational numbers.

Q. 77 Rational numbers are closed under addition and multiplication but not under subtraction.

Sol. ***False***

Rational numbers are closed under addition, subtraction and multiplication.

Q. 78 Subtraction of rational number is commutative.

Sol. ***False***

Subtraction of rational numbers is not commutative.

i.e. $a - b \neq b - a$

where, a and b are rational numbers.

Q. 79 $-\frac{3}{4}$ is smaller than -2.

Sol. ***False***

Here, $\frac{-3}{4}$ and -2 (like)

First, we do same denominator.

We get, $-\frac{3}{4}$ and $\frac{-2\times 4}{1\times 4}$

$\Rightarrow \quad \frac{-3}{4}$ and $\frac{-8}{4}$

Now, comparing both numbers,

$$\frac{-3}{4}>\frac{-8}{4} \Rightarrow \frac{-3}{4}>-2$$

So, $-\frac{3}{4}$ is greater than -2.

Q. 80 0 is a rational number.

Sol. ***True***

$0=\frac{0}{1}$ is a rational number.

Q. 81 All positive rational numbers lie between 0 and 1000.

Sol. ***False***

Infinite positive rational numbers lie on the right side of 0 on the number line.

Q. 82 The population of India in 2004–05 is a rational number.

Sol. ***True***

The population of India in 2004-05 is a rational number.

Q. 83 There are countless rational numbers between $\frac{5}{6}$ and $\frac{8}{9}$.

Sol. ***True***

$\frac{5}{6}$ and $\frac{8}{9}$ are rational numbers and there are infinite (countless) rational numbers lie between $\frac{5}{6}$ and $\frac{8}{9}$.

Note *We know that there are infinite rational numbers lie between two rational numbers.*

Q. 84 The reciprocal of x^{-1} is $\frac{1}{x}$.

Sol. ***False***

$x^{-1} = \frac{1}{x}$

$\therefore$ Reciprocal of $\frac{1}{x}$ is x.

Q. 85 The rational number $\frac{57}{23}$ lies to the left of zero on the number line.

Sol. ***False***

Since, $\frac{57}{23}$ is a positive rational number.

So, it lies on the right of zero on the number line.

Q. 86 The rational number $\frac{7}{-4}$ lies to the right of zero on the number line.

Sol. ***False***

Since, $\frac{-7}{4}$ is a negative rational number.

So, it lies on the left of zero on the number line.

Q. 87 The rational number $\frac{-8}{-3}$ lies neither to the right nor to the left of zero on the number line.

Sol. ***False***

$\frac{-8}{-3} = \frac{8}{3}$ is a positive rational number.

Hence, it lies on the right of zero on the number line.

Q. 88 The rational numbers $\frac{1}{2}$ and -1 are on the opposite sides of zero on the number line.

Sol. ***True***

Since, positive rational number and negative rational number are on the opposite sides of zero on the number line.

Hence, $\frac{1}{2}$ and -1 are on the opposite sides of zero on the number line.

Q. 89 Every fraction is a rational number.

Sol. ***True***

A fraction is a part or portion of the whole which can be expressed in the form of $\frac{p}{q}$. (positive rational number) where $p, q \in I^+$.
Hence, every fraction is a rational number but *vice-versa* is not true.

Q. 90 Every integer is a rational number.

Sol. ***True***

Every integer is a rational number whose denominator remain 1.

Q. 91 The rational numbers can be represented on the number line.

Sol. ***True***

The rational numbers can be represented on the number line.

Q. 92 The negative of a negative rational number is a positive rational number.

Sol. ***True***

Let x be a positive rational number.

Then, $-x$ be the negative rational number.

Hence, negative of negative rational number $= -(-x) = x =$ Positive rational number

Q. 93 If x and y are two rational numbers such that $x > y$, then $x - y$ is always a positive rational number.

Sol. ***True***

If x and y are two rational numbers such that $x > y$.

Then, there are three possible cases, i.e.

Case I x and y both are positive.

Case II x is positive and y is negative.

Case III x and y both are negative.

In all three cases, $x - y$ is always a positive rational number.

Q. 94 0 is the smallest rational number.

Sol. ***False***

As the smallest rational number does not exist.

Q. 95 Every whole number is an integer.

Sol. ***True***

W (whole numbers) = {0, 1, 2, 3, ...}

Z (integers) = {... − 3, − 2, − 1, 0, 1, 2, 3, ...}

Every whole number is an integer, but every integer is not a whole number.

Q. 96 Every whole number is a rational number.

Sol. ***True***

Every whole number can be written in the form of $\frac{p}{q}$, where p, q are integers and $q \neq 0$.

Hence, every whole number is a rational number.

Q. 97 0 is whole number but it is not a rational number.

Sol. ***False***

0 is a whole number and also a rational number.

Q. 98 The rational numbers $\frac{1}{2}$ and $-\frac{5}{2}$ are on the opposite sides of zero on the number line.

Sol. ***True***

Positive rational number and negative rational number remain on opposite sides of zero on the number line.

Q. 99 Rational numbers can be added (or multiplied) in any order
$\frac{-4}{5} \times \frac{-6}{5} = \frac{-6}{5} \times \frac{-4}{5}$

Sol. ***True***

We know, $\frac{-4}{5} \times \frac{-6}{5} = \frac{-6}{5} \times \frac{-4}{5} \Rightarrow \frac{24}{25} = \frac{24}{25}$

So, rational number can be added (or multiplied) in any order.

Note *Let a and b are two rational numbers.*

Then, $ab = ba$ *[commutative under multiplication]*

$a + b = b + a$ *[commutative under addition]*

Hence, rational numbers can be added (or multiplied) in any order.

Q. 100 Solve the following, select the rational numbers from the list which are also the integers.

$\frac{9}{4}, \frac{8}{4}, \frac{7}{4}, \frac{6}{4}, \frac{9}{3}, \frac{8}{3}, \frac{7}{3}, \frac{6}{3}, \frac{5}{2}, \frac{4}{2}, \frac{3}{1}, \frac{3}{2}, \frac{1}{1}, \frac{0}{1}, \frac{-1}{1}, \frac{-2}{2}, \frac{-3}{2}, \frac{-4}{2}, \frac{-5}{2}, \frac{-6}{2}$

Sol. From the given rational numbers, the numbers whose denominator is 1 and the numbers whose numerator is the multiple of denominator are the integers.

Hence, $\frac{8}{4}, \frac{9}{3}, \frac{6}{3}, \frac{4}{2}, \frac{3}{1}, \frac{1}{1}, \frac{-1}{1}, \frac{-2}{2}, \frac{-4}{2}, \frac{-6}{2}$ are the integers.

Q. 101 **Select those which can be written as a rational number with denominator 4 in their lowest form**

$$\frac{7}{8}, \frac{64}{16}, \frac{36}{-12}, \frac{-16}{17}, \frac{5}{-4}, \frac{140}{28}$$

Sol. From the given rational numbers, the number with denominator 4 in their lowest form is $\frac{5}{-4}$.

Q. 102 **Using suitable rearrangement and find the sum**

(a) $\frac{4}{7} + \left(\frac{-4}{9}\right) + \frac{3}{7} + \left(\frac{-13}{9}\right)$

(b) $-5 + \frac{7}{10} + \frac{3}{7} + (-3) + \frac{5}{14} + \frac{-4}{5}$

Sol. (a) Here, $\frac{4}{7} + \left(\frac{-4}{9}\right) + \frac{3}{7} + \left(\frac{-13}{9}\right) = \frac{4}{7} + \frac{3}{7} + \left(\frac{-4}{9}\right) + \left(\frac{-13}{9}\right)$

$= \frac{7}{7} - \frac{17}{9} = 1 - \frac{17}{9} = \frac{9-17}{9} = \frac{-8}{9}$

(b) Here, $-5 + \frac{7}{10} + \frac{3}{7} + (-3) + \frac{5}{14} + \left(\frac{-4}{5}\right) = -5 + (-3) + \frac{7}{10} + \left(\frac{-4}{5}\right) + \frac{3}{7} + \frac{5}{14}$

$= -8 + \frac{7-8}{10} + \frac{6+5}{14} = -8 - \frac{1}{10} + \frac{11}{14}$

$= \frac{-560 - 7 + 55}{70} = \frac{-512}{70} = \frac{-256}{35}$

Q. 103 **Verify $-(-x) = x$ for**

(i) $x = \frac{3}{5}$ (ii) $x = \frac{-7}{9}$ (iii) $x = \frac{13}{-15}$

Sol. (i) Given, $x = \frac{3}{5} \Rightarrow -x = \frac{-3}{5} \Rightarrow -(-x) = -\left(\frac{-3}{5}\right) \Rightarrow -(-x) = \frac{3}{5} = x$

(ii) Given, $x = \frac{-7}{9} \Rightarrow -x = -\left(\frac{-7}{9}\right) \Rightarrow -x = \frac{7}{9} \Rightarrow -(-x) = \frac{-7}{9} = x$

(iii) Given, $x = \frac{13}{-15} \Rightarrow -x = -\left(\frac{13}{-15}\right) \Rightarrow -x = \frac{13}{15} \Rightarrow -(-x) = \frac{-13}{15} = x$

Q. 104 **Give one example each to show that the rational numbers are closed under addition, subtraction and multiplication. Are rational numbers closed under division? Give two examples in support of your answer.**

Sol. We know that, rational numbers are closed under addition, subtraction and multiplication. We can understand this from the following examples.

Rational numbers are closed under addition

e.g. $\frac{4}{7} + \frac{1}{2} = \frac{8+7}{14} = \frac{15}{14}$, which is a rational number.

Subtraction

e.g. $\frac{4}{7}-\frac{1}{2}=\frac{8-7}{14}=\frac{1}{14}$, which is a rational number.

Multiplication

e.g. $\frac{4}{7}\times\frac{1}{2}=\frac{4}{14}=\frac{2}{7}$, which is a rational number.

But rational are not closed under division. If zero is excluded from the collection of rational numbers, then we can say that rational numbers are closed under division.

Now, we see the examples given below:

$$\frac{4}{7}\div\frac{1}{2}=\frac{4}{7}\times 2=\frac{8}{7}, \text{ which is a rational number.}$$

But $\frac{4}{7}\div 0=\frac{4}{7}\times\frac{1}{0}$,

which is not defined and so, it is not a rational number.

Also, $\frac{1}{2}\div 0=\frac{1}{2}\times\frac{1}{0}$,

which is not defined and so, it is not a rational number.

Q. 105 Verify the property $x+y=y+x$ of rational numbers by taking

(a) $x=\frac{1}{2}$ and $y=\frac{1}{2}$ (b) $x=\frac{-2}{3}$ and $y=\frac{-5}{6}$

(c) $x=\frac{-3}{7}$ and $y=\frac{20}{21}$ (d) $x=\frac{-2}{5}$ and $y=\frac{-9}{10}$

Sol. (a) Given, $x=\frac{1}{2}$ and $y=\frac{1}{2}$

Then, $\text{LHS}=x+y=\frac{1}{2}+\frac{1}{2}=1$

$\text{RHS}=y+x=\frac{1}{2}+\frac{1}{2}=1$

$\therefore$ LHS = RHS

Hence, $x+y=y+x$

(b) Given, $x=\frac{-2}{3}$ and $y=\frac{-5}{6}$

Then, $\text{LHS}=x+y=\frac{-2}{3}+\frac{-5}{6}=\frac{-2}{3}-\frac{5}{6}=\frac{-4-5}{6}=\frac{-9}{6}$

and $\text{RHS}=y+x=\frac{-5}{6}+\frac{-2}{3}=\frac{-5}{6}-\frac{2}{3}=\frac{-5-4}{6}=\frac{-9}{6}$

$\therefore$ LHS = RHS

Hence, $x+y=y+x$

(c) Given, $x=\frac{-3}{7}$ and $y=\frac{20}{21}$

Then, $\text{LHS}=x+y=\frac{-3}{7}+\frac{20}{21}=\frac{-9+20}{21}=\frac{11}{21}$

$\text{RHS}=y+x=\frac{20}{21}-\frac{3}{7}=\frac{20-9}{21}=\frac{11}{21}$

$\therefore$ LHS = RHS

Hence, $x+y=y+x$

(d) Given, $x = \frac{-2}{5}$ and $y = \frac{-9}{10}$

Then, $\text{LHS} = x + y = \frac{-2}{5} + \frac{-9}{10} = \frac{-2}{5} - \frac{9}{10} = \frac{-4-9}{10} = \frac{-13}{10}$

$\text{RHS} = y + x = \frac{-9}{10} + \frac{-2}{5} = \frac{-9}{10} - \frac{2}{5} = \frac{-9-4}{10} = \frac{-13}{10}$

$\therefore$ LHS = RHS

Hence, $x + y = y + x$

Q. 106 Simplify each of the following by using suitable property. Also, name the property.

(a) $\left[\frac{1}{2} \times \frac{1}{4}\right] + \left[\frac{1}{2} \times 6\right]$ (b) $\left[\frac{1}{5} \times \frac{2}{15}\right] - \left[\frac{1}{5} \times \frac{2}{5}\right]$

(c) $\frac{-3}{5} \times \left\{\frac{3}{7} + \left(\frac{-5}{6}\right)\right\}$

Sol. (a) Given, $\left[\frac{1}{2} \times \frac{1}{4}\right] + \left[\frac{1}{2} \times 6\right] = \frac{1}{2}\left[\frac{1}{4} + 6\right] = \frac{1}{2}\left[\frac{1+24}{4}\right] = \frac{25}{8}$

[using distributive property over addition]

(b) Given, $\left[\frac{1}{5} \times \frac{2}{15}\right] - \left[\frac{1}{5} \times \frac{2}{5}\right] = \frac{1}{5}\left[\frac{2}{15} - \frac{2}{5}\right]$ [using distributive property over addition]

$= \frac{1}{5}\left[\frac{2-6}{15}\right] = \frac{-4}{75}$

(c) Given, $\frac{-3}{5} \times \left\{\frac{3}{7} + \left(\frac{-5}{6}\right)\right\} = \frac{-3}{5} \times \frac{3}{7} + \left(\frac{-3}{5}\right) \times \left(\frac{-5}{6}\right)$

[using distributive property of multiplication over addition]

$= \frac{-9}{35} + \frac{15}{30} = \frac{-54+105}{210} = \frac{51}{210} = \frac{17}{70}$

Q. 107 Tell which property allows you to compute $\frac{1}{5} \times \left[\frac{5}{6} \times \frac{7}{9}\right]$ as $\left[\frac{1}{5} \times \frac{5}{6}\right] \times \frac{7}{9}$.

Sol. $\frac{1}{5} \times \left[\frac{5}{6} \times \frac{7}{9}\right]$ can be written as $\left[\frac{1}{5} \times \frac{5}{6}\right] \times \frac{7}{9}$ by the help of associative property for multiplication.

Q. 108 Verify the property $x \times y = y \times x$ of rational numbers by using

(a) $x = 7$ and $y = \frac{1}{2}$ (b) $x = \frac{2}{3}$ and $y = \frac{9}{4}$

(c) $x = \frac{-5}{7}$ and $y = \frac{14}{15}$ (d) $x = \frac{-3}{8}$ and $y = \frac{-4}{9}$

Sol. (a) Given, $x = 7$ and $y = \frac{1}{2}$

Then, $\text{LHS} = x \times y = 7 \times \frac{1}{2} = \frac{7}{2}$

$$RHS = y \times x = \frac{1}{2} \times 7 = \frac{7}{2}$$

$\therefore$ $LHS = RHS$

Hence, $xy = yx$

(b) Given, $x = \frac{2}{3}$ and $y = \frac{9}{4}$

Then, $LHS = x \times y = \frac{2}{3} \times \frac{9}{4} = \frac{18}{12} = \frac{3}{2}$

$$RHS = y \times x = \frac{9}{4} \times \frac{2}{3} = \frac{18}{12} = \frac{3}{2}$$

$\therefore$ $LHS = RHS$

Hence, $xy = yx$

(c) Given, $x = \frac{-5}{7}$ and $y = \frac{14}{15}$

Then, $LHS = x \times y = \frac{-5}{7} \times \frac{14}{15} = \frac{-2}{3}$

$$RHS = y \times x = \frac{14}{15} \times \frac{-5}{7} = \frac{-2}{3}$$

$\therefore$ $LHS = RHS$

Hence, $xy = yx$

(d) Given, $x = \frac{-3}{8}$ and $y = \frac{-4}{9}$

Then, $LHS = x \times y = \frac{-3}{8} \times \frac{-4}{9} = \frac{1}{3 \times 2} = \frac{1}{6}$

$$RHS = y \times x = \frac{-4}{9} \times \frac{-3}{8} = \frac{1}{6}$$

$\therefore$ $LHS = RHS$

Hence, $xy = yx$

Q. 109 Verify the property $x \times (y \times z) = (x \times y) \times z$ of rational numbers by using

(a) $x = 1, y = \frac{-1}{2}$ and $z = \frac{1}{4}$ (b) $x = \frac{2}{3}, y = \frac{-3}{7}$ and $z = \frac{1}{2}$

(c) $x = \frac{-2}{7}, y = \frac{-5}{6}$ and $z = \frac{1}{4}$ (d) $x = 0, y = \frac{1}{2}$ and $z = \frac{1}{4}$

and what is the name of this property?

Sol. (a) Given, $x = 1, y = \frac{-1}{2}$ and $z = \frac{1}{4}$

Now, $LHS = x \times (y \times z) = 1 \times \left(\frac{-1}{2} \times \frac{1}{4}\right) = 1 \times \frac{-1}{8} = \frac{-1}{8}$

and $RHS = (x \times y) \times z = \left(1 \times \frac{-1}{2}\right) \times \frac{1}{4} = \frac{-1}{2} \times \frac{1}{4} = \frac{-1}{8}$

$LHS = RHS$

Hence, $x \times (y \times z) = (x \times y) \times z$

(b) Given, $x = \frac{2}{3}$, $y = \frac{-3}{7}$ and $z = \frac{1}{2}$

Now, $\text{LHS} = x \times (y \times z) = \frac{2}{3} \times \left(\frac{-3}{7} \times \frac{1}{2}\right) = \frac{2}{3} \times \left(\frac{-3}{14}\right) = \frac{-2}{14} = \frac{-1}{7}$

and $\text{RHS} = (x \times y) \times z = \left(\frac{2}{3} \times \frac{-3}{7}\right) \times \frac{1}{2} = \frac{-2}{7} \times \frac{1}{2} = \frac{-1}{7}$

LHS = RHS

Hence, $x \times (y \times z) = (x \times y) \times z$

(c) Given, $x = \frac{-2}{7}$, $y = \frac{-5}{6}$ and $z = \frac{1}{4}$

Now, $\text{LHS} = x \times (y \times z) = \frac{-2}{7} \times \left(\frac{-5}{6} \times \frac{1}{4}\right) = \frac{-2}{7} \times \frac{-5}{24} = \frac{5}{84}$

and $\text{RHS} = (x \times y) \times z = \left(\frac{-2}{7} \times \frac{-5}{6}\right) \times \frac{1}{4} = \frac{5}{21} \times \frac{1}{4} = \frac{5}{84}$

LHS = RHS

Hence, $x \times (y \times z) = (x \times y) \times z$

(d) Question is incomplete.

The name of the verified property is associative property for multiplication.

Q. 110 Verify the property $x \times (y + z) = x \times y + x \times z$ of rational numbers by taking

(a) $x = \frac{-1}{2}, y = \frac{3}{4}$ and $z = \frac{1}{4}$ (b) $x = \frac{-1}{2}$, $y = \frac{2}{3}$ and $z = \frac{3}{4}$

(c) $x = \frac{-2}{3}$, $y = \frac{-4}{6}$ and $z = \frac{-7}{9}$ (d) $x = \frac{-1}{5}$, $y = \frac{2}{15}$ and $z = \frac{-3}{10}$

Sol. (a) Given, $x = \frac{-1}{2}$, $y = \frac{3}{4}$ and $z = \frac{1}{4}$

Now, $\text{LHS} = x \times (y + z) = \frac{-1}{2} \times \left(\frac{3}{4} + \frac{1}{4}\right) = \frac{-1}{2} \times \frac{4}{4} = \frac{-1}{2}$

and $\text{RHS} = x \times y + x \times z = \frac{-1}{2} \times \frac{3}{4} + \left(\frac{-1}{2}\right) \times \frac{1}{4} = \frac{-3}{8} - \frac{1}{8} = \frac{-3-1}{8} = \frac{-4}{8} = \frac{-1}{2}$

LHS = RHS

Hence, $x \times (y + z) = x \times y + x \times z$

(b) Given, $x = \frac{-1}{2}$, $y = \frac{2}{3}$ and $z = \frac{3}{4}$

Now, $\text{LHS} = x \times (y + z) = \frac{-1}{2} \times \left(\frac{2}{3} + \frac{3}{4}\right) = \frac{-1}{2} \times \left(\frac{8+9}{12}\right) = \frac{-1}{2} \times \frac{17}{12} = \frac{-17}{24}$

and $\text{RHS} = x \times y + x \times z = \frac{-1}{2} \times \frac{2}{3} + \left(\frac{-1}{2}\right) \times \frac{3}{4} = \frac{-1}{3} - \frac{3}{8} = \frac{-8-9}{24} = \frac{-17}{24}$

LHS = RHS

Hence, $x \times (y + z) = x \times y + x \times z$

(c) Given, $x = \frac{-2}{3}$, $y = \frac{-4}{6}$ and $z = \frac{-7}{9}$

Now, LHS $= x \times (y + z) = \frac{-2}{3} \times \left(\frac{-4}{6} + \frac{-7}{9}\right) = \frac{-2}{3} \times \left(\frac{-4}{6} - \frac{7}{9}\right)$

$= \frac{-2}{3} \times \left(\frac{-12-14}{18}\right) = \frac{-2}{3} \times \frac{-26}{18} = \frac{26}{27}$

and RHS $= x \times y + x \times z = \frac{-2}{3} \times \left(\frac{-4}{6}\right) + \left(\frac{-2}{3}\right) \times \left(\frac{-7}{9}\right) = \frac{4}{9} + \frac{14}{27} = \frac{12+14}{27} = \frac{26}{27}$

LHS = RHS

Hence, $x \times (y + z) = x \times y + x \times z$

(d) Given, $x = \frac{-1}{5}$, $y = \frac{2}{15}$ and $z = \frac{-3}{10}$

Now, LHS $= x \times (y + z) = \frac{-1}{5} \times \left(\frac{2}{15} + \frac{-3}{10}\right) = \frac{-1}{5} \times \left(\frac{2}{15} - \frac{3}{10}\right) = \frac{-1}{5} \times \left(\frac{4-9}{30}\right)$

$= \frac{-1}{5} \times \frac{-5}{30} = \frac{1}{30}$

and RHS $= x \times y + x \times z = \frac{-1}{5} \times \frac{2}{15} + \left(\frac{-1}{5}\right) \times \left(\frac{-3}{10}\right)$

$= \frac{-2}{75} + \frac{3}{50} = \frac{-4+9}{150} = \frac{5}{150} = \frac{1}{30}$

LHS = RHS

Hence, $x \times (y + z) = x \times y + x \times z$

Q. 111 Use the distributivity of multiplication of rational numbers over addition to simplify

(a) $\frac{3}{5} \times \left[\frac{35}{24} + \frac{10}{1}\right]$ (b) $\frac{-5}{4} \times \left[\frac{8}{5} + \frac{16}{15}\right]$

(c) $\frac{2}{7} \times \left[\frac{7}{16} - \frac{21}{4}\right]$ (d) $\frac{3}{4} \times \left[\frac{8}{9} - 40\right]$

Sol. (a) Given, $\frac{3}{5} \times \left(\frac{35}{24} + \frac{10}{1}\right) = \frac{3}{5} \times \frac{35}{24} + \frac{3}{5} \times \frac{10}{1}$ [by using distributive property over addition]

$= \frac{7}{8} + \frac{6}{1} = \frac{7+48}{8} = \frac{55}{8}$

(b) Given, $\frac{-5}{4} \times \left(\frac{8}{5} + \frac{16}{15}\right) = \frac{-5}{4} \times \frac{8}{5} + \left(\frac{-5}{4}\right) \times \left(\frac{16}{15}\right)$

[by using distributive property over addition]

$= -2 - \frac{4}{3} = \frac{-6-4}{3} = \frac{-10}{3}$

(c) Given, $\frac{2}{7} \times \left(\frac{7}{16} - \frac{21}{4}\right) = \frac{2}{7} \times \frac{7}{16} - \frac{2}{7} \times \frac{21}{4}$ [by using distributive property over addition]

$= \frac{1}{8} - \frac{3}{2} = \frac{1-12}{8} = \frac{-11}{8}$

(d) Given, $\frac{3}{4} \times \left(\frac{8}{9} - 40\right) = \frac{3}{4} \times \frac{8}{9} + \left(\frac{3}{4}\right) \times (-40)$

[by using distributive property over addition]

$= \frac{2}{3} - 30 = \frac{2-90}{3} = \frac{-88}{3}$

Q. 112 Simplify

(a) $\frac{32}{5}+\frac{23}{11}\times\frac{22}{15}$ (b) $\frac{3}{7}\times\frac{28}{15}\div\frac{14}{5}$

(c) $\frac{3}{7}+\frac{-2}{21}\times\frac{-5}{6}$ (d) $\frac{7}{8}+\frac{1}{16}-\frac{1}{12}$

Sol. (a) Given, $\frac{32}{5}+\frac{23}{11}\times\frac{22}{15}=\frac{32}{5}+\frac{46}{15}=\frac{96+46}{15}=\frac{142}{15}$

(b) Given, $\frac{3}{7}\times\frac{28}{15}\div\frac{14}{5}=\frac{4}{5}\div\frac{14}{5}=\frac{4}{5}\times\frac{5}{14}=\frac{2}{7}$

(c) Given, $\frac{3}{7}+\frac{-2}{21}\times\frac{-5}{6}=\frac{3}{7}+\frac{5}{63}=\frac{27+5}{63}=\frac{32}{63}$

(d) Given, $\frac{7}{8}+\frac{1}{16}-\frac{1}{12}=\frac{14+1}{16}-\frac{1}{12}=\frac{15}{16}-\frac{1}{12}=\frac{45-4}{48}=\frac{41}{48}$

Q. 113 Identify the rational number that does not belong with the other three. Explain your reasoning $\frac{-5}{11},\frac{-1}{2},\frac{-4}{9},\frac{-7}{3}$.

Sol. $\frac{-7}{3}$ does not belong with the other three. Since, $\frac{-7}{3}$ as it is smaller than –1 whereas rest of the numbers are greater than –1.

Q. 114 The cost of $\frac{19}{4}$ m of wire is ₹ $\frac{171}{2}$. Find the cost of one metre of the wire.

Sol. The cost of $\frac{19}{4}$ m of wire = ₹ $\frac{171}{2}$.

$\therefore$ Cost of 1 m of wire $=\frac{171}{2}\div\frac{19}{4}=\frac{171}{2}\times\frac{4}{19}=9\times2=$ ₹ 18

Hence, the cost of 1 m of wire is ₹ 18.

Q. 115 A train travels $\frac{1445}{2}$ km in $\frac{17}{2}$ h. Find the speed of the train in km/h.

Sol. Here, distance travelled by trian $=\frac{1445}{2}$ km

Time taken by trian $=\frac{17}{2}$ h

$\because$ Speed of train $=\frac{\text{Distance travelled by train}}{\text{Time taken by train}}$

$$=\frac{\frac{1445}{2}}{\frac{17}{2}}=\frac{1445}{2}\times\frac{2}{17}\text{ km/h}$$

$$=85\text{ km/h}$$

Hence, the speed of the train is 85 km/h.

Q. 116 **If 16 shirts of equal size can be made out of 24m of cloth, how much cloth is needed for making one shirt?**

Sol. If 16 shirts are to be made by cloth of 24 m

Then, 1 shirt is to be made by cloth of $= \frac{24}{16}\text{m} = \frac{3}{2}\text{m} = 1.5\text{m}$

Hence, 1.5 m cloth is needed for making one shirt.

Q. 117 $\frac{7}{11}$ **of all the money in Hamid's bank account is ₹ 77000. How much money does Hamid have in his bank account?**

Sol. Let money in Hamid's bank account be ₹ x.

Given, $\frac{7}{11}$ of all the money in Hamid's bank account = ₹ 77000

$$\Rightarrow \quad \frac{7}{11} \times x = 77000$$

$$\Rightarrow \quad x = \frac{77000 \times 11}{7}$$

$$\Rightarrow \quad x = 11000 \times 11$$

$$\Rightarrow \quad x = 121000$$

Hence, Hamid has ₹ 121000 in his bank account.

Q. 118 **A $117\frac{1}{3}$ m long rope is cut into equal pieces measuring $7\frac{1}{3}$ m each. How many such small pieces are these?**

Sol. We have, length of rope $= 117\frac{1}{3}$ m

$$= \frac{117 \times 3 + 1}{3}\text{m} = \frac{352}{3}\text{m}$$

Length of each piece $= 7\frac{1}{3}\text{m} = \frac{22}{3}\text{m}$

So, the number of pieces of the rope $= \frac{\text{Total length of the rope}}{\text{Length of each piece}}$

$$= \frac{\frac{352}{3}}{\frac{22}{3}} = \frac{352}{3} \div \frac{22}{3} = \frac{352}{3} \times \frac{3}{22} = 16$$

Hence, number of small pieces cut from the $117\frac{1}{3}$ m long rope is 16.

Q. 119 $\frac{1}{6}$ **of the class students are above average,** $\frac{1}{4}$ **are average and rest are below average. If there are 48 students in all, how many students are below average in the class?**

Sol. Number of above average students $= \frac{1}{6}$ of the class students

Number of average students $= \frac{1}{4}$ of the class students

$\therefore$ Number of below average students $= 1 - \left[\frac{1}{6} + \frac{1}{4}\right]$ of the class students

$$= 1 - \left[\frac{2+3}{12}\right]$$

$$= 1 - \frac{5}{12} = \frac{7}{12} \text{ of the class students}$$

Since, number of students in the class = 48 [given]

$\therefore$ Number of below average students $= \frac{7}{12} \times 48 = 28$

So, number of below average students are 28.

Q. 120 $\frac{2}{5}$ **of total number of students of a school come by car while** $\frac{1}{4}$ **of students come by bus to school. All the other students walk to school of which** $\frac{1}{3}$ **walk on their own and the rest are escorted by their parents. If 224 students come to school walking on their own, how many students study in that school?**

Sol. Let the number of students study in school be x.

Number of students come by car $= \frac{2}{5} \times x = \frac{2}{5}x$

Number of students come by bus $= \frac{1}{4} \times x = \frac{1}{4}x$

Remaining students walk to school $= x - \left(\frac{2}{5}x + \frac{1}{4}x\right) = x - \left(\frac{8x + 5x}{20}\right)$

$$= x - \frac{13x}{20} = \frac{20x - 13x}{20} = \frac{7x}{20}$$

Now, number of students walk to school on their own $= \frac{1}{3}$ of $\frac{7x}{20} = \frac{7x}{60}$.

Since, 224 students come to school on their own.

According to the question,

$$\frac{7x}{60} = 224$$

$$\Rightarrow \quad x = \frac{224 \times 60}{7}$$

$$= 32 \times 60 = 1920$$

Hence, 1920 students study in that school.

Q. 121 Huma, Hubna and Seema received a total of ₹ 2016 as monthly allowance from their mother such that Seema gets $\frac{1}{2}$ **of what Hubna gets and Huma gets** $1\frac{2}{3}$ **times Seema's share. How much money do the three sisters get individually?**

Sol. Seema gets allowance = $\frac{1}{2}$ of Huma's share

Hubna gets allowance $= 1\frac{2}{3}$ of Seema's share

$= \frac{5}{3}$ of Seema's share

$= \frac{5}{3}$ of $\frac{1}{2}$ of Huma's share [$\because$ Seema's share = $\frac{1}{2}$ of Huma's share]

$= \frac{5}{3} \times \frac{1}{2}$ of Huma's share

$= \frac{5}{6}$ of Huma's share

But Huma, Hubna and Seema received total monthly allowance from their mother = ₹ 2016

$\therefore$ Huma's share + Hubna's share + Seema's share = ₹ 2016

1 of Huma's share + $\frac{5}{6}$ of Huma's share + $\frac{1}{2}$ of Huma's share = ₹ 2016

So, $\left(1 + \frac{5}{6} + \frac{1}{2}\right)$ of Huma's share = ₹ 2016

$\Rightarrow$ $\left(\frac{6+5+3}{6}\right)$ of Huma's share = ₹ 201 6

$\Rightarrow$ $\frac{14}{6}$ of Huma's share = ₹ 2016

$\therefore$ Huma's share = ₹ 2016 $\div \frac{14}{6}$

= ₹ 2016 $\times \frac{6}{14} = 144 \times 6 =$ ₹ 864

So, Seema's share = $\frac{1}{2}$ of 864 = $\frac{1}{2} \times 864$ = ₹ 432

and share = $\frac{5}{6}$ of 864 = 5×144 = ₹ 720

Hence, Huma, Hubna and Seema get ₹ 864, ₹ 432 and ₹ 720, respectively.

Q. 122 A mother and her two daughters got a room constructed for ₹ 62000. The elder daughter contributes $\frac{3}{8}$ of her mother's contribution while the younger daughter contributes $\frac{1}{2}$ of her mother's share. How much do the three contribute individually?

Sol. Let the mother's share be ₹ x.

Now, elder daughter's share = ₹ $\frac{3}{8}x$

and younger daughter's share = ₹ $\frac{1}{2}x$

According to the question,

$$x + \frac{3}{8}x + \frac{x}{2} = 62000$$

$$\Rightarrow \quad \frac{8x + 3x + 4x}{8} = 62000$$

$$\Rightarrow \quad 15x = 62000 \times 8$$

$$\Rightarrow \quad x = \frac{62000 \times 8}{15}$$

$$\Rightarrow \quad x = \frac{12400 \times 8}{3}$$

$$\Rightarrow \quad x = \frac{99200}{3} = 33066.6$$

So, mother's share = ₹ 33066.6

Elder daughter's share = $\frac{3}{8} \times \frac{99200}{3}$ = ₹ 12400

Younger daughter's share = $\frac{1}{2} \times \frac{99200}{3}$ = ₹ 16533.3

Hence, mother and her two daughters contributed ₹ 33066.6, ₹ 12400 and ₹ 16533.3, respectively.

Q. 123 Tell which property allows you to compare $\frac{2}{3} \times \left[\frac{3}{4} \times \frac{5}{7}\right]$ and $\left[\frac{2}{3} \times \frac{5}{7}\right] \times \frac{3}{4}$.

Sol. $\frac{2}{3} \times \left[\frac{3}{4} \times \frac{5}{7}\right] = \frac{2}{3} \times \left(\frac{5}{7} \times \frac{3}{4}\right)$ [by commutative property over multiplication]

$= \left(\frac{2}{3} \times \frac{5}{7}\right) \times \frac{3}{4}$ [by associative property over multiplication]

Hence, $\frac{2}{3} \times \left(\frac{3}{4} \times \frac{5}{7}\right)$ can be compared with $\left(\frac{2}{3} \times \frac{5}{7}\right) \times \frac{3}{4}$ with the help of associative and commutative property.

Q. 124 Name the property used in each of the following:

(i) $-\frac{7}{11} \times \frac{-3}{5} = \frac{-3}{5} \times \frac{-7}{11}$

(ii) $-\frac{2}{3} \times \left[\frac{3}{4} + \frac{-1}{2}\right] = \left[\frac{-2}{3} \times \frac{3}{4}\right] + \left[\frac{-2}{3} \times \frac{-1}{2}\right]$

(iii) $\frac{1}{3} + \left[\frac{4}{9} + \left(\frac{-4}{3}\right)\right] = \left[\frac{1}{3} + \frac{4}{9}\right] + \left[\frac{-4}{3}\right]$

(iv) $\frac{-2}{7} + 0 = 0 + \frac{-2}{7} = -\frac{2}{7}$

(v) $\frac{3}{8} \times 1 = 1 \times \frac{3}{8} = \frac{3}{8}$

Sol. (i) Commutative property over multiplication

(ii) Distributive property over addition

(iii) Associative property over addition

(iv) Existence of additive identity

(v) Existence of multiplicative identity

Q. 125 Find the multiplicative inverse of

(i) $-1\frac{1}{8}$ (ii) $3\frac{1}{3}$

Sol. (i) Given number is $-1\frac{1}{8}$, i.e. $\frac{-9}{8}$.

The multiplicative inverse of $\frac{-9}{8}$ is $\frac{-8}{9}$.

(ii) Given number is $3\frac{1}{3}$, i.e. $\frac{10}{3}$.

The multiplicative inverse of $\frac{10}{3}$ is $\frac{3}{10}$.

Q. 126 Arrange the numbers $\frac{1}{4}, \frac{13}{16}, \frac{5}{8}$ in the descending order.

Sol. Given numbers are $\frac{1}{4}, \frac{13}{16}$ and $\frac{5}{8}$.

First, we convert the number as like denominator.

Taking LCM of 4, 16, 8 = $2 \times 2 \times 2 \times 2 = 16$

2	4, 16, 8
2	2, 8, 4
2	1, 4, 2
2	1, 2, 1
	1, 1, 1

Now,
$$\frac{1}{4} = \frac{1}{4} \times \frac{4}{4} = \frac{4}{16},$$
$$\frac{5}{8} = \frac{5}{8} \times \frac{2}{2} = \frac{10}{16}$$
$$\frac{13}{16} > \frac{10}{16} > \frac{4}{16}$$

i.e.
$$\frac{13}{16} > \frac{5}{8} > \frac{1}{4}$$

Q. 127 The product of two rational numbers is $\frac{-14}{27}$. If one of the numbers be $\frac{7}{9}$, find the other.

Sol. Let other number be x.

Given, one number = $\frac{7}{9}$

According to the question,

One number × Other number = Product of two numbers

$$\frac{7x}{9} = \frac{-14}{27}$$
$$x = \frac{-14}{27} \times \frac{9}{7}$$
$$x = \frac{-2}{3}$$

Hence, the other number is $\frac{-2}{3}$.

Q. 128 **By what numbers should we multiply $\frac{-15}{20}$ so that the product may be $\frac{-5}{7}$?**

Sol. Let the required number be x.

According to the question,

$$x \times \frac{-15}{20} = \frac{-5}{7}$$

$$x = \frac{-5}{7} \times \frac{20}{-15} = \frac{20}{21}$$

Hence, the required number is $\frac{20}{21}$.

Q. 129 **By what number should we multiply $\frac{-8}{13}$ so that the product may be 24?**

Sol. Let the required number be x.

According to the question,

$$\frac{-8x}{13} = 24$$

$$x = -\frac{13 \times 24}{8}$$

$$x = -13 \times 3 = -39$$

Hence, $\frac{-8}{13}$ should be multiplied by –39 to get the product 24.

Q. 130 **The product of two rational numbers is –7. If one of the number is –5, find the other?**

Sol. Given, one number = – 5

Suppose, the other number be x.

According to the question,

$$-5x = -7$$

$$\Rightarrow \quad x = \frac{-7}{-5} \Rightarrow x = \frac{7}{5}$$

Hence, the other number is $\frac{7}{5}$.

Q. 131 **Can you find a rational number whose multiplicative inverse is –1?**

Sol. No, we cannot find a rational number whose multiplicative inverse is –1.

Q. 132 **Find five rational numbers between 0 and 1.**

Sol. $\because \quad 0 < 1 < 2 < 3 < 4 < 5 < 6$

$$\Rightarrow \quad 0 < \frac{1}{6} < \frac{2}{6} < \frac{3}{6} < \frac{4}{6} < \frac{5}{6} < \frac{6}{6}$$

Hence, $\frac{1}{6}, \frac{2}{6}, \frac{3}{6}, \frac{4}{6}, \frac{5}{6}$ are the rational numbers lying between 0 and 1.

Q. 133 Find the two rational numbers whose absolute value is $\frac{1}{5}$.

Sol. Given, absolute value of two rational numbers is $\frac{1}{5}$.

One rational number is $\frac{1}{5}$, so $\left|\frac{1}{5}\right| = \frac{1}{5}$

and other rational number is $-\frac{1}{5}$, so $\left|\frac{-1}{5}\right| = \frac{1}{5}$

Q. 134 From a rope 40 m long, pieces of equal size are cut. If the length of one piece is $\frac{10}{3}$ m, find the number of such pieces.

Sol. Total length of rope = 40 m

Length of one piece = $\frac{10}{3}$ m

Let the number of pieces be x.

Then, according to the question,

$$\frac{10x}{3} = 40$$

$$\Rightarrow \quad x = \frac{40 \times 3}{10}$$

$$\Rightarrow \quad x = 12$$

Hence, number of pieces cut from the rope are 12.

Q. 135 $5\frac{1}{2}$ m long rope is cut into 12 equal pieces. What is the length of each piece?

Sol. Total length of the rope = $5\frac{1}{2}$ m = $\frac{11}{2}$ m

Total number of pieces = 12

Let the length of each piece be x m.

According to the question,

$$12x = \frac{11}{2}$$

$$x = \frac{11}{2 \times 12}$$

$$x = \frac{11}{24} \text{ m}$$

Hence, the length of each piece is $\frac{11}{24}$ m.

Q. 136 Write the following rational numbers in the descending order.

$$\frac{8}{7}, \frac{-9}{8}, \frac{-3}{2}, 0, \frac{2}{5}$$

Sol. Given numbers are $\frac{8}{7}, \frac{-9}{8}, \frac{-3}{2}, 0, \frac{2}{5}$

First, we convert the given numbers as like denominators.

LCM of 7, 8, 2, 5 = $2 \times 7 \times 4 \times 5 = 280$

Now,
$$\frac{8}{7} = \frac{8}{7} \times \frac{40}{40} = \frac{320}{280}$$
$$\frac{-9}{8} = \frac{-9}{8} \times \frac{35}{35} = \frac{-315}{280}$$
$$\frac{-3}{2} = \frac{-3}{2} \times \frac{140}{140} = \frac{-420}{280}$$
$$\frac{2}{5} = \frac{2}{5} \times \frac{56}{56} = \frac{112}{280}$$

In descending order,
$$\because \quad \frac{320}{280} > \frac{112}{280} > 0 > \frac{-315}{280} > \frac{-420}{280}$$
$$\Rightarrow \quad \frac{8}{7} > \frac{2}{5} > 0 > \frac{-9}{8} > \frac{-3}{2}$$

Q. 137 Find

(i) $0 \div \frac{2}{3}$

(ii) $\frac{1}{3} \times \frac{-5}{7} \times \frac{-21}{10}$

Sol. (i) $0 \div \frac{2}{3} = \frac{0}{2} \times 3 = 0$

(ii) $\frac{1}{3} \times \frac{-5}{7} \times \frac{-21}{10} = \frac{1}{3} \times \frac{3}{2} = \frac{1}{2}$

Q. 138 On a winter day the temperature at a place in Himachal Pradesh was −16°C. Convert it in degree Fahrenheit (°F) by using the formula
$$\frac{C}{5} = \frac{F-32}{9}$$

Sol. Given, temperature of Himachal Pradesh = − 16 °C
$$\because \quad \frac{C}{5} = \frac{F-32}{9}$$
$$\Rightarrow \quad \frac{-16}{5} = \frac{F-32}{9}$$
$$\Rightarrow \quad F - 32 = -\frac{144}{5}$$
$$\Rightarrow \quad F = 32 - \frac{144}{5}$$
$$\Rightarrow \quad F = \frac{160-144}{5}$$
$$= \frac{16}{5} = 3.2°F$$

Q. 139 Find the sum of additive inverse and multiplicative inverse of 7.

Sol. The additive inverse of 7 = – 7

The multiplicative inverse of 7 = $\frac{1}{7}$

∴ Required sum = $-7 + \frac{1}{7} = \frac{-49+1}{7}$

$= \frac{-48}{7} = -6\frac{6}{7}$

Q. 140 Find the product of additive inverse and multiplicative inverse of $-\frac{1}{3}$.

Sol. The additive inverse of $\frac{-1}{3} = \frac{1}{3}$

The multiplicative inverse of $\frac{-1}{3} = -3$

∴ Required product = $\frac{1}{3} \times -3 = -1$

Q. 141 The diagram shows the wingspans of different species of birds. Use the diagram to answer the question given below

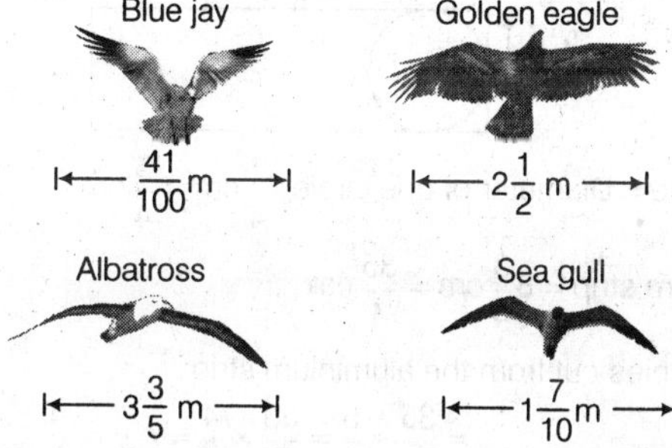

(a) How much longer is the wingspan of an Albatross than the wingspan of a Sea gull?

(b) How much longer is the wingspan of a Golden eagle than the wingspan of a Blue jay?

Sol. (a) We have, length of the wingspan of Albatross = $3\frac{3}{5}$ m

and length of the wingspan of a Sea gull = $1\frac{7}{10}$ m

∴ Difference = $3\frac{3}{5} - 1\frac{7}{10}$

$= \frac{18}{5} - \frac{17}{10}$

$= \frac{36-17}{10} = \frac{19}{10}$ m

Hence, the wingspan of an Albatross is $\frac{19}{10}$ m longer than the wingspan of a Sea gull.

(b) We have, length of the wingspan of Golden eagle $= 2\frac{1}{2}$ m

and the length the wingspan of a Blue jay $= \frac{41}{100}$ m

$$\therefore \quad \text{Difference} = 2\frac{1}{2} - \frac{41}{100}$$

$$= \frac{5}{2} - \frac{41}{100}$$

$$= \frac{250 - 41}{100}$$

$$= \frac{209}{100} \text{ m}$$

Hence, the wingspan of a Golden eagle is $\frac{209}{100}$ m longer than the wingspan of a Blue jay.

Q. 142 Shalini has to cut out circles of diameter $1\frac{1}{4}$ cm from an aluminium strip of dimensions $8\frac{3}{4}$ cm by $1\frac{1}{4}$ cm. How many full circles can Shalini cut? Also, calculate the wastage of the aluminium strip.

$8\frac{3}{4}$ cm

$1\frac{1}{4}$ cm

Sol. Breadth of the circle = Diameter of one circle $1\frac{1}{4}$ cm $= \frac{5}{4}$ cm

Length of aluminium strip $= 8\frac{3}{4}$ cm $= \frac{35}{4}$ cm

$\therefore$ Number of full circles cut from the aluminium strip

$$= \frac{35}{4} \div \frac{5}{4} = \frac{35}{4} \times \frac{4}{5} = 7$$

Hence, the number of circle 7.

$8\frac{3}{4}$ cm

$1\frac{1}{4}$ cm

Now, diameter of circle $= \frac{5}{4}$ cm

Radius of circle $= \frac{5}{4 \times 2} = \frac{5}{8}$ cm

Now, area to be cut by one circle $= \pi r^2 = \frac{22}{7} \times \left(\frac{5}{8}\right)^2$

$$= \frac{22}{7} \times \frac{25}{64} \text{ cm}^2$$

$\therefore$ Area to be cut by 7 full circles $= 7 \times \frac{22}{7} \times \frac{25}{64} = \frac{22 \times 25}{64}$

Also, area of the aluminium strip = Length × Breadth

$$= \frac{35}{4} \times \frac{5}{4} \text{ cm}^2$$

$\therefore$ Wastage of aluminium strip $= \left(\frac{35}{4} \times \frac{5}{4}\right) - \left(\frac{22 \times 25}{64}\right)$

$$= \frac{175}{16} - \frac{550}{64}$$

$$= \frac{700 - 550}{64} = \frac{150}{64}$$

$$= \frac{75}{32} = 2\frac{11}{32} \text{ cm}^2$$

Hence, the wastage of aluminium strip is $2\frac{11}{32}$ cm^2.

Q. 143 **One fruit salad recipe requires $\frac{1}{2}$ cup of sugar. Another recipe for the same fruit salad requires 2 tablespoons of sugar. If 1 tablespoon is equivalent to $\frac{1}{16}$ cup, how much more sugar does the first recipe require?**

Sol. Given, sugar required for one fruit salad $= \frac{1}{2}$ cup

Sugar required for another salad $= 2 \times \frac{1}{16} = \frac{2}{16}$ cup

$\therefore$ Required sugar $= \frac{1}{2} - \frac{2}{16} = \frac{8-2}{16} = \frac{6}{16} = \frac{3}{8}$ cup

Q. 144 **Four friends had a competition to see how far could they hop on one foot. The table given shows the distance covered by each.**

Name	**Distance covered** (in km)
Seema	$\frac{1}{25}$
Nancy	$\frac{1}{32}$
Megha	$\frac{1}{40}$
Soni	$\frac{1}{20}$

(a) How farther did Soni hop than Nancy?

(b) What is the total distance covered by Seema and Megha?

(c) Who walked farther, Nancy or Megha?

Sol. We have, $\frac{1}{25}, \frac{1}{32}, \frac{1}{40}, \frac{1}{20}$

First, we convert the numbers as like denominators.

Taking LCM of 25, 32, 40 and 20 = $2 \times 2 \times 2 \times 5 \times 5 \times 4 = 800$

2	25, 32, 40, 20
2	25, 16, 20, 10
2	25, 8, 10, 5
5	25, 4, 5, 5
	5, 4, 1, 1

we get

$$\frac{1}{25} = \frac{1 \times 32}{25 \times 32} = \frac{32}{800}, \frac{1}{32} = \frac{1 \times 25}{32 \times 25} = \frac{25}{800}; \frac{1}{40} = \frac{1 \times 20}{40 \times 20} = \frac{20}{800}$$

and $\frac{1}{20} = \frac{1 \times 40}{20 \times 40} = \frac{40}{800}$

(a) Soni hop more than Nancy $= \frac{40}{800} - \frac{25}{800} = \frac{40-25}{800} = \frac{15}{800} = \frac{3}{160}$ km

(b) Total distance covered by Seema and Megha

$$= \frac{32}{800} + \frac{20}{800} = \frac{32+20}{800} = \frac{52}{800} = \frac{13}{200} \text{ km}$$

(c) Clearly, Nancy walked farther than Megha.

Q. 145 The table given below shows the distances, in kilometres, between four villages of a state. To find the distance between two villages, locate the square, where the row for one village and the column for the other village intersect.

	Sonapur	Ramgarh	Himgaon	Rawalpur
Sonapur		$40\frac{2}{3}$	$100\frac{5}{6}$	$16\frac{1}{2}$
Ramgarh	$40\frac{2}{3}$		$210\frac{3}{8}$	$16\frac{2}{3}$
Himgaon	$100\frac{5}{6}$	$210\frac{3}{8}$		$98\frac{3}{4}$
Rawalpur	$16\frac{1}{2}$	$30\frac{2}{3}$	$98\frac{3}{4}$	

(a) Compare the distance between Himgaon and Rawalpur to Sonapur and Ramgarh?

(b) If you drove from Himgaon to Sonapur and then from Sonapur to Rawalpur, how far would you drive?

Sol. (a) The distance between Himgaon and Rawalpur = $98\frac{3}{4}$ km

and the distance between Sonapur and Ramgarh = $40\frac{2}{3}$ km

Difference of the distance between Himgaon and Rawalpur to Sonapur and Ramgarh

$$= \left(98\frac{3}{4} - 40\frac{2}{3}\right) = \left(\frac{395}{4} - \frac{122}{3}\right)$$

$$= \left(\frac{1185 - 488}{12}\right) = \frac{697}{12} = 58\frac{1}{12} \text{ km}$$

(b) Distance between Himgaon and Sonapur = $100\frac{5}{6}$ km

and distance between Sonapur and Rawalpur = $16\frac{1}{2}$ km

Total distance that he would drive

$$= 100\frac{5}{6} + 16\frac{1}{2} = \frac{605}{6} + \frac{33}{2}$$

$$= \frac{605 + 99}{6} = \frac{704}{6}$$

$$= \frac{352}{3} = 117\frac{1}{3} \text{ km}$$

Q. 146 The table shows the portion of some common materials that are recycled.

Material	**Recycled**
Paper	$\frac{5}{11}$
Aluminium cans	$\frac{5}{8}$
Glass	$\frac{2}{5}$
Scrap	$\frac{3}{4}$

(a) Is the rational number expressing the amount of paper recycled more than $\frac{1}{2}$ or less than $\frac{1}{2}$?

(b) Which items have a recycled amount less than $\frac{1}{2}$?

(c) Is the quantity of aluminium cans recycled more (or less) than half of the quantity of aluminium cans?

(d) Arrange the rate of recycling the materials from the greatest to the smallest.

Sol. (a) Here, $\frac{1}{2} = \frac{1}{2} \times \frac{11}{11} = \frac{11}{22}$

and $\frac{5}{11} = \frac{5}{11} \times \frac{2}{2} = \frac{10}{22}$

So, paper recycled is less than $\frac{1}{2}$.

(b) Similarly, $\frac{5}{8}$ is greater than $\frac{1}{2}\left(=\frac{4}{8}\right)$.

Also, $\frac{2}{5} = \frac{2 \times 2}{5 \times 2} = \frac{4}{10} < \frac{1}{2}\left(=\frac{5}{10}\right)$

and $\frac{3}{4} > \frac{1}{2}\left(=\frac{2}{4}\right)$

So, the quantity of paper and glass recycled is less than $\frac{1}{2}$.

(c) Quantity of aluminium cans $= \frac{5}{8}\left(=\frac{10}{16}\right)$ is more than $\frac{1}{2}$ of the quantity of aluminium cans

$$= \frac{5}{8} \times \frac{1}{2} = \frac{5}{16}$$

(d) Taking LCM of 11, 8, 5, 4 = 440

Now,
$$\frac{5}{11} = \frac{5}{11} \times \frac{40}{40} = \frac{200}{440}$$
$$\frac{5}{8} = \frac{5}{8} \times \frac{55}{55} = \frac{275}{440}$$
$$\frac{2}{5} = \frac{2}{5} \times \frac{88}{88} = \frac{176}{440}$$
$$\frac{3}{4} = \frac{3}{4} \times \frac{110}{110} = \frac{330}{440}$$

As,
$$\frac{330}{440} > \frac{275}{440} > \frac{200}{440} > \frac{176}{440}$$

i.e.
$$\frac{3}{4} > \frac{5}{8} > \frac{5}{11} > \frac{2}{5}$$

That means, Scrap > Aluminium cans> Paper > Glass

Q. 147 The overall width in cm of several wide-screen televisions are 97.28 cm, $98\frac{4}{9}$ cm, $98\frac{1}{25}$ cm and 97.94 cm. Express these numbers as rational numbers in the form $\frac{p}{q}$ and arrange the widths in ascending order.

Sol. We have,width of televisions screen are 97.28 cm, $98\frac{4}{9}$ cm, $98\frac{1}{25}$ cm and 97.94 cm.

Then, firstly, we convert all widths in the rational numbers.

(i) $97.28\,\text{cm} = \frac{9728}{100}$ [remove decimal]

$\therefore \quad \frac{p}{q} = \frac{2432}{25}$ cm [numerator and denominator both dividing by 4]

(ii) $98\frac{4}{9}\,\text{cm} = \frac{886}{9}$ cm [convert mixed fraction into simple fraction]

$\therefore \quad \frac{p}{q} = \frac{886}{9}$ cm

(iii) $98\frac{1}{25}\,\text{cm} = \frac{2451}{25}$ cm [convert mixed fraction into simple fraction]

$\therefore \quad \frac{p}{q} = \frac{2451}{25}$ cm

(iv) $97.94\,\text{cm} = \frac{9794}{100}$ [remove decimal]

$\therefore \quad \frac{p}{q} = \frac{4897}{50}$ cm [numerator and denominator both dividing by 2]

To arrange in ascending order, firstly we convert all the denominators same, then we get

2	25, 9, 25, 50
25	25, 9, 25, 25
9	1, 9, 1, 1
	1, 1, 1, 1

$\therefore$ LCM of 25, 9, 25, 50 $= 2 \times 25 \times 9 = 450$

So, $\frac{2432}{25} = \frac{2432 \times 18}{25 \times 18} = \frac{43776}{450}; \frac{886}{9} = \frac{886 \times 50}{9 \times 50} = \frac{44300}{450}$

$\frac{2451}{25} = \frac{2451 \times 18}{25 \times 18} = \frac{44118}{450}; \frac{4897}{50} = \frac{4897 \times 9}{50 \times 9} = \frac{44073}{450}$

In ascending order, $\frac{43776}{450} > \frac{44073}{450} > \frac{44118}{450} > \frac{44300}{450}$

i.e. $97.28 \text{ cm} > 97.94 \text{ cm} < 98\frac{1}{25} \text{ cm} < 98\frac{4}{9} \text{ cm}$

Q. 148 Roller coaster at an amusement park is $\frac{2}{3}$ m high. If a new roller coaster is built that is $\frac{3}{5}$ times the height of the existing coaster, what will be the height of the new roller coaster?

Sol. Given, height of the existing roller coaster $= \frac{2}{3}$ m

Height of new roller coaster $= \frac{3}{5}$ of height of the existing roller coaster

$$= \frac{3}{5} \times \frac{2}{3} = \frac{2}{5} \text{ m}$$

Q. 149 Here is a table which gives the information about the total rainfall for several months compared to the average monthly rains of a town. Write each decimal in the form of rational number $\frac{p}{q}$.

Months	**Above/Below normal** (in cm)
May	2.6924
June	0.6096
July	−6.0988
August	−8.636

Sol. (i) May $= 2.6924 = \frac{26924}{10000}$ [remove decimal]

$\Rightarrow \frac{p}{q} = \frac{6731}{2500}$ cm [after dividing numerator and denominator by 4]

(ii) June $= 0.6096 = \frac{6096}{10000}$ [remove decimal]

$\Rightarrow \frac{p}{q} = \frac{381}{625}$ cm [after dividing numerator and denominator by 16]

(iii) July $= -6.9088$

$= -\frac{69088}{10000}$ [remove decimal]

$\Rightarrow \frac{p}{q} = -\frac{4318}{625}$ cm [after dividing numerator and denomiator by 16]

(iv) August $= -8.636 = -\frac{8636}{1000}$ [remove decimal]

$\Rightarrow \frac{p}{q} = -\frac{2159}{250}$ cm [after dividing numerator and denominator by 4]

Q. 150 The average life expectancies of males for several states are shown in the table. Express each decimal in the form $\frac{p}{q}$ and arrange the states from the least to the greatest male life expectancy.

State-wise data are included below; more indicators can be found in the "FACTFILE" section on the homepage for each state.

State	**Male**	$\frac{p}{q}$ **form**	**Lowest terms**
Andhra Pradesh	61.6		
Assam	57.1		
Bihar	60.7		
Gujarat	61.9		
Haryana	64.1		
Himachal Pradesh	65.1		
Karnataka	62.4		
Kerala	70.6		
Madhya Pradesh	56.5		
Maharashtra	64.5		
Orissa	57.6		
Punjab	66.9		
Rajasthan	59.8		
Tamil Nadu	63.7		
Uttar Pradesh	58.9		
West Bengal	62.8		

Source Registrar General of India (2003) SRS Based Abridged Lefe Tables. SRS Analytical Studies, Report No. 3 of 2003, New Delhi: Registrar General of India.

The data are for the 1995-99 period; states subsequently divided are therefore included in their pre-partition states (Chhatisgarh in MP, Uttaranchal in UP and Jharkhand in Bihar)

Sol.

State	Male	$\frac{p}{q}$ form	Lowest term
Andhra Pradesh	61.6	$\frac{616}{10}$	$\frac{308}{5}$
Assam	57.1	$\frac{571}{10}$	$\frac{571}{10}$
Bihar	60.7	$\frac{607}{10}$	$\frac{607}{10}$
Gujarat	61.9	$\frac{619}{10}$	$\frac{619}{10}$
Haryana	64.1	$\frac{641}{10}$	$\frac{641}{10}$
Himachal Pradesh	65.1	$\frac{651}{10}$	$\frac{651}{10}$
Karnataka	62.4	$\frac{624}{10}$	$\frac{312}{5}$
Kerala	70.6	$\frac{706}{10}$	$\frac{353}{5}$
Madhya Pradesh	56.5	$\frac{565}{10}$	$\frac{113}{2}$
Maharashtra	64.5	$\frac{645}{10}$	$\frac{129}{2}$
Orissa	57.6	$\frac{576}{10}$	$\frac{288}{5}$
Punjab	66.9	$\frac{669}{10}$	$\frac{669}{10}$
Rajasthan	59.8	$\frac{598}{10}$	$\frac{299}{5}$
Tamil Nadu	63.7	$\frac{637}{10}$	$\frac{637}{10}$
Uttar Pradesh	58.9	$\frac{589}{10}$	$\frac{589}{10}$
West Bengal	62.8	$\frac{628}{10}$	$\frac{314}{5}$

Arrangement of the states from the least to the greatest male life expectancy, Haryana, Tamil Nadu, West Bengal, Karnataka, Gujarat, Andhra Pradesh, Bihar, Rajasthan, Uttar Pradesh, Orissa, Assam, Madhya Pradesh.

Q. 151 A skirt that is $35\frac{7}{8}$ cm long has a hem of $3\frac{1}{8}$ cm. How long will the skirt be if the hem is let down?

Sol. Length of the skirt $= 35\frac{7}{8}$ cm $= \frac{287}{8}$ cm

Dimension of hem $= 3\frac{1}{8}$ cm $= \frac{25}{8}$ cm

Length of skirt, if hem is let down $= \left(\frac{287}{8} + \frac{25}{8}\right)$ cm $= \frac{312}{8}$ cm $= 39$ cm

Hence, the length of the skirt, if the hem is let down, is 39 cm.

Q. 152 Manavi and Kuber each receives an equal allowance. The table shows the fraction of their allowance each deposits into his/her saving account and the fraction each spends at the mall. If allowance of each is ₹1260, find the amount left with each.

Where money goes	**Fraction of allowance**	
	Manavi	Kuber
Saving account	$\frac{1}{2}$	$\frac{1}{3}$
Spend at mall	$\frac{1}{4}$	$\frac{3}{5}$
Left over	?	?

Sol. Let total cost be ₹1.

For Manavi,

Left over = Total cost − All spends $= 1-\left(\frac{1}{2}+\frac{1}{4}\right) = 1-\frac{3}{4} = \frac{1}{4}$

$\therefore$ Amount $= 1260 \times \frac{1}{4} =$ ₹ 315

For Kuber,

Left over = Total cost − All spends $= 1-\left(\frac{1}{3}+\frac{3}{5}\right) = 1-\frac{14}{15} = \frac{1}{15}$

$\therefore$ Amount $= 1260 \times \frac{1}{15} =$ ₹ 84

Alternate Method

Allowance given to Manavi = ₹ 1260

Left over amount of Manavi = Allowance − Saving − Spend at mall

$$= 1260 - \frac{1}{2} \times 1260 - \frac{1}{4} \times 1260$$

$$= 1260\left(1-\frac{1}{2}-\frac{1}{4}\right) = 1260 \times \left(\frac{4-2-1}{4}\right)$$

$$= 1260 \times \left(\frac{4-3}{4}\right) = 1260 \times \frac{1}{4} = ₹\ 315$$

Hence, the amount left with Manavi is ₹ 315.

Allowance given to Kuber = ₹ 1260

Left over amount of Kuber = Allowance − Saving − Spend at mall

$$= 1260 - \frac{1}{3} \times 1260 - \frac{3}{5} \times 1260$$

$$= 1260\left(1-\frac{1}{3}-\frac{3}{5}\right) = 1260\left(\frac{15-5-9}{15}\right)$$

$$= 1260\left(\frac{15-14}{15}\right)$$

$$= 1260 \times \frac{1}{15} = ₹\ 84$$

Hence, the amount left with Kuber is ₹ 84.

2

Data Handling

Multiple Choice Questions (MCQs)

Q. 1 The height of a rectangle in a histogram shows the

(a) width of the class
(b) upper limit of the class
(c) lower limit of the class
(d) frequency of the class

Sol. ***(d)*** The height of a rectangle in a histogram shows the frequency of the class.

Note *The number of times a particular observation occurs in a given data, is called its* ***frequency****.*

Q. 2 A geometric representation showing the relationship between a whole and its parts, is a

(a) pie chart
(b) histogram
(c) bar graph
(d) pictograph

Sol. ***(a)*** Data can also be represented by using a pie chart (circle graph). It shows the relationship between a whole and its parts.

Q. 3 In a pie chart, the total angle at the centre of the circle is

(a) 180°
(b) 360°
(c) 270°
(d) 90°

Sol. ***(b)*** The total angle at the centre of the circle is 360°.

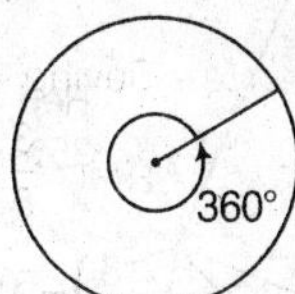

Q. 4 The range of the data 30, 61, 55, 56, 60, 20, 26, 46, 28, 56 is

(a) 26
(b) 30
(c) 41
(d) 61

Sol. ***(c)*** Range of data = Maximum value − Minimum value

$= 61 - 20 = 41$

Q. 5 Which of the following is not a random experiment?

(a) Tossing a coin
(b) Rolling a die
(c) Choosing a card from a deck of 52 cards
(d) Throwing a stone from the roof of a building

Sol. ***(d)*** Tossing a coin, rolling a die and choosing a card from a deck of 52 cards are the random experiments, as we don't have an idea about the output of these experiments. But if we throw a stone from the roof of a building, we know the output, it will fall on the ground.

Q. 6 What is the probability of choosing a vowel from the alphabets?

(a) $\frac{21}{26}$ (b) $\frac{5}{26}$
(c) $\frac{1}{26}$ (d) $\frac{3}{26}$

Sol. ***(b)*** Total number of alphabets = 26

Total number of vowels = 5

$$\text{Probability of choosing a vowel from the alphabets} = \frac{\text{Total number of vowels}}{\text{Total number of alphabets}} = \frac{5}{26}$$

Q. 7 In a school, only 3 out of 5 students can participate in a competition. What is the probability of the students who do not make it to the competition?

(a) 0.65 (b) 0.4
(c) 0.45 (d) 0.6

Sol. ***(b)*** Given, 3 out of 5 students can participate in a competition, i.e. 2 out of 5 students cannot participate in a competition.

Hence, probability of students who do not make it to competition $= \frac{2}{5} = 0.4$

Students of a class voted for their favourite colour and a pie chart was prepared based on the data collected.

Observe the pie chart given below and answer the questions 8-10 based on it.

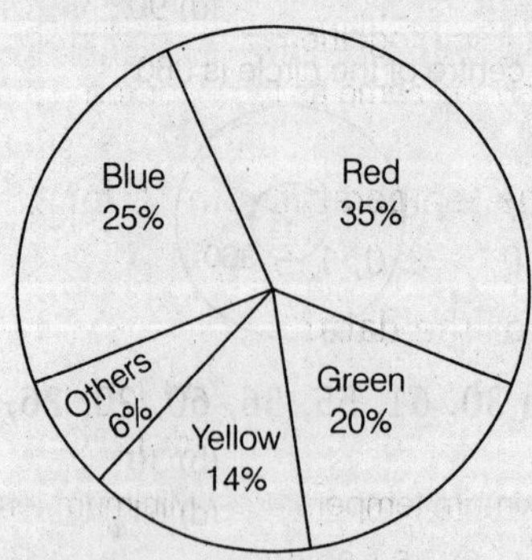

Q. 8 Which colour received $\frac{1}{5}$ of the votes?

(a) Red (b) Blue
(c) Green (d) Yellow

Sol. *(c)* Blue (25%), i.e. $\frac{25}{100} = \frac{1}{4}$ of votes received by blue.

Red (35%), i.e. $\frac{35}{100} = \frac{7}{20}$ of votes received by red.

Green (20%), i.e. $\frac{20}{100} = \frac{1}{5}$ of votes received by green.

Yellow (14%), i.e. $\frac{14}{100} = \frac{7}{50}$ of votes received by yellow.

Others (6%), i.e. $\frac{6}{100} = \frac{3}{50}$ of votes received by others.

Hence, green is the required colour.

Q. 9 If 400 students voted in all, then how many did vote 'Others' colour as their favourite?

(a) 6 (b) 20
(c) 24 (d) 40

Sol. *(c)* If total number of votes = 400

Then, number of votes in favour of 'Others' = 6% of 400 = $\frac{6}{100} \times 400 = \frac{3}{50} \times 400 = 24$

Q. 10 Which of the following is a reasonable conclusion for the given data?

(a) $\frac{1}{20}$ th student voted for blue colour

(b) Green is the least popular colour

(c) The number of students who voted for red colour, is two times the number of students who voted for yellow colour

(d) Number of students liking together yellow and green colours is approximately the same as those for red colour

Sol. *(d)* Number of students liking together yellow and green colours is (14 + 20)% i.e. 34%, which is approximately the same as those for red (35%).

Q. 11 Listed below are the temperatures in °C for 10 days.

$$-6, -8, 0, 3, 2, 0, 1, 5, 4, 4$$

What is the range of the data?

(a) 8°C (b) 13°C
(c) 10°C (d) 12°C

Sol. *(b)* Range of data = Maximum temperature – Minimum temperature

$= 5 - (-8) = 5 + 8 = 13$

Hence, the range of data is 13°C.

Q. 12 **Ram put some buttons on the table. There were 4 blue, 7 red, 3 black and 6 white buttons in all. All of a sudden, a cat jumped on the table and knocked out one button on the floor. What is the probability that the button on the floor is blue?**

(a) $\frac{7}{20}$ (b) $\frac{3}{5}$ (c) $\frac{1}{5}$ (d) $\frac{1}{4}$

Sol. *(c)* Total number of buttons = 4 + 7 + 3 + 6 = 20

Probability that button on the floor is blue $= \frac{\text{Number of blue buttons}}{\text{Total number of buttons}} = \frac{4}{20} = \frac{1}{5}$

Q. 13 **Rahul, Varun and Yash are playing a game of spinning a coloured wheel. Rahul wins, if spinner lands on red. Varun wins, if spinner lands on blue. Yash wins, if it lands on green. Which of the following spinners should be used to make the game fair?**

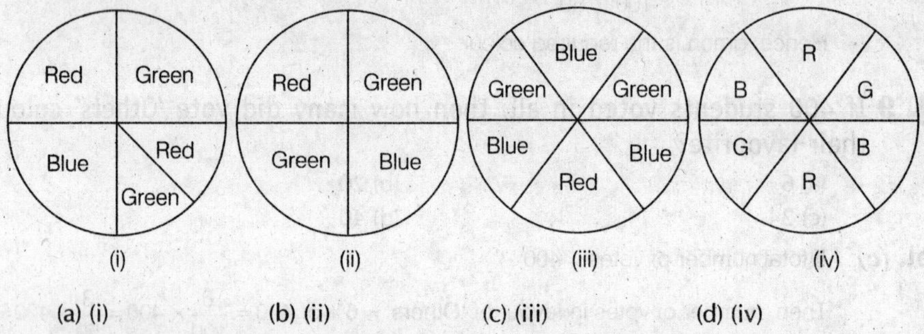

(a) (i) (b) (ii) (c) (iii) (d) (iv)

Sol. *(d)* The figure (iv) should be selected to make the game fair as the area occupied by each colour is equal. Hence, the chance of winning for each person is equal.

Q. 14 **In a frequency distribution with classes 0-10, 10-20 etc., the size of the class intervals is 10. The lower limit of fourth class is**

(a) 40 (b) 50 (c) 20 (d) 30

Sol. *(d)* Given classes are 0-10 and 10-20.

As, the class of given classes is 10, so the next classes will be 20-30 and 30-40.

As, the fourth class is 30-40.

Hence, the lower limit of fourth class is 30.

Q. 15 **A coin is tossed 200 times and head appeared 120 times. The probability of getting a head in this experiment is**

(a) $\frac{2}{5}$ (b) $\frac{3}{5}$ (c) $\frac{1}{5}$ (d) $\frac{4}{5}$

Sol. *(b)* Given, head appeared 120 times, if a coin is tossed 200 times.

Then, probability of getting a head in this experiment

$$= \frac{\text{Number of times head appeared}}{\text{Number of times coin is tossed}} = \frac{120}{200} = \frac{3}{5}$$

Q. 16 Data collected in a survey shows that 40% of the buyers are interested in buying a particular brand of toothpaste. The central angle of the sector of the pie chart representing this information is

(a) 120° (b) 150°
(c) 144° (d) 40°

Sol. *(c)* Percentage of buyers who selected the particular brand of toothpaste = 40%

Central angle of the sector of pie chart representing the above information

$$= 40\% \text{ of central angle}$$

$$= \frac{40}{100} \times 360° = 144°$$

Q. 17 Monthly salary of a person is ₹ 15000. The central angle of the sector representing his expenses on food and house rent on a pie chart is 60°. The amount he spends on food and house rent, is

(a) ₹ 5000 (b) ₹ 2500
(c) ₹ 6000 (d) ₹ 9000

Sol. *(b)* Central angle of the sector representing his expenses on food and house rent on a pie chart = 60°

Part of the monthly salary he is expending on food and house rent $= \frac{60°}{360°} = \frac{1}{6}$

Hence, the amount he spends on food and house rent $= \frac{1}{6} \times$ Monthly salary

$$= \frac{1}{6} \times 15000 = ₹\ 2500$$

Q. 18 The following pie chart gives the distribution of constituents in the human body. The central angle of the sector showing the distribution of protein and other constituents is

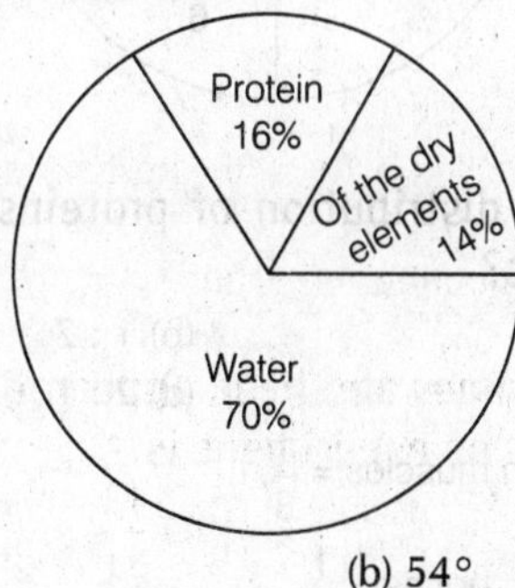

(a) 108° (b) 54°
(c) 30° (d) 216°

Sol. *(a)* Distribution of protein and other constituents in human body = 16 + 14 = 30%

Central angle of the sector showing the distribution of protein and other constituents

$$= \frac{30}{100} \times 360° = 108°$$

Q. 19 Rohan and Shalu are playing with 5 cards as shown in the given figure. What is the probability of Rohan picking a card without seeing, that has the number 2 on it?

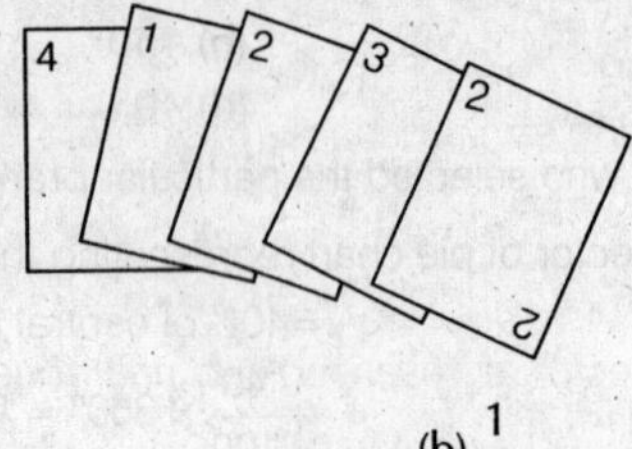

(a) $\frac{2}{5}$ (b) $\frac{1}{5}$

(c) $\frac{3}{5}$ (d) $\frac{4}{5}$

Sol. *(a)* Total number of cards = 5

Number of cards having 2 on it = 2

$\therefore$ Probability of Rohan picking a card without seeing, that has the number 2 on it

$$= \frac{2}{5}$$

In questions 20 to 22, the following pie chart represents the distribution of proteins in parts of human body.

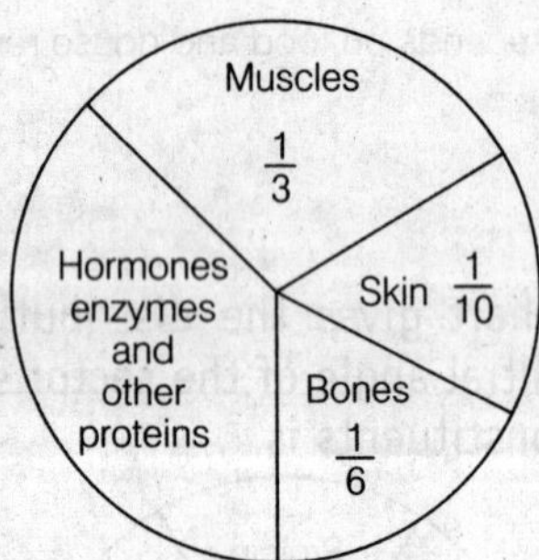

Q. 20 What is the ratio of distribution of proteins in the muscles to that of proteins in the bones?

(a) 3 : 1 (b) 1 : 2

(c) 1 : 3 (d) 2 : 1

Sol. *(d)* Distribution of protein in muscles $= \frac{1}{3}$

Distribution of protein in bones $= \frac{1}{6}$

Ratio of distribution of proteins in the muscles to that of proteins in the bones

$$= \frac{1}{3} : \frac{1}{6} = \frac{1}{3} \times \frac{6}{1}$$

$$= 2 : 1$$

Q. 21 **What is the central angle of the sector (in the above pie chart) representing skin and bones together?**

(a) 36° (b) 60° (c) 90° (d) 96°

Sol. *(d)* The portion representing skin and bones together $= \frac{1}{10} + \frac{1}{6}$

$$= \frac{3+5}{30} = \frac{8}{30}$$

Central angle of the sector representing skin and bones together

$$= \frac{8}{30} \times 360° = 96°$$

Q. 22 **What is the central angle of the sector representing hormones enzymes and other proteins?**

(a) 120° (b) 144° (c) 156° (d) 176°

Sol. *(b)* The portion representing hormones enzymes and other proteins $= 1 - \left(\frac{1}{3} + \frac{1}{10} + \frac{1}{6}\right)$

$$= 1 - \left(\frac{20+6+10}{60}\right) = 1 - \frac{36}{60} = \frac{60-36}{60} = \frac{2}{5}$$

Central angle of the sector representing hormones enzymes and other proteins

$$= \frac{2}{5} \times 360° = 144°$$

Q. 23 **A coin is tossed 12 times and the outcomes are observed as shown below:**

The chance of occurrence of head is

(a) $\frac{1}{2}$ (b) $\frac{5}{12}$ (c) $\frac{7}{12}$ (d) $\frac{5}{7}$

Sol. *(b)* Total number of times a coin is tossed = 12

Total number of occurrence of head = 5

The chance of occurrence of head $= \frac{\text{Number of times head appeared}}{\text{Number of times a coin is tossed}} = \frac{5}{12}$

Q. 24 **Total number of outcomes, when a ball is drawn from a bag which contains 3 red, 5 black and 4 blue balls, is**

(a) 8 (b) 7 (c) 9 (d) 12

Sol. *(d)* Given, a bag contains 3 red, 5 black and 4 blue balls.

Then, total number of outcomes = Total number of balls = 3 + 5 + 4 = 12

Q. 25 A graph showing two sets of data simultaneously is known as

(a) pictograph (b) histogram
(c) pie chart (d) double bar graph

Sol. *(d)* A graph showing two sets of data simultaneously is known as double bar graph.

Q. 26 Size of the class 150-175 is

(a) 150 (b) 175
(c) 25 (d) −25

Sol. *(c)* Size of the class 150-175 = Upper limit − Lower limit = 175 − 150 = 25

Q. 27 In a throw of a die, the probability of getting the number 7 is

(a) $\frac{1}{2}$ (b) $\frac{1}{6}$
(c) 1 (d) 0

Sol. *(d)* In a die, there are only 6 numbers, which are 1, 2, 3, 4, 5 and 6.
Hence, there is no possibility of number 7.
Therefore, probability of getting the number 7 is 0.

Q. 28 Data represented using circles is known as

(a) bar graph (b) histogram
(c) pictograph (d) pie chart

Sol. *(d)* Data represented using circles is known as pie chart.

Note ***Bar graph*** *Data using bars of different heights in a graphical display is known as bar graph (bar chart).*

Histogram *Grouped data can be represented by a histogram.*

Pictograph *Data using pictures and symbols to represent the statistical information is known as pictograph.*

Q. 29 Tally marks are used to find

(a) class intervals (b) range (c) frequency (d) upper limit

Sol. *(c)* Tally marks are used to find the frequency of the observations.

Q. 30 Upper limit of class interval 75-85 is

(a) 10 (b) −10 (c) 75 (d) 85

Sol. *(d)* Upper limit of class interval 75-85 is 85.

Note *The upper value of class interval is called its* ***upper class limit*** *and lower value of a class interval is called* ***lower class limit.***

Q. 31 Numbers 1 to 5 are written on separate slips, i.e. one number on one slip and put in a box. Wahida pick a slip from the box without looking at it. What is the probability that the slip bears an odd number?

(a) $\frac{1}{5}$ (b) $\frac{2}{5}$ (c) $\frac{3}{5}$ (d) $\frac{4}{5}$

Sol. *(c)* Numbers on the slips are 1, 2, 3, 4 and 5.

Odd numbers = 1, 3, 5

Number of slips bears an odd number = 3

Probability that the slip bears an odd number = $\frac{\text{Number of slips wtih odd numbers}}{\text{Total number of slips}} = \frac{3}{5}$

Q. 32 **A glass jar contains 6 red, 5 green, 4 blue and 5 yellow marbles of same size. Hari takes out a marble from the jar at random. What is the probability that the chosen marble is of red colour?**

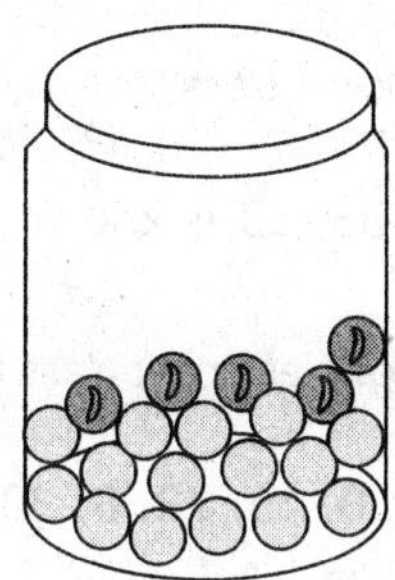

(a) $\frac{7}{10}$ (b) $\frac{3}{10}$ (c) $\frac{4}{5}$ (d) $\frac{2}{5}$

Sol. *(b)* As, jar contains 6 red, 5 green, 4 blue and 5 yellow marbles of same size. Then, probability that the chosen marble is of red colour

$$= \frac{\text{Number of red marbles}}{\text{Total number of marbles}} = \frac{6}{6+5+4+5} = \frac{6}{20} = \frac{3}{10}$$

Q. 33 **A coin is tossed two times. The number of possible outcomes is**

(a) 1 (b) 2 (c) 3 (d) 4

Sol. *(d)* Number of possible outcomes is 4, i.e. *HH, HT, TH, TT.*

Q. 34 **A coin is tossed three times. The number of possible outcomes is**

(a) 3 (b) 4 (c) 6 (d) 8

Sol. *(d)* Number of possible outcomes is 8, i.e. *HHH, HHT, HTH, THH, TTH, THT, HTT, TTT.*

Q. 35 **A die is tossed two times. The number of possible outcomes is**

(a) 12 (b) 24 (c) 36 (d) 30

Sol. *(c)* Number of possible outcomes is 36,

i.e. (1, 1), (1, 2), (1, 3), (1, 4), (1, 5), (1, 6)
(2, 1), (2, 2), (2, 3), ...,(2, 6)
(3, 1), (3, 2), (3, 3),.....,(3, 6)
(4, 1), (4, 2),.....,(4, 6)
(5, 1), (5, 2),.....,(5, 6)
(6, 1), (6, 2),.....,(6, 6)

Fill in the Blanks

In questions 36 to 58, fill in the blanks to make the statements true.

Q. 36 Data available in an unorganised form is called_____data.

Sol. **raw**

Data available in an unorganised form is called raw data.

Q. 37 In the class interval 20-30, the lower class limit is____.

Sol. **20**

In the class interval 20-30, the lower class limit is 20.

Q. 38 In the class interval 26-33, 33 is known as___.

Sol. **upper class limit**

In class interval 26-33, 33 is known as upper class limit.

Q. 39 The range of the data 6, 8, 16, 22, 8, 20, 7, 25 is___.

Sol. **19**

Range of the given data = Maximum value – Minimum value = 25 – 6 = 19

Q. 40 A pie chart is used to compare____to a whole.

Sol. **a part**

A pie chart is used to compare a part to a whole.

Q. 41 In the experiment of tossing a coin one time, the outcome is either _____or_____.

Sol. **head, tail**

On tossing a coin one time, the outcome can be head or tail.

Q. 42 When a die is rolled, the six possible outcomes are___.

Sol. **1, 2, 3, 4, 5, 6**

When a die is rolled, then the six possible outcomes are 1, 2, 3, 4, 5 and 6.

Q. 43 Each outcome or a collection of outcomes in an experiment makes an____.

Sol. **event**

Each outcome or a collection of outcomes in an experiment makes an event.

Q. 44 An experiment whose outcomes cannot be predicted exactly in advance, is called a _____experiment.

Sol. **random**

An experiment whose outcomes cannot be predicted exactly in advance, is called a random experiment.

Q. 45 The difference between the upper and lower limits of a class interval is called the _____ of the class interval.

Sol. size

The difference between the upper and lower limits of a class interval is called the size of the class interval.

Q. 46 The sixth class interval for a grouped data whose first two class intervals are 10-15 and 15-20 is _____.

Sol. 35-40

From the first two intervals, we can observe that the class size is 5. So, the sixth class interval will be 35-40.

Histogram given below shows the number of people owning the different number of books. Answer 47 to 50 based on it.

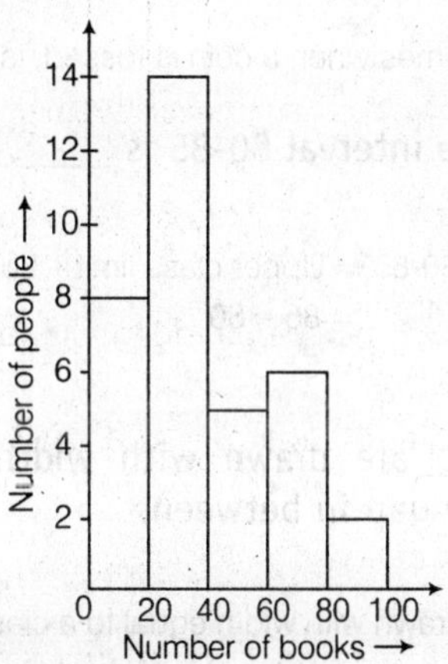

Q. 47 The total number of people surveyed is _____.

Sol. 35

Total number of people surveyed = 8 + 14 + 5 + 6 + 2 = 35

Q. 48 The number of people owning books more than 60 is _____.

Sol. 8

The number of people owning books more than 60 = 6 + 2 = 8

Q. 49 The number of people owning books less than 40 is _____.

Sol. 22

The number of people owning books less than 40 = 8 + 14 = 22

Q. 50 The number of people having books more than 20 and less than 40 is _____.

Sol. 14

The number of people having books more than 20 but less than 40 = 14

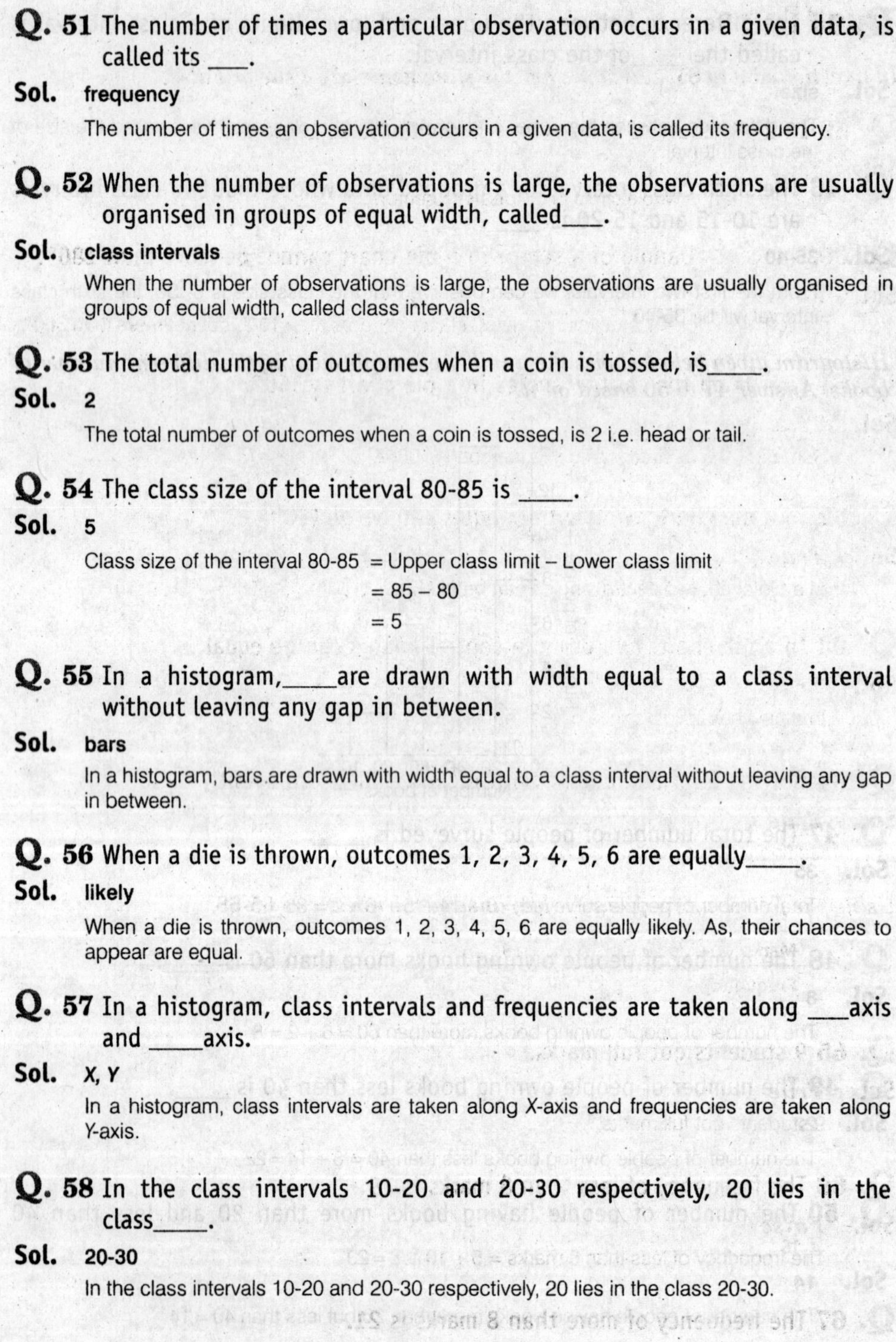

Q. 51 The number of times a particular observation occurs in a given data, is called its ___.

Sol. **frequency**

The number of times an observation occurs in a given data, is called its frequency.

Q. 52 When the number of observations is large, the observations are usually organised in groups of equal width, called___.

Sol. **class intervals**

When the number of observations is large, the observations are usually organised in groups of equal width, called class intervals.

Q. 53 The total number of outcomes when a coin is tossed, is____.

Sol. **2**

The total number of outcomes when a coin is tossed, is 2 i.e. head or tail.

Q. 54 The class size of the interval 80-85 is ____.

Sol. **5**

Class size of the interval 80-85 = Upper class limit – Lower class limit

= 85 – 80

= 5

Q. 55 In a histogram,____are drawn with width equal to a class interval without leaving any gap in between.

Sol. **bars**

In a histogram, bars are drawn with width equal to a class interval without leaving any gap in between.

Q. 56 When a die is thrown, outcomes 1, 2, 3, 4, 5, 6 are equally_____.

Sol. **likely**

When a die is thrown, outcomes 1, 2, 3, 4, 5, 6 are equally likely. As, their chances to appear are equal.

Q. 57 In a histogram, class intervals and frequencies are taken along ___axis and _____axis.

Sol. ***X, Y***

In a histogram, class intervals are taken along *X*-axis and frequencies are taken along *Y*-axis.

Q. 58 In the class intervals 10-20 and 20-30 respectively, 20 lies in the class_____.

Sol. **20-30**

In the class intervals 10-20 and 20-30 respectively, 20 lies in the class 20-30.

True / False

In questions 59 to 81, state whether the statements are True or False.

Q. 59 In a pie chart, a whole circle is divided into sectors.

Sol. *True*

In a pie chart, a whole circle is divided into sectors.

Q. 60 The central angle of a sector in a pie chart cannot be more than 180°.

Sol. *False*

The central angle of a sector in a pie chart can be more than 180°, but not more than 360°.

Q. 61 Sum of all the central angles in a pie chart is 360°.

Sol. *True*

Sum of all the central angles in a pie chart is 360°.

Q. 62 In a pie chart, two central angles can be of 180°.

Sol. *True*

In a pie chart, two central angles can be of 180°.

Q. 63 In a pie chart, two or more central angles can be equal.

Sol. *True*

In a pie chart, two or more central angles can be equal.

Q. 64 Getting a prime number on throwing a die is an event.

Sol. *True*

Getting a prime number on throwing a die is an event.

Using the following frequency table, answer the questions 65-68.

Marks (obtained out of 10)	4	5	7	8	9	10
Frequency	5	10	8	6	12	9

Q. 65 9 students got full marks.

Sol. *True*

9 students got full marks.

Q. 66 The frequency of less than 8 marks is 29.

Sol. *False*

The frequency of less than 8 marks = 5 + 10 + 8 = 23

Q. 67 The frequency of more than 8 marks is 21.

Sol. *True*

The frequency of more than 8 marks = 12 + 9 = 21

Q. 68 10 marks has the highest frequency.

Sol. ***False***

9 Marks has the highest frequency.

Q. 69 If the fifth class interval is 60-65 and fourth class interval is 55-60, then the first class interval is 45-50.

Sol. ***False***

If fifth class interval is 60-65 and fourth class interval is 55-60, then third class interval is 50-55, second class interval is 45-50 and first class interval is 40-45.

Q. 70 From the histogram given below, we can say that 1500 males above the age of 20 are literate.

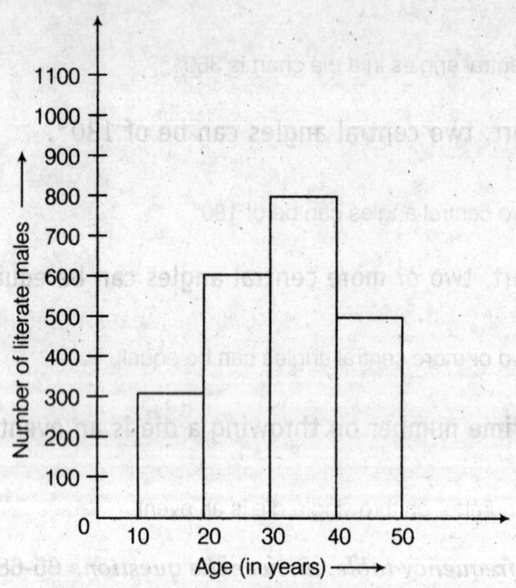

Sol. ***False***

Number of literate males above the age of 20 yr

$$= 600 + 800 + 500$$
$$= 1900$$

Q. 71 The class size of the class interval 60-58 is 8.

Sol. ***True***

Class size of the class interval 60-68 = Upper class limit – Lower class limit = 68 – 60 = 8

Q. 72 If a pair of coins is tossed, then the number of outcomes are 2.

Sol. ***False***

When a pair of coins is tossed, then the number of outcomes are 4, i.e. *HH*, *HT*, *TH* and *TT*.

Q. 73 On throwing a die once, the probability of occurrence of an even number is $\frac{1}{2}$.

Sol. ***True***

On throwing a die, the occurrence of even numbers can be as 2, 4 and 6.

Hence, probability of occurrence of an even number $= \frac{\text{Number of even numbers on a die}}{\text{Total numbers on a die}}$

$$= \frac{3}{6} = \frac{1}{2}$$

Q. 74 On throwing a die once, the probability of occurrence of a composite number is $\frac{1}{2}$.

Sol. ***False***

On throwing a die, the occurrence of composite numbers can be as 4, 6.

Hence, probability of occurrence of a composite number

$$= \frac{\text{Number of composite numbers on a die}}{\text{Total numbers on a die}} = \frac{2}{6} = \frac{1}{3}$$

Q. 75 From the given pie chart, we can infer that production of Manganese is least in state *B*.

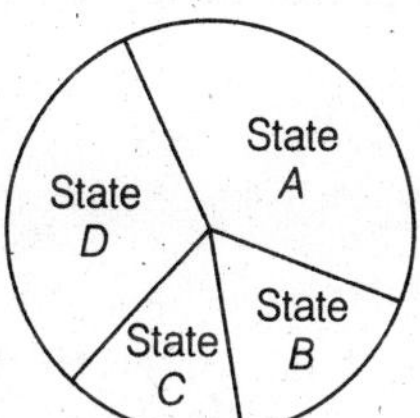

Production of manganese in 4 different states

Sol. ***False***

From the given pie chart, we cannot infer that production of manganese is least in state *B*. Unless we know the central angle for it.

Q. 76 One or more outcomes of an experiment make an event.

Sol. ***True***

One or more outcomes of an experiment make an event.

Q. 77 The probability of getting number 6 in a throw of a die is $\frac{1}{6}$. Similarly, the probability of getting a number 5 is $\frac{1}{5}$.

Sol. ***False***

The probability of getting number 6 or number 5 on a throw of a die $= \frac{1}{6}$

Q. 78 The probability of getting a prime number is the same as that of a composite number in a throw of die.

Sol. ***False***

In throw of a die, the occurrence of prime numbers can be as 2, 3, 5 and occurrence of composite numbers can be as 4, 6.

Hence, the probability of getting a prime number is 3/6 and of getting is 2/61, which is a composite not same.

Q. 79 In a throw of a die, the probability of getting an even number is the same as that of getting an odd number.

Sol. ***True***

In throw of a die, the occurrence of even numbers can be as 2, 4, 6 and the occurrence of odd numbers can be as 1, 3, 5.

Hence, probability of getting an even number is same as that of getting an odd number on a throw of a die.

Q. 80 To verify Pythagoras theorem is a random experiment.

Sol. ***False***

Verifying Pythagoras theorem is not a random experiment, because we already know the result.

Q. 81 The following pictorial representation of data is a histogram.

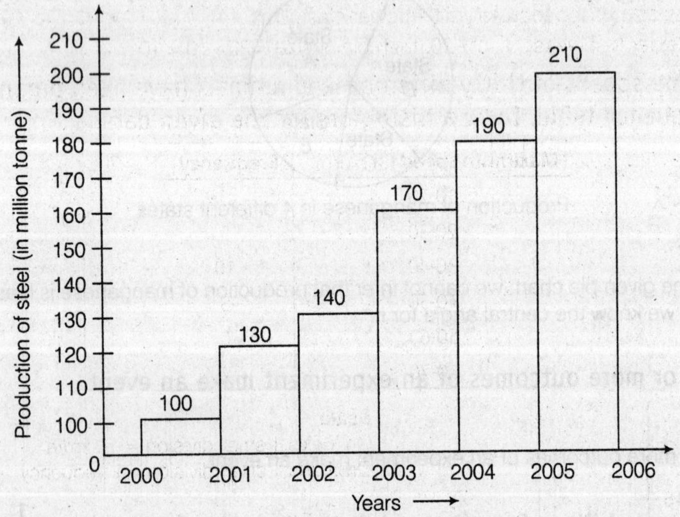

Sol. ***True***

The following pictorial representation of data is a histogram.

Q. 82 Given below is a frequency distribution table. Read it and answer the questions that follow.

Class interval	Frequency
10-20	5
20-30	10
30-40	4
40-50	15
50-60	12

(a) What is the lower limit of the second class interval?

(b) What is the upper limit of the last class interval?

(c) What is the frequency of the third class?

(d) Which interval has a frequency of 10?

(e) Which interval has the lowest frequency?

(f) What is the class size?

Sol. (a) The lower limit of second class interval (20-30) is 20.

(b) The upper limit of the last class interval (50-60) is 60.

(c) The frequency of the third class (30-40) is 4.

(d) The interval (20-30) has a frequency of 10.

(e) The interval (30-40) has the lowest frequency, i.e. 4.

(f) We know that,

Class size = Upper class limit – Lower class limit

Consider first class, i.e. 10-20, then class size $= 20 - 10 = 10$

Q. 83 The top speeds of thirty different land animals have been organised into a frequency table. Draw a histogram for the given data.

Maximum speed (in km/h)	**Frequency**
10-20	5
20-30	5
30-40	10
40-50	8
50-60	0
60-70	2

Sol.

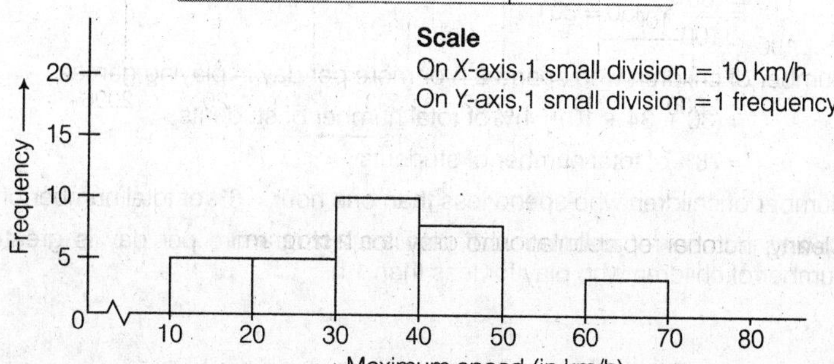

Q. 84 Given below is a pie chart showing the time spend by a group of 350 children in different games. Observe it and answer the questions that follow.

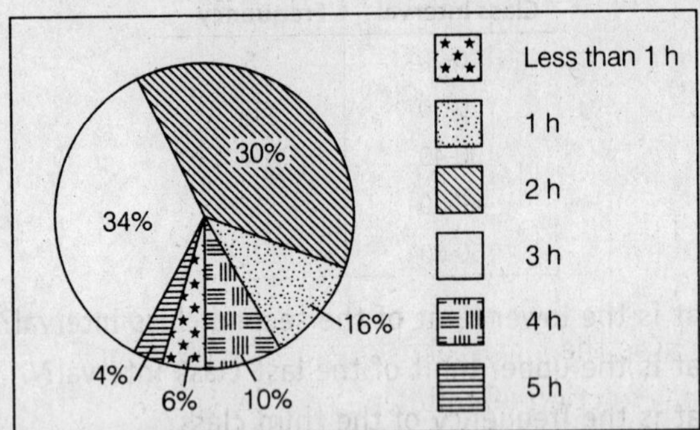

(a) How many children spend atleast one hour in playing games?

(b) How many children spend more than 2 h in playing games?

(c) How many children spend 3 or lesser hours in playing games?

(d) Which is greater, number of children who spend 2 hours or more per day or number of children who play for less than one hour?

Sol. (a) Number of children who spend atleast 1 h in playing games i.e. the number of children playing 1 h or more than 1 h

= (Total number of children) – (Number of children spend less than 1 h)

$= 350 - 6\%$ of 350

$= 350 - \dfrac{6}{100} \times 350$

$= 350 - 21 = 329$

(b) Number of children who spend more than 2 h in playing games

$= (34 + 10 + 4)\%$ of the total number of students

$= 48\%$ of 350

$= \dfrac{48}{100} \times 350 = 168$

(c) Number of children who spend 3 or lesser hours in playing games

$= (34 + 30 + 16 + 6)\%$ of total number of students

$= 86\%$ of 350

$= \dfrac{86}{100} \times 350 = 301$

(d) Number of children who spend 2 h or more per day in playing games

$= (30 + 34 + 10 + 4)\%$ of total number of students

$= 78\%$ of total number of students

Number of children who spend less than one hour = 6% of total number of students

Clearly, number of children who play for 2 h or more per day is greater than the number of children who play for less than 1 h.

Q. 85 The pie chart given below shows the result of a survey carried out to find the modes of travel used by the children to go to school. Study the pie chart and answer the questions that follow.

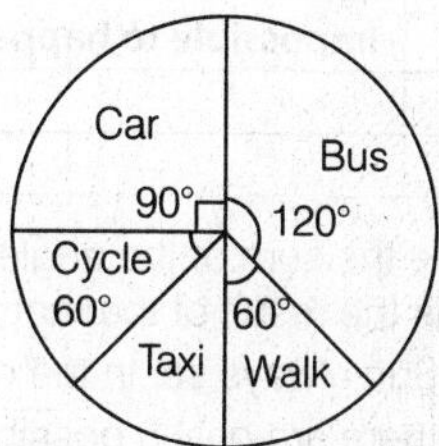

(a) What is the most common mode of transport?

(b) What fraction of children travel by car?

(c) If 18 children travel by car, how many children took part in the survey?

(d) By which two modes of transport are equal number of children travelling?

Sol. (a) The central angle is maximum for bus, hence bus is the most common mode of transport.

(b) Fraction of children travelled by car $= \frac{\text{Central angle}}{360°} = \frac{90°}{360°} = \frac{1}{4}$

(c) We know that, fraction of children travel by car $= \frac{1}{4}$

Hence, total number of children travelled by car $= \frac{1}{4} \times$ Total number of children

$\Rightarrow$ $18 = \frac{1}{4} \times$ Total number of children

$\therefore$ Total number of children $= 18 \times 4 = 72$

(d) The central angle made up the sectors representing cycle and walk are same. Hence, the cycle and walk are two modes of transport, by which equal number of children are travelling.

Q. 86 A die is rolled once. What is the probability that the number on top will be

(a) odd (b) greater than 5 (c) a multiple of 3

(d) less than 1 (e) a factor of 36 (f) a factor of 6

Sol. When a die is rolled once, then the possible outcomes are 1, 2, 3, 4, 5 and 6.

$\therefore$ Probability that number on top will be

(a) odd $= \frac{3}{6} = \frac{1}{2}$

(b) greater than 5 $= \frac{1}{6}$

(c) a multiple of 3 $= \frac{2}{6} = \frac{1}{3}$

(d) less than 1 = 0

(e) a factor of 36 $= \frac{5}{6}$

(f) a factor of 6 $= \frac{4}{6} = \frac{2}{3}$

Q. 87 Classify the following statements under appropriate headings.

(a) Getting the sum of angles of a triangle as 180°.

(b) India winning a cricket match against Pakistan.

(c) Sun setting in the evening.

(d) Getting 7 when a die is thrown.
(e) Sun rising from the West.
(f) Winning a racing competition by you.

Certain to happen	Impossible to happen	May or may not happen

Sol. (a) Certain to happen, because the sum of the angles of a triangle is 180°.
(b) May or may not happen, as the result of the match is unpredictable.
(c) Certain to happen, as the Sun always set in the evening.
(d) Impossible to happen, as there are only 6 possible outcomes on throwing a die, i.e. 1, 2, 3, 4, 5 and 6.
(e) Impossible to happen, as the Sun rise from East.
(f) May or may not happen, as the winning of the competition is unpredictable.

Q. 88 Study the pie chart given below depicting the marks scored by a student in an examination out of 540. Find the marks obtained by him in each subject.

Sol. From the pie chart we see that, percentage of each subject are,

Hindi = 16.67%, English= 25%, Social Science = 5.55%, Mathematics = 33.33%, Science = 19.44%

Given, marks obtained by student in an examination = 540

∴ The marks obtained in each subject are,

Hindi $= \frac{16.67}{100} \times 540 = 90$

English $= \frac{25}{100} \times 540 = 135$

Social Science $= \frac{5.55}{100} \times 540 = 29.97 = 30$ (approx.)

Mathematics $= \frac{33.33}{100} \times 540$

$= 179.98 = 180$ (approx.)

Science $= \frac{19.44}{100} \times 540 = 104.97 = 105$ (approx.)

Q. 89 Ritwik draws a ball from a bag that contains white and yellow balls. The probability of choosing a white ball is $\frac{2}{9}$. If the total number of balls in the bag is 36, then find the number of yellow balls.

Sol. The probability of choosing a white ball $= \frac{2}{9}$

Then, the probability of choosing a yellow ball $= 1 - \frac{2}{9} = \frac{9-2}{9} = \frac{7}{9}$

Given, total number of balls in the bag = 36

∴ Number of yellow balls $= \frac{7}{9} \times 36 = 28$

Q. 90 Look at the histogram below and answer the questions that follow.

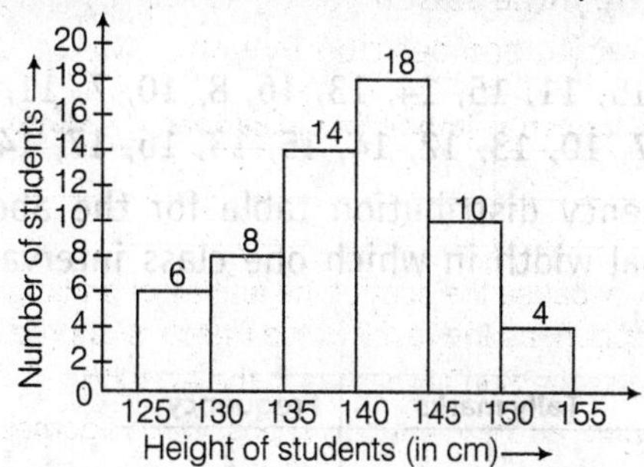

(a) How many students have height more than or equal to 135 cm, but less than 150 cm?

(b) Which class interval has the least number of students?

(c) What is class size?

(d) How many students have height less than 140 cm?

Sol. (a) Number of students who have height more than or equal to 135 cm, but less than 150 cm = 14 + 18 + 10 = 42

(b) The class interval 150-155 has the least number of students, i.e. 4.

(c) We know, class size = Upper class limit – Lower class limit
Consider any class, say (125-130), then class size = 130 – 125 = 5
Hence, the class size is 5.

(d) Number of students who have height less than 140 cm = 6 + 8 + 14 = 28

Q. 91 Following are the numbers of members in 25 families of a village:

6, 8, 7, 7, 6, 5, 3, 2, 5, 6, 8, 7, 7, 4, 3, 6, 6,6, 7, 5, 4, 3, 3, 2, 5

Prepare a frequency distribution table for the data using class intervals 0-2, 2-4 etc.

Sol.

Class interval	Tally marks	Frequency
0-2		0
2-4	~~||||~~ |	6
4-6	~~||||~~ |	6
6-8	~~||||~~ ~~||||~~ |	11
8-10	||	2
Total		**25**

Q. 92 Draw a histogram to represent the frequency distribution in question 91.

Sol.

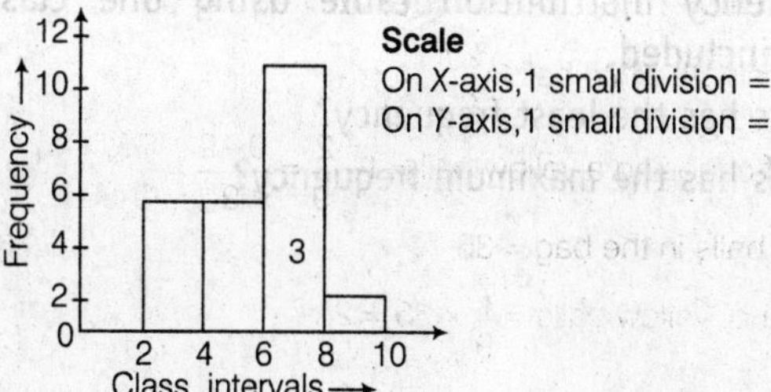

Q. 93 The marks obtained (out of 20) by 30 students of a class in a test are as follows:

14, 16, 15, 11, 15, 14, 13, 16, 8, 10, 7, 11, 18, 15, 14,
19, 20, 7, 10, 13, 12, 14, 15, 13, 16, 17, 14, 11, 10, 20.

Prepare a frequency distribution table for the above data using class intervals of equal width in which one class interval is 4-8 (excluding 8 and including 4).

Sol.

Class interval	Tally marks	Frequency
4-8	||	2
8-12	𝍸 ||	7
12-16	𝍸 𝍸 |||	13
16-20	𝍸 |	6
20-24	||	2
Total		**30**

Q. 94 Prepare a histogram from the frequency distribution table obtained in question 93.

Sol.

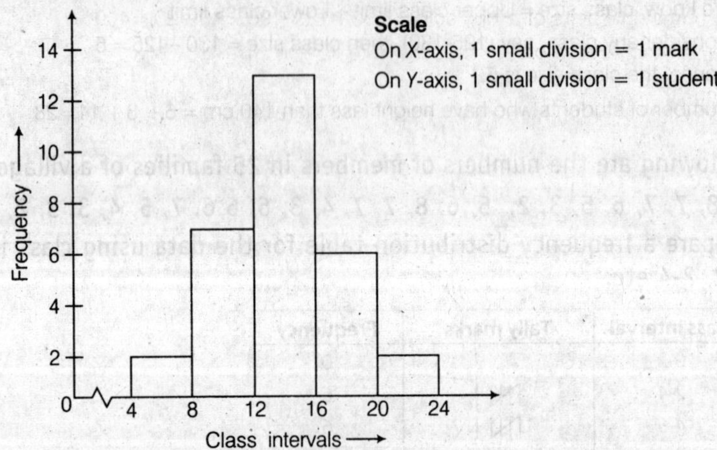

Q. 95 The weights (in kg) of 30 students of a class are as follows:

39, 38, 36, 38, 40, 42, 43, 44, 33, 33, 31, 45, 46, 38, 37,
31, 30, 39, 41, 41, 46, 36, 35, 34, 39, 43, 32, 37, 29, 26

Prepare a frequency distribution table using one class interval as (30-35), 35 not included.

(i) Which class has the least frequency?

(ii) Which class has the maximum frequency?

Sol.

Class interval	Tally marks	Frequency
25-30	||	2
30-35	卌 ||	7
35-40	卌 卌 |	11
40-45	卌 ||	7
45-50	|||	3
Total		**30**

(i) The class interval 25-30 has the least frequency, i.e. 2.

(ii) The class interval 35-40 has the maximum frequency, i.e. 11.

Q. 96 Shoes of the following brands are sold in November 2007 at a shoe store. Construct a pie chart for the given data.

Brand	Number of pairs of shoes sold
A	130
B	120
C	90
D	40
E	20

Sol. Total number of pairs of shoes sold = (130 + 120 + 90 + 40 + 20) = 400

∴ *Central angle of pie chart representing the brand*

(i) $A = \frac{130}{400} \times 360° = 117°$

(ii) $B = \frac{120}{400} \times 360° = 108°$

(iii) $C = \frac{90}{40} \times 360° = 81°$

(iv) $D = \frac{40}{400} \times 360° = 36°$

(v) $E = \frac{20}{400} \times 360° = 18°$

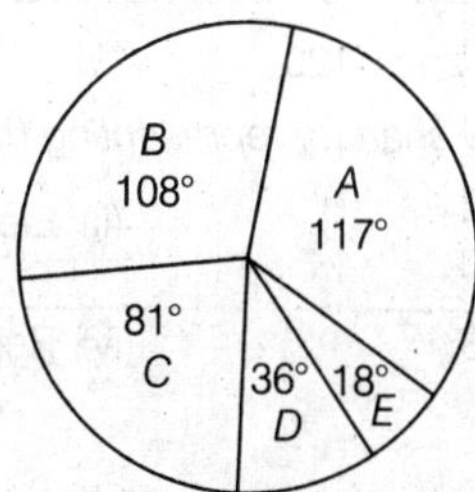

Q. 97 The following pie chart depicts the expenditure of a state government under different heads:

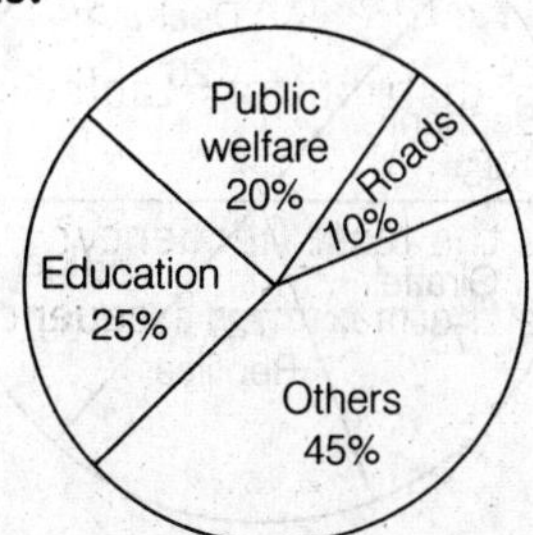

(i) If the total spending is 10 crore, how much money was spent on roads?

(ii) How many times is the amount of money spents on education compared to the amount spent on roads?

(iii) What fraction of the total expenditure is spents on both roads and public welfare together?

Sol. (i) Money spent on roads = 10% of total spending $= \frac{10}{100} \times 10$ crore $= 1$ crore

(ii) Money spent on education = 25% of total spending $= \frac{25}{100} \times$ Total spending

Money spent on roads = 10% of total spending $= \frac{10}{100} \times$ Total spending

Now, $\frac{\text{money spent on education}}{\text{money spent on roads}} = \frac{25}{10}$

$\Rightarrow$ Money spent on education = 2.5 × Money spent on roads

(iii) Fraction of the total expenditure spent on both roads and public welfare

$= 10\% + 20\% = \frac{10}{100} + \frac{20}{100} = \frac{(10+20)}{100} = \frac{30}{100} = \frac{3}{10}$

Q. 98 The following data represents the different number of animals in a zoo. Prepare a pie chart for the given data.

Animals	Number of animals
Deer	42
Elephant	15
Giraffe	26
Reptiles	24
Tiger	13

Sol. Total number of animals in a zoo = 120

∴ *Central angle made in pie chart for representing the animals like*

(i) Deer $= \frac{42}{120} \times 360° = 126°$

(ii) Elephant $= \frac{15}{120} \times 360° = 45°$

(iii) Giraffe $= \frac{26}{120} \times 360° = 78°$

(iv) Reptiles $= \frac{24}{120} \times 360° = 72°$

(v) Tiger $= \frac{13}{120} \times 360° = 39°$

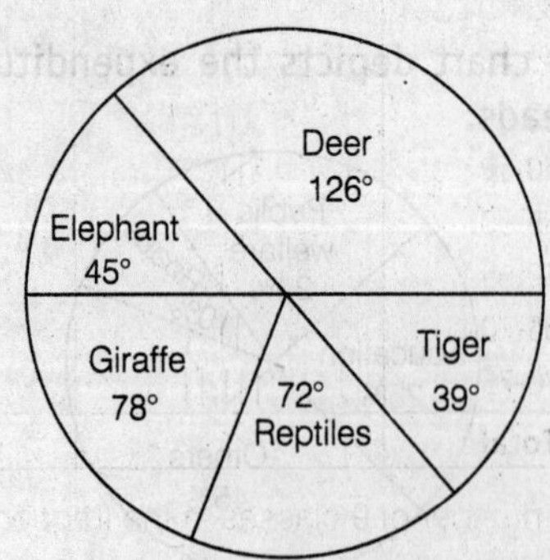

Q. 99 Playing cards

(a) From a pack of cards, the following cards are kept face down:

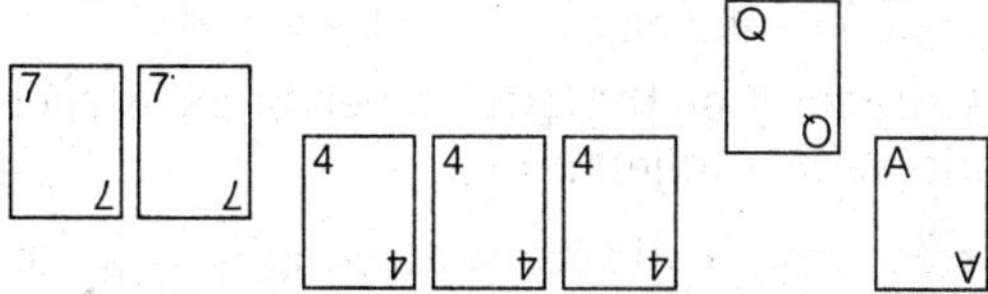

Suhail wins if he picks up face card. Find probability of Suhail winning?

(b) Now, the following cards are added to the above cards:

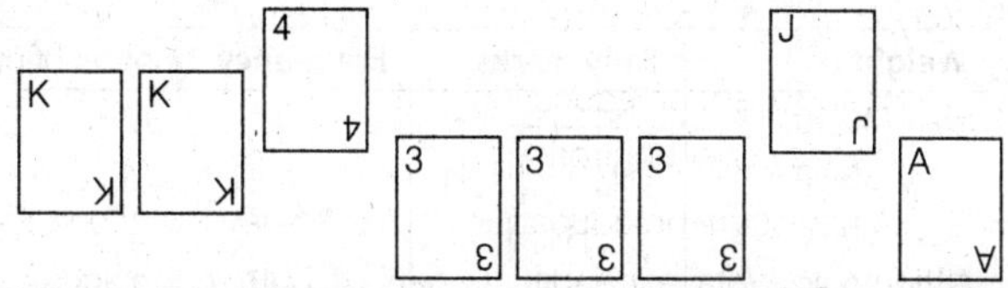

What is the probability of Suhail winning now? Reshma wins, if she picks up a 4. What is the probability of Reshma winning?

[Queen, King and Jack cards are called face cards.]

Sol. (a) P (Suhail winning) $= \frac{1}{7}$ [as there is only one face card]

(b) P (Suhail winning now) $= \frac{4}{15}$ [as there are 4 face cards]

P (Reshma winning) $= \frac{4}{15}$ [as there are four 4-number cards]

Q. 100 Construct a frequency distribution table for the following weights (in grams) of 35 mangoes, using the equal class intervals, one of them is 40-45 (45 not included):

30, 40, 45, 32, 43, 50, 55, 62, 70, 70, 61, 62, 53, 52, 50, 42, 35, 37, 53, 55, 65, 70, 73, 74, 45, 46, 58, 59, 60, 62, 74, 34, 35, 70, 68

(a) How many classes are there in the frequency distribution table?

(b) Which weight group has the highest frequency?

Sol.

Class interval	Tally marks	Frequency
30-35	|||	3
35-40	|||	3
40-45	|||	3
45-50	|||	3
50-55	~~||||~~	5
55-60	||||	4
60-65	~~||||~~	5
65-70	||	2
70-75	~~||||~~ ||	7
Total		**35**

(a) There are total number of 9 classes in the frequency distribution table.

(b) The weight group 70-75 has the highest frequency, i.e. 7.

Q. 101 **Complete the following table.**

Weight (in kg)	**Tally marks**	**Frequency** (Number of persons)
40-50	||||̸ ||||̸ ||	
50-60	||||̸ ||||̸ ||||	
60-70	||||̸ |	
70-80	||	
80-90	|	

Find the total number of persons, whose weights are given in the above table.

Sol.

Weight (in kg)	**Tally marks**	**Frequency** (Number of persons)
40-50	||||̸ ||||̸ ||	12
50-60	||||̸ ||||̸ ||||	14
60-70	||||̸ |	6
70-80	||	2
80-90	|	1

$\therefore$ Total number of persons $= 12 + 14 + 6 + 2 + 1 = 35$

Q. 102 **Draw a histogram for the following data.**

Class interval	10-15	15-20	20-25	25-30	30-35	35-40
Frequency	30	98	80	58	29	50

Sol.

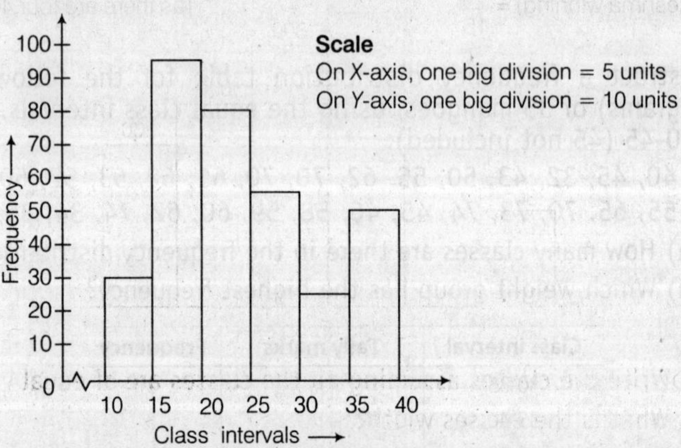

Q. 103 **In a hypothetical sample of 20 people, the amount of money (in ₹ thousands) with each was found to be as follows:**

114, 108, 100, 98, 101, 109, 117, 119, 126, 131,

136, 143, 156, 169, 182, 195, 207, 219, 235, 118

Draw a histogram of the frequency distribution, taking one of the class intervals as 50-100.

Sol. Before preparing histogram of the given data, we will prepare the frequency distribution table.

Amount (in ₹ thousand)	Tally marks	Frequency (Number of persons)
50-100	|	1
100-150	~~||||~~ ~~||||~~ ||	12
150-200	||||	4
200-250	|||	3

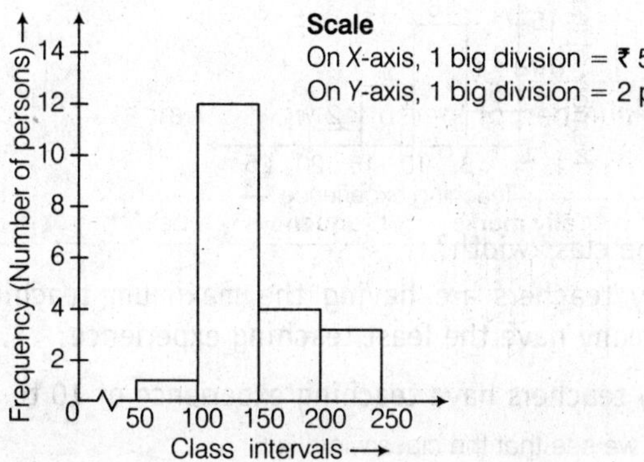

Q. 104 The below histogram shows the number of literate females in the age group of 10 yr to 40 yr in a town.

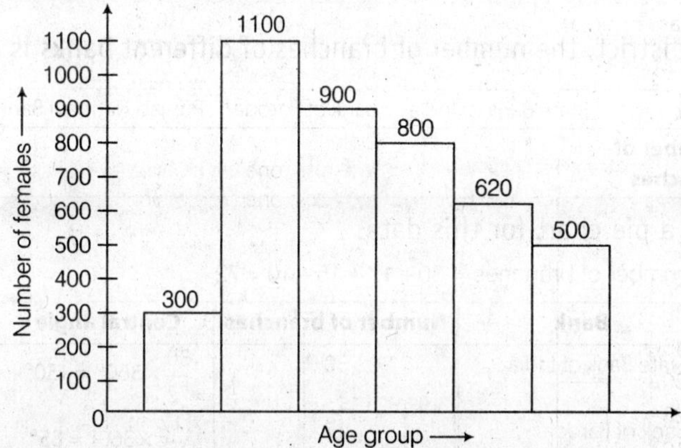

(a) Write the classes assuming all the classes are of equal width.
(b) What is the classes width?
(c) In which age group, are literate females the least?
(d) In which age group, is the number of literate females the highest?

Sol. (a) As we know that; the age group of 10 yr to 40 yr is to be divided into classes of equal width, starting with 10. Then, the classes of equal width can be written as 10-15, 15-20, 20-25, 25-30, 30-35, 35-40

(b) The width of the classes is 5, as the difference between upper class limit and lower class limit is 5.

(c) In the age group of 10-15, the number of literate females is the least.

(d) In the age group of 15-20, the number of literate females is the highest.

Q. 105 The following histogram shows the frequency distribution of teaching experiences of 30 teachers in various schools:

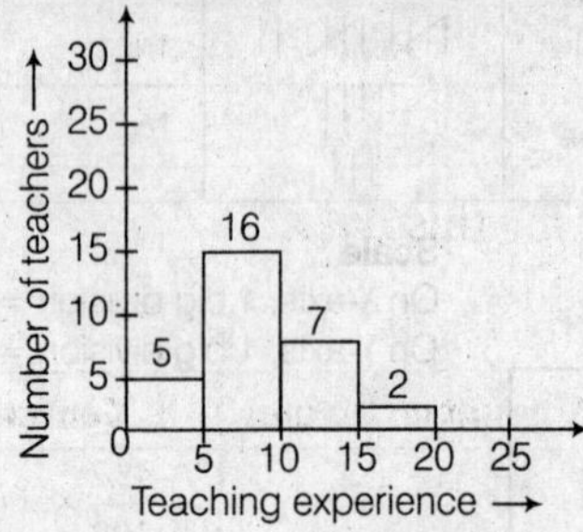

(a) What is the class width?

(b) How many teachers are having the maximum teaching experience and how many have the least teaching experience?

(c) How many teachers have teaching experience of 10 to 20 years?

Sol. (a) In the histogram, we see that the class width is 5.

(b) By the histogram, it is clear that two teachers have the maximum teaching experience, i.e. 15-20 years, and five teachers have the least teaching experience, i.e. 0-5 years.

(c) The number of teachers having experience from 10 to 20 years, is $7 + 2$, i.e. 9.

Q. 106 In a district, the number of branches of different banks is given below:

Bank	State Bank of India	Bank of Baroda	Punjab National Bank	Canara Bank
Number of branches	30	17	15	10

Draw a pie chart for this data.

Sol. Total number of branches $= 30 + 17 + 15 + 10 = 72$

Bank	**Number of branches**	**Central angle**
State Bank of India	30	$\frac{30}{72} \times 360° = 150°$
Bank of Baroda	17	$\frac{17}{72} \times 360° = 85°$
Punjab National Bank	15	$\frac{15}{72} \times 360° = 75°$
Canara Bank	10	$\frac{10}{72} \times 360° = 50°$

The pie chart is as follows:

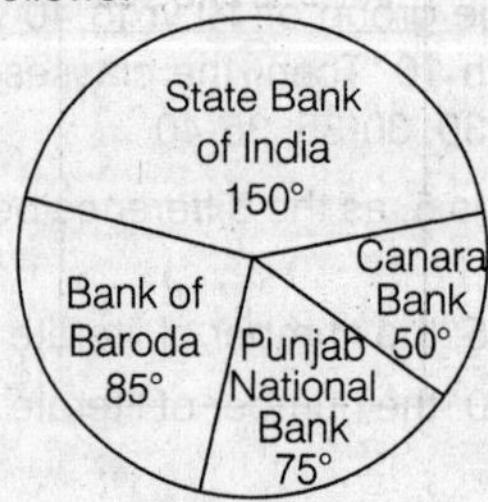

Q. 107 **For the development of basic infrastructure in a district, a project of ₹ 108 crore approved by Development Bank is as follows:**

Item head	Road	Electricity	Drinking water	Sewerage
Amount (in ₹ crore)	43.2	16.2	27.00	21.6

Draw a pie chart for this data.

Sol. Total amount = ₹ 108 crore

Item head	**Amount** (in ₹ crore)	**Central angle**
Road	43.2	$\frac{43.2}{108} \times 360° = 144°$
Electricity	16.2	$\frac{16.2}{108} \times 360° = 54°$
Drinking water	27. 00	$\frac{27}{108} \times 360° = 90°$
Sewerage	21.6	$\frac{21.6}{108} \times 360° = 72°$

The pie chart is as follows:

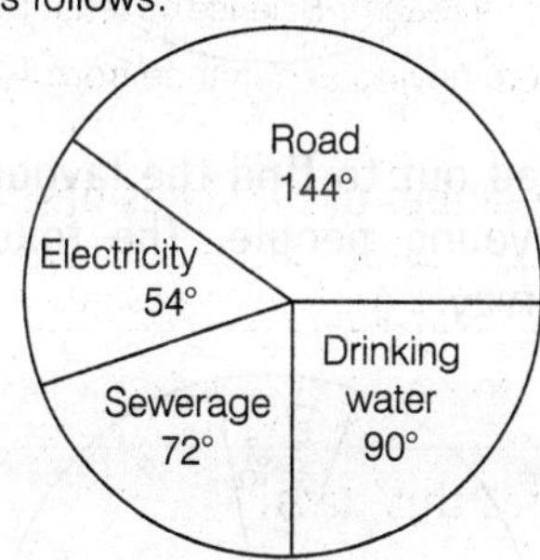

Q. 108 **In the time table of a school, periods allotted per week to different teaching subjects are given below.**

Subject	Hindi	English	Maths	Science	Social Science	Computer	Sanskrit
Periods allotted	7	8	8	8	7	4	3

Draw a pie chart for this data.

Sol. Total periods = 7 + 8 + 8 + 8 + 7 + 4 + 3 = 45

Subject	**Periods allotted**	**Central angle**
Hindi	7	$\frac{7}{45} \times 360° = 56°$
English	8	$\frac{8}{45} \times 360° = 64°$
Maths	8	$\frac{8}{45} \times 360° = 64°$

Subject	Periods allotted	Central angle
Science	8	$\frac{8}{45} \times 360° = 64°$
Social Science	7	$\frac{7}{45} \times 360° = 56°$
Computer	4	$\frac{4}{45} \times 360° = 32°$
Sanskrit	3	$\frac{3}{45} \times 360° = 24°$

The pie chart is as follows:

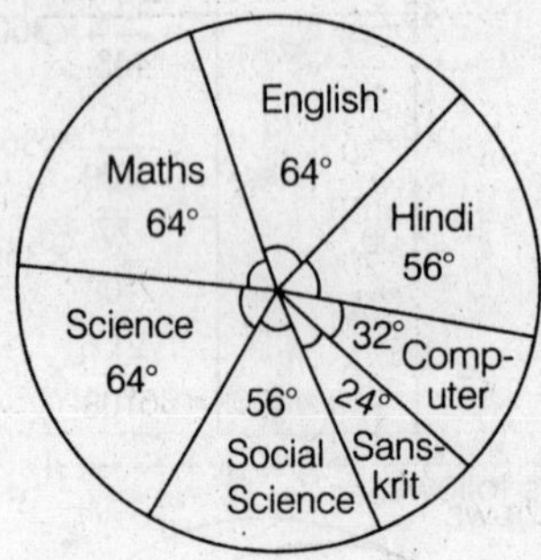

Q. 109 **A survey was carried out to find the favourite beverage preferred by a certain group of young people. The following pie chart shows the findings of this survey.**

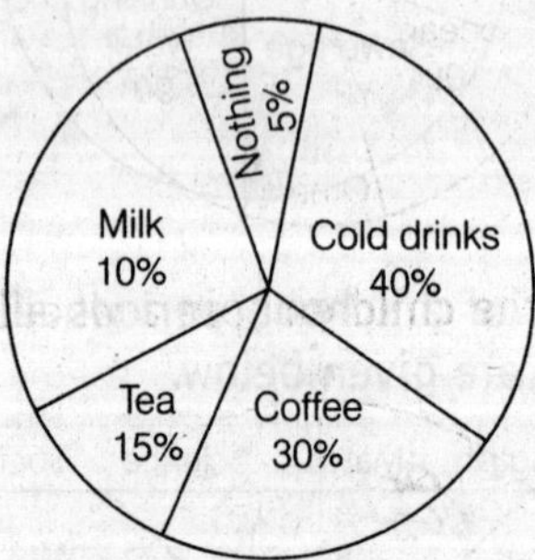

From this pie chart, answer the following:

(i) Which type of beverage is liked by the maximum number of people?

(ii) If 45 people like tea, how many people were surveyed?

Sol. (i) The percentage of people preferring cold drinks is maximum. So, cold drinks is liked by the maximum number of people.

(ii) From the pie chart, number of people who like tea = 45

$\Rightarrow$ 15% of total number of people surveyed = 45

$\Rightarrow$ $\frac{15}{100} \times$ Total number of people surveyed = 45

$\therefore$ Total number of people surveyed $= \frac{45 \times 100}{15} = 300$

Q. 110 The following data represents the approximate percentage of water in various oceans. Prepare a pie chart of the given data.

Ocean	Percentage of water
Pacific	40%
Atlantic	30%
Indian	20%
Others	10%

Sol.

Ocean	Central angle
Pacific	$\frac{40}{100} \times 360° = 144°$
Atlantic	$\frac{30}{100} \times 360° = 108°$
Indian	$\frac{20}{100} \times 360° = 72°$
Others	$\frac{10}{100} \times 360° = 36°$

The pie chart is as follows:

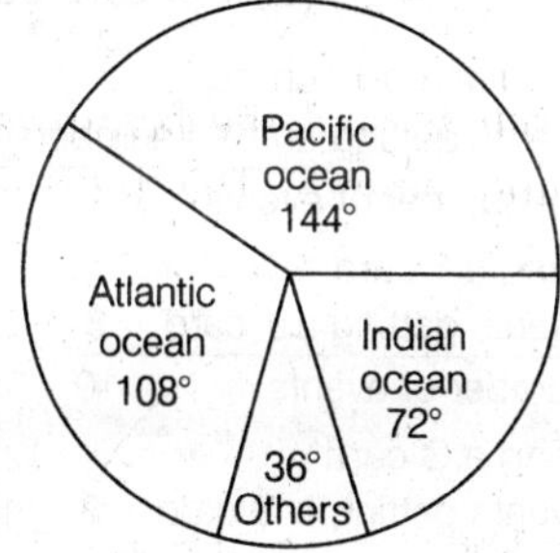

Q. 111 At a birthday party, the children spin a wheel to get a gift.

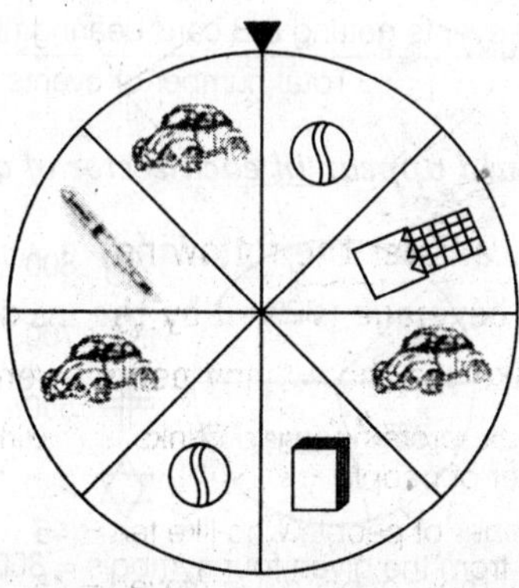

Find the probability of

(a) getting a ball (b) getting a toy car

(c) getting any toy except a chocolate.

Sol. (a) The probability of getting a ball

$$= \frac{\text{Number of events of getting a ball}}{\text{Total number of events}} = \frac{2}{8} = \frac{1}{4}$$

(b) The probability of getting a toy car

$$= \frac{\text{Number of events of getting a toy car}}{\text{Total number of events}} = \frac{3}{8}$$

(c) The probability of getting any gift except a chocolate

$$= \frac{\text{Number of events of getting any gift except a chocolate}}{\text{Total number of events}} = \frac{7}{8}$$

Q. 112 Sonia picks up a card from the given cards

R 1	Y 2	Y 3	R 4	B 5
B 6	G 7	Y 8	R 9	G 10

Find the probability of getting

(a) an odd number (b) a Y card

(c) a G card (d) a B card bearing number greater than 7.

Sol. (a) The probability of getting an odd number

$$= \frac{\text{Number of events getting an odd number}}{\text{Total number of events}} = \frac{5}{10} = \frac{1}{2}$$

(b) The probability of getting a Y card

$$= \frac{\text{Number of events getting a Y card}}{\text{Total number of events}} = \frac{3}{10}$$

(c) The probability of getting a G card

$$= \frac{\text{Number of events getting a G card}}{\text{Total number of events}} = \frac{2}{10} = \frac{1}{5}$$

(d) The probability of getting a B card bearing number greater than 7

$$= \frac{\text{Number of events getting a B card bearing number greater than 7}}{\text{Total number of events}} = \frac{0}{10} = 0$$

Identify which symbol should appear in each sector of questions **113 and 114.**

Q. 113

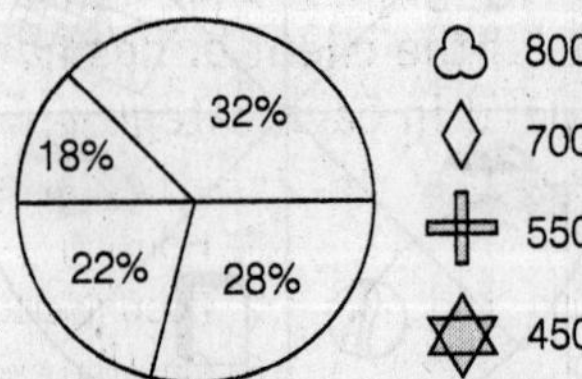

Sol. Total Quantity obtained from the given four symbols = 800 + 700 + 550 + 450 = 2500

From the pie chart,

$$28\% \text{ of } 2500 = \frac{28}{100} \times 2500 = 700$$

$$22\% \text{ of } 2500 = \frac{22}{100} \times 2500 = 550$$

$$18\% \text{ of } 2500 = \frac{18}{100} \times 2500 = 450$$

$$32\% \text{ of } 2500 = \frac{32}{100} \times 2500 = 800$$

Thus, 32% → ♧

28% → ◊

22% → ✢

18% → ✡

Q. 114

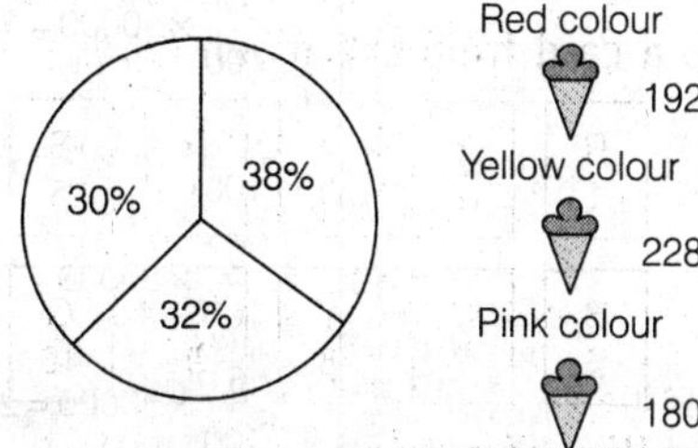

Sol. Total quantity obtained from the given three colours $= 192 + 228 + 180 = 600$

Also, $600 = 100\%$

or $1 = \frac{100}{600}\% = \frac{1}{6}\%$

or $192 = \frac{1}{6} \times 192 = 32\%$

or $228 = \frac{1}{6} \times 228 = 38\%$

or $180 = \frac{1}{6} \times 180 = 30\%$

∴ Red colour → 32%

Yellow colour → 38%

Pink colour → 30%

Q. 115 A financial counselor gave a client this pie chart describing how to budget his income. If the client brings home ₹ 50000 each month, how much should he spend in each category?

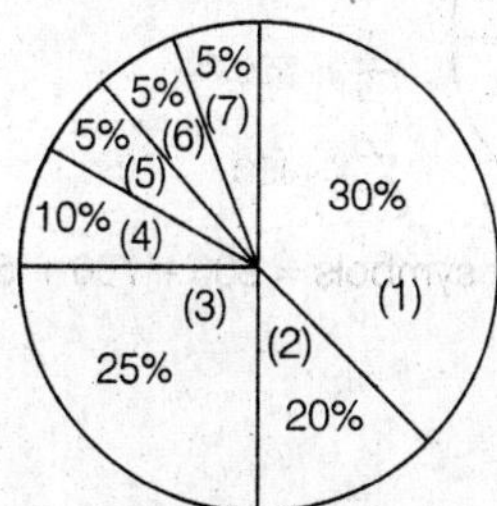

1. Housing
2. Food (including eating out)
3. Car loan and maintenance
4. Utilities
5. Phone
6. Clothing
7. Entertainment

Sol. Monthly income = ₹ 50000

Category	Money spent
Housing	$\frac{30}{100} \times 50000 = 15000$
Food (including eating out)	$\frac{20}{100} \times 50000 = 10000$
Car loan and maintenance	$\frac{25}{100} \times 50000 = 12500$
Utilities	$\frac{10}{100} \times 50000 = 5000$
Phone	$\frac{5}{100} \times 50000 = 2500$
Clothing	$\frac{5}{100} \times 50000 = 2500$
Entertainment	$\frac{5}{100} \times 50000 = 2500$

Q. 116 Following is a pie chart showing the amount spent (in ₹ thousands) by a company on various modes of advertising for a product.

Now, answer the following questions.

(i) Which type of media advertising is the greatest amount of the total?

(ii) Which type of media advertising is the least amount of the total?

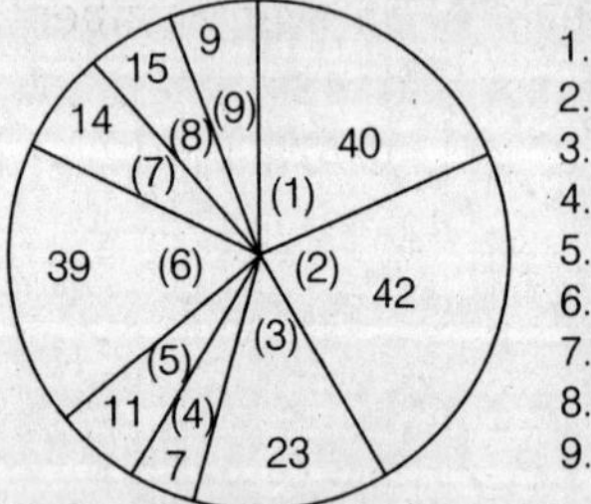

1. Television
2. Newspaper
3. Magazines
4. Radio
5. Business papers
6. Direct mail
7. Yellow page
8. Outdoor
9. Miscellaneous

Sol. (i) The greatest amount of the total is spent in the advertisement of newspaper, i.e. ₹ 42.

(ii) The least amount of the total is spent in the advertisement of radio, i.e. ₹ 7 thousand.

3

Square-Square Root and Cube-Cube Root

Multiple Choice Questions (MCQs)

Q. 1 196 is the square of

(a) 11 (b) 12
(c) 14 (d) 16

Sol. *(c)* Square of $11 = 11 \times 11 = 121$

Square of $12 = 12 \times 12 = 144$

Square of $14 = 14 \times 14 - 196$

Clearly, 196 is the square of 14.

Q. 2 Which of the following is a square of an even number?

(a) 144 (b) 169
(c) 441 (d) 625

Sol. *(a)* Here, $144 = (12)^2$

Similarly, $169 = (13)^2$

$441 = (21)^2$

$625 = (25)^2$

Thus, 144 is a square of an even number.

Alternate Method

We know that, square of an even number is always an even number. Hence, 169, 441 and 625 are not even numbers. So, only 144 is an even number, which is the square of 12.

Q. 3 A number ending in 9 will have the unit's place of its square as

(a) 3 (b) 9
(c) 1 (d) 6

Sol. *(c)* We know that, if a number is ending in 1 or 9 in the unit's place, then its square ends in 1.

The number ending in 9, will have the unit's place of its square as 1. $[\because 9 \times 9 = 81]$

Q. 4 **Which of the following will have 4 at the unit's place?**

(a) 14^2 (b) 62^2 (c) 27^2 (d) 35^2

Sol. ***(b)*** The unit place of the square of $14 = 4^2 = 16 = 6$

The unit place of the square of $62 = 2^2 = 4$ $[\because 2^2 = 4]$

The unit place of the square of $27 = 7^2 = 49 = 9$

The unit place of the square of $35 = 5^2 = 25 = 5$

Clearly, 62^2 has 4 at the unit's place.

Q. 5 **How many natural numbers lie between 5^2 and 6^2?**

(a) 9 (b) 10 (c) 11 (d) 12

Sol. ***(b)*** The natural numbers lying between 5^2 and 6^2, i.e. between 25 and 36 are 26, 27, 28, 29, 30, 31, 32, 33, 34 and 35.

Hence, 10 natural numbers lie between 5^2 and 6^2.

Q. 6 **Which of the following cannot be a perfect square?**

(a) 841 (b) 529 (c) 198 (d) All of these

Sol. ***(c)*** We know that, a number ending with digits 2, 3, 7 or 8 can never be a perfect square.

So, 198 cannot be written in the form of a perfect square.

Q. 7 **The one's digit of the cube of 23 is**

(a) 6 (b) 7 (c) 3 (d) 9

Sol. ***(b)*** We know that, the cubes of the numbers ending with digits 3 and 7, have 7 and 3 at one's digit, respectively.

So, the one's digit of the cube of 23 is 7.

Q. 8 **A square board has an area of 144 sq units. How long is each side of the board?**

(a) 11 units (b) 12 units (c) 13 units (d) 14 units

Sol. ***(b)*** Given, area of square board = 144 sq units

$\therefore$ $(\text{Side})^2 = 144$ $[\because \text{area of square} = (\text{side})^2]$

$\Rightarrow$ $(\text{Side})^2 = (12)^2$

$\Rightarrow$ Side = 12 units

Hence, the length of each side of the board is 12 units.

Q. 9 **Which letter best represents the location of $\sqrt{25}$ on a number line?**

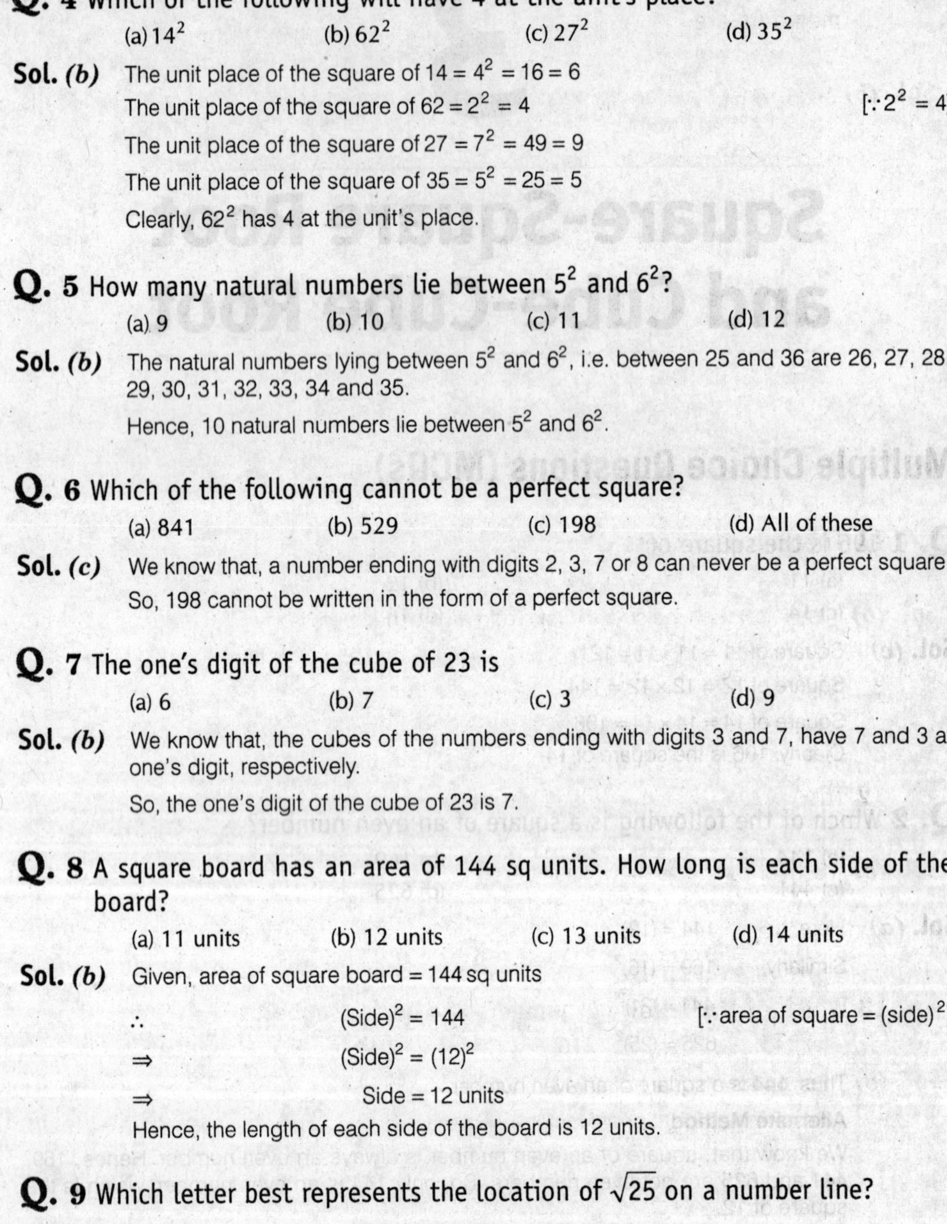

(a) A (b) B (c) C (d) D

Sol. ***(c)*** We have, $\sqrt{25} = 5$

Therefore, 5 at letter C represents the best location of $\sqrt{25}$ on number line.

Q. 10 If one member of a pythagorean triplet is $2m$, then the other two members are

(a) m, m^2+1 (b) m^2+1, m^2-1 (c) m^2, m^2-1 (d) $m^2, m+1$

Sol. *(b)* We know that, for any natural number m greater than 1, $(2m, m^2-1, m^2+1)$ is a pythagorean triplet.

So, one number is $2m$, then other two numbers are m^2+1 and m^2-1.

e.g. If one number is 4, then the pythagorean triplet,

$$2m = 4$$

$$\Rightarrow \quad m = 2$$

$$m^2+1 = 2^2+1 = 4+1 = 5$$

$$\text{and} \quad m^2-1 = 2^2-1 = 4-1 = 3$$

$$\text{Now,} \quad 3^2+4^2 = 5^2$$

$$\Rightarrow \quad 9+16 = 25$$

$$\Rightarrow \quad 25 = 25$$

So, 3, 4 and 5 are pythagorean triplets.

Q. 11 The sum of successive odd numbers 1, 3, 5, 7, 9, 11, 13 and 15 is

(a) 81 (b) 64 (c) 49 (d) 36

Sol. *(b)* We know that, the sum of first n odd natural numbers is n^2.

Given odd numbers are 1, 3, 5, 7, 9, 11, 13 and 15.

So, number of odd numbers, $n = 8$

$\therefore$ The sum of given odd numbers $= n^2 = (8)^2 = 64$

Q. 12 The sum of first n odd natural numbers is

(a) $2n+1$ (b) n^2 (c) n^2-1 (d) n^2+1

Sol. *(b)* Sum of first n odd natural numbers $= \Sigma(2n-1) = 2\,\Sigma n - n$

$$= \frac{2 \times n(n+1)}{2} - n = n(n+1) - n = n^2+n-n = n^2$$

Q. 13 Which of the following numbers is a perfect cube?

(a) 243 (b) 216 (c) 392 (d) 8640

Sol. *(b)* **For option (a)** We have, 243

Resolving 243 into prime factors, we have

$$243 = 3 \times 3 \times 3 \times 3 \times 3$$

Grouping the factors in triplets of equal factors, we get

$$243 = (3 \times 3 \times 3) \times 3 \times 3$$

Clearly, in grouping, the factors in triplets of equal factors, we are left with two factors 3×3.

Therefore, 243 is not a perfect cube.

For option (b) We have, 216

Resolving 216 into prime factors, we have

$$216 = 2 \times 2 \times 2 \times 3 \times 3 \times 3$$

Grouping the factors in triplets of equal factors, we get

$$216 = (2\times2\times2)\times(3\times3\times3)$$

Clearly, in grouping, the factors of triplets of equal factors, no factor is left over.

So, 216 is a perfect cube.

For option (c) We have, 392

Resolving 392 into prime factors, we get

$$392 = 2\times2\times2\times7\times7$$

Grouping the factors in triplets of equal factors, we get

$$392 = (2\times2\times2)\times7\times7$$

Clearly, in grouping, the factors in triplets of equal factors, we are left with two factors 7×7.

Therefore, 392 is not a perfect cube.

For option (d) We have, 8640

Resolving 8640 into prime factors, we get

$$8640 = 2\times2\times2\times2\times2\times2\times3\times3\times3\times5$$

Grouping the factors in triplets of equal factors, we get

$$8640 = (2\times2\times2)\times(2\times2\times2)\times(3\times3\times3)\times5$$

Clearly, in grouping, the factors in triplets of equal factors, we are left with one factor 5.

Therefore, 8640 in not a perfect cube.

After solving, it is clear that option (b) is correct.

Q. 14 The hypotenuse of a right angled triangle with its legs of lengths $3x \times 4x$ is

(a) $5x$ (b) $7x$ (c) $16x$ (d) $25x$

Sol. *(a)* Given, lengths of the legs of right angled triangle are $3x$ and $4x$.

Now, hypotenuse $= \sqrt{(3x)^2 + (4x)^2}$ [using Pythagoras theorem]

$$= \sqrt{9x^2 + 16x^2}$$

$$= \sqrt{25x^2} = 5x$$

Q. 15 The next two numbers in the number pattern 1, 4, 9, 16, 25,... are

(a) 35, 48 (b) 36, 49 (c) 36, 48 (d) 35, 49

Sol. *(b)* We have, 1, 4, 9, 16, 25, ...

The number pattern can be written as $(1)^2, (2)^2, (3)^2, (4)^2, (5)^2$, ...

Hence, the next two numbers are $(6)^2$ and $(7)^2$, i.e. 36 and 49.

Q. 16 Which among 43^2, 67^2, 52^2, 59^2 would end with digit 1?

(a) 43^2 (b) 67^2 (c) 52^2 (d) 59^2

Sol. *(d)* We know that, the unit's digit of the square of a natural number is the unit's digit of the square of the digit at unit's place of the given natural number.

$\therefore$ Unit's digit of $43^2 = 9$ [$\because 3^2 = 9$]

Unit's digit of $67^2 = 9$ [$\because$ unit's digit of 7^2 is 9]

Unit's digit of $52^2 = 4$ [$\because 2^2 = 4$]

Unit's digit of $59^2 = 1$ [$\because$ unit's digit of 9^2 is 1]

Clearly, the square of 59 end with digit 1.

Q. 17 A perfect square can never have the following digit in its one's place.

(a) 1 (b) 8 (c) 0 (d) 6

Sol. *(b)* We know that, a number ending with digits 2, 3, 7 or 8 can never be a perfect square.

Clearly, a perfect square can never have the digit 8 in its one's place.

Q. 18 Which of the following numbers is not a perfect cube?

(a) 216 (b) 567 (c) 125 (d) 343

Sol. *(b)* $216 = 6 \times 6 \times 6$, $567 = 3 \times 3 \times 3 \times 3 \times 7$

$125 = 5 \times 5 \times 5$, $343 = 7 \times 7 \times 7$

Clearly, 567 is not a perfect cube, because in grouping, the factors in triplets of equal factors, we are left with two factors 3×7.

Q. 19 $\sqrt[3]{1000}$ is equal to

(a) 10 (b) 100 (c) 1 (d) None of these

Sol. *(a)* We have, $\sqrt[3]{1000} = \sqrt[3]{10 \times 10 \times 10} = \sqrt[3]{(10)^3} = (10)^{3/3} = 10$

Q. 20 If m is the square of a natural number n, then n is

(a) the square of m (b) greater than m

(c) equal to m (d) $\sqrt{m}$

Sol. *(d)* Given, m is the square of n, i.e. $m = n^2$

Taking square root both sides, we get

$$n = \sqrt{m}$$

Q. 21 A perfect square number having n digits, where n is even, will have square root with

(a) $(n + 1)$ digit (b) $\frac{n}{2}$ digit (c) $\frac{n}{3}$ digit (d) $\left(\frac{n+1}{2}\right)$ digit

Sol. *(b)* A perfect square number having n digits, where n is even, will have square root with $\frac{n}{2}$ digit.

Q. 22 If m is the cube root of n, then n is

(a) m^3 (b) $\sqrt{m}$ (c) $\frac{m}{3}$ (d) $\sqrt[3]{m}$

Sol. *(a)* Given, m is the cube root of n, i.e. $m = \sqrt[3]{n}$

$$\Rightarrow \quad m = (n)^{1/3}$$

$$\Rightarrow \quad m^3 = (n)^{3/3} \quad \text{[taking cube on both sides]}$$

$$\therefore \quad m^3 = n$$

Q. 23 The value of $\sqrt{248+\sqrt{52+\sqrt{144}}}$ is

(a) 14 (b) 12 (c) 16 (d) 13

Sol. *(c)* We have, $\sqrt{248+\sqrt{52+\sqrt{144}}}$

$= \sqrt{248+\sqrt{52+12}}$ [$\because$ square root of 144 = 12]

$= \sqrt{248+\sqrt{64}}$

$= \sqrt{248+8}$ [$\because$ square root of 64 = 8]

$= \sqrt{256} = 16$ [$\because$ square root of 256 = 16]

Q. 24 Given that, $\sqrt{4096} = 64$, the value of $\sqrt{4096}+\sqrt{40.96}$ is

(a) 74 (b) 60.4 (c) 64.4 (d) 70.4

Sol. *(d)* Given, $\sqrt{4096} = 64$

So, $\sqrt{4096}+\sqrt{40.96}$

$= 64 + \sqrt{4096 \times 10^{-2}}$

$= 64 + \sqrt{4096}\sqrt{10^{-2}}$

$= 64 + 64 \times 10^{-1}$

$= 64 + 6.4 = 70.4$

Fill in the Blanks

In questions 25 to 48, fill in the blanks to make the statements true.

Q. 25 There are ______ perfect squares between 1 and 100.

Sol. 8

There are 8 perfect squares between 1 and 100, i.e. 4, 9, 16, 25, 36, 49, 64 and 81.

Q. 26 There are ______ perfect cubes between 1 and 1000.

Sol. 8

There are 8 perfect cubes between 1 and 1000, i.e. 8, 27, 64, 125, 216, 343 and 729.

Q. 27 The unit's digit in the square of 1294 is ______.

Sol. 6

We know that, the unit's digit of the square of a number having digit at unit's place as 4 or 6 is 6.

Hence, the units digit in the square of 1294 is 6 as $4 \times 4 = 16$.

Q. 28 The square of 500 will have ______ zeroes.

Sol. four

The square of 500 = $(500)^2$

$= 500 \times 500 = 250000$

Hence, the square of 500 will have four zeroes.

Q. 29 There are ______ natural numbers between n^2 and $(n+1)^2$.

Sol. $2n$

Natural numbers between n^2 and $(n+1)^2 = [(n+1)^2 - n^2] - 1$

$$= [n^2 + 2n + 1 - n^2] - 1$$

$$= 2n + 1 - 1 = 2n$$

Q. 30 The square root of 24025 will have ______ digits.

Sol. 3

Given number is 24025.

Here, number of digits, $n = 5$ (odd)

$\therefore$ Number of digits in the square root of $24025 = \frac{n+1}{2} = \frac{5+1}{2} = 3$

Q. 31 The square of 5.5 is ______.

Sol. 30.25

Square of $5.5 = (5.5)^2 = 5.5 \times 5.5 = 30.25$

Q. 32 The square root of 5.3×5.3 is ______.

Sol. 5.3

Square root of $5.3 \times 5.3 = \sqrt{(5.3)^2}$

$$= (5.3)^{2/2} = 5.3$$

Q. 33 The cube of 100 will have ______ zeroes.

Sol. 6

Cube of $100 = 100^3$

$$= 100 \times 100 \times 100$$

$$= 1000000$$

Q. 34 1m^2 = ______ cm^2.

Sol. 10000 cm^2

$$1\text{m}^2 = (100\text{ cm})^2 \quad [\because 1\text{ m} = 100\text{ cm}]$$

$$= 10000\text{ cm}^2$$

Q. 35 1m^3 = ______ cm^3.

Sol. 1000000 cm^3

$$1\text{m}^3 = (100\text{ cm})^3 \quad [\because 1\text{m} = 100\text{cm}]$$

$$= (100 \times 100 \times 100)\text{ cm}^3$$

$$= 1000000\text{ cm}^3$$

Q. 36 One's digit in the cube of 38 is ______.

Sol. 2

We know that, the cube of a number having 8 at one's place

$\therefore$ One's digit in cube of 38 = 2

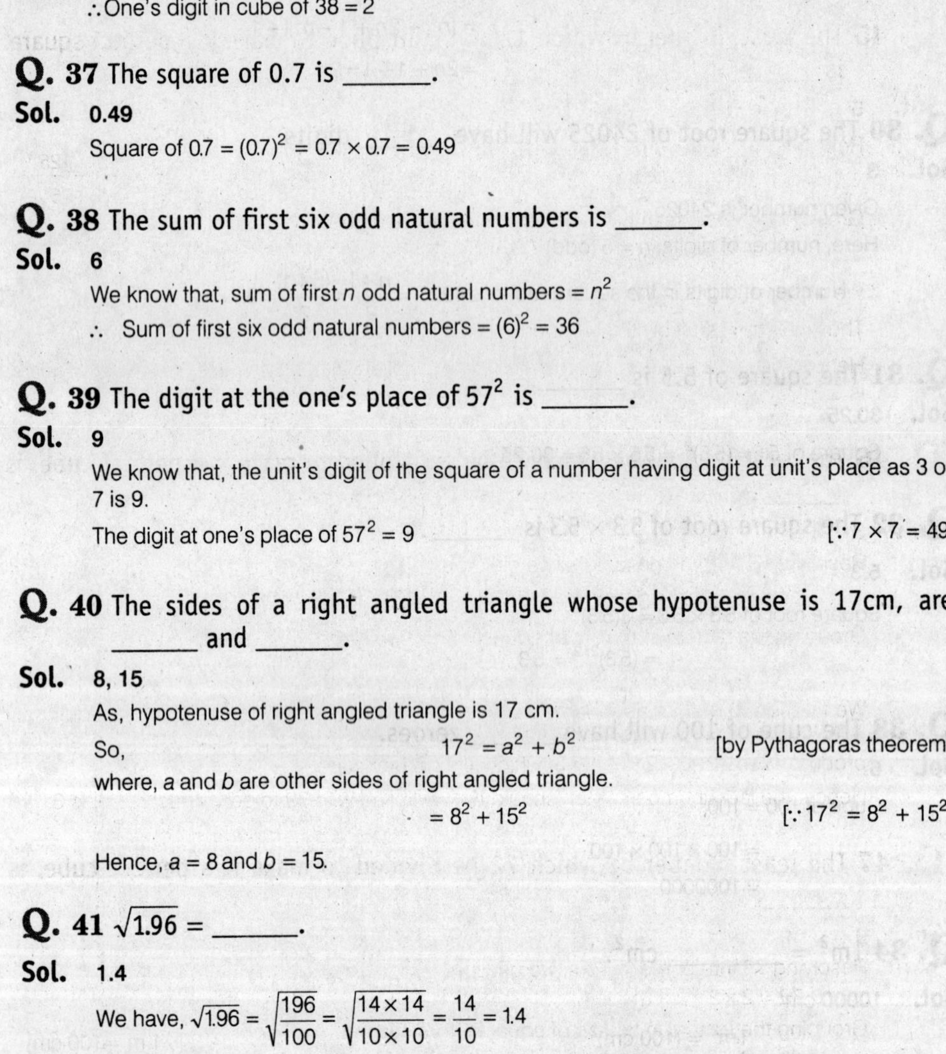

Q. 37 The square of 0.7 is ______.

Sol. 0.49

Square of 0.7 = $(0.7)^2 = 0.7 \times 0.7 = 0.49$

Q. 38 The sum of first six odd natural numbers is ______.

Sol. 6

We know that, sum of first n odd natural numbers = n^2

$\therefore$ Sum of first six odd natural numbers = $(6)^2 = 36$

Q. 39 The digit at the one's place of 57^2 is ______.

Sol. 9

We know that, the unit's digit of the square of a number having digit at unit's place as 3 or 7 is 9.

The digit at one's place of $57^2 = 9$ $[\because 7 \times 7 = 49]$

Q. 40 The sides of a right angled triangle whose hypotenuse is 17cm, are ______ and ______.

Sol. 8, 15

As, hypotenuse of right angled triangle is 17 cm.

So, $17^2 = a^2 + b^2$ [by Pythagoras theorem]

where, a and b are other sides of right angled triangle.

$= 8^2 + 15^2$ $[\because 17^2 = 8^2 + 15^2]$

Hence, $a = 8$ and $b = 15$.

Q. 41 $\sqrt{1.96}$ = ______.

Sol. 1.4

We have, $\sqrt{1.96} = \sqrt{\frac{196}{100}} = \sqrt{\frac{14 \times 14}{10 \times 10}} = \frac{14}{10} = 1.4$

Q. 42 $(1.2)^3$ = ______.

Sol. 1.728

We have, $(1.2)^3 = \left(\frac{12}{10}\right)^3 = \frac{12}{10} \times \frac{12}{10} \times \frac{12}{10} = \frac{1728}{1000} = 1.728$

Q. 43 The cube of an odd number is always an ______ number.

Sol. odd

We know that, the cubes of all odd natural numbers are odd.

Q. 44 The cube root of a number x is denoted by ______.

Sol. $\sqrt[3]{x}$ or $x^{1/3}$

The cube root of a number x is denoted by $\sqrt[3]{x}$ or $x^{1/3}$.

Q. 45 The least number by which 125 be multiplied to make it a perfect square, is ______.

Sol. 5

Resolving 125 into prime factors, we get

$$125 = 5 \times 5 \times 5$$

5	125
5	25
5	5
	1

Grouping the factors in triplets of equal factors, we get

$$125 = (5 \times 5) \times 5$$

We observe that 5 is without a pair.

Thus, we must multiply the number by 5, so that the product is a perfect square.

Hence, the least number, which should be multiplied with 125 to make it a perfect square, is 5.

Q. 46 The least number by which 72 be multiplied to make it a perfect cube, is ______.

Sol. 3

Resolving 72 into prime factors, we get

$$72 = 2 \times 2 \times 2 \times 3 \times 3$$

Grouping the factors in triplets of equal factors, we get

$$72 = (2 \times 2 \times 2) \times 3 \times 3$$

We find that 2 occurs as a prime factor of 72 thrice, but 3 occurs as a prime factor only twice. Thus, if we multiply 72 by 3, 3 will also occurs as a prime factor thrice and the product will be $2 \times 2 \times 2 \times 3 \times 3 \times 3$, which is a perfect cube.

Hence, the least number, which should be multiplied with 72 to get perfect cube, is 3.

Q. 47 The least number by which 72 be divided to make it a perfect cube, is ______.

Sol. 9

Resolving 72 into prime factors, we get

$$72 = 2 \times 2 \times 2 \times 3 \times 3$$

Grouping the factors in triplets of equal factors, we get

$$72 = (2 \times 2 \times 2) \times 3 \times 3$$

Clearly, if we divide 72 by 3×3, the quotient would be $2 \times 2 \times 2$, which is a perfect cube.

Hence, the least number by which 72 be divided to make it, a perfect cube, is 9.

Q. 48 Cube of a number ending in 7 will end in the digit ______.

Sol. 3

We know that, the cubes of the numbers ending in digits 3 or 7 ends in digits 7 or 3, respectively.

i.e $\quad 7 \times 7 \times 7 = 343$

Hence, the cube of a number ending in 7 will end in the digit 3.

True / False

In questions 49 to 86, state whether the statements are True or False.

Q. 49 The square of 86 will have 6 at the unit's place.

Sol. ***True***

We know that, the unit's digit of the square of a number having digit at unit's place as 4 or 6 is 6.

Q. 50 The sum of two perfect squares is a perfect square.

Sol. ***False***

e.g. 16 and 25 are the perfect squares, but $16 + 25 = 41$ is not a perfect square.

Q. 51 The product of two perfect squares is a perfect square.

Sol. ***True***

e.g. If 4 and 25 are the perfect square, then $4 \times 25 = 100$ is also a perfect square.
Clearly, the product of two perfect squares is a perfect square.

Q. 52 There is no square number between 50 and 60.

Sol. ***True***

Numbers between 50 and 60 are 51, 52, 53, 54, 55, 56, 57, 58 and 59.
We observed that there is no square number between 50 and 60.

Q. 53 The square root of 1521 is 31.

Sol. ***False***

As, the square of $31 = (31)^2 = 31 \times 31 = 961$

Q. 54 Each prime factor appears 3 times in its cube.

Sol. ***True***

If a^3 is the cube and m is one of the prime factors of a. Then, m appears three times in a^3.

Q. 55 The square of 2.8 is 78.4.

Sol. ***False***

The square of $2.8 = (2.8)^2 = 2.8 \times 2.8 = 7.84$

Q. 56 The cube of 0.4 is 0.064.

Sol. ***True***

Cube of $0.4 = (0.4)^3 = 0.4 \times 0.4 \times 0.4 = 0.064$

Q. 57 The square root of 0.9 is 0.3.

Sol. ***False***

As, the square of $0.3 = (0.3)^2 = 0.3 \times 0.3 = 0.09$

Q. 58 The square of every natural number is always greater than the number itself.

Sol. ***False***

1 is a natural number and square of 1 is not greater than 1.

Q. 59 The cube root of 8000 is 200.

Sol. ***False***

We have, $\sqrt[3]{8000} = \sqrt[3]{(2\times2\times2)\times(2\times2\times2)\times(5\times5\times5)}$
$= 2\times2\times5 = 20$

Q. 60 There are five perfect cubes between 1 and 100.

Sol. ***False***

There are eight perfect cubes between 1 and 100, i.e. 8, 27, 64, 125, 216, 343, 512 and 729.

Q. 61 There are 200 natural numbers between 100^2 and 101^2.

Sol. ***True***

Natural numbers between 100^2 and 101^2

$= 101^2 - 100^2 - 1$ [$\because$ natural numbers between a and $b = b - a - 1$]

$= (101 + 100)(101 - 100) - 1 = 201 - 1 = 200$

Q. 62 The sum of first n odd natural numbers is n^2.

Sol. ***True***

Sum of odd natural numbers $= \Sigma(2n - 1) = \dfrac{2\times n\times(n+1)}{2} - n$

$= n^2 + n - n = n^2$

Q. 63 1000 is a perfect square.

Sol. ***False***

$1000 = 2\times2\times2\times5\times5\times5 = 2^2\times5^2\times2\times5$

Clearly, it is not a perfect square, because it has two unpaired factors 2 and 5.

Q. 64 A perfect square can have 8 as its unit's digit.

Sol. ***False***

A perfect square can never have 8 as its unit's digit.

Q. 65 For every natural number m, $(2m - 1, 2m^3 - 2m, 2m^2 - 2m + 1)$ is a pythagorean triplet.

Sol. ***False***

$\because \quad (2m-1)^2 \neq (2m^3 - 2m)^2 + (2m^2 - 2m + 1)^2$

$(2m^3 - 2m)^2 \neq (2m-1)^2 + (2m^2 - 2m + 1)^2$

and $(2m^2 - 2m + 1)^2 \neq (2m - 1)^2 + (2m^3 - 2m)^2$

Q. 66 All numbers of a pythagorean triplet are odd.

Sol. ***False***

3, 4 and 5 are the numbers of Pythagorean triplet as $5^2 = 4^2 + 3^2$

where, 4 is not an odd number.

Q. 67 For an integer a, a^3 is always greater than a^2.

Sol. ***False***

e.g. – 1 is an integer and $(-1)^3$, i.e. – 1 is not greater than $(-1)^2$, i.e. 1.

Q. 68 If x and y are integers such that $x^2 > y^2$, then $x^3 > y^3$.

Sol. ***False***

Suppose, – 1 and – 2 are integers.

Then, $(-2)^2 > (-1)^2 = 4 > 1$

and $(-2)^3 < (-1)^3 = -8 < -1$

Q. 69 Let x and y be natural numbers. If x divides y, then x^3 divides y^3.

Sol. ***True***

If x divides y, then $\frac{y}{x}$ is a natural number.

$\Rightarrow$ $\left(\frac{y}{x}\right)^3$ is also a natural number.

$\Rightarrow$ $\frac{y^3}{x^3}$ is a natural number.

$\Rightarrow$ x^3 divides y^3.

Q. 70 If a^2 ends in 5, then a^3 ends in 25.

Sol. ***False***

$\because (35)^2 = 1225$ ends in 5 and $(35)^3$, i.e. 42875 does not end in 25.

Q. 71 If a^2 ends in 9, then a^3 ends in 7.

Sol. ***False***

$\because (7)^2 = 49$ ends in 9 and $(7)^3$, i.e. 343 does not end in 7.

Q. 72 The square root of a perfect square of n digits will have $\left(\frac{n+1}{2}\right)$ digits, if n is odd.

Sol. ***True***

If the square has 3 digits, then its square root has 2 i.e. $\left(\frac{3+1}{2}\right)$ digits.

Similarly, if the square has 5 digits, then its square root has 3 i.e. $\left(\frac{5+1}{2}\right)$ digits.

Q. 73 Square root of a number x is denoted by $\sqrt{x}$.

Sol. ***True***

Square root of a number x is denoted by $\sqrt{x}$.

Q. 74 A number having 7 at its one's place will have 3 at the unit's place of its square.

Sol. ***False***

Square of $7 = 7 \times 7 = 49$

Square of $17 = 17 \times 17 = 289$

Square of $27 = 27 \times 27 = 729$

and so on.

Q. 75 A number having 7 at its one's place will have 3 at the one's place of its cube.

Sol. ***True***

Cube of $7 = 7 \times 7 \times 7 = 343$

Cube of $17 = 17 \times 17 \times 17 = 4913$

Cube of $27 = 27 \times 27 \times 27 = 19683$

and so on.

Q. 76 The cube of a one-digit number cannot be a two-digit number.

Sol. ***False***

e.g. 3 is a one-digit number and $(3)^3$, i.e. 27 is a two-digit number.

Q. 77 Cube of an even number is odd.

Sol. ***False***

We know that, the cube of an even number is always an even number.

e.g. 2 is an even number. Then, $2^3 = 2 \times 2 \times 2 = 8$

Clearly, 8 is also an even number.

Q. 78 Cube of an odd number is even.

Sol. ***False***

We know that, the cube of an odd number is always an odd number.

e.g. 3 is an odd number. Then, $3^3 = 3 \times 3 \times 3 = 27$

Clearly, 27 is not an even number.

Q. 79 Cube of an even number is even.

Sol. ***True***

We know that, the cube of an even number is always an even number.

e.g. 4 is an even number. Then, $4^3 = 4 \times 4 \times 4 = 64$

Clearly, 64 is also an even number.

Q. 80 Cube of an odd number is odd.

Sol. ***True***

We know that, the cube of an odd number is always an odd number.

e.g. 9 is an odd number.

Then, $9^3 = 9 \times 9 \times 9 = 729$

Clearly, 729 is also an odd number.

Q. 81 999 is a perfect cube.

Sol. ***False***

Resolving 999 into prime factors, we get

$$999 = 3 \times 3 \times 3 \times 37$$

3	999
3	333
3	111
37	37
	1

Grouping the factors in triplets of equal factors, we get

$$999 = (3 \times 3 \times 3) \times 37$$

Clearly, in grouping, the factors in triplets of equal factors, we are left with one factor 37.

Therefore, 999 is not a perfect cube.

Q. 82 363×81 is a perfect cube.

Sol. ***False***

$$\because \quad 363 \times 81 = 3 \times 11 \times 11 \times 3 \times 3 \times 3 \times 3$$
$$= 3 \times 3 \times 3 \times 3 \times 3 \times 11 \times 11$$

Grouping the factors in triplets of equal factors, we have

$$363 \times 81 = (3 \times 3 \times 3) \times 3 \times 3 \times 11 \times 11$$

Clearly, in grouping, the factors in triplets of equal factors, we are left with two factors 3×3 and 11×11.

Hence, 363×81 is not a perfect cube.

Q. 83 Cube roots of 8 are $+2$ and -2.

Sol. ***False***

Cube root of 8 is 2 only and cube root of -8 is -2.

Q. 84 $\sqrt[3]{8+27} = \sqrt[3]{8} + \sqrt[3]{27}$

Sol. ***False***

We have, $\sqrt[3]{8+27} \neq \sqrt[3]{8} + \sqrt[3]{27}$

$\because \quad \sqrt[3]{8} + \sqrt[3]{27} = \sqrt[3]{2 \times 2 \times 2} + \sqrt[3]{3 \times 3 \times 3} = 2 + 3 = 5$

But $\quad \sqrt[3]{8+27} = \sqrt[3]{35} \neq \sqrt[3]{125} = 5$

Q. 85 There is no cube root of a negative integer.

Sol. ***False***

e.g. Let -8 be a negative number.

Then, cube root of $-8 = \sqrt[3]{-8} = \sqrt[3]{(-2) \times (-2)(-2)} = -2$

Q. 86 Square of a number is positive, so the cube of that number will also be positive.

Sol. ***False***

e.g. $(-2)^2$, i.e. 4 is a positive number and $(-2)^3$. i.e. -8 is a negative number.

Q. 87 Write the first five square numbers.

Sol. First five square numbers are $1^2, 2^2, 3^2, 4^2$ and 5^2, i.e. 1, 4, 9, 16 and 25.

Q. 88 Write cubes of first three multiples of 3.

Sol. Since, the first three multiples of 3 are 3, 6 and 9.

Hence, the cubes of first three multiples of 3 are $(3)^3$, $(6)^3$ and $(9)^3$, i.e. 27, 216 and 729.

Q. 89 Show that 500 is not a perfect square.

Sol. Resolving 500 into prime factors, we have

2	500
2	250
5	125
5	25
5	5
	1

$$500 = 2 \times 2 \times 5 \times 5 \times 5$$

Grouping the factors into pairs of equal factors, we get

$$500 = (2 \times 2) \times (5 \times 5 \times 5)$$

Clearly, by grouping into pairs of equal factors, we are left with one factor 5, which cannot be paired.

Hence, 500 is not a perfect square.

Q. 90 Express 81 as the sum of first nine consecutive odd numbers.

Sol. $81 = (9)^2 = 1 + 3 + 5 + 7 + 9 + 11 + 13 + 15 + 17$

= Sum of first nine consecutive odd numbers

Q. 91 Using prime factorisation, find which of the following are perfect squares.

(a) 484
(b) 11250
(c) 841
(d) 729

Sol. (a) Prime factors of $484 = (2 \times 2) \times (11 \times 11)$

As grouping, there is no unpaired factor left over.

2	484
2	242
11	121
11	11
	1

So, 484 is a perfect square.

(b) Prime factors of $11250 = 2 \times (3 \times 3) \times (5 \times 5) \times (5 \times 5)$

As grouping, 2 has no pair.

2	11250
3	5625
3	1875
5	625
5	125
5	25
5	5
5	1

So, 11250 is not a perfect square.

(c) Prime factors of $841 = (29 \times 29)$

29	841
29	29
	1

As grouping, there is no unpaired factor left over.

So, 841 is a perfect square.

(d) Prime factors of $729 = (3 \times 3) \times (3 \times 3) \times (3 \times 3)$

As grouping, there is no unpaired factor left over.

3	729
3	243
3	81
3	27
3	9
3	3
3	1

So, 729 is a perfect square.

Q. 92 Using prime factorisation, find which of the following are perfect cubes.

(a) 128 (b) 343 (c) 729 (d) 1331

Sol. (a) We have, $128 = 2 \times 2 \times 2 \times 2 \times 2 \times 2 \times 2$

Since, 2 remains after grouping in triplets.

So, 128 is not a perfect cube.

(b) We have, $343 = 7 \times 7 \times 7$

Since, the prime factors appear in triplets.

So, 343 is a perfect cube.

(c) We have, $729 = 3 \times 3 \times 3 \times 3 \times 3 \times 3$

Since, the prime factors appear in triplets.

So, 729 is a perfect cube.

(d) We have, $1331 = 11 \times 11 \times 11$

Since, the prime factors appear in triplets.

So, 1331 is a perfect cube.

Q. 93 Using distributive law, find the squares of

(a) 101 (b) 72

Sol. (a) We have, $101^2 = 101 \times 101$

$$= 101\,(100 + 1) = 10100 + 101 = 10201$$

(b) We have, $72^2 = 72 \times 72 = 72 \times (70 + 2)$

$$= 5040 + 144 = 5184$$

Q. 94 Can a right angled triangle with sides 6cm, 10cm and 8cm be formed? Give reason.

Sol. We know that, the sum of the squares of two smaller sides is equal to the square of longer side.

$\because 10^2 = 100 = 64 + 36 = 8^2 + 6^2$

Hence, 6 cm, 8 cm and 10 cm are the sides of a right angled triangle.

Q. 95 Write the pythagorean triplet whose one of the numbers is 4.

Sol. We know that, for any natural number greater than 1, $(2m, m^2 - 1, m^2 + 1)$ is a pythagorean triplet.

So, one number is $2m$, then other two numbers are m^2+1 and $m^2 - 1$.

Hence, one number is 4, then pythagorean triplet,

$$2m = 4 \Rightarrow m = 2$$

$\therefore \quad m^2 + 1 = 2^2 + 1 = 4 + 1 = 5$

and $\quad m^2 - 1 = 2^2 - 1 = 4 - 1 = 3$

Now, $\quad 3^2 + 4^2 = 5^2$

$\Rightarrow \quad 9 + 16 = 25 \Rightarrow 25 = 25$

So, 3, 4 and 5 are pythagorean triplets.

Q. 96 Using prime factorisation, find the square roots of

(a) 11025 (b) 4761

Sol. (a) We have, 11025

3	11025
3	3675
5	1225
5	245
7	49
7	7
	1

Now, $\quad 11025 = \underline{3 \times 3} \times \underline{5 \times 5} \times \underline{7 \times 7}$

$\therefore$ Square root of $11025 = \sqrt{11025} = 3 \times 5 \times 7 = 105$

(b) We have, 4761

3	4761
3	1587
23	529
23	23
	1

Now, $\quad 4761 = \underline{3 \times 3} \times \underline{23 \times 23}$

$\therefore$ Square root of $4761 = \sqrt{4761} = 3 \times 23 = 69$

Q. 97 Using prime factorisation, find the cube roots of

(a) 512

(b) 2197

Sol. (a) We have, 512

2	512
2	256
2	128
2	64
2	32
2	16
2	8
2	4
2	2
	1

Now, $512 = 2 \times 2 \times 2 \times 2 \times 2 \times 2 \times 2 \times 2 \times 2$

$\therefore$ $\sqrt[3]{512} = 2 \times 2 \times 2$

$= 8$

(b) We have, 2197

13	2197
13	169
13	13
	1

Now, $2197 = 13 \times 13 \times 13$

$\therefore$ $\sqrt[3]{2197} = 13$

Q. 98 Is 176 a perfect square? If not, find the smallest number by which it should be multiplied to get a perfect square.

Sol. Prime factors of $176 = 2 \times 2 \times 2 \times 2 \times 11$

Here, 11 has no pair.

So, it is not a perfect square and 11 is the smallest number by which 176 should be multiplied to get a perfect square.

Then, $176 \times 11 = 2^2 \times 2^2 \times 11 \times 11$

$= 2^2 \times 2^2 \times 11^2$

$= 1936 = (44)^2$

which is a perfect square of 44.

Hence, the smallest number is 11 by which it should be multiplied to get a perfect square.

Q. 99 Is 9720 a perfect cube? If not, find the smallest number by which it should be divided to get a perfect cube.

Sol. Prime factors of $9720 = 2 \times 2 \times 2 \times 3 \times 3 \times 3 \times 3 \times 3 \times 5$

The prime factors 3 and 5 do not appear in group of triplets.

So, 9720 is not a perfect cube.

If we divide the number by $3\times3\times5$, then the prime factorisation of the quotient will not contain $3\times3\times5=45$.

2	9720
2	4860
2	2430
3	1215
3	405
3	135
3	45
3	15
5	5
	1

$\therefore\ 9720\div45=\underline{2\times2\times2}\times\underline{3\times3\times3}$

$=216$

$=(6)^3$

Hence, the smallest number by which 9720 should be divided to get a perfect cube, is 45.

Q. 100 Write two pythagorean triplets, each having one of the numbers as 5.

Sol. As, $5^2=3^2+4^2$

and $13^2=12^2+5^2$

Hence, 3, 4, 5 and 12, 5, 13 are the two pythagorean triplets.

Q. 101 By what smallest number should 216 be divided, so that the quotient is a perfect square? Also, find the square root of the quotient.

Sol. Prime factors of $216=2\times2\times2\times3\times3\times3$

Grouping the factors into pairs of equal factors, we get

$216=2\times2\times2\times3\times3\times3$

We find that there is no prime factor to form a pair with 2 and 3.

Therefore, we must divide the number by 6, so that the quotient becomes a perfect square.

If we divide the given number by 2×3 i.e.6, then

New number $=\dfrac{216}{6}=36$

Taking one factor from each, we get square root of new number (quotient)

$=2\times3=6$

Q. 102 By what smallest number should 3600 be multiplied, so that the quotient is a perfect cube. Also, find the cube root of the quotient.

Sol. Prime factors of $3600=2\times2\times2\times2\times3\times3\times5\times5$

Grouping the factors into triplets of equal factors, we get

$3600 = \underline{2 \times 2 \times 2} \times 2 \times 3 \times 3 \times 5 \times 5$

2	3600
2	1800
2	900
2	450
3	225
3	75
5	25
5	5
	1

We know that, if a number is to be a perfect cube, then each of its prime factors must occur thrice.

We find that 2 occurs once 3 and 5 occurs twice only.

Hence, the smallest number, by which the given number must be multiplied in order that the product is a perfect cube $= 2 \times 2 \times 3 \times 5 = 60$

Also, product $= 3600 \times 60 = 216000$

Now, arranging into triplets of equal prime factors, we have

$$216000 = \underline{2 \times 2 \times 2} \times \underline{2 \times 2 \times 2} \times \underline{3 \times 3 \times 3} \times \underline{5 \times 5 \times 5}$$

Taking one factor from each triplets, we get

$$\sqrt[3]{216000} = 2 \times 2 \times 3 \times 5 = 60$$

Q. 103 **Find the square root of the following by long division method.**

(a) 1369 **(b) 5625**

Sol. (a) We have, 1369

	37
3	$\overline{13}\,\overline{69}$
	9
67	469
	469
	0

$\therefore \quad \sqrt{1369} = 37$

(b) We have, 5625

	75
7	$\overline{56}\,\overline{25}$
	49
145	725
	725
	0

$\therefore \quad \sqrt{5625} = 75$

Q. 104 **Find the square root of the following by long division method.**

(a) 27.04 **(b) 1.44**

Sol. (a) We have, 27.04

	5.2
5	$\overline{27}.\overline{04}$
	25
102	204
	204
	0

(b) We have, 1.44

	1.2
1	$\overline{1}.\overline{44}$
	1
22	44
	44
	0

$\therefore \quad \sqrt{1.44} = 1.2$

Q. 105 What is the least number, that should be subtracted from 1385 to get a perfect square? Also, find the square root of the perfect square.

Sol. First, find the square root of 1385 by long division method.

	37
3	$\overline{13}\,\overline{85}$
	9
67	485
	469
	16

Hence, the least number is 16, which should be subtracted from 1385 to get a perfect square and the required perfect square number = 1385 – 16 = 1369

$\therefore$ Square root of 1369 = $\sqrt{37 \times 37} = 37$

Q. 106 What is the least number that should be added to 6200 to make it a perfect square?

Sol. First, find the square root of 6200 by long division method.

	79
7	$\overline{62}\,\overline{00}$
	49
149	1300
	1341
	– 41

Hence, the least number is 41, which should be added to 6200 to make it a perfect square and the perfect square number = 6200 + 41 = 6241

$\therefore$ Square root of 6241 = $\sqrt{79 \times 79} = 79$

Q. 107 Find the least number of four digits that is a perfect square.

Sol. Since, the least number of four digits is 1000.

Now, find the square root of 1000 by long division method.

	32
3	$\overline{10}\,\overline{00}$
	9
62	100
	124
	– 24

Hence, the least number of four digits, i.e. a perfect square = 1000 + 24 = 1024

Q. 108 Find the greatest number of three digits that is a perfect square.

Sol. Since, the greatest number of three digits is 1000.

Now, find the square root of 1000 by long division method.

	31
3	$\overline{10}\,\overline{00}$
	9
61	100
	61
	39

Hence, the greatest number of three digits, i.e. a perfect square = 1000 − 39 = 961

Q. 109 Find the least square number, which is exactly divisible by 3, 4, 5, 6 and 8.

Sol. The least square number divisible by each of 3, 4, 5, 6 and 8, is equal to the LCM of 3, 4, 5, 6 and 8.

2	3, 4, 5, 6, 8
2	3, 2, 5, 3, 4
2	3, 1, 5, 3, 2
3	3, 1, 5, 3, 1
5	1, 1, 5, 1, 1
	1, 1, 1, 1, 1

$\therefore$ LCM of 3, 4, 5, 6 and 8 = $2\times2\times2\times3\times5 = 120$

The prime factorisation of 120 = $(2\times2)\times2\times3\times5$

Here, prime factors 2, 3 and 5 are unpaired. Clearly, to make it a perfect square, it must be multiplied by $2\times3\times5$, i.e. 30.

Therefore, required number = $120\times30 = 3600$

Hence, the least square number is 3600.

Q. 110 Find the length of the side of a square, if the length of its diagonal is 10 cm.

Sol. Given, length of diagonal = 10 cm

Suppose, the length of side of a square is x cm.

By using Pythagoras theorem,

$$(10)^2 = x^2 + x^2$$

$\Rightarrow$ $100 = 2x^2$

$\Rightarrow$ $x^2 = 50$

$\Rightarrow$ $x = \sqrt{50}$ [taking square root on both sides]

$\therefore$ $x = 5\sqrt{2}$ cm

Hence, the length of the side of square is $\sqrt{50}$ or $5\sqrt{2}$ cm.

Q. 111 A decimal number is multiplied by itself. If the product is 51.84, then find the number.

Sol. Let the number be x. Then, product $= x \times x = x^2$

But product = 51.84 [given]

$\therefore \quad x^2 = 51.84$

$\Rightarrow \quad x = \sqrt{51.84}$

Now, place the bar over the numbers, then square root is given below.

$\therefore \quad x = \sqrt{51.84} = 7.2$

	7.2
7	$\overline{51}.\overline{84}$
	49
142	284
	284
	0

Hence, the required number is 7.2.

Q. 112 Find the decimal fraction, which when multiplied by itself, gives 84.64.

Sol. Let the decimal fraction be x.

When a decimal fraction is multiplied by itself, then product $= x \times x = x^2$

But product = 84.64 [given]

$\therefore \quad x^2 = 84.64$

$\Rightarrow \quad x = \sqrt{84.64}$

Now, place the bar over the numbers, then square root is given below.

	9.2
9	$\overline{84}.\overline{64}$
	81
182	364
	364
	0

$\therefore \quad x = \sqrt{84.64} = 9.2$

Hence, the required decimal is 9.2.

Q. 113 A farmer wants to plough his square field of side 150m. How much area will he have to plough?

Sol. Given, side of square field = 150 m

$\therefore$ Area of square field = Side $\times$ Side $= 150 \times 150 = 22500 \text{ m}^2$

Q. 114 What will be the number of unit squares on each side of a square graph paper, if the total number of unit squares is 256?

Sol. Let the number be x. Then, number of unit squares $= x \times x = x^2$

But total number of unit squares = 256

$\therefore \quad x^2 = 256$

$\Rightarrow \quad x = \sqrt{256} = \sqrt{16 \times 16} = 16$

Hence, the required number of squares is 16.

Q. 115 If one side of a cube is 15m in length, then find its volume.

Sol. Given, one side of a cube = 15 m

$\therefore$ Volume of cube = $(\text{Side})^3 = (15)^3 = 3375\ \text{m}^3$

Hence, the volume of cube is $3375\ \text{m}^3$.

Q. 116 The dimensions of a rectangular field are 80m and 18m. Find the length of its diagonal.

Sol. Here, length of a rectangular field (l) = 80 m

and breadth of a rectangular field (b) = 18 m

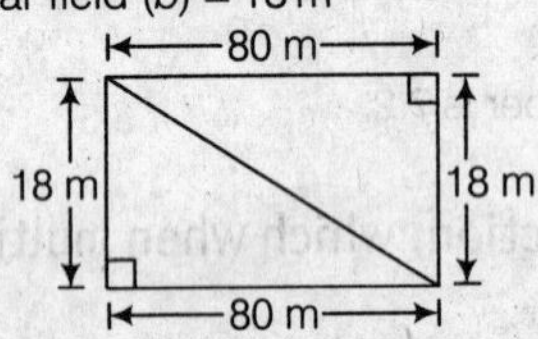

$\therefore$ Length of diagonal $= \sqrt{l^2 + b^2}$

$= \sqrt{(80)^2 + (18)^2}$

$= \sqrt{6400 + 324}$

$= \sqrt{6724} = 82\ \text{m}$

Q. 117 Find the area of a square field, if its perimeter is 96 m.

Sol. Given, perimeter of square field = 96 m

$\because$ Perimeter of square = 4 × Side

$\Rightarrow$ 4 × (Side) = 96

$\Rightarrow$ Side = 24 m

$\therefore$ Area of square field = $(\text{Side})^2 = (24)^2 = 576\ \text{m}^2$

Q. 118 Find the length of each side of a cube, if its volume is 512 cm^3.

Sol. Given, volume of a cube = 512 cm^3

$\Rightarrow$ $(\text{Side of a cube})^3 = 8 \times 8 \times 8 = (8)^3$

$\therefore$ Side of a cube = 8 cm

Hence, the length of each side of the cube is 8 cm.

Q. 119 Three numbers are in the ratio 1 : 2 : 3 and the sum of their cubes is 4500. Find the numbers.

Sol. Let the three numbers be x, $2x$ and $3x$.

According to the question,

$$(x)^3 + (2x)^3 + (3x)^3 = 4500$$

$$\Rightarrow \quad x^3 + 8x^3 + 27x^3 = 4500$$

$$\Rightarrow \quad 36x^3 = 4500$$

$$\Rightarrow \quad x^3 = \frac{4500}{36}$$

$\Rightarrow \quad x^3 = 125$ [taking cube root on both sides]

$\Rightarrow \quad x = \sqrt[3]{125}$

$\Rightarrow \quad x = \sqrt[3]{5 \times 5 \times 5}$

$\therefore \quad x = 5$

Hence, the numbers are 5, 2×5 and 3×5, i.e. 5, 10 and 15.

Q. 120 How many square metres of carpet will be required for a square room of side 6.5m to be carpeted?

Sol. Given, side of a square room = 6.5 m

$\therefore$ Area of carpet to be required = (Side of square room)^2

$= (6.5)^2 = 6.5 \times 6.5$

$= 42.25 \text{ m}^2$

Q. 121 Find the side of a square, whose area is equal to the area of a rectangle with sides 6.4m and 2.5m.

Sol. Given dimensions of a rectangle are 6.4 m and 2.5 m.

Area of a rectangle = Length $\times$ Breadth = $6.4 \times 2.5 = 16 \text{ m}^2$

Let the side of square be x m.

According to the question,

Area of square = Area of rectangle

$\Rightarrow \quad x^2 = 16$

$\Rightarrow \quad x = \sqrt{16}$

$\Rightarrow \quad x = \sqrt{4 \times 4}$

$\therefore \quad x = 4 \text{ m}$

Hence, the side of a square is 4 m.

Q. 122 Difference of two perfect cubes is 189. If the cube root of the smaller of the two numbers is 3, then find the cube root of the larger number.

Sol. Given different of two perfect cubes = 189

and cube root of the smaller number = 3

$\therefore$ Cube of smaller number = $(3)^3 = 27$

Let cube root of the larger number be x.

Then, cube of larger number = x^3

According to the question,

$x^3 - 27 = 189$

$\Rightarrow \quad x^3 = 189 + 27$

$\Rightarrow \quad x^3 = 216$

$\Rightarrow \quad x = \sqrt[3]{216} = \sqrt[3]{6 \times 6 \times 6}$

$\therefore \quad x = 6$

Hence, the cube root of the larger number is 6.

Q. 123 Find the number of plants in each row, if 1024 plants are arranged, so that number of plants in a row is the same as the number of rows.

Sol. Let the number of plants in each row be x.

Then, number of rows = Number of plants in each row = x

$\therefore$ Total plants = $x \times x = x^2$

According to the question,

$$x^2 = 1024$$

$$\Rightarrow \quad x = \sqrt{1024} = \sqrt{32 \times 32}$$

$$\therefore \quad x = 32$$

	32
3	$\overline{10}\,\overline{24}$
	9
62	124
	124
	0

Hence, there are 32 plants in each row.

Q. 124 A hall has a capacity of 2704 seats. If the number of rows is equal to the number of seats in each row, then find the number of seats in each row.

Sol. Let the number of seats in each row be x.

Then, number of rows = Number of seats in each row = x

$\therefore$ Total seats = $x \times x = x^2$

According to the question,

$$x^2 = 2704$$

$$\Rightarrow \quad x = \sqrt{2704} = \sqrt{52 \times 52}$$

$$\Rightarrow \quad x = 52$$

	52
5	$\overline{27}\,\overline{04}$
	25
102	204
	204
	0

Hence, there are 52 seats in each row.

Q. 125 A General wishes to draw up his 7500 soldiers in the form of a square. After arranging, he found out that some of them are left out. How many soldiers were left out?

Sol. Given, total number of soldiers = 7500

	86
8	$\overline{75}\,\overline{00}$
	64
166	1100
	996
	104

Hence, 104 soldiers were left out.

Q. 126 8649 students were sitting in a lecture room in such a manner that there were as many students in the row as there were rows in the lecture room. How many students were there in each row of the lecture room?

Sol. Let number of students in each row of the lecture room be x.

Then, number of rows = x

$\therefore$ Total students = $x \times x = x^2$

According to the question,

$$x^2 = 8649$$

$$\Rightarrow \quad x = \sqrt{8649}$$

$$\therefore \quad x = 93$$

	93
9	$\overline{86}\,\overline{49}$
	81
183	549
	549
	0

Hence, there are 93 students in each row of the lecture room.

Q. 127 **Rahul walks 12m North from his house and turns West to walk 35m to reach his friend's house. While returning, he walks diagonally from his friend's house to reach back to his house. What distance did he walk, while returning?**

Sol. Let Rahul walked x m, while returning home.

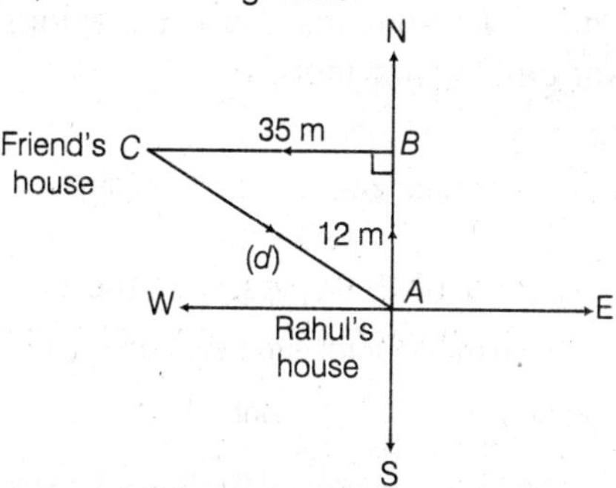

In ΔABC, by using Pythagoras theorem, we get

$$AC^2 = AB^2 + BC^2$$

$\Rightarrow$ $$AC^2 = (12)^2 + (35)^2$$

$\Rightarrow$ $$AC^2 = 144 + 1225 = 1369$$

$\Rightarrow$ $$AC = \sqrt{1369}$$

$\Rightarrow$ $$AC = 37 \text{ m}$$

	37
3	$\overline{13}\,\overline{69}$
	9
67	469
	469
	0

Hence, Rahul walked 37m distance for returning to his house diagonally.

Q. 128 **A 5.5m long ladder is leaned against a wall. The ladder reaches the wall to a height of 4.4m. Find the distance between the wall and the foot of the ladder.**

Sol. Let the distance between the wall and the foot of the ladder be x m

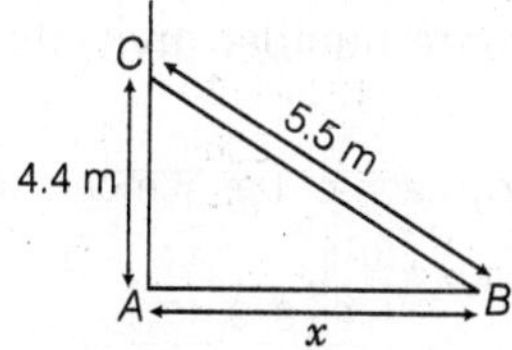

In right angled ΔABC, by using Pythagoras theorem, we get

$$BC^2 = AB^2 + AC^2$$

$\Rightarrow$ $$(5.5)^2 = x^2 + (4.4)^2$$

$\Rightarrow$ $$x^2 = (5.5)^2 - (4.4)^2$$

$\Rightarrow$ $$x^2 = 30.25 - 19.36$$

$\Rightarrow$ $$x^2 = 10.89$$

$\Rightarrow$ $$x = \sqrt{10.89}$$

$\therefore$ $$x = 3.3 \text{ m}$$

	3.3
3	$\overline{10}\,.\,\overline{89}$
	9
63	189
	189
	0

Hence, the distance between the wall and the foot of the ladder is 3.3 m.

Q. 129 **A king wanted to reward his advisor, a wiseman of the kingdom. So, he asked the wiseman to name his own reward. The wiseman thanked the king, but said that he would ask only for some gold coins each day for a month. The coins were to be counted out in a pattern of one coin for the first day, 3 coins for the second day, 5 coins for the third day and so on for 30 days. Without making calculations, find how many coins will the advisor get in that month?**

Sol. Let the advisor get x coins in that month.

According to the question, advisor get coins upto 30 days as pattern

$$1+3+5+\ldots$$

Here, $n = 30$

We know that, sum of first n odd natural numbers $= n^2 = (30)^2 = 30 \times 30 = 900$

Hence, the advisor get 900 coins in that month.

Q. 130 **Find three numbers in the ratio 2 : 3 : 5, the sum of whose squares is 608.**

Sol. Let the three numbers be $2x$, $3x$ and $5x$, respectively.

According to the question,

$$(2x)^2 + (3x)^2 + (5x)^2 = 608 \quad \text{[given]}$$

$$\Rightarrow \quad 4x^2 + 9x^2 + 25x^2 = 608$$

$$\Rightarrow \quad 38x^2 = 608$$

$$\Rightarrow \quad x^2 = \frac{608}{38}$$

$$\Rightarrow \quad x^2 = 16 = (4)^2$$

$$\therefore \quad x = 4$$

Hence, the numbers are 2×4, 3×4, 5×4, i.e. 8, 12 and 20.

Q. 131 **Find the smallest square number divisible by each of the numbers 8, 9 and 10.**

Sol. The least number divisible by each of the numbers 8, 9 and 10 is equal to the LCM of 8, 9 and 10.

2	8, 9, 10
2	4, 9, 5
2	2, 9, 5
3	1, 9, 5
3	1, 3, 5
5	1, 1, 5
	1, 1, 1

$\therefore$ LCM of 8, 9 and 10 $= 2 \times 2 \times 2 \times 3 \times 3 \times 5 = 360$

Prime factors of 360 $= (2 \times 2) \times 2 \times (3 \times 3) \times 5$

Here, prime factors 2 and 5 are unpaired. Clearly, to make it a perfect square, it must be multiplied by 2×5, i.e. 10.

Therefore, required number $= 360 \times 10 = 3600$

Hence, the smallest square number divisible by each of the numbers 8, 9 and 10 is 3600.

Q. 132 The area of a square plot is $101\frac{1}{400}$ m^2. Find the length of one side of the plot.

Sol. Let length of the square plot be a. Then, the area of square = a^2

According to the question,

$$\text{Area} = 101\frac{1}{400}\,\text{m}^2 \qquad \text{[given]}$$

$$\therefore \quad a^2 = 101\frac{1}{400} \Rightarrow a^2 = \frac{40401}{400}$$

$$\Rightarrow \quad a = \sqrt{\frac{40401}{400}} \Rightarrow a = \sqrt{\frac{201\times 201}{20\times 20}}$$

$$\therefore \quad a = \frac{201}{20} = 10\frac{1}{20}\,\text{m} \qquad \text{[taking square root on both sides]}$$

Hence, the length of one side of the plot is $10\frac{1}{20}$ m.

Q. 133 Find the square root of 324 by the method of repeated subtraction.

Sol. Given number is 324.

Now, we subtract successive odd numbers starting from 1 as follows:

Here, $324 - 1 = 323,\ 323 - 3 = 320$

$320 - 5 = 315,\ 315 - 7 = 308$

$308 - 9 = 299,\ 299 - 11 = 288$

$288 - 13 = 275,\ 275 - 15 = 260$

$260 - 17 = 243,\ 243 - 19 = 224$

$224 - 21 = 203,\ 203 - 23 = 180$

$180 - 25 = 155,\ 155 - 27 = 128$

$128 - 29 = 99,\ 99 - 31 = 68$

$68 - 33 = 35,\ 35 - 35 = 0$

We observe that the number 324 reduced to zero (0) after subracting 18 odd numbers.

So, 324 is a perfect square of 18.

$\therefore \sqrt{324} = 18$

Hence, the square root of 324 is 18.

Q. 134 Three numbers are in the ratio 2 : 3 : 4. The sum of their cubes is 0.334125. Find the numbers.

Sol. Let the numbers be $2x$, $3x$ and $4x$, respectively.

$\because$ Sum of their cubes = 0.334125 [given]

According to the question,

$$(2x)^3 + (3x)^3 + (4x)^3 = 0.334125$$

$$\Rightarrow \quad 8x^3 + 27x^3 + 64x^3 = 0.334125$$

$$\Rightarrow \quad 99x^3 = 0.334125$$

$$\Rightarrow \quad x^3 = \frac{0.334125}{99}$$

$$\Rightarrow \quad x^3 = 0.003375$$

$\Rightarrow \quad x^3 = \dfrac{3375}{1000000}$

$\Rightarrow \quad x = \sqrt[3]{\dfrac{15\times15\times15}{10\times10\times10\times10\times10\times10}}$ [taking cube root on both sides]

$\Rightarrow \quad x = \dfrac{15}{10\times10\times10}$

$\therefore \quad x = 0.015$

Hence, the required numbers are 2×0.015, 3×0.015 and 4×0.015, i.e. 0.03, 0.045 and 0.06.

Q. 135 **Evaluate: $\sqrt[3]{27}+\sqrt[3]{0.008}+\sqrt[3]{0.064}$**

Sol. We have, $\sqrt[3]{27}+\sqrt[3]{0.008}+\sqrt[3]{0.064}$

$= (27)^{1/3} + (0.008)^{1/3} + (0.064)^{1/3}$

$= (3\times3\times3)^{\frac{1}{3}} + (0.2\times0.2\times0.2)^{\frac{1}{3}} + (0.4\times0.4\times0.4)^{\frac{1}{3}}$

$= (3)^{3\times\frac{1}{3}} + (0.2)^{3\times\frac{1}{3}} + (0.4)^{3\times\frac{1}{3}}$

$= 3 + 0.2 + 0.4 = 3.6$

Q. 136 **Evaluate: $\{5^2 + (12^2)^{1/2}\}^3$**

Sol. We have, $\{5^2 + (12^2)^{1/2}\}^3 = \{25 + 12\}^3$

$= (37)^3 = 37\times37\times37 = 50653$

Q. 137 **Evaluate: $\{6^2 + (8^2)^{1/2}\}^3$**

Sol. We have, $\{6^2 + (8^2)^{1/2}\}^3 = \{36 + 8\}^3 = (44)^3 = 44\times44\times44 = 85184$

Q. 138 **A perfect square number has four digits, none of which is zero. The digits from left to right have values, that are even, even, odd, even. Find the number.**

Sol. Suppose *abcd* is a perfect square.

where, a = even number

b = even number

c = odd number

d = even number

Hence, 8836 is one of the number which satisfies the given condition.

Q. 139 **Put three different numbers in the circles, so that when you add the numbers at the end of each line, you always get a perfect square.**

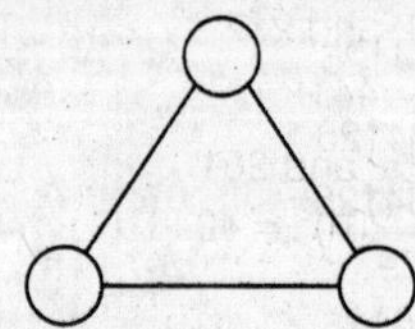

Sol. $\because$ $6 + 19 = 25$ (perfect square)
$19 + 30 = 49$ (perfect square)
and $30 + 6 = 36$ (perfect square)

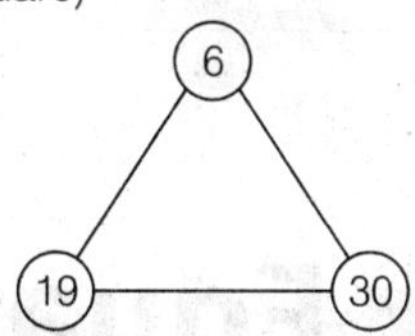

Q. 140 **The perimeters of two squares are 40m and 96m, respectively. Find the perimeter of another square equal in area to the sum of the first two squares.**

Sol. Let the side of two squares be a_1 and a_2.
Then, perimeter of first square $= 4a_1$
Given, perimeter of first square = 40
According to the question,

$$4a_1 = 40 \Rightarrow a_1 = 10$$

Similarly, perimeter of second square $= 4a_2$
Given, perimeter of second square = 96
According to the question,

$$4a_2 = 96 \Rightarrow a_2 = 24$$

Let a be the side of another square.
Then, area of another square $= a^2$
$\therefore$ Area of another square = Sum of the areas of first and second squares
= Area of first square + Area of second square
$= a_1^2 + a_2^2$

$$\Rightarrow a^2 = (10)^2 + (24)^2 = 100 + 576 = 676 \Rightarrow a = \sqrt{676} = 26 \text{ m}$$

[taking square root on both sides]

Perimeter of another square $= 4a = 4 \times 26 = 104$ m
So, the perimeter of another square is 104 m.

Q. 141 **A three-digit perfect square is such that, if it is viewed upside down, the number seen is also a perfect square. What is the number?**
[Hint **The digits 1, 0 and 8 stay the same when viewed upside down, whereas 9 becomes 6 and 6 becomes 9]**

Sol. Three-digit perfect squares are 196 and 961, which looks same when viewed upside down.

Q. 142 **13 and 31 is a strange pair of numbers, such that their squares 169 and 961 are also mirror of each other. Can you find two other such pairs?**

Sol. (i) Let a pair of numbers be 12 and 21.
Also, $(12)^2 = 144$ and $(21)^2 = 441$

(ii) Let a pair of numbers be 102 and 201.
Also, $(102)^2 = 10404$ and $(201)^2 = 40401$

4

Linear Equations in One Variable

Multiple Choice Questions (MCQs)

Q. 1 The solution of which of the following equations is neither a fraction nor an integer?

(a) $3x + 2 = 5x + 2$ (b) $4x - 18 = 2$ (c) $4x + 7 = x + 2$ (d) $5x - 8 = x + 4$

Sol. *(c)* **For option (a)**

Given linear equation is $3x + 2 = 5x + 2$

$\Rightarrow$ $3x - 5x = 2 - 2$ [transposing $5x$ to LHS and 2 to RHS]

$\Rightarrow$ $-2x = 0$

$\Rightarrow$ $\frac{-2x}{-2} = \frac{0}{-2}$ [dividing both sides by −2]

$\therefore$ $x = 0$

Hence, $x = 0$ is an integer.

For option (b)

Given linear equation is $4x - 18 = 2$

$\Rightarrow$ $4x = 2 + 18$ [transposing −18 to RHS]

$\Rightarrow$ $4x = 20$

$\Rightarrow$ $\frac{4x}{4} = \frac{20}{4}$ [dividing both sides by 4]

$\therefore$ $x = 5$

Hence, $x = 5$ is a positive integer.

For option (c)

Given linear equation is $4x + 7 = x + 2$

$\Rightarrow$ $4x - x = 2 - 7$ [transposing x to LHS and 7 to RHS]

$\Rightarrow$ $3x = -5$

$\therefore$ $x = \frac{-5}{3}$ [dividing both sides by 3]

Hence, $x = \frac{-5}{3}$ is neither a fraction nor an integer.

For option (d)

Given linear equation is $5x - 8 = x + 4$

$\Rightarrow$ $5x - x = 4 + 8$ [transposing x to LHS and -8 to RHS]

$\Rightarrow$ $4x = 12$

$\Rightarrow$ $\frac{4x}{4} = \frac{12}{4}$ [dividing both sides by 4]

$\therefore$ $x = 3$

Hence, $x = 3$ is a positive integer.

From the above it is clear that, option (c) satisfies the condition.

Q. 2 The solution of the equation $ax + b = 0$ is

(a) $x = \frac{a}{b}$ (b) $x = -b$

(c) $x = \frac{-b}{a}$ (d) $x = \frac{b}{a}$

Sol. *(c)* Given equation is $ax + b = 0$

$\Rightarrow$ $ax = -b$ [transposing b to RHS]

$\Rightarrow$ $\frac{ax}{a} = \frac{-b}{a}$ [dividing both sides by a]

$\therefore$ $x = \frac{-b}{a}$

Hence, the solution of the equation $ax + b = 0$ is $x = -\frac{b}{a}$.

Q. 3 If $8x - 3 = 25 + 17x$, then x is

(a) a fraction (b) an integer

(c) a rational number (d) Cannot be solved

Sol. *(c)* Given, $8x - 3 = 25 + 17x$

$\Rightarrow$ $8x - 17x = 25 + 3$ [transposing $17x$ to LHS and -3 to RHS]

$\Rightarrow$ $-9x = 28$

$\therefore$ $x = \frac{-28}{9}$ [dividing both sides by -9]

Hence, x is a rational number.

Q. 4 The shifting of a number from one side of an equation to other is called

(a) transposition (b) distributivity

(c) commutativity (d) associativity

Sol. *(a)* The shifting of a number from one side of an equation to other side is called transposition.

e.g. $x + a = 0$ is the equation.

$\therefore x = -a$

Here, number 'a' shifts from left hand side to right hand side.

Q. 5 If $\frac{5x}{3} - 4 = \frac{2x}{5}$, then the numerical value of $2x - 7$ is

(a) $\frac{19}{13}$ (b) $-\frac{13}{19}$

(c) 0 (d) $\frac{13}{19}$

Sol. *(b)* Given, $\frac{5x}{3} - 4 = \frac{2x}{5}$

$\Rightarrow \frac{5x}{3} - \frac{2x}{5} = 4$ $\left[\text{transposing } \frac{2x}{5} \text{ to LHS and } -4 \text{ to RHS}\right]$

$\Rightarrow \frac{25x - 6x}{15} = 4$ [taking LCM in LHS]

$\Rightarrow 19x = 60$

$\Rightarrow \frac{19x}{19} = \frac{60}{19}$ [dividing both sides by 19]

$\therefore x = \frac{60}{19}$

Now, $2x - 7 = 2 \times \frac{60}{19} - 7$ [putting the value of x]

$= \frac{120 - 133}{19} = -\frac{13}{19}$ [taking LCM]

Hence, the numerical value of $2x - 7$ is $-\frac{13}{19}$.

Q. 6 The value of x, for which the expressions $3x - 4$ and $2x + 1$ become equal, is

(a) -3 (b) 0

(c) 5 (d) 1

Sol. *(c)* Given expressions $3x - 4$ and $2x + 1$ are equal.

Then, $3x - 4 = 2x + 1$

$\Rightarrow 3x - 2x = 1 + 4$ [transposing $2x$ to LHS and -4 to RHS]

$\therefore x = 5$

Hence, the value of x is 5.

Q. 7 If a and b are positive integers, then the solution of the equation $ax = b$ has to be always

(a) positive (b) negative (c) one (d) zero

Sol. *(a)* If $ax = b$, then $x = \frac{b}{a}$

Since, a and b are positive integers.

So, $\frac{b}{a}$ is also positive integer.

Hence, the solution of the given equation has to be always positive.

Q. 8 Linear equation in one variable has

(a) only one variable with any power
(b) only one term with a variable
(c) only one variable with power 1
(d) only constant term

Sol. (c) Linear equation in one variable has only one variable with power 1.

e.g. $3x+1=0$, $2y-3=7$ and $z+9=-2$ are the linear equations in one variable.

Q. 9 Which of the following is a linear expression?

(a) x^2+1 (b) $y+y^2$
(c) 4 (d) $1+z$

Sol. (d) We know that, the algebraic expression in one variable having the highest power of the variable as 1, is known as the linear expression.

Here, $1+z$ is the only linear expression, as the power of the variable z is 1.

Q. 10 A linear equation in one variable has

(a) only one solution (b) two solutions
(c) more than two solutions (d) no solution

Sol. (a) A linear equation in one variable has only one solution.

e.g. Solution of the linear equation $ax+b=0$ is unique, i.e. $x=-\frac{b}{a}$.

Q. 11 The value of S in $\frac{1}{3}+S=\frac{2}{5}$ is

(a) $\frac{4}{5}$ (b) $\frac{1}{15}$
(c) 10 (d) 0

Sol. (b) Given, $\frac{1}{3}+S=\frac{2}{5}$

$\Rightarrow$ $S=\frac{2}{5}-\frac{1}{3}$ $\left[\text{transposing } \frac{1}{3} \text{ to RHS}\right]$

$\Rightarrow$ $S=\frac{6-5}{15}$ [taking LCM in RHS]

$\therefore$ $S=\frac{1}{15}$

Q. 12 If $\frac{-4}{3}y=-\frac{3}{4}$, then y is equal to

(a) $-\left(\frac{3}{4}\right)^2$ (b) $-\left(\frac{4}{3}\right)^2$
(c) $\left(\frac{3}{4}\right)^2$ (d) $\left(\frac{4}{3}\right)^2$

Sol. *(c)* Given, $-\frac{4}{3}y = \frac{-3}{4}$

$\Rightarrow \quad y = \frac{-3}{4} \times \frac{-3}{4}$ [by cross-multiplication]

$\Rightarrow \quad y = \left(\frac{3}{4}\right)^2$

Hence, the value of y is $\left(\frac{3}{4}\right)^2$.

Q. 13 The digit in the ten's place of a two-digit number is 3 more than the digit in the unit's place. Let the digit at unit's place be *b*. Then, the number is

(a) $11b + 30$ (b) $10b + 30$
(c) $11b + 3$ (d) $10b + 3$

Sol. *(a)* Let digit at unit's place be b.

Then, digit at ten's place = $(3 + b)$

$\therefore$ Number $= 10(3 + b) + b = 30 + 10b + b = 11b + 30$

Q. 14 Arpita's present age is thrice of Shilpa. If Shilpa's age three years ago was *x*, then Arpita's present age is

(a) $3(x - 3)$ (b) $3x + 3$
(c) $3x - 9$ (d) $3(x + 3)$

Sol. *(d)* Given, Shilpa's age three years ago = x

Then, Shilpa's present age = $(x + 3)$

$\therefore$ Arpita's present age = $3\times$ Shilpa's present age = $3(x + 3)$

Q. 15 The sum of three consecutive multiples of 7 is 357. Find the smallest multiple.

(a) 112 (b) 126
(c) 119 (d) 116

Sol. *(a)* Let the three consecutive multiples of 7 be $7x$, $(7x + 7)$, $(7x + 14)$ where x is a natural number.

According to the question,

$$7x + (7x + 7) + (7x + 14) = 357$$

$\Rightarrow \quad 21x + 21 = 357$

$\Rightarrow \quad 21(x + 1) = 357$

$\Rightarrow \quad \frac{21(x+1)}{21} = \frac{357}{21}$ [dividing both sides by 21]

$\Rightarrow \quad x + 1 = 17$

$\Rightarrow \quad x = 17 - 1$ [transposing 1 to RHS]

$\therefore \quad x = 16$

Hence, the smallest multiple of 7 is 7×16, i.e. 112.

Fill in the Blanks

In questions 16 to 32, fill in the blanks to make each statement true.

Q. 16 In a linear equation, the ______ power of the variable appearing in the equation is one.

Sol. **highest**

e.g. $x + 3 = 0$ and $x + 2 = 4$ are the linear equations.

Q. 17 The solution of the equation $3x - 4 = 1 - 2x$ is ______ .

Sol. **1**

Given, $3x - 4 = 1 - 2x$

$\Rightarrow$ $3x + 2x = 1 + 4$ [transposing $-2x$ to LHS and -4 to RHS]

$\Rightarrow$ $5x = 5$

$\Rightarrow$ $\frac{5x}{5} = \frac{5}{5}$ [dividing both sides by 5]

$\therefore$ $x = 1$

Hence, the solution of the given equation is 1.

Q. 18 The solution of the equation $2y = 5y - \frac{18}{5}$ is______ .

Sol. $\frac{6}{5}$

Given, $2y = 5y - \frac{18}{5}$

$\Rightarrow$ $2y - 5y = \frac{-18}{5}$ [transposing $5y$ to LHS]

$\Rightarrow$ $-3y = -\frac{18}{5}$

$\Rightarrow$ $\frac{-3y}{-3} = \frac{-18}{-3 \times 5}$ [dividing both sides by -3]

$\therefore$ $y = \frac{6}{5}$

Hence, the solution of the given equation is $\frac{6}{5}$.

Q. 19 Any value of the variable, which makes both sides of an equation equal, is known as a _____ of the equation.

Sol. **solution**

e.g. $x + 2 = 3 \Rightarrow x = 3 - 2 = 1$ [transposing 2 to RHS]

Hence, $x = 1$ satisfies the equation and it is a solution of the equation.

Q. 20 $9x -$ _____ $= -21$ has the solution (-2).

Sol. **3**

Let $9x - m = -21$ has the solution (-2).

Since, $x = -2$ is the solution of the equation.

$\therefore \quad 9 \times (-2) - m = -21$

$\Rightarrow \quad -18 - m = -21$ [transposing -21 to LHS and $-m$ to RHS]

$-18 + 21 = m$

$\Rightarrow \quad m = 3$

Hence, $9x - 3 = -21$ has the solution (-2).

Q. 21 **Three consecutive numbers whose sum is 12 are _____ , _____ and _____ .**

Sol. **3, 4, 5**

Let the three consecutive numbers be x, $x + 1$ and $x + 2$.

According to the question,

$$x + x + 1 + x + 2 = 12$$

$\Rightarrow \quad 3x + 3 = 12$

$\Rightarrow \quad 3(x + 1) = 12$

$\Rightarrow \quad \dfrac{3(x+1)}{3} = \dfrac{12}{3}$ [dividing both sides by 3]

$\Rightarrow \quad x + 1 = 4$

$\Rightarrow \quad x = 4 - 1$ [transposing 1 to RHS]

$\Rightarrow \quad x = 3$

Hence, the consecutive numbers are 3, 3 + 1 and 3 + 2, i.e. 3, 4 and 5.

Q. 22 **The share of *A* when ₹ 25 are divided between *A* and *B*, so that *A* gets ₹ 8 more than *B*, is _____ .**

Sol. **₹ 16.5**

Let, *B*'s share be ₹ x. Then, *A*'s share = ₹ $(x + 8)$

According to the question,

$$x + x + 8 = 25$$

$\Rightarrow \quad 2x + 8 = 25$

$\Rightarrow \quad 2x = 25 - 8$ [transposing 8 to RHS]

$\Rightarrow \quad 2x = 17$

$\Rightarrow \quad \dfrac{2x}{2} = \dfrac{17}{2}$ [dividing both sides by 2]

$\Rightarrow \quad x = 8.5$

Hence, *A*'s share = 8.5 + 8 = ₹ 16.5

Q. 23 **A term of an equation can be transposed to the other side by changing its _____ .**

Sol. **sign**

e.g. $x + a = 0$ is a linear equation.

$\Rightarrow \quad x = -a$

Hence, the term of an equation can be transposed to the other side by changing its sign.

Q. 24 On subtracting 8 from x, the result is 2. The value of x is _____.

Sol. 10

Given, $x - 8 = 2$

$\Rightarrow$ $x = 8 + 2$ [transposing -8 to RHS]

$\therefore$ $x = 10$

Hence, the value of x is 10.

Q. 25 $\frac{x}{5} + 30 = 18$ has the solution as _____.

Sol. -60

Given, $\frac{x}{5} + 30 = 18$

$\Rightarrow$ $\frac{x}{5} = 18 - 30$ [transposing 30 to RHS]

$\Rightarrow$ $\frac{x}{5} = -12$

$\frac{x}{5} \times 5 = -12 \times 5$ [multiplying both sides by 5]

$\Rightarrow$ $x = -60$

Hence, the solution is -60.

Q. 26 When a number is divided by 8, the result is -3. The number is _____.

Sol. -24

Let the number be x.

According to the question,

$$\frac{x}{8} = -3$$

$\Rightarrow$ $x = 8 \times (-3)$

$\Rightarrow$ $x = -24$ [by cross-multiplication]

Hence, the required number is -24.

Q. 27 When 9 is subtracted from the product of p and 4, the result is 11. The value of p is _____.

Sol. 5

Given, 9 is subtracted from the product of p and 4.

Then, $4p - 9 = 11$

$\Rightarrow$ $4p = 11 + 9$ [transposing -9 to RHS]

$\Rightarrow$ $4p = 20$

$\Rightarrow$ $\frac{4p}{4} = \frac{20}{4}$ [dividing both sides by 4]

$\therefore$ $p = 5$

Hence, the value of p is 5.

Q. 28 If $\frac{2}{5}x - 2 = 5 - \frac{3}{5}x$, then $x =$ _____ .

Sol. 7

Given, $$\frac{2}{5}x - 2 = 5 - \frac{3}{5}x$$

$$\Rightarrow \quad \frac{2x}{5} + \frac{3x}{5} = 5 + 2 \quad \left[\text{transposing } -\frac{3x}{5} \text{ to LHS and } -2 \text{ to RHS}\right]$$

$$\Rightarrow \quad \frac{5x}{5} = 7$$

$$\Rightarrow \quad x = 7$$

Hence, the value of x is 7.

Q. 29 After 18 years, Swarnim will be 4 times as old as he is now. His present age is _____ .

Sol. 6 years

Let Swarnim's present age be x yr.

After 18 yr, Swarnim's age = $(x + 18)$ yr

According to the question,

$$x + 18 = 4x$$

$$\Rightarrow \quad x - 4x = -18 \quad \text{[transposing } 4x \text{ to LHS and 18 to RHS]}$$

$$\Rightarrow \quad -3x = -18$$

$$\Rightarrow \quad \frac{-3x}{-3} = \frac{-18}{3} \quad \text{[dividing both sides by } -3]$$

$$\therefore \quad x = 6$$

Hence, Swarnim's present age is 6 yr.

Q. 30 Convert the statement 'adding 15 to 4 times x is 39' into an equation.

Sol. $4x + 15 = 39$

To convert the given statement into an equation, first x is multiplied by 4 and then 15 is added to get the result 39.

i.e. $$4x + 15 = 39$$

Q. 31 The denominator of a rational number is greater than the numerator by 10. If the numerator is increased by 1 and the denominator is decreased by 1, then expression for new denominator is _____ .

Sol. $x + 9$

Let numerator be x. Then, denominator = $x + 10$

$\therefore$ Rational number = $\frac{x}{x + 10}$

According to the question,

New rational number = $\frac{\text{Numerator} + 1}{\text{Denominator} - 1} = \frac{x + 1}{x + 10 - 1} = \frac{x + 1}{x + 9}$

Hence, the new denominator is $x + 9$.

Q. 32 The sum of two consecutive multiples of 10 is 210. The smaller multiple is _____ .

Sol. 100

Let the two consecutive multiples of 10 be $10x$ and $10x+10$.

According to the question,

$$10x + 10x + 10 = 210$$

$$\Rightarrow \quad 20x + 10 = 210$$

$$\Rightarrow \quad 20x = 210 - 10 \quad \text{[transposing 10 to RHS]}$$

$$\Rightarrow \quad 20x = 200$$

$$\Rightarrow \quad \frac{20x}{20} = \frac{200}{20} \quad \text{[dividing both sides by 20]}$$

$$\therefore \quad x = 10$$

Hence, the smaller multiple is 10×10, i.e. 100.

True/False

In questions 33 to 48, state whether the statements are True or False.

Q. 33 3 years ago, the age of boy was y years. His age 2 years ago was $(y-2)$ years.

Sol. *False*

Given, 3 yr ago, age of boy = y yr

Then, present age of boy = $(y+3)$ yr

$\therefore$ 2 yr ago, age of boy = $y+3-2=(y+1)$ yr

Q. 34 Shikha's present age is p years. Reemu's present age is 4 times the present age of Shikha. After 5 years, Reemu's age will be $15p$ years.

Sol. *False*

Given, Shikha's present age = p yr

Then, Reemu's present age = $4 \times$ (Shikha's present age) = $4p$ yr

$\therefore$ After 5 yr, Reemu's age = $(4p+5)$ yr

Q. 35 In a 2-digit number, the unit's place digit is x. If the sum of digits be 9, then the number is $(10x-9)$.

Sol. *False*

Given, unit's digit = x

and sum of digits = 9

$\therefore$ Ten's digit = $9-x$

Hence, the number = $10(9-x)+x = 90-10x+x = 90-9x$

Q. 36 Sum of the ages of Anju and her mother is 65 years. If Anju's present age is y years, then her mother's age before 5 years is $(60 - y)$ years.

Sol. ***True***

Given, Anju's present age = y yr

Then, Anju's mother age = $(65 - y)$ yr

Before 5 yr, Anju's mother age = $65 - y - 5 = (60 - y)$ yr

Q. 37 The number of boys and girls in a class are in the ratio 5 : 4. If the number of boys is 9 more than the number of girls, then number of boys is 9.

Sol. ***False***

Let the number of boys be $5x$ and the number of girls be $4x$.

According to the question,

$$5x - 4x = 9$$

$$\Rightarrow \quad x = 9$$

Hence, number of boys = $5 \times 9 = 45$

Q. 38 A and B are together 90 years old. Five years ago, A was thrice as old as B was. Hence, the ages of A and B five years back would be $(x - 5)$ years and $(85 - x)$ years, respectively.

Sol. ***True***

Let the age of A be x yr.

Then, age of $B = (90 - x)$ yr

Five years ago, the age of $A = (x - 5)$ yr

The age of $B = 90 - x - 5 = (85 - x)$ yr

Hence, the ages of A and B five years back would be $(x - 5)$ yr and $(85 - x)$ yr, respectively.

Q. 39 Two different equations can never have the same answer.

Sol. ***False***

Two different equations may have the same answer.

e.g. $2x + 1 = 2$ and $2x - 5 = -4$ are the two linear equations whose solution is $\frac{1}{2}$.

Q. 40 In the equation $3x - 3 = 9$, transposing -3 to RHS, we get $3x = 9$.

Sol. ***False***

Given, $3x - 3 = 9$

$\Rightarrow \quad 3x = 9 + 3$ [transposing -3 to RHS]

$\Rightarrow \quad 3x = 12$

Q. 41 In the equation $2x = 4 - x$, transposing $-x$ to LHS, we get $x = 4$.

Sol. ***False***

Given, $2x = 4 - x$

$\Rightarrow \quad 2x + x = 4$ [transposing $-x$ to LHS]

$\Rightarrow \quad 3x = 4$

Q. 42 If $\frac{15}{8} - 7x = 9$, then $-7x = 9 + \frac{15}{8}$.

Sol. ***False***

Given, $$\frac{15}{8} - 7x = 9$$

$\Rightarrow$ $$-7x = 9 - \frac{15}{8}$$ $\left[\text{transposing } \frac{15}{8} \text{ to RHS}\right]$

Q. 43 If $\frac{x}{3} + 1 = \frac{7}{15}$, then $\frac{x}{3} = \frac{6}{15}$.

Sol. ***False***

Given, $$\frac{x}{3} + 1 = \frac{7}{15}$$

$\Rightarrow$ $$\frac{x}{3} = \frac{7}{15} - 1$$ [transposing 1 to RHS]

$\Rightarrow$ $$\frac{x}{3} = \frac{7 - 15}{15}$$

$\Rightarrow$ $$\frac{x}{3} = \frac{-8}{15}$$

Q. 44 If $6x = 18$, then $18x = 54$.

Sol. ***True***

Given, $$6x = 18$$

$\Rightarrow$ $$3 \times 6x = 18 \times 3$$ [multiplying both sides by 3]

$\Rightarrow$ $$18x = 54$$

Q. 45 If $\frac{x}{11} = 15$, then $x = \frac{11}{15}$.

Sol. ***False***

Given, $$\frac{x}{11} = 15$$

$\Rightarrow$ $$x = 11 \times 15$$ [by cross-multiplication]

Q. 46 If x is an even number, then the next even number is $2(x + 1)$.

Sol. ***False***

Given, x is an even number. Then, the next even number is $(x + 2)$.

Q. 47 If the sum of two consecutive numbers is 93 and one of them is x, then the other number is $93 - x$.

Sol. ***True***

Given, one of the consecutive number = x

Then, the next consecutive number = $x + 1$

According to the question,

$$x + x + 1 = 93$$

$\Rightarrow$ $2x = 93 - 1$ [transposing 1 to RHS]

$\Rightarrow$ $2x = 92$

$\Rightarrow$ $\dfrac{2x}{2} = \dfrac{92}{2}$ [dividing both sides by 2]

$\therefore$ $x = 46$

Hence, the other consecutive number $= 46 + 1 = 47 = 93 - 46 = 93 - x$

Q. 48 **Two numbers differ by 40. When each number is increased by 8, the bigger becomes thrice the lesser number. If one number is x, then the other number is $(40 - x)$.**

Sol. ***False***

Given, one number $= x$

and other number $= 40 - x$

Let $(40 - x) > x$

Then, according to the question,

$$40 - x + 8 = 3(x + 8)$$

$\Rightarrow$ $48 - x = 3x + 24$

$\Rightarrow$ $-x - 3x = 24 - 48$ [transposing $3x$ to LHS and 48 to RHS]

$\Rightarrow$ $-4x = -24$

$\Rightarrow$ $x = -24 \times \left(-\dfrac{1}{4}\right)$

$\therefore$ $x = 6$

Hence, one number $= x = 6$

and other number $= 40 - x = 40 - 6 = 34$

Now, difference between numbers $= 34 - 6 = 28 \neq 40$

which is not satisfy the condition given in question.

In Questins 49 to 78, solve the following.

Q. 49 $\dfrac{3x - 8}{2x} = 1$

Sol. Given, $\dfrac{3x - 8}{2x} = 1$

$\Rightarrow$ $3x - 8 = 2x$ [by cross-multiplication]

$\Rightarrow$ $3x - 2x = 8$ [transposing $2x$ to LHS and 8 to RHS]

$\therefore$ $x = 8$

Q. 50 $\frac{5x}{2x-1} = 2$

Sol. Given, $\frac{5x}{2x-1} = 2$

$5x = 2(2x-1)$ [by cross-multiplication]

$\Rightarrow$ $5x = 4x - 2$

$\Rightarrow$ $5x - 4x = -2$ [transposing $4x$ to LHS]

$\therefore$ $x = -2$

Q. 51 $\frac{2x-3}{4x+5} = \frac{1}{3}$

Sol. Given, $\frac{2x-3}{4x+5} = \frac{1}{3}$

$\Rightarrow$ $3(2x-3) = 4x + 5$ [by cross-multiplication]

$\Rightarrow$ $6x - 9 = 4x + 5$

$\Rightarrow$ $6x - 4x = 9 + 5$ [transposing $4x$ to LHS and -9 to RHS]

$\Rightarrow$ $2x = 14$

$\Rightarrow$ $\frac{2x}{2} = \frac{14}{2}$ [dividing both sides by 2]

$\therefore$ $x = 7$

Q. 52 $\frac{8}{x} = \frac{5}{x-1}$

Sol. Given, $\frac{8}{x} = \frac{5}{x-1}$

$\Rightarrow$ $8(x-1) = 5x$ [by cross-multiplication]

$\Rightarrow$ $8x - 8 = 5x$

$\Rightarrow$ $8x - 5x = 8$ [transposing $5x$ to LHS and -8 to RHS]

$\Rightarrow$ $3x = 8$

$\Rightarrow$ $\frac{3x}{3} = \frac{8}{3}$ [dividing both sides by 3]

$\therefore$ $x = \frac{8}{3}$

Q. 53 $\frac{5(1-x) + 3(1+x)}{1-2x} = 8$

Sol. Given, $\frac{5(1-x) + 3(1+x)}{1-2x} = 8$

$\Rightarrow$ $5(1-x) + 3(1+x) = 8(1-2x)$ [by cross-multiplication]

$\Rightarrow$ $5 - 5x + 3 + 3x = 8 - 16x$

$\Rightarrow$ $8 - 2x = 8 - 16x$

$\Rightarrow$ $16x - 2x = 8 - 8$ [transposing $-16x$ to LHS and 8 to RHS]

$\Rightarrow$ $14x = 0$

$\Rightarrow$ $\frac{14x}{14} = \frac{0}{14}$ [dividing both sides by 14]

$\therefore$ $x = 0$

Q. 54 $\frac{0.2x+5}{3.5x-3}=\frac{2}{5}$

Sol. Given, $\frac{0.2x+5}{3.5x-3}=\frac{2}{5}$

$\Rightarrow$ $5(0.2x+5)=2(3.5x-3)$ [by cross-multiplication]

$\Rightarrow$ $x+25=7x-6$

$\Rightarrow$ $x-7x=-6-25$ [transposing $7x$ to LHS and 25 to RHS]

$\Rightarrow$ $-6x=-31$

$\Rightarrow$ $\frac{-6x}{-6}=\frac{-31}{-6}$ [dividing both sides by -6]

$\therefore$ $x=\frac{31}{6}$

Q. 55 $\frac{y-(4-3y)}{2y-(3+4y)}=\frac{1}{5}$

Sol. Given, $\frac{y-(4-3y)}{2y-(3+4y)}=\frac{1}{5}$

$\Rightarrow$ $5(y-4+3y)=2y-3-4y$ [by cross-multiplication]

$\Rightarrow$ $5(4y-4)=-3-2y$

$\Rightarrow$ $20y-20=-3-2y$

$\Rightarrow$ $20y+2y=20-3$ [transposing -20 to RHS and $-2y$ to LHS]

$\Rightarrow$ $22y=17$

$\Rightarrow$ $\frac{22y}{22}=\frac{17}{22}$ [dividing both sides by 22]

$\therefore$ $y=\frac{17}{22}$

Q. 56 $\frac{x}{5}=\frac{x-1}{6}$

Sol. Given, $\frac{x}{5}=\frac{x-1}{6}$

$\Rightarrow$ $6x=5(x-1)$ [by cross-multiplication]

$\Rightarrow$ $6x=5x-5$

$\Rightarrow$ $6x-5x=-5$ [transposing $5x$ to LHS]

$\therefore$ $x=-5$

Q. 57 $0.4(3x-1)=0.5x+1$

Sol. Given, $0.4(3x-1)=0.5x+1$

$\Rightarrow$ $1.2x-0.4=0.5x+1$

$\Rightarrow$ $1.2x-0.5x=1+0.4$ [transposing $0.5x$ to LHS and -0.4 to RHS]

$\Rightarrow$ $0.7x=1.4$

$\Rightarrow$ $\frac{0.7x}{0.7}=\frac{1.4}{0.7}$ [dividing both sides by 0.7]

$\therefore$ $x=2$

Q. 58 $8x - 7 - 3x = 6x - 2x - 3$

Sol. Given, $8x - 7 - 3x = 6x - 2x - 3$

$\Rightarrow 8x - 3x - 6x + 2x = -3 + 7$ [transposing $6x$, $-2x$ to LHS and -7 to RHS]

$\therefore x = 4$

Q. 59 $10x - 5 - 7x = 5x + 15 - 8$

Sol. Given, $10x - 5 - 7x = 5x + 15 - 8$

$\Rightarrow 10x - 7x - 5x = 5 + 15 - 8$ [transposing $5x$ to LHS and -5 to RHS]

$\Rightarrow -2x = 12$

$\Rightarrow \frac{-2x}{-2} = \frac{12}{-2}$ [dividing both sides by -2]

$\therefore x = -6$

Q. 60 $4t - 3 - (3t + 1) = 5t - 4$

Sol. Given, $4t - 3 - (3t + 1) = 5t - 4$

$\Rightarrow 4t - 3 - 3t - 1 = 5t - 4$

$\Rightarrow t - 4 = 5t - 4$

$\Rightarrow t - 5t = -4 + 4$ [transposing $5t$ to LHS and -4 to RHS]

$\Rightarrow -4t = 0$

$\Rightarrow \frac{-4t}{-4} = \frac{0}{-4}$ [dividing both sides by -4]

$\therefore t = 0$

Q. 61 $5(x - 1) - 2(x + 8) = 0$

Sol. Given, $5(x - 1) - 2(x + 8) = 0$

$\Rightarrow 5x - 5 - 2x - 16 = 0$

$\Rightarrow 3x - 21 = 0$

$\Rightarrow 3x = 21$ [transposing -21 to RHS]

$\Rightarrow \frac{3x}{3} = \frac{21}{3}$ [dividing both sides by 3]

$\therefore x = 7$

Q. 62 $\frac{x}{2} - \frac{1}{4}\left(x - \frac{1}{3}\right) = \frac{1}{6}(x + 1) + \frac{1}{12}$

Sol. Given, $\frac{x}{2} - \frac{1}{4}\left(x - \frac{1}{3}\right) = \frac{1}{6}(x + 1) + \frac{1}{12}$

$\Rightarrow \frac{x}{2} - \frac{x}{4} + \frac{1}{12} = \frac{x}{6} + \frac{1}{6} + \frac{1}{12}$

$\Rightarrow \frac{2x - x}{4} + \frac{1}{12} = \frac{x}{6} + \frac{2 + 1}{12}$

$\Rightarrow \frac{x}{4} + \frac{1}{12} = \frac{x}{6} + \frac{3}{12}$

$\Rightarrow \quad \frac{x}{4} - \frac{x}{6} = \frac{3}{12} - \frac{1}{12}$ $\left[\text{transposing } \frac{x}{6} \text{ to LHS and } \frac{1}{12} \text{ to RHS}\right]$

$\Rightarrow \quad \frac{6x - 4x}{24} = \frac{3 - 1}{12}$

$\Rightarrow \quad \frac{2x}{24} = \frac{2}{12}$

$\Rightarrow \quad 2 \times 12x = 2 \times 24$ [by cross-multiplication]

$\Rightarrow \quad 24x = 48$

$\Rightarrow \quad \frac{24x}{24} = \frac{48}{24}$ [dividing both sides by 24]

$\therefore \quad x = 2$

Q. 63 $\frac{1}{2}(x + 1) + \frac{1}{3}(x - 1) = \frac{5}{12}(x - 2)$

Sol. Given, $\frac{1}{2}(x + 1) + \frac{1}{3}(x - 1) = \frac{5}{12}(x - 2)$

$\Rightarrow \quad \frac{x}{2} + \frac{1}{2} + \frac{x}{3} - \frac{1}{3} = \frac{5x}{12} - \frac{5}{6}$

$\Rightarrow \quad \frac{x}{2} + \frac{x}{3} - \frac{5x}{12} = \frac{1}{3} - \frac{1}{2} - \frac{5}{6}$ $\left[\text{transposing } \frac{1}{2}, \frac{1}{3} \text{ to RHS and } \frac{5x}{12} \text{ to LHS}\right]$

$\Rightarrow \quad \frac{6x + 4x - 5x}{12} = \frac{2 - 3 - 5}{6}$

$\Rightarrow \quad \frac{5x}{12} = \frac{-6}{6}$

$\Rightarrow \quad 5x \times 6 = (-6) \times 12$ [by cross-multiplication]

$\Rightarrow \quad x = \frac{(-6) \times 12}{5 \times 6}$

$\therefore \quad x = \frac{-12}{5}$

Q. 64 $\frac{x + 1}{4} = \frac{x - 2}{3}$

Sol. Given, $\frac{x + 1}{4} = \frac{x - 2}{3}$

$\Rightarrow \quad 3(x + 1) = 4(x - 2)$ [by cross-multiplication]

$\Rightarrow \quad 3x + 3 = 4x - 8$

$\Rightarrow \quad 3x - 4x = -8 - 3$ [transposing $4x$ to LHS and 3 to RHS]

$\Rightarrow \quad -x = -11$ [dividing both sides by −1]

$\Rightarrow \quad \frac{-x}{-1} = \frac{-11}{-1}$

$\therefore \quad x = 11$

Q. 65 $\frac{2x - 1}{5} = \frac{3x + 1}{3}$

Sol. Given, $\frac{2x - 1}{5} = \frac{3x + 1}{3}$

$$\Rightarrow \quad 3(2x-1) = 5(3x+1) \quad \text{[by cross-multiplication]}$$
$$\Rightarrow \quad 6x - 3 = 15x + 5$$
$$\Rightarrow \quad 6x - 15x = 3 + 5 \quad \text{[transposing } 15x \text{ to LHS and } -3 \text{ to RHS]}$$
$$\Rightarrow \quad -9x = 8$$
$$\Rightarrow \quad \frac{-9x}{-9} = \frac{8}{-9} \quad \text{[dividing both sides by } -9]$$
$$\therefore \quad x = \frac{-8}{9}$$

Q. 66 $1-(x-2)-[(x-3)-(x-1)]=0$

Sol. Given, $1-(x-2)-[(x-3)-(x-1)]=0$

$$\Rightarrow \quad 1-x+2-[x-3-x+1]=0$$
$$\Rightarrow \quad 3-x-[-2]=0$$
$$\Rightarrow \quad 3-x+2=0$$
$$\Rightarrow \quad -x+5=0$$
$$\Rightarrow \quad -x=-5 \quad \text{[transposing 5 to RHS]}$$
$$\Rightarrow \quad \frac{-x}{-1}=\frac{-5}{-1} \quad \text{[dividing both sides by } -1]$$
$$\therefore \quad x=5$$

Q. 67 $3x-\frac{x-2}{3}=4-\frac{x-1}{4}$

Sol. Given, $3x-\frac{x-2}{3}=4-\frac{x-1}{4}$

$$\Rightarrow \quad \frac{9x-(x-2)}{3}=\frac{16-(x-1)}{4}$$
$$\Rightarrow \quad 4(9x-x+2)=3(16-x+1) \quad \text{[by cross-multiplication]}$$
$$\Rightarrow \quad 4(8x+2)=3(-x+17)$$
$$\Rightarrow \quad 32x+8=-3x+51$$
$$\Rightarrow \quad 32x+3x=51-8 \quad \text{[transposing } -3x \text{ to LHS and 8 to RHS]}$$
$$\Rightarrow \quad 35x=43$$
$$\Rightarrow \quad \frac{35x}{35}=\frac{43}{35} \quad \text{[dividing both sides by 35]}$$
$$\therefore \quad x=\frac{43}{35}$$

Q. 68 $\frac{3t+5}{4}-1=\frac{4t-3}{5}$

Sol. Given, $\frac{3t+5}{4}-1=\frac{4t-3}{5}$

$$\Rightarrow \quad \frac{3t+5-4}{4}=\frac{4t-3}{5}$$
$$\Rightarrow \quad 5(3)t+5-4)=4(4t-3) \quad \text{[by cross-multiplication]}$$

$\Rightarrow \quad 5(3t + 1) = 4(4t - 3)$

$\Rightarrow \quad 15t + 5 = 16t - 12$

$\Rightarrow \quad 15t - 16t = -12 - 5$ [transposing 16t to LHS and 5 to RHS]

$\Rightarrow \quad -t = -17$

$\Rightarrow \quad \frac{-t}{-1} = \frac{-17}{-1}$ [dividing both sides by –1]

$\therefore \quad t = 17$

Q. 69 $\frac{2y-3}{4} - \frac{3y-5}{2} = y + \frac{3}{4}$

Sol. Given, $\frac{2y-3}{4} - \frac{3y-5}{2} = y + \frac{3}{4}$

$\Rightarrow \quad \frac{2y - 3 - 2(3y-5)}{4} = \frac{4y+3}{4}$

$\Rightarrow \quad 2y - 3 - 6y + 10 = 4y + 3$

$\Rightarrow \quad -4y + 7 = 4y + 3$ [transposing 4y to LHS and 7 to RHS]

$\Rightarrow \quad -4y - 4y = 3 - 7$

$\Rightarrow \quad -8y = -4$

$\Rightarrow \quad \frac{-8y}{-8} = \frac{-4}{-8}$ [dividing both sides by –8]

$\therefore \quad y = \frac{1}{2}$

Q. 70 $0.25(4x - 5) = 0.75x + 8$

Sol. Given, $0.25(4x - 5) = 0.75x + 8$

$\Rightarrow \quad x - 1.25 = 0.75x + 8$

$\Rightarrow \quad x - 0.75x = 1.25 + 8$ [transposing 0.75x to LHS and 1.25 to RHS]

$\Rightarrow \quad 0.25x = 9.25$

$\Rightarrow \quad \frac{0.25x}{0.25} = \frac{9.25}{0.25}$ [dividing both sides by 0.25]

$\therefore \quad x = 37$

Q. 71 $\frac{9-3y}{1-9y} = \frac{8}{5}$

Sol. Given, $\frac{9-3y}{1-9y} = \frac{8}{5}$

$\Rightarrow \quad 5(9 - 3y) = 8(1 - 9y)$ [by cross-multiplication]

$\Rightarrow \quad 45 - 15y = 8 - 72y$

$\Rightarrow \quad 72y - 15y = 8 - 45$ [transposing –72y to LHS and 45 to RHS]

$\Rightarrow \quad 57y = -37$

$\Rightarrow \quad \frac{57y}{57} = \frac{-37}{57}$ [dividing both sides by 57]

$\therefore \quad y = \frac{-37}{57}$

Q. 72 $\frac{3x+2}{2x-3} = -\frac{3}{4}$

Sol. Given, $\frac{3x+2}{2x-3} = -\frac{3}{4}$

$\Rightarrow$ $4(3x+2) = -3(2x-3)$ [by cross-multiplication]

$\Rightarrow$ $12x + 8 = -6x + 9$

$\Rightarrow$ $12x + 6x = 9 - 8$ [transposing $-6x$ to LHS and 8 to RHS]

$\Rightarrow$ $18x = 1$

$\Rightarrow$ $\frac{18x}{18} = \frac{1}{18}$ [dividing both sides by 18]

$\therefore$ $x = \frac{1}{18}$

Q. 73 $\frac{5x+1}{2x} = -\frac{1}{3}$

Sol. Given, $\frac{5x+1}{2x} = -\frac{1}{3}$

$\Rightarrow$ $3(5x+1) = -2x$ [by cross-multiplication]

$\Rightarrow$ $15x + 3 = -2x$

$\Rightarrow$ $15x + 2x = -3$ [transposing $-2x$ to LHS and 3 to RHS]

$\Rightarrow$ $17x = -3$

$\Rightarrow$ $\frac{17x}{17} = \frac{-3}{17}$ [dividing both sides by 17]

$\therefore$ $x = \frac{-3}{17}$

Q. 74 $\frac{3t-2}{3} + \frac{2t+3}{2} = t + \frac{7}{6}$

Sol. Given, $\frac{3t-2}{3} + \frac{2t+3}{2} = t + \frac{7}{6}$

$\Rightarrow$ $\frac{2(3t-2) + 3(2t+3)}{6} = \frac{6t+7}{6}$

$\Rightarrow$ $6t - 4 + 6t + 9 = 6t + 7$

$\Rightarrow$ $12t + 5 = 6t + 7$

$\Rightarrow$ $12t - 6t = 7 - 5$ [transposing $6t$ to LHS and 5 to RHS]

$\Rightarrow$ $6t = 2$

$\Rightarrow$ $\frac{6t}{6} = \frac{2}{6}$ [dividing both sides by 6]

$\therefore$ $t = \frac{1}{3}$

Q. 75 $m - \frac{m-1}{2} = 1 - \frac{m-2}{3}$

Sol. Given, $m - \frac{m-1}{2} = 1 - \frac{m-2}{3}$

$\Rightarrow \quad \frac{2m-(m-1)}{2} = \frac{3-(m-2)}{3}$

$\Rightarrow \quad 3(2m-m+1) = 2(3-m+2)$ [by cross multiplication]

$\Rightarrow \quad 3(m+1) = 2(5-m)$

$\Rightarrow \quad 3m+3 = 10-2m$

$\Rightarrow \quad 3m+2m = 10-3$ [transposing $-2m$ to LHS and 3 to RHS]

$\Rightarrow \quad 5m = 7$

$\Rightarrow \quad \frac{5m}{5} = \frac{7}{5}$ [dividing both sides by 5]

$\therefore \quad m = \frac{7}{5}$

Q. 76 $4(3p+2)-5(6p-1) = 2(p-8)-6(7p-4)$

Sol. Given, $4(3p+2)-5(6p-1) = 2(p-8)-6(7p-4)$

$\Rightarrow \quad 12p+8-30p+5 = 2p-16-42p+24$

$\Rightarrow \quad -18p+13 = -40p+8$

$\Rightarrow \quad -18p+40p = 8-13$ [transposing $-40p$ to LHS and 13 to RHS]

$\Rightarrow \quad 22p = -5$

$\Rightarrow \quad \frac{22p}{22} = \frac{-5}{22}$ [dividing both sides by 22]

$\therefore \quad p = \frac{-5}{22}$

Q. 77 $3(5x-7)+2(9x-11) = 4(8x-7)-111$

Sol. Given, $3(5x-7)+2(9x-11) = 4(8x-7)-111$

$\Rightarrow \quad 15x-21+18x-22 = 32x-28-111$

$\Rightarrow \quad 33x-43 = 32x-139$

$\Rightarrow \quad 33x-32x = -139+43$ [transposing $32x$ to LHS and -43 to RHS]

$\therefore \quad x = -96$

Q. 78 $0.16(5x-2) = 0.4x+7$

Sol. Given, $0.16(5x-2) = 0.4x+7$

$\Rightarrow \quad 0.8x-0.32 = 0.4x+7$

$\Rightarrow \quad 0.8x-0.4x = 0.32+7$ [transposing $0.4x$ to LHS and -0.32 to RHS]

$\Rightarrow \quad 0.4x = 7.32$

$\Rightarrow \quad \frac{0.4x}{0.4} = \frac{7.32}{0.4}$ [dividing both sides by 0.4]

$\therefore \quad x = 18.3$

Q. 79 Radha takes some flowers in a basket and visits three temples one-by-one. At each temple, she offers one half of the flowers from the basket. If she is left with 3 flowers at the end, then find the number of flowers she had in the beginning.

Sol. Let total number of the flowers be x.

Then, flowers offered in first temple $= \frac{x}{2}$

Flowers offered in second temple $= \frac{x}{4}$

Flowers offered in third temple $= \frac{x}{8}$

Number of flowers left at the end $= 3$

According to the question,

$$x - \left(\frac{x}{2} + \frac{x}{4} + \frac{x}{8}\right) = 3$$

$$\Rightarrow \quad \frac{8x - (4x + 2x + x)}{8} = 3$$

$$\Rightarrow \quad 8x - 7x = 24$$

$$\therefore \quad x = 24$$

Hence, total number of flowers she had in the beginning is 24.

Q. 80 ₹ 13500 are to be distributed among Salma, Kiran and Jenifer in such a way that Salma gets ₹ 1000 more than Kiran and Jenifer gets ₹ 500 more than Kiran. Find the money received by Jenifer.

Sol. Let the money received by Kiran be ₹ x.

Then, the money received by Salma = ₹ $(x + 1000)$

and the money received by Jenifer = ₹ $(x + 500)$

According to the question,

$$x + x + 1000 + x + 500 = 13500$$

$$\Rightarrow \quad 3x + 1500 = 13500$$

$$\Rightarrow \quad 3x = 13500 - 1500$$

$$\Rightarrow \quad 3x = 12000$$

$$\Rightarrow \quad x = \frac{12000}{3}$$

$$\therefore \quad x = 4000$$

Hence, the money received by Jenifer = ₹ 4000 + 500 = ₹4500

Q. 81 The volume of water in a tank is twice of that in the other. If we draw out 25 litres from the first and add it to the other, the volumes of the water in each tank will be the same. Find the volumes of water in each tank.

Sol. Let volume of water in one tank be x L.

Then, volume of the water in another tank = $2x$ L.

According to the question,

Volume of the water in first tank + 25 = Volume of the water in another tank − 25

$$\Rightarrow \quad x + 25 = 2x - 25$$

$$\Rightarrow \quad 2x - x = 25 + 25$$

$$\therefore \quad x = 50$$

Hence, volume of water in one tank = 50 L

and volume of the water in another tank = 2 × 50 = 100 L

Q. 82 **Anushka and Aarushi are friends. They have equal amount of money in their pockets. Anushka gave $\frac{1}{3}$ of her money to Aarushi as her birthday gift. Then, Aarushi gave a party at a restaurant and cleared the bill by paying half of the total money with her. If the remaining money in Aarushi's pocket is ₹ 1600, then find the sum gifted by Anushka.**

Sol. Let Anushka and Aarushi have equal amount of money in their packet, which is ₹ x.

After giving $\frac{1}{3}$ of the money of Anushka to Aarushi,

Amount of Aarushi = ₹ $\left(x + \frac{x}{3}\right)$

According to the question,

$$\left(x + \frac{x}{3}\right) - \frac{1}{2} \times \left(x + \frac{x}{3}\right) = 1600$$

$$\Rightarrow \quad \left(x + \frac{x}{3}\right)\left(1 - \frac{1}{2}\right) = 1600$$

$$\Rightarrow \quad \left(x + \frac{x}{3}\right) \times \frac{1}{2} = 1600$$

$$\Rightarrow \quad \frac{3x + x}{3} = 1600 \times 2$$

$$\Rightarrow \quad \frac{4x}{3} = 3200$$

$$\therefore \quad x = 3200 \times \frac{3}{4} = 2400$$

So, money gifted by Anushka = $\frac{1}{3}$ of $2400 = \frac{1}{3} \times 2400 =$ ₹ 800

Q. 83 **Kaustubh had 60 flowers. He offered some flowers in temple and found that the ratio of the number of remaining flowers to that of flowers in the beginning is 3 : 5. Find the number of flowers offered by him in the temple.**

Sol. Let number of flowers offered by Kaustubh in the temple be x.

Then, remaining flowers = $60 - x$

According to the question,

$$\frac{\text{Number of remaining flowers}}{\text{Number of flowers in beginning}} = \frac{3}{5} \quad \text{[given]}$$

$$\Rightarrow \quad \frac{60 - x}{60} = \frac{3}{5}$$

$$\Rightarrow \quad 300 - 5x = 180$$

$$\Rightarrow \quad 5x = 300 - 180$$

$$\Rightarrow \quad 5x = 120$$

$$\Rightarrow \quad x = \frac{120}{5}$$

$$\therefore \quad x = 24$$

Hence, the number of flowers offered by Kaustubh in the temple is 24.

Q. 84 The sum of three consecutive even natural numbers is 48. Find the greatest of these numbers.

Sol. Let the three consecutive even natural numbers be x, $(x + 2)$ and $(x + 4)$.

According to the question,

$$x + (x + 2) + (x + 4) = 48 \quad \text{[given]}$$

$$\Rightarrow \quad 3x + 6 = 48$$

$$\Rightarrow \quad 3x = 48 - 6$$

$$\Rightarrow \quad 3x = 42 \Rightarrow x = \frac{42}{3}$$

$$\therefore \quad x = 14$$

Hence, the three consecutive even natural numbers are 14, (14+2) and (14 + 4), i.e.14,16 and 18.

Therefore, the greatest number is 18.

Q. 85 The sum of three consecutive odd natural numbers is 69. Find the prime number out of these numbers.

Sol. Let the three consecutive odd natural numbers be x, $(x + 2)$ and $(x + 4)$.

According to the question,

$$x + (x + 2) + (x + 4) = 69 \quad \text{[given]}$$

$$\Rightarrow \quad 3x + 6 = 69$$

$$\Rightarrow \quad 3x = 69 - 6 \Rightarrow 3x = 63$$

$$\therefore \quad x = 63 \times \frac{1}{3} = 21$$

Thus, the three consecutive odd natural numbers are 21, (21 + 2) and (21 + 4), i.e. 21, 23 and 25. Out of these, only 23 is the prime number.

Q. 86 The sum of three consecutive numbers is 156. Find the number which is a multiple of 13 out of these numbers.

Sol. Let three consecutive numbers be x, $(x + 1)$ and $(x + 2)$.

According to the question,

$$x + (x + 1) + (x + 2) = 156 \quad \text{[given]}$$

$$\Rightarrow \quad 3x + 3 = 156 \Rightarrow 3x = 156 - 3 = 153$$

$$\therefore \quad x = 153 \times \frac{1}{3} = 51$$

Thus, we get the numbers 51, 51 + 1 and 51 + 2, i.e. 51, 52 and 53. Out of these, only 52 is a multiple of 13.

Q. 87 Find a number whose fifth part increased by 30 is equal to its fourth part decreased by 30.

Sol. Let the number be x.

According to the question,

$$\frac{x}{5} + 30 = \frac{x}{4} - 30$$

$$\Rightarrow \quad \frac{x}{5} - \frac{x}{4} = -30 - 30 \quad \left[\text{transposing } \frac{x}{4} \text{ to LHS and 30 to RHS}\right]$$

$$\Rightarrow \quad \frac{4x - 5x}{20} = -60$$

$$\Rightarrow \quad -x = -60 \times 20 \quad \text{[by cross-multiplication]}$$

$$\therefore \quad x = 1200$$

Hence, the required number is 1200.

Q. 88 Divide 54 into two parts, such that one part is $\frac{2}{7}$ of the other.

Sol. Let the other part be x. Then, first part will be $\frac{2x}{7}$.

According to the question,

$$x + \frac{2x}{7} = 54$$

$$\Rightarrow \quad \frac{7x + 2x}{7} = 54$$

$$\Rightarrow \quad 9x = 7 \times 54 \quad \text{[by cross-multiplication]}$$

$$\Rightarrow \quad x = \frac{7 \times 54}{9}$$

$$\Rightarrow \quad x = 7 \times 6$$

$$\Rightarrow \quad x = 42$$

Hence, the first part $= \frac{2 \times 42}{7} = 12$

and the other part = 42

Q. 89 Sum of the digits of a two-digit number is 11. The given number is less than the number obtained by interchanging the digits by 9. Find the number.

Sol. Let the unit's digit be x. Then, the ten's digit $= 11 - x$

$\therefore$ Number $= 10(11 - x) + x = 110 - 10x + x = 110 - 9x$

Number obtained by interchanging the digits $= 10x + (11 - x) = 9x + 11$

According to the question,

$$9x + 11 - (110 - 9x) = 9$$

$$\Rightarrow \quad 9x + 11 - 110 + 9x = 9$$

$$\Rightarrow \quad 18x = 9 - 11 + 110$$

$$\Rightarrow \quad 18x = 108$$

$$\Rightarrow \quad x = \frac{108}{18}$$

$$\Rightarrow \quad x = 6$$

Hence, unit's digit = 6 and ten's digit = 11 − 6 = 5

Therefore, the required number is 56.

Q. 90 Two equal sides of a triangle are each 4 m less than three times the third side. Find the dimensions of the triangle, if its perimeter is 55 m.

Sol. Let the third side of triangle be x m.

Then, two equal sides of triangle = $(3x - 4)$m

Given, perimeter of triangle = 55m

$\because$ Perimeter of a triangle = Sum of the sides of the triangle

$$\therefore \quad x + 3x - 4 + 3x - 4 = 55$$

$$\Rightarrow \quad 7x - 8 = 55 \Rightarrow 7x = 55 + 8$$

$$\Rightarrow \quad 7x = 63 \Rightarrow x = \frac{63}{7}$$

$$\therefore \quad x = 9$$

Hence, the dimensions of the triangle are 9 m, $(3 \times 9 - 4)$ m and $(3 \times 9 - 4)$m, i.e. 9, $(27 - 4)$, and $(27 - 4)$ m, i.e. 9 m, 23 m and 23m.

Q. 91 After 12 years, Kanwar shall be 3 times as old as he was 4 years ago. Find his present age.

Sol. Let Kanwar's present age be x yr.

After 12 yr, Kanwar's age = $(x + 12)$y

and 4 yr ago, Kanwar's age = $(x - 4)$yr

According to the question,

$$x + 12 = 3(x - 4) \Rightarrow x + 12 = 3x - 12$$

$$\Rightarrow \quad 3x - x = 12 + 12 \Rightarrow 2x = 24$$

$$\Rightarrow \quad x = \frac{24}{2}$$

$$\therefore \quad x = 12$$

Hence, Kanwar's present age is 12 yr.

Q. 92 Anima left one-half of her property to her daughter, one-third to her son and donated the rest to an educational institute. If the donation was worth ₹ 100000, how much money did Anima have?

Sol. Let Anima's property be ₹ x.

Property left for her daughter = ₹ $\frac{x}{2}$

Remaining property = $x - \frac{x}{2} = \frac{2x - x}{2}$ = ₹ $\frac{x}{2}$

Property left for her son = $\frac{1}{3}$ of remaining property = $\frac{1}{3} \times \frac{x}{2}$ = ₹ $\frac{x}{6}$

Remaining property = $\left[x - \left(\frac{x}{2} + \frac{x}{6}\right)\right] = x - \left(\frac{3x + x}{6}\right) = \frac{6x - 4x}{6} = \frac{2x}{6}$ = ₹ $\frac{x}{3}$

Since, the remaining property donated to an educational institute.

But donation property = ₹ 100000

$$\therefore \quad \frac{x}{3} = 100000 \Rightarrow x = 300000$$

Hence, Anima had ₹ 300000.

Q. 93 **If $\frac{1}{2}$ is subtracted from a number and the difference is multiplied by 4, the result is 5. What is the number?**

Sol. Let the number be x.

According to the question,

$$4\left(x-\frac{1}{2}\right)=5 \Rightarrow 4x-2=5$$

$$\Rightarrow \quad 4x=5+2 \Rightarrow 4x=7$$

$$\therefore \quad x=\frac{7}{4}$$

Hence, the required number is $\frac{7}{4}$.

Q. 94 **The sum of four consecutive integers is 266. What are the integers?**

Sol. Let the four consecutive integers be x, $x+1$, $x+2$ and $x+3$.

According to the question,

$$x+x+1+x+2+x+3=266 \quad \text{[given]}$$

$$\Rightarrow \quad 4x+6=266$$

$$\Rightarrow \quad 4x=266-6$$

$$\Rightarrow \quad 4x=260$$

$$\Rightarrow \quad x=\frac{260}{4}$$

$$\therefore \quad x=65$$

Hence, the four consecutive integers are 65, 65 + 1, 65 + 2 and 65 + 3, i.e. 65, 66, 67 and 68.

Q. 95 **Hamid has three boxes of different fruits. Box *A* weighs $2\frac{1}{2}$ kg more than box *B* and Box *C* weighs $10\frac{1}{4}$ kg more than box *B*. The total weight of the three boxes is $48\frac{3}{4}$ kg. How many kilograms does box *A* weigh?**

Sol. Let the weight of box A be x kg.

According to the question,

$$\text{Weight of Box } A=\text{Weight of Box B}+\frac{5}{2}\text{ kg} \quad \text{[given]}$$

$$\Rightarrow \quad \text{Weight of box } B=\left(x-\frac{5}{2}\right)\text{kg}$$

$$\text{and weight of Box } C=\text{Weight of box } B+\frac{41}{4}\text{ kg} \quad \text{[given]}$$

$$\Rightarrow \quad \text{Weight of Box } C=x-\frac{5}{2}+\frac{41}{4}\text{ kg}=x+\left(\frac{-10+41}{4}\right)\text{kg}=\left(x+\frac{31}{4}\right)\text{kg}$$

$$\text{As, total weight of three boxes}=48\frac{3}{4}\text{ kg}=\frac{195}{4}\text{ kg} \quad \text{[given]}$$

$\because$ Total weight of three boxes = Weight of box A + Weight of box B + Weight of box C

$\therefore$ $$\frac{195}{4} = x + x - \frac{5}{2} + x + \frac{31}{4}$$

$\Rightarrow$ $$\frac{195}{4} = 3x + \frac{31-10}{4}$$

$\Rightarrow$ $$\frac{195}{4} = 3x + \frac{21}{4} \Rightarrow 3x = \frac{195}{4} - \frac{21}{4}$$

$\Rightarrow$ $$3x = \frac{195-21}{4} \Rightarrow 3x = \frac{174}{4}$$

$\Rightarrow$ $$x = \frac{174}{3 \times 4} \Rightarrow x = \frac{29}{2}$$

$\therefore$ $$x = 14\frac{1}{2} \text{ kg}$$

Hence, box A weighs $14\frac{1}{2}$ kg.

Q. 96 The perimeter of a rectangle is 240 cm. If its length is increased by 10% and its breadth is decreased by 20%, then we get the same perimeter. Find the length and breadth of the rectangle.

Sol. Given, perimeter of rectangle = 240 cm

$\Rightarrow$ $2 \times (\text{Length} + \text{Breadth}) = 240$ cm

$\Rightarrow$ Length + Breadth = 120 cm

Let the length of rectangle be x cm.

Then, the breadth of rectangle = $(120 - x)$ cm

$\therefore$ New length of rectangle = x + 10% of $x = x + \frac{10}{100} \times x = \frac{110}{100} x$ cm

and new breadth of rectangle = $(120 - x)$ − 20% of $(120 - x)$ cm

$$= (120 - x) - \frac{20}{100} \times (120 - x)$$

$$= (120 - x)\left(1 - \frac{20}{100}\right) = \frac{80}{100}(120 - x) \text{ cm}$$

It is given that, perimeter of new rectangle is 240 cm.

According to the question,

$$2 \times (\text{New length} + \text{New breadth}) = 240$$

$\Rightarrow$ $$2 \times \left[\frac{110x}{100} + \frac{80}{100}(120 - x)\right] = 240$$

$\Rightarrow$ $$\frac{110x + 9600 - 80x}{100} = \frac{240}{2}$$

$\Rightarrow$ $$30x + 9600 = \frac{240}{2} \times 100$$

$\Rightarrow$ $$30x + 9600 = 12000$$

$\Rightarrow$ $$30x = 12000 - 9600$$

$\Rightarrow$ $$30x = 2400$$

$\Rightarrow$ $$x = \frac{2400}{30} = 80$$

Hence, length of rectangle = 80 cm

and breadth of rectangle = 120 − 80 = 40 cm

Q. 97 The age of A is five years more than that of B. 5 years ago, the ratio of their ages was 3 : 2. Find their present ages.

Sol. Let the present age of B be x yr.

Then, the present age of $A = (x + 5)$ yr

Five years ago, age of $A = x + 5 - 5 = x$ yr

and age of $B = (x - 5)$ yr

According to the question,

$$\frac{x}{x-5} = \frac{3}{2}$$

$$\Rightarrow \quad 2x = 3(x - 5)$$

$$\Rightarrow \quad 2x = 3x - 15$$

$$\Rightarrow \quad 3x - 2x = 15$$

$$\therefore \quad x = 15$$

Hence, the present age of B is 15 yr and the present age of A is (15 + 5), i.e. 20 yr.

Q. 98 If numerator is 2 less than denominator of a rational number and when 1 is subtracted from numerator and denominator both, the rational number in its simplest form is $\frac{1}{2}$. What is the rational number?

Sol. Suppose denominator of a rational number be x.

Numerator = Denominator − 2 = $x - 2$

According to the question,

$$\frac{(x-2)-1}{x-1} = \frac{1}{2}$$

$$\Rightarrow \quad 2(x - 2 - 1) = x - 1$$

$$\Rightarrow \quad 2(x - 3) = x - 1$$

$$\Rightarrow \quad 2x - 6 = x - 1$$

$$\Rightarrow \quad 2x - x = 6 - 1$$

$$\therefore \quad x = 5$$

Hence, denominator = 5 and numerator = 5 − 2 = 3

Thus, the rational number is $\frac{3}{5}$.

Q. 99 In a two-digit number, digit in unit's place is twice the digit in ten's place. If 27 is added to it, digits are reversed. Find the number.

Sol. Let ten's digit of two-digit number be x.

Then, unit's digit = $2x$

$\therefore$ Number = $10 \times x + 2x = 10x + 2x = 12x$

On reversing the digits,

New number = $10 \times (2x) + x = 20x + x = 21x$

According to the question,

$$12x + 27 = 21x$$

$\Rightarrow$ $21x - 12x = 27$

$\Rightarrow$ $9x = 27$

$\Rightarrow$ $x = 3$

Hence, the required number is 12×3, i.e. 36.

Q. 100 A man was engaged as typist for the month of February in 2009. He was paid ₹ 500 per day, but ₹ 100 per day were deducted for the days he remained absent. He received ₹ 9100 as salary for the month. For how many days did he work?

Sol. Let the man worked as a typist for x days in the month of February 2009.

Then, absent in the month of February 2009 = $(29 - x)$ days

[we know that, number of days in month of February 2009 is 29]

Per day payment = ₹ 500 [given]

Total paid amount for working days = ₹ $500x$

And per day deduction, when he remained absent = ₹ 100 [given]

Total amount deducted for being absent = ₹ $100 \times (29 - x)$

Given, salary received by man for the month of February is ₹ 9100.

According to the question,

$$500\,x - 100\,(29 - x) = 9100$$

$\Rightarrow$ $500\,x - 2900 + 100\,x = 9100$

$\Rightarrow$ $600\,x = 9100 + 2900$

$\Rightarrow$ $600\,x = 12000$

$\Rightarrow$ $x = \frac{12000}{600}$

$\therefore$ $x = 20$

Therefore, the man worked for 20 days.

Q. 101 A steamer goes downstream and covers the distance between two ports in 3 hours. It covers distance in 5 hours, when it goes upstream. If the stream flows at 3 km/h, then find what is the speed of the steamer upstream?

Sol. Let speed of the steamer in still water be x km/h.

Speed of the stream = 3 km/h [given]

Now, speed of the steamer downstream = $(x + 3)$ km/h

and speed of the steamer upstream = $(x - 3)$ km/h

According to the question,

Distance covered in 3 h by steamer downstream

= Distance covered in 5 h by steamer upstream

$\therefore$ $3\,(x + 3) = 5(x - 3)$ [$\because$ distance = speed $\times$ time]

$\Rightarrow$ $3x + 9 = 5x - 15$

$\Rightarrow \quad 3x - 5x = -15 - 9$

$\Rightarrow \quad -2x = -24$

$\Rightarrow \quad x = -24 \times \left(\frac{-1}{2}\right) = 12 \text{ km/h}$

Hence, the speed of the steamer upstream is (12 – 3), i.e. 9 km/h.

Q. 102 A lady went to a bank with ₹ 100000. She asked the cashier to give her ₹ 500 and ₹1000 currency notes in return. She got 175 currency notes in all. Find the number of each kind of currency notes.

Sol. Given, total number of currency notes = 175

Let the total number of notes of ₹ 500 be x.

Then, total number of notes of ₹ 1000 = 175 – x

$\because$ Total amount which lady had = ₹ 100000 [given]

According to the question,

$$500x + (175 - x)\,1000 = 100000$$

$\Rightarrow \quad 500x + 175000 - 1000x = 100000$

$\Rightarrow \quad -500x = 100000 - 175000$

$\Rightarrow \quad -500x = -75000$

$\Rightarrow \quad x = -75000 \times \left(\frac{-1}{500}\right)$

$\therefore \quad x = 150$

Therefore, total number of notes of ₹ 500 = 150

and total number of notes of ₹ 1000 = 175 – 150 = 25

Q. 103 There are 40 passengers in a bus, some with ₹ 3 tickets and remaining with ₹ 10 tickets. The total collection from these passengers is ₹ 295. Find how many passengers have tickets worth ₹ 3?

Sol. Given, total number of passengers = 40

Let the number of passengers having tickets worth ₹ 3 be x.

Then, the number of passengers having tickets worth ₹ 10 = (40 – x)

Total collection from passengers = ₹ 295 [given]

According to the question,

$$3x + 10(40 - x) = 295$$

$\Rightarrow \quad 3x + 400 - 10x = 295$

$\Rightarrow \quad -7x = 295 - 400$

$\Rightarrow \quad -7x = -105$

$\Rightarrow \quad x = -105 \times \left(\frac{-1}{7}\right)$

$\therefore \quad x = 15$

Hence, the number of passengers having tickets worth ₹ 3 is 15.

Q. 104 **Denominator of a number is 4 less than its numerator. If 6 is added to the numerator, it becomes thrice the denominator. Find the fraction.**

Sol. Let the numerator of the number be x.

Then, denominator of the number = $x - 4$

$$\therefore \quad \text{Fraction} = \frac{x}{x-4} \quad \ldots(i)$$

According to the question, if 6 is added to numerator, it becomes thrice the denominator.

$$\therefore \quad x + 6 = 3(x - 4)$$

$$\Rightarrow \quad 3x - 12 = x + 6$$

$$\Rightarrow \quad 3x - x = 6 + 12$$

$$\Rightarrow \quad 2x = 18$$

$$\Rightarrow \quad x = \frac{18}{2}$$

$$\therefore \quad x = 9$$

Hence, fraction $= \dfrac{x}{x-4} = \dfrac{9}{9-4} = \dfrac{9}{5}$

Q. 105 **An employee works in a company on a contract of 30 days on the condition that he will receive ₹ 120 for each day he works and he will be fined ₹ 10 for each day he is absent. If he receives ₹ 2300 in all, for how many days did he remain absent?**

Sol. Given, total number of days in contract = 30

Money received per day for working = ₹ 120

Money deducted per day for being absent = ₹ 10

and amount received by employee as salary = ₹ 2300

Let the employee remained absent for x days. Then, employee worked for $(30 - x)$ days.

According to the question,

$$120(30 - x) - 10x = 2300$$

$$\Rightarrow \quad 3600 - 120x - 10x = 2300$$

$$\Rightarrow \quad -130x = -3600 + 2300$$

$$\Rightarrow \quad -130x = -1300$$

$$\Rightarrow \quad x = -1300 \times \left(\frac{-1}{130}\right)$$

$$\therefore \quad x = 10$$

Therefore, employee remained absent for 10 days.

Q. 106 **Kusum buys some chocolates at the rate of ₹ 10 per chocolate. She also buys an equal number of candies at the rate of ₹ 5 per candy. She makes a 20% profit on chocolates and 8% profit on candies. At the end of the day, all chocolates and candies are sold out and her profit is ₹ 240. Find the number of chocolates purchased.**

Sol. Let Kusum purchased x chocolates.

Then, total cost of chocolates = ₹ $10x$

Similarly, she purchased x candies.

Then, total cost of candies = ₹ $5x$

According to the question,

Profit on chocolates = 20% of $10x = \frac{20}{100} \times 10x =$ ₹ $2x$

and profit on candies = 8% of $5x = \frac{8}{100} \times 5x =$ ₹ $0.4x$

$\therefore$ Total profit = $2x + 0.4x =$ ₹ $2.4x$

But it is given that total profit is ₹ 240.

Again, according to the question,

$$2.4x = 240 \Rightarrow x = \frac{240}{2.4} = 100$$

Hence, she purchased 100 chocolates.

Q. 107 **A steamer goes downstream and covers the distance between two ports in 5 hours, while it covers the same distance upstream in 6 hours. If the speed of the stream is 1 km/h, then find the speed of the steamer in still water.**

Sol. Given, speed of stream = 1 km/h

Let speed of the steamer in still water be x km/h.

Then, speed of steamer downstream = $(x + 1)$ km/h

and speed of steamer upstream = $(x - 1)$ km/h

According to the question,

Distance covered upstream = Distance covered downstream

$\Rightarrow$ (Speed of steamer in upstream) × Time taken upstream

= (Speed of steamer downstream) × Time taken downstream

[$\because$ distance = speed × time]

$$\Rightarrow (x - 1) \times 6 = (x + 1) \times 5$$

$$\Rightarrow 6x - 6 = 5x + 5$$

$$\Rightarrow 6x - 5x = 6 + 5$$

$$\therefore x = 11$$

Therefore, the speed of steamer in still water is 11 km/h.

Q. 108 **Distance between two places A and B is 210 km. Two cars start simultaneously from A and B in opposite directions and distance between them after 3 hours is 54 km. If speed of one car is less than that of other by 8 km/h, then find the speed of each.**

Sol. Let the speed of car starts from A be x km/h.

Then, speed of car starts from $B = (x + 8)$ km/h

Given, distance between the cars after 3 h = 54 km

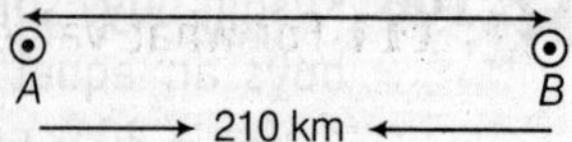

According to the question,

Total distance between A and B – Total distance covered by both cars in 3 h = 54

$\Rightarrow$ $210 - [3x + 3(x + 8)] = 54$ [$\because$ distance = speed × time]

$\Rightarrow \quad 210 - 3x - 3x - 24 = 54$

$\Rightarrow \quad -6x = -210 + 24 + 54$

$\Rightarrow \quad -6x = -210 + 78$

$\Rightarrow \quad -6x = -132$

$\Rightarrow \quad x = -132 \times \left(\frac{-1}{6}\right)$

$\therefore \quad x = 22$

Hence, the speed of car starts from $A = 22$ km/h

and the speed of car starts from $B = 22 + 8 = 30$ km/h

Q. 109 A carpenter charged ₹ 2500 for making a bed. The cost of materials used is ₹ 1100 and the labour charge is ₹ 200 per hour. For how many hours did the carpenter work?

Sol. Let the carpenter worked for x h.

Given, labour charge = ₹ 200 per hour

Then, total labour charge = ₹ $200x$

As, amount charged by carpenter for making a bed

= Cost of materials + Total labour charge

$\therefore \quad 2500 = 1100 + 200x \Rightarrow 200x = 2500 - 1100$

$\Rightarrow \quad 200x = 1400 \Rightarrow x = \frac{1400}{200} = 7$

Hence, the carpenter worked for 7 h.

Q. 110 For what value of x is the perimeter of shape 77cm?

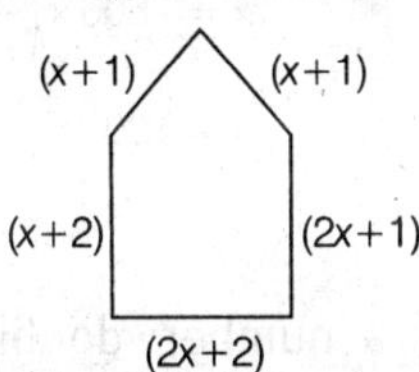

Sol. Given, perimeter of shape = 77 cm

$\therefore$ Sum of all sides of the shape = 77

$\Rightarrow (x + 1) + (x + 1) + (x + 2) + (2x + 1) + (2x + 2) = 77$

$\Rightarrow \quad 7x + 7 = 77 \Rightarrow 7x = 77 - 7$

$\Rightarrow \quad 7x = 70 \Rightarrow x = \frac{70}{7} = 10$

Hence, the value of x is 10 cm.

Q. 111 For what value of x is the perimeter of shape 186 cm?

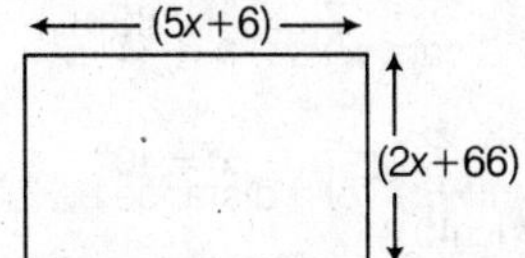

Sol. Given, length of the given figure = $(5x + 6)$

and breadth of the given figure = $(2x + 66)$

$\because$ Perimeter of shape = 186 cm [given]

$\therefore \quad 2 \times (\text{Length} + \text{Breadth}) = 186$

$\Rightarrow \quad 2 \times [(5x + 6) + (2x + 66)] = 186$

$\Rightarrow \quad 2 \times [7x + 72] = 186$

$\Rightarrow \quad 14x + 144 = 186$

$\Rightarrow \quad 14x = 186 - 144$

$\Rightarrow \quad 14x = 42$

$\Rightarrow \quad x = \dfrac{42}{14}$

$\therefore \quad x = 3$

Hence, the value of x is 3 cm.

Q. 112 On dividing ₹ 200 between *A* and *B*, such that twice of *A*'s share is less than 3 times *B*'s share by 200, what is *B*'s share?

Sol. Let *B*'s share be ₹ x. Then, *A*'s share = ₹ $(200 - x)$

According to the question,

$2 \times (A\text{'s share}) = 3 \times (B\text{'s share}) - 200$

$\Rightarrow \quad 2 \times (200 - x) = 3x - 200$

$\Rightarrow \quad 400 - 2x = 3x - 200$

$\Rightarrow \quad -2x - 3x = -200 - 400$

$\Rightarrow \quad -5x = -600$

$\Rightarrow \quad x = -600 \times \left(-\dfrac{1}{5}\right)$

$\therefore \quad x = 120$

Hence, *B*'s share is ₹ 120.

Q. 113 Madhulika thought of a number, doubled it and added 20 to it. On dividing the resulting number by 25, she gets 4. What is the number?

Sol. Let the number be x.

According to the question,

$$\frac{2x + 20}{25} = 4$$

$\Rightarrow \quad 2x + 20 = 25 \times 4$

$\Rightarrow \quad 2x + 20 = 100$

$\Rightarrow \quad 2x = 100 - 20$

$\Rightarrow \quad 2x = 80$

$\Rightarrow \quad x = \dfrac{80}{2}$

$\therefore \quad x = 40$

Hence, the required number is 40.

5

Understanding Quadrilaterals and Practical Geometry

Multiple Choice Questions (MCQs)

Q. 1 If three angles of a quadrilateral are each equal to 75°, then, the fourth angle is

(a) 150° (b) 135°
(c) 45° (d) 75°

Sol. *(b)* Given, three angles of quadrilateral = 75°
Let the fourth angle be $x°$.

Then, according to the property, $75° + 75° + 75° + x° = 360°$, since sum of the angles of a quadrilateral is 360°.

So, $225° + x° = 360°$ or $x° = 360° - 225° = 135°$

Hence, the fourth angle is 135°.

Q. 2 For which of the following, diagonals bisect each other?

(a) Square (b) Kite
(c) Trapezium (d) Quadrilateral

Sol. *(a)* We know that, the diagonals of a square bisect each other but the diagonals of kite, trapezium and quadrilateral do not bisect each other.

Q. 3 In which of the following figures, all angles are equal?

(a) Rectangle (b) Kite
(c) Trapezium (d) Rhombus

Sol. *(a)* In a rectangle, all angles are equal, i.e. all equal to 90°.

Q. 4 For which of the following figures, diagonals are perpendicular to each other?

(a) Parallelogram
(b) Kite
(c) Trapezium
(d) Rectangle

Sol. ***(b)*** The diagonals of a kite are perpendicular to each other.

Q. 5 For which of the following figures, diagonals are equal?

(a) Trapezium
(b) Rhombus
(c) Parallelogram
(d) Rectangle

Sol. ***(d)*** By the property of a rectangle, we know that its diagonals are equal.

Q. 6 Which of the following figures satisfy the following properties?

All sides are congruent.

All angles are right angles.

Opposite sides are parallel.

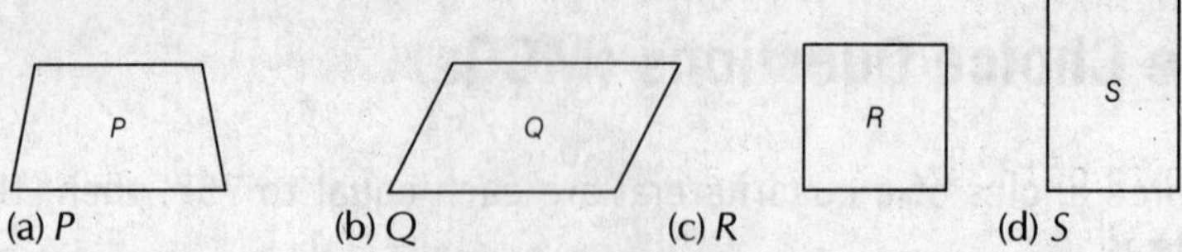

(a) *P* (b) *Q* (c) *R* (d) *S*

Sol. ***(c)*** We know that all the properties mentioned above are related to square and we can observe that figure *R* resembles a square.

Q. 7 Which of the following figures satisfy the following property?
Has two pairs of congruent adjacent sides.

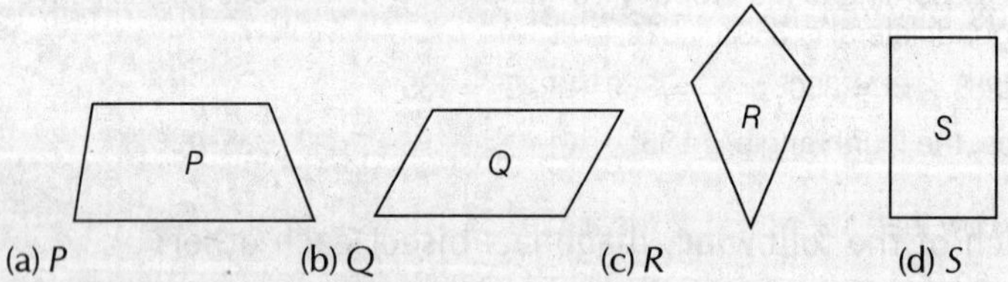

(a) *P* (b) *Q* (c) *R* (d) *S*

Sol. ***(c)*** We know that, a kite has two pairs of congruent adjacent sides and we can observe that figure *R* resembles a kite.

Q. 8 Which of the following figures satisfy the following property?
Only one pair of sides are parallel.

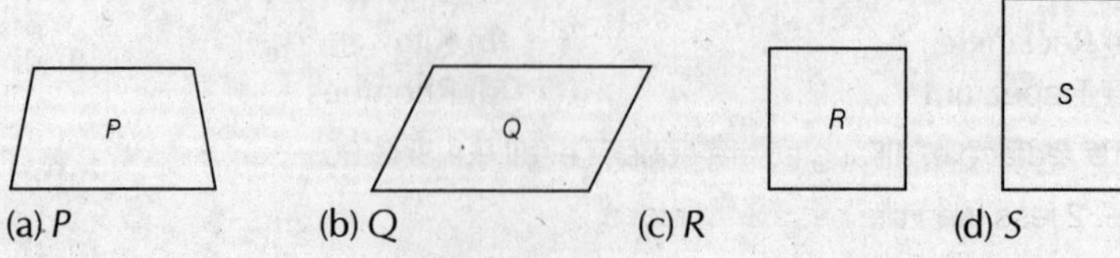

(a) *P* (b) *Q* (c) *R* (d) *S*

Sol. ***(a)*** We know that, in a trapezium, only one pair of sides are parallel and we can observe that figure *P* resembles a trapezium.

Q. 9 Which of the following figures do not satisfy any of the following properties?

All sides are equal.

All angles are right angles.

Opposite sides are parallel.

(a) P (b) Q (c) R (d) S

Sol. ***(a)*** On observing the above figures, we conclude that the figure P does not satisfy any of the given properties.

Q. 10 Which of the following properties describe a trapezium?

(a) A pair of opposite sides is parallel
(b) The diagonals bisect each other
(c) The diagonals are perpendicular to each other
(d) The diagonals are equal

Sol. ***(a)*** We know that, in a trapezium, a pair of opposite sides are parallel.

Q. 11 Which of the following is a property of a parallelogram?

(a) Opposite sides are parallel
(b) The diagonals bisect each other at right angles
(c) The diagonals are perpendicular to each other
(d) All angles are equal

Sol. ***(a)*** We know that, in a parallelogram, opposite sides are parallel.

Q. 12 What is the maximum number of obtuse angles that a quadrilateral can have?

(a) 1 (b) 2
(c) 3 (d) 4

Sol. ***(c)*** We know that, the sum of all the angles of a quadrilateral is $360°$.

Also, an obtuse angle is more than $90°$ and less than $180°$.

Thus, all the angles of a quadrilateral cannot be obtuse.

Hence, atmost 3 angles can be obtuse.

Q. 13 How many non-overlapping triangles can we make in a n-gon (polygon having n sides), by joining the vertices?

(a) $n-1$ (b) $n-2$
(c) $n-3$ (d) $n-4$

Sol. ***(b)*** The number of non-overlapping triangles in a n-gon $= n-2$,

i.e. 2 less than the number of sides.

Q. 14 What is the sum of all the angles of a pentagon?

(a) 180° (b) 360° (c) 540° (d) 720°

Sol. *(c)* We know that, the sum of angles of a polygon is $(n-2) \times 180°$, where n is the number of sides of the polygon.

In pentagon, $n = 5$

$\therefore$ Sum of the angles $= (n-2) \times 180° = (5-2) \times 180°$

$= 3 \times 180° = 540°$

Q. 15 What is the sum of all angles of a hexagon?

(a) 180° (b) 360° (c) 540° (d) 720°

Sol. *(d)* Sum of all angles of a n-gon is $(n-2) \times 180°$.

In hexagon, $n = 6$, therefore the required sum $= (6-2) \times 180° = 4 \times 180° = 720°$

Q. 16 If two adjacent angles of a parallelogram are $(5x - 5)$ and $(10x + 35)$, then the ratio of these angles is

(a) 1 : 3 (b) 2 : 3 (c) 1 : 4 (d) 1 : 2

Sol. *(a)* We know that, adjacent angles of a parallelogram are supplementary, i.e. their sum equals 180°.

$\therefore (5x - 5) + (10x + 35) = 180°$

$\Rightarrow 15x + 30° = 180°$

$\Rightarrow 15x = 150°$

$\Rightarrow x = 10°$

Thus, the angles are $(5 \times 10 - 5)$ and $(10 \times 10 + 35)$, i.e. 45° and 135°.

Hence, the required ratio is 45° : 135°, i.e. 1 : 3.

Q. 17 A quadrilateral whose all sides are equal, opposite angles are equal and the diagonals bisect each other at right angles is a ______ .

(a) rhombus (b) parallelogram (c) square (d) rectangle

Sol. *(a)* We know that, in rhombus, all sides are equal, opposite angles are equal and diagonals bisect each other at right angles.

Q. 18 A quadrilateral whose opposite sides and all the angles are equal is a

(a) rectangle (b) parallelogram (c) square (d) rhombus

Sol. *(a)* We know that, in a rectangle, opposite sides and all the angles are equal.

Q. 19 A quadrilateral whose all sides, diagonals and angles are equal is a

(a) square (b) trapezium (c) rectangle (d) rhombus

Sol. *(a)* These are the properties of a square, i.e. in a square, all sides, diagonals and angles are equal.

Q. 20 How many diagonals does a hexagon have?

(a) 9 (b) 8 (c) 2 (d) 6

Sol. *(a)* We know that, the number of diagonals in a polygon of n sides is $\frac{n(n-3)}{2}$.

In hexagon, $n = 6$

$\therefore$ Number of diagonals in a hexagon $= \frac{6(6-3)}{2} = \frac{6 \times 3}{2} = 3 \times 3 = 9$

Q. 21 If the adjacent sides of a parallelogram are equal, then parallelogram is a

(a) rectangle (b) trapezium (c) rhombus (d) square

Sol. *(c)* We know that, in a parallelogram, opposite sides are equal.

But according to the question, adjacent sides are also equal.

Thus, the parallelogram in which all the sides are equal is known as rhombus.

Q. 22 If the diagonals of a quadrilateral are equal and bisect each other, then the quadrilateral is a

(a) rhombus (b) rectangle (c) square (d) parallelogram

Sol. *(b)* Since, diagonals are equal and bisect each other, therefore it will be a rectangle.

Q. 23 The sum of all exterior angles of a triangle is

(a) 180° (b) 360° (c) 540° (d) 720°

Sol. *(b)* We know that, the sum of exterior angles, taken in order of any polygon is 360° and triangle is also a polygon.

Hence, the sum of all exterior angles of a triangle is 360°.

Q. 24 Which of the following is an equiangular and equilateral polygon?

(a) Square (b) Rectangle (c) Rhombus (d) Right triangle

Sol. *(a)* In a square, all the sides and all the angles are equal.

Hence, square is an equiangular and equilateral polygon.

Q. 25 Which one has all the properties of a kite and a parallelogram?

(a) Trapezium (b) Rhombus (c) Rectangle (d) Parallelogram

Sol. *(b)* **In a kite**

Two pairs of equal sides.

Diagonals bisect at 90°.

One pair of opposite angles are equal.

In a parallelogram

Opposite sides are equal.

Opposite angles are equal.

Diagonals bisect each other.

So, from the given options, all these properties are satisfied by rhombus.

Q. 26 **The angles of a quadrilateral are in the ratio 1 : 2 : 3 : 4. The smallest angle is**

(a) 72° (b) 144° (c) 36° (d) 18°

Sol. *(c)* Let the angles of the given quadrilateral be $x°, 2x°, 3x°$ and $4x°$.

$\therefore x° + 2x° + 3x° + 4x° = 360°$ [$\because$ sum of the angles of a quadrilateral is 360°]

$\Rightarrow \quad 10x = 360°$

$\Rightarrow \quad x = \dfrac{360°}{10} = 36°$

Hence, the smallest angle = 36°

Q. 27 **In the trapezium *ABCD*, the measure of $\angle D$ is**

(a) 55° (b) 115° (c) 135° (d) 125°

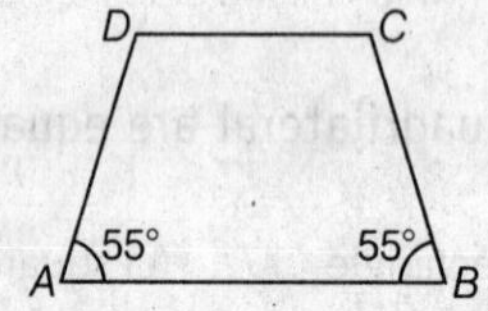

Sol. *(d)* We know that, in a trapezium, the angles on either sides of base are supplementary angle.

In trapezium *ABCD*,

$\therefore \quad \angle A + \angle D = 180°$

$\Rightarrow \quad 55° + \angle D = 180°$

$\Rightarrow \quad \angle D = 180° - 55°$

$\Rightarrow \quad \angle D = 125°$

Q. 28 **A quadrilateral has three acute angles. If each measures 80°, then the measure of the fourth angle is**

(a) 150° (b) 120° (c) 105° (d) 140°

Sol. *(b)* Let the fourth angle be x, then $80° + 80° + 80° + x = 360°$

[$\because$ sum of all the angles of quadrilateral is 360°]

$\Rightarrow \quad 240° + x = 360°$

$\Rightarrow \quad x = 360° - 240°$

$\Rightarrow \quad x = 120°$

Q. 29 **The number of sides of a regular polygon where each exterior angle has a measure of 45° is**

(a) 8 (b) 10 (c) 4 (d) 6

Sol. *(a)* We know that, the sum of exterior angles taken in an order of a polygon is 360°.

Since, each exterior angle measures 45°, therefore the number of sides

$$= \frac{\text{Sum of exterior angles}}{\text{Measure of an exterior angle}}$$

$$= \frac{360°}{45°} = 8$$

Q. 30 In a parallelogram $PQRS$, if $\angle P = 60°$, then other three angles are

(a) 45°, 135°, 120° (b) 60°, 120°, 120°
(c) 60°, 135°, 135° (d) 45°, 135°, 135°

Sol. *(b)* Given, $\angle P = 60°$

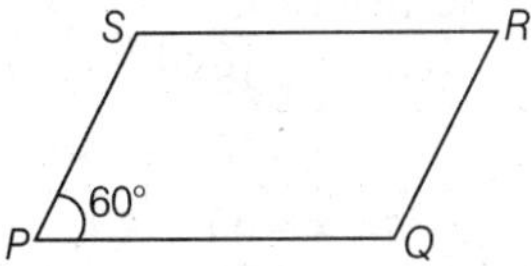

Since, in a parallelogram, adjacent angles are supplementary,

$\angle P + \angle Q = 180° \Rightarrow 60° + \angle Q = 180° \quad \Rightarrow \quad \angle Q = 120°$

Also, opposite angles are equal in a parallelogram.

Therefore, $\angle R = \angle P = 60°$, $\angle S = \angle Q = 120°$

Hence, other three angles are 60°, 120°, 120°.

Q. 31 If two adjacent angles of a parallelogram are in the ratio 2 : 3, then the measure of angles are

(a) 72°, 108° (b) 36°, 54° (c) 80°, 120° (d) 96°, 144°

Sol. *(a)* Let the angles be $2x$ and $3x$.

Then, $2x + 3x = 180°$ [$\because$ adjacent angles of a parallelogram are supplementary]

$\Rightarrow \quad 5x = 180°$

$\Rightarrow \quad x = 36°$

Hence, the measures of angles are $2x = 2 \times 36° = 72°$ and $3x = 3 \times 36° = 108°$

Q. 32 If $PQRS$ is a parallelogram, then $\angle P - \angle R$ is equal to

(a) 60° (b) 90° (c) 80° (d) 0°

Sol. *(d)* Since, in a parallelogram, opposite angles are equal. Therefore, $\angle P - \angle R = 0$, as $\angle P$ and $\angle R$ are opposite angles.

Q. 33 The sum of adjacent angles of a parallelogram is

(a) 180° (b) 120° (c) 360° (d) 90°

Sol. *(a)* By property of the parallelogram, we know that, the sum of adjacent angles of a parallelogram is 180°.

Q. 34 The angle between the two altitudes of a parallelogram through the same vertex of an obtuse angle of the parallelogram is 30°. The measure of the obtuse angle is

(a) 100° (b) 150° (c) 105° (d) 120°

Sol. *(b)* Let EC and FC be altitudes and $\angle ECF = 30°$.

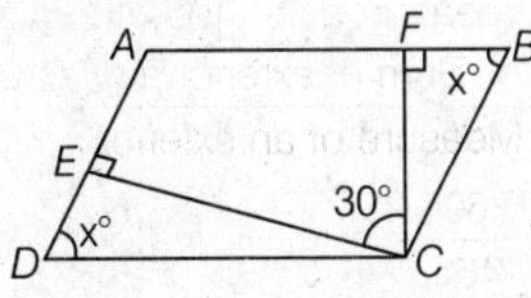

Let $\angle EDC = x = \angle FBC$

So, $\angle ECD = 90 - x°$ and $\angle BCF = 90° - x$

So, by property of the parallelogram,

$$\angle ADC + \angle DCB = 180°$$

$$\angle ADC + (\angle ECD + \angle ECF + \angle BCF) = 180°$$

$$\Rightarrow \quad x + 90° - x + 30° + 90° - x = 180°$$

$$\Rightarrow \quad -x = 180° - 210° = -30°$$

$$\Rightarrow \quad x = 30°$$

Hence, $\angle DCB = 30° + 60° + 60° = 150°$

Q. 35 In the given figure, $ABCD$ and $BDCE$ are parallelograms with common base DC. If $BC \perp BD$, then $\angle BEC$ is equal to

 (a) 60° 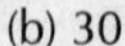 (b) 30° (c) 150° (d) 120°

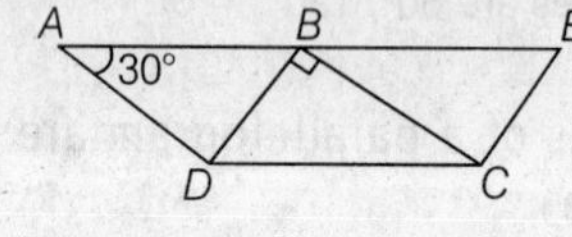

Sol. *(a)* $\angle BAD = 30°$ [given]

$\therefore \quad \angle BCD = 30°$ [$\because$ opposite angles of a parallelogram are equal]

In ΔCBD, by angle sum property of a triangle, we have

$\angle DBC + \angle BCD + \angle CDB = 180°$

$\Rightarrow \quad 90° + 30° + \angle CDB = 180°$

$\Rightarrow \quad \angle CDB = 180° - 120° = 60°$

$\therefore \quad \angle BEC = 60°$ [$\because$ opposite angles of a parallelogram are equal]

Q. 36 Length of one of the diagonals of a rectangle whose sides are 10 cm and 24 cm is

(a) 25 cm (b) 20 cm (c) 26 cm (d) 3.5 cm

Sol. *(c)* In ΔBCD,

$\angle BDC = 90°$

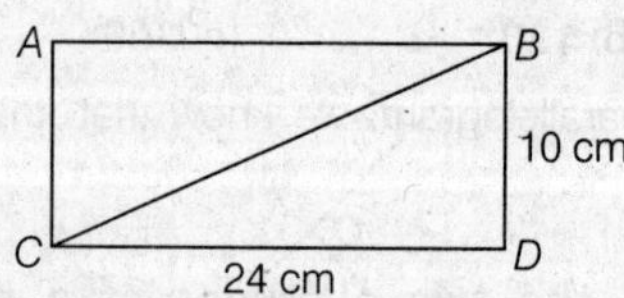

$\therefore$ Using Pythagoras theorem,

we have, $BC^2 = BD^2 + CD^2$

$\Rightarrow \quad BC^2 = 10^2 + 24^2 = 100 + 576$

$\Rightarrow \quad BC^2 = 676$

$\Rightarrow \quad BC = \sqrt{676}$

$\Rightarrow \quad BC = 26 \text{ cm}$

Q. 37 If the adjacent angles of a parallelogram are equal, then the parallelogram is a

(a) rectangle (b) trapezium (c) rhombus (d) None of these

Sol. *(a)* We know that, the adjacent angles of a parallelogram are supplementary, i.e. their sum equals 180° and given that both the angles are same. Therefore, each angle will be of measure 90°.

Hence, the parallelogram is a rectangle.

Q. 38 Which of the following can be four interior angles of a quadrilateral?

(a) 140°, 40°, 20°, 160° (b) 270°, 150°, 30°, 20°

(c) 40°, 70°, 90°, 60° (d) 110°, 40°, 30°, 180°

Sol. *(a)* We know that, the sum of interior angles of a quadrilateral is 360°.
Thus, the angles in option (a) can be four interior angles of a quadrilateral as their sum is 360°.

Q. 39 The sum of angles of a concave quadrilateral is

(a) more than 360° (b) less than 360°

(c) equal to 360° (d) twice of 360°

Sol. *(c)* We know that, the sum of interior angles of any polygon (convex or concave) having n sides is $(n-2) \times 180°$.

$\therefore$ The sum of angles of a concave quadrilateral is $(4-2) \times 180°$, i.e. 360°

Q. 40 Which of the following can never be the measure of exterior angle of a regular polygon?

(a) 22° (b) 36° (c) 45° (d) 30°

Sol. *(a)* Since, we know that, the sum of measures of exterior angles of a polygon is 360°, i.e. measure of each exterior angle $= \frac{360°}{n}$, where n is the number of sides/angles.

Thus, measure of each exterior angle will always divide 360° completely.

Hence, 22° can never be the measure of exterior angle of a regular polygon.

Q. 41 In the figure, *BEST* is a rhombus, then the value of $y - x$ is

(a) 40° (b) 50° (c) 20° (d) 10°

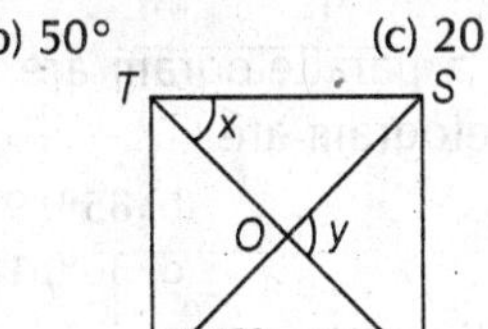

Sol. *(a)* Given, a rhombus *BEST*.

$TS \parallel BE$ and BS is transversal.

$\therefore \angle SBE = \angle TSB = 40°$ [alternate interior angles]

Also, $\angle y = 90°$ [diagonals bisect at 90°]

In ΔTSO, $\angle STO + \angle TSO = \angle SOE$

$x + 40° = 90° \Rightarrow x = 50°$ [exterior angle property of triangle]

$\therefore y - x = 90° - 50° = 40°$

Q. 42 The closed curve which is also a polygon, is

(a) 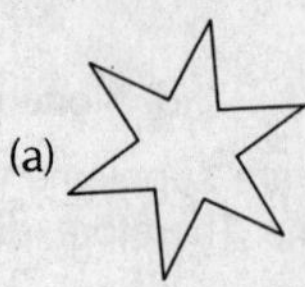 (b) 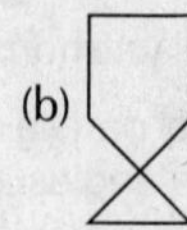 (c) 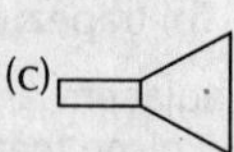 (d) 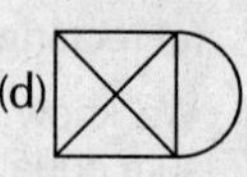

Sol. ***(a)*** Figure (a) is polygon as no two line segments intersect each other.

Q. 43 Which of the following is not true for an exterior angle of a regular polygon with n sides?

(a) Each exterior angle $= \dfrac{360°}{n}$ (b) Exterior angle $= 180° -$ Interior angle

(c) $n = \dfrac{360°}{\text{Exterior angle}}$ (d) Each exterior angle $= \dfrac{(n-2) \times 180°}{n}$

Sol. ***(d)*** We know that, (a) and (b) are the formulae to find the measure of each exterior angle, when number of sides and measure of an interior angle respectively are given and (c) is the formula to find number of sides of polygon when exterior angle is given.

Hence, the formula given in option (d) is not true for an exterior angle of a regular polygon with n sides.

Q. 44 $PQRS$ is a square. PR and SQ intersect at O. Then, $\angle POQ$ is a

(a) right angle (b) straight angle (c) reflex angle (d) complete angle

Sol. ***(a)***

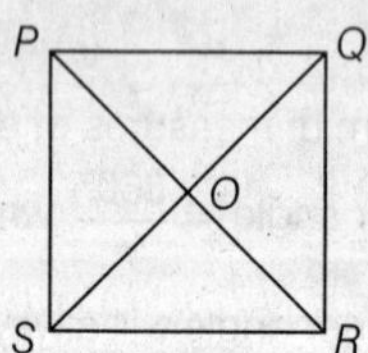

We know that, the diagonals of a square intersect each other at right angle.

Hence, $\angle POQ = 90°$, i.e. right angle.

Q. 45 Two adjacent angles of a parallelogram are in the ratio 1 : 5. Then, all the angles of the parallelogram are

(a) 30°, 150°, 30°, 150° (b) 85°, 95°, 85°, 95°

(c) 45°, 135°, 45°, 135° (d) 30°, 180°, 30°, 180°

Sol. ***(a)*** Let the adjacent angles of a parallelogram be x and $5x$, respectively.

Then, $x + 5x = 180°$ [$\because$ adjacent angles of a parallelogram are supplementary]

$\Rightarrow 6x = 180°$

$\Rightarrow x = 30°$

$\therefore$ The adjacent angles are 30° and 150°.

Hence, the angles are 30°, 150°, 30°, 150° [$\because$ opposite angles are equal]

Q. 46 A parallelogram $PQRS$ is constructed with sides $QR = 6$ cm, $PQ = 4$ cm and $\angle PQR = 90°$. Then, $PQRS$ is a

(a) square (b) rectangle (c) rhombus (d) trapezium

Sol. *(b)* We know that, if in a parallelogram one angle is of 90°, then all angles will be of 90° and a parallelogram with all angles equal to 90° is called a rectangle.

Q. 47 The angles P, Q, R and S of a quadrilateral are in the ratio $1:3:7:9$. Then, $PQRS$ is a

(a) parallelogram (b) trapezium with $PQ \parallel RS$
(c) trapezium with $QR \parallel PS$ (d) kite

Sol. *(b)*

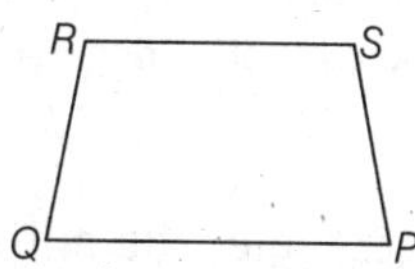

Let the angles be x, $3x$, $7x$ and $9x$, then

$x + 3x + 7x + 9x = 360°$ [$\because$ sum of angles in any quadrilateral is 360°]

$\Rightarrow \quad 20x = 360°$

$\Rightarrow \quad x = \dfrac{360°}{20}$

$\Rightarrow \quad x = 18°$

Then, the angles P, Q, R and S are 18°, 54°, 126° and 162°, respectively.

Since, $\angle P + \angle S = 18° + 162° = 180°$ and $\angle Q + \angle R = 54° + 126° = 180°$

$\therefore$ The quadrilateral $PQRS$ is a trapezium with $PQ \parallel RS$.

Q. 48 $PQRS$ is a trapezium in which $PQ \parallel SR$ and $\angle P = 130°$, $\angle Q = 110°$. Then, $\angle R$ is equal to

(a) 70° (b) 50° (c) 65° (d) 55°

Sol. *(a)* Since, $PQRS$ is a trapezium and $PQ \parallel SR$.

$\therefore \angle Q + \angle R = 180°$ [$\because$ angles between the pair of parallel sides are supplementary]

$\Rightarrow \quad \angle R = 180° - 110° = 70°$

Q. 49 The number of sides of a regular polygon whose each interior angle is of 135° is

(a) 6 (b) 7 (c) 8 (d) 9

Sol. *(c)* We know that, the measures of each exterior angle of a polygon having n sides is given by $\dfrac{360°}{n}$.

$\therefore$ The number of sides, $n = \dfrac{360°}{\text{Exterior angle}} = \dfrac{360°}{180° - 135°}$

[$\because$ exterior angle + interior angle = 180°]

$= \dfrac{360°}{45°} = 8$

Q. 50 If a diagonal of a quadrilateral bisects both the angles, then it is a

(a) kite (b) parallelogram (c) rhombus (d) rectangle

Sol. *(c)* If a diagonal of a quadrilateral bisects both the angles, then it is a rhombus.

Q. 51 To construct a unique parallelogram, the minimum number of measurements required is

(a) 2 (b) 3 (c) 4 (d) 5

Sol. *(b)* We know that, in a parallelogram, opposite sides are equal and parallel. Also, opposite angles are equal.

So, to construct a parallelogram uniquely, we require the measure of any two non-parallel sides and the measure of an angle.

Hence, the minimum number of measurements required to draw a unique parallelogram is 3.

Q. 52 To construct a unique rectangle, the minimum number of measurements required is

(a) 4 (b) 3 (c) 2 (d) 1

Sol. *(c)* Since, in a rectangle, opposite sides are equal and parallel, so we need the measurement of only two adjacent sides, i.e. length and breadth.

Also, each angle measures 90°.

Hence, we require only two measurements to construct a unique rectangle.

Fill in the Blanks

In questions 53 to 91, fill in the blanks to make the statements true.

Q. 53 In quadrilateral *HOPE*, the pairs of opposite sides are ______ .

Sol.

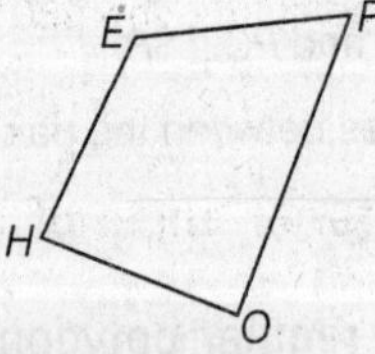

EH, *PO* and *HO*, *EP* are pairs of opposite sides.

Q. 54 In quadrilateral *ROPE*, the pairs of adjacent angles are ______ .

Sol.

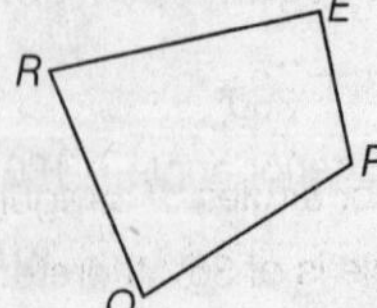

The pairs of adjacent angles are $\angle R$, $\angle O$; $\angle O$, $\angle P$; $\angle P$, $\angle E$; $\angle E$, $\angle R$

Q. 55 In quadrilateral *WXYZ*, the pairs of opposite angles are ______ .

Sol.

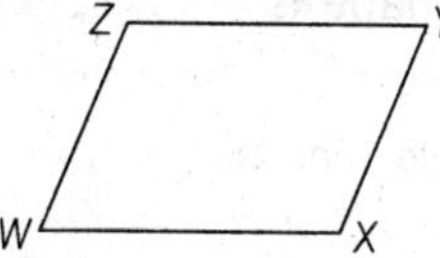

The pairs of opposite angles are $\angle W$, $\angle Y$; $\angle X$, $\angle Z$.

Q. 56 The diagonals of the quadrilateral *DEFG* are ______ and ______ .

Sol.

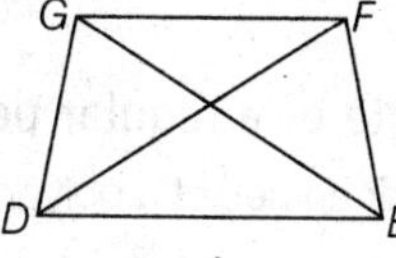

The diagonals are ***GE*** and ***FD***.

Q. 57 The sum of all ______ of a quadrilateral is 360°.

Sol. **angles**

We know that, the sum of all angles of a quadrilateral is 360°.

Q. 58 The measure of each exterior angle of a regular pentagon is ______ .

Sol. 72°

$$\text{Measure of exterior angle} = \frac{360°}{\text{Number of sides}} = \frac{360°}{5} = 72°$$

[$\because$ in pentagon, number of sides, $n = 5$]

Q. 59 Sum of the angles of a hexagon is ______ .

Sol. 720°

Since, the sum of angles of an *n*-gon = $(n - 2) \times 180°$

$\therefore$ Sum of the angles of a hexagon = $(6 - 2) \times 180° = 4 \times 180° = 720°$

[$\because$ in hexagon, number of sides, $n = 6$]

Q. 60 The measure of each exterior angle of a regular polygon of 18 sides is ______ .

Sol. 20°

We know that, measure of each exterior angle $= \frac{360°}{\text{Number of sides}} = \frac{360°}{18} = 20°$

Q. 61 The number of sides of a regular polygon, where each exterior angle has a measure of 36°, is ______ .

Sol. 10°

We know that, the sum of exterior angles of a regular polygon is 360°.

Further, since each exterior angle is of 36°, therefore number of sides $= \frac{360°}{\text{Exterior angle}}$

$$= \frac{360°}{36°} = 10°$$

Q. 62 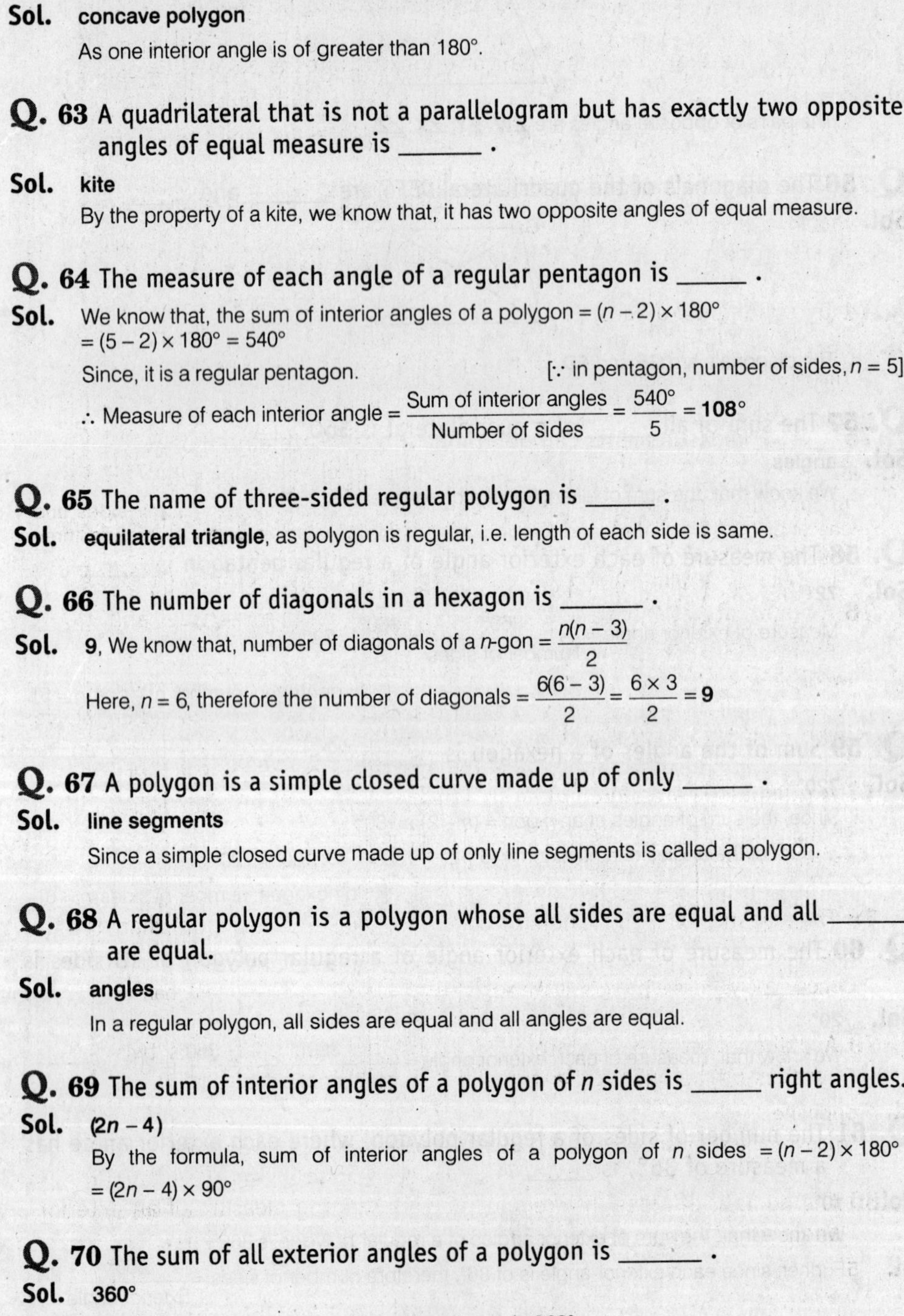 is a closed curve entirely made up of line segments. The another name for this shape is ______ .

Sol. **concave polygon**

As one interior angle is of greater than 180°.

Q. 63 A quadrilateral that is not a parallelogram but has exactly two opposite angles of equal measure is ______ .

Sol. **kite**

By the property of a kite, we know that, it has two opposite angles of equal measure.

Q. 64 The measure of each angle of a regular pentagon is ______ .

Sol. We know that, the sum of interior angles of a polygon $= (n-2) \times 180°$

$= (5-2) \times 180° = 540°$

Since, it is a regular pentagon. [$\because$ in pentagon, number of sides, $n = 5$]

$\therefore$ Measure of each interior angle $= \dfrac{\text{Sum of interior angles}}{\text{Number of sides}} = \dfrac{540°}{5} = \mathbf{108°}$

Q. 65 The name of three-sided regular polygon is ______ .

Sol. **equilateral triangle**, as polygon is regular, i.e. length of each side is same.

Q. 66 The number of diagonals in a hexagon is ______ .

Sol. **9**, We know that, number of diagonals of a n-gon $= \dfrac{n(n-3)}{2}$

Here, $n = 6$, therefore the number of diagonals $= \dfrac{6(6-3)}{2} = \dfrac{6 \times 3}{2} = \mathbf{9}$

Q. 67 A polygon is a simple closed curve made up of only ______ .

Sol. **line segments**

Since a simple closed curve made up of only line segments is called a polygon.

Q. 68 A regular polygon is a polygon whose all sides are equal and all ______ are equal.

Sol. **angles**

In a regular polygon, all sides are equal and all angles are equal.

Q. 69 The sum of interior angles of a polygon of n sides is ______ right angles.

Sol. $(2n-4)$

By the formula, sum of interior angles of a polygon of n sides $= (n-2) \times 180°$

$= (2n-4) \times 90°$

Q. 70 The sum of all exterior angles of a polygon is ______ .

Sol. **360°**

As the sum of all exterior angles of a polygon is 360°.

Q. 71 ______ is a regular quadrilateral.

Sol. **Square**

Since in square, all the sides are of equal length and all angles are equal.

Q. 72 A quadrilateral in which a pair of opposite sides is parallel is ______ .

Sol. **trapezium**

We know that, in a trapezium, one pair of sides is parallel.

Q. 73 If all sides of a quadrilateral are equal, it is a ______ .

Sol. **rhombus or square**

As in both the quadrilaterals all sides are of equal length.

Q. 74 In a rhombus, diagonals intersect at ______ angles.

Sol. **right**

The diagonals of a rhombus intersect at right angles.

Q. 75 ______ measurements can determine a quadrilateral uniquely.

Sol. **5**

To construct a unique quadrilateral, we require 5 measurements, i.e. four sides and one angle or three sides and two included angles or two adjacent sides and three angles are given.

Q. 76 A quadrilateral can be constructed uniquely, if its three sides and ______ angles are given.

Sol. **two included**

We can determine a quadrilateral uniquely, if three sides and two included angles are given.

Q. 77 A rhombus is a parallelogram in which ______ sides are equal.

Sol. **all**

As length of each side is same in a rhombus.

Q. 78 The measure of ______ angle of concave quadrilateral is more than 180°.

Sol. **one**

Concave polygon is a polygon in which atleast one interior angle is more than 180°.

Q. 79 A diagonal of a quadrilateral is a line segment that joins two ______ vertices of the quadrilateral.

Sol. **opposite**

Since the line segment connecting two opposite vertices is called diagonal.

Q. 80 The number of sides in a regular polygon having measure of an exterior angle as 72° is ______ .

Sol. **5**

We know that,

the sum of exterior angles of any polygon is 360°.

The number of sides in a regular polygon $= \dfrac{360°}{\text{Exterior angle}}$

$\therefore$ The number of sides in given polygon $= \dfrac{360°}{72°} = 5$

Q. 81 If the diagonals of a quadrilateral bisect each other, it is a _____ .

Sol. **parallelogram**

Since in a parallelogram, the diagonals bisect each other.

Q. 82 The adjacent sides of a parallelogram are 5 cm and 9 cm. Its perimeter is _____ .

Sol. **28 cm**

Perimeter of a parallelogram = 2 (Sum of lengths of adjacent sides)

$= 2(5 + 9) = 2 \times 14 = 28\text{cm}$

Q. 83 A nonagon has _____ sides.

Sol. **9**

Nonagon is a polygon which has 9 sides.

Q. 84 Diagonals of a rectangle are _____ .

Sol. **equal**

We know that, in a rectangle, both the diagonals are of equal length.

Q. 85 A polygon having 10 sides is known as _____ .

Sol. **decagon**

A polygon with 10 sides is called decagon.

Q. 86 A rectangle whose adjacent sides are equal becomes a _____ .

Sol. **square**

If in a rectangle, adjacent sides are equal, then it is called a square.

Q. 87 If one diagonal of a rectangle is 6 cm long, length of the other diagonal is _____ .

Sol. **6 cm**

Since both the diagonals of a rectangle are equal. Therefore, length of other diagonal is also 6 cm.

Q. 88 Adjacent angles of a parallelogram are _____ .

Sol. **supplementary**

By property of a parallelogram, we know that, the adjacent angles of a parallelogram are supplementary.

Q. 89 If only one diagonal of a quadrilateral bisects the other, then the quadrilateral is known as _____ .

Sol. **kite**

This is a property of kite, i.e. only one diagonal bisects the other.

Q. 90 In trapezium $ABCD$ with $AB \parallel CD$, if $\angle A = 100°$, then $\angle D =$ _____ .

Sol. 80°

In a trapezium, we know that, the angles on either side of the base are supplementary.

So, in trapezium $ABCD$, given $AB \parallel CD$

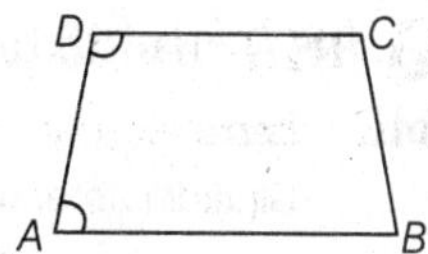

$\therefore \quad \angle A + \angle D = 180°$

$\Rightarrow \quad 100° + \angle D = 180°$

$\Rightarrow \quad \angle D = 180° - 100°$

$\therefore \quad \angle D = 80°$

Q. 91 The polygon in which sum of all exterior angles is equal to the sum of interior angles is called _____ .

Sol. quadrilateral

We know that, the sum of exterior angles of a polygon is 360° and in a quadrilateral, sum of interior angles is also 360°. Therefore, a quadrilateral is a polygon in which the sum of both interior and exterior angles are equal.

True/False

In questions 92 to 131, state whether the statements are True or False.

Q. 92 All angles of a trapezium are equal.

Sol. *False*

As all angles of a trapezium are not equal.

Q. 93 All squares are rectangles.

Sol. *True*

Since squares possess all the properties of rectangles. Therefore, we can say that, all squares are rectangles but *vice-versa* is not true.

Q. 94 All kites are squares.

Sol. *False*

As kites do not satisfy all the properties of a square.

e.g. In square, all the angles are of 90° but in kite, it is not the case.

Q. 95 All rectangles are parallelograms.

Sol. *True*

Since rectangles satisfy all the properties of parallelograms. Therefore, we can say that, all rectangles are parallelograms but *vice-versa* is not true.

Q. 96 All rhombuses are squares.

Sol. *False*

As in a rhombus, each angle is not a right angle, so rhombuses are not squares.

Q. 97 Sum of all the angles of a quadrilateral is 180°.

Sol. ***False***

Since sum of all the angles of a quadrilateral is 360°.

Q. 98 A quadrilateral has two diagonals.

Sol. ***True***

A quadrilateral has two diagonals.

Q. 99 Triangle is a polygon whose sum of exterior angles is double the sum of interior angles.

Sol. ***True***

As the sum of interior angles of a triangle is 180° and the sum of exterior angles is 360°, i.e. double the sum of interior angles.

Q. 100 [figure: star] is a polygon.

Sol. ***False***

Because it is not a simple closed curve as it intersects with itself more than once.

Q. 101 A kite is not a convex quadrilateral.

Sol. ***False***

A kite is a convex quadrilateral as the line segment joining any two opposite vertices inside it, lies completely inside it.

Q. 102 The sum of interior angles and the sum of exterior angles taken in an order are equal in case of quadrilaterals only.

Sol. ***True***

Since the sum of interior angles as well as of exterior angles of a quadrilateral are 360°.

Q. 103 If the sum of interior angles is double the sum of exterior angles taken in an order of a polygon, then it is a hexagon.

Sol. ***True***

Since the sum of exterior angles of a hexagon is 360° and the sum of interior angles of a hexagon is 720°, i.e. double the sum of exterior angles.

Q. 104 A polygon is regular, if all of its sides are equal.

Sol. ***False***

By definition of a regular polygon, we know that, a polygon is regular, if all sides and all angles are equal.

Q. 105 Rectangle is a regular quadrilateral.

Sol. ***False***

As its all sides are not equal.

Q. 106 If diagonals of a quadrilateral are equal, it must be a rectangle.

Sol. ***True***

If diagonals are equal, then it is definitely a rectangle.

Q. 107 If opposite angles of a quadrilateral are equal, it must be a parallelogram.

Sol. ***True***

If opposite angles are equal, it has to be a parallelogram.

Q. 108 The interior angles of a triangle are in the ratio 1 : 2 : 3, then the ratio of its exterior angles is 3 : 2 : 1.

Sol. ***False***

Given, ratio of interior angles = 1:2:3

Let the interior angles be x, $2x$ and $3x$.

So, $x + 2x + 3x = 180°$ [angle sum property of triangle]

$\Rightarrow \quad 6x = 180°$

$\Rightarrow \quad x = \frac{180°}{6} = 30°$

$\therefore$ The interior angles are 30°, 60° and 90°.

Now, the exterior angles will be (180° – 30°), (180° – 60°) and (180° – 90°),

i.e. 150°, 120° and 90°.

The ratio of exterior angles = 150° : 120° : 90° = 15 : 12 : 9 = 5 : 4 : 3

Q. 109 [figure] is a concave pentagon.

Sol. ***False***

As it has 6 sides, therefore it is a concave hexagon.

Q. 110 Diagonals of a rhombus are equal and perpendicular to each other.

Sol. ***False***

As diagonals of a rhombus are perpendicular to each other but not equal.

Q. 111 Diagonals of a rectangle are equal.

Sol. ***True***

The diagonals of a rectangle are equal.

Q. 112 Diagonals of rectangle bisect each other at right angles.

Sol. ***False***

Diagonals of a rectangle does not bisect each other.

Q. 113 Every kite is a parallelogram.

Sol. ***False***

Kite is not a parallelogram as its opposite sides are not equal and parallel.

Q. 114 Every trapezium is a parallelogram.

Sol. ***False***

Since in a trapezium, only one pair of sides is parallel.

Q. 115 Every parallelogram is a rectangle.

Sol. ***False***

As in a parallelogram, all angles are not right angles, while in a rectangle, all angles are equal and are right angles.

Q. 116 Every trapezium is a rectangle.

Sol. ***False***

Since in a rectangle, opposite sides are equal and parallel but in a trapezium, it is not so.

Q. 117 Every rectangle is a trapezium.

Sol. ***True***

As a rectangle satisfies all the properties of a trapezium. So, we can say that, every rectangle is a trapezium but *vice-versa* is not true.

Q. 118 Every square is a rhombus.

Sol. ***True***

As a square possesses all the properties of a rhombus. So, we can say that, every square is a rhombus but *vice-versa* is not true.

Q. 119 Every square is a parallelogram.

Sol. ***True***

Every square is also a parallelogram as it has all the properties of a parallelogram but *vice-versa* is not true.

Q. 120 Every square is a trapezium.

Sol. ***True***

As a square has all the properties of a trapezium. So, we can say that, every square is a trapezium but *vice-versa* is not true.

Q. 121 Every rhombus is a trapezium.

Sol. ***True***

Since a rhombus satisfies all the properties of a trapezium. So, we can say that, every rhombus is a trapezium but *vice-versa* is not true.

Q. 122 A quadrilateral can be drawn if only measures of four sides are given.

Sol. ***False***

As we require atleast five measurements to determine a quadrilateral uniquely.

Q. 123 **A quadrilateral can have all four angles as obtuse.**

Sol. ***False***

If all angles will be obtuse, then their sum will exceed 360°. This is not possible in case of a quadrilateral.

Q. 124 **A quadrilateral can be drawn, if all four sides and one diagonal is known.**

Sol. ***True***

A quadrilateral can be constructed uniquely, if four sides and one diagonal is known.

Q. 125 **A quadrilateral can be drawn, when all the four angles and one side is given.**

Sol. ***False***

We cannot draw a unique quadrilateral, if four angles and one side is known.

Q. 126 **A quadrilateral can be drawn, if all four sides and one angle is known.**

Sol. ***True***

A quadrilateral can be drawn, if all four sides and one angle is known.

Q. 127 **A quadrilateral can be drawn, if three sides and two diagonals are given.**

Sol. ***True***

A quadrilateral can be drawn, if three sides and two diagonals are given.

Q. 128 **If diagonals of a quadrilateral bisect each other, it must be a parallelogram.**

Sol. ***True***

It is the property of a parallelogram.

Q. 129 **A quadrilateral can be constructed uniquely, if three angles and any two included sides are given.**

Sol. ***True***

We can construct a unique quadrilateral with given three angles given and two included sides.

Q. 130 **A parallelogram can be constructed uniquely, if both diagonals and the angle between them is given.**

Sol. ***True***

We can draw a unique parallelogram, if both diagonals and the angle between them is given.

Q. 131 **A rhombus can be constructed uniquely, if both diagonals are given.**

Sol. ***True***

A rhombus can be constructed uniquely, if both diagonals are given.

Q. 132 The diagonals of a rhombus are 8 cm and 15 cm. Find its side.

Sol. Given, $AC = 15$ cm, $BD = 8$ cm

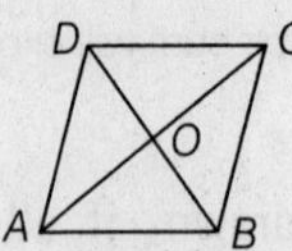

Since, the diagonals of a rhombus bisect each other at 90°, therefore in the ΔAOB, we have

$$AB^2 = OA^2 + OB^2$$

$$\Rightarrow \quad AB^2 = \left(\frac{15}{2}\right)^2 + \left(\frac{8}{2}\right)^2 = (7.5)^2 + (4)^2 = 56.25 + 16$$

$$\Rightarrow \quad AB^2 = 72.25$$

$$\Rightarrow \quad AB = \sqrt{72.25}$$

$$\Rightarrow \quad AB = 8.5 \text{ cm}$$

Since it is a rhombus, the length of each side is 8.5 cm.

Q. 133 Two adjacent angles of a parallelogram are in the ratio 1 : 3. Find its angles.

Sol. Let the adjacent angles of a parallelogram be x and $3x$.

Then, we have $x + (3x) = 180°$ [$\because$ adjacent angles of parallelogram are supplementary]

$$\Rightarrow \quad 4x = 180°$$

$$\Rightarrow \quad x = 45°$$

Thus, the angles are 45°, 135°.

Hence, the angles are 45°, 135, 45°, 135°. [$\because$ opposite angles in a parallelogram are equal]

Q. 134 Of the four quadrilaterals - square, rectangle, rhombus and trapezium-one is somewhat different from the others because of its design. Find it and give justification.

Sol. In square, rectangle and rhombus, opposite sides are parallel and equal. Also, opposite angles are equal. i.e. they all are parallelograms.

But in trapezium, there is only one pair of parallel sides, i.e. it is not a parallelogram.

Therefore, trapezium has different design.

Q. 135 In a rectangle *ABCD*, *AB* = 25 cm and *BC* = 15 cm. In what ratio, does the bisector of ∠*C* divide *AB*?

Sol. Given, $AB = 25$ cm and $BC = 15$ cm

Now, in rectangle $ABCD$,

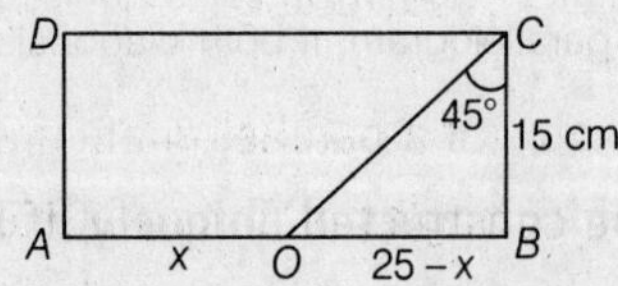

CO is the bisector of $\angle C$ and it divides AB.

$$\therefore \quad \angle OCB = \angle OCD = 45°$$

$\therefore \quad \angle OCB = \angle OCD = 45°$

In ΔOCB, we have

$\angle CBO + \angle OCB + \angle COB = 180°$ [angle sum property of triangle]

$90° + 45° + \angle COB = 180°$

$\angle COB = 180° - 90° + 45°$

$\angle COB = 180° - 135° = 45°$

Now, in ΔOCB,

$\angle OCB = \angle COB$

Then, $OB = BC$

$\Rightarrow \quad OB = 15\text{ cm}$

CO divides AB in the ratio $AO : OB$.

Let AO be x, then

$OB = AB - x = 25 - x$

Hence, $AO : OB = x : 25 - x$

$\Rightarrow 10 : 15 \quad \Rightarrow \quad 2 : 3$

Q. 136 ***PQRS* is a rectangle. The perpendicular *ST* from *S* on *PR* divides ∠*S* in the ratio 2 : 3. Find ∠*TPQ*.**

Sol. Given, $ST \perp PR$ and ST divides $\angle S$ in the ratio 2 : 3.

So, sum of ratio = 2 + 3 = 5

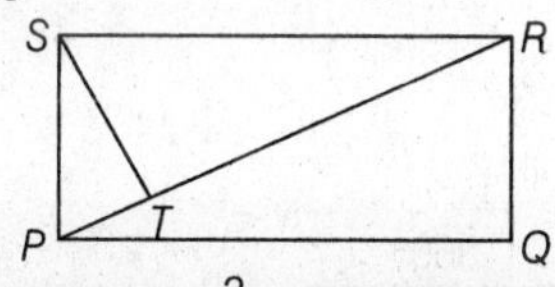

Now, $\angle TSP = \frac{2}{5} \times 90° = 36°$, $\angle TSR = \frac{3}{5} \times 90° = 54°$

Also, by the angle sum property of a triangle,

$\angle TPS = 180° - (\angle STP + \angle TSP)$

$= 180° - (90° + 36°) = 54°$

We know that, $\angle SPQ = 90°$

$\Rightarrow \angle TPS + \angle TPQ = 90°$

$\Rightarrow \quad 54° + \angle TPQ = 90°$

$\Rightarrow \quad \angle TPQ = 90° - 54° = 36°$

Q. 137 **A photo frame is in the shape of a quadrilateral, with one diagonal longer than the other. Is it a rectangle? Why or why not?**

Sol. No, it cannot be a rectangle, as in rectangle, both the diagonals are of equal lengths.

Q. 138 **The adjacent angles of a parallelogram are (2x – 4)° and (3x – 1)°. Find the measures of all angles of the parallelogram.**

Sol. Since, the adjacent angles of a parallelogram are supplementary.

$\therefore (2x - 4)° + (3x - 1)° = 180°$

$\Rightarrow \quad 5x - 5° = 180°$

$\Rightarrow \quad 5x = 185°$

$\Rightarrow \quad x = \frac{185°}{5} \quad \Rightarrow \quad x = 37°$

Thus, the adjacent angles are

$2x - 4 = 2 \times 37° - 4 = 74 - 4 = 70°$

and $3x - 1 = 3 \times 37° - 1 = 111 - 1 = 110°$

Hence, the angles are 70°, 110°, 70°, 110°

[$\because$ opposite angles in a parallelogram are equal]

Q. 139 The point of intersection of diagonals of a quadrilateral divides one diagonal in the ratio 1 : 2. Can it be a parallelogram? Why or why not?

Sol. No, it can never be a parallelogram, as the diagonals of a parallelogram intersect each other in the ratio 1 : 1.

Q. 140 The ratio between exterior angle and interior angle of a regular polygon is 1 : 5. Find the number of sides of the polygon.

Sol. Let the exterior angle and interior angle be x and $5x$, respectively.

Then, $x + 5x = 180°$

[$\because$ exterior angle and corresponding interior angle are supplementary]

$\Rightarrow \quad 6x = 180°$

$\Rightarrow \quad x = \frac{180°}{6}$

$\Rightarrow \quad x = 30°$

$\therefore$ The number of sides $= \frac{360°}{\text{Exterior angle}}$

$= \frac{360°}{30°} = 12$

Q. 141 Two sticks each of length 5 cm are crossing each other such that they bisect each other. What shape is formed by joining their end points? Give reason.

Sol. Sticks can be taken as the diagonals of a quadrilateral.

Now, since they are bisecting each other, therefore the shape formed by joining their end points will be a parallelogram.

Hence, it may be a rectangle or a square depending on the angle between the sticks.

Q. 142 Two sticks each of length 7 cm are crossing each other such that they bisect each other at right angles. What shape is formed by joining their end points? Give reason.

Sol. Sticks can be treated as the diagonals of a quadrilateral.

Now, since the diagonals (sticks) are bisecting each other at right angles, therefore the shape formed by joining their end points will be a rhombus.

Q. 143 A playground in the town is in the form of a kite. The perimeter is 106 m. If one of its sides is 23 m, what are the lengths of other three sides?

Sol. Let the length of other non-consecutive side be x cm.

Then, we have, perimeter of playground $= 23 + 23 + x + x$

$\Rightarrow \quad 106 = 2(23 + x)$

$\Rightarrow \quad 46 + 2x = 106$

$\Rightarrow \quad 2x = 106 - 46$

$\Rightarrow \quad 2x = 60$

$\Rightarrow \quad x = 30$ m

Hence, the lengths of other three sides are 23m, 30m and 30m. As a kite has two pairs of equal consecutive sides.

Q. 144 In rectangle *READ*, find $\angle EAR$, $\angle RAD$ and $\angle ROD$.

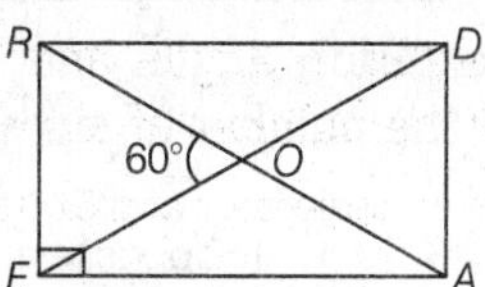

Sol. Given, a rectangle *READ*, in which $\angle ROE = 60°$

$\therefore \quad \angle EOA = 180° - 60° = 120°$ [linear pair]

Now, in ΔEOA, $\angle OEA = \angle OAE = 30°$ [$\because$ $OE = OA$ and equal sides make equal angles]

$\therefore \quad \angle EAR = 30°$, $\angle RAD = 90° - \angle EAR = 60°$ and $\angle ROD = \angle EOA = 120°$

Q. 145 In rectangle *PAIR*, find $\angle ARI$, $\angle RMI$ and $\angle PMA$.

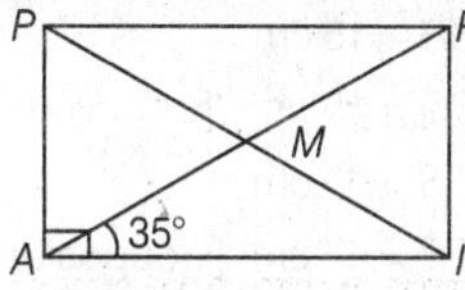

Sol. Given, $\angle RAI = 35°$

$\therefore \quad \angle PRA = 35°$ [$PR \parallel AI$ and AR is transversal]

$\Rightarrow \quad \angle ARI = 90° - \angle PRA = 90° - 35° = 55°$

$\because \quad AM = IM$, $\angle MIA = \angle MAI = 35°$

In ΔAMI, $\angle RMI = \angle MAI + \angle MIA = 70°$ [exterior angle]

Also, $\angle RMI = \angle PMA$

$\Rightarrow \quad \angle PMA = 70°$ [vertically opposite angles]

Q. 146 In parallelogram *ABCD*, find $\angle B$, $\angle C$ and $\angle D$.

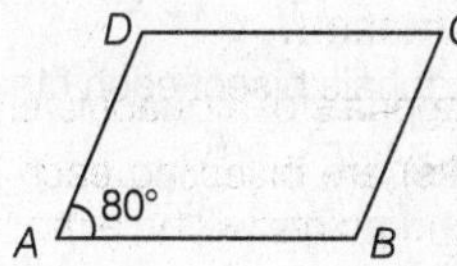

Sol. In a parallelogram, the opposite angles are equal, therefore $\angle C = \angle A = 80^\circ$

Also, adjacent angles are supplementary.

$\therefore \quad \angle A + \angle B = 180^\circ$

$80^\circ + \angle B = 180^\circ$

$\angle B = 180^\circ - 80^\circ \Rightarrow \angle B = 100^\circ$

Now, $\angle B = \angle D$

$\therefore \quad \angle D = 100^\circ$

Q. 147 **In parallelogram *PQRS*, *O* is the mid-point of *SQ*. Find $\angle S$, $\angle R$, *PQ*, *QR* and diagonal *PR*.**

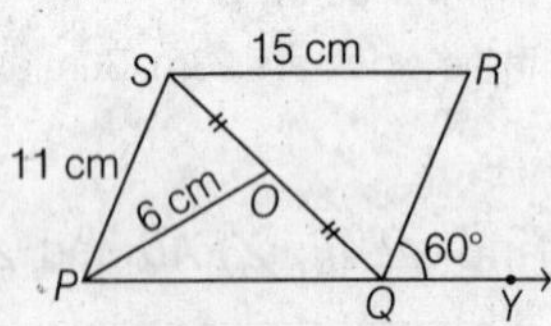

Sol. Given, $\angle RQY = 60^\circ$

$\therefore \quad \angle RQP = 120^\circ$ [linear pair]

$\therefore \quad \angle S = 120^\circ$ [$\because$ opposite angles are equal in a parallelogram]

By the angle sum property of a quadrilateral, $\angle P + \angle R + \angle S + \angle Q = 360^\circ$

$\Rightarrow \quad \angle P + \angle R + 120^\circ + 120^\circ = 360^\circ$

$\Rightarrow \quad \angle P + \angle R = 120^\circ$

$\Rightarrow \quad 2\angle P = 120^\circ$

$\Rightarrow \quad \angle P = 60^\circ$ [$\because$ opposite angles are equal in parallelogram]

$\Rightarrow \quad \angle P = \angle R = 60^\circ$

Also, $SR = 15$ cm

$\therefore \quad PQ = 15$ cm [$\because$ opposite sides of a parallelogram are equal]

And $PS = 11$ cm

$\therefore \quad QR = 11$ cm [$\because$ opposite sides of a parallelogram are equal]

and $PR = 2 \times PO = 2 \times 6 = 12$ [$\because$ diagonals of a parallelogram bisect each other]

Q. 148 **In rhombus *BEAM*, find $\angle AME$ and $\angle AEM$.**

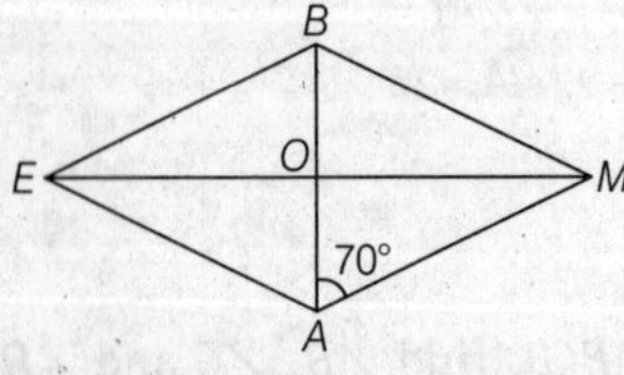

Sol. Given, $\angle BAM = 70^\circ$

We know that, in rhombus, diagonals bisect each other at right angles.

$\therefore \quad \angle BOM = \angle BOE = \angle AOM = \angle AOE = 90^\circ$

Now, in ΔAOM,

$\angle AOM + \angle AMO + \angle OAM = 180^\circ$ [angle sum property of triangle]

$\Rightarrow$ $90^\circ + \angle AMO + 70^\circ = 180^\circ$

$\Rightarrow$ $\angle AMO = 180^\circ - 90^\circ - 70^\circ$

$\Rightarrow$ $\angle AMO = 20^\circ$

Also, $AM = BM = BE = EA$

In ΔAME, we have,

$AM = EA$

$\therefore$ $\angle AME = \angle AEM = 20^\circ$ [$\because$ equal sides make equal angles]

Q. 149 In parallelogram *FIST*, find $\angle SFT$, $\angle OST$ and $\angle STO$.

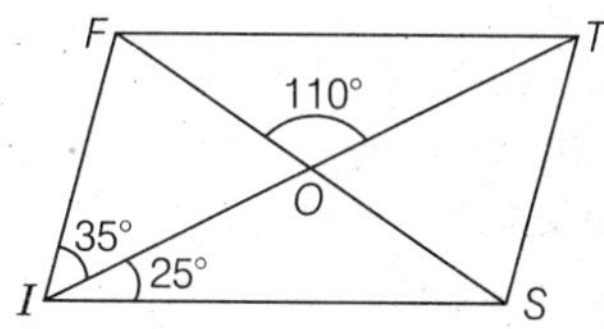

Sol. Given, $\angle FIS = 60^\circ$

Now, $\angle FTS = \angle FIS = 60^\circ$ [$\because$ opposite angles of a parallelogram are equal]

Now, $FT \parallel IS$ and TI is a transversal, therefore $\angle FTO = \angle SIO = 25^\circ$ [alternate angles]

$\therefore$ $\angle STO = \angle FTS - \angle FTO = 60^\circ - 25^\circ = 35^\circ$

Also, $\angle FOT + \angle SOT = 180^\circ$ [linear pair]

$\Rightarrow$ $110^\circ + \angle SOT = 180^\circ$

$\Rightarrow$ $\angle SOT = 180^\circ - 110^\circ = 70^\circ$

In ΔTOS, $\angle TSO + \angle OTS + \angle TOS = 180^\circ$ [angle sum property of triangle]

$\therefore$ $\angle OST = 180^\circ - (70^\circ + 35^\circ) = 75^\circ$

In ΔFOT, $\angle FOT + \angle FTO + \angle OFT = 180^\circ$

$\Rightarrow$ $\angle SFT = \angle OFT = 180^\circ - (\angle FOT + \angle FTO) = 180^\circ - (110^\circ + 25^\circ) = 45^\circ$

Q. 150 In the given parallelogram *YOUR*, $\angle RUO = 120^\circ$ and *OY* is extended to point *S*, such that $\angle SRY = 50^\circ$. Find $\angle YSR$.

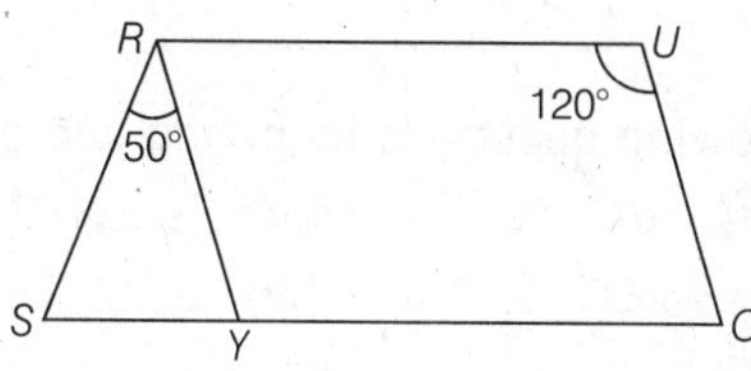

Sol. Given, $\angle RUO = 120^\circ$ and $\angle SRY = 50^\circ$

$\angle RYO = \angle RUO = 120^\circ$ [$\because$ opposite angles of a parallelogram]

Now, $\angle SYR = 180^\circ - \angle RYO$ [linear pair]

$= 180^\circ - 120^\circ = 60^\circ$

In ΔSRY,

By the angle sum property of a triangle, $\angle SRY + \angle RYS + \angle YSR = 180^\circ$

$\Rightarrow$ $50^\circ + 60^\circ + \angle YSR = 180^\circ$

$\Rightarrow$ $\angle YSR = 180^\circ - (50^\circ + 60^\circ) = 70^\circ$

Q. 151 In kite $WEAR$, $\angle WEA = 70°$ and $\angle ARW = 80°$. Find the remaining two angles.

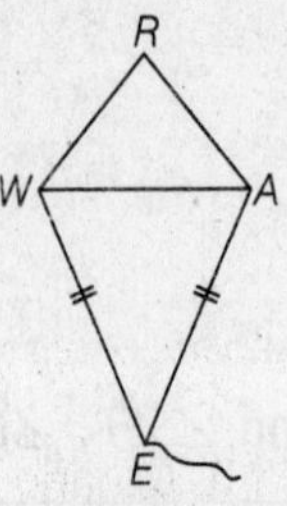

Sol. Given, in a kite $WEAR$, $\angle WEA = 70°$, $\angle ARW = 80°$

Now, by the interior angle sum property of a quadrilateral,

$$\angle RWE + \angle WEA + \angle EAR + \angle ARW = 360°$$

$$\Rightarrow \quad \angle RWE + 70° + \angle EAR + 80° = 360°$$

$$\Rightarrow \quad \angle RWE + \angle EAR = 360° - 150°$$

$$\Rightarrow \quad \angle RWE + \angle EAR = 210° \quad \text{...(i)}$$

Now, $\angle RWA = \angle RAW$ [$\because RW = RA$] ...(ii)

and $\angle AWE = \angle WAE$ [$\because WE = AE$] ...(iii)

On adding Eqs. (ii) and (iii), we get $\angle RWA + \angle AWE = \angle RAW + \angle WAE$

$$\Rightarrow \quad \angle RWE = \angle RAE$$

From Eq. (i),

$$2\angle RWE = 210°$$

$$\angle RWE = 105° \Rightarrow \angle RWE = \angle RAE = 105°$$

Q. 152 A rectangle $MORE$ is shown below.

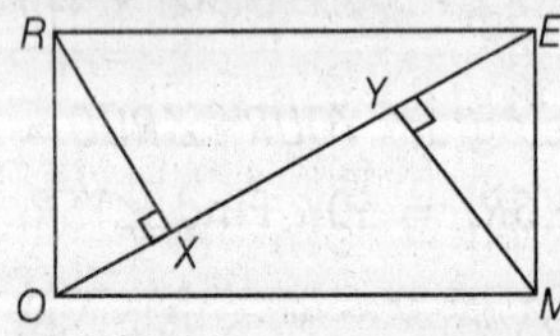

Answer the following questions by giving appropriate reason.

(i) Is $RE = OM$?
(ii) Is $\angle MYO = \angle RXE$?
(iii) Is $\angle MOY = \angle REX$?
(iv) Is $\Delta MYO \cong \Delta RXE$?
(v) Is $MY = RX$?

Sol. (i) Yes, $RE = OM$

Given, $MORE$ is a rectangle. Therefore, opposite sides are equal.

(ii) Yes, $\angle MYO = \angle RXE$

Here, MY and RX are perpendicular to OE.

Since, $\angle RXO = 90° \Rightarrow \angle RXE = 90°$ and $\angle MYE = 90° \Rightarrow \angle MYO = 90°$

(iii) Yes, $\angle MOY = \angle REX$

$\because$ $RE \parallel OM$ and EO is a transversal.

$\therefore$ $\angle MOE = \angle OER$ [$\because$ alternate interior angles]

$\Rightarrow \angle MOY = \angle REX$

(iv) Yes, $\Delta MYO \cong \Delta RXE$

In ΔMYO and ΔRXE

$MO = RE$ [proved in (i)]

$\angle MOY = \angle REX$ [proved in (iii)]

$\angle MYO = \angle RXE$ [proved in (ii)]

$\therefore$ $\Delta MYO \cong \Delta RXE$ [by AAS]

(v) Yes, $MY = RX$

Since, these are corresponding parts of congruent triangles.

Q. 153 In parallelogram $LOST$, $SN \perp OL$ and $SM \perp LT$. Find $\angle STM$, $\angle SON$ and $\angle NSM$.

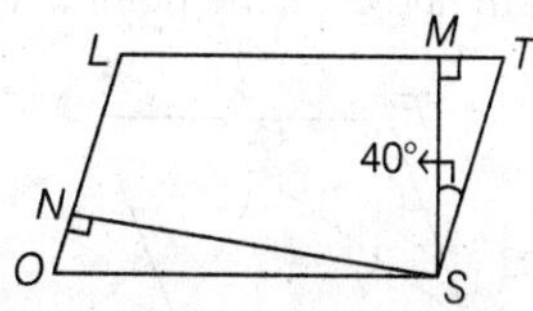

Sol. Given, $\angle MST = 40°$

In ΔMST,

By the angle sum property of a triangle, $\angle TMS + \angle MST + \angle STM = 180°$

$\Rightarrow$ $\angle STM = 180° - (90° + 40°)$ [$\because SM \perp LT$, $\angle TMS = 90°$]

$= 50°$

$\therefore$ $\angle SON = \angle STM = 50°$ [$\because$ opposite angles of a parallelogram are equal]

Now, in the ΔONS,

$\angle ONS + \angle OSN + \angle SON = 180°$ [angle sum property of triangle]

$\angle OSN = 180° - (90° + 50°)$

$= 180° - 140° = 40°$

Moreover, $\angle SON + \angle TSO = 180°$

[$\because$ adjacent angles of a parallelogram are supplementary]

$\Rightarrow$ $\angle SON + \angle TSM + \angle NSM + \angle OSN = 180°$

$\Rightarrow$ $50° + 40° + \angle NSM + 40° = 180°$

$\Rightarrow$ $90° + 40° + \angle NSM = 180°$

$\Rightarrow$ $130° + \angle NSM = 180°$

$\Rightarrow$ $\angle NSM = 180° - 130° = 50°$

Q. 154 In trapezium $HARE$, EP and RP are bisectors of $\angle E$ and $\angle R$, respectively. Find $\angle HAR$ and $\angle EHA$.

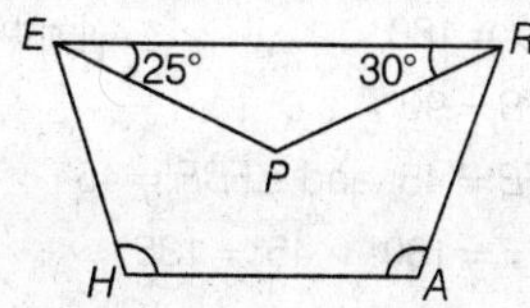

Sol. Given, $\angle PER = 25°$ and $\angle PRE = 30°$

Also, $\angle PEH = 25°$ and $\angle PRA = 30°$,

As EP and PR are angle bisectors of $\angle REH$, and $\angle ARE$ respectively. [given]

Since, $HARE$ is a trapezium,

Therefore, $\angle E + \angle H = 180°$ and $\angle R + \angle A = 180°$

$\Rightarrow \angle PER + \angle PEH + \angle H = 180°$ and $\angle ERP + \angle PRA + \angle RAH = 180°$

$\Rightarrow 25° + 25° + \angle H = 180°$ and $30° + 30° + \angle A = 180°$

$\Rightarrow 50° + \angle H = 180°$ and $60° + \angle A = 180°$

$\Rightarrow \angle H = 130°$ and $\angle A = 120°$, i.e. $\angle EHA = 130°$ and $\angle HAR = 120°$

Q. 155 In parallelogram *MODE*, the bisectors of $\angle M$ and $\angle O$ meet at *Q*. Find the measure of $\angle MQO$.

Sol. Let $MODE$ be a parallelogram and Q be the point of intersection of the bisector of $\angle M$ and $\angle O$.

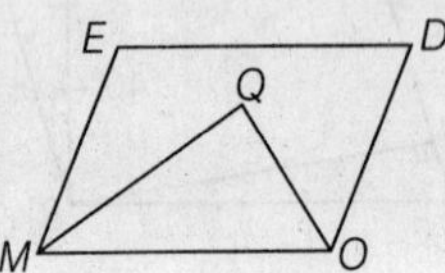

Since, $MODE$ is a parallelogram.

$\therefore \quad \angle EMO + \angle DOM = 180°$ [$\because$ adjacent angles are supplementary]

$\Rightarrow \quad \frac{1}{2}\angle EMO + \frac{1}{2}\angle DOM = 90°$ [dividing both sides by 2]

$\Rightarrow \quad \angle QMO + \angle QOM = 90°$ ...(i)

Now, in ΔMOQ,

$\angle QOM + \angle QMO + \angle MQO = 180°$ [angle sum property of triangle]

$\Rightarrow \quad 90° + \angle MQO = 180°$ [from Eq. (i)]

$\therefore \quad \angle MQO = 180° - 90° = 90°$

Q. 156 A playground is in the form of a rectangle *ATEF*. Two players are standing at the points *F* and *B*, where *EF* = *EB*. Find the values of *x* and *y*.

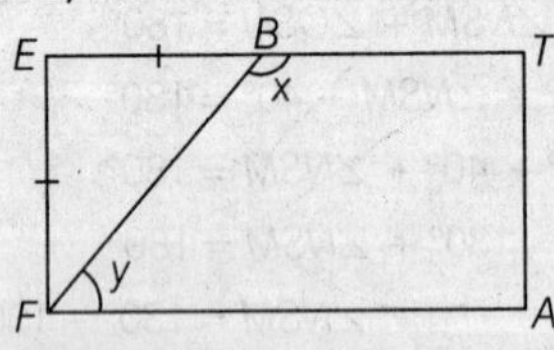

Sol. Given, a rectangle $ATEF$ in which $EF = EB$. Then, ΔFEB is an isosceles triangle. Therefore, by the angle sum property of a triangle, we have

$\angle EFB + \angle EBF + \angle FEB = 180°$ [angle sum property of triangle]

$\Rightarrow \quad \angle EFB + \angle EBF + 90° = 180°$ [$\because$ in a rectangle, each angle is of 90°]

$\Rightarrow \quad 2\angle EFB = 90°$ [$\because \angle EFB = \angle EBF$]

$\angle EFB = 45°$ and $\angle EBF = 45°$

Now, $\angle x = 180° - 45° = 135°$ [linear pair]

and $\angle EFB + \angle y = 90°$ [$\because$ in a rectangle, each angle is of 90°]

$\Rightarrow \quad \angle y = 90° - 45° = 45°$

Q. 157 In the following figure of a ship, *ABDH* and *CEFG* are two parallelograms. Find the value of *x*.

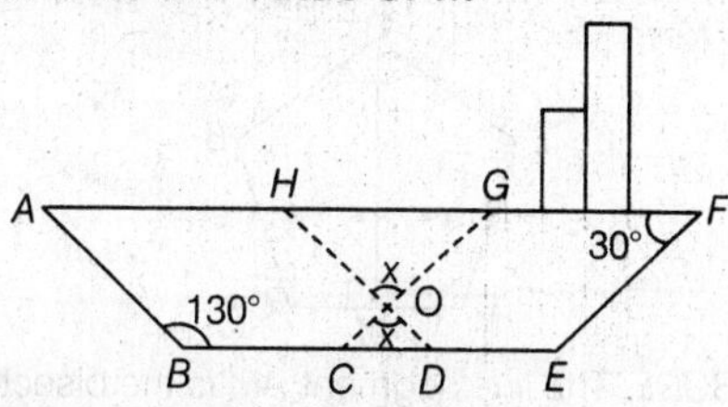

Sol. We have, two parallelograms *ABDH* and *CEFG*.

Now, in *ABDH*,

$\therefore \quad \angle ABD = \angle AHD = 130°$ [∵ opposite angles of a parallelogram are equal]

and $\angle GHD = 180° - \angle AHD = 180° - 130°$ [linear pair]

$\Rightarrow \quad 50° = \angle GHO$

Also, $\angle EFG + \angle FGC = 180°$ [∵ adjacent angles of a parallelogram are supplementary]

$\Rightarrow \quad 30° + \angle FGC = 180° \Rightarrow \angle FGC = 180° - 30° = 150°$

and $\angle HGC + \angle FGC = 180°$ [linear pair]

$\therefore \quad \angle HGC = 180° - \angle FGC = 180° - 150° = 30° = \angle HGO$

In ΔHGO, by using angle sum property, $\angle OHG + \angle HGO + \angle HOG = 180°$

$\Rightarrow \quad 50° + 30° + x = 180° \Rightarrow x = 180° - 80° = 100°$

Q. 158 A rangoli has been drawn on the floor of a house. *ABCD* and *PQRS* both are in the shape of a rhombus. Find the radius of semi-circle drawn on each side of rhombus *ABCD*.

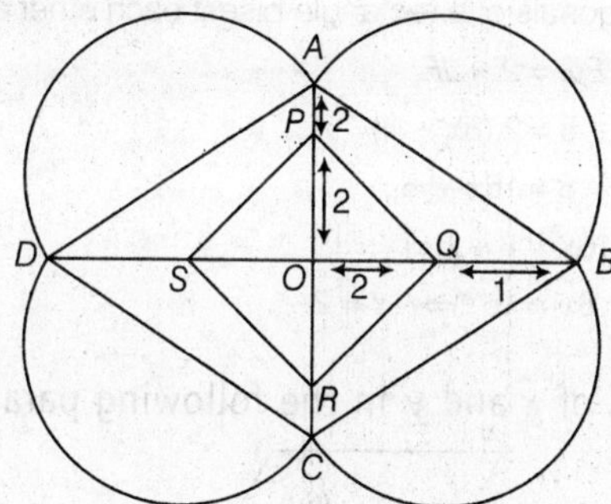

Sol. In rhombus *ABCD*,

$AO = OP + PA = 2 + 2 = 4$ units and $OB = OQ + QB = 2 + 1 = 3$ units

We know that, diagonals of rhombus bisect each other at 90°.

Now,

In ΔOAB, $(AB)^2 = (OA)^2 + (OB)^2$ [by Pythagoras theorem]

$\Rightarrow \quad (AB)^2 = (4)^2 + (3)^2 = 25$

$\Rightarrow \quad AB = \sqrt{25} \quad \Rightarrow \quad AB = 5$ units

Since, *AB* is diameter of semi-circle.

$\therefore \quad \text{Radius} = \frac{\text{Diameter}}{2} = \frac{AB}{2} = \frac{5}{2} = 2.5$ units

Hence, radius of the semi-circle is 2.5 units.

Q. 159 *ABCDE* is a regular pentagon. The bisector of angle *A* meets the sides *CD* at *M*. Find $\angle AMC$

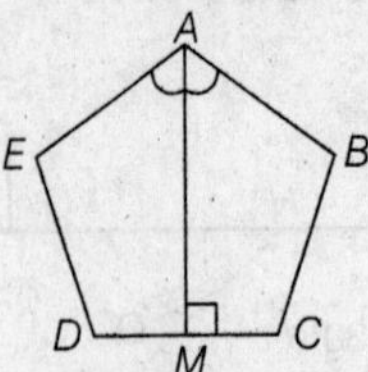

Sol. Given, a pentagon *ABCDE*. The line segment *AM* is the bisector of the $\angle A$.

Now, since the measure of each interior angle of a regular pentagon is 108°.

$$\therefore \quad \angle BAM = \frac{1}{2} \times 108° = 54°$$

By the angle sum property of a quadrilateral, we have (in quadrilateral *ABCM*)

$$\angle BAM + \angle ABC + \angle BCM + \angle AMC = 360°$$

$$\Rightarrow \quad 54° + 108° + 108° + \angle AMC = 360°$$

$$\Rightarrow \quad \angle AMC = 360° - 270° \Rightarrow \angle AMC = 90°$$

Q. 160 Quadrilateral *EFGH* is a rectangle in which *J* is the point of intersection of the diagonals. Find the value of *x*, if $JF = 8x + 4$ and $EG = 24x - 8$.

Sol. Given, *EFGH* is a rectangle in which diagonals are intersecting at the point *J*.

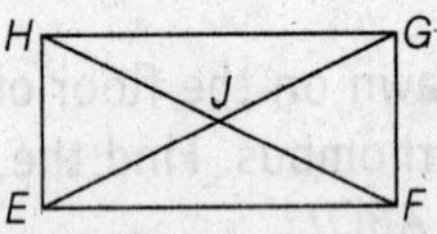

We know that, the diagonals of a rectangle bisect each other and are equal.

Then, $EG = 2 \times JF$

$$\Rightarrow \quad 24x - 8 = 2(8x + 4)$$

$$\Rightarrow \quad 24x - 8 = 16x + 8$$

$$\Rightarrow \quad 24x - 16x = 8 + 8$$

$$\Rightarrow \quad 8x = 16 \Rightarrow x = 2$$

Q. 161 Find the values of *x* and *y* in the following parallelogram.

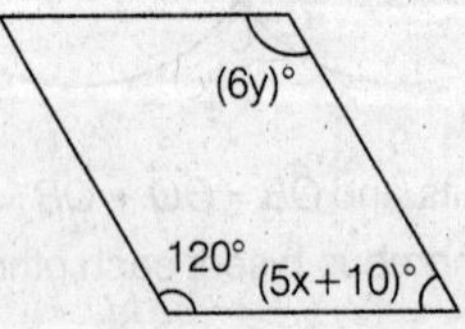

Sol. In a parallelogram, adjacent angles are supplementary.

$$\therefore \quad 120° + (5x + 10)° = 180°$$

$$\Rightarrow \quad 5x + 10° + 120° = 180°$$

$$\Rightarrow \quad 5x = 180° - 130°$$

$$\Rightarrow \quad 5x = 50°$$

$$\Rightarrow \quad x = 10°$$

Also, opposite angles are equal in a parallelogram.

Therefore, $6y = 120° \Rightarrow y = 20°$

Q. 162 **Find the values of x and y in the following kite.**

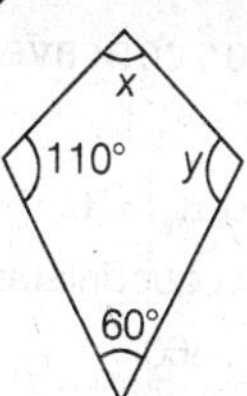

Sol. The given figure is a kite.

In a kite, one pair of opposite angles are equal.

$\therefore \quad y = 110°$

Now, by the angle sum property of a quadrilateral, we have

$$110° + 60° + 110° + x = 360°$$

$\Rightarrow \quad x = 360° - 280° \Rightarrow x = 80°$

Q. 163 **Find the value of x in the trapezium $ABCD$ given below.**

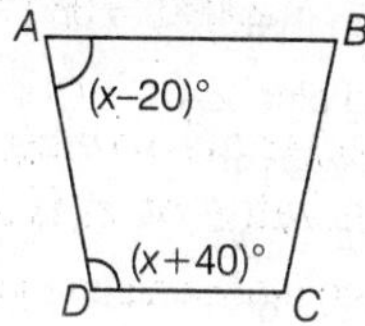

Sol. Given, a trapezium $ABCD$ in which $\angle A = (x - 20)°$, $\angle D = (x + 40)°$

Since, in a trapezium, the angles on either side of the base are supplementary, therefore

$$(x - 20) + (x + 40) = 180°$$

$\Rightarrow \quad x - 20 + x + 40 = 180°$

$\Rightarrow \quad 2x + 20° = 180°$

$\Rightarrow \quad 2x = (180° - 20°) = 160° \Rightarrow x = 80°$

Q. 164 **Two angles of a quadrilateral are each of measure 75° and the other two angles are equal. What is the measure of these two angles? Name the possible figures so formed.**

Sol. Let $ABCD$ be a quadrilateral,

where $\angle A = \angle C = 75°$ and $\angle B = \angle D = x$ [say]

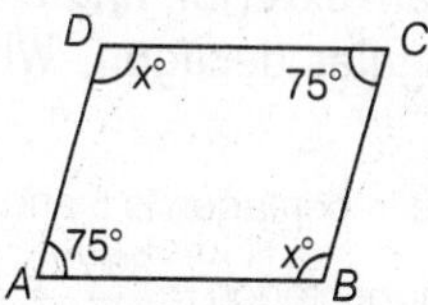

Then, by the angle sum property of a quadrilateral, we have

$$\angle A + \angle B + \angle C + \angle D = 360°$$

$\Rightarrow \quad 75° + x + 75° + x = 360°$

$\Rightarrow \quad 2x = 360° - 150°$

$\Rightarrow \quad 2x = 210° \Rightarrow x = 105°$

Thus, other two angles are of 105° each.

Since, opposite angles are equal, therefore the quadrilateral is a parallelogram.

Q. 165 **In a quadrilateral *PQRS*, $\angle P = 50°$, $\angle Q = 50°$, $\angle R = 60°$. Find $\angle S$. Is this quadrilateral convex or concave?**

Sol. Given a quadrilateral *PQRS*, where

$$\angle P = 50°, \angle Q = 50° \text{ and } \angle R = 60°$$

Now, by the angle sum property of a quadrilateral, we have

$$\angle P + \angle Q + \angle R + \angle S = 360°$$

$$\Rightarrow \quad 50° + 50° + 60° + \angle S = 360°$$

$$\Rightarrow \quad \angle S = 360° - 160°$$

$$\Rightarrow \quad \angle S = 200°$$

Since, one interior angle of the given quadrilateral is obtuse, therefore the quadrilateral is concave.

Q. 166 **Both the pairs of opposite angles of a quadrilateral are equal and supplementary. Find the measure of each angle.**

Sol. Let *ABCD* be a quadrilateral, such that

$$\angle A = \angle C, \angle B = \angle D \text{ and also } \angle A + \angle C = 180°, \ \angle B + \angle D = 180°$$

Now, $\angle A + \angle A = 180°$ $\quad [\because \angle C = \angle A]$

$$\Rightarrow \quad 2\angle A = 180°$$

$$\Rightarrow \quad \angle A = 90°$$

Similarly, $\angle B = 90°$

Hence, each angle is a right angle.

Q. 167 **Find the measure of each angle of a regular octagon.**

Sol. Number of sides(n) in octagon = 8

Now, the sum of interior angles of a regular octagon $= (n-2)\times 180°$

$$= (8-2) \times 180°$$

$$= 6 \times 180° = 1080°$$

Since, the octagon is regular, measure of each angle $= \dfrac{1080°}{8} = 135°$

Q. 168 **Find the measure of an exterior angle of a regular pentagon and an exterior angle of a regular decagon. What is the ratio between these two angles?**

Sol. We know that, number of sides in pentagon is 5 and in decagon is 10.

Now, exterior angle of a regular pentagon $= \dfrac{360°}{5} = 72°$

Exterior angle of a regular decagon $= \dfrac{360°}{10} = 36°$

$\therefore$ Required ratio $= \dfrac{72}{36} = 2:1$

So, the ratio between these two angles is 2:1.

Q. 169 In the figure, find the value of x.

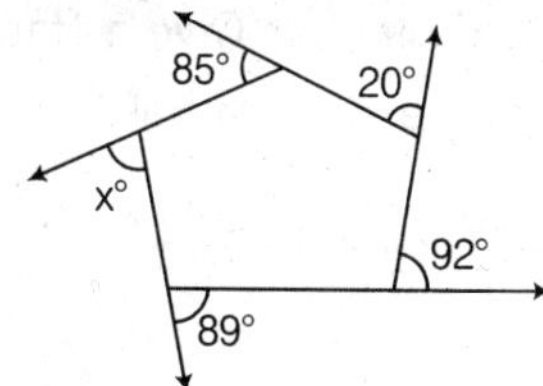

Sol. We observe that, the given figure is a pentagon.

Now, we know that, sum of all the exterior angles of a pentagon is 360°.

$\therefore \quad 92° + 20° + 85° + x° + 89° = 360°$

$\Rightarrow \quad 286° + x° = 360°$

$\Rightarrow \quad x° = 360° - 286° = 74°$

Q. 170 Three angles of a quadrilateral are equal. Fourth angle is of measure 120°. What is the measure of equal angles?

Sol. Let the measures of equal angles be $x°$ each.

Then, by the angle sum property of a quadrilateral, we have

$$x° + x° + x° + 120° = 360°$$

$\Rightarrow \quad 3x° + 120° = 360°$

$\Rightarrow \quad 3x° = 240°$

$\Rightarrow \quad x° = 80°$

Q. 171 In a quadrilateral *HOPE*, *PS* and *ES* are bisectors of $\angle P$ and $\angle E$ respectively. Give reason.

Sol. Data insufficient.

Q. 172 *ABCD* is a parallelogram. Find the values of x, y and z.

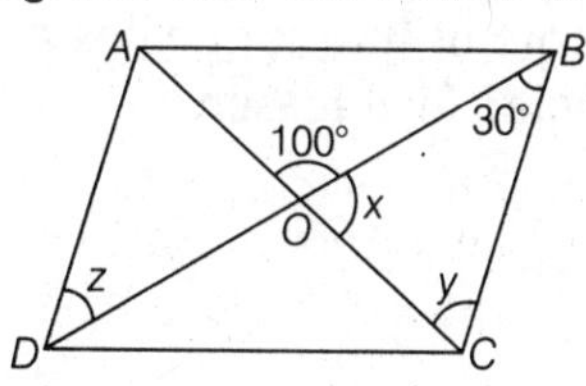

Sol. Given, a parallelogram *ABCD*.

In the ΔOBC, we have

$y + 30° = 100°$ [exterior angle property of triangle]

$\Rightarrow \quad y = 70°$

By the angle sum property of a triangle,

we have, $x + y + 30 = 180°$

$\Rightarrow \quad x + 70° + 30° = 180° \quad \Rightarrow \quad x = 180° - 100° = 80°$

Now, since $AD \parallel BC$ and BD is transversal, therefore

$\angle ADO = \angle OBC$ [alternate interior angles]

$\Rightarrow \quad z = 30°$

Q. 173 Diagonals of a quadrilateral are perpendicular to each other. Is such a quadrilateral always a rhombus? Give a figure to justify your answer.

Sol. False, it is not necessary that a quadrilateral having perpendicular diagonals is a rhombus.

e.g. Consider a trapezium *ABCD* in which $AB \parallel CD$.

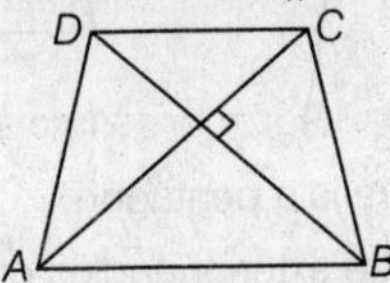

Q. 174 *ABCD* is a trapezium such that $AB \parallel CD$, $\angle A : \angle D = 2:1$, $\angle B : \angle C = 7:5$. Find the angles of the trapezium.

Sol. Let *ABCD* be a trapezium, where $AB \parallel CD$.

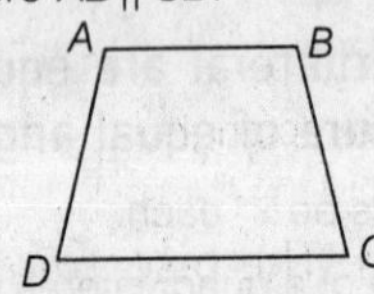

Let the angles *A* and *D* be of measures $2x$ and x, respectively.

Then, $2x + x = 180°$

[$\because$ in trapezium, the angles on either side of the base are supplementary]

$\Rightarrow \quad 3x = 180° \quad \Rightarrow \quad x = 60°$

$\therefore \quad \angle A = 2 \times 60° = 120°, \angle D = 60°$

Again, let the angles *B* and *C* be $7x$ and $5x$ respectively. Then, $7x + 5x = 180°$

$\Rightarrow \quad 12x = 180° \quad \Rightarrow \quad x = 15°$

Thus, $\quad \angle B = 7 \times 15 = 105°$ and $\angle C = 5 \times 15 = 75°$

Q. 175 A line *l* is parallel to line *m* and a transversal *p* intersects them at *X*, *Y* respectively. Bisectors of interior angles at *X* and *Y* intersect at *P* and *Q*. Is *PXQY* a rectangle? Give reason.

Sol. Given, $l \parallel m$

$\therefore \quad \angle DXY = \angle XYA$ [alternate interior angles]

$\Rightarrow \quad \dfrac{\angle DXY}{2} = \dfrac{\angle XYA}{2}$ [dividing both the sides by 2]

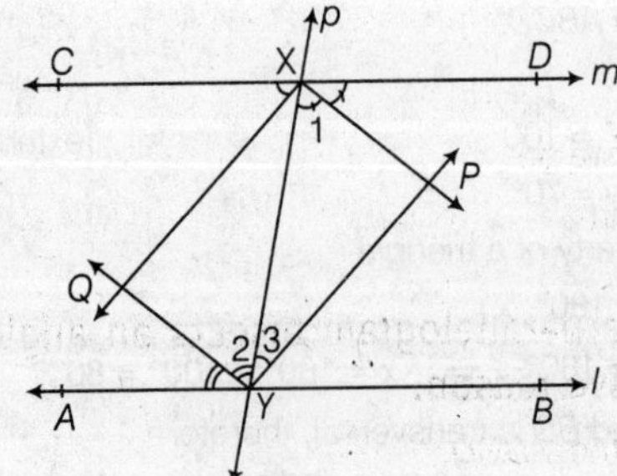

Now, $\quad \angle 1 = \angle 2$ [$\because$ *XP* and *YQ* are bisectors]

$\because$ Alternate angles are equal, i.e. $\angle 1 = \angle 2$

$\therefore \quad XP \parallel QY$ ...(i)

Similarly, $\quad XQ \parallel PY$ ...(ii)

From Eqs. (i) and (ii), we get

PXQY is a parallelogram. ...(iii)

$\Rightarrow \quad \angle DXY + \angle XYB = 180^\circ$

[$\because$ interior angles on the same side of transversal are supplementary]

$$\frac{\angle DXY}{2} + \frac{\angle XYB}{2} = \frac{180^\circ}{2}$$ [dividing both the sides by 2]

$$\angle 1 + \angle 3 = 90^\circ$$ ...(iv)

In ΔXYP,

$$\angle 1 + \angle 3 + \angle P = 180^\circ$$

$$90^\circ + \angle P = 180^\circ$$ [from Eq. (iv)]

$$\angle P = 90^\circ$$ ...(v)

From Eqs. (iii) and (v), *PXQY* is a rectangle.

Q. 176 ***ABCD* is a parallelogram. The bisector of angle *A* intersects *CD* at *X* and bisector of angle *C* intersects *AB* at *Y*. Is *AXCY* a parallelogram? Give reason.**

Sol. Given, *ABCD* is a parallelogram.

So, $\angle A = \angle C$ [$\because$ opposite angles of a parallelogram are equal]

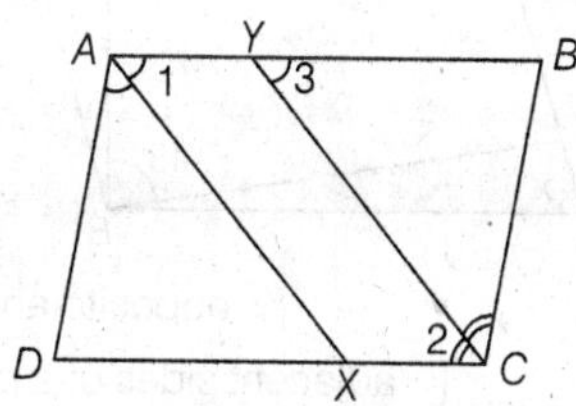

$\therefore \quad \frac{\angle A}{2} = \frac{\angle C}{2}$ [dividing both the sides by 2]

$\angle 1 = \angle 2$ [alternate angles]

But $\quad \angle 2 = \angle 3$ [$\because$ $AB \parallel CD$ and *CY* is the transversal]

$\therefore \quad \angle 1 = \angle 3$

But they are pair of corresponding angles.

$\therefore \quad AX \parallel YC$ ...(i)

$AY \parallel XC$ [$\because$ $AB \parallel DC$] ...(ii)

From Eqs. (i) and (ii), we get

AXCY is a parallelogram.

Q. 177 **A diagonal of a parallelogram bisects an angle. Will it also bisect the other angle? Give reason.**

Sol. Consider a parallelogram *ABCD*.

Given, $\angle 1 = \angle 2$

Since, $ABCD$ is a parallelogram.

$AB \parallel CD$ and AC is the transversal.

$\therefore \quad \angle 1 = \angle 4$ [alternate angles] ...(i)

Similarly,

$\angle 2 = \angle 3$ [alternate angles]...(ii)

But given, $\angle 1 = \angle 2$

$\therefore \quad \angle 3 = \angle 4$ [from Eqs. (i) and (ii)]

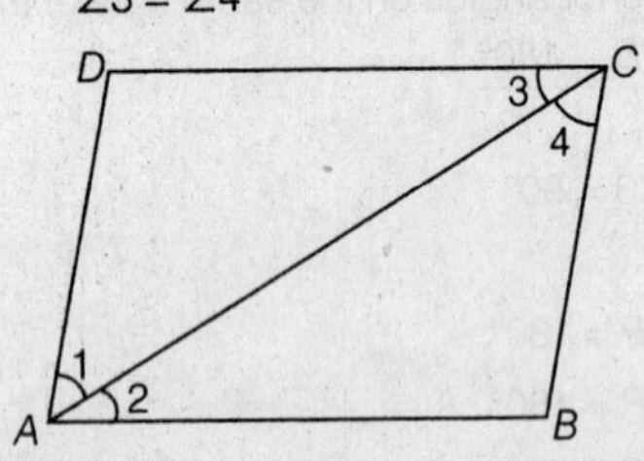

Q. 178 The angle between the two altitudes of a parallelogram through the vertex of an obtuse angle of the parallelogram is 45°. Find the angles of the parallelogram.

Sol. Let $ABCD$ be a parallelogram, where BE and BF are the perpendiculars through the vertex B to the sides DC and AD, respectively.

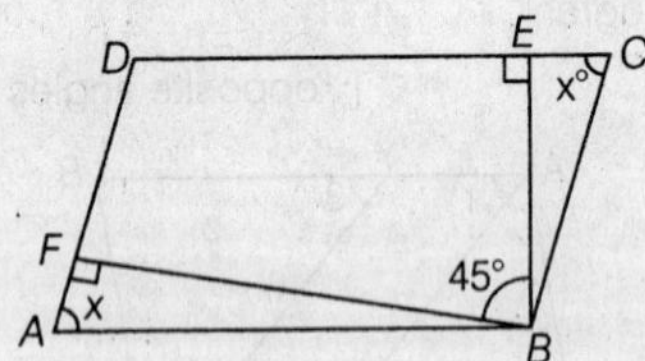

Let $\angle A = \angle C = x$, $\angle B = \angle D = y$ [$\because$ opposite angles are equal in parallelogram]

Now, $\angle A + \angle B = 180°$ [$\because$ adjacent sides of a parallelogram are supplementary]

$\Rightarrow \quad x + \angle ABF + \angle FBE + \angle EBC = 180°$

$\Rightarrow \quad x + 90° - x + 45° + 90° - x = 180°$

[$\because$ In ΔABF, $\angle ABF = 90° - x$ and in ΔBEC, $\angle EBC = 90° - x$]

$\Rightarrow \quad -x = 180° - 225°$

$\Rightarrow \quad x = 45°$

$\therefore \quad \angle A = \angle C = 45°$

$\angle B = 45° + 45° + 45° = 135°$

$\Rightarrow \quad \angle D = 135°$

Hence, the angles are 45°, 135°, 45°, 135°.

Q. 179 *ABCD* is a rhombus such that the perpendicular bisector of *AB* passes through *D*. Find the angles of the rhombus.

[Hint Join *BD*. Then, ΔABD is equilateral.]

Sol. Let $ABCD$ be a rhombus in which

DE is perpendicular bisector of AB.

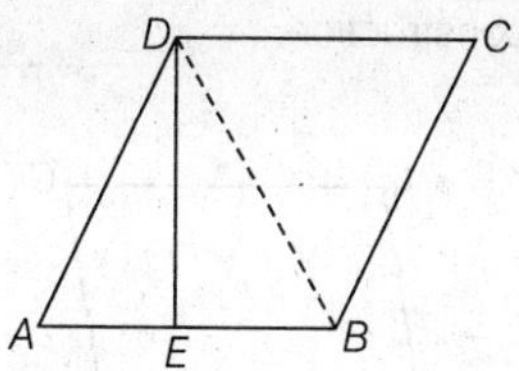

Join BD. Then, in ΔAED and ΔBED, we have

$AE = EB$

$ED = ED$ [common side]

$\angle AED = \angle DEB = 90°$

Then, by SAS rule, $\Delta AED \cong BED$

$\therefore$ $AD = DB = AB$ [$\because$ $ABCD$ is a rhombus. So, $AD = AB$]

Thus, ΔADB is an equilateral triangle.

$\therefore$ $\angle DAB = \angle DBA = \angle ADB = 60°$

$\Rightarrow$ $\angle DCB = 60°$ [opposite angles of a rhombus are equal]

Now, $\angle DAB + \angle ABC = 180°$ [adjacent angles of a rhombus are supplementary]

$\Rightarrow$ $60° + \angle ABD + \angle DBC = 180°$

$\Rightarrow$ $60° + 60° + \angle DBC = 180°$

$\Rightarrow$ $\angle DBC = 60°$

$\therefore$ $\angle ABC = \angle ABD + \angle DBC = 60° + 60° = 120°$

$\therefore$ $\angle ADC = 120°$ [opposite angles of a rhombus are equal]

Hence, the angles of the rhombus arc 60°, 120°, 60°, 120°.

Q. 180 ***ABCD* is a parallelogram. Point *P* and *Q* are taken on the sides *AB* and *AD*, respectively and the parallelogram *PRQA* is formed. If $\angle C = 45°$, find $\angle R$.**

Sol. Let $ABCD$ be a parallelogram, where $\angle C = 45°$

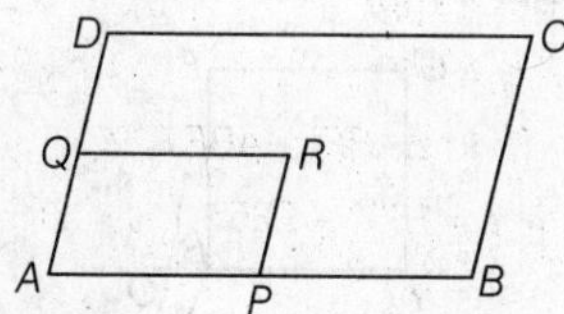

Since, $ABCD$ is a parallelogram,

$\angle A = \angle C$ [opposite angles of parallelogram are equal]

Again, since $PRQA$ is a parallelogram,

$\angle A = \angle R$ [opposite angles of parallelogram are equal]

$\Rightarrow$ $\angle R = 45°$ [$\because \angle A = \angle C = 45°$]

Q. 181 **In parallelogram *ABCD*, the angle bisector of $\angle A$ bisects *BC*. Will angle bisector of *B* also bisect *AD*? Give reason.**

Sol. Given, $ABCD$ is a parallelogram, bisector of $\angle A$, bisects BC at F, i.e. $\angle 1 = \angle 2$, $CF = FB$

Draw $FE \parallel BA$

ABFE is a parallelogram by construction [$\because FE \parallel BA$]

$\Rightarrow$ $\angle 1 = \angle 6$ [alternate angle]

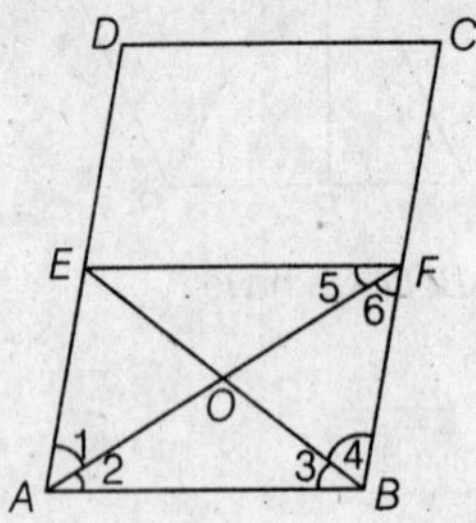

But $\angle 1 = \angle 2$ [given]

$\therefore$ $\angle 2 = \angle 6$

$AB = FB$ [opposite sides to equal angles are equal] ...(i)

$\therefore$ *ABFE* is a rhombus.

Now, in ΔABO and ΔBOF, $AB = BF$ [from Eq. (i)]

$BO = BO$ [common]

$AO = FO$ [diagonals of rhombus bisect each other]

$\therefore$ $\Delta ABO \cong \Delta BOF$ [by SSS]

$\angle 3 = \angle 4$ [by CPCT]

Now, $BF = \frac{1}{2} BC$ [given]

$\Rightarrow$ $BF = \frac{1}{2} AD$ [$BC = AD$]

$\Rightarrow$ $AE = \frac{1}{2} AD$ [$BF = AE$]

$\therefore$ *E* is the mid-point of *AD*.

Q. 182 A regular pentagon *ABCDE* and a square *ABFG* are formed on opposite sides of *AB*. Find $\angle BCF$?

Sol.

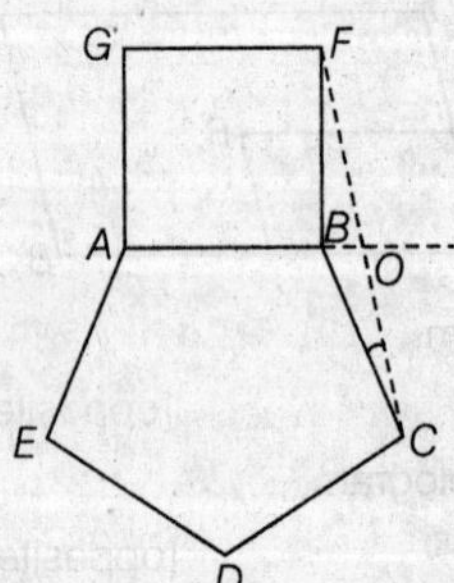

Given, *ABCDE* is a regular pentagon.

Then, measure of each interior angle of the regular pentagon

$$= \frac{\text{Sum of interior angles}}{\text{Number of sides}} = \frac{(x-2)\times 180^\circ}{5}$$

$$= \frac{(5-2)\times 180^\circ}{5} = \frac{540^\circ}{5} = 108^\circ$$

$\therefore \quad \angle CBA = 108°$

Join CF.

Now, $\angle FBC = 360° - (90° + 108°) = 360° - 198° = 162°$

In ΔFBC, by the angle sum property, we have

$$\angle FBC + \angle BCF + \angle BFC = 180°$$

$$\Rightarrow \quad \angle BCF + \angle BFC = 180° - 162°$$

$$\Rightarrow \quad \angle BCF + \angle BFC = 18°$$

Since, ΔFBC is an isosceles triangle and $BF = BC$.

$$\therefore \quad \angle BCF = \angle BFC = 9°$$

Q. 183 Find maximum number of acute angles which a convex quadrilateral, a pentagon and a hexagon can have. Observe the pattern and generalise the result for any polygon.

Sol. If an angle is acute, then the corresponding exterior angle is greater than 90°. Now, suppose a convex polygon has four or more acute angles. Since, the polygon is convex, all the exterior angles are positive, so the sum of the exterior angle is atleast the sum of the interior angles. Now, supplementary of the four acute angles, which is greater than $4 \times 90° = 360°$

However, this is impossible. Since, the sum of exterior angle of a polygon must equal to 360° and cannot be greater than it. It follows that the maximum number of acute angle in convex polygon is 3.

Q. 184 In the following figure, $FD \parallel BC \parallel AE$ and $AC \parallel ED$. Find the value of x.

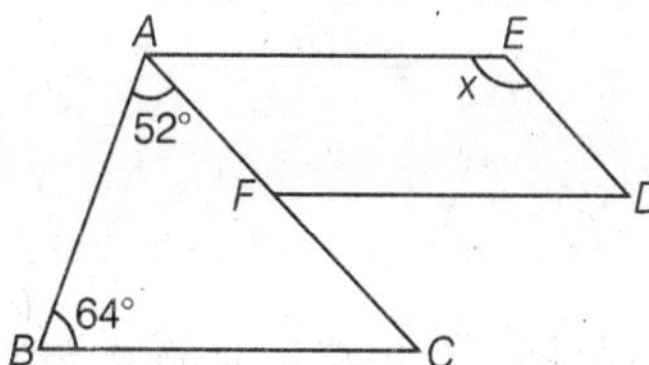

Sol. Produce DF such that it intersects AB at G.

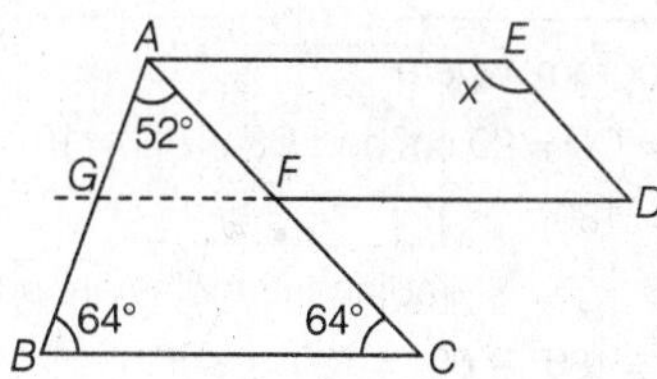

In ΔABC,

$$\angle A + \angle B + \angle C = 180° \quad \text{[angle sum property of triangle]}$$

$$\Rightarrow \quad 52° + 64° + \angle C = 180°$$

$$\angle C = 180° - (52° + 64°) = 180° - 116° = 64°$$

Now, we see that, $DG \parallel BC$ and $DG \parallel AE$

$\therefore \quad \angle ACB = \angle AFG$ [$\because$ $FG \parallel BC$ and FC is a transversal, so corresponding angles]

$\Rightarrow \quad 64° = \angle AFG$

Also, GFD is a straight line.

$\therefore \quad \angle GFA + \angle AFD = 180°$ [linear pair]

$\Rightarrow \quad 64° + \angle AFD = 180°$

$\Rightarrow \quad \angle AFD = 180° - 64° = 116°$

Also, $FD \parallel AE$ and $AF \parallel ED$

So, $AEDF$ is a parallelogram.

$\therefore \quad \angle AFD = \angle AED$ [$\because$ opposite angles in a parallelogram are equal]

$\Rightarrow \quad \angle AED = x = 116°$

Q. 185 In the following figure, $AB \parallel DC$ and $AD = BC$. Find the value of x.

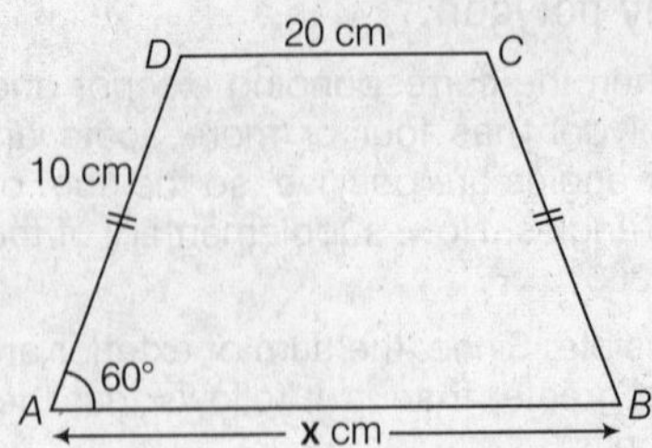

Sol. Given, an isosceles trapezium, where $AB \parallel DC$, $AD = BC$ and $\angle A = 60°$.

Then, $\angle B = 60°$.

Draw a line parallel to BC through D which intersects the line AB at E (say).

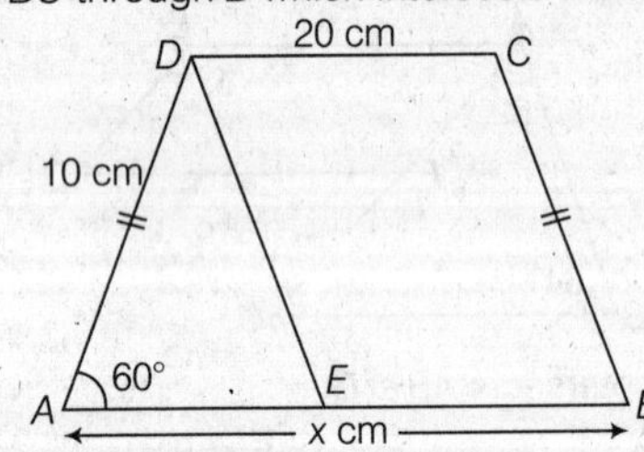

Then, $DEBC$ is a parallelogram, where

$$BE = CD = 20 \text{ cm and } DE = BC = 10 \text{ cm}$$

Now, $\quad \angle DEB + \angle CBE = 180°$

[adjacent angles are supplementary in parallelogram]

$\Rightarrow \quad \angle DEB = 180° - 60° = 120°$

$\therefore$ In ΔADE, $\angle ADE = 60°$ [exterior angle]

Also, $\quad \angle DEA = 60°$ [$\because$ $AD = DE = 10$ cm and $\angle DAE = 60°$]

Then, ΔADE is an equilateral triangle.

$\therefore \quad AE = 10$ cm

$\Rightarrow \quad AB = AE + EB = 10 + 20 = 30$ cm

Hence, $x = 30$ cm

Q. 186 Construct a trapezium $ABCD$ in which $AB \parallel DC$, $\angle A = 105°$, $AD = 3$ cm, $AB = 4$ cm and $CD = 8$ cm.

Sol. We know that.

$$\angle A + \angle D = 180 \qquad [\because \text{ sum of adjacent angle of a trapezium is } 180°]$$

$$105° + \angle D = 180°$$

$$\angle D = 75°$$

Steps of Construction

***Step* I** Draw $AB = 4$ cm.

***Step* II** Draw $\overline{AX}$ such that $\angle BAX = 105°$.

***Step* III** Mark a point D on AX such that $AD = 3$cm.

***Step* IV** Draw $\overline{DY}$ such that $\angle ADY = 75°$.

***Step* V** Mark a point C such that $CD = 8$cm.

***Step* VI** Join BC.

Hence, $ABCD$ is the required trapezium.

Q. 187 Construct a parallelogram $ABCD$ in which $AB = 4$ cm, $BC = 5$ cm and $\angle B = 60°$.

Sol. We know that, the opposite sides of a parallelogram are equal.

So,
$$AB = DC = 4 \text{ cm}$$

$$BC = AD = 5 \text{ cm}$$

$$\angle B = 60°$$

$$\angle A + \angle B = 180° \qquad [\text{sum of cointerior angles}]$$

$$\angle A = 120°$$

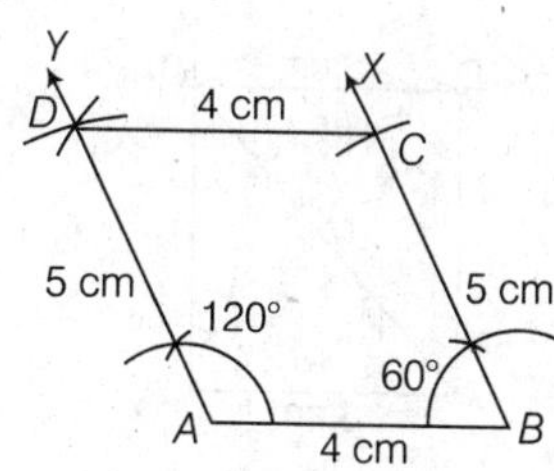

Steps of Construction

***Step* I** Draw $AB = 4$cm.

***Step* II** Draw ray BX such that $\angle ABX = 60°$.

***Step* III** Mark a point C such that $BC = 5$ cm.

***Step* IV** Draw a ray AY such that $\angle YAB = 120°$.

***Step* V** Mark a point D such that $AD = 5$ cm.

***Step* VI** Join C and D.

Hence, $ABCD$ is required parallelogram.

Q. 188 Construct a rhombus whose side is 5 cm and one angle is of 60°.

Sol.

$\angle B = 60°$ [suppose]

$\angle A + \angle B = 180°$ [sum of cointerior angles]

$\angle A + 60° = 180°$

$\angle A = 120°$

$AB = BC = CD = DA = 5\text{ cm}$

Steps of Construction

***Step* I** Draw $AB = 5\text{cm}$.

***Step* II** Draw a ray AY such that $\angle BAY = 120°$.

***Step* III** Mark a point D such that $AD = 5\text{cm}$.

***Step* IV** Draw a ray BX such that $\angle ABX = 60°$

***Step* V** Mark a point C such that $BC = 5\text{cm}$.

***Step* VI** Joint C and D.

$\therefore ABCD$ is the required rhombus.

Q. 189 Construct a rectangle whose one side is 3 cm and a diagonal is equal to 5 cm.

Sol. We know that, diagonals of a rectangle and opposite sides are equal.

All the angles of rectangle are right angle.

So, $AC = 5\text{cm}$

$AB = 3\text{cm}$

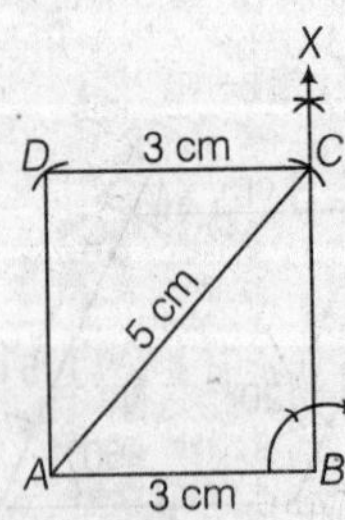

Steps of Construction

***Step* I** Draw $AB = 3\text{cm}$.

***Step* II** Draw a ray BX such that $\angle ABX = 90°$

***Step* III** Draw an arc such that $AC = 5\text{cm}$.

Step IV With B as centre, draw an arc of radius 5 cm. With C as centre, draw an another arc of radius 3 cm which intersect first arc at a point, suppose D.

Step V Join CD and AD.

Thus, $ABCD$ is the required rectangle.

Q. 190 Construct a square of side 4 cm.

Sol. We know that, all sides of a square are equal and each side is perpendicular to adjacent side.

So, $AB = BC = CD = DA = 4$ cm

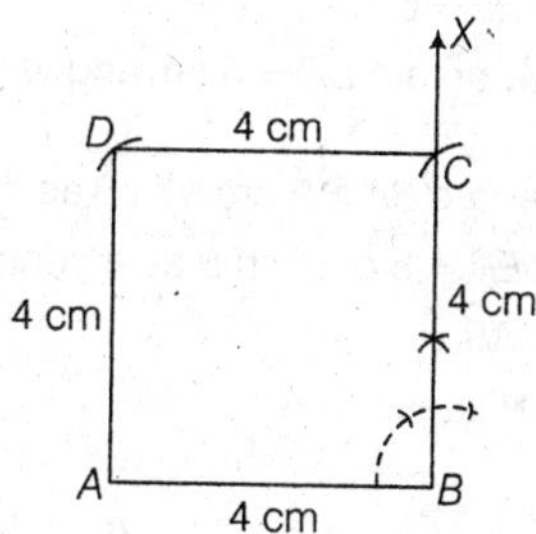

Steps of Construction

Step I Draw $\overline{AB} = 4$ cm.

Step II At B, draw $\overline{BX}$ such that $\angle ABX = 90°$.

Step III From $\overline{BX}$, cut-off $BC = 4$ cm.

Step IV With centre C and radius = 4 cm, drawn an arc.

Step V With centre A and radius = 4 cm, draw another arc to intersect the previous arc at D.

Step VI Join DA and CD.

Thus, $ABCD$ is the required square.

Q. 191 Construct a rhombus $CLUE$ in which $CL = 7.5$ cm and $LE = 6$ cm.

Sol. We know that, all sides of a rhombus are equal and opposite sides are parallel to each other.

Steps of Construction

Step I Draw a line segment $CL = 7.5$ cm.

Step II With C as a centre, draw an arc $CE = 7.5$ cm.

Step III With L as a centre, draw an another arc $LU = 7.5$ cm.

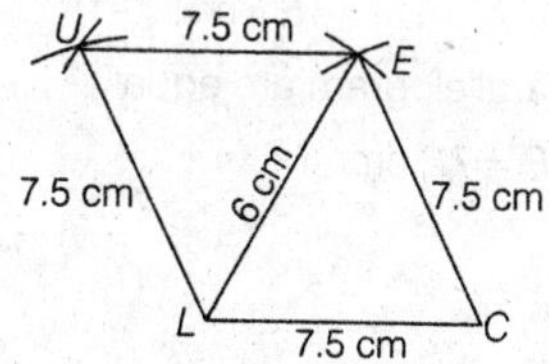

Step IV Now, with centre L, draw an arc $LE = 6$ cm, which cut-off previous arc CE.

Step V With E as a centre, draw an arc $UE = 7.5$ cm, which cut-off previous arc LU.

Step VI Now join UL, CE and EU.

Thus, we have required rhombus $CLUE$.

Q. 192 Construct a quadrilateral *BEAR* in which $BE = 6$ cm, $EA = 7$ cm, $RB = RE = 5$ cm and $BA = 9$ cm. Measure its fourth side.

Sol. ***Steps of Construction***

***Step* I** Draw a line segment $BE = 6$ cm.

***Step* II** With *B* as center, draw an arc $BR = 5$ cm and with *E* as a centre, draw an arc $EA = 7$ cm.

***Step* III** Now, draw an another arc $BA = 9$ cm with *B* as a centre, which cut-off arc *AE*.

***Step* IV** Draw an another arc $ER = 5$ cm with *E* as a centre, which cut-off arc *BR*.

***Step* V** Now join *BR*, *EA* and *AR*.

Thus, we have required quadrilateral *BEAR*.

Also, $AR = 5$ cm.

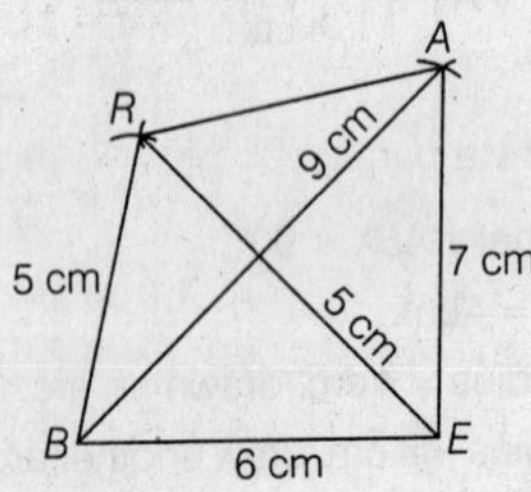

Q. 193 Construct a parallelogram *POUR* in which $PO = 5.5$ cm, $OU = 7.2$ cm and $\angle O = 70°$.

Sol. Since,

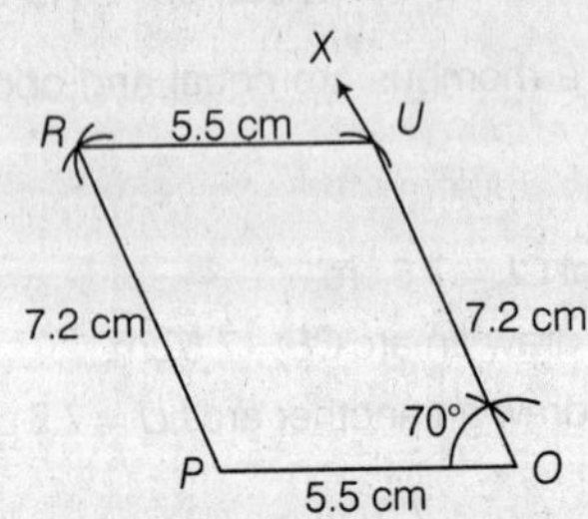

Since, opposite sides of a parallelogram are equal.

$\therefore PO = RU = 5.5$ cm, $OU = RP = 7.2$ cm

Steps of Construction

***Step* I** Draw $PO = 5.5$ cm.

***Step* II** Construct $\angle POX = 70°$.

***Step* III** With *O* as centre and radius $OU = 7.2$ cm, draw an arc.

***Step* IV** With *U* as centre and radius $UR = 5.5$ cm, draw an arc.

***Step* V** With *P* as centre and radius $PR = 7.2$ cm, draw an arc to cut the arc drawn in Step IV.

***Step* VI** Join *PR* and *UR*.

Hence, *POUR* is the required parallelogram.

Q. 194 Draw a circle of radius 3 cm and draw its diameter and label it as AC. Construct its perpendicular bisector and let it intersect the circle at B and D. What type of quadrilateral is $ABCD$? Justify your answer.

Sol.

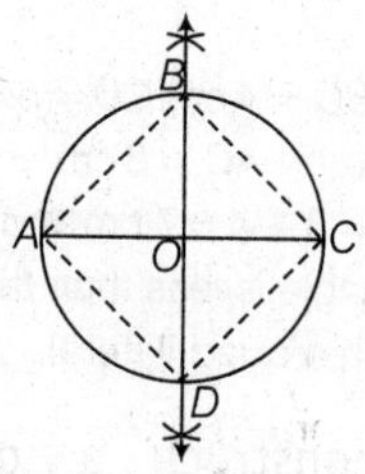

Steps of Construction

Step I Taking centre $OC = 3$ cm, draw a circle.

Step II Join A to C and draw a perpendicular bisector of AC that cuts the circumference of circle at B and D.

Step III Join B and D.

Step IV Thus, $ABCD$ is a cyclic quadrilateral.

Justification

In cyclic quadrilateral,

$\angle B = \angle D = 90°$ [angle in a semi-circle]

$\angle A = \angle C = 90°$

$\angle B + \angle D = 180°$

and $\angle A + \angle C = 180°$

[opposite angles are supplementary]

Since, opposite angles are supplementary, thus quadrilateral is a cyclic quadrilateral.

Q. 195 Construct a parallelogram $HOME$ with $HO = 6$ cm, $HE = 4$ cm and $OE = 3$ cm.

Sol.

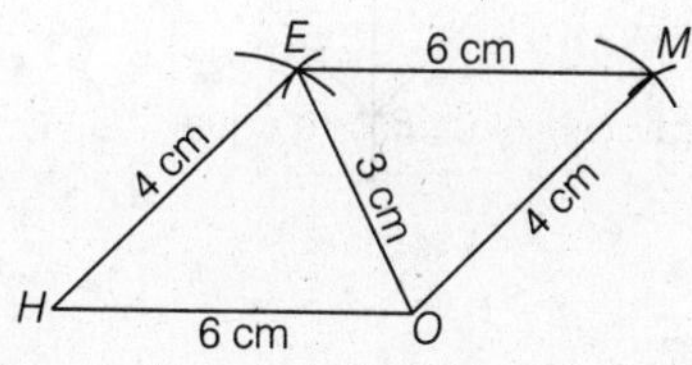

Steps of Construction

Step I Draw $HO = 6$cm.

Step II With H as centre and radius $HE = 4$cm, draw an arc.

Step III With O as centre and radius $OE = 3$cm, draw an arc, intersecting the arc drawn in step II at E.

Step IV With E as centre and radius $EM = 6$cm, draw an arc opposite to the side HE.

Step V With O as centre and radius $OM = 4$cm, draw an arc, intersecting the arc drawn in step IV at M.

Step VI Join HE, OE, EM and OM.

Hence, $HOME$ is the required parallelogram.

Q. 196 Is it possible to construct a quadrilateral $ABCD$ in which $AB = 3$ cm, $BC = 4$ cm, $CD = 5.4$ cm, $DA = 5.9$ cm and diagonal $AC = 8$ cm? If not, why?

Sol. No,

Given measures are $AB = 3$ cm, $BC = 4$ cm, $CD = 5.4$ cm,

$DA = 5.9$ cm and $AC = 8$ cm

Here, we observe that $AB + BC = 3 + 4 = 7$ cm and $AC = 8$ cm

i.e. the sum of two sides of a triangle is less than the third side, which is absurd.

Hence, we cannot construct such a quadrilateral.

Q. 197 Is it possible to construct a quadrilateral $ROAM$ in which $RO = 4$ cm, $OA = 5$ cm, $\angle O = 120°$, $\angle R = 105°$ and $\angle A = 135°$? If not, why?

Sol. No,

Given measures are

$OA = 5$ cm, $\angle O = 120°$, $\angle R = 105°$ and $\angle A = 135°$

Here, we see that, $\angle O + \angle R + \angle A = 120° + 105° + 135° = 360°$

i.e. the sum of three angles of a quadrilateral is 360°.

This is impossible, as the total sum of angles is 360° in a quadrilateral.

Hence, this quadrilateral cannot be constructed.

Q. 198 Construct a square in which each diagonal is 5 cm long.

Sol.

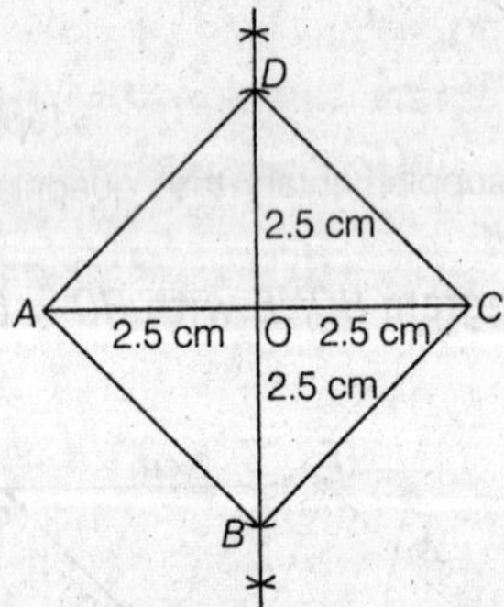

Steps of Construction

***Step* I** Draw $AC = 5$ cm.

***Step* II** With A as centre, draw arc of length slightly greater than $\frac{1}{2}$ AC above and below the line segment AC.

***Step* III** With C as centre, draw an arc of same length as in step II above and below the line segment AC which intersect the arcs drawn in step II.

***Step* IV** Join both the intersection points obtained in step III by a line segment which intersects AC at O (say).

***Step* V** With O as centre cut-off $OB = OD = 2.5$ cm along the bisector line.

***Step* VI** Join AD, CD, AB and CB.

This is the required square $ABCD$.

Q. 199 Construct a quadrilateral *NEWS* in which $NE = 7$ cm, $EW = 6$ cm, $\angle N = 60°$, $\angle E = 110°$ and $\angle S = 85°$

Sol.

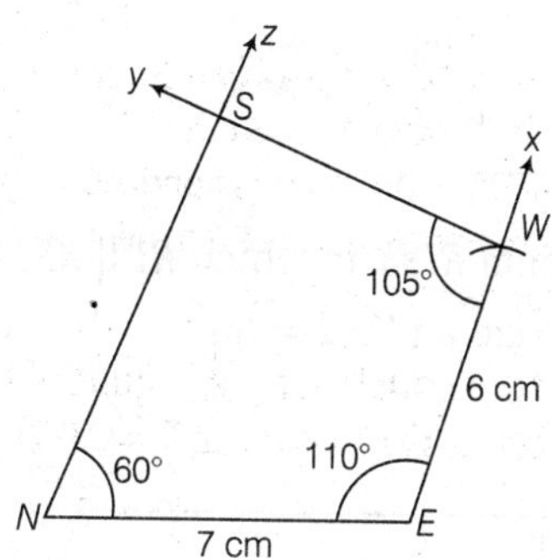

Fourth angle = 360° – (60° + 110° + 85°) = 360° – 255° = 105°

Steps of Construction

***Step* I** Draw $NE = 7$ cm.

***Step* II** Make $\angle NEX = 110°$.

***Step* III** With *E* as centre and radius 6 cm, draw an arc, cutting *EX* at *W*.

***Step* IV** Make $\angle EWY = 105°$

***Step* V** Make $\angle ENZ = 60°$, so that *NZ* and *WY* intersect each other at point *S*.

Thus, *NEWS* is the required quadrilateral.

Q. 200 Construct a parallelogram when one of its side is 4cm and its two diagonals are 5.6 cm and 7cm. Measure the other side.

Sol.

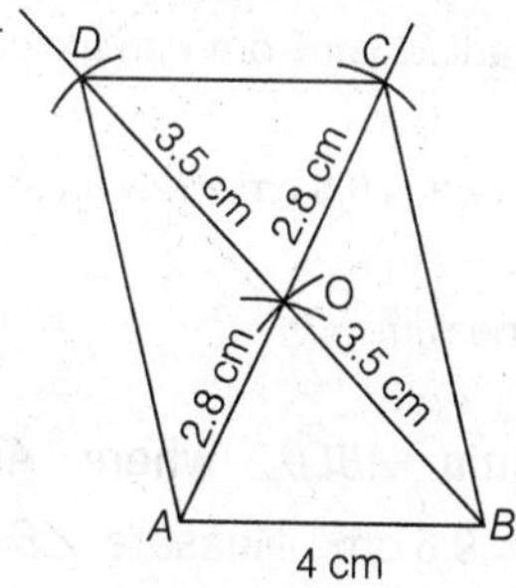

Steps of Construction

Step I Draw $AB = 4$cm.

Step II With *A* as centre and radius 2.8 cm, draw an arc.

Step III With *B* as centre and radius 3.5 cm, draw another arc cutting the previous arc at *O*.

Step IV Join *OA* and *OB*.

Step V Produce *AO* to *C* such that $OC = AO$ and produce *BO* to *D* such that $OD = BD$.

Step VI Join *AD*, *BC* and *CD*.

Thus, *ABCD* is the required parallelogram.

and other side = 5 cm.

Q. 201 **Find the measure of each angle of a regular polygon of 20 sides?**

Sol. We know that, the sum of interior angles of an n polygon $= (n-2) \times 180°$

Here, $n = 20$, then

$$\text{Sum} = (20-2) \times 180° = 18 \times 180° = 3240°$$

$\therefore$ The measure of each interior angle $= \dfrac{3240}{20} = 162°$

Q. 202 **Construct a trapezium *RISK* in which $RI \parallel KS$, $RI = 7$ cm, $IS = 5$ cm, $RK = 6.5$ cm and $\angle I = 60°$.**

Sol.

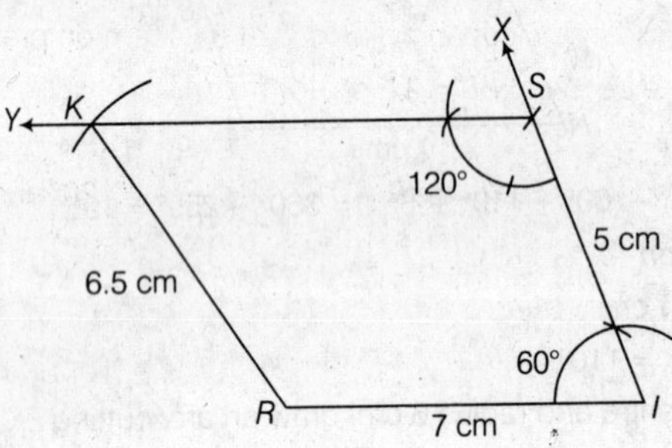

$$\angle I + \angle S = 180° \quad \text{[cointerior angles]}$$
$$60° + \angle S = 180°$$
$$\angle S = 120°$$

Steps of Construction

***Step* I** Draw an arc $RI = 7$ cm.

***Step* II** Make $\angle RIX = 60°$.

***Step* III** With I as centre and radius 5 cm, draw an arc cutting IX at S.

***Step* IV** Make $\angle ISY = 120°$

***Step* V** With R as centre and radius 6.5 cm, draw an arc cutting SY at K.

***Step* VI** Join KR.

Thus, *RISK* is the required trapezium.

Q. 203 **Construct a trapezium *ABCD*, where $AB \parallel CD$, $AD = BC = 3.2$ cm, $AB = 6.4$ cm and $CD = 9.6$ cm. Measure $\angle B$ and $\angle A$.**

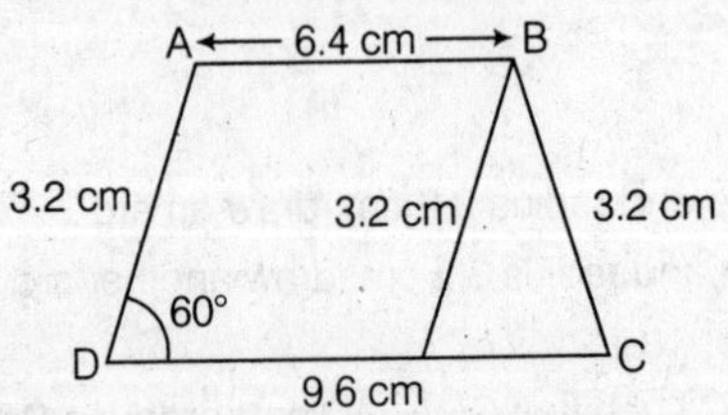

[Hint Difference of two parallel sides gives an equilateral triangle.**]**

Sol.

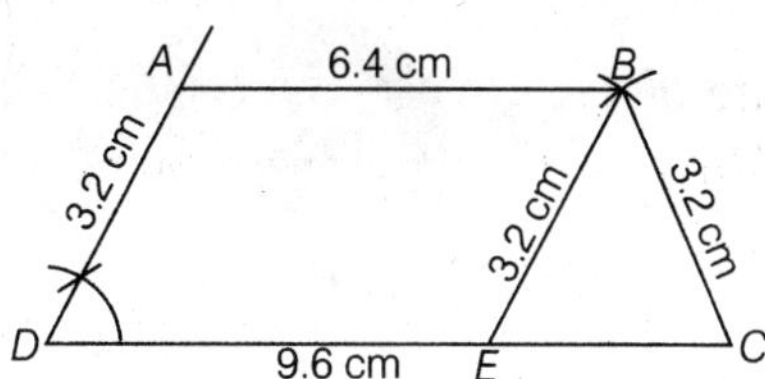

Steps of Construction

***Step* I** Draw a line segment $DC = 9.6$ cm.

***Step* II** With D as center, draw an angle measure 60°. Now, cut-off it with an arc 3.2 cm called point A.

***Step* III** Now, draw a parallel AB to CD.

***Step* IV** Talking C as center, cut an arc B measure 3.2 cm on previous parallel line.

***Step* V** Draw a line segment $BE = 3.2$ cm from arc B.

***Step* VI** Join B to E and C.

Thus, we have required trapezium $ABCD$ in which $\angle A = 120°$ and $\angle B = 60°$.

6

Visualising Solid Shapes

Multiple Choice Questions (MCQs)

Q. 1 Which amongst the following is not a polyhedron?

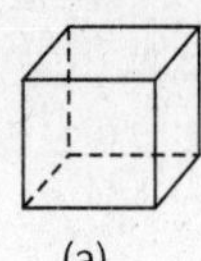
(a)

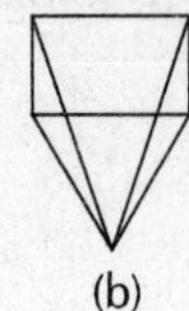
(b)

(c)

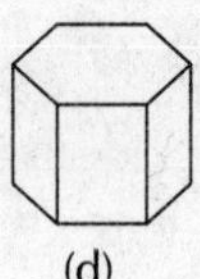
(d)

Sol. *(c)* According to the definition of a polyhedron, option (c) figure does not satisfies the condition of a polyhedron.
Since, a solid is a polyhedron if it is made up of only polygonal-faces, the faces meet at edges with one line segment and the edges meeting at a point. The point is generally called as vertex. But all the faces of option (c) are not polygons, there is a circular base, so the figure is not a polyhedron.

Q. 2 Which of the following will not form a polyhedron?

(a) 3 triangles
(b) 2 triangles and 3 parallelograms
(c) 8 triangles
(d) 1 pentagon and 5 triangles

Sol. *(a)* A polyhedron is bounded by more than four polygonal faces. But in case of 3 triangles, it is not possible. So, option (a) does not form a polyhedron.

Q. 3 Which of the following is a regular polyhedron?

(a) Cuboid
(b) Triangular prism
(c) Cube
(d) Square prism

Sol. *(c)* A polyhedron is regular, if its faces are congruent regular polygons and the same number of faces meet at each vertex. Hence, a cube satisfies all the properties for a regular polyhedron.

Q. 4 Which of the following is a two dimensional figure?

(a) Rectangle
(b) Rectangle prism
(c) Square pyramid
(d) Square prism

Sol. *(a)* A two dimensional figure have two dimensions (measurements) like length and breadth. In the given options, only rectangle has two dimensions, i.e. length and breadth.

Q. 5 Which of the following can be the base of a pyramid?

(a) Line segment (b) Circle (c) Octagon (d) Oval

Sol. ***(c)*** Since, a pyramid is a polyhedron whose base is a polygon and lateral faces are triangles.

Hence, octagon can be the base of a pyramid.

Q. 6 Which of the following 3-D shapes does not have a vertex?

(a) Pyramid (b) Prism (c) Cone (d) Sphere

Sol. ***(d)*** As we know that, a vertex is a meeting point of two or more edges. Since, a sphere has only one curved face, so it has no vertex and no edges.

Q. 7 Solid having only line segments as its edges is a

(a) Polyhedron (b) Cone (c) Cylinder (d) Polygon

Sol. ***(a)*** In polyhedron, the faces meet at edges which are line segments and edges meet at vertex.

Q. 8 In a solid, if $F = V = 5$, then the number of edges in this shape is

(a) 6 (b) 4 (c) 8 (d) 2

Sol. ***(c)*** Euler's formula for any polyhedron is

$$F + V - E = 2$$

Given, $F = V = 5$

On putting the values of F and V in the Euler's formula, we get

$$5 + 5 - E = 2$$

$\Rightarrow$ $10 - E = 2 \Rightarrow E = 8$

Note *F = faces, V = vertices and E = edges.*

Q. 9 Which of the following is the top view of the given shape?

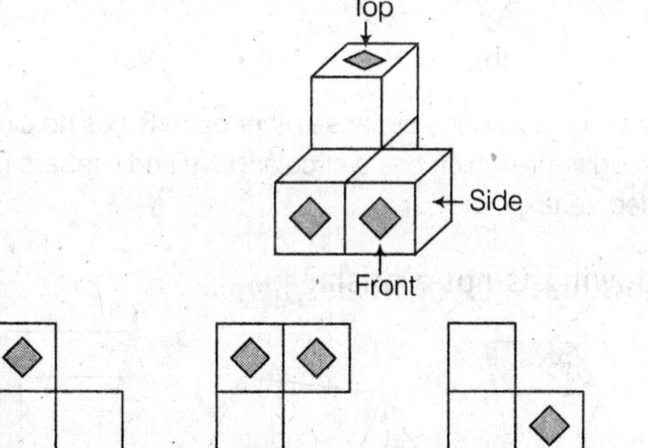

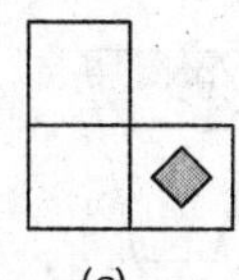

(a) (b) (c) (d)

Sol. ***(a)*** Since, top view is the picture of the solid which is seen from the top of the given figure. Therefore, the option (a) figure will be the top view, i.e.

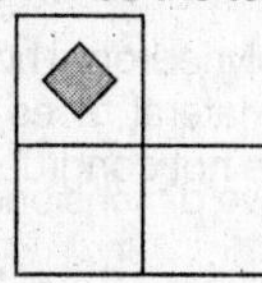

Top view

Q. 10 **The net shown below can be folded into the shape of a cube. The face marked with the letter L is opposite to the face marked with which letter?**

(a) M
(b) N
(c) Q
(d) O

Sol. (a) Clearly, the given net is a cube. If we fold it into a cube, then N will face opposite to P, Q on the top and O on the bottom. So, L faces opposite to M.

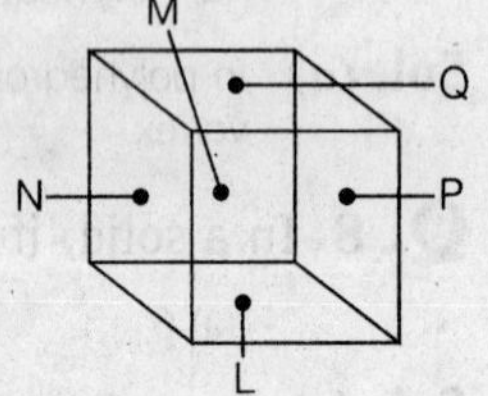

Q. 11 **Which of the nets given below will generate a cone?**

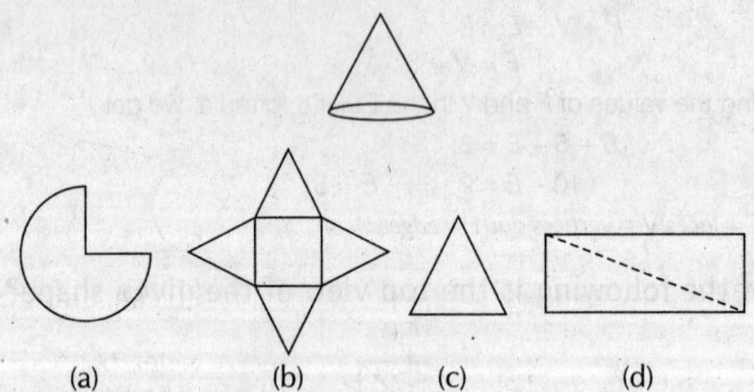

Sol. (a) Option (a) net diagram gives a cone because other options has no circular base. Since, a cone is a solid figure which has a circular base and it tapers from a circular base to a point called vertex.

Q. 12 **Which of the following is not a prism?**

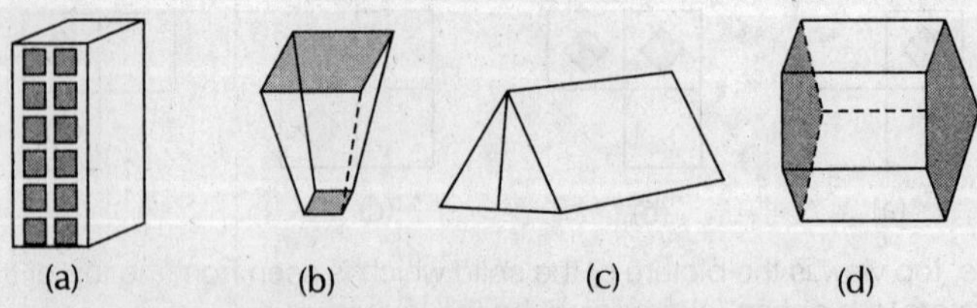

Sol. (b) We know that, a prism is a polyhedron whose bottom and top faces are congruent polygons and faces known as lateral faces are parallelograms. Clearly in option (b) figure, bottom and top faces are not congruent polygons and also lateral faces are not parallelograms.

Q. 13 **We have 4 congruent equilateral triangles. What do we need more to make a pyramid?**

(a) An equilateral triangle.

(b) A square with same side length as of triangle.

(c) 2 equilateral triangles with side length same as triangle.

(d) 2 squares with side length same as triangle.

Sol. *(b)* We know that, a pyramid is a polyhedron, whose base is a polygon and lateral faces are triangles. But in the question, we have only 4 congruent equilateral triangles. Thus, we have to add a polygon in the base of atleast a four-sided figure.

Hence, option (b) is required to make a pyramid.

Q. 14 **Side of a square garden is 30 m. If the scale used to draw its picture is 1 cm : 5 m, the perimeter of the square in the picture is**

(a) 20 cm (b) 24 cm (c) 28 cm (d) 30 cm

Sol. *(b)* Given, side of a square garden = 30 m

$\because$ Perimeter of a square = 4 × Side

$\therefore$ Perimeter of a square garden = 4 × 30 m = 120 m

Scale used to draw its picture = 1 cm : 5 m

Hence, the perimeter of a square in the picture $= \frac{120}{5} = 24$ cm

Q. 15 **Which of the following shapes has a vertex?**

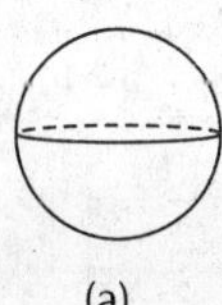

(a)

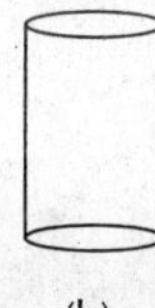

(b)

(c)

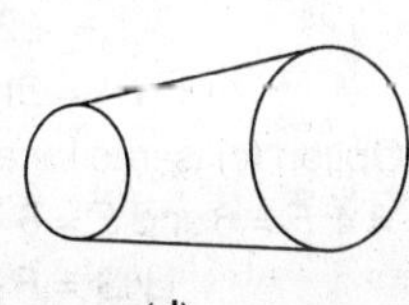

(d)

Sol. *(c)* Figures given in options (a),(b) and (d) have no vertex but figure given in option (c), is a cone having a vertex. Since, vertex is a point where two or more edges meet.

Q. 16 **In the given map, the distance between the places is shown using the scale 1 cm: 0.5 km. Then the actual distance (in km) between school and the book shop is**

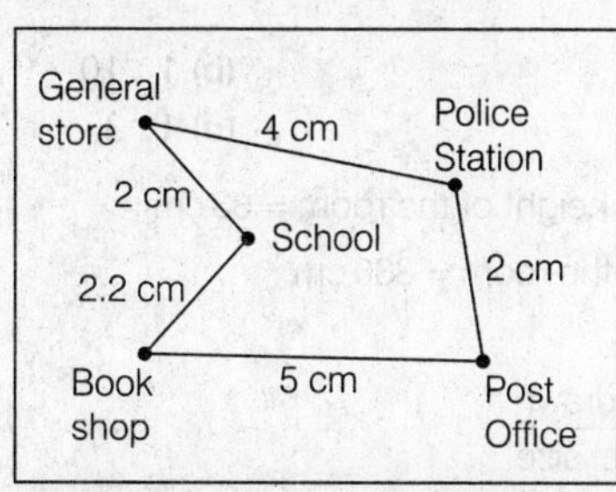

(a) 1.25 (b) 2.5 (c) 2 (d) 1.1

Sol. *(d)* Given, scale 1 cm = 0·5 km

The distance between school and the book shop shown in map is equal to 2.2 cm.

So, the actual distance between them will be = 2.2 × 0.5 km

= 1.1 km

Q. 17 Which of the following cannot be true for a polyhedron?

(a) $V = 4, F = 4, E = 6$ (b) $V = 6, F = 8, E = 12$

(c) $V = 20, F = 12, E = 30$ (d) $V = 4, F = 6, E = 6$

Sol. ***(d)*** We know that, Euler's formula for any polyhedron is $F + V - E = 2$

where, F = faces, V = vertices

and E = edges

(a) $V = 4$, $F = 4$ and $E = 6$

$$\text{LHS} = F + V - E = 4 + 4 - 6 = 8 - 6 = 2 = \text{RHS}$$

$\therefore$ Option (a) is true for a polyhedron.

(b) $V = 6$, $F = 8$ and $E = 12$

$$\text{LHS} = F + V - E = 8 + 6 - 12 = 14 - 12 = 2 = \text{RHS}$$

$\therefore$ Option (b) is true for a polyhedron.

(c) $V = 20$, $F = 12$ and $E = 30$

$$\text{LHS} = F + V - E = 12 + 20 - 30 = 32 - 30 = 2 = \text{RHS}$$

$\therefore$ Option (c) is true for a polyhedron.

(d) $V = 4$, $F = 6$ and $E = 6$

$$\text{LHS} = F + V - E = 6 + 4 - 6 = 10 - 6 = 4 \neq \text{RHS}$$

$\therefore$ Option (d) is not true for a polyhedron.

Q. 18 In a blueprint of a room, an architect has shown the height of the room as 33 cm. If the actual height of the room is 330 cm, then the scale used by her is

(a) 1 : 11 (b) 1 : 10

(c) 1 : 100 (d) 1 : 3

Sol. ***(b)*** Given, in a blueprint height of the room = 33 cm,

and actual height of the room = 330 cm

We know that,

$$\text{Scale of map} = \frac{\text{Size drawn}}{\text{Actual size}} = \frac{33}{330} = \frac{1}{10}$$

i.e. Scale = 1 : 10

Q. 19 The following is the map of a town. Based on it answer questions 19-21.

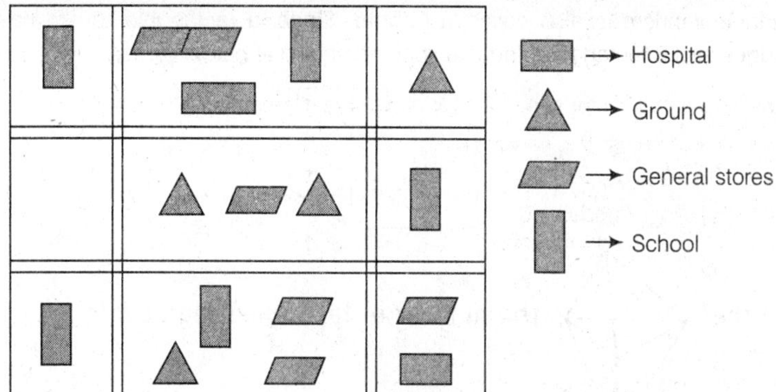

The number of hospitals in the town is

(a) 1 (b) 2 (c) 3 (d) 4

Sol. *(b)* Clearly, represent hospital. So, we will count in the given map. Hence, the number of in the map is 2.

Q. 20 The ratio of the number of general stores and that of the ground is

(a) 1 : 2 (b) 2 : 1
(c) 2 : 3 (d) 3 : 2

Sol. *(d)* Clearly, represent general stores and represent ground in the given map.

∴ Total number is 6

and total number is 4.

Hence, ratio of the number of general stores and that of the ground is

$$\frac{6}{4} = \frac{3}{2} = 3:2$$

Q. 21 According to the map, the number of schools in the town is

(a) 4 (b) 3
(c) 5 (d) 12

Sol. *(c)* Clearly, represent school. So we count in the given map.

Hence, the number of in the map is 5.

Fill in the Blanks

In questions 22 to 41, fill in the blanks to make the statements true.

Q. 22 Square prism is also called a ____.

Sol. Square prism is called a **cube**.

We know that, a square prism has a square base, a congruent square top and the sides are parallelograms. So, it is also a cube.

Q. 23 Rectangular prism is also called a_____.

Sol. Rectangular prism is also called a **cuboid**. Since, a rectangular prism has 8 vertices, 12 edges and 6 rectangular faces as cuboid shown in below figure.

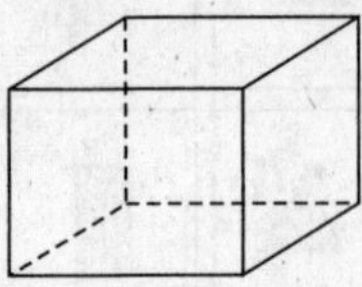

Q. 24 In the 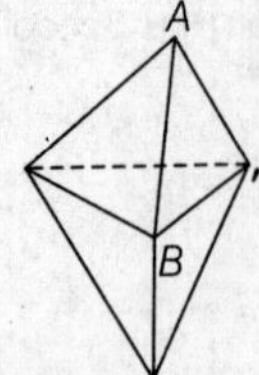 , the number of faces meeting at B is_____.

Sol. In the given figure, the number of faces meeting at B is **4**.

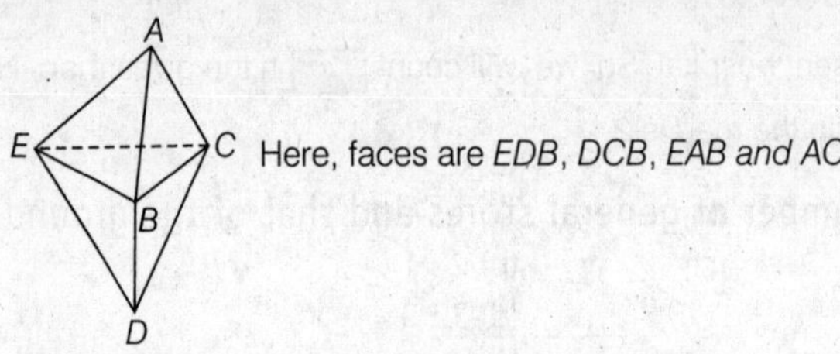

Here, faces are EDB, DCB, EAB and ACB.

Q. 25 A pyramid on an n sided polygon has_____ faces.

Sol. A pyramid on an n sided polygon has $\boldsymbol{n+1}$ faces.

We know that, in a pyramid, the number of faces is 1 more than the number of sides of the polygonal base.

Q. 26 If a solid shape has 12 faces and 20 vertices,then the number of edges in this solid is_____.

Sol. We know that, Euler's formula for any polyhedron is, $F + V - E = 2$

Given, faces, $F = 12$, vertices, $V = 20$

Now, on putting the value of F and V in the Euler's formula, we get $12 + 20 - E = 2$

$\Rightarrow \quad 32 - E = 2 \quad \Rightarrow \quad 32 - 2 = E \quad \Rightarrow \quad E = 30$

Hence, the number of edges = **30**

Q. 27 The given net 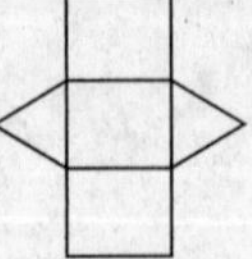 can be folded to make a_____.

Sol. The given net can be folded to make a **prism**, i.e.

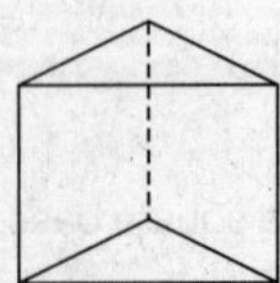

Q. 28 A solid figure with only 1 vertex is a_____.

Sol. A solid figure, with only 1 vertex is a **cone**. We know that, cone is a solid figure which has a circular base and its all other surfaces comes to a point called vertex.

Q. 29 Total number of faces in a pyramid which has eight edges is _____.

Sol. Total number of faces in a pyramid which has eight edges is **5**, i.e.

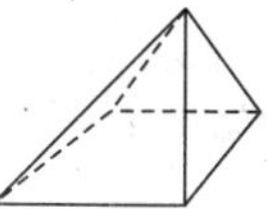

Q. 30 The net of a rectangular prism has _____ rectangles.

[**Hint** Every square is a rectangle but every rectangle is not a square]

Sol. The net of a rectangular prism is

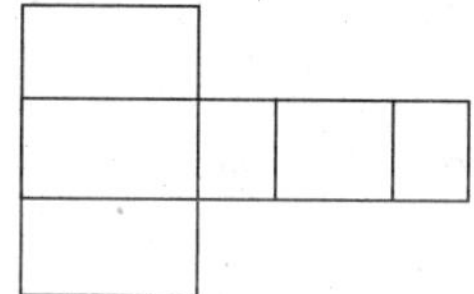

Hence, net of a rectangular prism has **6** rectangles.

Q. 31 In a three-dimensional shape, diagonal is a line segment that joins two vertices that do not lie on the _____ face.

Sol. In a three-dimensional shape, diagonal is a line segment that joins two vertices that do not lie on the **same** face.

Q. 32 If 4 km on a map is represented by 1 cm, then 16 km is represented by _____ cm.

Sol. Given, 4 km on a map is represented by 1 cm, then 1 km on a map is represented by $\frac{1}{4}$ cm.

Hence, 16 km on a map is represented by $\frac{1}{4} \times 16 = \mathbf{4}$ cm

Q. 33 If actual distance between two places A and B is 110 km and it is represented on a map by 25 mm. Then the scale used is _____.

Sol. $\because$ Scale of map $= \frac{\text{Size drawn}}{\text{Actual size}} = \frac{25 \text{ mm}}{110 \text{ km}}$

$$= \frac{25 \text{ mm}}{110000000} \qquad [\because 1 \text{ km} = 110000000 \text{ mm}]$$

$$= \frac{1}{4400000}$$

Hence, the scale used is **1 : 4400000**.

Q. 34 A pentagonal prism has ______ faces.

Sol. A pentagonal prism has **7** faces as shown in below figure

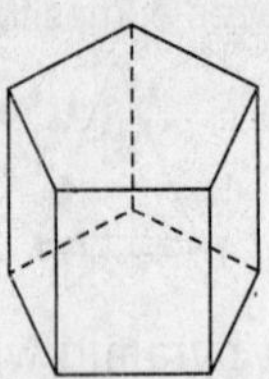

Q. 35 If a pyramid has a hexagonal base, then the number of vertices is ______.

Sol. If a pyramid has a hexagonal base, then the number of vertices is **7**.

We know that, in a pyramid the number of vertices is 1 more than the number of sides of the polygonal base.

Q. 36 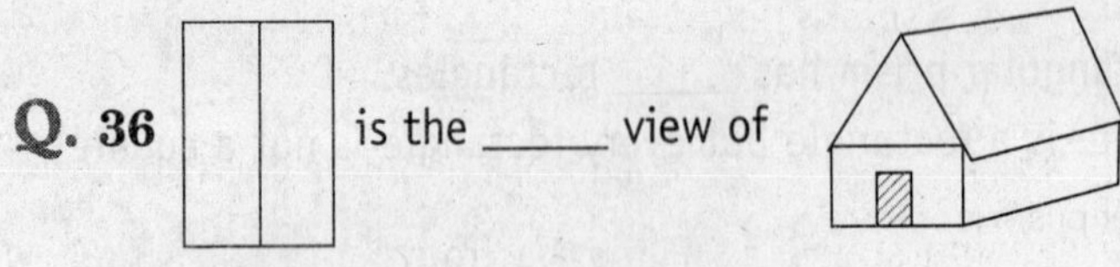 is the ______ view of

Sol. is the **top** view of the given figure.

Note *If we see the given figure from the top, then view is,*

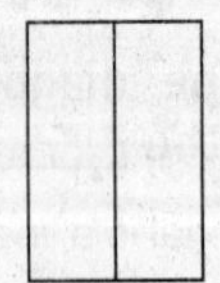

Q. 37 The number of cubes in ______ are ______.

Sol. The number of cubes in the given figure are **8**.

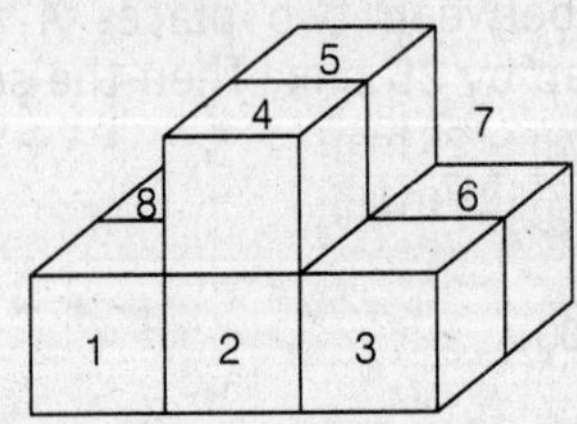

[7th cube is below the 5th cube]

Q. 38 **If the sum of number of vertices and faces in a polyhedron is 14, then the number of edges in that shape is _____.**

Sol. Given, the sum of number of vertices and faces in a polyhedron is 14, i.e. $V + F = 14$

We know that, Euler's formula, $F + V - E = 2$ for any polyhedron.

$$\Rightarrow \quad 14 - E = 2$$
$$\Rightarrow \quad 14 - 2 = E$$
$$\Rightarrow \quad E = 12$$

Hence, the number of edges are **12**.

Q. 39 **Total number of regular polyhedron is _____.**

Sol. Total number of regular polyhedron is **five**, i.e. cube, octahedron, tetrahedron, dodecahedron and icosahedron.

Q. 40 **A regular polyhedron is a solid made up of _____ faces.**

Sol. A regular polyhedron is a solid made up of **congruent** faces.

[according to the definition of regular polyhedron]

Q. 41 **For each of the following solids, identify the front, side and top views and write it in the space provided.**

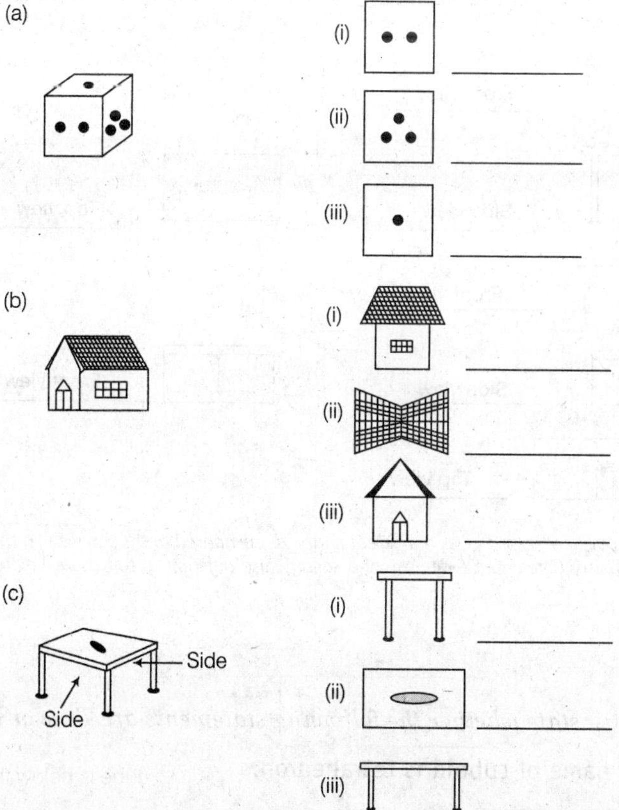

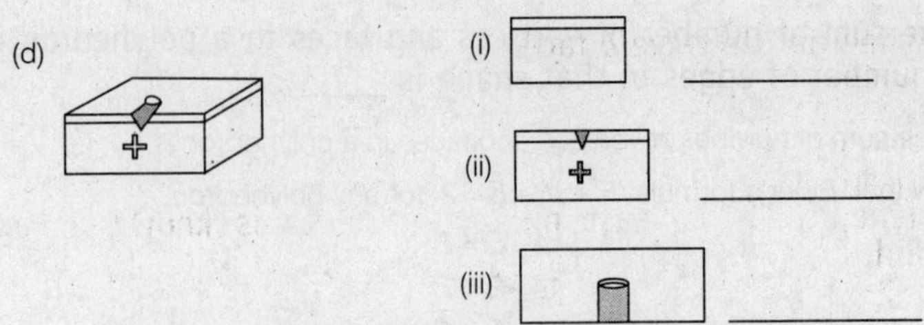

Note *Top view is the picture of the solid as seen from the top.*

Sol. (a) (i)  Front view

(ii) 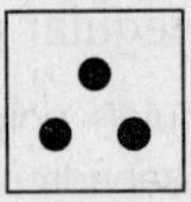 Side view

(iii) 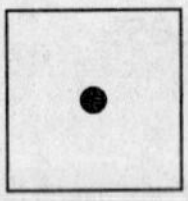 Top view

(b) (i)  Side view

(ii)  Top view

(iii)  Front view

(c) (i)  Side view

(ii)  Top view

(iii) 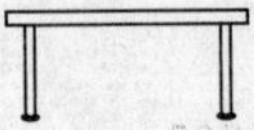 Front view

(d) (i) 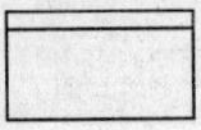 Side view

(ii) 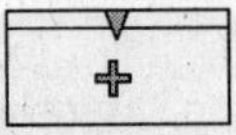 Front view

(iii) 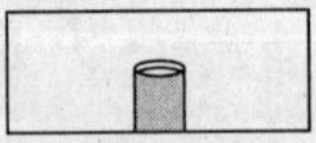 Top view

Note *Front view of a solid gives a different shape as compared to the top view in the solid symmetry (like cube). Side view of a solid is also different to top as well as to front view.*

True/False

In questions 42 to 61, state whether the following statements are True or False.

Q. 42 The other name of cuboid is tetrahedron.

Sol. ***False***

The other name of cuboid is rectangular prism.

Q. 43 A polyhedron can have 4 faces.

Sol. ***False***

A polyhedron can have atleast 4 faces.

Q. 44 A polyhedron with least number of faces is known as a triangular pyramid.

Sol. ***True***

A polyhedron have atleast 4 faces and a four faced polyhedron is known as pyramid.

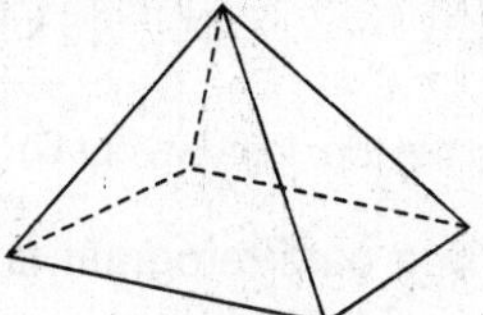

Q. 45 Regular octahedron has 8 congruent faces which are isosceles triangles.

Sol. ***False***

A regular octahedron is obtained by joining two congruent square pyramids such that the vertices of the two square pyramids coincide. It has eight congruent equilateral triangular faces.

Q. 46 Pentagonal prism has 5 pentagons.

Sol. ***False***

Pentagonal prism has 2 pentagons, one on the top and other on the base.

Q. 47 Every cylinder has 2 opposite faces as congruent circles, so it is also a prism.

Sol. ***False***

The cylinder has a congruent cross-section which is a circle, so it could be called as a circular prism.

Q. 48 Euler's formula is true for all three-dimensional shapes.

Sol. ***False***

Euler's formula is true only for polyhedrons.

i.e. $F + V - E = 2$

Where $F =$ faces, $V =$ vertices

and $E =$ edges

Q. 49 A polyhedron can have 10 faces, 20 edges and 15 vertices.

Sol. ***False***

We know that, Euler's formula satisfies for every polyhedron.

i.e. $F + V - E = 2$

Here, $F = 10, E = 20$

and $V = 15$

On putting these values in the Euler's formula, we get

$$10 + 15 - 20 = 2$$

$\Rightarrow$ $25 - 20 = 2$

$\Rightarrow$ $5 \neq 2$

Hence,the given values does not satisfy the Euler's formula.

Q. 50 The top view of

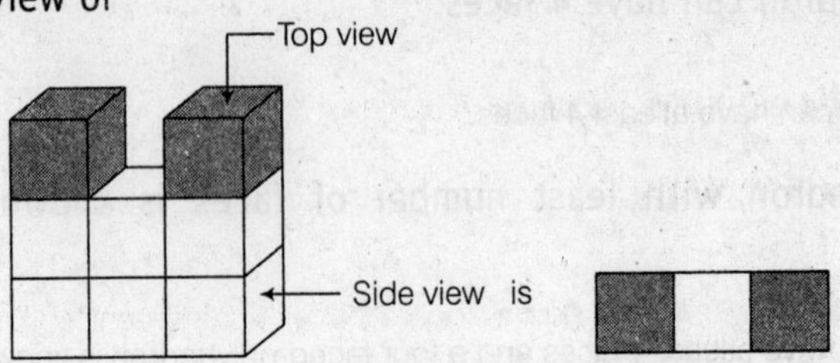

Sol. ***True***

If we see the given figure from the top, then we obtain 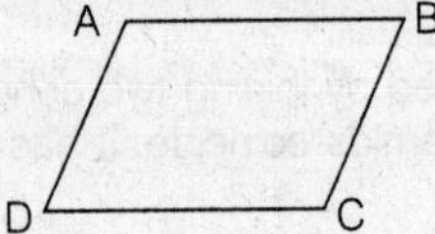.

Q. 51 The number of edges in a parallelogram is 4.

Sol. ***True***

AB, *BC*, *CD* and *DA* are the edges of a parallelogram *ABCD*.

Q. 52 Every solid shape has a unique net.

Sol. ***False***

A net is a flat figure that can be folded to form a closed, three-dimensional object. So, for an object, more than one net is possible but it is not true for the objects of all shapes.

Q. 53 Pyramids do not have a diagonal.

Sol. ***True***

Pyramids are polyhedron with a polygon as its base and other faces as triangles meeting at a common vertex and diagonal is a line joining the two opposite vertex.

So, in pyramids, two opposite vertex cannot be formed.

So, we can say pyramids has no diagonal.

Q. 54 The given shape is a cylinder.

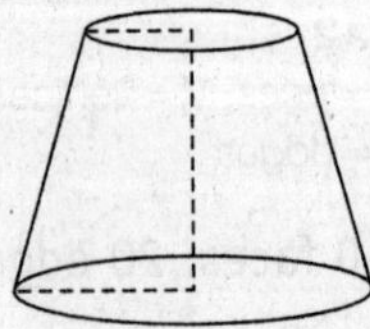

Sol. ***False***

The give shape is a frustum. The shape of a cylinder is,

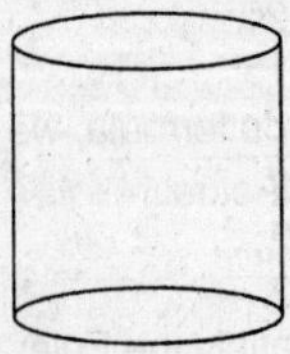

Q. 55 A cuboid has atleast 4 diagonals.

Sol. ***True***

In a cuboid, the number of diagonals is not least then 4.

Q. 56. All cubes are prism.

Sol. ***True***

A cube is a prism because it has a square base, a congruent square top and the lateral sides are parallelograms.

Q. 57 A cylinder is a 3-D shape having two circular faces of different radii.

Sol. ***False***

In a cylinder, the radii of the two circular faces are same. If the radii of two circular faces are different, then it will become frustum.

Q. 58 On the basis of the given figure, the length of a rectangle in the net of a cylinder is same as circumference of circles in its net.

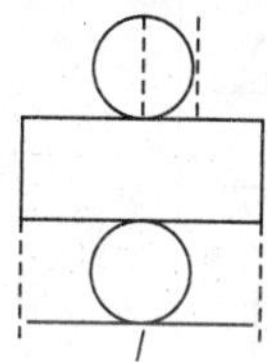

Sol. ***True***

Since, the length of a rectangle in the net of a cylinder is same as circumference of circle in the given net.

Q. 59 If a length of 100 m is represented on a map by 1 cm, then the actual distance corresponding to 2 cm is 200 m.

Sol. ***True***

When a length 100 m is respresented on a map by 1 cm.

Then, actual distance corresponding to 2 cm $= 2 \times 100 = 200$ m

Q. 60 The model of a ship shown is of height 3.5 cm. The actual height of the ship is 210 cm, if the scale chosen is 1 : 60.

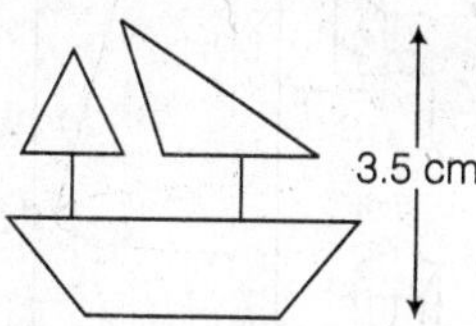

Sol. ***True***

Given, actual height = 210 cm and shown height = 3.5 cm

Scale chosen is 1 : 60.

So,
$$\text{Scale} = \frac{\text{Shown height}}{\text{Actual height}} = \frac{3.5}{210}$$
$$= \frac{35}{2100} = \frac{1}{60} = 1 : 60$$

Q. 61 The actual width of a store room is 280 cm. If the scale chosen to make its drawing is 1 : 7, then the width of the room in the drawing will be 40 cm.

Sol. ***True***

Actual width of a store room = 280 cm

Given, scale = 1 : 7

Width of the room in the drawing will be = Actual Size × Scale $\left[\because \text{scale} = \dfrac{\text{size drawing}}{\text{actual size}}\right]$

$$= 280 \times \frac{1}{7} = \frac{280}{7} = 40 \text{ cm}$$

Q. 62 Complete the table given below :

S. No.	Solid	Shape of Solid	Number of faces (F)	Number of vertices (V)	Number of edges (E)	F + V	E + 2
a.	Cuboid	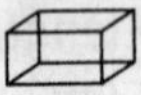					
b.	Triangular Pyramid						
c.	Square Pyramid						
d.	Rectangular Pyramid						
e.	Pentagonal Pyramid						
f.	Hexagonal Pyramid						
g.	Triangular Prism	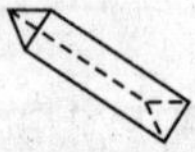					
h.	Square Prism	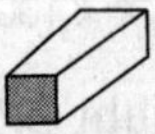					
i.	Cube	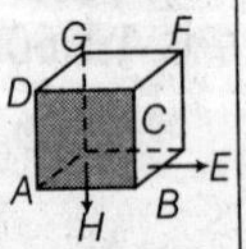 G F D C A E B H					
j.	Pentagonal Prism						
k.	Octagonal Prism						
l.	Heptagonal Prism	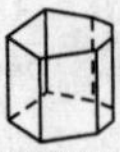					

Sol. By using Euler's formula for polyhedron,

S. No.	Solid	Shape of Solid	Number of faces (F)	Number of Vertices (V)	Number of edges (E)	F + V	E + 2
a.	Cuboid		6	8	12	6 + 8 = 14	12 + 2=14
b.	Triangular Pyramid		4	4	6	4 + 4 = 8	6 + 2 = 8
c.	Square Pyramid		5	5	8	5 + 5 = 10	8 + 2 = 10
d.	Rectangular Pyramid		5	5	8	5 + 5 = 10	8 + 2 = 10
e.	Pentagona l Pyramid		6	6	10	6 + 6 = 12	10+2 = 12
f.	Hexagonal Pyramid		7	7	12	7 + 7 = 14	12+2=14
g.	Triangular Prism		5	6	9	5 + 6 = 11	9+2=11
h.	Square Prism		6	8	12	6+8=14	12 + 2 = 14
i.	Cube	G F D C A E B H	6	8	12	6 + 8=14	12+2=14
j.	Pentagona l Prism		7	10	15	7+ 10=17	15+2=17
k.	Octagonal Prism		10	16	24	10+ 16=26	24+2=26
l.	Heptagona l Prism		9	14	21	9+ 14=23	21+2=23

Q. 63 How many faces does each of the following solids have?

(a) Tetrahedron (b) Hexahedron

(c) Octagonal pyramid (d) Octahedron

Sol. (a) Tetrahedron has 4 faces.

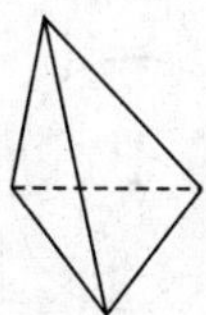

(b) Hexahedron has 6 faces.

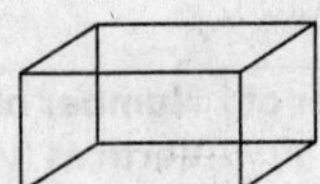

(c) Octagonal pyramid has 9 faces.

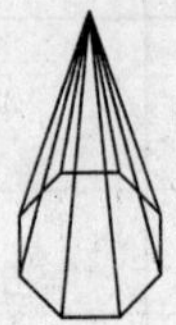

(d) Octahedron has 8 faces.

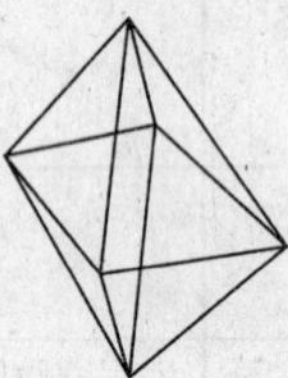

Q. 64 Draw a prism with its base as regular hexagon with one of its face facing you. Now draw the top view, front view and side view of this solid.

Sol. The following figure shows a prism with its base as regular hexagon with one of its face to us. And also, we shows the top view, front view and side view of the prism.

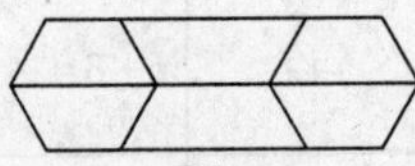

Prism

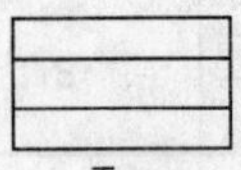

Top

Front

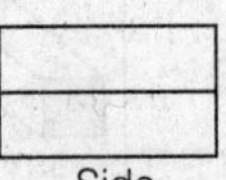

Side

Q. 65 How many vertices does each of the following solids have?

(a) Cone (b) Cylinder

(c) Sphere (d) Octagonal Pyramid

(e) Tetrahedron (f) Hexagonal Prism

Sol. (a) Cone has one vertex.

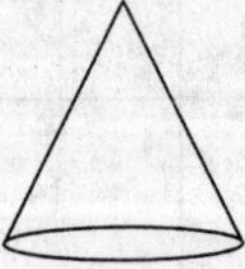

(b) Cylinder has no vertex.

(c) Sphere has no vertex.

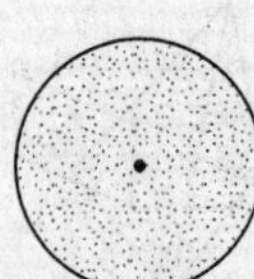

(d) Octagonal pyramid has one vertex.

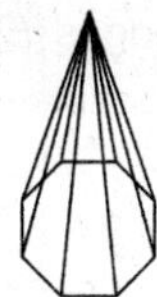

(e) Tetrahedron has 4 vertices.

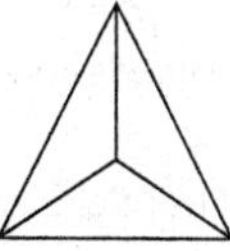

(f) Hexagonal prism has 12 vertices.

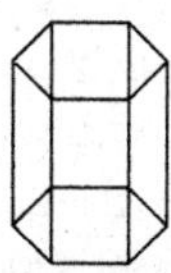

Q. 66 How many edges does each of following solids have?

(a) Cone
(b) Cylinder
(c) Sphere
(d) Octagonal Pyramid
(e) Hexagonal Prism
(f) Kaleidoscope

Sol. (a) Cone has one edge.

(b) Cylinder has two edges.

(c) Sphere has no edge.

(d) Octagonal pyramid has 16 edges.

(e) Hexagonal prism has 18 edges.

(f) Kaleidoscope has 9 edges.

Note *See edges in previous question's solution figures.*

Q. 67 Look at the shapes given below and state which of these are polyhedra using Euler's formula.

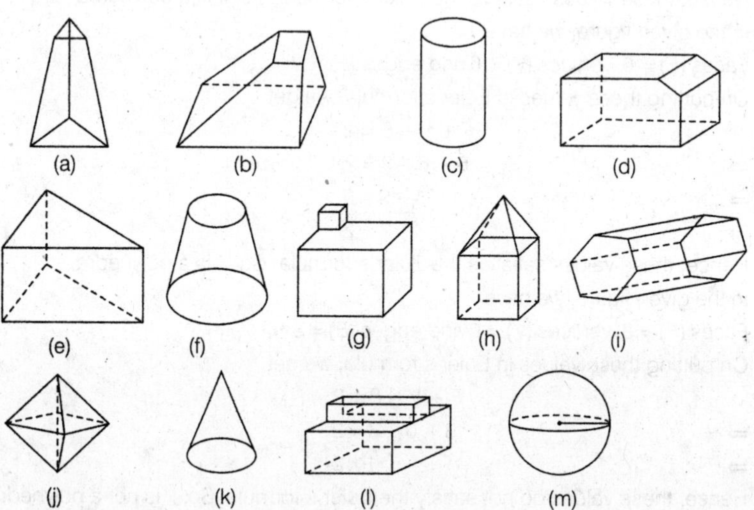

Sol. (a) In the given figure, we have

Faces $(F) = 5$, Vertices $(V) = 6$ and edges $(E) = 9$

On putting these values in Euler's formula, we get

$$F + V - E = 2$$
$$\Rightarrow \quad 5 + 6 - 9 = 2$$
$$\Rightarrow \quad 11 - 9 = 2$$
$$\Rightarrow \quad 2 = 2$$

Hence, these values satisfies the Euler's formula. So, it is a polyhedra.

(b) In the given figure, we have

Faces $(F) = 6$, vertices $(V) = 8$ and edges $(E) = 12$

On putting these values in Euler's formula, we get

$$F + V - E = 2$$
$$\Rightarrow \quad 6 + 8 - 12 = 2$$
$$\Rightarrow \quad 14 - 12 = 2$$
$$\Rightarrow \quad 2 = 2$$

Hence, these values satisfies the Euler's formula. So, it is a polyhedra.

(c) In the given figure, we have

Faces $(F) = 3$, vertices $(V) = 0$ and edges $(E) = 2$

On putting these values in Euler's formula, we get

$$F + V - E = 2$$
$$\Rightarrow \quad 3 + 0 - 2 = 2$$
$$\Rightarrow \quad 1 \neq 2$$

Hence, these values do not satisfy the Euler's formula. So, it is not a polyhedra.

(d) In the given figure, we have

Faces $(F) = 7$, vertices $(V) = 10$ and edges $(E) = 15$

On putting these values in Euler's formula, we get

$$F + V - E = 2$$
$$\Rightarrow \quad 7 + 10 - 15 = 2$$
$$\Rightarrow \quad 17 - 15 = 2$$
$$\Rightarrow \quad 2 = 2$$

Hence, these values satisfies the Euler's formula. So, it is a polyhedra.

(e) In the given figure, we have

Faces $(F) = 5$, vertices $(V) = 6$ and edges $(E) = 9$

On putting these values in Euler's formula, we get

$$F + V - E = 2$$
$$\Rightarrow \quad 5 + 6 - 9 = 2$$
$$\Rightarrow \quad 11 - 9 = 2$$
$$\Rightarrow \quad 2 = 2$$

Hence, these values satisfies the Euler's formula. So, it is a polyhedra.

(f) In the given figure, we have

Faces $(F) = 3$, vertices $(V) = 0$ and edges $(E) = 2$

On putting these values in Euler's formula, we get

$$F + V - E = 2$$
$$\Rightarrow \quad 3 + 0 - 2 = 2$$
$$\Rightarrow \quad 1 \neq 2$$

Hence, these values do not satisfy the Euler's formula. So, it is not a polyhedra.

(g) In the given figure, we have

Faces $(F) = 11$, vertices $(V) = 11$ and edges $(E) = 20$

On putting these values in Euler's formula, we get

$$F + V - E = 2$$

$\Rightarrow$ $11 + 11 - 20 = 2$

$\Rightarrow$ $22 - 20 = 2$

$\Rightarrow$ $2 = 2$

Hence, these values satisfies the Euler's formula. So, it is a polyhedra.

(h) In the given figure, we have

Faces $(F) = 9$, vertices $(V) = 9$ and edges $(E) = 16$

On putting these values in Euler's formula, we get

$$F + V - E = 2$$

$\Rightarrow$ $9 + 9 - 16 = 2$

$\Rightarrow$ $18 - 16 = 2$

$\Rightarrow$ $2 = 2$

Hence, these values satisfies the Euler's formula. So, it is a polyhedra.

(i) In the given figure, we have

Faces $(F) = 8$, vertices $(V) = 12$ and edges $(E) = 18$

On putting these values in Euler's formula, we get

$$F + V - E = 2$$

$\Rightarrow$ $8 + 12 - 18 = 2$

$\Rightarrow$ $20 - 18 = 2$

$\Rightarrow$ $2 = 2$

Hence, these values satisfies the Euler's formula. So, it is a polyhedra.

(j) In the given figure, we have

Faces $(F) = 8$, vertices $(V) = 6$ and edges $(E) = 12$

On putting these values in Euler's formula, we get

$$F + V - E = 2$$

$\Rightarrow$ $8 + 6 - 12 = 2$

$\Rightarrow$ $14 - 12 = 2$

$\Rightarrow$ $2 = 2$

Hence, these values satisfies the Euler's formula. So, it is a polyhedra.

(k) In the given figure, we have

Faces $(F) = 2$, vertices $(V) = 1$ and edges $(E) = 0$

On putting these values in Euler's formula, we get

$$F + V - E = 2$$

$\Rightarrow$ $2 + 1 - 0 = 2$

$\Rightarrow$ $3 \neq 2$

Hence, these values do not satisfy the Euler's formula. So, it is not a polyhedra.

(l) In the given figure, we have

faces $(F) = 10$, vertices $(V) = 16$ and edges $(E) = 24$

On putting these values in Euler's formula, we get

$$F + V - E = 2$$

$\Rightarrow$ $10 + 16 - 24 = 2$

$\Rightarrow$ $26 - 24 = 2$

$\Rightarrow$ $2 = 2$

Hence, these values satisfies the Euler's formula. So, it is a polyhedra.

(m) In the given figure, we have

Faces $(F) = 1$, vertices $(V) = 0$ and edges $(E) = 1$

On putting these values in Euler's formula, we get

$$F + V - E = 2$$

$$\Rightarrow \quad 1 + 0 - 1 = 2$$

$$\Rightarrow \quad 0 \neq 2$$

Hence, these values do not satisfy the Euler's formula. So, it is not a polyhedra.

Q. 68 Count the number of cubes in the given shapes.

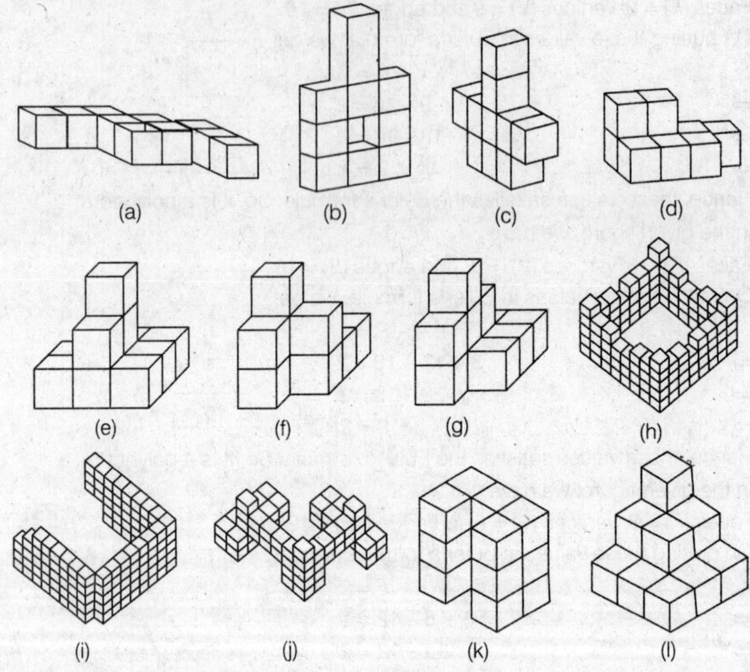

Sol. For finding the number of cubes in the given shapes you have to count all cubes which are visible or not. Hence, we have the total number of cubes for the given figures as:

(a) 10 cubes
(b) 10 cubes
(c) 10 cubes
(d) 9 cubes
(e) 11 cubes
(f) 9 cubes
(g) 11 cubes
(h) 110 cubes
(i) 113 cubes
(j) 66 cubes
(k) 15 cubes
(l) 14 cubes

Q. 69 Draw the front, side and top view of the given shapes.

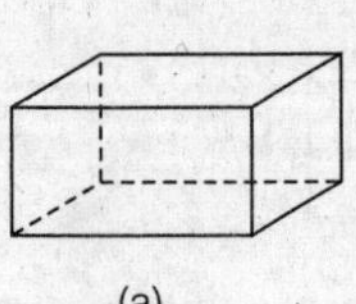
(a)

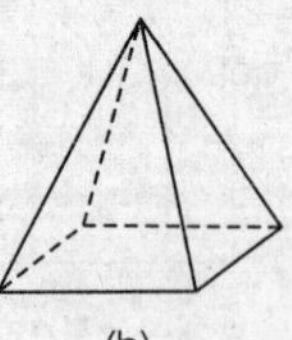
(b)

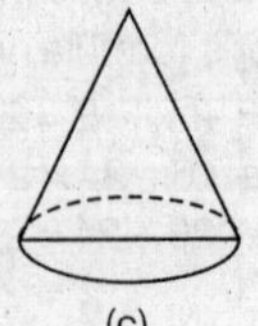
(c)

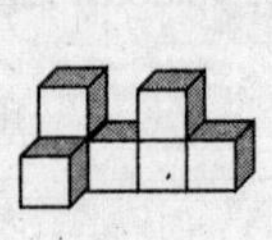
(d)

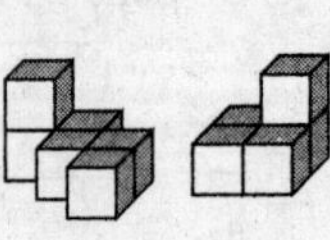
(e) (f)

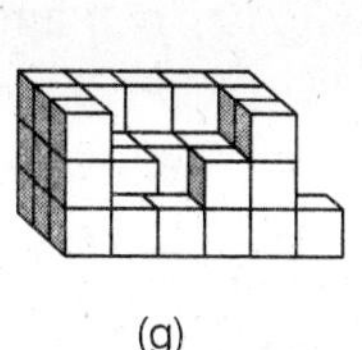
(g)

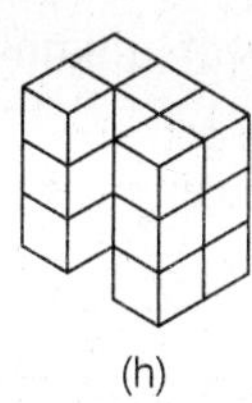
(h)

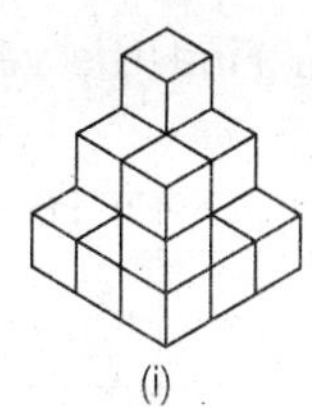
(i)

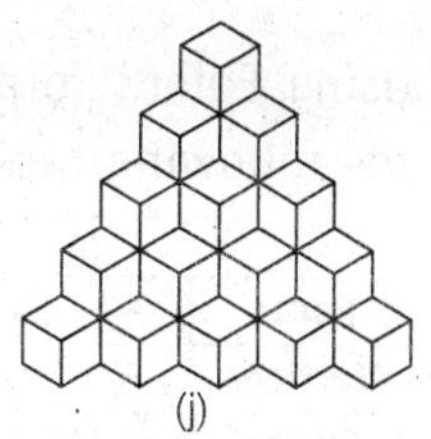
(j)

Sol. On the basis of properties and features of front view, top view and side view, we can draw all the three views of the given figures as:

	Front	Side	Top
Figure (a)			
Figure (b)			
Figure (c)			
Figure (d)			
Figure (e)			
Figure (f)			
Figure (g)			
Figure (h)			
Figure (i)			
Figure (j)			

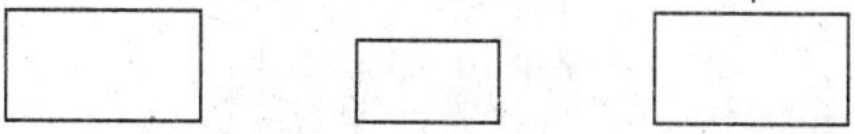

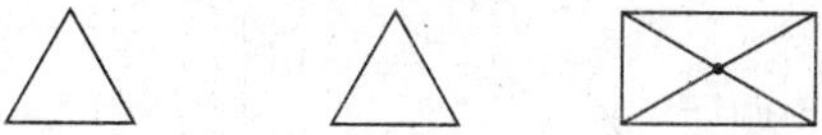

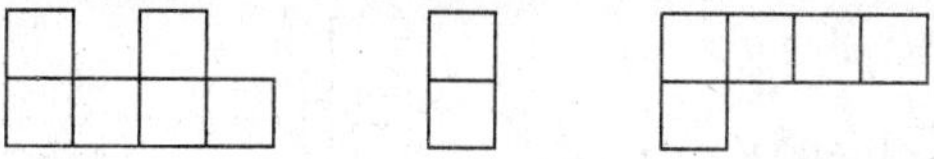

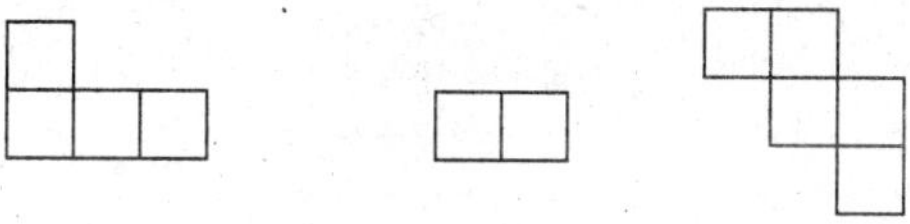

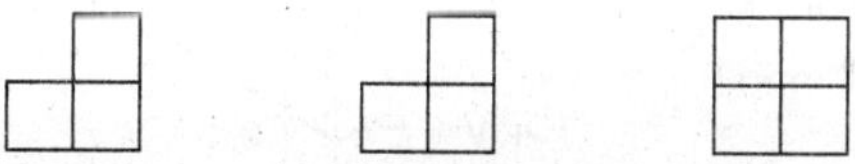

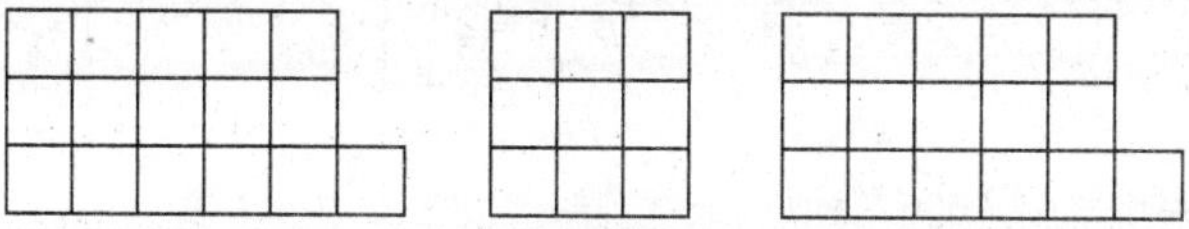

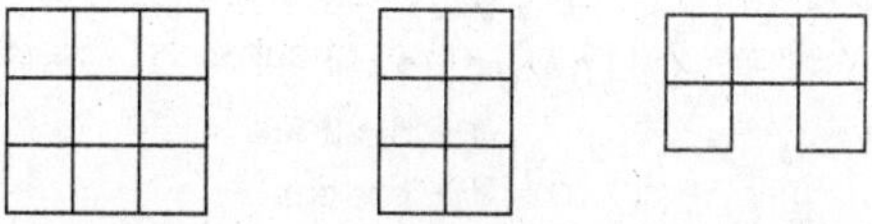

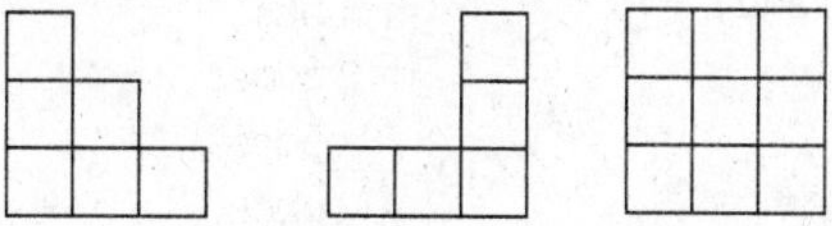

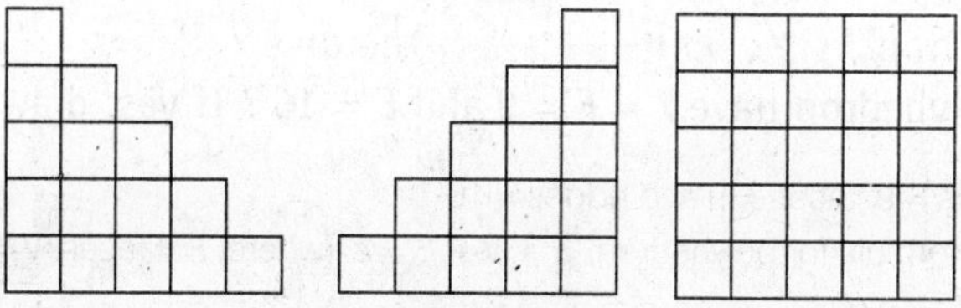

Q. 70 Using Euler's formula. Find the value of unknown x, y, z, p, q and r in the following table.

	(i)	(ii)	(iii)	(iv)	(v)	(vi)
Faces	7	y	9	p	6	8
Vertices	10	12	z	6	q	11
Edges	x	18	16	12	12	r

Sol. By using Euler's formula for polyhedron

From (i), $F = 7$, $V = 10$ and $E = x$

So, $F + V - E = 2$

$\Rightarrow$ $7 + 10 - x = 2$

$\Rightarrow$ $17 - x = 2$

$\Rightarrow$ $17 - 2 = x$

$\Rightarrow$ $x = 15$

From (ii), $V = 12$, $E = 18$ and $F = y$

So, $F + V - E = 2$

$\Rightarrow$ $y + 12 - 18 = 2$

$\Rightarrow$ $y - 6 = 2$

$\Rightarrow$ $y = 2 + 6$

$\Rightarrow$ $y = 8$

From (iii), $F = 9$, $E = 16$, and $V = z$

So, $F + V - E = 2$

$\Rightarrow$ $9 + z - 16 = 2$

$z - 7 = 2$

$\Rightarrow$ $z = 2 + 7$

$\Rightarrow$ $z = 9$

From (iv), $V = 6$, $E = 12$ and $F = p$

So, $F + V - E = 2$

$\Rightarrow$ $p + 6 - 12 = 2$

$\Rightarrow$ $p - 6 = 2$

$\Rightarrow$ $p = 2 + 6$

$\Rightarrow$ $p = 8$

From (v), $F = 6$, $E = 12$ and $V = q$

So, $F + V - E = 2$

$\Rightarrow$ $6 + q - 12 = 2$

$\Rightarrow$ $q - 6 = 2$

$\Rightarrow$ $q = 2 + 6 = 8$

From (vi), $F = 8$, $V = 11$ and $E = r$

So, $F + V - E = 2$

$\Rightarrow$ $8 + 11 - r = 2$

$\Rightarrow$ $19 - r = 2$

$\Rightarrow$ $r = 19 - 2$

$\Rightarrow$ $r = 17$

Q. 71 Can a polyhedron have $V = F = 9$ and $E = 16$? If yes, draw its figure.

Sol. Given, vertices = 9, faces = 9 and edges = 16

Using Euler's formula for polyhedron, $F + V - E = 2$ [where, F = faces, V = vertices and E = edges]

$\Rightarrow$ $9 + 9 - 16 = 2$

$\Rightarrow$ $18 - 16 = 2$

$\Rightarrow$ $2 = 2$

Hence, the given values satisfies the Euler's formula. So, a polyhedron can have $V = F = 9$ and $E = 16$

Thus, we can draw a octagonal pyramid.

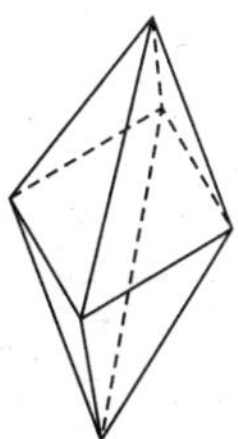

Q. 72 Check whether a polyhedron can have $V = 12, E = 6$ and $F = 8$.

Sol. By using Euler's formula for polyhedron,

$$F + V - E = 2 \quad \text{[where, } F = \text{faces, } V = \text{vertices, } E = \text{edges]}$$

$$\Rightarrow \quad 8 + 12 - 6 = 2$$

$$\Rightarrow \quad 20 - 6 = 2$$

$$\Rightarrow \quad 14 \neq 2$$

$\therefore$ Given values do not satisfy the Euler's formula. Its mean this type of polyhedron cannot be possible.

Q. 73 A polyhedron has 60 edges and 40 vertices. Find the number of its faces.

Sol. By using Euler's formula for polyhedron,

$$F + V - E = 2 \quad \text{[where, } F = \text{faces, } V = \text{vertices, } E = \text{edges]}$$

$$\Rightarrow \quad F + 40 - 60 = 2 \quad [\because E = 60 \text{ and } V = 40, \text{ given}]$$

$$\Rightarrow \quad F - 20 = 2$$

$$\Rightarrow \quad F = 2 + 20$$

$$\Rightarrow \quad F = 22$$

Hence, the number of faces are 22.

Q. 74 Find the number of faces in the given shapes.

 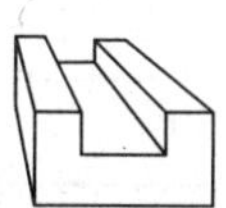 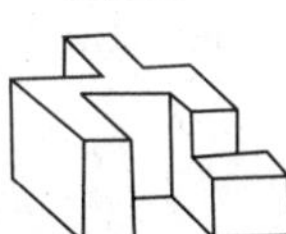

Sol. In the first figure, the number of faces are equal to 14.

In the second figure, the number of faces are equal to 10.

In the third figure, the number of faces are equal to 16.

Q. 75 A polyhedron has 20 faces and 12 vertices. Find the edges of the polyhedron.

Sol. By using Euler's formula for polyhedron,

$$F + V - E = 2 \quad \text{[where, } F = \text{faces, } V = \text{vertices, } E = \text{edges]}$$

Given, faces $(F) = 20$, vertices $(V) = 12$

$$\Rightarrow \quad 20 + 12 - E = 2$$

$$\Rightarrow \quad 32 - E = 2$$

$$\Rightarrow \quad E = 32 - 2$$

$$\Rightarrow \quad E = 30$$

Hence, the edges of the polyhedron are 30.

Q. 76 **A solid has forty faces and sixty edges. Find the number of vertices of the solid.**

Sol. By using Euler's formula for polyhedron

$$F + V - E = 2$$

Given, faces $(F) = 40$, edges $(E) = 60$.

$\Rightarrow \quad 40 + V - 60 = 2$

$\Rightarrow \quad V - 20 = 2$

$\Rightarrow \quad V = 2 + 20 = 22$

Hence, the vertices of the solid are 22.

Q. 77 **Draw the net of a regular hexahedron with side 3 cm.**

[Hint Regular hexahedron cube]

Sol. The net of a regular hexahedron with side 3 cm is given below:

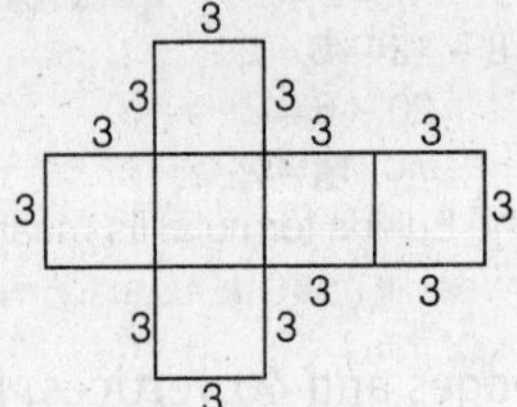

Q. 78 **Draw the net of a regular tetrahedron with side 6 cm.**

Sol. The net of a regular tetrahedron with side 6 cm is given below:

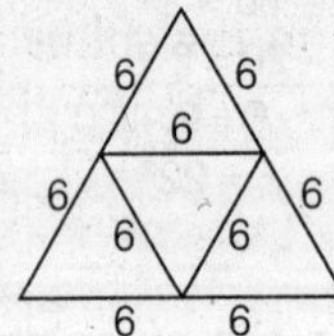

Q. 79 **Draw the net of the following cuboid:**

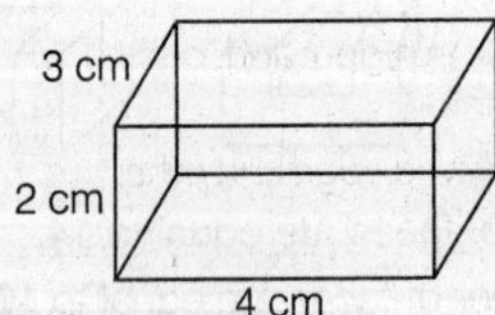

Sol. The net of the given cuboid is shown below:

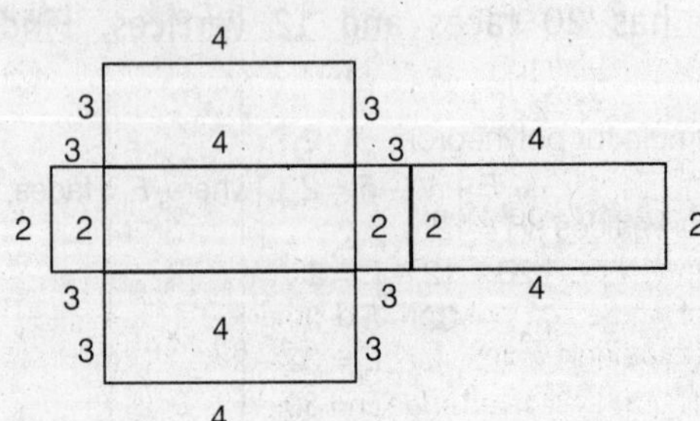

Q. 80 Match the following

	Figure	Name	
(i)		(a)	Hexahedron
(ii)		(b)	Hexagonal prism
(iii)		(c)	Square pyramid
(iv)		(d)	Cone

Sol. In figure (i), the base and top both are the hexagonal polygons.
So, it is a hexagonal prism.
In figure (ii), only one vertex is available.
So, it is a cone.
In figure (iii), the base is square and rest four faces are equilateral triangles.
So, it is a square pyramid.
In figure (iv), the base is square and it has 6 faces and 8 vertices. So, it is a hexahedron (cube).
*[**Note** Cube is also known as Hexahedron.]*
Hence, the correct matching is as:
(i) → (b) (ii) → (d) (iii) → (c) (iv) → (a)

Q. 81 Complete the table given below by putting tick mark across the respective property found in the solids mentioned.

	Properties	Cone	Cylinder	Prism	Pyramid
1.	The figure is a polyhedron.				
2.	The figure has diagonals.				
3.	The shape has curved edges.				
4.	The base of figure is a polygon.				
5.	The bases are congruent.				
6.	The base of figure is a polygon and other faces meet at a single point.				
7.	The base of figure is a curved edge and other faces meet at a single point.				

Sol. On the basis of properties and features of cone, cylinder, prism and pyramid, we can fill the given table as follows:

	Properties	Cone	Cylinder	Prism	Pyramid
1.	The figure is a polyhedron.	×	×	✓	✓
2.	The figure has diagonals.	×	×	×	✓
3.	The shape has curved edges	✓	✓	×	×
4.	The base of figure is a polygon.	×	×	✓	✓
5.	The bases are congruent	×	✓	✓	×
6.	The base of figure is a polygon and other faces meet at a single point.	×	×	×	✓
7.	The base of figure is a curved edge and other faces meet at a single point.	✓	×	×	×

Q. 82 **Draw the net of the following shape.**

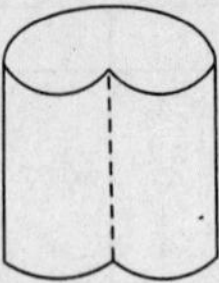

Sol. The net of the given shape is shown below:

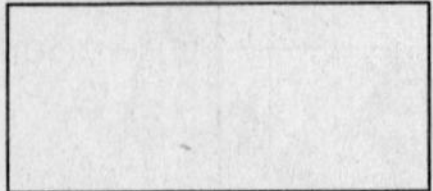

Note *If we open this shape from dotted line, we will find above net.*

Q. 83 **Draw the net of the following solid.**

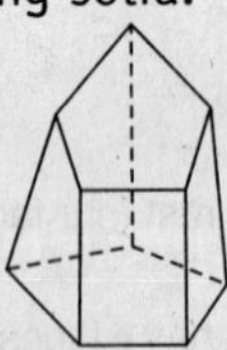

[Hint Pentagons are not congruent.**]**

Sol. The net of the given solid is shown below:

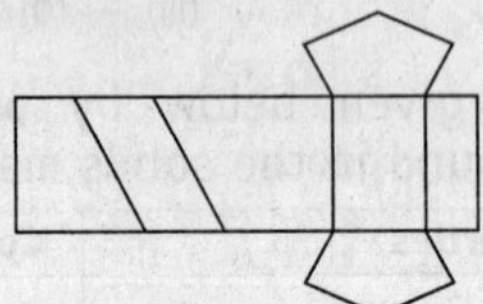

Note *If we open this solid shape, we will find above net.*

Q. 84 **Find the number of cubes in the base layer of the following figure.**

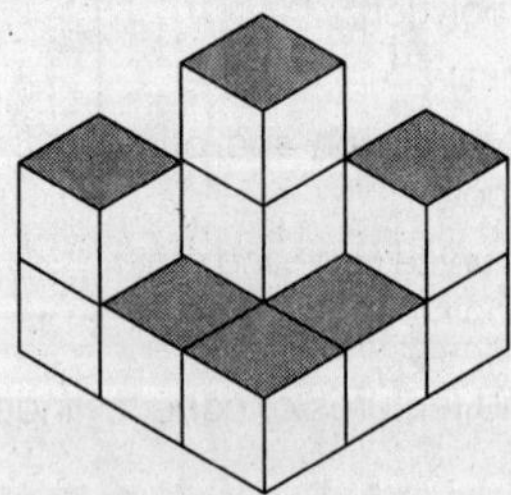

Sol. The number of cubes in the the base layer of the given figure is 6.

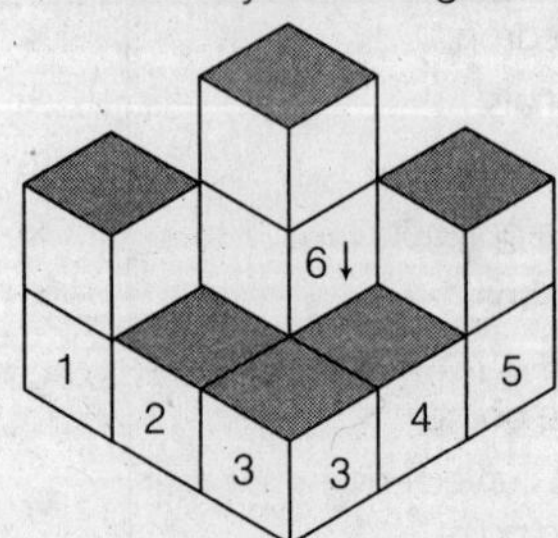

Q. 85 **In the figure given in Q.84, if only the shaded cubes are visible from the top, draw the base layer.**

Sol. The top view of the figure is shown below:

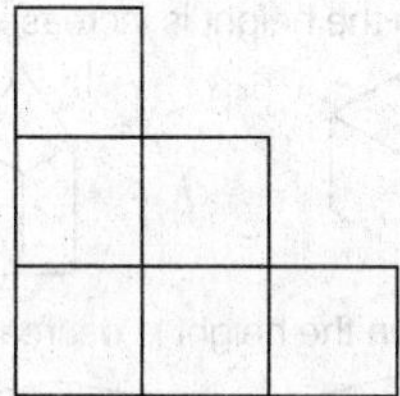

Note *If we see the given figure from top, we will only see upper layer not base layer.*

Q. 86 **How many faces, edges and vertices does a pyramid have with n sided polygon as its base?**

Sol. In a pyramid, the number of vertices is 1 more than the number of sides of the polygon base, i.e. vertices $= n + 1$

Also, the number of faces is 1 more than the number of sides of the polygonal base, i.e. faces $= n + 1$

But the number of edges is 2 times the number of sides of the polygonal base, i.e. edges $= 2n$

Q. 87 **Draw a figure that represents your mathematics textbook. What is the name of this figure? Is it a prism?**

Sol. The figure of our mathematics textbook is cuboid which is shown below. Also, we know that the another name of cuboid is a rectangular prism.

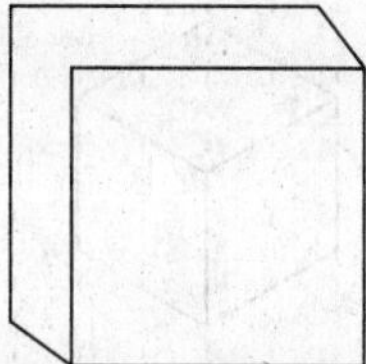

Q. 88 **In the given figures, identify the different shapes involved.**

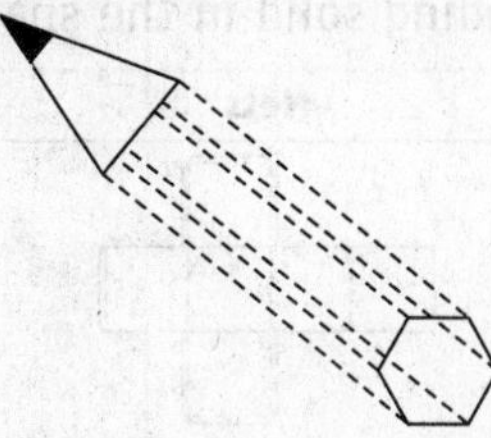

Sol. First figure is made by using a hemisphere and cylinder. In this figure, cylinder is mounted by hemisphere.

The second figure is made by using a cone and hexagonal prism. In this figure, hexagonal prism is mounted by a cone.

Q. 89 What figure is formed if only the height of a cube is increased or decreased?

Sol. If we only increase on decrease the height of a cube, the obtained figure is cuboid.

When the height is increased

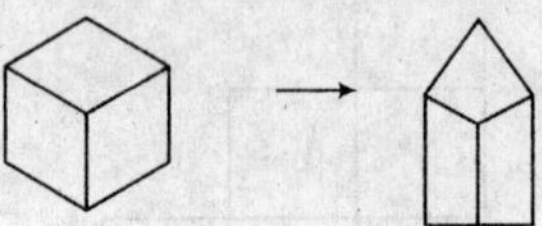

When the height is decreased

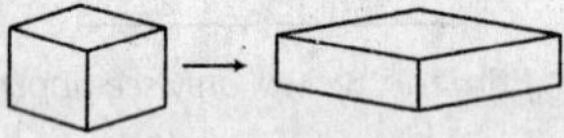

Q. 90 Use isometric dot paper to draw each figure.

(a) A tetrahedron.

(b) A rectangular prism with length 4 units, width 2 units and height 2 units.

Sol. (a) The following tetrahedron figure is made by using isometric dot paper.

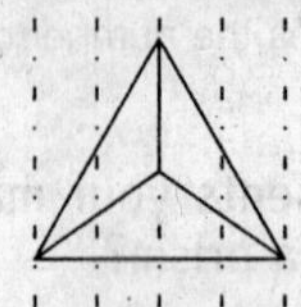

(b) The following rectangular prism with length 4 units, width 2 units and height 2 units is made by using isometric dot paper.

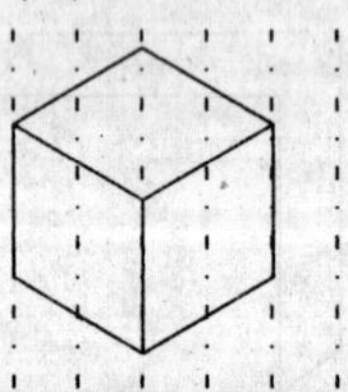

Q. 91 Identify the nets given below and mention the name of the corresponding solid in the space provided.

	Nets	Name of solid
(a)		
(b)		

	Nets	Name of solid
(c)	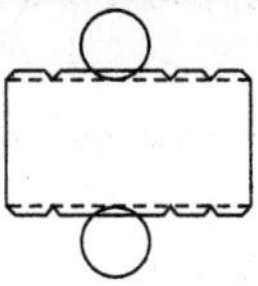	
(d)		
(e)	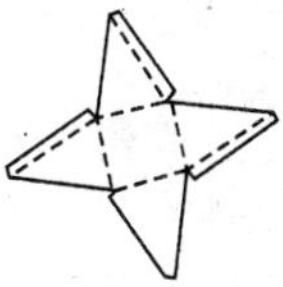	
(f)	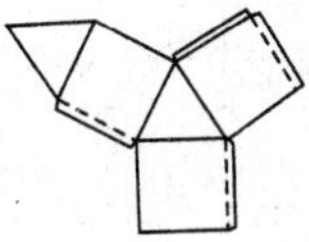	

Sol. On the basis of properties regarding drawing a net diagram of a solid figure, we can easily name the solid by using the net.

	Nets	Name of solid
(a)	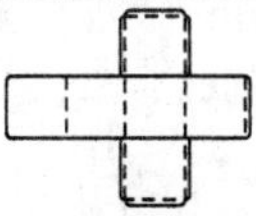	Cube
(b)	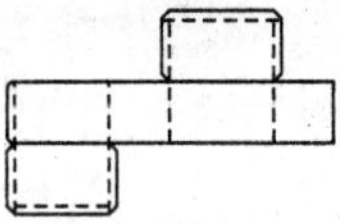	Cuboid
(c)	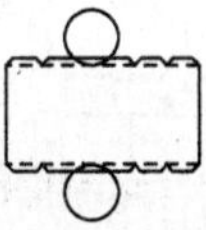	Cylinder
(d)		Cone
(e)	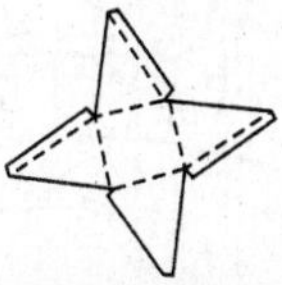	Square pyramid
(f)	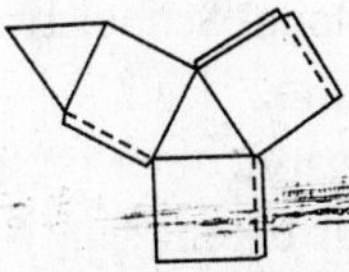	Triangular prism

Q. 92 Draw a map of your school playground. Mark all necessary places like 2 Library, Playground, Medical Room, Classrooms, Assembly area, etc.

Sol. A number of maps can be drawn for a school from which one map is given below :

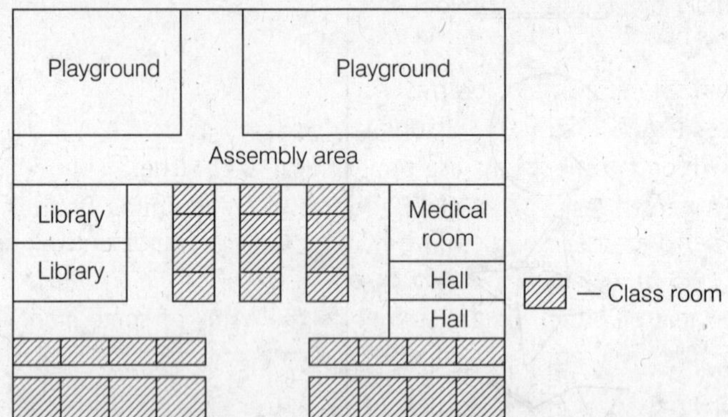

Q. 93 Refer to the given map to answer the following questions.

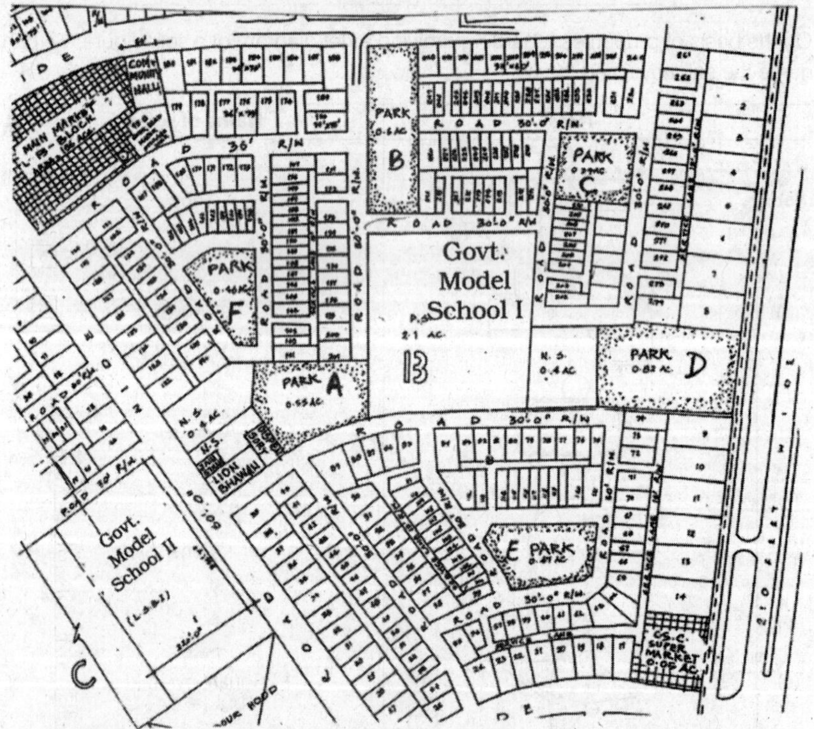

(a) What is the built-up area of Govt. Model School I?

(b) Name the schools shown in the picture.

(c) Which park is nearest to the dispensary?

(d) To which block does the main market belong?

(e) How many parks have been represented in the map?

Sol. If we see the given map, we can answer the given questions as:

(a) The built-up area of Govt. Model School I is equal to 2.1 acre.
(b) Two schools shown in the picture, Govt. Model School I and II.
(c) Part A is nearest to the dispensary.
(d) The main market belongs to block *A*.
(e) 6 parks have been represented in the map.

Q. 94 Look at the map given below.

Answer the following questions.

(a) Which two hospitals are opposite to each other?
(b) A person residing at Niti Bagh has to go to Chirag Delhi after dropping her daughter at Asiad Tower. Mention the important landmarks he will pass alongwith the roads taken.
(c) Name of which road is similar to the name of some month.

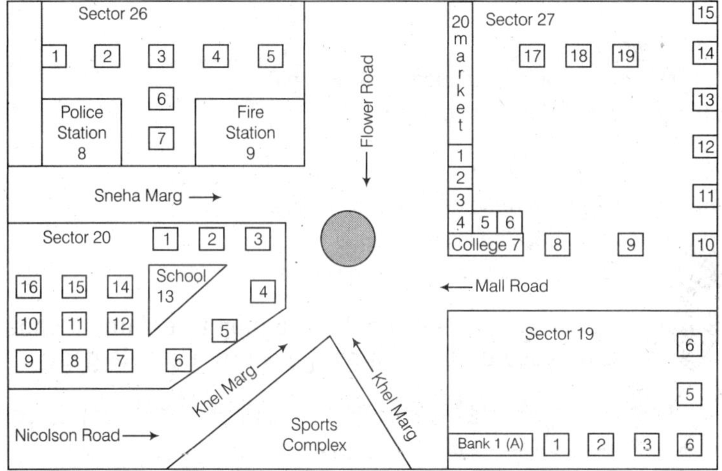

Sol. The given map is not sufficient to answer these questions.

Q. 95 Loot at the map given below.

B Town, India

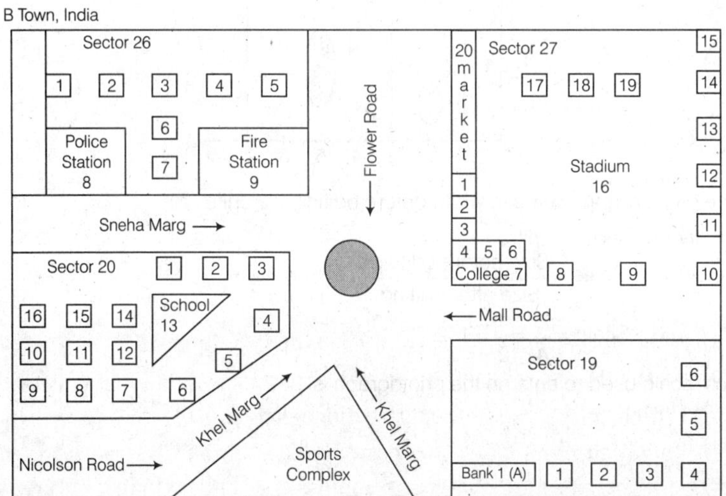

Now, answer the following questions.

(a) Name the roads that meet at round about.

(b) What is the address of the stadium?

(c) On which road is the Police Station situated?

(d) If Ritika stays adjacent to bank and you have to send her a card. What address will you write?

(e) Which sector has maximum number of houses?

(f) In which sector is Fire Station Located?

(g) In the map, how many sectors have been shown?

Sol. Carefully see the map.

(a) Flower road, Khel marg, Mall road and Sneha marg meet at round.

(b) The address of the stadium is given below:

Sector 27.

B Town, India

(c) The police station is situated on Sneha marg.

(d) Sneha's address is given below :

H.N-1Nr. Bank 1 (A)

Sector 19, B town, India

(e) Sector 27 has maximum number of houses.

(f) Fire station is located in sector 26.

(g) In the map, four sectors have been shown.

Q. 96 A photographer uses a computer program to enlarge a photograph. What is the scale according to which the width has enlarged?

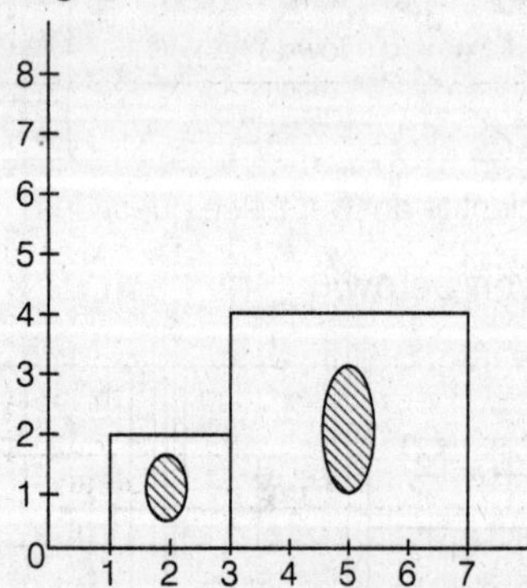

Sol. By the given graph, we have width before editing = 2 units

Width after editing = 4 units

We know that, $\text{Scale} = \dfrac{\text{Size before editing}}{\text{Size after editing}}$

$\therefore \quad \text{Scale} = \dfrac{2}{4} = \dfrac{1}{2} = 1:2$

Hence, scale used to enlarge the photograph is 1 : 2.

Q. 97 **The side of a square board is 50 cm. A student has to draw its image in her notebook. If the drawing of the square board in the notebook has perimeter of 40 cm, then by which scale the figure has been drawn?**

Sol. Given, the side of a square board is 50 cm.

So, perimeter of the square board = 4 × Side = 4 × 50 = 200 cm

On drawing in the notebook, the perimeter of a square board = 40 cm

$$\therefore \quad \text{Scale} = \frac{\text{Size of actual square board}}{\text{Size in notebook}} = \frac{200}{40} = 5:1$$

Hence, the used scale is 5 : 1.

Q. 98 **The distance between school and house of a girl is given by 5 cm in a picture, using the scale 1cm : 5 km. Find the actual distance between the two places?**

Sol. Given scale = 1 cm : 5 km, i.e. 1 cm in picture = 5 km of actual distance

∴ 5 cm in picture = 5 × 5 km of actual distance

Hence, the actual distance between the two places is 25 km.

So, 5 cm represent = 5 × 5 = 25 km distance

Q. 99 **Use a ruler to measure the distance in cm between the places joined by dotted lines. If the map has been drawn using the scale, 1 cm : 10 km, find the actual distances between**

(a) School and Library

(b) College and Complex

(c) House and School

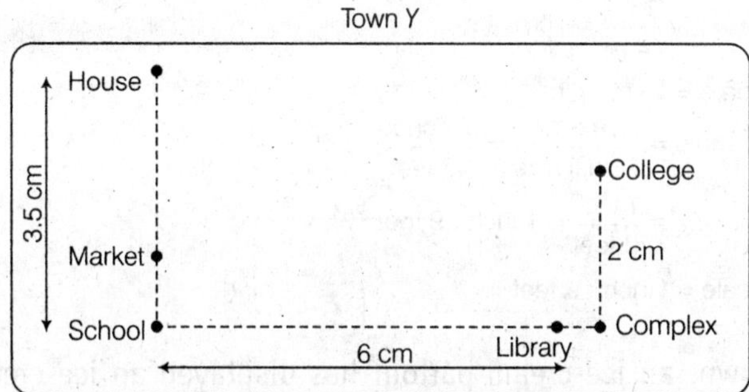

Sol. Given scale is 1 cm : 10 km, i.e. 1 cm in a picture = 10 km of actual distance

(a) The distance between the school and libarary in the picture = 6 cm
Hence, the actual distance between the school and library = 6 × 10 = 60 km

(b) Distance between the college and complex in the picture = 2 cm
Hence, the actual distance between the college and complex = 2 × 10 = 20 km

(c) Distance between the house and school in the picture = 3.5 cm
Hence, the actual distance between the house and school = 3.5 × 10 = 35 km

Q. 100 The actual length of a painting was 2m. What is the length in the photograph if the scale used is 1 mm : 20 cm.

Sol. The actual length of the painting was 2 m or $2 \times 100 = 200$ cm [$\because 1 \text{ m} = 100 \text{ cm}$]

Scale used in the painting = 1 mm : 20 cm

Hence, length of painting in photograph = Scale × Actual Size $\left[\because \text{scale} = \dfrac{\text{size drawn}}{\text{actual size}}\right]$

$$= \frac{1}{20} \times 200 = 10 \text{ mm}$$

Q. 101 Find the scale,

(a) Actual size 12 m
Drawing size 3 cm

(b) Actual size 45 feet
Drawing size 5 inches

Sol. (a) By using, scale $= \dfrac{\text{Size drawn}}{\text{Actual size}}$

$$= \frac{3 \text{ cm}}{12 \text{ m}}$$

$$= \frac{1 \text{ cm}}{4 \text{ m}} = 1 \text{ cm} : 4 \text{ m}$$

Hence, scale = 1 cm : 4 m

(b) By using, scale $= \dfrac{\text{Size drawn}}{\text{Actual size}} = \dfrac{5 \text{ inches}}{45 \text{ feet}}$

$$= \frac{1 \text{ inch}}{9 \text{ feet}} = 1 \text{ inch} : 9 \text{ feet}$$

Hence, scale = 1 inch : 9 feet

Q. 102 In a town, an ice-cream parlour has displayed an ice-cream sculpture of height 360 cm. The parlour claims that these ice-creams and the sculpture are in the scale 1 : 30. What is the height of the ice-creams served?

Sol. Given, height of ice-cream sculpture = 360 cm

Scale used for ice-cream and sculpture = 1 : 30

The height of the ice-creams served = Scale × Actual size $\left[\because \text{scale} = \dfrac{\text{size drawn}}{\text{actual size}}\right]$

$$= \frac{1 \times 360}{30} = 12 \text{ cm}$$

Hence, the height of thel ice-cream served is 12 cm.

7

Algebraic Expressions, Identities and Factorisation

Multiple Choice Questions (MCQs)

Q. 1 The product of a monomial and a binomial is a

(a) monomial (b) binomial
(c) trinomial (d) None of these

Sol. ***(b)*** Monomial consists of only single term and binomial contains two terms. So, the multiplication of a binomial by a monomial will always produce a binomial, whose first term is the product of monomial and the binomial's first term and second term is the product of monomial and the binomial's second term.

Q. 2 In a polynomial, the exponents of the variables are always

(a) integers (b) positive integers
(c) non-negative integers (d) non-positive integers

Sol. ***(c)*** In a polynomial, the exponents of the variables are either positive integers or 0. Constant term C can be written as $C \cdot x^0$. We do not consider the expressions as a polynomial which consist of the variables having negative/fractional exponent.

Q. 3 Which of the following is correct?

(a) $(a-b)^2 = a^2 + 2ab - b^2$ (b) $(a-b)^2 = a^2 - 2ab + b^2$
(c) $(a-b)^2 = a^2 - b^2$ (d) $(a+b)^2 = a^2 + 2ab - b^2$

Sol. ***(b)*** We have,

$$(a-b)^2 = (a-b)(a-b)$$
$$= a(a-b) - b(a-b)$$
$$= a \cdot a - a \cdot b - b \cdot a + b \cdot b$$
$$= a^2 - ab - ab + b^2 \quad [\because a \cdot b = b \cdot a]$$
$$= a^2 - 2ab + b^2$$

and
$$(a+b)^2 = (a+b)(a+b)$$
$$= a \cdot a + a \cdot b + b \cdot a + b \cdot b$$
$$= a^2 + 2ab + b^2$$

Q. 4 The sum of $-7pq$ and $2pq$ is

(a) $-9pq$ (b) $9pq$
(c) $5pq$ (d) $-5pq$

Sol. ***(d)*** Given, monomials are $-7pq$ and $2pq$.

$\therefore$ Their sum $= -7pq + 2pq = (-7 + 2)\,pq$

[both monomials consist of like terms, so adding their numerical coefficient]

$= -5pq$

Q. 5 If we subtract $-3x^2y^2$ from x^2y^2, then we get

(a) $-4x^2y^2$ (b) $-2x^2y^2$
(c) $2x^2y^2$ (d) $4x^2y^2$

Sol. ***(d)*** Given, monomials are $-3x^2y^2$ and x^2y^2. Now, we have to subtract the first one from the second one.

i.e. $x^2y^2 - (-3x^2y^2) = x^2y^2 - (-3)x^2y^2$

$= x^2y^2 + 3x^2y^2$

$= (1 + 3)\,x^2y^2$

$= 4x^2y^2$

Q. 6 Like term as $4m^3n^2$ is

(a) $4m^2n^2$ (b) $-6m^3n^2$
(c) $6pm^3n^2$ (d) $4m^3n$

Sol. ***(b)*** We know that, the like terms contain the same literal factor. So, the like term as $4m^3n^2$ is $-6m^3n^2$, as it contains the same literal factor m^3n^2.

Q. 7 Which of the following is a binomial?

(a) $7 \times a + a$ (b) $6a^2 + 7b + 2c$
(c) $4a \times 3b \times 2c$ (d) $6\,(a^2 + b)$

Sol. ***(d)*** Binomials are algebraic expressions consisting of two unlike terms.

(a) $7 \times a + a = 7a + a = 8a$ [monomial]

(b) $6a^2 + 7b + 2c$ [trinomial]

(c) $4a \times 3b \times 2c = 24\,abc$ [monomial]

(d) $6\,(a^2 + b) = 6a^2 + 6b$ [binomial]

Q. 8 Sum of $a - b + ab$, $b + c - bc$ and $c - a - ac$ is

(a) $2c + ab - ac - bc$ (b) $2c - ab - ac - bc$
(c) $2c + ab + ac + bc$ (d) $2c - ab + ac + bc$

Sol. ***(a)*** Required sum $= (a - b + ab) + (b + c - bc) + (c - a - ac)$

$= a - b + ab + b + c - bc + c - a - ac$

$= 2c + ab - ac - bc$ [adding the like terms and retaining others]

Q. 9 Product of the monomials $4p, -7q^3, -7pq$ is

(a) $196\ p^2q^4$ (b) $196\ pq^4$
(c) $-196\ p^2q^4$ (d) $196\ p^2q^3$

Sol. ***(a)*** Required product $= 4p \times (-7q^3) \times (-7\ pq)$

$= 4 \times (-7) \times (-7)\ p \times q^3 \times pq$ [multiplying the numerical coefficients]

$= 196\ p^2q^4$ [multiplying the literal factors having same variables]

Q. 10 Area of a rectangle with length $4ab$ and breadth $6b^2$ is

(a) $24a^2b^2$ (b) $24\ ab^3$
(c) $24\ ab^2$ (d) $24ab$

Sol. ***(b)*** We know that, area of a rectangle = Length × Breadth $= 4ab \times 6b^2$

This is the product of two monomials.

$\therefore$ Area of rectangle $= (4 \times 6)\ ab \times b^2$

$= 24\ ab^3$

Q. 11 Volume of a rectangular box (cuboid) with length $= 2ab$, breadth $= 3ac$ and height $= 2ac$ is

(a) $12\ a^3bc^2$ (b) $12\ a^3bc$
(c) $12\ a^2bc$ (d) $2\ ab + 3\ ac + 2ac$

Sol. ***(a)*** We know that, volume of a cuboid = Length × Breadth × Height $= 2ab \times 3ac \times 2ac$

$= (2 \times 3 \times 2)\ ab \times ac \times ac = 12\ a \times a \times a \times b \times c \times c = 12a^3bc^2$

Q. 12 Product of $6a^2 - 7b + 5ab$ and $2ab$ is

(a) $12a^3b - 14ab^2 + 10ab$ (b) $12a^3b - 14ab^2 + 10a^2b^2$
(c) $6a^2 - 7b + 7ab$ (d) $12a^2b - 7ab^2 + 10ab$

Sol. ***(b)*** Required product $= 2ab \times (6a^2 - 7b + 5ab)$

This is the product of a trinomial by a monomial, so we multiply monomial with each term of the trinomial.

$\therefore 2ab \times (6a^2 - 7b + 5ab) = 2ab \times 6a^2 + 2ab\ (-7b) + 2ab \times 5ab$

$= 12a^3b - 14ab^2 + 10a^2b^2$

Q. 13 Square of $3x - 4y$ is

(a) $9x^2 - 16y^2$ (b) $6x^2 - 8y^2$
(c) $9x^2 + 16y^2 + 24xy$ (d) $9x^2 + 16y^2 - 24xy$

Sol. ***(d)*** Square of $(3x - 4y)$ will be $(3x - 4y)^2$.

Comparing $(3x - 4y)^2$ with $(a - b)^2$, we get $a = 3x$ and $b = 4y$.

Now, using the identity $(a - b)^2 = a^2 - 2ab + b^2$

$(3x - 4y)^2 = (3x)^2 - 2 \cdot 3x \cdot 4y + (4y)^2$

$= 9x^2 - 24xy + 16y^2$

Q. 14 Which of the following are like terms?

(a) $5xyz^2, -3xy^2z$ (b) $-5xyz^2, 7xyz^2$
(c) $5xyz^2, 5x^2yz$ (d) $5xyz^2, x^2y^2z^2$

Sol. *(b)* We know that, the terms having same algebraic (literal) factors are called like terms.

(a) $5\,xyz^2, -3\,xy^2z$ [unlike terms]

(b) $-5\,xyz^2, 7\,xyz^2$ [like terms]

(c) $5\,xyz^2, 5\,x^2yz$ [unlike terms]

(d) $5\,xyz^2, x^2y^2z^2$ [unlike terms]

Q. 15 Coefficient of y in the term of $\frac{-y}{3}$ is

(a) -1 (b) -3 (c) $\frac{-1}{3}$ (d) $\frac{1}{3}$

Sol. *(c)* We can write $\frac{-y}{3}$ as $-\frac{1}{3} \times y$.

So, the coefficient of y is $-\frac{1}{3}$.

Q. 16 $a^2 - b^2$ is equal to

(a) $(a-b)^2$ (b) $(a-b)(a-b)$ (c) $(a+b)(a-b)$ (d) $(a+b)(a+b)$

Sol. *(c)* (a) $(a-b)^2 = a^2 - 2ab + b^2$

(b) $(a-b)(a-b) = (a-b)^2 = a^2 - 2ab + b^2$

(c) $(a+b)(a-b) = a(a-b) + b(a-b) = a^2 - ab + ba - b^2 = a^2 - b^2$ $[\because ab = ba]$

(d) $(a+b)(a+b) = (a+b)^2 = a^2 + 2ab + b^2$

Q. 17 Common factor of $17abc$, $34ab^2$, $51a^2b$ is

(a) $17abc$ (b) $17ab$ (c) $17ac$ (d) $17a^2b^2c$

Sol. *(b)* Given, $17abc = 17 \times a \times b \times c$

$34ab^2 = 2 \times 17 \times a \times b \times b$

$51a^2b = 3 \times 17 \times a \times a \times b$

Now, collecting the common factors, we get $17 \times a \times b = 17ab$

Q. 18 Square of $9x - 7xy$ is

(a) $81x^2 + 49x^2y^2$ (b) $81x^2 - 49x^2y^2$
(c) $81x^2 + 49x^2y^2 - 126x^2y$ (d) $81x^2 + 49x^2y^2 - 63x^2y$

Sol. *(c)* Square of $(9x - 7xy) = (9x - 7xy)^2$

Comparing with $(a-b)^2$, we get $a = 9x$ and $b = 7xy$

$(9x - 7xy)^2 = (9x)^2 - 2 \cdot 9x \cdot 7xy + (7xy)^2$ [using the identity, $(a-b)^2 = a^2 - 2ab + b^2$]

$= 81x^2 - 126x^2y + 49x^2y^2$

$= 81x^2 + 49x^2y^2 - 126x^2y$

Q. 19 Factorised form of $23xy - 46x + 54y - 108$ is

(a) $(23x + 54)(y - 2)$ (b) $(23x + 54y)(y - 2)$
(c) $(23xy + 54y)(-46x - 108)$ (d) $(23x + 54)(y + 2)$

Sol. *(a)* We have, $23xy - 46x + 54y - 108 = 23xy - 2 \times 23x + 54y - 2 \times 54$

$= 23x(y - 2) + 54(y - 2)$

[taking common out in I and II expressions]

$= (y - 2)(23x + 54)$ [taking $(y - 2)$ common]

$= (23x + 54)(y - 2)$

Q. 20 Factorised form of $r^2 - 10r + 21$ is

(a) $(r - 1)(r - 4)$ (b) $(r - 7)(r - 3)$
(c) $(r - 7)(r + 3)$ (d) $(r + 7)(r + 3)$

Sol. *(b)* We have, $r^2 - 10r + 21$

$= r^2 - 7r - 3r + 21 = r(r - 7) - 3(r - 7)$

[by splitting the middle term, so that the product of their numerical coefficients is equal constant term]

$= (r - 7)(r - 3)$ [$\because x^2 + (a + b)x + ab = (x + a)(x + b)$]

Q. 21 Factorised form of $p^2 - 17p - 38$ is

(a) $(p - 19)(p + 2)$ (b) $(p - 19)(p - 2)$
(c) $(p + 19)(p + 2)$ (d) $(p + 19)(p - 2)$

Sol. *(a)* We have, $p^2 - 17p - 38 = p^2 - 19p + 2p - 38$

[by splitting the middle term, so that the product of their numerical coefficients is equal constant term]

$= p(p - 19) + 2(p - 19) = (p - 19)(p + 2)$ [$\because x^2 + (a + b)x + ab = (x + a)(x + b)$]

Q. 22 On dividing $57p^2qr$ by $114pq$, we get

(a) $\frac{1}{4}pr$ (b) $\frac{3}{4}pr$ (c) $\frac{1}{2}pr$ (d) $2pr$

Sol. *(c)* Required value $= \frac{57p^2qr}{114pq} = \frac{57 \times p \times p \times q \times r}{114 \times p \times q} = \frac{57}{114}pr = \frac{1}{2}pr$

Q. 23 On dividing $p(4p^2 - 16)$ by $4p(p - 2)$, we get

(a) $2p + 4$ (b) $2p - 4$ (c) $p + 2$ (d) $p - 2$

Sol. *(c)* We have,

$$\frac{p(4p^2 - 16)}{4p(p - 2)} = \frac{p[(2p)^2 - 4^2]}{4p(p - 2)}$$

$$= \frac{(2p - 4)(2p + 4)}{4(p - 2)} \quad [\because a^2 - b^2 = (a + b)(a - b)]$$

$$= \frac{2(p - 2) \cdot 2(p + 2)}{4(p - 2)} = \frac{4(p - 2)(p + 2)}{4(p - 2)} = p + 2$$

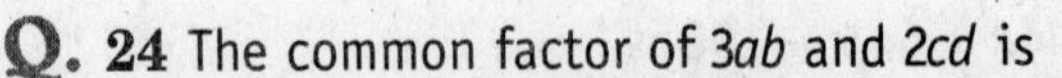

Q. 24 The common factor of $3ab$ and $2cd$ is

(a) 1 (b) -1 (c) a (d) c

Sol. *(a)* We have, monomials $3ab$ and $2cd$

Now, $3ab = 3 \times a \times b$

$2cd = 2 \times c \times d$

Observing the monomials, we see that, there is no common factor (neither numerical nor literal) between them except 1.

Q. 25 An irreducible factor of $24x^2y^2$ is

(a) x^2 (b) y^2 (c) x (d) $24x$

Sol. *(c)* A factor is said to be irreducible, if it cannot be factorised further.

We have, $24x^2y^2 = 2 \times 2 \times 2 \times 3 \times x \times x \times y \times y$

Hence, an irreducible factor of $24x^2y^2$ is x.

Q. 26 Number of factors of $(a + b)^2$ is

(a) 4 (b) 3 (c) 2 (d) 1

Sol. *(c)* We can write $(a + b)^2$ as, $(a + b)(a + b)$ and this cannot be factorised further.

Hence, number of factors of $(a + b)^2$ is 2.

Q. 27 The factorised form of $3x - 24$ is

(a) $3x \times 24$ (b) $3(x - 8)$ (c) $24(x - 3)$ (d) $3(x - 12)$

Sol. *(b)* We have,

$3x - 24 = 3 \times x - 3 \times 8 = 3(x - 8)$ [taking 3 as common]

Q. 28 The factors of $x^2 - 4$ are

(a) $(x - 2), (x - 2)$ (b) $(x + 2), (x - 2)$

(c) $(x + 2), (x + 2)$ (d) $(x - 4), (x - 4)$

Sol. *(b)* We have,

$x^2 - 4 = x^2 - 2^2 = (x + 2)(x - 2)$ $[\because a^2 - b^2 = (a + b)(a - b)]$

Hence, $(x + 2), (x - 2)$ are factors of $x^2 - 4$.

Q. 29 The value of $(-27x^2y) \div (-9xy)$ is

(a) $3xy$ (b) $-3xy$

(c) $-3x$ (d) $3x$

Sol. *(d)* We have,

$$(-27x^2y) \div (-9xy) = \frac{-27x^2y}{-9xy} = \frac{27 \times x \times x \times y}{9 \times x \times y} = \frac{27}{9}x = 3x$$

Q. 30 The value of $(2x^2 + 4) \div 2$ is

(a) $2x^2 + 2$ (b) $x^2 + 2$ (c) $x^2 + 4$ (d) $2x^2 + 4$

Sol. ***(b)*** We have,

$$(2x^2+4)\div 2=\frac{2x^2+4}{2}=\frac{2(x^2+2)}{2}$$ [taking 2 as common]

$$=x^2+2$$

Q. 31 The value of $(3x^3+9x^2+27x)\div 3x$ is

(a) $x^2+9+27x$
(b) $3x^2+3x^2+27x$
(c) $3x^3+9x^2+9$
(d) x^2+3x+9

Sol. ***(d)*** We have,

$$(3x^3+9x^2+27x)\div 3x=\frac{3x^3+9x^2+27x}{3x}=\frac{3x^3}{3x}+\frac{9x^2}{3x}+\frac{27x}{3x}=x^2+3x+9$$

Q. 32 The value of $(a+b)^2+(a-b)^2$ is

(a) $2a+2b$
(b) $2a-2b$
(c) $2a^2+2b^2$
(d) $2a^2-2b^2$

Sol. ***(c)*** We have,

$$(a+b)^2+(a-b)^2=(a^2+b^2+2ab)+(a^2+b^2-2ab)$$

$[\because (a+b)^2=a^2+b^2+2ab$ and $(a-b)^2=a^2+b^2-2ab]$

$$=(a^2+a^2)+(b^2+b^2)+(2ab-2ab)$$ [combining the like terms]

$$=2a^2+2b^2$$

Q. 33 The value of $(a+b)^2-(a-b)^2$ is

(a) $4ab$
(b) $-4ab$
(c) $2a^2+2b^2$
(d) $2a^2-2b^2$

Sol. ***(a)*** We have,

$$(a+b)^2-(a-b)^2=a^2+b^2+2ab-(a^2+b^2-2ab)$$

$[\because (a+b)^2=a^2+b^2+2ab$ and $(a-b)^2=a^2+b^2-2ab]$

$$=a^2+b^2+2ab-a^2-b^2+2ab=a^2-a^2+b^2-b^2+2ab+2ab=2ab+2ab=4ab$$

[combining the like terms]

Fill in the Blanks

In questions 34 to 58, fill in the blanks to make the statements true.

Q. 34 The product of two terms with like signs is a _______ term.

Sol. **Positive**

If both the like terms are either positive or negative, then the resultant term will always be positive.

Q. 35 The product of two terms with unlike signs is a _______ term.

Sol. **Negative**

As the product of a positive term and a negative term is always negative.

Q. 36 $a(b+c) = a \times$ ______ $+ a \times$ ______

Sol. ***b*, *c***

We have,

$$a(b+c) = a \times b + a \times c \quad \text{[using left distributive law]}$$

Q. 37 $(a-b)$ ______ $= a^2 - 2ab + b^2$

Sol. $(a-b)$

We know that, $(a-b)(a-b) = (a-b)^2$

$$= a^2 - 2ab + b^2 \quad [\because (a-b)^2 = a^2 - 2ab + b^2]$$

Q. 38 $a^2 - b^2 = (a+b)$ ______

Sol. $(a-b)$

We have, $a^2 - b^2 = (a+b)(a-b)$ $\quad [\because a^2 - b^2 = (a+b)(a-b)]$

Alternative Method

Let $\quad (a^2 - b^2) = (a+b)x$

$$\Rightarrow \quad x = \frac{a^2 - b^2}{a+b} = \frac{(a+b)(a-b)}{a+b} = a - b$$

Q. 39 $(a-b)^2 +$ ______ $= a^2 - b^2$

Sol. $2ab - 2b^2$

Let $(a-b)^2 + x = a^2 - b^2$

$\Rightarrow a^2 + b^2 - 2ab + x = a^2 - b^2$ $\quad [\because (a-b)^2 = a^2 + b^2 - 2ab]$

$$\Rightarrow \quad x = a^2 - b^2 - (a^2 + b^2 - 2ab) = a^2 - b^2 - a^2 - b^2 + 2ab = 2ab - 2b^2$$

Q. 40 $(a+b)^2 - 2ab =$ ______ $+$ ______

Sol. $a^2 + b^2$

We have,

$$(a+b)^2 - 2ab = a^2 + b^2 + 2ab - 2ab \quad [\because (a+b)^2 = a^2 + b^2 + 2ab]$$
$$= a^2 + b^2$$

Q. 41 $(x+a)(x+b) = x^2 + (a+b)x +$ ______.

Sol. ab

We have,

$$(x+a)(x+b) = x^2 + bx + ax + ab$$
$$= x^2 + (a+b)x + ab$$

Q. 42 The product of two polynomials is a ______.

Sol. **Polynomial**

As the product of two polynomials is again a polynomial.

Q. 43 Common factor of $ax^2 + bx$ is ______.

Sol. x

We have, $ax^2 + bx = x(ax + b)$ [taking x as common]

Q. 44 Factorised form of $18mn + 10mnp$ is ______.

Sol. $2mn(9 + 5p)$

We have, $18mn + 10mnp = 2 \times 9 \times m \times n + 2 \times 5 \times m \times n \times p$

$= 2mn(9 + 5p)$ [taking $2mn$ as common]

Q. 45 Factorised form of $4y^2 - 12y + 9$ is ______.

Sol. $(2y - 3)(2y - 3)$

Let

$$4y^2 - 12y + 9 = (2y)^2 - 2 \times 2y \times 3 + 3^2$$

$$= (2y - 3)^2 \quad [\because (a - b)^2 = a^2 - 2ab + b^2]$$

$$= (2y - 3)(2y - 3)$$

Q. 46 $38x^3y^2z \div 19xy^2$ is equal to ______.

Sol. $2x^2z$

We have, $38x^3y^2z \div 19xy^2$

i.e. $$\frac{38x^3y^2z}{19xy^2} = \frac{38 \times x \times x \times x \times y \times y \times z}{19 \times x \times y \times y} = \frac{38}{19}x^2z = 2x^2z$$

Q. 47 Volume of a rectangular box with length $2x$, breadth $3y$ and height $4z$ is ______.

Sol. $24xyz$

We know that, the volume of a rectangular box,

$$V = \text{Length} \times \text{Breadth} \times \text{Height} = 2x \times 3y \times 4z = (2 \times 3 \times 4)xyz = 24xyz$$

Q. 48 $67^2 - 37^2 = (67 - 37) \times$ ______ $=$ ______

Sol. $67 + 37$, 3120

We have, $67^2 - 37^2 = (67 - 37)(67 + 37)$ $[\because a^2 - b^2 = (a - b)(a + b)]$

$= 30 \times 104 = 3120$

Q. 49 $103^2 - 102^2 =$ ______ $\times (103 - 102) =$ ______ .

Sol. $(103 + 102)$, 205

We have,

$$103^2 - 102^2 = (103 + 102)(103 - 102) \quad [\because a^2 - b^2 = (a + b)(a - b)]$$

$$= 205 \times 1 = 205$$

Q. 50 Area of a rectangular plot with sides $4x^2$ and $3y^2$ is ________.

Sol. $12x^2y^2$

We know that, area of rectangle = Length × Breadth

$\therefore$ Area of a rectangular plot $= 4x^2 \times 3y^2 = (4 \times 3)x^2y^2 = 12x^2y^2$

Q. 51 Volume of a rectangular box with $l = b = h = 2x$ is ________.

Sol. $8x^3$

Volume of a rectangular box $= l \times b \times h = 2x \times 2x \times 2x$

$= (2 \times 2 \times 2)\, x^3$

$= 8x^3$

Q. 52 The numerical coefficient in $-37abc$ is ________.

Sol. -37

The constant term (with their sign) involved in term of an algebraic expression is called the numerical coefficient of that term.

Q. 53 Number of terms in the expression $a^2 + bc \times d$ is ________.

Sol. We have, $a^2 + bc \times d = a^2 + bcd$

$\therefore$ The number of terms in this expression is **2** as bcd is treated as a single term.

Q. 54 The sum of areas of two squares with sides $4a$ and $4b$ is ________.

Sol. $16(a^2 + b^2)$

$\because$ Area of a square = (Side)^2

$\therefore$ Area of the square whose one side is $4a = (4a)^2 = 16a^2$

Area of the square with side $4b = (4b)^2 = 16b^2$

$\therefore$ Sum of areas $= 16a^2 + 16b^2 = 16(a^2 + b^2)$

Q. 55 The common factor method of factorisation for a polynomial is based on ________ property.

Sol. **Distributive**

In this method, we regroup the terms in such a way, so that each term in the group contains a common literal or number or both.

Q. 56 The side of the square of area $9y^2$ is ________.

Sol. $3y$

Given, area of a square $= 9y^2$

We know that, the area of a square with side $a = a^2$

$\therefore \quad a^2 = 9y^2$

$\Rightarrow \quad a^2 = (3y)^2$

$\Rightarrow \quad a = 3y$ [taking square root both sides]

Q. 57 On simplification, $\frac{3x+3}{3} =$ ______.

Sol. $x+1$

We have, $\frac{3x+3}{3} = \frac{3x}{3} + \frac{3}{3} = x+1$

Q. 58 The factorisation of $2x+4y$ is ______

Sol. $2(x+2y)$

We have, $2x + 4y = 2x + 2 \times 2y = 2(x+2y)$

True/False

In questions 59 to 80, state whether the statements are True or False

Q. 59 $(a+b)^2 = a^2 + b^2$

Sol. ***False***

We have, $(a+b)^2 = a^2 + b^2 + 2ab$ [an algebraic identity]

Q. 60 $(a-b)^2 = a^2 - b^2$

Sol. ***False***

We have, $(a-b)^2 = a^2 + b^2 - 2ab$ [an algebraic identity]

Q. 61 $(a+b)(a-b) = a^2 - b^2$

Sol. ***True***

We know that, $(a+b)(a-b) = a \times a - a \times b + b \times a - b \times b$

$$= a^2 - b^2$$

$$= a^2 - ab + ba - b^2$$

Q. 62 The product of two negative terms is a negative term.

Sol. ***False***

Since, the product of two negative terms is always a positive term, i.e. $(-) \times (-) = (+)$.

Q. 63 The product of one negative and one positive term is a negative term.

Sol. ***True***

When we multiply a negative term by a positive term, the resultant will be a negative term. i.e. $(-) \times (+) = (-)$.

Q. 64 The numerical coefficient of the term $-6x^2y^2$ is -6.

Sol. ***True***

Since, the constant term (i.e. a number) present in the expression $-6x^2y^2$ is -6.

Q. 65 $p^2q + q^2r + r^2q$ is a binomial.

Sol. ***False***

Since, the given expression contains three unlike terms, so it is a trinomial.

Q. 66 The factors of $a^2 - 2ab + b^2$ are $(a + b)$ and $(a + b)$.

Sol. ***False***

We have, $a^2 - 2ab + b^2 = (a - b)^2 = (a - b)(a - b)$ [an algebraic identity]

Q. 67 h is a factor of $2\pi(h + r)$.

Sol. ***False***

h is not a factor of $2\pi(h + r)$.

This expression has only two factors 2π and $(h + r)$.

Q. 68 Some of the factors of $\frac{n^2}{2} + \frac{n}{2}$ are $\frac{1}{2}n$ and $(n + 1)$.

Sol. ***True***

We have, $\frac{n^2}{2} + \frac{n}{2} = \frac{n^2 + n}{2} = \frac{1}{2}n(n + 1)$

$\therefore$ The factors are $\frac{1}{2}n$ and $(n + 1)$.

Q. 69 An equation is true for all values of its variables.

Sol. ***False***

As equation is true only for some values of its variables.

e.g. $2x - 4 = 0$ is true, only for $x = 2$.

Q. 70 $x^2 + (a + b)x + ab = (a + b)(x + ab)$

Sol. ***False***

As we know that,

$$x^2 + (a + b)x + ab = (x + a)(x + b)$$

Q. 71 Common factors of $11pq^2$, $121p^2q^3$, $1331p^2q$ is $11p^2q^2$.

Sol. ***False***

We have,

$$11pq^2 = 11 \times p \times q \times q$$

$$121p^2q^3 = 11 \times 11 \times p \times p \times q \times q \times q$$

$$1331p^2q = 11 \times 11 \times 11 \times p \times p \times q$$

$\therefore$ Common factor $= 11 \times p \times q = 11pq$

Q. 72 Common factor of $12a^2b^2 + 4ab^2 - 32$ is 4.

Sol. ***True***

As we have,

$$12a^2b^2 + 4ab^2 - 32 = 2 \times 2 \times 3 \times a \times a \times b \times b + 2 \times 2 \times a \times b \times b - 2^2 \times 2^3$$
$$= 4(3a^2b^2 + ab^2 - 8)$$

Thus, the common factor is 4.

Q. 73 Factorisation of $-3a^2 + 3ab + 3ac$ is $3a(-a - b - c)$.

Sol. ***False***

We have,

$$-3a^2 + 3ab + 3ac = 3a(-a + b + c)$$

Q. 74 Factorised form of $p^2 + 30p + 216$ is $(p + 18)(p - 12)$.

Sol. ***False***

We have,

$$p^2 + 30p + 216 = p^2 + (12 + 18)p + 216$$
$$= p^2 + 12p + 18p + 216 \quad \text{[by splitting the middle term]}$$
$$= p(p + 12) + 18(p + 12)$$
$$= (p + 18)(p + 12)$$

Q. 75 The difference of the squares of two consecutive numbers is their sum.

Sol. ***True***

Let n and $n + 1$ be any two consecutive numbers, then their sum $= n + n + 1 = 2n + 1$

Now, the difference of their squares,

$$(n + 1)^2 - n^2 = n^2 + 1 + 2n - n^2$$
$$= 2n + 1 \quad [\because (a + b)^2 = a^2 + 2ab + b^2]$$

Q. 76 $abc + bca + cab$ is a monomial.

Sol. ***True***

The given expression seems to be a trinomial but it is not as it contains three like terms which can be added to form a monomial, i.e. $abc + abc + abc = 3abc$

Q. 77 On dividing $\frac{p}{3}$ by $\frac{3}{p}$, the quotient is 9.

Sol. ***False***

We have, $\frac{p}{3} \div \frac{3}{p} = \frac{p}{3} \times \frac{p}{3} = \frac{1}{9}p^2$ $\quad \left[\because \text{reciprocal of } \frac{3}{p} \text{ is } \frac{p}{3}\right]$

Hence, the quotient is $\frac{1}{9}p^2$.

Q. 78 The value of p for $51^2 - 49^2 = 100p$ is 2.

Sol. ***True***

We have, $51^2 - 49^2 = 100p$

$\Rightarrow (51 + 49)(51 - 49) = 100p$ $[\because a^2 - b^2 = (a+b)(a-b)]$

$\Rightarrow 100 \times 2 = 100p$

$\Rightarrow p = 2$

Q. 79 $(9x - 51) \div 9$ is $x - 51$.

Sol. ***False***

We have, $(9x - 51) \div 9 = \dfrac{9x - 51}{9} = \dfrac{9x}{9} - \dfrac{51}{9} = x - \dfrac{51}{9}$

Q. 80 The value of $(a + 1)(a - 1)(a^2 + 1)$ is $a^4 - 1$.

Sol. ***True***

We have, $(a + 1)(a - 1)(a^2 + 1) = (a^2 - 1)(a^2 + 1)$

[using the identity, $(a + b)(a - b) = a^2 - b^2$ in first two factors]

$= (a^2)^2 - 1^2$ [again using the same identity]

$= a^4 - 1$

Q. 81 Add :

(i) $7a^2bc, -3abc^2, 3a^2bc, 2abc^2$

(ii) $9ax + 3by - cz, -5by + ax + 3cz$

(iii) $xy^2z^2 + 3x^2y^2z - 4x^2yz^2, -9x^2y^2z + 3xy^2z^2 + x^2yz^2$

(iv) $5x^2 - 3xy + 4y^2 - 9, 7y^2 + 5xy - 2x^2 + 13$

(v) $2p^4 - 3p^3 + p^2 - 5p + 7, -3p^4 - 7p^3 - 3p^2 - p - 12$

(vi) $3a(a - b + c), 2b(a - b + c)$

(vii) $3a(2b + 5c), 3c(2a + 2b)$

Sol. (i) We have,

$7a^2bc + (-3abc^2) + 3a^2bc + 2abc^2 = 7a^2bc - 3abc^2 + 3a^2bc + 2abc^2$

$= (7a^2bc + 3a^2bc) + (-3abc^2 + 2abc^2)$ [grouping like terms]

$= 10a^2bc + (-abc^2)$

$= 10a^2bc - abc^2$

(ii) We have,

$(9ax + 3by - cz) + (-5by + ax + 3cz)$

$= 9ax + 3by - cz - 5by + ax + 3cz$

$= (9ax + ax) + (3by - 5by) + (-cz + 3cz)$ [grouping like terms]

$= 10ax - 2by + 2cz$

(iii) We have,

$(xy^2z^2 + 3x^2y^2z - 4x^2yz^2) + (-9x^2y^2z + 3xy^2z^2 + x^2yz^2)$

$= xy^2z^2 + 3x^2y^2z - 4x^2yz^2 - 9x^2y^2z + 3xy^2z^2 + x^2yz^2$

$= (xy^2z^2 + 3xy^2z^2) + (3x^2y^2z - 9x^2y^2z) + (-4x^2yz^2 + x^2yz^2)$

[grouping like terms]

$= 4xy^2z^2 - 6x^2y^2z - 3x^2yz^2$

(iv) We have,

$(5x^2 - 3xy + 4y^2 - 9) + (7y^2 + 5xy - 2x^2 + 13)$

$= 5x^2 - 3xy + 4y^2 - 9 + 7y^2 + 5xy - 2x^2 + 13$

$= (5x^2 - 2x^2) + (-3xy + 5xy) + (4y^2 + 7y^2) + (-9 + 13)$

[grouping like terms]

$= 3x^2 + 2xy + 11y^2 + 4$

(v) We have,

$(2p^4 - 3p^3 + p^2 - 5p + 7) + (-3p^4 - 7p^3 - 3p^2 - p - 12)$

$= 2p^4 - 3p^3 + p^2 - 5p + 7 - 3p^4 - 7p^3 - 3p^2 - p - 12$

$= (2p^4 - 3p^4) + (-3p^3 - 7p^3) + (p^2 - 3p^2) + (-5p - p) + (7 - 12)$

[grouping like terms]

$= -p^4 - 10p^3 - 2p^2 - 6p - 5$

(vi) We have,

$3a(a - b + c) + 2b(a - b + c)$

$= (3a^2 - 3ab + 3ac) + (2ab - 2b^2 + 2bc)$

$= 3a^2 - 3ab + 2ab + 3ac + 2bc - 2b^2 = 3a^2 - ab + 3ac + 2bc - 2b^2$

[grouping like terms]

(vii) We have,

$3a(2b + 5c) + 3c(2a + 2b)$

$= (6ab + 15ac) + (6ac + 6bc) = 6ab + 15ac + 6ac + 6bc$

[grouping like terms]

$= 6ab + 21ac + 6bc$

Q. 82 Subtract

(i) $5a^2b^2c^2$ from $-7a^2b^2c^2$

(ii) $6x^2 - 4xy + 5y^2$ from $8y^2 + 6xy - 3x^2$

(iii) $2ab^2c^2 + 4a^2b^2c - 5a^2bc^2$ from $-10a^2b^2c + 4ab^2c^2 + 2a^2bc^2$

(iv) $3t^4 - 4t^3 + 2t^2 - 6t + 6$ from $-4t^4 + 8t^3 - 4t^2 - 2t + 11$

(v) $2ab + 5bc - 7ac$ from $5ab - 2bc - 2ac + 10abc$

(vi) $7p(3q + 7p)$ from $8p(2p - 7q)$

(vii) $-3p^2 + 3pq + 3px$ from $3p(-p - a - r)$

Sol. (i) We have, $5a^2b^2c^2$ and $-7a^2b^2c^2$

The required difference is given by $-7a^2b^2c^2 - 5a^2b^2c^2$

$= (-7 - 5)a^2b^2c^2 = -12a^2b^2c^2$

(ii) We have, $6x^2 - 4xy + 5y^2$ and $8y^2 + 6xy - 3x^2$

The required difference is given by $(8y^2 + 6xy - 3x^2) - (6x^2 - 4xy + 5y^2)$

$= 8y^2 + 6xy - 3x^2 - 6x^2 + 4xy - 5y^2$

$= (8y^2 - 5y^2) + (6xy + 4xy) - (3x^2 + 6x^2) = 3y^2 + 10xy - 9x^2$

(iii) We have,

$2ab^2c^2 + 4a^2b^2c - 5a^2bc^2$ and $-10a^2b^2c + 4ab^2c^2 + 2a^2bc^2$

The required difference is given by

$(-10a^2b^2c + 4ab^2c^2 + 2a^2bc^2) - (2ab^2c^2 + 4a^2b^2c - 5a^2bc^2)$

$= -10a^2b^2c + 4ab^2c^2 + 2a^2bc^2 - 2ab^2c^2 - 4a^2b^2c + 5a^2bc^2$

$= (-10a^2b^2c - 4a^2b^2c) + (4ab^2c^2 - 2ab^2c^2) + (2a^2bc^2 + 5a^2bc^2)$

[grouping like terms]

$= -14a^2b^2c + 2ab^2c^2 + 7a^2bc^2$

(iv) We have, $3t^4 - 4t^3 + 2t^2 - 6t + 6$ and $-4t^4 + 8t^3 - 4t^2 - 2t + 11$

The required difference is given by

$(-4t^4 + 8t^3 - 4t^2 - 2t + 11) - (3t^4 - 4t^3 + 2t^2 - 6t + 6)$

$= -4t^4 + 8t^3 - 4t^2 - 2t + 11 - 3t^4 + 4t^3 - 2t^2 + 6t - 6$

$= (-4t^4 - 3t^4) + (8t^3 + 4t^3) + (-4t^2 - 2t^2) + (-2t + 6t) + (11 - 6)$

[grouping like terms]

$= -7t^4 + 12t^3 - 6t^2 + 4t + 5$

(v) We have, $2ab + 5bc - 7ac$ and $5ab - 2bc - 2ac + 10abc$

The required difference is given by $(5ab - 2bc - 2ac + 10abc) - (2ab + 5bc - 7ac)$

$= 5ab - 2bc - 2ac + 10abc - 2ab - 5bc + 7ac$

$= (5ab - 2ab) + (-2bc - 5bc) + (-2ac + 7ac) + 10abc$

[groupting like terms]

$= 3ab - 7bc + 5ac + 10abc$

(vi) We have, $7p(3q + 7p)$ and $8p(2p - 7q)$

The required difference is given by $8p(2p - 7q) - 7p(3q + 7p)$

$= 16p^2 - 56pq - 21pq - 49p^2 = (16p^2 - 49p^2) + (-56pq - 21pq)$

[grouping like terms]

$= -33p^2 - 77pq$

(vii) We have, $-3p^2 + 3pq + 3px$ and $3p(-p - a - r)$

The required difference is given by

$3p(-p - a - r) - (-3p^2 + 3pq + 3px) = -3p^2 - 3ap - 3pr + 3p^2 - 3pq - 3px$

$= (-3p^2 + 3p^2) - 3ap - 3pr - 3pq - 3px = -3ap - 3pr - 3pq - 3px$

[grouping like terms]

Q. 83 Multiply the following:

(i) $-7pq^2r^3, -13p^3q^2r$ (ii) $3x^2y^2z^2, 17xyz$

(iii) $15xy^2, 17yz^2$ (iv) $-5a^2bc, 11ab, 13abc^2$

(v) $-3x^2y, (5y - xy)$ (vi) $abc, (bc + ca)$

(vii) $7pqr, (p - q + r)$ (viii) $x^2y^2z^2, (xy - yz + zx)$

(xi) $(p + 6), (q - 7)$ (x) $6mn, 0mn$

(xi) a, a^5, a^6 (xii) $-7st, -1, -13st^2$

(xiii) $b^3, 3b^2, 7ab^5$ (xiv) $-\frac{100}{9}rs; \frac{3}{4}r^3s^2$

(xv) $(a^2 - b^2), (a^2 + b^2)$ (xvi) $(ab + c), (ab + c)$

(xvii) $(pq - 2r), (pq - 2r)$ (xviii) $\left(\frac{3}{4}x - \frac{4}{3}y\right), \left(\frac{2}{3}x + \frac{3}{2}y\right)$

(xix) $\frac{3}{2}p^2 + \frac{2}{3}q^2, (2p^2 - 3q^2)$ (xx) $(x^2 - 5x + 6), (2x + 7)$

(xxi) $(3x^2 + 4x - 8), (2x^2 - 4x + 3)$

(xxii) $(2x - 2y - 3), (x + y + 5)$

Sol. (i) We have, $-7pq^2r^3$ and $-13p^3q^2r$

$\therefore (-7pq^2r^3) \times (-13p^3q^2r) = (-7) \times (-13)\, p^4q^4r^4 = 91p^4q^4r^4$

(ii) We have, $3x^2y^2z^2$ and $17xyz$

$\therefore 3x^2y^2z^2 \times 17\, xyz = (3 \times 17)x^2y^2z^2 \times xyz = 51\, x^3y^3z^3$

(iii) We have, $15xy^2$ and $17yz^2$

$15xy^2 \times 17yz^2 = (15 \times 17)xy^2 \times yz^2 = 255xy^3z^2$

(iv) We have, $-5a^2bc$, $11ab$ and $13abc^2$

$\therefore -5a^2bc \times 11\, ab \times 13abc^2 = (-5 \times 11 \times 13)\, a^2bc \times ab \times abc^2 = -715a^4b^3c^3$

(v) We have, $-3x^2y$ and $(5y - xy)$

$\therefore -3x^2y \times (5y - xy) = -3x^2y \times 5y + 3x^2y \times xy = -15x^2y^2 + 3x^3y^2$

(vi) We have, abc and $(bc + ca)$

$\therefore abc \times (bc + ca) = abc \times bc + abc \times ca = ab^2c^2 + a^2bc^2$

(vii) We have, $7pqr$ and $(p - q + r)$

$\therefore 7pqr \times (p - q + r) = 7pqr \times p - 7pqr \times q + 7pqr \times r = 7p^2qr - 7pq^2r + 7pqr^2$

(viii) We have, $x^2y^2z^2$ and $(xy - yz - zx)$

$\therefore x^2y^2z^2 \times (xy - yz + zx) = x^2y^2z^2 \times xy - x^2y^2z^2 \times yz + x^2y^2z^2 \times zx$

$= x^3y^3z^2 - x^2y^3z^3 + x^3y^2z^3$

(ix) We have, $(p + 6)$ and $(q - 7)$

$\therefore (p + 6) \times (q - 7) = p(q - 7) + 6(q - 7) = pq - 7p + 6q - 42$

(x) We have, 6mn and 0mn

$\therefore 6mn \times 0mn = (6 \times 0)\, mn \times mn = 0 \times m^2n^2 = 0$

(xi) We have, a, a^5 and a^6

$\therefore a \times a^5 \times a^6 = a^{1+5+6} = a^{12}$

(xii) We have, $-7st$, -1 and $-13st^2$

$\therefore -7st \times (-1) \times (-13st^2) = [-7 \times (-1) \times (-13)]st \times (st^2) = -91s^2t^3$

(xiii) We have, b^3, $3b^2$ and $7ab^5$

$\therefore b^3 \times 3b^2 \times 7ab^5 = (1 \times 3 \times 7) b^3 \times b^2 \times ab^5 = 21ab^{10}$

(xiv) We have, $\frac{-100}{9} rs$ and $\frac{3}{4} r^3 s^2$

$\therefore \frac{-100}{9} rs \times \frac{3}{4} r^3 s^2 = \left(\frac{-100}{9} \times \frac{3}{4}\right) rs \times r^3 s^2 = \frac{-25}{3} \times r^4 s^3$

(xv) We have, $(a^2 - b^2)$ and $(a^2 + b^2)$

$\therefore (a^2 - b^2)(a^2 + b^2) = a^2(a^2 + b^2) - b^2(a^2 + b^2) = a^4 + a^2b^2 - b^2a^2 - b^4 = a^4 - b^4$

(xvi) We have, $(ab + c)$ and $(ab + c)$

$\therefore (ab + c)(ab + c) = ab(ab + c) + c(ab + c)$

$= a^2b^2 + abc + cab + c^2 = a^2b^2 + 2abc + c^2$

(xvii) We have, $(pq - 2r)$ and $(pq - 2r)$

$\therefore (pq - 2r)(pq - 2r) = pq(pq - 2r) - 2r(pq - 2r)$

$= p^2q^2 - 2pqr - 2rpq + 4r^2 = p^2q^2 - 4pqr + 4r^2$

(xviii) We have, $\left(\frac{3}{4}x - \frac{4}{3}y\right)$ and $\left(\frac{2}{3}x + \frac{3}{2}y\right)$

$\therefore \left(\frac{3}{4}x - \frac{4}{3}y\right)\left(\frac{2}{3}x + \frac{3}{2}y\right) = \frac{3}{4}x\left(\frac{2}{3}x + \frac{3}{2}y\right) - \frac{4}{3}y\left(\frac{2}{3}x + \frac{3}{2}y\right)$

$= \frac{3}{4} \times \frac{2}{3}x^2 + \frac{3}{4} \times \frac{3}{2}xy - \frac{4}{3} \times \frac{2}{3}yx - \frac{4}{3} \times \frac{3}{2}y^2$

$= \frac{1}{2}x^2 + \frac{9}{8}xy - \frac{8}{9}xy - 2y^2$

$= \frac{1}{2}x^2 + \left(\frac{9}{8} - \frac{8}{9}\right)xy - 2y^2$

$= \frac{1}{2}x^2 + \left(\frac{81 - 64}{72}\right)xy - 2y^2$

$= \frac{1}{2}x^2 + \frac{17}{72}xy - 2y^2$

(xix) We have, $\left(\frac{3}{2}p^2 + \frac{2}{3}q^2\right)$ and $(2p^2 - 3q^2)$

$\therefore \left(\frac{3}{2}p^2 + \frac{2}{3}q^2\right)(2p^2 - 3q^2) = \frac{3}{2}p^2(2p^2 - 3q^2) + \frac{2}{3}q^2(2p^2 - 3q^2)$

$= \frac{3}{2}p^2 \times 2p^2 - \frac{9}{2}p^2q^2 + \frac{4}{3}q^2p^2 - 2q^4$

$= 3p^4 + \left(\frac{4}{3} - \frac{9}{2}\right)p^2q^2 - 2q^4$

$= 3p^4 + \left(\frac{8 - 27}{6}\right)p^2q^2 - 2q^4$

$= 3p^4 - \frac{19}{6}p^2q^2 - 2q^4$

(xx) We have, $(x^2 - 5x + 6)$ and $(2x + 7)$

$\therefore (x^2 - 5x + 6)(2x + 7) = x^2(2x + 7) - 5x(2x + 7) + 6(2x + 7)$

$= 2x^3 + 7x^2 - 10x^2 - 35x + 12x + 42$

$= 2x^3 - 3x^2 - 23x + 42$

(xxi) We have, $(3x^2 + 4x - 8)$ and $(2x^2 - 4x + 3)$

$\therefore (3x^2 + 4x - 8)(2x^2 - 4x + 3)$

$= 3x^2(2x^2 - 4x + 3) + 4x(2x^2 - 4x + 3) - 8(2x^2 - 4x + 3)$

$= 6x^4 - 12x^3 + 9x^2 + 8x^3 - 16x^2 + 12x - 16x^2 + 32x - 24$

$= 6x^4 - 12x^3 + 8x^3 + 9x^2 - 16x^2 - 16x^2 + 12x + 32x - 24$

[grouping like terms]

$= 6x^4 - 4x^3 - 23x^2 + 44x - 24$

(xxii) We have, $(2x - 2y - 3)$ and $(x + y + 5)$

$\therefore (2x - 2y - 3)(x + y + 5)$

$= 2x(x + y + 5) - 2y(x + y + 5) - 3(x + y + 5)$

$= 2x^2 + 2xy + 10x - 2yx - 2y^2 - 10y - 3x - 3y - 15$

$= 2x^2 + 2xy - 2yx + 10x - 3x - 2y^2 - 10y - 3y - 15$

[grouping like terms]

$= 2x^2 + 7x - 13y - 2y^2 - 15$

Q. 84 Simplify

(i) $(3x + 2y)^2 + (3x - 2y)^2$

(ii) $(3x + 2y)^2 - (3x - 2y)^2$

(iii) $\left(\frac{7}{9}a + \frac{9}{7}b\right)^2 - ab$

(iv) $\left(\frac{3}{4}x - \frac{4}{3}y\right)^2 + 2xy$

(v) $(1.5p + 1.2q)^2 - (1.5p - 1.2q)^2$

(vi) $(2.5m + 1.5q)^2 + (2.5m - 1.5q)^2$

(vii) $(x^2 - 4) + (x^2 + 4) + 16$

(viii) $(ab - c)^2 + 2abc$

(ix) $(a - b)(a^2 + b^2 + ab) - (a + b)(a^2 + b^2 - ab)$

(x) $(b^2 - 49)(b + 7) + 343$

(xi) $(4.5a + 1.5b)^2 + (4.5b + 1.5a)^2$

(xii) $(pq - qr)^2 + 4pq^2r$

(xiii) $(s^2t + tq^2)^2 - (2stq)^2$

Sol. (i) We have,

$(3x + 2y)^2 + (3x - 2y)^2 = (3x)^2 + (2y)^2 + 2 \times 3x \times 2y + (3x)^2 + (2y)^2 - 2 \times 3x \times 2y$

[using the identities, $(a + b)^2 = a^2 + b^2 + 2ab$

and $(a - b)^2 = a^2 + b^2 - 2ab$]

$$= 9x^2 + 4y^2 + 12xy + 9x^2 + 4y^2 - 12xy$$
$$= (9x^2 + 9x^2) + (4y^2 + 4y^2) + 12xy - 12xy$$
$$= 18x^2 + 8y^2$$

(ii) We have,

$$(3x + 2y)^2 - (3x - 2y)^2$$
$$= [(3x + 2y) + (3x - 2y)] [(3x + 2y) - (3x - 2y)]$$

[using the identity, $a^2 - b^2 = (a + b)(a - b)$]

$$= (3x + 2y + 3x - 2y)(3x + 2y - 3x + 2y) = 6x \times 4y = (6 \times 4) \times xy = 24xy$$

(iii) We have, $\left(\frac{7}{9}a + \frac{9}{7}b\right)^2 - ab$

$$= \left(\frac{7}{9}a\right)^2 + \left(\frac{9}{7}b\right)^2 + 2 \times \frac{7}{9}a \times \frac{9}{7}b - ab$$

[using the identity, $(a + b)^2 = a^2 + b^2 + 2ab$]

$$= \frac{49}{81}a^2 + \frac{81}{49}b^2 + 2ab - ab$$
$$= \frac{49}{81}a^2 + ab + \frac{81}{49}b^2$$

(iv) We have,

$$\left(\frac{3}{4}x - \frac{4}{3}y\right)^2 + 2xy$$
$$= \left(\frac{3}{4}x\right)^2 + \left(\frac{4}{3}y\right)^2 - 2 \times \frac{3}{4}x \times \frac{4}{3}y + 2xy$$

[using the identity, $(a - b)^2 = a^2 + b^2 - 2ab$]

$$= \frac{9}{16}x^2 + \frac{16}{9}y^2 - 2xy + 2xy = \frac{9}{16}x^2 + \frac{16}{9}y^2$$

(v) We have,

$$(1.5p + 1.2q)^2 - (1.5p - 1.2q)^2$$
$$= [(1.5p + 1.2q) + (1.5p - 1.2q)] [(1.5p + 1.2q) - (1.5p - 1.2q)]$$

[using the identity, $a^2 - b^2 = (a + b)(a - b)$]

$$= [(1.5p + 1.5p) + (1.2q - 1.2q)][(1.5p - 1.5p) + (1.2q + 1.2q)]$$
$$= 3p \times 2.4q = 7.2pq$$

(vi) We have,

$$(2.5m + 1.5q)^2 + (2.5m - 1.5q)^2$$
$$= (2.5m)^2 + (1.5q)^2 + 2 \times 2.5m \times 1.5q + (2.5m)^2 + (1.5q)^2 - 2 \times (2.5m) \times (1.5q)$$

[using the identities, $(a + b)^2 = a^2 + b^2 + 2ab$ and $(a - b)^2 = a^2 + b^2 - 2ab$]

$$= 6.25m^2 + 2.25q^2 + 6.25m^2 + 2.25q^2$$
$$= (6.25 + 6.25)m^2 + (2.25 + 2.25)q^2$$
$$= 12.5m^2 + 4.5q^2$$

(vii) We have,

$$(x^2 - 4) + (x^2 + 4) + 16$$
$$= x^2 - 4 + x^2 + 4 + 16 = 2x^2 + 16$$

(viii) $(ab-c)^2+2abc$

$= (ab)^2+c^2-2abc+2abc$ [using the identity, $(a-b)^2=a^2+b^2-2ab$]
$= a^2b^2+c^2$

(ix) $(a-b)(a^2+b^2+ab)-(a+b)(a^2+b^2-ab)$

$= a(a^2+b^2+ab)-b(a^2+b^2+ab)-a(a^2+b^2-ab)-b(a^2+b^2-ab)$
$= a^3+ab^2+a^2b-ba^2-b^3-ab^2-a^3-ab^2+a^2b-ba^2-b^3+ab^2$
$= (a^3-a^3)+(-b^3-b^3)+(ab^2-ab^2)+(a^2b-a^2b+a^2b-a^2b)$
$= 0-2b^3+0+0+0$
$= -2b^3$

(x) We have,

$(b^2-49)(b+7)+343$
$= b^2(b+7)-49(b+7)+343$
$= b^3+7b^2-49b-343+343$
$= b^3-49b+7b^2$

(xi) We have, $(4.5a+1.5b)^2+(4.5b+1.5a)^2$

$= (4.5a)^2+(1.5b)^2+2\times 4.5a\times 1.5b+(4.5b)^2+(1.5a)^2+2\times 4.5b\times 1.5a$

[using the identity, $(a+b)^2=a^2+b^2+2ab$]

$= 20.25a^2+2.25b^2+13.5ab+20.25b^2+2.25a^2+13.5ab$
$= 40.5a^2+4.5b^2+27ab$

(xii) We have, $(pq-qr)^2+4pq^2r$

$= p^2q^2+q^2r^2-2pq^2r+4pq^2r$

[using the identity, $(a-b)^2=a^2+b^2-2ab$]

$= p^2q^2+q^2r^2+2pq^2r$

(xiii) We have, $(s^2t+tq^2)^2-(2stq)^2$

$= (s^2t)^2+(tq^2)^2+2\times s^2t\times tq^2-4s^2t^2q^2$

[using the identity, $(a+b)^2=a^2+b^2+2ab$]

$= s^4t^2+t^2q^4+2s^2t^2q^2-4s^2t^2q^2$
$= s^4t^2+t^2q^4-2s^2t^2q^2$

Q. 85 Expand the following, using suitable identities.

(i) $(xy+yz)^2$

(ii) $(x^2y-xy^2)^2$

(iii) $\left(\frac{4}{5}a+\frac{5}{4}b\right)^2$

(iv) $\left(\frac{2}{3}x-\frac{3}{2}y\right)^2$

(v) $\left(\frac{4}{5}p+\frac{5}{3}q\right)^2$

(vi) $(x+3)(x+7)$

(vii) $(2x+9)(2x-7)$

(viii) $\left(\frac{4x}{5}+\frac{y}{4}\right)\left(\frac{4x}{5}+\frac{3y}{4}\right)$

(ix) $\left(\frac{2x}{3}-\frac{2}{3}\right)\left(\frac{2x}{3}+\frac{2a}{3}\right)$ (x) $(2x-5y)(2x-5y)$

(xi) $\left(\frac{2a}{3}+\frac{b}{3}\right)\left(\frac{2a}{3}-\frac{b}{3}\right)$ (xii) $(x^2+y^2)(x^2-y^2)$

(xiii) $(a^2+b^2)^2$ (xiv) $(7x+5)^2$

(xv) $(0.9p-0.5q)^2$

Sol. (i) We have,

$$(xy+yz)^2=(xy)^2+(yz)^2+2\times xy\times yz$$

[using the identity, $(a+b)^2=a^2+b^2+2ab$]

$$=x^2y^2+y^2z^2+2xy^2z$$

(ii) We have,

$$(x^2y-xy^2)^2=(x^2y)^2+(xy^2)^2-2x^2y\times xy^2$$
$$=x^4y^2+x^2y^4-2x^3y^3$$

[using the identity, $(a-b)^2=a^2+b^2-2ab$]

(iii) We have,

$$\left(\frac{4}{5}a+\frac{5}{4}b\right)^2=\left(\frac{4}{5}a\right)^2+\left(\frac{5}{4}b\right)^2+2\times\frac{4}{5}a\times\frac{5}{4}b$$

$$=\frac{16}{25}a^2+\frac{25}{16}b^2+2ab$$ [using the identity, $(a+b)^2=a^2+b^2+2ab$]

(iv) We have,

$$\left(\frac{2}{4}x-\frac{3}{2}y\right)^2=\left(\frac{2}{3}x\right)^2+\left(\frac{3}{2}y\right)^2-2\times\frac{2}{3}x\times\frac{3}{2}y$$

[using the identity, $(a-b)^2=a^2+b^2-2ab$]

$$=\frac{4}{9}x^2+\frac{9}{4}y^2-2xy$$

(v) We have,

$$\left(\frac{4}{5}p+\frac{5}{3}q\right)^2=\left(\frac{4}{5}p\right)^2+\left(\frac{5}{3}q\right)^2+2\times\frac{4}{5}p\times\frac{5}{3}q$$
$$=\frac{16}{25}p^2+\frac{25}{9}q^2+\frac{8}{3}pq$$

[using the identity, $(a+b)^2=a^2+b^2+2ab$]

(vi) We have,

$$(x+3)(x+7)=x^2+(3+7)x+3\times7$$

[using the identity, $(x+a)(x+b)=x^2+(a+b)x+ab$]

$$=x^2+10x+21$$

(vii) We have,

$$(2x+9)(2x-7)=(2x+9)[2x+(-7)]$$
$$=(2x)^2+[9+(-7)]2x+9\times(-7)$$

[using the identity, $(x+a)(x+b)=x^2+(a+b)x+ab$]

$$=4x^2+4x-63$$

(viii) We have,

$$\left(\frac{4x}{5}+\frac{y}{4}\right)\left(\frac{4x}{5}+\frac{3y}{4}\right)=\left(\frac{4x}{5}\right)^2+\left(\frac{y}{4}+\frac{3y}{4}\right)\frac{4x}{5}+\frac{y}{4}\times\frac{3y}{4}$$

[using the identity, $(x+a)(x+b)=x^2+(a+b)x+ab$]

$$=\frac{16}{25}x^2+\frac{4xy}{5}+\frac{3y^2}{16}$$

(ix) We have,

$$\left(\frac{2x}{3}-\frac{2}{3}\right)\left(\frac{2x}{3}+\frac{2a}{3}\right)=\left(\frac{2x}{3}\right)^2+\left(\frac{-2}{3}+\frac{2a}{3}\right)\frac{2x}{3}+\left(\frac{-2}{3}\times\frac{2a}{3}\right)$$

[using the identity, $(x+a)(x+b)=x^2+(a+b)x+ab$]

$$=\frac{4x^2}{9}+\frac{2a-2}{3}\times\frac{2}{3}x-\frac{4}{9}a=\frac{4x^2}{9}+\frac{4}{9}(a-1)x-\frac{4}{9}a$$

(x) We have,

$$(2x-5y)(2x-5y)=(2x-5y)^2$$

$$=(4x)^2+(5y)^2-2\times 2x\times 5y$$

[using the identity, $(a-b)^2=a^2+b^2-2ab$]

$$=16x^2+25y^2-20xy$$

(xi) We have,

$$\left(\frac{2a}{3}+\frac{b}{3}\right)\left(\frac{2a}{3}-\frac{b}{3}\right)=\left(\frac{2a}{3}\right)^2-\left(\frac{b}{3}\right)^2$$

[using the identity, $(a+b)(a-b)-a^2-b^2$]

$$=\frac{4}{9}a^2-\frac{1}{9}b^2$$

(xii) We have,

$$(x^2+y^2)(x^2-y^2)=(x^2)^2-(y^2)^2$$

[using the identity, $(a+b)(a-b)=a^2-b^2$]

$$=x^4-y^4$$

(xiii) We have,

$$(a^2+b^2)^2=(a^2)^2+(b^2)^2+2a^2\times b^2$$

$$=a^4+b^4+2a^2b^2$$

[using the identity, $(a+b)^2=a^2+b^2+2ab$]

(xiv) We have,

$$(7x+5)^2=(7x)^2+5^2+2\times 7x\times 5$$

$$=49x^2+25+70x$$

[using the identity, $(a+b)^2=a^2+b^2+2ab$]

(xv) We have,

$$(0.9p-0.5q)^2=(0.9p)^2+(0.5q)^2-2\times 0.9p\times 0.5q$$

[using the identity, $(a-b)^2=a^2+b^2-2ab$]

$$=0.81p^2+025q^2-0.9pq$$

Q. 86 Using suitable identities, evaluate the following:

(i) $(52)^2$ (ii) $(49)^2$
(iii) $(103)^2$ (iv) $(98)^2$
(v) $(1005)^2$ (vi) $(995)^2$
(vii) 47×53 (viii) 52×53
(ix) 105×95 (x) 104×97
(xi) 101×103 (xii) 98×103
(xiii) $(9.9)^2$ (xiv) 9.8×10.2
(xv) 10.1×10.2 (xvi) $(35.4)^2 - (14.6)^2$
(xvii) $(69.3)^2 - (30.7)^2$ (xviii) $(9.7)^2 - (0.3)^2$
(xix) $(132)^2 - (68)^2$ (xx) $(339)^2 - (161)^2$
(xxi) $(729)^2 - (271)^2$

Sol. (i) We have,

$(52)^2 = (50 + 2)^2$
$= (50)^2 + (2)^2 + 2 \times 50 \times 2$ [using the identity, $(a + b)^2 = a^2 + b^2 + 2ab$]
$= 2500 + 4 + 200$
$= 2704$

(ii) We have,

$(49)^2 = (50 - 1)^2$
$= (50)^2 + 1^2 - 2 \times 50 \times 1$ [using the identity, $(a - b)^2 = a^2 + b^2 - 2ab$]
$= 2500 + 1 - 100$
$= 2401$

(iii) We have,

$(103)^2 = (100 + 3)^2$
$= (100)^2 + 3^2 + 2 \times 100 \times 3$
$= 10000 + 9 + 600$
$= 10609$ [using the identity, $(a + b)^2 = a^2 + b^2 + 2ab$]

(iv) We have,

$(98)^2 = (100 - 2)^2$
$= (100)^2 + (2)^2 - 2 \times 100 \times 2$
$= 10000 + 4 - 400$
$= 9604$ [using the identity, $(a - b)^2 = a^2 + b^2 - 2ab$]

(v) We have,

$(1005)^2 = (1000 + 5)^2$
$= (1000)^2 + 5^2 + 2 \times 1000 \times 5$
$= 1000000 + 25 + 10000$
$= 1010025$ [using the identity, $(a + b)^2 = a^2 + b^2 + 2ab$]

(vi) We have,

$(995)^2 = (1000 - 5)^2$

$= (1000)^2 + (5)^2 - 2 \times 1000 \times 5$

$= 1000000 + 25 - 10000$

$= 990025$ [using the identity, $(a-b)^2 = a^2 + b^2 - 2ab$]

(vii) We have,

$47 \times 53 = (50 - 3)(50 + 3)$

$= (50)^2 - (3)^2$ [using the identity, $(a - b)(a + b) = a^2 - b^2$]

$= 2500 - 9$

$= 2491$

(viii) We have,

$52 \times 53 = (50 + 2)(50 + 3)$

$= (50)^2 + (2 + 3)\,50 + 2 \times 3$

[using the identity, $(x + a)(x + b) = x^2 + (a + b)\,x + ab$]

$= 2500 + 250 + 6 = 2756$

(ix) We have,

$105 \times 95 = (100 + 5)(100 - 5)$

$= (100)^2 - (5)^2$ [using the identity, $(a + b)(a - b) = a^2 - b^2$]

$= 10000 - 25$

$= 9975$

(x) Wc have,

$104 \times 97 = (100 + 4)(100 - 3)$

$= (100)^2 + (4 - 3)100 + 4 \times (-3)$

$= 10000 + 100 - 12$

$= 10088$ [using the identity, $(x + a)(x + b) = x^2 + (a + b)\,x + ab$]

(xi) We have,

$101 \times 103 = (100 + 1)(100 + 3)$

$= (100)^2 + (1 + 3)\,100 + 3 \times 1$

$= 10000 + 400 + 3$

$= 10403$ [using the identity, $(x + a)(x + b) = x^2 + (a + b)\,x + ab$]

(xii) We have,

$98 \times 103 = (100 - 2)(100 + 3)$

$= (100)^2 + (-2 + 3)\,100 + (-2) \times 3$

$= 10000 + 100 - 6$

$= 10094$ [using the identity, $(x + a)(x + b) = x^2 + (a + b)\,x + ab$]

(xiii) We have,

$(9.9)^2 = (10 - 0.1)^2$

$= 10^2 + (0.1)^2 - 2 \times 10 \times 0.1$

$= 100 + 0.01 - 2 = 98.01$

[using the identity, $(a-b)^2 = a^2 + b^2 - 2ab$]

(xiv) We have,

$$9.8 \times 10.2 = (10 - 0.2)(10 + 0.2)$$
$$= 10^2 - (0.2)^2$$
$$= 100 - 0.04$$
$$= 100 - 0.04$$
$$= 99.96 \quad \text{[using the identity, } (a+b)(a-b) = a^2 - b^2\text{]}$$

(xv) We have,

$$10.1 \times 10.2 = (10 + 0.1)(10 + 0.2)$$
$$= (10)^2 + (0.1 + 0.2)10 + (0.1)(0.2)$$
$$= 100 + 0.3 \times 10 + 0.02$$
$$= 103.02 \quad \text{[using the identity, } (x+a)(x+b) = x^2 + (a+b)x + ab\text{]}$$

(xvi) We have,

$$(35.4)^2 - (14.6)^2 = (35.4 + 14.6)(35.4 - 14.6)$$
$$= 50 \times 20.8$$
$$= 1040 \quad \text{[using the identity, } (a+b)(a-b) = a^2 - b^2\text{]}$$

(xvii) We have,

$$(69.3)^2 - (30.7)^2 = (69.3 + 30.7)(69.3 - 30.7)$$
$$= 100 \times 38.6$$
$$= 3860 \quad \text{[using the identity, } (a+b)(a-b) = a^2 - b^2\text{]}$$

(xviii) We have,

$$(9.7)^2 - (0.3)^2 = (9.7 + 0.3)(9.7 - 0.3)$$
$$= 10 \times 9.4$$
$$= 94 \quad \text{[using the identity, } a^2 - b^2 = (a+b)(a-b)\text{]}$$

(xix) We have,

$$(132)^2 - (68)^2 = (132 + 68)(132 - 68)$$
$$= 200 \times 64$$
$$= 12800 \quad \text{[using the identity, } a^2 - b^2 = (a+b)(a-b)\text{]}$$

(xx) We have,

$$(339)^2 - (161)^2 = (339 + 161)(339 - 161)$$
$$= 500 \times 178$$
$$= 89000 \quad \text{[using the identity, } a^2 - b^2 = (a+b)(a-b)\text{]}$$

(xxi) We have,

$$(729)^2 - (271)^2 = (729 + 271)(729 - 271)$$
$$= 1000 \times 458$$
$$= 458000 \quad \text{[using the identity, } a^2 - b^2 = (a+b)(a-b)\text{]}$$

Q. 87 Write the greatest common factor in each of the following terms.

(i) $-18a^2, 108a$

(ii) $3x^2y, 18xy^2, -6xy$

(iii) $2xy, -y^2, 2x^2y$

(iv) $l^2m^2n, lm^2n^2, l^2mn^2$

(v) $21pqr, -7p^2q^2r^2, 49p^2qr$

(vi) $qrxy, pryz, rxyz$

(vii) $3x^3y^2z, -6xy^3z^2, 12x^2yz^3$

(viii) $63p^2a^2r^2s, -9pq^2r^2s^2, 15p^2qr^2s^2, -60p^2a^2rs^2$

(ix) $13x^2y, 169xy$

(x) $11x^2, 12y^2$

Sol. (i) We have,

$$-18a^2 = -18 \times a \times a$$

$$108a = 18 \times 10 \times a$$

$\therefore$ The greatest common factor i.e. GCF is $18a$.

(ii) We have,

$$3x^2y = 3 \times x \times x \times y$$

$$18xy^2 = 3 \times 6 \times x \times y \times y$$

$$-6xy = -1 \times 3 \times 2 \times x \times y$$

$\therefore$ GCF $= 3xy$

(iii) We have, $2xy = 2 \times x \times y$

$$-y^2 = -y \times y$$

$$2x^2y = 2 \times x \times x \times y$$

$\therefore$ GCF $= y$

(iv) We have,

$$l^2m^2n = l \times l \times m \times m \times n$$

$$lm^2n^2 = l \times m \times m \times n \times n$$

$$l^2mn^2 = l \times l \times m \times n \times n$$

$\therefore$ GCF $= lmn$

(v) We have,

$$21pqr = 7 \times 3 \times p \times q \times r$$

$$-7p^2q^2r^2 = -7 \times p \times p \times q \times q \times r \times r$$

$$49p^2qr = 7 \times 7 \times p \times p \times q \times r$$

$\therefore$ GCF $= 7pqr$

(vi) We have,

$$qrxy = q \times r \times x \times y$$

$$pryz = p \times r \times y \times z$$

$$rxyz = r \times x \times y \times z$$

$\therefore$ GCF $= ry$

(vii) We have,

$$3x^3y^2z = 3 \times x \times x \times x \times y \times y \times z$$

$$-6xy^3z^2 = -3 \times 2 \times x \times y \times y \times y \times z \times z$$

$$12x^2yz^3 = 3 \times 4 \times x \times x \times y \times z \times z \times z$$

$\therefore$ GCF $= 3xyz$

(viii) We have,

$$63p^2a^2r^2s = 3 \times 3 \times 7 \times p \times p \times a \times a \times r \times r \times s$$
$$-9pq^2r^2s^2 = -3 \times 3 \times p \times q \times q \times r \times r \times s \times s$$
$$15p^2qr^2s^2 = 3 \times 5 \times p \times p \times q \times r \times r \times s \times s$$
$$-60p^2a^2rs^2 = -2 \times 2 \times 3 \times 5 \times p \times p \times a \times a \times r \times s \times s$$

$\therefore$ GCF = $3prs$

(ix) We have,

$$13x^2y = 13 \times x \times x \times y$$
$$169xy = 13 \times 13 \times x \times y$$

$\therefore$ GCF = $13xy$

(x) We have, $11x^2$, $12y^2$

The GCF of 11, 12 is 1.

Also, there is no common factor between x^2 and y^2.

Hence, the GCF of $11x^2$ and $12y^2$ is 1.

Q. 88 Factorise the following expressions.

(i) $6ab + 12bc$

(ii) $-xy - ay$

(iii) $ax^3 - bx^2 + cx$

(iv) $l^2m^2n - lm^2n^2 - l^2mn^2$

(v) $3pqr - 6p^2q^2r^2 - 15r^2$

(vi) $x^3y^2 + x^2y^3 - xy^4 + xy$

(vii) $4xy^2 - 10x^2y + 16x^2y^2 + 2xy$

(viii) $2a^3 - 3a^2b + 5ab^2 - ab$

(ix) $63p^2q^2r^2s - 9pq^2r^2s^2 + 15p^2qr^2s^2 - 60p^2q^2rs^2$

(x) $24x^2yz^3 - 6xy^3z^2 + 15x^2y^2z - 5xyz$

(xi) $a^3 + a^2 + a + 1$

(xii) $lx + my + mx + ly$

(xiii) $a^3x - x^4 + a^2x^2 - ax^3$

(xiv) $2x^2 - 2y + 4xy - x$

(xv) $y^2 + 8zx - 2xy - 4yz$

(xvi) $ax^2y - bxyz - ax^2z + bxy^2$

(xvii) $a^2b + a^2c + ab + ac + b^2c + c^2b$

(xviii) $2ax^2 + 4axy + 3bx^2 + 2ay^2 + 6bxy + 3by^2$

Sol. (i) We have,

$$6ab + 12bc = 6ab + 6 \times 2 \times bc = 6b\,(a + 2c)$$

(ii) We have,

$$-xy - ay = -y(x + a)$$

(iii) We have,

$$ax^3 - bx^2 + cx = x(ax^2 - bx + c)$$

(iv) We have,

$$l^2m^2n - lm^2n^2 - l^2mn^2 = lmn(lm - mn - ln)$$

(v) We have, $3pqr - 6p^2q^2r^2 - 15r^2$

$$= 3pqr - 3 \times 2p^2q^2r^2 - 3 \times 5r^2 = 3r(pq - 2p^2q^2r - 5r)$$

(vi) We have, $x^3y^2 + x^2y^3 - xy^4 + xy$

$$= xy(x^2y + xy^2 - y^3 + 1)$$

(vii) We have, $4xy^2 - 10x^2y + 16x^2y^2 + 2xy$

$$= 2 \times 2xy^2 - 2 \times 5 \times x^2y + 2 \times 8 \times x^2y^2 + 2xy$$

$$= 2xy(2y - 5x + 8xy + 1)$$

(viii) We have, $2a^3 - 3a^2b + 5ab^2 - ab$

$$= a(2a^2 - 3ab + 5b^2 - b)$$

(ix) We have, $63p^2q^2r^2s - 9pq^2r^2s^2 + 15p^2qr^2s^2 - 60p^2q^2rs^2$

$$= 3 \times 21p^2q^2r^2s - 3 \times 3pq^2r^2s^2 + 3 \times 5p^2qr^2s^2 - 3 \times 20p^2q^2rs^2$$

$$= 3pqrs(21pqr - 3qrs + 5prs - 20pqs)$$

(x) We have, $24x^2yz^3 - 6xy^3z^2 + 15x^2y^2z - 5xyz$

$$= xyz(24xz^2 - 6y^2z + 15xy - 5)$$

(xi) We have, $a^3 + a^2 + a + 1$

$$= a^2(a + 1) + 1(a + 1) = (a + 1)(a^2 + 1)$$

(xii) We have, $lx + my + mx + ly$

$$= lx + mx + my + ly = x(l + m) + y(m + l) = (l + m)(x + y)$$

(xiii) We have, $a^3x - x^4 + a^2x^2 - ax^3$

$$= x(a^3 - x^3 + a^2x - ax^2) = x(a^3 + a^2x - x^3 - ax^2)$$

$$= x[a^2(a + x) - x^2(x + a)]$$

$$= x[(x + a)(a^2 - x^2)] = x(a^2 - x^2)(a + x)$$

(xiv) We have, $2x^2 - 2y + 4xy - x$

$$= 2x^2 - x - 2y + 4xy = x(2x - 1) - 2y(1 - 2x)$$

$$= x(2x - 1) + 2y(2x - 1) = (2x - 1)(x + 2y)$$

(xv) We have, $y^2 + 8zx - 2xy - 4yz$

$$= y^2 - 2xy + 8zx - 4yz = y(y - 2x) - 4z(y - 2x)$$

$$= (y - 2x)(y - 4z)$$

(xvi) We have, $ax^2y - bxyz - ax^2z + bxy^2$

$$= x(axy - byz - axz + by^2)$$

$$= x(axy - axz - byz + by^2)$$

$$= x[ax(y - z) + by(-z + y)]$$

$$= x[(ax + by)(y - z)]$$

(xvii) We have, $a^2b + a^2c + ab + ac + b^2c + c^2b$

$= (a^2b + ab + b^2c) + (a^2c + ac + c^2b)$

$= b(a^2 + a + bc) + c(a^2 + a + bc)$

$= (a^2 + a + bc)(b + c)$

(xviii) We have, $2ax^2 + 4axy + 3bx^2 + 2ay^2 + 6bxy + 3by^2$

$= (2ax^2 + 2ay^2 + 4axy) + (3bx^2 + 3by^2 + 6bxy)$

$= 2a(x^2 + y^2 + 2xy) + 3b(x^2 + y^2 + 2xy)$

$= (2a + 3b)(x + y)^2$

Q. 89 Factorise the following, using the identity, $a^2 + 2ab + b^2 = (a + b)^2$

(i) $x^2 + 6x + 9$

(ii) $x^2 + 12x + 36$

(iii) $x^2 + 14x + 49$

(iv) $x^2 + 2x + 1$

(v) $4x^2 + 4x + 1$

(vi) $a^2x^2 + 2ax + 1$

(vii) $a^2x^2 + 2abx + b^2$

(viii) $a^2x^2 + 2abxy + b^2y^2$

(ix) $4x^2 + 12x + 9$

(x) $16x^2 + 40x + 25$

(xi) $9x^2 + 24x + 16$

(xii) $9x^2 + 30x + 25$

(xiii) $2x^3 + 24x^2 + 72x$

(xiv) $a^2x^3 + 2abx^2 + b^2x$

(xv) $4x^4 + 12x^3 + 9x^2$

(xvi) $\frac{x^2}{4} + 2x + 4$

(xvii) $9x^2 + 2xy + \frac{y^2}{9}$

Sol. (i) We have,

$x^2 + 6x + 9 = x^2 + 2 \cdot 3 \cdot x + 3^2$

$= (x + 3)^2$ $[\because a^2 + 2ab + b^2 = (a + b)^2]$

$= (x + 3)(x + 3)$

(ii) We have, $x^2 + 12x + 36$

$= x^2 + 2 \cdot 6 \cdot x + 6^2$

$= (x + 6)^2$ $[\because a^2 + 2ab + b^2 = (a + b)^2]$

$= (x + 6)(x + 6)$

(iii) We have, $x^2 + 14x + 49$

$= x^2 + 2 \cdot 7 \cdot x + 7^2 = (x + 7)^2 = (x + 7)(x + 7)$

(iv) We have, $x^2 + 2x + 1$

$= x^2 + 2 \cdot 1 \cdot x + 1^2 = (x + 1)^2 = (x + 1)(x + 1)$

(v) We have, $4x^2 + 4x + 1$

$= (2x)^2 + 2 \cdot 2x \cdot 1 + 1^2 = (2x + 1)^2 = (2x + 1)(2x + 1)$

(vi) We have, $a^2x^2 + 2ax + 1$

$= (ax)^2 + 2 \cdot ax \cdot 1 + (1)^2 = (ax + 1)^2 = (ax + 1)(ax + 1)$

(vii) We have, $a^2x^2 + 2abx + b^2$

$$= (ax)^2 + 2\cdot ax\cdot b + b^2 = (ax + b)^2 = (ax + b)(ax + b)$$

(viii) We have, $a^2x^2 + 2abxy + b^2y^2$

$$= (ax)^2 + 2\cdot ax\cdot by + (by)^2 = (ax + by)^2 = (ax + by)(ax + by)$$

(ix) We have, $4x^2 + 12x + 9$

$$= (2x)^2 + 2\cdot 2x\cdot 3 + 3^2 = (2x + 3)^2 = (2x + 3)(2x + 3)$$

(x) We have, $16x^2 + 40x + 25$

$$= (4x)^2 + 2\cdot 4x\cdot 5 + 5^2 = (4x + 5)^2 = (4x + 5)(4x + 5)$$

(xi) We have, $9x^2 + 24x + 16$

$$= (3x)^2 + 2\cdot 3x\cdot 4 + 4^2 = (3x + 4)^2 = (3x + 4)(3x + 4)$$

(xii) We have, $9x^2 + 30x + 25$

$$= (3x)^2 + 2\cdot 3x\cdot 5 + 5^2 = (3x + 5)^2 = (3x + 5)(3x + 5)$$

(xiii) We have, $2x^3 + 24x^2 + 72x$

$$= 2x(x^2 + 12x + 36) = 2x(x^2 + 2\cdot 6\cdot x + 6^2)$$
$$= 2x(x + 6)^2 = 2x(x + 6)(x + 6)$$

(xiv) We have, $a^2x^3 + 2abx^2 + b^2x$

$$= x(a^2x^2 + 2abx + b^2) = x[(ax)^2 + 2\cdot ax\cdot b + b^2]$$
$$= x(ax + b)^2 = x(ax + b)(ax + b)$$

(xv) We have, $4x^4 + 12x^3 + 9x^2$

$$= x^2(4x^2 + 12x + 9) = x^2[(2x)^2 + 2\cdot 2x\cdot 3 + 3^2]$$
$$= x^2(2x + 3)^2 = x^2(2x + 3)(2x + 3)$$

(xvi) We have, $\frac{x^2}{4} + 2x + 4$

$$= \left(\frac{x}{2}\right)^2 + 2\cdot\frac{x}{2}\cdot 2 + 2^2 = \left(\frac{x}{2} + 2\right)^2 = \left(\frac{x}{2} + 2\right)\left(\frac{x}{2} + 2\right)$$

(xvii) We have, $9x^2 + 2xy + \frac{y^2}{9}$

$$= (3x)^2 + 2\cdot 3x\cdot\frac{y}{3} + \left(\frac{y}{3}\right)^2 = \left(3x + \frac{y}{3}\right)^2 = \left(3x + \frac{y}{3}\right)\left(3x + \frac{y}{3}\right)$$

Q. 90 Factorise the following, using the identity, $a^2 - 2ab + b^2 = (a - b)^2$.

(i) $x^2 - 8x + 16$

(ii) $x^2 - 10x + 25$

(iii) $y^2 - 14y + 49$

(iv) $p^2 - 2p + 1$

(v) $4a^2 - 4ab + b^2$

(vi) $p^2y^2 - 2py + 1$

(vii) $a^2y^2 - 2aby + b^2$

(viii) $9x^2 - 12x + 4$

(ix) $4y^2 - 12y + 9$

(x) $\frac{x^2}{4} - 2x + 4$

(xi) $a^2y^3 - 2aby^2 + b^2y$

(xii) $9y^2 - 4xy + \frac{4x^2}{9}$

Sol. (i) We have,

$$x^2 - 8x + 16 = x^2 - 2 \cdot x \cdot 4 + 4^2$$
$$= (x-4)^2 \quad [\because a^2 - 2ab + b^2 = (a-b)^2]$$
$$= (x-4)(x-4)$$

(ii) We have,

$$x^2 - 10x + 25 = x^2 - 2 \cdot x \cdot 5 + 5^2$$
$$= (x-5)^2 = (x-5)(x-5)$$

(iii) We have,

$$y^2 - 14y + 49 = y^2 - 2 \cdot y \cdot 7 + 7^2$$
$$= (y-7)^2 = (y-7)(y-7)$$

(iv) We have,

$$p^2 - 2p + 1 = p^2 - 2 \cdot p \cdot 1 + 1^2$$
$$= (p-1)^2 = (p-1)(p-1)$$

(v) We have,

$$4a^2 - 4ab + b^2 = (2a)^2 - 2 \cdot 2a \cdot b + b^2$$
$$= (2a-b)^2 = (2a-b)(2a-b)$$

(vi) We have,

$$p^2y^2 - 2py + 1 = (py)^2 - 2 \cdot py \cdot 1 + 1^2$$
$$= (py-1)^2 = (py-1)(py-1)$$

(vii) We have,

$$a^2y^2 - 2aby + b^2 = (ay)^2 - 2 \cdot ay \cdot b + b^2$$
$$= (ay-b)^2 = (ay-b)(ay-b)$$

(viii) We have,

$$9x^2 - 12x + 4 = (3x)^2 - 2 \cdot 3x \cdot 2 + 2^2$$
$$= (3x-2)^2 = (3x-2)(3x-2)$$

(ix) We have,

$$4y^2 - 12y + 9 = (2y)^2 - 2 \cdot 2y \cdot 3 + 3^2$$
$$= (2y-3)^2 = (2y-3)(2y-3)$$

(x) We have,

$$\frac{x^2}{4} - 2x + 4 = \left(\frac{x}{2}\right)^2 - 2 \cdot \frac{x}{2} \cdot 2 + 2^2$$
$$= \left(\frac{x}{2} - 2\right)^2 = \left(\frac{x}{2} - 2\right)\left(\frac{x}{2} - 2\right)$$

(xi) We have,

$$a^2y^3 - 2aby^2 + b^2y = y(a^2y^2 - 2aby + b^2) = y[(ay)^2 - 2 \cdot ay \cdot b + b^2]$$
$$= y(ay-b)^2 = y(ay-b)(ay-b)$$

(xii) We have,

$$9y^2 - 4xy + \frac{4x^2}{9} = (3y)^2 - 2 \cdot 3y \cdot \frac{2}{3}x + \left(\frac{2}{3}x\right)^2$$
$$= \left(3y - \frac{2}{3}x\right)^2 = \left(3y - \frac{2x}{3}\right)\left(3y - \frac{2x}{3}\right)$$

Q. 91 Factorise the following:

(i) $x^2 + 15x + 26$ (ii) $x^2 + 9x + 20$

(iii) $y^2 + 18y + 65$ (iv) $p^2 + 14p + 13$

(v) $y^2 + 4y - 21$ (vi) $y^2 - 2y - 15$

(vii) $18 + 11x + x^2$ (viii) $x^2 - 10x + 21$

(ix) $x^2 - 17x + 60$ (x) $x^2 + 4x - 77$

(xi) $y^2 + 7y + 12$ (xii) $p^2 - 13p - 30$

(xiii) $p^2 - 16p - 80$

Sol. (i) We have, $x^2 + 15x + 26$

$= x^2 + 2x + 13x + 2 \times 13 = x(x + 2) + 13(x + 2) = (x + 2)(x + 13)$

(ii) We have, $x^2 + 9x + 20$

$= x^2 + 5x + 4x + 5 \times 4 = x(x + 5) + 4(x + 5) = (x + 5)(x + 4)$

(iii) We have, $y^2 + 18y + 65$

$= y^2 + 13y + 5y + 5 \times 13 = y(y + 13) + 5(y + 13) = (y + 13)(y + 5)$

(iv) We have, $p^2 + 14p + 13$

$= p^2 + 13p + p + 13 \times 1 = p(p + 13) + 1(p + 13) = (p + 13)(p + 1)$

(v) We have, $y^2 + 4y - 21$

$= y^2 + (7 - 3)y - 21 = y^2 + 7y - 3y - 21 = y(y + 7) - 3(y + 7) = (y + 7)(y - 3)$

(vi) We have, $y^2 - 2y - 15$

$= y^2 + (3 - 5)y - 15 = y^2 + 3y - 5y - 15 = y(y + 3) - 5(y + 3) = (y + 3)(y - 5)$

(vii) We have, $18 + 11x + x^2$

$= x^2 + 11x + 18 = x^2 + (9 + 2)x + 18 = x^2 + 9x + 2x + 18$

$= x(x + 9) + 2(x + 9) = (x + 9)(x + 2)$

(viii) We have, $x^2 - 10x + 21$

$= x^2 - (7 + 3)x + 21 = x^2 - 7x - 3x + 21 = x(x - 7) - 3(x - 7)$

$= (x - 7)(x - 3)$

(ix) We have, $x^2 - 17x + 60$

$= x^2 - (12 + 5)x + 60 = x^2 - 12x - 5x + 60 = x(x - 12) - 5(x - 12)$

$= (x - 12)(x - 5)$

(x) We have, $x^2 + 4x - 77$

$x^2 + (11 - 7)x - 77 = x^2 + 11x - 7x - 77 = x(x + 11) - 7(x + 11)$

$= (x + 11)(x - 7)$

(xi) We have, $y^2 + 7y + 12$

$y^2 + (4 + 3)y + 12 = y^2 + 4y + 3y + 12 = y(y + 4) + 3(y + 4) = (y + 4)(y + 3)$

(xii) We have, $p^2 - 13p - 30$

$= p^2 - (15 - 2)p - 30 = p^2 - 15p + 2p - 30 = p(p - 15) + 2(p - 15)$

$= (p - 15)(p + 2)$

(xiii) We have, $p^2 - 16p - 80$

$= p^2 - (20 - 4)p - 80 = p^2 - 20p + 4p - 80 = p(p - 20) + 4(p - 20)$

$= (p - 20)(p + 4)$

Q. 92 Factorise the following using the identity $a^2 - b^2 = (a + b)(a - b)$.

(i) $x^2 - 9$ (ii) $4x^2 - 25y^2$

(iii) $4x^2 - 49y^2$ (iv) $3a^2b^3 - 27a^4b$

(v) $28ay^2 - 175ax^2$ (vi) $9x^2 - 1$

(vii) $25ax^2 - 25a$ (viii) $\frac{x^2}{9} - \frac{y^2}{25}$

(ix) $\frac{2p^2}{25} - 32q^2$ (x) $49x^2 - 36y^2$

(xi) $y^3 - \frac{y}{9}$ (xii) $\frac{x^2}{25} - 625$

(xiii) $\frac{x^2}{8} - \frac{y^2}{18}$ (xiv) $\frac{4x^2}{9} - \frac{9y^2}{16}$

(xv) $\frac{x^3y}{9} - \frac{xy^3}{16}$ (xvi) $1331x^3y - 11y^3x$

(xvii) $\frac{1}{36}a^2b^2 - \frac{16}{49}b^2c^2$ (xviii) $a^4 - (a - b)^4$

(xix) $x^4 - 1$ (xx) $y^4 - 625$

(xxi) $p^5 - 16p$ (xxii) $16x^4 - 81$

(xxiii) $x^4 - y^4$ (xxiv) $y^4 - 81$

(xxv) $16x^4 - 625y^4$ (xxvi) $(a - b)^2 - (b - c)^2$

(xxvii) $(x + y)^4 - (x - y)^4$ (xxviii) $x^4 - y^4 + x^2 - y^2$

(xxix) $8a^3 - 2a$ (xxx) $x^2 - \frac{y^2}{100}$

(xxxi) $9x^2 - (3y + z)^2$

Sol. (i) We have,

$$x^2 - 9 = x^2 - 3^2 = (x - 3)(x + 3) \quad [\because a^2 - b^2 = (a - b)(a + b)]$$

(ii) We have,

$$4x^2 - 25y^2 = (2x)^2 - (5y)^2 = (2x - 5y)(2x + 5y)$$

(iii) We have,

$$4x^2 - 49y^2 = (2x)^2 - (7y)^2 = (2x - 7y)(2x + 7y)$$

(iv) We have,

$$3a^2b^3 - 27a^4b = 3a^2b(b^2 - 9a^2) = 3a^2b[b^2 - (3a)^2]$$

$$= 3a^2b(b + 3a)(b - 3a)$$

(v) We have,

$$28ay^2 - 175ax^2 = 7a\,(4y^2 - 25x^2)$$
$$= 7a\,[(2y)^2 - (5x)^2] = 7a\,(2y - 5x)\,(2y + 5x)$$

(vi) We have,

$$9x^2 - 1 = (3x)^2 - 1^2 = (3x - 1)\,(3x + 1)$$

(vii) We have,

$$25ax^2 - 25a = 25a\,(x^2 - 1^2) = 25a\,(x - 1)\,(x + 1)$$

(viii) We have,

$$\frac{x^2}{9} - \frac{y^2}{25} = \left(\frac{x}{3}\right)^2 - \left(\frac{y}{5}\right)^2 = \left(\frac{x}{3} - \frac{y}{5}\right)\left(\frac{x}{3} + \frac{y}{5}\right)$$

(ix) We have,

$$\frac{2p^2}{25} - 32q^2 = 2\left(\frac{p^2}{25} - 16q^2\right) = 2\left[\left(\frac{p}{5}\right)^2 - (4q)^2\right] = 2\left(\frac{p}{5} + 4q\right)\left(\frac{p}{5} - 4q\right)$$

(x) We have,

$$49x^2 - 36y^2 = (7x)^2 - (6y)^2 = (7x - 6y)(7x + 6y)$$

(xi) We have,

$$y^3 - \frac{y}{9} = y\left(y^2 - \frac{1}{9}\right) = y\left[y^2 - \left(\frac{1}{3}\right)^2\right] = y\left(y + \frac{1}{3}\right)\left(y - \frac{1}{3}\right)$$

(xii) We have,

$$\frac{x^2}{25} - 625 = \left(\frac{x}{5}\right)^2 - (25)^2 = \left(\frac{x}{5} - 25\right)\left(\frac{x}{5} + 25\right)$$

(xiii) We have,

$$\frac{x^2}{8} - \frac{y^2}{18} = \frac{1}{2}\left(\frac{x^2}{4} - \frac{y^2}{9}\right) = \frac{1}{2}\left[\left(\frac{x}{2}\right)^2 - \left(\frac{y}{3}\right)^2\right]$$
$$= \frac{1}{2}\left(\frac{x}{2} + \frac{y}{3}\right)\left(\frac{x}{2} - \frac{y}{3}\right)$$

(xiv) We have,

$$\frac{4x^2}{9} - \frac{9y^2}{16} = \left(\frac{2x}{3}\right)^2 - \left(\frac{3y}{4}\right)^2 = \left(\frac{2x}{3} + \frac{3y}{4}\right)\left(\frac{2x}{3} - \frac{3y}{4}\right)$$

(xv) We have,

$$\frac{x^3y}{9} - \frac{xy^3}{16} = xy\left(\frac{x^2}{9} - \frac{y^2}{16}\right) = xy\left[\left(\frac{x}{3}\right)^2 - \left(\frac{y}{4}\right)^2\right] = xy\left(\frac{x}{3} + \frac{y}{4}\right)\left(\frac{x}{3} - \frac{y}{4}\right)$$

(xvi) We have,

$$1331x^3y - 11y^3x = (11)^3x^3y - 11y^3x = 11xy\,(11^2x^2 - y^2)$$
$$= 11xy\,[(11x)^2 - y^2] = 11xy\,(11x + y)\,(11x - y)$$

(xvii) We have,

$$\frac{1}{36}a^2b^2 - \frac{16}{49}b^2c^2 = \left(\frac{ab}{6}\right)^2 - \left(\frac{4bc}{7}\right)^2 = \left(\frac{ab}{6} + \frac{4bc}{7}\right)\left(\frac{ab}{6} - \frac{4bc}{7}\right)$$
$$= b^2\left(\frac{a}{6} + \frac{4c}{7}\right)\left(\frac{a}{6} - \frac{4c}{7}\right)$$

(xviii) We have,

$$a^4 - (a-b)^4 = (a^2)^2 - [(a-b)^2]^2 = [a^2 + (a-b)^2][a^2 - (a-b)^2]$$
$$= [a^2 + a^2 + b^2 - 2ab][a^2 - (a^2 + b^2 - 2ab)]$$
$$= [2a^2 + b^2 - 2ab][-b^2 + 2ab]$$
$$= (2a^2 + b^2 - 2ab)(2ab - b^2)$$

(xix) We have,

$$x^4 - 1 = (x^2)^2 - 1 = (x^2 + 1)(x^2 - 1)$$
$$= (x^2 + 1)(x + 1)(x - 1)$$

(xx) We have,

$$y^4 - 625 = (y^2)^2 - (25)^2$$
$$= (y^2 + 25)(y^2 - 25)$$
$$= (y^2 + 25)(y^2 - 5^2)$$
$$= (y^2 + 25)(y + 5)(y - 5)$$

(xxi) We have,

$$p^5 - 16p = p(p^4 - 16) = p[(p^2)^2 - 4^2]$$
$$= p(p^2 + 4)(p^2 - 4)$$
$$= p(p^2 + 4)(p^2 - 2^2)$$
$$= p(p^2 + 4)(p + 2)(p - 2)$$

(xxii) We have,

$$16x^4 - 81 = (4x^2)^2 - 9^2 = (4x^2 + 9)(4x^2 - 9)$$
$$= (4x^2 + 9)[(2x)^2 - 3^2]$$
$$= (4x^2 + 9)(2x + 3)(2x - 3)$$

(xxiii) We have,

$$x^4 - y^4 = (x^2)^2 - (y^2)^2$$
$$= (x^2 + y^2)(x^2 - y^2)$$
$$= (x^2 + y^2)(x + y)(x - y)$$

(xxiv) We have,

$$y^4 - 81 = (y^2)^2 - (9)^2 = (y^2 + 9)(y^2 - 9)$$
$$= (y^2 + 9)[(y)^2 - (3)^2]$$
$$= (y^2 + 9)(y + 3)(y - 3)$$

(xxv) We have,

$$16x^4 - 625y^4 = (4x^2)^2 - (25y^2)^2 = (4x^2 + 25y^2)(4x^2 - 25y^2)$$
$$= (4x^2 + 25y^2)[(2x)^2 - (5y)^2]$$
$$= (4x^2 + 25y^2)(2x + 5y)(2x - 5y)$$

(xxvi) We have,

$$(a-b)^2 - (b-c)^2 = (a - b + b - c)(a - b - b + c)(a - c)(a - 2b + c)$$

(xxvii) We have,

$$(x + y)^4 - (x - y)^4 = [(x + y)^2]^2 - [(x - y)^2]^2$$
$$= [(x + y)^2 + (x - y)^2][(x + y)^2 - (x - y)^2]$$

$= (x^2 + y^2 + 2xy + x^2 + y^2 - 2xy)(x + y + x - y)(x + y - x + y)$

$= (2x^2 + 2y^2)(2x)(2y) = 2(x^2 + y^2)(2x)(2y) = 8xy(x^2 + y^2)$

(xxviii) We have,

$x^4 - y^4 + x^2 - y^2 = (x^2)^2 - (y^2)^2 + (x^2 - y^2) = (x^2 + y^2)(x^2 - y^2) + (x^2 - y^2)$

$= (x^2 - y^2)(x^2 + y^2 + 1) = (x + y)(x - y)(x^2 + y^2 + 1)$

(xxix) We have,

$8a^3 - 2a = 2a(4a^2 - 1)$

$= 2a[(2a)^2 - (1)^2] = 2a(2a + 1)(2a - 1)$

(xxx) We have,

$$x^2 - \frac{y^2}{100} = x^2 - \left(\frac{y}{10}\right)^2 = \left(x + \frac{y}{10}\right)\left(x - \frac{y}{10}\right)$$

(xxxi) We have,

$9x^2 - (3y + z)^2 = (3x)^2 - (3y + z)^2 = (3x + 3y + z)(3x - 3y - z)$

Q. 93 The following expressions are the areas of rectangles. Find the possible lengths and breadths of these rectangles.

(i) $x^2 - 6x + 8$ (ii) $x^2 - 3x + 2$

(iii) $x^2 - 7x + 10$ (iv) $x^2 + 19x - 20$

(v) $x^2 + 9x + 20$

Sol. (i) Given, area of a rectangle $= x^2 - 6x + 8$

Now, we have to find the possible length and breadth of the rectangle.

So, we factorise the given expression.

i.e. $x^2 - 6x + 8 = x^2 - (4 + 2)x + 8 = x^2 - 4x - 2x + 8$

$= x(x - 4) - 2(x - 4) = (x - 4)(x - 2)$

Since, area of a rectangle = Length × Breadth. Hence, the possible length and breadth are $(x - 4)$ and $(x - 2)$.

(ii) We have,

Area of rectangle $= x^2 - 3x + 2$

$= x^2 - (2 + 1)x + 2 = x^2 - 2x - x + 2$

$= x(x - 2) - 1(x - 2) = (x - 2)(x - 1)$

∴ The possible length and breadth are $(x - 2)$ and $(x - 1)$.

(iii) We have,

Area of rectangle $= x^2 - 7x + 10$

$= x^2 - (5 + 2)x + 10 = x^2 - 5x - 2x + 10$

$= x(x - 5) - 2(x - 5) = (x - 5)(x - 2)$

∴ The possible length and breadth are $(x - 5)$ and $(x - 2)$.

(iv) We have,

Area of rectangle $= x^2 + 19x - 20$

$= x^2 + (20 - 1)x - 20 = x^2 + 20x - x - 20$

$= x(x + 20) - 1(x + 20) = (x + 20)(x - 1)$

∴ The possible length and breadth are $(x + 20)$ and $(x - 1)$.

(v) We have, area of rectangle

$$= x^2 + 9x + 20$$
$$= x^2 + (5+4)x + 20 = x^2 + 5x + 4x + 20$$
$$= x(x+5) + 4(x+5) = (x+5)(x+4)$$

$\therefore$ The possible length and breadth are $(x + 5)$ and $(x + 4)$.

Q. 94 Carry out the following divisions:

(i) $51x^3y^2z \div 17xyz$ (ii) $76x^3yz^3 \div 19x^2y^2$

(iii) $17ab^2c^3 \div (-abc^2)$ (iv) $-121p^3q^3r^3 \div (-11xy^2z^3)$

Sol. (i) We have,

$$51x^3y^2z \div 17xyz = \frac{51x^3y^2z}{17xyz}$$
$$= \frac{17\times 3\times x\times x\times x\times y\times y\times z}{17\times x\times y\times z} = 3x^2y$$

(ii) We have,

$$76x^3yz^3 \div 19x^2y^2 = \frac{76x^3yz^3}{19x^2y^2}$$
$$= \frac{4\times 19\times x\times x\times x\times y\times z\times z\times z}{19\times x\times x\times y\times y} = \frac{4xz^3}{y}$$

(iii) We have,

$$17ab^2c^3 \div (-abc^2) = \frac{17ab^2c^3}{-abc^2} = \frac{17\times a\times b\times b\times c\times c\times c}{-a\times b\times c\times c} = -17bc$$

(iv) We have,

$$-121p^3q^3r^3 \div (-11xy^2z^3) = \frac{-121p^3q^3r^3}{-11xy^2z^3}$$
$$= \frac{-11\times 11\times p\times p\times p\times q\times q\times q\times r\times r\times r}{-11\times x\times y\times y\times z\times z\times z} = \frac{11p^3q^3r^3}{xy^2z^3}$$

Q. 95 Perform the following divisions:

(i) $(3pqr - 6p^2q^2r^2) \div 3pq$

(ii) $(ax^3 - bx^2 + cx) \div (-dx)$

(iii) $(x^3y^3 + x^2y^3 - xy^4 + xy) \div xy$

(iv) $(-qrxy + pryz - rxyz) \div (-xyz)$

Sol. (i) We have,

$$(3pqr - 6p^2q^2r^2) \div 3pq = \frac{3pqr - 6p^2q^2r^2}{3pq} = \frac{3pqr}{3pq} - \frac{6p^2q^2r^2}{3pq}$$
$$= r - \frac{2\times 3\times p\times p\times q\times q\times r\times r}{3\times p\times q}$$
$$= r - 2pqr^2$$

(ii) We have,

$$(ax^3 - bx^2 + cx) \div (-dx) = \frac{ax^3 - bx^2 + cx}{-dx}$$

$$= \frac{ax^3}{-dx} + \frac{bx^2}{dx} + \frac{cx}{-dx} = \frac{a \times x \times x \times x}{-d \times x} + \frac{b \times x \times x}{d \times x} + \frac{c \times x}{-d \times x}$$

$$= -\frac{a}{d}x^2 + \frac{b}{d}x - \frac{c}{d}$$

(iii) We have,

$$(x^3y^3 + x^2y^3 - xy^4 + xy) \div xy$$

$$= \frac{x^3y^3 + x^2y^3 - xy^4 + xy}{xy} = \frac{x^3y^3}{xy} + \frac{x^2y^3}{xy} - \frac{xy^4}{xy} + \frac{xy}{xy}$$

$$= \frac{x \times x \times x \times y \times y \times y}{x \times y} + \frac{x \times x \times y \times y \times y}{x \times y} - \frac{x \times y \times y \times y \times y}{x \times y} + \frac{x \times y}{x \times y}$$

$$= x^2y^2 + xy^2 - y^3 + 1$$

(iv) We have,

$$(-qrxy + pryz - rxyz) \div (-xyz)$$

$$= \frac{-qrxy + pryz - rxyz}{-xyz} = \frac{-qrxy}{-xyz} + \frac{pryz}{-xyz} - \frac{rxyz}{-xyz} = \frac{qr}{z} - \frac{pr}{x} + r$$

Q. 96 Factorise the expressions and divide them as directed.

(i) $(x^2 - 22x + 117) \div (x - 13)$

(ii) $(x^3 + x^2 - 132x) \div x(x - 11)$

(iii) $(2x^3 - 12x^2 + 16x) \div (x - 2)(x - 4)$

(iv) $(9x^2 - 4) \div (3x + 2)$

(v) $(3x^2 - 48) \div (x - 4)$

(vi) $(x^4 - 16) \div x^3 + 2x^2 + 4x + 8$

(vii) $(3x^4 - 1875) \div (3x^2 - 75)$

Sol. (i) We have,

$$(x^2 - 22x + 117) \div (x - 13)$$

$$= \frac{x^2 - 22x + 117}{x - 13} = \frac{x^2 - 13x - 9x + 117}{x - 13} = \frac{x(x - 13) - 9(x - 13)}{x - 13}$$

$$= \frac{(x - 13)(x - 9)}{x - 13} = x - 9$$

(ii) We have,

$$(x^3 + x^2 - 132x) \div x(x - 11)$$

$$= \frac{x^3 + x^2 - 132x}{x(x - 11)} = \frac{x(x^2 + x - 132)}{x(x - 11)} = \frac{x^2 + 12x - 11x - 132}{x - 11}$$

$$= \frac{x(x + 12) - 11(x + 12)}{x - 11} = \frac{(x + 12)(x - 11)}{x - 11}$$

$$= x + 12$$

(iii) We have,

$(2x^3 - 12x^2 + 16x) \div (x-2)(x-4)$

$$= \frac{2x^3 - 12x^2 + 16x}{(x-2)(x-4)} = \frac{2x(x^2 - 6x + 8)}{(x-2)(x-4)}$$

$$= \frac{2x(x^2 - 4x - 2x + 8)}{(x-2)(x-4)}$$

$$= \frac{2x[x(x-4) - 2(x-4)]}{(x-2)(x-4)} = \frac{2x(x-4)(x-2)}{(x-2)(x-4)} = 2x$$

(iv) We have,

$$(9x^2 - 4) \div (3x+2) = \frac{9x^2 - 4}{3x+2} = \frac{(3x)^2 - (2)^2}{3x+2}$$

$$= \frac{(3x+2)(3x-2)}{3x+2} \qquad [\because a^2 - b^2 = (a+b)(a-b)]$$

$$= 3x - 2$$

(v) We have,

$$(3x^2 - 48) \div (x-4) = \frac{3x^2 - 48}{x-4} = \frac{3(x^2 - 16)}{x-4}$$

$$= \frac{3(x^2 - 4^2)}{x-4}$$

$$= \frac{3(x+4)(x-4)}{x-4} \qquad [\because a^2 - b^2 = (a+b)(a-b)]$$

$$= 3(x+4)$$

(vi) We have,

$(x^4 - 16) \div x^3 + 2x^2 + 4x + 8$

$$= \frac{x^4 - 16}{x^3 + 2x^2 + 4x + 8} = \frac{(x^2)^2 - 4^2}{x^2(x+2) + 4(x+2)}$$

$$[\because a^2 - b^2 = (a+b)(a-b)]$$

$$= \frac{(x^2+4)(x^2-4)}{(x^2+4)(x+2)} = \frac{x^2 - 2^2}{x+2} = \frac{(x+2)(x-2)}{x+2} = x - 2$$

(vii) We have,

$$(3x^4 - 1875) \div (3x^2 - 75) = \frac{3x^4 - 1875}{3x^2 - 75} = \frac{x^4 - 625}{x^2 - 25} = \frac{(x^2)^2 - (25)^2}{x^2 - 25}$$

$$= \frac{(x^2 + 25)(x^2 - 25)}{(x^2 - 25)} = x^2 + 25$$

Q. 97 **The area of a square is given by $4x^2 + 12xy + 9y^2$. Find the side of the square.**

Sol. We have,

Area of square $= 4x^2 + 12xy + 9y^2$

So, we factorise the given expression.

$\therefore \quad 4x^2 + 12xy + 9y^2 = (2x)^2 + 2 \times 2x \times 3y + (3y)^2$ $\quad [\because a^2 + 2ab + b^2 = (a+b)^2]$

$= (2x + 3y)^2$

Since, area of a square having side length a is a^2. Hence, side of the given square is $2x + 3y$.

Q. 98 **The area of a square is $9x^2 + 24xy + 16y^2$. Find the side of the square.**

Sol. We have,

Area of a square $= 9x^2 + 24xy + 16y^2 = (3x)^2 + 2 \times 3x \times 4y + (4y)^2$

$[\because a^2 + 2ab + b^2 = (a+b)^2]$

$= (3x + 4y)^2$

$\therefore$ The side of the square $= 3x + 4y$ $\quad [\because \text{area of square} = (\text{side})^2]$

Q. 99 **The area of a rectangle is $x^2 + 7x + 12$. If its breadth is $(x + 3)$, then find its length.**

Sol. Let the length of the rectangle be l.

Given, area of a rectangle $= x^2 + 7x + 12$

and breadth $= x + 3$

We know that,

Area of rectangle = Length × Breadth

$\Rightarrow \quad x^2 + 7x + 12 = l \times (x + 3)$

$$\Rightarrow \quad l = \frac{x^2 + 7x + 12}{x + 3} = \frac{x^2 + 4x + 3x + 12}{x + 3} = \frac{x(x+4) + 3(x+4)}{x+3} = \frac{(x+4)(x+3)}{x+3} = x + 4$$

Hence, the length of rectangle $= x + 4$

Q. 100 **The curved surface area of a cylinder is $2\pi(y^2 - 7y + 12)$ and its radius is $(y - 3)$. Find the height of the cylinder (CSA of cylinder $= 2\pi rh$)**

Sol. Let the height of cylinder be h.

Given, the curved surface area of a cylinder $= 2\pi(y^2 - 7y + 12)$

and radius of cylinder $= y - 3$

We know that,

Curved surface area of cylinder $= 2\pi rh$

$\therefore \quad 2\pi rh = 2\pi(y^2 - 7y + 12)$

$\Rightarrow \quad 2\pi rh = 2\pi(y^2 - 4y - 3y + 12) = 2\pi[y(y-4) - 3(y-4)] = 2\pi(y-3)(y-4)$

$\Rightarrow \quad 2\pi rh = 2\pi r(y - 4)$ $\quad [\because r = (y - 3), \text{ given}]$

On comparing the both sides, we get $h = y - 4$

Hence, the height of the cylinder is $y - 4$.

Q. 101 **The area of a circle is given by the expression $\pi x^2 + 6\pi x + 9\pi$. Find the radius of the circle.**

Sol. We have,

Area of a circle $= \pi x^2 + 6\pi x + 9\pi = \pi(x^2 + 6x + 9)$

$\Rightarrow \quad \pi r^2 = \pi(x^2 + 3x + 3x + 9)$ [$\because$ area of a circle $= \pi r^2$, where r is the radius]

$\Rightarrow \quad \pi r^2 = \pi[x(x + 3) + 3(x + 3)] = \pi(x + 3)(x + 3) = \pi(x + 3)^2$

$\Rightarrow \quad \pi r^2 = \pi(x + 3)^2$

On comparing both sides, $r^2 = (x + 3)^2 \Rightarrow r = x + 3$

Hence, the radius of circle is $x + 3$.

Q. 102 **The sum of first n natural numbers is given by the expression $\frac{n^2}{2} + \frac{n}{2}$. Factorise this expression.**

Sol. We have, the sum of first n natural numbers

$$= \frac{n^2}{2} + \frac{n}{2}$$

Factorisation of given expression $= \frac{1}{2}(n^2 + n) = \frac{1}{2}n(n + 1)$ [taking n as common]

Q. 103 **The sum of $(x + 5)$ observations is $x^4 - 625$. Find the mean of the observations.**

Sol. We have, the sum of $(x + 5)$ observations $= x^4 - 625$

We know that, the mean of the n observations $x_1, x_2, \ldots x_n$ is given by $\frac{x_1 + x_2 + \ldots x_n}{n}$.

$\therefore$ The mean of $(x + 5)$ observations

$$= \frac{\text{Sum of } (x + 5) \text{ observations}}{x + 5} = \frac{x^4 - 625}{x + 5} = \frac{(x^2)^2 - (25)^2}{x + 5}$$

$$= \frac{(x^2 + 25)(x^2 - 25)}{x + 5} \quad [\because a^2 - b^2 = (a + b)(a - b)]$$

$$= \frac{(x^2 + 25)[(x)^2 - (5)^2]}{x + 5}$$

$$= \frac{(x^2 + 25)(x + 5)(x - 5)}{(x + 5)} = (x^2 + 25)(x - 5)$$

Q. 104 **The height of a triangle is $x^4 + y^4$ and its base is $14xy$. Find the area of the triangle.**

Sol. Given, the height of a triangle and its base are $x^4 + y^4$ and $14xy$, respectively.

We know that, the area of a triangle $= \frac{1}{2} \times \text{Base} \times \text{Height} = \frac{1}{2} \times 14xy \times (x^4 + y^4)$

$$= 7xy(x^4 + y^4)$$

Q. 105 **The cost of a chocolate is ₹ $(x+4)$ and Rohit bought $(x+4)$ chocolates. Find the total amount paid by him in terms of x. If $x = 10$, find the amount paid by him.**

Sol. Given, cost of a chocolate = ₹ $(x + 4)$

Rohit bought $(x + 4)$ chocolates.

$\therefore$ The cost of $(x + 4)$ chocolates

= Cost of one chocolate × Number of chocolates = $(x + 4)(x + 4) = (x + 4)^2$

$= x^2 + 8x + 16$ $\quad [\because (a + b)^2 = a^2 + 2ab + b^2]$

$\therefore$ The total amount paid by Rohit = ₹$(x^2 + 8x + 16)$

Now, if $x = 10$. Then, the amount paid by Rohit = $10^2 + 8 \times 10 + 16 = 100 + 80 + 16 =$ ₹196

Q. 106 **The base of a parallelogram is $(2x + 3)$ units and the corresponding height is $(2x - 3)$ units. Find the area of the parallelogram in terms of x. What will be the area of a parallelogram of $x = 30$ units?**

Sol. We have, the base and the corresponding height of a parallelogram are $(2x + 3)$ units and $(2x - 3)$ units, respectively.

$\because$ Area of a parallelogram = Base × Height

$= (2x + 3) \times (2x - 3) = (2x)^2 - (3)^2$ $\quad [\because (a + b)(a - b) = a^2 - b^2]$

$= (4x^2 - 9)$ sq units

Now, if $x = 10$. Then, the area of the parallelogram = $4 \times (10)^2 - 9 = 400 - 9 = 391$ sq units

Q. 107 **The radius of a circle is $7ab - 7bc - 14ac$. Find the circumference of the circle, $\left(\pi = \frac{22}{7}\right)$.**

Sol. We have, radius of the circle = $7ab - 7bc - 14ac = r$ [say]

We know that,

$\because$ The circumference of the circle = $2\pi r$

$$= 2 \times \frac{22}{7} \times (7ab - 7bc - 14ac)$$

$$= \frac{44}{7} \times 7\,(ab - bc - 2ac)$$

$$= 44[ab - c(b + 2a)]$$

Q. 108 **If $p + q = 12$ and $pq = 22$, then find $p^2 + q^2$.**

Sol. Given, $p + q = 12$ and $pq = 22$

Since,

$(p + q)^2 = p^2 + q^2 + 2pq$ $\quad$ [using the identity, $(a + b)^2 = a^2 + b^2 + 2ab$]

$\therefore \quad (12)^2 = p^2 + q^2 + 2 \times 22$

$\Rightarrow \quad p^2 + q^2 = (12)^2 - 44$

$\Rightarrow \quad p^2 + q^2 = 144 - 44 = 100$

Q. 109 If $a+b=25$ and $a^2+b^2=225$, then find ab.

Sol. Given, $a+b=25$ and $a^2+b^2=225$

We know that,

$$(a+b)^2 = a^2+b^2+2ab \quad \text{[an algebraic identity]}$$

$\Rightarrow \quad (25)^2 = 225 + 2ab$

$\Rightarrow \quad 2ab = (25)^2 - 225$

$\Rightarrow \quad 2ab = 625 - 225$

$\Rightarrow \quad 2ab = 400$

$\Rightarrow \quad ab = \dfrac{400}{2}$

$\Rightarrow \quad ab = 200$

Q. 110 If $x-y=13$ and $xy=28$, then find x^2+y^2.

Sol. Given, $x-y=13$ and $xy=28$

Since, $(x-y)^2 = x^2+y^2-2xy$

[using the identity, $(a-b)^2 = a^2+b^2-2ab$]

$\therefore \quad (13)^2 = x^2+y^2-2\times 28$

$\Rightarrow \quad x^2+y^2 = (13)^2 + 56$

$\Rightarrow \quad x^2+y^2 = 169+56$

$\Rightarrow \quad x^2+y^2 = 225$

Q. 111 If $m-n=16$ and $m^2+n^2=400$, then find mn.

Sol. Given, $m-n=16$ and $m^2+n^2=400$.

Since, $(m-n)^2 = m^2+n^2-2mn$

[using the identity, $(a-b)^2 = a^2+b^2-2ab$]

$\therefore \quad (16)^2 = 400 - 2mn$

$\Rightarrow \quad 2mn = 400 - (16)^2$

$\Rightarrow \quad 2mn = 400 - 256$

$\Rightarrow \quad 2mn = 144$

$\Rightarrow \quad mn = \dfrac{144}{2}$

$\Rightarrow \quad mn = 72$

Q. 112 If $a^2+b^2=74$ and $ab=35$, then find $a+b$.

Sol. Given, $a^2+b^2=74$ and $ab=35$

Since, $(a+b)^2 = a^2+b^2+2ab$

[using the identity, $(a+b)^2 = a^2+b^2+2ab$]

$\therefore \quad (a+b)^2 = 74 + 2\times 35$

$\therefore \quad (a+b)^2 = 74 + 2 \times 35$

$\Rightarrow \quad (a+b)^2 = 144$

$\Rightarrow \quad a + b = \sqrt{144}$ [taking square root]

$\Rightarrow \quad a + b = 12$ [rejecting –ve sign]

Q. 113 Verify the following:

(i) $(ab+bc)(ab-bc)+(bc+ca)(bc-ca)+(ca+ab)(ca-ab)=0$

(ii) $(a+b+c)(a^2+b^2+c^2-ab-bc-ca)=a^3+b^3+c^3-3abc$

(iii) $(p-q)(p^2+pq+q^2)=p^3-q^3$

(iv) $(m+n)(m^2-mn+n^2)=m^3+n^3$

(v) $(a+b)(a+b)(a+b)=a^3+3a^2b+3ab^2+b^3$

(vi) $(a-b)(a-b)(a-b)=a^3-3a^2b+3ab^2-b^3$

(vii) $(a^2-b^2)(a^2+b^2)+(b^2-c^2)(b^2+c^2)+(c^2-a^2)(c^2+a^2)=0$

(viii) $(5x+8)^2-160x=(5x-8)^2$

(ix) $(7p-13q)^2+364pq=(7p+13q)^2$

(x) $\left(\frac{3p}{7}+\frac{7}{6p}\right)^2-\left(\frac{3p}{7}-\frac{7}{6p}\right)^2=2$

Sol. (i) Taking LHS $= (ab+bc)(ab-bc)+(bc+ca)(bc-ca)+(ca+ab)(ca-ab)$

$= [(ab)^2-(bc)^2]+[(bc)^2-(ca)^2]+[(ca)^2-(ab)^2]$

[using the identity, $(a+b)(a-b)=a^2-b^2$]

$= a^2b^2-b^2c^2+b^2c^2-c^2a^2+c^2a^2-a^2b^2=0$

= RHS [cancelling the like terms having opposite signs]

Hence verified.

(ii) Taking LHS $= (a+b+c)(a^2+b^2+c^2-ab-bc-ca)$

$= a(a^2+b^2+c^2-ab-bc-ca)+b(a^2+b^2+c^2-ab-bc-ca)$
$+c(a^2+b^2+c^2-ab-bc-ca)$

[distributive law]

$= a^3+ab^2+ac^2-a^2b-abc-a^2c+ba^2+b^3+bc^2$
$-b^2a-b^2c-bca+ca^2+cb^2+c^3-cab-c^2b-c^2a$

$= a^3+b^3+c^3-3abc =$ RHS **Hence verified.**

(iii) Taking LHS $= (p-q)(p^2+pq+q^2)$

$= p(p^2+pq+q^2)-q(p^2+pq+q^2)$

$= p^3+p^2q+pq^2-qp^2-pq^2-q^3 = p^3-q^3 =$ RHS **Hence verified.**

(iv) Taking LHS $= (m+n)(m^2-mn+n^2)$

$= m(m^2-mn+n^2)+n(m^2-mn+n^2)$

$= m^3-m^2n+mn^2+nm^2-mn^2+n^3 = m^3+n^3 =$ RHS **Hence verified.**

(v) Taking LHS $= (a+b)(a+b)(a+b)$

$= (a+b)(a+b)^2$

$= (a+b)(a^2+b^2+2ab)$ [using the identity, $(a+b)^2 = a^2+2ab+b^2$]

$= a(a^2+2ab+b^2)+b(a^2+2ab+b^2)$

$= a^3+2a^2b+ab^2+ba^2+2ab^2+b^3$

$= a^3+3a^2b+3ab^2+b^3$ [adding like terms]

$=$ RHS **Hence verified.**

(vi) Taking LHS $= (a-b)(a-b)(a-b)$

$= (a-b)(a-b)^2$

$= (a-b)(a^2-2ab+b^2)$ [using the identity, $(a-b)^2 = a^2-2ab+b^2$]

$= a(a^2-2ab+b^2)-b(a^2-2ab+b^2)$

$= a^3-2a^2b+ab^2-ba^2+2ab^2-b^3$

$= a^3-3a^2b+3ab^2-b^3$ [adding like terms]

$=$ RHS **Hence verified.**

(vii) Taking LHS $= (a^2-b^2)(a^2+b^2)+(b^2-c^2)(b^2+c^2)+(c^2-a^2)(c^2+a^2)$

$= (a^4-b^4+b^4-c^4+c^4-a^4)$ [using the identity, $(a-b)(a+b) = a^2-b^2$]

$= 0 =$ RHS **Hence verified.**

(viii) Taking LHS $= (5x+8)^2-160x$

$= (5x)^2+(8)^2+2\times 5x\times 8-160x$ [using the identity, $(a+b)^2 = a^2+2ab+b^2$]

$= (5x)^2+(8)^2+80x-160x$

$= (5x)^2+(8)^2-80x$

$= (5x)^2+(8)^2-2\times 5x\cdot 8$

$= (5x-8)^2$ [$\because a^2+b^2-2ab = (a-b)^2$]

$=$ RHS **Hence verified.**

(ix) Taking LHS $= (7p-13q)^2+364pq$

$= (7p)^2+(13q)^2-2\times 7p\times 13q+364pq$

$= (7p)^2+(13q)^2-182pq+364pq$

$= (7p)^2+(13q)^2+182pq$

$= (7p)^2+(13q)^2+2\times 7p\times 13q = (7p+13q)^2 =$ RHS **Hence verified.**

(x) Taking LHS $= \left(\frac{3p}{7}+\frac{7}{6p}\right)^2-\left(\frac{3p}{7}-\frac{7}{6p}\right)^2$

$= \left[\left(\frac{3p}{7}+\frac{7}{6p}\right)+\left(\frac{3p}{7}-\frac{7}{6p}\right)\right]\left[\left(\frac{3p}{7}+\frac{7}{6p}\right)-\left(\frac{3p}{7}-\frac{7}{6p}\right)\right]$

[using the identity, $a^2-b^2 = (a+b)(a-b)$]

$= \left(\frac{3p}{7}+\frac{7}{6p}+\frac{3p}{7}-\frac{7}{6p}\right)\left(\frac{3p}{7}+\frac{7}{6p}-\frac{3p}{7}+\frac{7}{6p}\right) = \frac{6p}{7}\times\frac{14}{6p} = 2 =$ RHS

Hence verified.

Q. 114 Find the value of a, if

(i) $8a = 35^2 - 27^2$

(ii) $9a = 76^2 - 67^2$

(iii) $pqa = (3p + q)^2 - (3p - q)^2$

(iv) $pq^2a = (4pq + 3q)^2 - (4pq - 3q)^2$

Sol. (i) We have,

$$8a = 35^2 - 27^2$$

$\Rightarrow$ $8a = (35 + 27)(35 - 27)$ [using the identity, $a^2 - b^2 = (a + b)(a - b)$]

$\Rightarrow$ $8a = 62 \times 8$

$\Rightarrow$ $a = \dfrac{62 \times 8}{8}$

$\Rightarrow$ $a = 62$

(ii) We have, $9a = (76)^2 - (67)^2$

$\Rightarrow$ $9a = (76 + 67)(76 - 67)$ [using the identity, $a^2 - b^2 = (a + b)(a - b)$]

$\Rightarrow$ $9a = 143 \times 9$

$\Rightarrow$ $a = \dfrac{143 \times 9}{9}$

$\Rightarrow$ $a = 143$

(iii) We have, $pqa = (3p + q)^2 - (3p - q)^2$

$\Rightarrow$ $pqa = [(3p + q) + (3p - q)][(3p + q) - (3p - q)]$

[using the identity, $a^2 - b^2 = (a + b)(a - b)$]

$\Rightarrow$ $pqa = [(3p + q + 3p - q)][3p + q - 3p + q]$

$\Rightarrow$ $pqa = 6p \times 2q$

$\Rightarrow$ $a = \dfrac{6p \times 2q}{pq} = \dfrac{(6 \times 2)pq}{pq}$

$\Rightarrow$ $a = 12$

(iv) We have,

$$pq^2a = (4pq + 3q)^2 - (4pq - 3q)^2$$

$\Rightarrow$ $= [(4pq + 3q) + (4pq - 3q)][(4pq + 3q) - (4pq - 3q)]$

[using the identity, $a^2 - b^2 = (a + b)(a - b)$]

$= (4pq + 3q + 4pq - 3q)(4pq + 3q - 4pq + 3q)$

$= 8pq \times 6q$

$\Rightarrow$ $pq^2a = 48pq^2$

$\Rightarrow$ $a = \dfrac{48pq^2}{pq^2}$

$\Rightarrow$ $a = 48$

Q. 115 What should be added to $4c(-a + b + c)$ to obtain $3a(a + b + c) - 2b(a - b + c)$?

Sol. Let x be added to the given expression $4c(-a + b + c)$ to obtain $3a(a + b + c) - 2b(a - b + c)$

i.e. $x + 4c(-a + b + c) = 3a(a + b + c) - 2b(a - b + c)$

$\Rightarrow$ $x = 3a(a + b + c) - 2b(a - b + c) - 4c(-a + b + c)$

$= 3a^2 + 3ab + 3ac - 2ba + 2b^2 - 2bc + 4ca - 4cb - 4c^2$

$\Rightarrow$ $x = 3a^2 + ab + 7ac + 2b^2 - 6bc - 4c^2$ [adding the like terms]

Q. 116 Subtract $b(b^2 + b - 7) + 5$ from $3b^2 - 8$ and find the value of expression obtained for $b = -3$.

Sol. We have,

Required difference $= (3b^2 - 8) - [b(b^2 + b - 7) + 5]$

$= 3b^2 - 8 - b(b^2 + b - 7) - 5$

$= 3b^2 - 8 - b^3 - b^2 + 7b - 5 = -b^3 + 2b^2 + 7b - 13$

Now, if $b = -3$

The value of above expression $= -(-3)^3 + 2(-3)^2 + 7(-3) - 13$

$= -(-27) + 2 \times 9 - 21 - 13$

$= 27 + 18 - 21 - 13$

$= 45 - 34 = 11$

Q. 117 If $x - \frac{1}{x} = 7$, then find the value of $x^2 + \frac{1}{x^2}$.

Sol. Given, $x - \frac{1}{x} = 7$.

Since, $\left(x - \frac{1}{x}\right)^2 = x^2 + \frac{1}{x^2} - 2 \cdot x \cdot \frac{1}{x}$ [using the identity, $(a - b)^2 = a^2 + b^2 - 2ab$]

$\therefore$ $7^2 = x^2 + \frac{1}{x^2} - 2$

$\Rightarrow$ $x^2 + \frac{1}{x^2} = 49 + 2$

$\Rightarrow$ $x^2 + \frac{1}{x^2} = 51$

Q. 118 Factorise $x^2 + \frac{1}{x^2} + 2 - 3x - \frac{3}{x}$.

Sol. We have, $x^2 + \frac{1}{x^2} + 2 - 3x - \frac{3}{x}$

$= x^2 + \frac{1}{x^2} + 2 \cdot x \cdot \frac{1}{x} - 3\left(x + \frac{1}{x}\right)$

$= \left(x + \frac{1}{x}\right)^2 - 3\left(x + \frac{1}{x}\right)$

[using the identity, $a^2 + b^2 + 2ab = (a + b)^2$]

$= \left(x + \frac{1}{x}\right)\left(x + \frac{1}{x} - 3\right)$ $\left[\text{taking } \left(x + \frac{1}{x}\right) \text{ as common}\right]$

Q. 119 Factorise $p^4 + q^4 + p^2q^2$

Sol. We have, $p^4 + q^4 + p^2q^2$

$= p^4 + q^4 + 2p^2q^2 - 2p^2q^2 + p^2q^2$ [adding and subtracting $2p^2q^2$]

$= p^4 + q^4 + 2p^2q^2 - p^2q^2$

$= [(p^2)^2 + (q^2)^2 + 2p^2q^2] - p^2q^2$

[using the identity, $a^2 + b^2 + 2ab = (a+b)^2$]

$= (p^2 + q^2)^2 - (pq)^2$

$= (p^2 + q^2 + pq)(p^2 + q^2 - pq)$ [using the identity, $a^2 - b^2 = (a+b)(a-b)$]

Q. 120 Find the value of

(i) $\dfrac{6.25 \times 6.25 - 1.75 \times 1.75}{4.5}$ (ii) $\dfrac{198 \times 198 - 102 \times 102}{96}$

Sol. (i) We have, $\dfrac{6.25 \times 6.25 - 1.75 \times 1.75}{4.5} = \dfrac{(6.25)^2 - (1.75)^2}{4.5}$

$= \dfrac{(6.25 + 1.75)(6.25 - 1.75)}{4.5}$ [using the identity, $a^2 - b^2 = (a+b)(a-b)$]

$= \dfrac{8 \times 4.5}{4.5} = 8$

(ii) We have,

$\dfrac{198 \times 198 - 102 \times 102}{96} = \dfrac{(198)^2 - (102)^2}{96} = \dfrac{(198 + 102)(198 - 102)}{96}$

$= \dfrac{300 \times 96}{96} = 300$ [using the identity, $a^2 - b^2 = (a-b)(a+b)$]

Q. 121 The product of two expressions is $x^5 + x^3 + x$. If one of them is $x^2 + x + 1$, find the other.

Sol. We have, product of two expressions $x^5 + x^3 + x$ and one is $x^2 + x + 1$.

Let the other expression be A. Then,

$A \cdot (x^2 + x + 1) = x^5 + x^3 + x$

$\Rightarrow \quad A = \dfrac{x^5 + x^3 + x}{x^2 + x + 1} = \dfrac{x(x^4 + x^2 + 1)}{x^2 + x + 1}$

$\Rightarrow \quad A = \dfrac{x(x^4 + 2x^2 - x^2 + 1)}{x^2 + x + 1} = \dfrac{x(x^4 + 2x^2 + 1 - x^2)}{x^2 + x + 1}$

[adding and subtracting x^2 in numerator term]

$= \dfrac{x[(x^4 + 2x^2 + 1) - x^2]}{x^2 + x + 1} = \dfrac{x[(x^2 + 1)^2 - x^2]}{x^2 + x + 1}$

$= \dfrac{x(x^2 + 1 + x)(x^2 + 1 - x)}{x^2 + x + 1}$ [using the identity, $a^2 - b^2 = (a+b)(a-b)$]

$= x(x^2 + 1 - x)$

Hence, the other expression is $x(x^2 - x + 1)$.

Q. 122 Find the length of the side of the given square, if area of the square is 625sq units and then find the value of x.

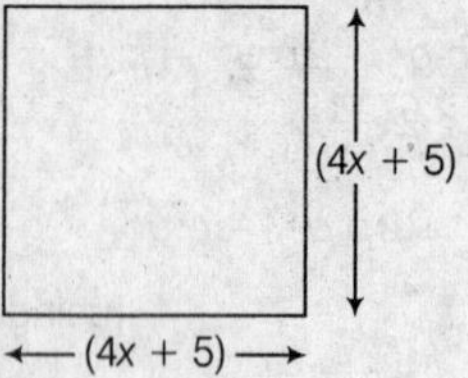

Sol. We have, a square having length of a side $(4x + 5)$ units and area is 625 sq units.

$\because$ Area of a square = $(\text{Side})^2$

$$(4x + 5)^2 = 625$$

$\Rightarrow (4x + 5)^2 = (25)^2$ [taking square root both sides and neglecting (–ve) sign]

$\Rightarrow 4x + 5 = 25$

$\Rightarrow 4x = 25 - 5$

$\Rightarrow 4x = 20$

$\Rightarrow x = 5$

Hence, side $= 4x + 5 = 4 \times 5 + 5 = 25$ units

Q. 123 Take suitable number of cards given in the adjoining diagram [G($x \times x$) representing x^2, R ($x \times 1$) representing x and Y (1×1) representing 1] to factorise the following expressions, by arranging to cards in the form of rectangles: (i) $2x^2 + 6x + 4$ (ii) $x^2 + 4x + 4$. Factorise $2x^2 + 6x + 4$ by using the figure.

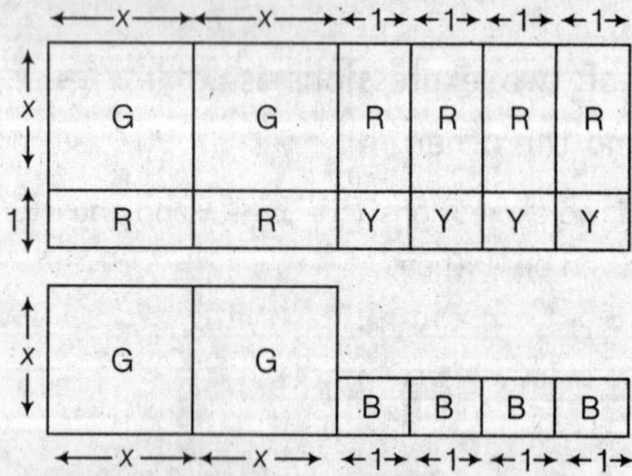

Calculate the area of figure.

Sol. The given information is incomplete for solution of this question.

Q. 124 The figure shows the dimensions of a wall having a window and a door of a room. Write an algebraic expression for the area of the wall to be painted.

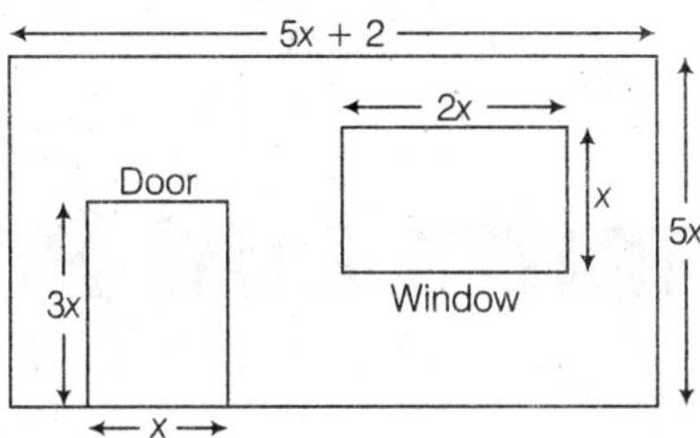

Sol. We have a wall of dimension $5x \times (5x + 2)$ having a window and a door of dimension $(2x \times x)$ and $(3x \times x)$, respectively.

Then, area of the window $= 2x \times x = 2x^2$ sq units

Area of the door $= 3x \times x = 3x^2$ sq units

and area of wall $= (5x + 2) \times 5x = (25x^2 + 10x)$ sq units

Now, area of the required part of the wall to be painted

$= \text{Area of the wall} - (\text{Area of the window} + \text{Area of the door})$

$= 25x^2 + 10x - (2x^2 + 3x^2)$

$= 25x^2 + 10x - 5x^2 = 20x^2 + 10x$

$= 2 \times 2 \times 5 \times x \times x + 2 \times 5 \times x$

$= 2 \times 5 \times x(2x + 1) = 10x(2x + 1)$ sq units

Q. 125 Match the expressions of column I with that of column II

	Column I		Column II
(i)	$(21x + 13y)^2$	(a)	$441x^2 - 169y^2$
(ii)	$(21x - 13y)^2$	(b)	$441x^2 + 169y^2 + 546xy$
(iii)	$(21x - 13y)(21x + 13y)$	(c)	$441x^2 + 169y^2 - 546xy$
		(d)	$441x^2 - 169y^2 + 546xy$

Sol. (i) We have,

$(21x + 13y)^2 = (21x)^2 + (13y)^2 + 2 \times 21x \times 13y$

[using the identity, $(a + b)^2 = a^2 + b^2 + 2ab$]

$= 441x^2 + 169y^2 + 546xy$

(ii) $(21x - 13y)^2 = (21x)^2 + (13y)^2 - 2 \times 21x \times 13y$

[using the identity, $(a - b)^2 = a^2 + b^2 - 2ab$]

$= 441x^2 + 169y^2 - 546xy$

(iii) $(21x - 13y)(21x + 13y)$

$= (21x)^2 - (13y)^2 = 441x^2 - 169y^2$

[using the identity, $(a - b)(a + b) = a^2 - b^2$]

Hence, (i) → (a), (ii) → (c), (iii) → (a)

8

Exponents and Powers

Multiple Choice Questions (MCQs)

Q. 1 In 2^n, n is known as

(a) base
(b) constant
(c) exponent
(d) variable

Sol. *(c)* We know that a^n is called the nth power of a; and is also read as a raised to the power n. The rational number a is called the base and n is called the exponent (power or index). In the same way in 2^n, n is known as exponent.

Q. 2 For a fixed base, if the exponent decreases by 1, the number becomes

(a) one-tenth of the previous number
(b) ten times of the previous number
(c) hundredth of the previous number
(d) hundred times of the previous number

Sol. *(a)* For a fixed base, if the exponent decreases by 1, the number becomes one-tenth of the previous number.

e.g. For 10^5, exponent decreases by 1.

i.e. $$10^{5-1} = 10^4$$

$$\therefore \quad \frac{10^4}{10^5} = \frac{1}{10}$$

Note *Option (a) is possible only, if we taken base as* 10.

Q. 3 3^{-2} can be written as

(a) 3^2
(b) $\frac{1}{3^2}$
(c) $\frac{1}{3^{-2}}$
(d) $-\frac{2}{3}$

Sol. *(b)* Using law of exponents, $a^{-m} = \frac{1}{a^m}$ [$\because a$ is non-zero integer]

So, we can write 3^{-2} as $\frac{1}{3^2}$.

Q. 4 The value of $\frac{1}{4^{-2}}$ is

(a) 16 (b) 8 (c) $\frac{1}{16}$ (d) $\frac{1}{8}$

Sol. ***(a)*** Using law of exponents, $a^{-m} = \frac{1}{a^m}$ [$\because a$ is non-zero integer]

$$\therefore \quad \frac{1}{4^{-2}} = \frac{1}{\frac{1}{4^2}} = \frac{1}{\frac{1}{16}} = 1 \times 16 = 16$$

Q. 5 The value of $3^5 \div 3^{-6}$ is

(a) 3^5 (b) 3^{-6} (c) 3^{11} (d) 3^{-11}

Sol. ***(c)*** Using law of exponents, $a^m \div a^n = a^{m-n}$ [$\because a$ is non-zero integer]

$$\therefore \quad 3^5 \div 3^{-6} = 3^{5-(-6)} = 3^{5+6} = 3^{11}$$

Q. 6 The value of $\left(\frac{2}{5}\right)^{-2}$ is

(a) $\frac{4}{5}$ (b) $\frac{4}{25}$ (c) $\frac{25}{4}$ (d) $\frac{5}{2}$

Sol. ***(c)*** Using law of exponents, $a^{-m} = \frac{1}{a^m}$ [$\because a$ is non-zero integer]

$$\therefore \quad \left(\frac{2}{5}\right)^{-2} = \frac{1}{\left(\frac{2}{5}\right)^2} = \frac{1}{\frac{4}{25}} = \frac{25}{4}$$

Q. 7 The reciprocal of $\left(\frac{2}{5}\right)^{-1}$ is

(a) $\frac{2}{5}$ (b) $\frac{5}{2}$ (c) $-\frac{5}{2}$ (d) $-\frac{2}{5}$

Sol. ***(b)*** Using law of exponents, $a^{-m} = \frac{1}{a^m}$ [$\because a$ is non-zero integer]

$$\therefore \quad \left(\frac{2}{5}\right)^{-1} = \frac{1}{\left(\frac{2}{5}\right)^1} = \frac{5}{2}$$

Q. 8 The multiplicative inverse of 10^{-100} is

(a) 10 (b) 100 (c) 10^{100} (d) 10^{-100}

Sol. ***(c)*** For multiplicative inverse, let a be the multiplicative inverse of 10^{-100}.

So, $\quad a \times b = 1$

$\therefore \quad a \times 10^{-100} = 1$

$$\Rightarrow \quad a = \frac{1}{10^{-100}} \frac{1}{\frac{1}{10^{100}}} = 10^{100} \quad \left[\because a^{-m} = \frac{1}{a^m}\right]$$

Q. 9 The value of $(-2)^{2 \times 3 - 1}$ is

(a) 32 (b) 64 (c) −32 (d) −64

Sol. (c) Given, $(-2)^{2 \times 3 - 1} = (-2)^{6-1} = (-2)^5$

$$= (-2) \times (-2) \times (-2) \times (-2) \times (-2) = -32$$

[for $(-a)^m$, if m is odd, then $(-a)^m$ is negative]

Q. 10 The value of $\left(-\frac{2}{3}\right)^4$ is equal to

(a) $\frac{16}{81}$ (b) $\frac{81}{16}$ (c) $\frac{-16}{81}$ (d) $\frac{81}{-16}$

Sol. (a) Given, $\left(\frac{-2}{3}\right)^4 = \left(\frac{-2}{3}\right) \times \left(\frac{-2}{3}\right) \times \left(\frac{-2}{3}\right) \times \left(\frac{-2}{3}\right) = \frac{16}{81}$

[for $(-a)^m$, if m is even, then $(-a)^m$ is positive]

Q. 11 The multiplicative inverse of $\left(-\frac{5}{9}\right)^{-99}$ is

(a) $\left(-\frac{5}{9}\right)^{99}$ (b) $\left(\frac{5}{9}\right)^{99}$ (c) $\left(\frac{9}{-5}\right)^{99}$ (d) $\left(\frac{9}{5}\right)^{99}$

Sol. (a) For multiplicative inverse, a is called multiplicative inverse of b, if $a \times b = 1$.

Put $b = \left(\frac{-5}{9}\right)^{-99}$ $\Rightarrow$ $a \times \left(\frac{-5}{9}\right)^{-99} = 1$

$\Rightarrow$ $a = \frac{1}{\left(\frac{-5}{9}\right)^{-99}}$ $\Rightarrow$ $a = \left(-\frac{5}{9}\right)^{99}$ $\left[\because a^{-m} = \frac{1}{a^m}\right]$

Q. 12 If x be any non-zero integer and m, n be negative integers, then $x^m \times x^n$ is equal to

(a) x^m (b) $x^{(m+n)}$ (c) x^n (d) $x^{(m-n)}$

Sol. (b) Using law of exponents,

$a^m \times a^n = (a)^{m+n}$ [$\because$ a is non-zero integer]

Similarly, $x^m \times x^n = (x)^{m+n}$

Q. 13 If y be any non-zero integer, then y^0 is equal to

(a) 1 (b) 0 (c) −1 (d) not defined

Sol. (a) Using law of exponents,

$a^0 = 1$ [$\because$ a is non-zero integer]

Similarly, $y^0 = 1$

Q. 14 If x be any non-zero integer, then x^{-1} is equal to

(a) x (b) $\frac{1}{x}$ (c) $-x$ (d) $\frac{-1}{x}$

Sol. ***(b)*** Using law of exponents, $a^{-m} = \frac{1}{a^m}$ [$\because$ a is non-zero integer]

Similarly, $x^{-1} = \frac{1}{x}$

Q. 15 If x be any integer different from zero and m be any positive integer, then x^{-m} is equal to

(a) x^m (b) $-x^m$ (c) $\frac{1}{x^m}$ (d) $\frac{-1}{x^m}$

Sol. ***(c)*** Using law of exponents, $a^{-m} = \frac{1}{a^m}$ [$\because$ a is non-zero integer]

Similarly, $x^{-m} = \frac{1}{x^m}$

Q. 16 If x be any integer different from zero and m, n be any integers, then $(x^m)^n$ is equal to

(a) $x^{(m+n)}$ (b) x^{mn} (c) $\frac{m}{x^n}$ (d) $x^{(m-n)}$

Sol. ***(b)*** Using law of exponents, $(a^m)^n = (a)^{m \times n}$ [$\because$ a is non-zero integer]

Similarly, $(x^m)^n = (x)^{m \times n} = (x)^{mn}$

Q. 17 Which of the following is equal to $\left(-\frac{3}{4}\right)^{-3}$?

(a) $\left(\frac{3}{4}\right)^{-3}$ (b) $-\left(\frac{3}{4}\right)^{-3}$ (c) $\left(\frac{4}{3}\right)^{3}$ (d) $\left(-\frac{4}{3}\right)^{3}$

Sol. ***(d)*** Given, $\left(\frac{-3}{4}\right)^{-3}$

Using law of exponents, $a^{-m} = \frac{1}{a^m}$ [$\because$ a is non-zero integer]

$$\therefore \quad \left(\frac{-3}{4}\right)^{-3} = \frac{1}{\left(\frac{-3}{4}\right)^{3}} = \left(-\frac{4}{3}\right)^{3}$$

Q. 18 $\left(-\frac{5}{7}\right)^{-5}$ is equal to

(a) $\left(\frac{5}{7}\right)^{-5}$ (b) $\left(\frac{5}{7}\right)^{5}$ (c) $\left(\frac{7}{5}\right)^{5}$ (d) $\left(\frac{-7}{5}\right)^{5}$

Sol. ***(d)*** Using law of exponents, $a^{-m} = \frac{1}{a^m}$ [$\because$ a is non-zero integer]

$$\therefore \quad \left(\frac{-5}{7}\right)^{-5} = \frac{1}{\left(\frac{-5}{7}\right)^{5}} = \left(-\frac{7}{5}\right)^{5}$$

Q. 19 $\left(\frac{-7}{5}\right)^{-1}$ is equal to

(a) $\frac{5}{7}$ (b) $-\frac{5}{7}$ (c) $\frac{7}{5}$ (d) $\frac{-7}{5}$

Sol. *(b)* Using law of exponents, $a^{-m} = \frac{1}{a^m}$ [$\because a$ is non-zero integer]

$$\therefore \quad \left(\frac{-7}{5}\right)^{-1} = \frac{1}{\left(\frac{-7}{5}\right)} = \left(-\frac{5}{7}\right)$$

Q. 20 $(-9)^3 \div (-9)^8$ is equal to

(a) $(9)^5$ (b) $(9)^{-5}$ (c) $(-9)^5$ (d) $(-9)^{-5}$

Sol. *(d)* Given, $(-9)^3 \div (-9)^8$

Using law of exponents, $a^m \div a^n = (a)^{m-n}$ [$\because a$ is non-zero integer]

$$\therefore \quad (-9)^3 \div (-9)^8 = (-9)^{3-8} = (-9)^{-5}$$

Q. 21 For a non-zero integer x, $x^7 \div x^{12}$ is equal to

(a) x^5 (b) x^{19} (c) x^{-5} (d) x^{-19}

Sol. *(c)* Using law of exponents, $a^m \div a^n = (a)^{m-n}$ [$\because a$ is non-zero integer]

Similarly, $x^7 \div x^{12} = (x)^{7-12} = (x)^{-5}$

Q. 22 For a non-zero integer x, $(x^4)^{-3}$ is equal to

(a) x^{12} (b) x^{-12} (c) x^{64} (d) x^{-64}

Sol. *(b)* Using law of exponents, $(a^m)^n = (a)^{m \times n} = (a)^{mn}$ [$\because a$ is non-zero integer]

Similarly, $(x^4)^{-3} = (x)^{4 \times (-3)} = (x)^{-12}$

Q. 23 The value of $(7^{-1} - 8^{-1})^{-1} - (3^{-1} - 4^{-1})^{-1}$ is

(a) 44 (b) 56 (c) 68 (d) 12

Sol. *(a)* Using law of exponents, $a^{-m} = \frac{1}{a^m}$ [$\because a$ is non-zero integer]

$$\therefore \quad (7^{-1} - 8^{-1})^{-1} - (3^{-1} - 4^{-1})^{-1}$$

$$= \left(\frac{1}{7} - \frac{1}{8}\right)^{-1} - \left(\frac{1}{3} - \frac{1}{4}\right)^{-1}$$

$$= \left(\frac{1}{56}\right)^{-1} - \left(\frac{1}{12}\right)^{-1} = 56 - 12 = 44$$

Q. 24 The standard form for 0.000064 is

(a) 64×10^4 (b) 64×10^{-4} (c) 6.4×10^5 (d) 6.4×10^{-5}

Sol. *(d)* Given, $0.000064 = 0.64 \times 10^{-4} = 6.4 \times 10^{-5}$

Hence, standard form of 0.000064 is 6.4×10^{-5}.

Q. 25 The standard form for 234000000 is

(a) 2.34×10^8 (b) 0.234×10^9
(c) 2.34×10^{-8} (d) 0.234×10^{-9}

Sol. *(a)* Given, $234000000 = 234 \times 10^6 = 2.34 \times 10^{6+2} = 2.34 \times 10^8$

Hence, standard form of 234000000 is 2.34×10^8.

Q. 26 The usual form for 2.03×10^{-5} is

(a) 0.203 (b) 0.00203 (c) 203000 (d) 0.0000203

Sol. *(d)* Given, $2.03 \times 10^{-5} = 0.0000203$

[$\because$ placing decimal five digit towards left of original position]

Q. 27 $\left(\frac{1}{10}\right)^0$ is equal to

(a) 0 (b) $\frac{1}{10}$ (c) 1 (d) 10

Sol. *(c)* Using law of exponents, $a^0 = 1$ [$\because$ *a* is non-zero integer]

$\therefore \left(\frac{1}{10}\right)^0 = 1$

Q. 28 $\left(\frac{3}{4}\right)^5 \div \left(\frac{5}{3}\right)^5$ is equal to

(a) $\left(\frac{3}{4} \div \frac{5}{3}\right)^5$ (b) $\left(\frac{3}{4} \div \frac{5}{3}\right)^1$ (c) $\left(\frac{3}{4} \div \frac{5}{3}\right)^0$ (d) $\left(\frac{3}{4} \div \frac{5}{3}\right)^{10}$

Sol. *(a)* Using law of exponents, $a^m \div b^m = (a \div b)^m$ [$\because$ *a* and *b* are non-zero integers]

$\therefore \left(\frac{3}{4}\right)^5 \div \left(\frac{5}{3}\right)^5 = \left(\frac{3}{4} \div \frac{5}{3}\right)^5$

Q. 29 For any two non-zero rational numbers x and y, $x^4 \div y^4$ is equal to

(a) $(x \div y)^0$ (b) $(x \div y)^1$
(c) $(x \div y)^4$ (d) $(x \div y)^8$

Sol. *(c)* Using law of exponents, $\frac{a^m}{b^m} = \left(\frac{a}{b}\right)^m = (a \div b)^m$ [$\because$ *a* and *b* are non-zero integers]

Similarly, $x^4 \div y^4 = \left(\frac{x}{y}\right)^4 = (x \div y)^4$

Q. 30 For a non-zero rational number p, $p^{13} \div p^8$ is equal to

(a) p^5 (b) p^{21}
(c) p^{-5} (d) p^{-19}

Sol. *(a)* Using law of exponents, $a^m \div a^n = (a)^{m-n}$ [$\because$ *a* is non-zero integer]

Similarly, $p^{13} \div p^8 = (p)^{13-8} = (p)^5$

Q. 31 For a non-zero rational number z, $(z^{-2})^3$ is equal to

(a) z^6 (b) z^{-6}
(c) z^1 (d) z^4

Sol. *(b)* Using law of exponents, $(a^m)^n = (a)^{mn}$ [$\because a$ is non-zero integer]

Similarly, $(z^{-2})^3 = (z)^{(-2)\times 3} = (z)^{-6}$

Q. 32 Cube of $-\frac{1}{2}$ is

(a) $\frac{1}{8}$ (b) $\frac{1}{16}$
(c) $-\frac{1}{8}$ (d) $-\frac{1}{16}$

Sol. *(c)* Cube of a is $(a)^3 = a \times a \times a$

Similarly, $\left(-\frac{1}{2}\right)^3 = \left(\frac{-1}{2}\right) \times \left(\frac{-1}{2}\right) \times \left(\frac{-1}{2}\right) = \left(-\frac{1}{8}\right)$

[for $(-a)^m$, if m is odd, then $(-a)^m$ is negative]

Q. 33 Which of the following is not the reciprocal of $\left(\frac{2}{3}\right)^4$?

(a) $\left(\frac{3}{2}\right)^4$ (b) $\left(\frac{3}{2}\right)^{-4}$
(c) $\left(\frac{2}{3}\right)^{-4}$ (d) $\frac{3^4}{2^4}$

Sol. *(b)* Reciprocal of a is $\frac{1}{a}$.

Similarly, $\left(\frac{2}{3}\right)^4 = \left(\frac{3}{2}\right)^4 = \frac{3^4}{2^4} = \left(\frac{2}{3}\right)^{-4}$

Hence, option (b) is not the reciprocal of $\left(\frac{2}{3}\right)^4$.

Fill in the Blanks

In questions 34 to 65, fill in the blanks to make the statements true.

Q. 34 The multiplicative inverse of 10^{10} is ______.

Sol. For multiplicative inverse, a is called the multiplicative inverse of b, if $a \times b = 1$.

Put $b = 10^{10}$

Then, $a \times 10^{10} = 1 \Rightarrow a = \frac{1}{10^{10}}$ $\left[\because \frac{1}{a^m} = a^{-m}\right]$

$\therefore$ $a = 10^{-10}$

Hence, the multiplicative inverse of 10^{10} is $\mathbf{10^{-10}}$

Q. 35 $a^3 \times a^{-10} =$ _____

Sol. Given, $a^3 \times a^{-10}$

Using law of exponents, $a^m \times a^n = (a)^{m+n}$ [$\because a$ is non-zero integer]

Similarly, $a^3 \times a^{-10} = (a)^{3-10} = (a)^{-7}$

Hence, $a^3 \times a^{-10} = \mathbf{a^{-7}}$

Q. 36 $5^0 =$ _____

Sol. Using law of exponents, $a^0 = 1$ [$\because a$ is non-zero integer]

$\therefore$ $5^0 = 1$

Hence, $5^0 = \mathbf{1}$

Q. 37 $5^5 \times 5^{-5} =$ _____

Sol. Using law of exponents, $a^m \times a^n = (a)^{m+n}$ [$\because a$ is non-zero integer]

$\therefore$ $5^5 \times 5^{-5} = (5)^{5-5} = (5)^0 = 1$ [$\because a^0 = 1$]

Hence, $5^5 \times 5^{-5} = \mathbf{1}$

Q. 38 The value of $\left(\frac{1}{2^3}\right)^2$ is equal to _____.

Sol. Using law of exponents, $(a^m)^n = (a)^{mn}$ [$\because a$ is non-zero integer]

$\because$ $\left(\frac{1}{2^3}\right)^2 = \left(\frac{1^3}{2^3}\right)^2 = \left(\frac{1}{2}\right)^{3\times 2} = \left(\frac{1}{2}\right)^6 = \frac{1}{2^6}$ [$\because (1)^m = 1$]

Hence, $\left(\frac{1}{2^3}\right)^2 = \mathbf{\frac{1}{2^6}}$

Q. 39 The expression for 8^{-2} as a power with the base 2 is _____.

Sol. Given, 8^{-2}, where we can write $8 = 2 \times 2 \times 2$

$\therefore$ $(2 \times 2 \times 2)^{-2} = (2)^{3\times(-2)} = (2)^{-6}$

Hence, $8^{-2} = \mathbf{(2)^{-6}}$

Q. 40 Very small numbers can be expressed in standard form by using _____ exponents.

Sol. Very small numbers can be expressed in standard form by using **negative** exponents.

i.e. $0.000023 = 2.3 \times 10^{-3}$.

Q. 41 Very large numbers can be expressed in standard form by using _____ exponents.

Sol. Very large numbers can be expressed in standard form by using **positive** exponents.

i.e. $23000 = 23 \times 10^3 = 2.3 \times 10^3 \times 10^1 = 2.3 \times 10^4$

Q. 42 By multiplying $(10)^5$ by $(10)^{-10}$, we get ______.

Sol. Using law of exponents, $(a)^m \times (a)^n = (a)^{m+n}$ [$\because a$ is non-zero integer]

Similarly, $(10)^5 \times (10)^{-10} = (10)^{5-10} = (10)^{-5}$

Hence, $(10)^5 \times (10)^{-10} = \mathbf{(10)^{-5}}$

Q. 43 $\left[\left(\frac{2}{13}\right)^{-6} \div \left(\frac{2}{13}\right)^3\right]^3 \times \left(\frac{2}{13}\right)^{-9} =$ ______

Sol. Using laws of exponents, $a^m \div a^n = (a)^{m-n}$ and $a^m \times a^n = (a)^{m+n}$ [$\because a$ is non-zero integer]

$$\therefore \left[\left(\frac{2}{13}\right)^{-6} \div \left(\frac{2}{13}\right)^3\right]^3 \times \left(\frac{2}{13}\right)^{-9} = \left[\left(\frac{2}{13}\right)^{-6-3}\right]^3 \times \left(\frac{2}{13}\right)^{-9}$$

$$= \left(\frac{2}{13}\right)^{-27} \times \left(\frac{2}{13}\right)^{-9}$$

$$= \left(\frac{2}{13}\right)^{-27-9} = \left(\frac{2}{13}\right)^{-36}$$

Hence, $\left[\left(\frac{2}{13}\right)^{-6} \div \left(\frac{2}{13}\right)^3\right]^3 \times \left(\frac{2}{13}\right)^{-9} = \left(\frac{\mathbf{2}}{\mathbf{13}}\right)^{\mathbf{-36}}$

Q. 44 $[4^{-1} + 3^{-1} + 6^{-2}]^{-1} =$ ______

Sol. Using law of exponents, $a^{-m} = \frac{1}{a^m}$ [$\because a$ is non-zero integer]

$$\therefore [4^{-1} + 3^{-1} + 6^{-2}]^{-1} = \left(\frac{1}{4} + \frac{1}{3} + \frac{1}{36}\right)^{-1} = \left(\frac{9+12+1}{36}\right)^{-1}$$ [$\because$ LCM of 4, 3 and 36 = 36]

$$= \left(\frac{22}{36}\right)^{-1} = \frac{36}{22} = \frac{18}{11}$$

Hence, $[4^{-1} + 3^{-1} + 6^{-2}]^{-1} = \mathbf{\frac{18}{11}}$

Q. 45 $[2^{-1} + 3^{-1} + 4^{-1}]^0 =$ ______

Sol. Using law of exponents, $a^0 = 1$ [$\because a$ is non-zero integer]

$\therefore \quad [2^{-1} + 3^{-1} + 4^{-1}]^0 = 1$

Hence, $[2^{-1} + 3^{-1} + 4^{-1}]^0 = \mathbf{1}$

Q. 46 The standard form of $\left(\frac{1}{100000000}\right)$ is ______.

Sol. For standard form, $\frac{1}{100000000} = \frac{1}{1 \times 10^8} = \frac{1}{10^8} = 1 \times 10^{-8} = 1.0 \times 10^{-8}$

Hence, standard form of $\frac{1}{100000000}$ is $\mathbf{1.0 \times 10^{-8}}$.

Q. 47 The standard form of 12340000 is _____.

Sol. For standard form, $12340000 = 1234 \times 10^4$

$$= 1234 \times 10^4 \times 10^3 = 1234 \times 10^7$$

Hence, the standard form of 12340000 is $\mathbf{1.234 \times 10^7}$.

Q. 48 The usual form of 3.41×10^6 is _____.

Sol. For usual form, $3.41 \times 10^6 = 3.41 \times 10 \times 10 \times 10 \times 10 \times 10 \times 10 = 3410000$

Hence, the usual form of 3.41×10^6 is **3410000**.

Q. 49 The usual form of 2.39461×10^6 is _____.

Sol. For usual form, $2.39461 \times 10^6 = 2.39461 \times 10 \times 10 \times 10 \times 10 \times 10 \times 10 = 2394610$

Hence, the usual form of 2.39461×10^6 is **2394610**.

Q. 50 If $36 = 6 \times 6 = 6^2$, then $\frac{1}{36}$ expressed as a power with the base 6 is _____.

Sol. Given, $36 = 6 \times 6 = 6^2$

So, $\frac{1}{36} = \frac{1}{6 \times 6} = \frac{1}{(6)^2} = \mathbf{(6)^{-2}}$ $\left[\because a^{-m} = \frac{1}{a^m}\right]$

Q. 51 By multiplying $\left(\frac{5}{3}\right)^4$ by _____, we get 5^4.

Sol. Let x be multiplied with $\left(\frac{5}{3}\right)^4$ to get 5^4.

So, $\left(\frac{5}{3}\right)^4 \times x = 5^4$

$\therefore$ $x = \frac{5^4}{\left(\frac{5}{3}\right)^4} = 5^4 \times 3^4 \times 5^{-4} = (5)^{4-4} \times 3^4$ $\left[\because a^{-m} = \frac{1}{a^m}, a^m \times a^n = (a)^{m+n}\right]$

$= 5^0 \times 3^4 = 1 \times 81 = \mathbf{81}$ $[\because a^0 = 1]$

Q. 52 $3^5 \div 3^{-6}$ can be simplified as _____.

Sol. Given, $3^5 \div 3^{-6} = (3)^{5-(-6)} = (3)^{5+6} = (3)^{11}$ $[\because a^m \div a^n = (a)^{m-n}]$

Hence, $3^5 \div 3^{-6}$ can be simplified as $\mathbf{(3)^{11}}$.

Q. 53 The value of 3×10^{-7} is equal to _____.

Sol. Given, $3 \times 10^{-7} = 3.0 \times 10^{-7}$

Now, placing decimal seven place towards left of original position, we get 0.0000003.

Hence, the value of 3×10^{-7} is equal to **0.0000003**.

Q. 54 To add the numbers given in standard form, we first convert them into number with _____ exponents.

Sol. To add the numbers given in standard form, we first convert them into numbers with **equal** exponents.

e.g. $2.46 \times 10^6 + 24.6 \times 10^5 = 2.46 \times 10^6 + 2.46 \times 10^6 = 4.92 \times 10^6$

Q. 55 The standard form for 32500000000 is _____.

Sol. For standard form, $32500000000 = 3250 \times 10^2 \times 10^2 \times 10^3$

$= 3250 \times 10^7 = 3.250 \times 10^{10}$ or 3.25×10^{10}

Hence, the standard form for 32500000000 is $\mathbf{3.25 \times 10^{10}}$.

Q. 56 The standard form for 0.000000008 is _____.

Sol. For standard form, $0.000000008 = 0.8 \times 10^{-8} = 8 \times 10^{-9} = 8.0 \times 10^{-9}$

Hence, the standard form for 0.000000008 is $\mathbf{8.0 \times 10^{-9}}$.

Q. 57 The usual form for 2.3×10^{-10} is _____.

Sol. For usual form, $2.3 \times 10^{-10} = 0.23 \times 10^{-11}$

$= 0.00000000023$

Hence, the usual form for 2.3×10^{-10} is **0.00000000023.**

Q. 58 On dividing 8^5 by _____, we get 8.

Sol. Let 8^5 be divided by x to get 8.

So, $8^5 \div x = 8$

$\Rightarrow \quad 8^5 \times \frac{1}{x} = 8$

$\Rightarrow \quad \frac{8^5}{8} = x$

$\therefore \quad x = \frac{8^5}{8^1} = 8^{5-1} = \mathbf{8^4}$ $\quad [\because a^m \div a^n = (a)^{m-n}]$

Q. 59 On multiplying _____ by 2^{-5}, we get 2^5.

Sol. Let x be multiplied by 2^{-5} to get 2^5.

So, $x \times 2^{-5} = 2^5$

$\Rightarrow \quad x \times \frac{1}{2^5} = 2^5$ $\quad \left[\because a^{-m} = \frac{1}{a^m}\right]$

$\therefore \quad x = 2^5 \times 2^5 = (2)^{5+5} = \mathbf{2^{10}}$ $\quad [\because a^m \times a^n = (a)^{m+n}]$

Q. 60 The value of $[3^{-1} \times 4^{-1}]^2$ is _____.

Sol. Using law of exponents, $a^{-m} = \frac{1}{a^m}$ $\quad [\because a$ is non-zero integer$]$

$$\therefore \quad [3^{-1} \times 4^{-1}]^2 = \left(\frac{1}{3} \times \frac{1}{4}\right)^2 = \left(\frac{1}{12}\right)^2$$

$$= 12^{-2} = \frac{1}{144}$$

Hence, $[3^{-1} \times 4^{-1}]^2 = \mathbf{\frac{1}{144}}$

Q. 61 The value of $[2^{-1} \times 3^{-1}]^{-1}$ is ______.

Sol. Using law of exponents, $a^{-m} = \frac{1}{a^m}$ [$\because a$ is non-zero integer]

$$\therefore \quad [2^{-1} \times 3^{-1}]^{-1} = \left(\frac{1}{2} \times \frac{1}{3}\right)^{-1} = \left(\frac{1}{6}\right)^{-1} = 6$$

Hence, $[2^{-1} \times 3^{-1}]^{-1} = \mathbf{6}$

Q. 62 By solving $(6^0 - 7^0) \times (6^0 + 7^0)$, we get ______.

Sol. Using law of exponents, $a^0 = 1$ [$\because a$ is non-zero integer]

$$\therefore \quad (6^0 - 7^0) \times (6^0 + 7^0) = (1 - 1) \times (1 + 1) = 0 \times 2 = 0$$

Hence, $(6^0 - 7^0) \times (6^0 + 7^0) = \mathbf{0}$

Q. 63 The expression for 3^5 with a negative exponent is ______.

Sol. Using law of exponents, $a^{-m} = \frac{1}{a^m}$ [$\because a$ is non-zero integer]

$$\therefore \quad 3^5 = \frac{1}{3^{-5}}$$

Hence, the expression for 3^5 with a negative exponents is $\mathbf{\frac{1}{3^{-5}}}$.

Q. 64 The value for $(-7)^6 \div 7^6$ is ______.

Sol. Using law of exponents, $a^m \div a^n = (a)^{m-n}$ [$\because a$ is non-zero integer]

$$\therefore \quad (-7)^6 \div 7^6 = (7)^6 \div (7)^6 \quad [(-a^m) = (a^m), \text{ if } m \text{ is an even number}]$$

$$= (7)^{6-6} = (7)^0 = 1 \quad [\because a^0 = 1]$$

Hence, $(-7)^6 \div 7^6 = \mathbf{1}$

Q. 65 The value of $[1^{-2} + 2^{-2} + 3^{-2}] \times 6^2$ is ______.

Sol. Using law of exponents, $a^{-m} = \frac{1}{a^m}$ [$\because a$ is non-zero integer]

$$\therefore \quad [1^{-2} + 2^{-2} + 3^{-2}] \times 6^2 = \left[\frac{1}{1^2} + \frac{1}{2^2} + \frac{1}{3^2}\right] \times 6^2 = \left[1 + \frac{1}{4} + \frac{1}{9}\right] \times 6^2$$

$$= \left(\frac{36 + 9 + 4}{36}\right) \times 6^2$$

$$= \left(\frac{49}{36}\right) \times 6^2 = \left(\frac{7}{6}\right)^2 \times 6^2 = (7)^2 \times 6^{-2} \times 6^2$$

$$= (7)^2 \times 6^{2-2} = (7)^2 \times 6^0 = 49 \quad [a^\circ = 1]$$

Hence, $[1^{-2} + 2^{-2} + 3^{-2}] \times 6^2 = \mathbf{49}$

True / False

In questions 66 to 90, state whether the given statements are True or False.

Q. 66 The multiplicative inverse of $(-4)^{-2}$ is $(4)^{-2}$.

Sol. ***False***

a is called the multiplicative inverse of b, if $a \times b = 1$.

Put $b = (-4)^{-2}$

$\therefore \quad a \times (-4)^{-2} = 1$

$$\Rightarrow \quad a = \frac{1}{(-4)^{-2}} = (-4)^2 \qquad \left[\because a^{-m} = \frac{1}{a^m}\right]$$

Q. 67 The multiplicative inverse of $\left(\frac{3}{2}\right)^2$ is not equal to $\left(\frac{2}{3}\right)^2$.

Sol. ***True***

a is called the multiplicative inverse of b, if $a \times b = 1$.

Put $b = \left(\frac{3}{2}\right)^2$

So, $a \times \left(\frac{3}{2}\right)^2 = 1 \Rightarrow a = \left(\frac{3}{2}\right)^{-2}$

Q. 68 $10^{-2} = \frac{1}{100}$

Sol. ***True***

Using law of exponents, $a^{-m} = \frac{1}{a^m}$ [$\because a$ is non-zero integer]

$$\therefore \quad 10^{-2} = \frac{1}{10^2} = \frac{1}{10 \times 10} = \frac{1}{100} \qquad [\because 10^2 = 10 \times 10]$$

Q. 69 $24.58 = 2 \times 10 + 4 \times 1 + 5 \times 10 + 8 \times 100$

Sol. ***False***

RHS $= 2 \times 10 + 4 \times 1 + 5 \times 10 + 8 \times 100 = 20 + 4 + 50 + 800 = 874$

LHS $\neq$ RHS

Q. 70 $329.25 = 3 \times 10^2 + 2 \times 10^1 + 9 \times 10^0 + 2 \times 10^{-1} + 5 \times 10^{-2}$

Sol. ***True***

RHS $= 3 \times 10^2 + 2 \times 10^1 + 9 \times 10^0 + 2 \times 10^{-1} + 5 \times 10^{-2}$

$$= 3 \times 10 \times 10 + 2 \times 10 + 9 \times 1 + \frac{2}{10} + \frac{5}{10 \times 10} \qquad [\because a^0 = 1]$$

$$= 300 + 20 + 9 + 0.2 - 0.05 = 329.25$$

$\therefore$ LHS = RHS

Q. 71 $(-5)^{-2} \times (-5)^{-3} = (-5)^{-6}$

Sol. ***False***

LHS $= (-5)^{-2} \times (-5)^{-3}$

Using law of exponents, $a^m \times a^n = (a)^{m+n}$ [$\because a$ is non-zero integer]

$\therefore \quad (-5)^{-2} \times (-5)^{-3} = (-5)^{-2-3} = (-5)^{-5}$

LHS $\neq$ RHS

Q. 72 $(-4)^{-4} \times (4)^{-1} = (4)^5$

Sol. ***False***

LHS $= (-4)^{-4} \times (4)^{-1}$

Using law of exponents, $a^m \times a^n = (a)^{m+n}$ [$\because a$ is non-zero integer]

$\therefore \quad (-4)^{-4} \times (4)^{-1} = (4)^{-4} \times (4)^{-1}$

$= (4)^{-4-1}$

$= (4)^{-5}$

LHS $\neq$ RHS

Q. 73 $\left(\frac{2}{3}\right)^{-2} \times \left(\frac{2}{3}\right)^{-5} = \left(\frac{2}{3}\right)^{10}$

Sol. ***False***

LHS $= \left(\frac{2}{3}\right)^{-2} \times \left(\frac{2}{3}\right)^{-5}$

Using law of exponents, $a^m \times a^n = (a)^{m+n}$ [$\because a$ is non-zero integer]

$\therefore \quad \left(\frac{2}{3}\right)^{-2} \times \left(\frac{2}{3}\right)^{-5} = \left(\frac{2}{3}\right)^{-2-5} = \left(\frac{2}{3}\right)^{-7}$

LHS $\neq$ RHS

Q. 74 $5^0 = 5$

Sol. ***False***

LHS $= 5^0$

Using law of exponents, $a^0 = 1$ [$\because a$ is non-zero integer]

$\therefore \quad 5^0 = 1$

LHS $\neq$ RHS

Q. 75 $(-2)^0 = 2$

Sol. ***False***

LHS $= (-2)^0$

Using law of exponents, $a^0 = 1$ [$\because a$ is non-zero integer]

$\therefore \quad (-2)^0 = 1$

LHS $\neq$ RHS

Q. 76 $\left(-\frac{8}{2}\right)^0 = 0$

Sol. ***False***

LHS $= \left(-\frac{8}{2}\right)^0$

Using law of exponents, $a^0 = 1$ [$\because a$ is non-zero integer]

$\therefore \quad \left(-\frac{8}{2}\right) = 1$

LHS $\neq$ RHS

Q. 77 $(-6)^0 = -1$

Sol. ***False***

LHS $= (-6)^0$

Using law of exponents, $a^0 = 1$ [$\because a$ is non-zero integer]

$\therefore \quad (-6)^0 = 1$

LHS $\neq$ RHS

Q. 78 $(-7)^{-4} \times (-7)^2 = (-7)^{-2}$

Sol. ***True***

LHS $= (-7)^{-4} \times (-7)^2$

Using law of exponents, $a^m \times a^n = (a)^{m+n}$ [$\because a$ is non-zero integer]

$$\therefore \quad (-7)^{-4} \times (-7)^2 = (-7)^{-4+2} = (-7)^{-2}$$

LHS = RHS

Q. 79 The value of $\frac{1}{4^{-2}}$ is equal to 16.

Sol. ***True***

Using law of exponents, $a^{-m} = \frac{1}{a^m}$ [$\because a$ is non-zero integer]

$\therefore \frac{1}{4^{-2}} = 4^2 = 4 \times 4 = 16$

Q. 80 The expression for 4^{-3} as a power with the base 2 is 2^6.

Sol. ***False***

Using law of exponents, $a^{-m} = \frac{1}{a^m}$

$\therefore \quad 4^{-3} = \frac{1}{4^3} = \frac{1}{(2^2)^3} = \frac{1}{(2)^6}$ [$\because 2 \times 2 = 4, (a^m)^n = (a)^{mn}$]

Q. 81 $a^p \times b^q = (ab)^{pq}$

Sol. ***False***

RHS $= (ab)^{pq}$

Using law of exponents, $(ab)^m = a^m \times b^m$ [$\because a$ is non-zero integer]

$\therefore \quad (ab)^{pq} = (a)^{pq} \times (b)^{pq}$

LHS $\neq$ RHS

Q. 82 $\dfrac{x^m}{y^m} = \left(\dfrac{y}{x}\right)^{-m}$

Sol. ***True***

RHS $= \left(\dfrac{y}{x}\right)^{-m}$

Using laws of exponents, $\left(\dfrac{a}{b}\right)^m = \dfrac{a^m}{b^m}$ and $a^{-m} = \dfrac{1}{a^m}$ [$\because$ a and b are non-zero integers]

$\therefore \quad \left(\dfrac{y}{x}\right)^{-m} = \dfrac{y^{-m}}{x^{-m}} = \dfrac{x^m}{y^m}$

LHS = RHS

Q. 83 $a^m = \dfrac{1}{a^{-m}}$

Sol. ***True***

Using law of exponents,

$$a^m = \frac{1}{a^{-m}}$$

LHS = RHS

Q. 84 The exponential form for $(-2)^4 \times \left(\dfrac{5}{2}\right)^4$ is 5^4.

Sol. ***True***

Using laws of exponents, $a^m \div a^n = (a)^{m-n}$ and $\left(\dfrac{a}{b}\right)^m = \dfrac{a^m}{b^m}$

[$\because a$ and b are non-zero integers]

$\therefore \quad (-2)^4 \times \left(\dfrac{5}{2}\right)^4 = (2)^4 \times \dfrac{(5)^4}{(2)^4} = (2)^{4-4} \times 5^4$

$= 2^0 \times 5^4 = 5^4$ [$\because (-a^m) = (a^m)$, if m is an even number]

Q. 85 The standard form for 0.000037 is 3.7×10^{-5}.

Sol. ***True***

For standard form, $0.000037 = 0.37 \times 10^{-4} = 3.7 \times 10^{-5}$

Q. 86 The standard form for 203000 is 2.03×10^5.

Sol. ***True***

For standard form, $203000 = 203 \times 10 \times 10 \times 10 = 203 \times 10^3$

$$= 2.03 \times 10^2 \times 10^3 = 2.03 \times 10^5$$

Q. 87 The usual form for 2×10^{-2} is not equal to 0.02.

Sol. ***False***

For usual form , $2 \times 10^{-2} = 2 \times \frac{1}{10^2}$ $\left[\because a^{-m} = \frac{1}{a^m}\right]$

$$= \frac{2}{100} = 0.02$$

Q. 88 The value of 5^{-2} is equal to 25.

Sol. ***False***

Using law of exponents, $a^{-m} = \frac{1}{a^m}$ [$\because$ a is non-zero integer]

$\therefore$ $$5^{-2} = \frac{1}{5^2} = \frac{1}{25}$$

Q. 89 Large numbers can be expressed in the standard form by using positive exponents.

Sol. ***True***

e.g. $2360000 = 236 \times 10 \times 10 \times 10 \times 10 = 236 \times 10^4$

$$= 2.36 \times 10^4 \times 10^2 = 2.36 \times 10^6$$

Q. 90 $a^m \times b^m = (ab)^m$

Sol. ***True***

$\text{LHS} = a^m \times b^m = (a \times b)^m = (ab)^m$ [by law of exponents]

Q. 91 Solve the following.

(i) 100^{-10}

(ii) $2^{-2} \times 2^{-3}$

(iii) $\left(\frac{1}{2}\right)^{-2} \div \left(\frac{1}{2}\right)^{-3}$

Sol. (i) $100^{-10} = \frac{1}{100^{10}}$ $\left[\because a^{-m} = \frac{1}{a^m}\right]$

(ii) $2^{-2} \times 2^{-3} = (2)^{-2-3} = (2)^{-5}$ [$\because a^m \times a^n = (a)^{m+n}$]

(iii) $\left(\frac{1}{2}\right)^{-2} \div \left(\frac{1}{2}\right)^{-3} = \left(\frac{1}{2}\right)^{-2+3} = \frac{1}{2}$ [$\because a^m \div a^n = (a)^{m-n}$]

Q. 92 Express $3^{-5} \times 3^{-4}$ as a power of 3 with positive exponent.

Sol. Using laws of exponents, $a^m \times a^n = (a)^{m+n}$ and $a^{-m} = \frac{1}{a^m}$ [$\because a$ is non-zero integer]

$\therefore$ $$3^{-5} \times 3^{-4} = (3)^{-5-4} = (3)^{-9} = \frac{1}{3^9}$$

Q. 93 Express 16^{-2} as a power with the base 2.

Sol. $\because$ $2 \times 2 \times 2 \times 2 = 16 = 2^4$

$\therefore$ $$16^{-2} = (2^4)^{-2} = (2)^{4 \times (-2)}$$ [$\because (a^m)^n = (a)^{mn}$]

$$= (2)^{-8}$$

Q. 94 Express $\frac{27}{64}$ and $\frac{-27}{64}$ as powers of a rational number.

Sol. $\because$ $27 = 3 \times 3 \times 3 = 3^3$, $(-27) = (-3) \times (-3) \times (-3) = (-3)^3$

and $64 = 4 \times 4 \times 4 = 4^3$

$\therefore$ $$\frac{27}{64} = \frac{3^3}{4^3} = \left(\frac{3}{4}\right)^3 \text{ and } \frac{-27}{64} = \frac{(-3)^3}{(4)^3} = \left(\frac{-3}{4}\right)^3$$

Q. 95 Express $\frac{16}{81}$ and $\frac{-16}{81}$ as powers of a rational number.

Sol. $\because$ $16 = 4 \times 4 = 4^2$

and $81 = 9 \times 9 = 9^2$

$\therefore$ $$\frac{16}{81} = \frac{(4)^2}{(9)^2} = \left(\frac{4}{9}\right)^2 \text{ and } \frac{-16}{81} = \frac{-(4)^2}{(9)^2} = -\left(\frac{4}{9}\right)^2$$

Q. 96 Express as a power of a rational number with negative exponent.

(a) $\left(\left(\frac{-3}{2}\right)^{-2}\right)^{-3}$ (b) $(2^5 \div 2^8) \times 2^{-7}$

Sol. (a) Using laws of exponents, $(a^m)^n = (a)^{m \times n}$ and $a^{-m} = \frac{1}{a^m}$ [$\because a$ is non-zero integer]

$\therefore$ $$\left(\left(\frac{-3}{2}\right)^{-2}\right)^{-3} = \left(\frac{-3}{2}\right)^{-2\times(-3)} = \left(\frac{-3}{2}\right)^6 = \left(\frac{2}{3}\right)^{-6}$$

Using laws of exponents, $a^m \div a^n = a^{m-n}$

and $a^m \times a^n = a^{m+n}$ [$\because a$ is non-zero integer]

$\therefore$ $$(2^5 \div 2^8) \times 2^{-7} = (2^{5-8}) \times 2^{-7} = 2^{-3} \times 2^{-7} = 2^{-3-7} = 2^{-10}$$

Q. 97 Find the product of the cube of (–2) and the square of (+4).

Sol. $\because$ Cube of $(-2) = (-2)^3$

and square of $(+4) = (+4)^2$

$\therefore$ The product $= (-2)^3 \times (4)^2 = (-8) \times 16 = -128$

Q. 98 Simplify

(i) $\left(\frac{1}{4}\right)^{-2}+\left(\frac{1}{2}\right)^{-2}+\left(\frac{1}{3}\right)^{-2}$ (ii) $\left(\left(\frac{-2}{3}\right)^{-2}\right)^{3}\times\left(\frac{1}{3}\right)^{-4}\times 3^{-1}\times\frac{1}{6}$

(iii) $\frac{49\times z^{-3}}{7^{-3}\times 10\times z^{-5}}\ (z\neq 0)$ (iv) $(2^5\div 2^8)\times 2^{-7}$

Sol. (i) Using law of exponents, $a^{-m}=\frac{1}{a^m}$ [$\because a$ is non-zero integer]

$$\therefore \left(\frac{1}{4}\right)^{-2}+\left(\frac{1}{2}\right)^{-2}+\left(\frac{1}{3}\right)^{-2}=(4)^2+(2)^2+(3)^2=16+4+9=29$$

(ii) Using laws of exponents, $(a^m)^n=(a)^{m\times n}$, $a^{-m}=\frac{1}{a^m}$, $a^m\times a^n=a^{m+n}$ and $a^m\div a^n=a^{m-n}$

[$\because a$ is non-zero integer]

$$\therefore \left(\left(\frac{-2}{3}\right)^{-2}\right)^{3}\times\left(\frac{1}{3}\right)^{-4}\times 3^{-1}\times\frac{1}{6}=\left(\frac{-2}{3}\right)^{(-2)\times 3}\times(3)^4\times\frac{1}{3}\times\frac{1}{6}$$

$$=\left(\frac{-2}{3}\right)^{-6}\times 3^4\times\frac{1}{3}\times\frac{1}{2\times 3} \quad [\because 6=2\times 3]$$

$$=\left(\frac{3}{-2}\right)^{6}\times 3^4\times\frac{1}{3\times 2\times 3}=\frac{(3)^6}{(-2)^6}\times 3^4\times\frac{1}{2^1\times 3^2}$$

$$=\frac{(3)^{6+4}}{(2)^{6+1}\times 3^2} \quad [(-a^m)=a^m,\text{ if } m \text{ is an even number}]$$

$$=\frac{(3)^{10}}{2^7\times 3^2}=\frac{3^{10-2}}{2^7}=\frac{3^8}{2^7}$$

(iii) $$\frac{49\times z^{-3}}{7^{-3}\times 10\times z^{-5}}=\frac{(7)^2\times z^{-3}}{7^{-3}\times 10\times z^{-5}}=\frac{(7)^{2+3}\times z^{-3+5}}{10} \quad [\because a^m\div a^n=(a)^{m-n}]$$

$$=\frac{(7)^5 z^2}{10}=\frac{7^5}{10}z^2$$

(iv) Using laws of exponents, $a^m\div a^n=(a)^{m-n}$ and $a^m\times a^n=(a)^{m+n}$

[$\because a$ is non-zero integer]

$$\therefore (2^5\div 2^8)\times(2)^{-7}=(2)^{5-8}\times(2)^{-7}$$

$$=(2)^{-3}\times(2)^{-7}$$

$$=(2)^{-3-7}=(2)^{-10}=\frac{1}{2^{10}}=\frac{1}{1024} \quad \left[\because a^{-m}=\frac{1}{a^m}\right]$$

Q. 99 Find the value of *x*, so that

(i) $\left(\frac{5}{3}\right)^{-2}\times\left(\frac{5}{3}\right)^{-14}=\left(\frac{5}{3}\right)^{8x}$ (ii) $(-2)^3\times(-2)^{-6}=(-2)^{2x-1}$

(iii) $(2^{-1}+4^{-1}+6^{-1}+8^{-1})^x=1$

Sol. (i) We have, $\left(\frac{5}{3}\right)^{-2}\times\left(\frac{5}{3}\right)^{-14}=\left(\frac{5}{3}\right)^{8x}$

Using law of exponents, $a^m\times a^n=(a)^{m+n}$ [$\because a$ is non-zero integer]

Then, $\left(\frac{5}{3}\right)^{-2} \times \left(\frac{5}{3}\right)^{-14} = \left(\frac{5}{3}\right)^{8x}$

$\Rightarrow \left(\frac{5}{3}\right)^{-2-14} = \left(\frac{5}{3}\right)^{8x}$

$\Rightarrow \left(\frac{5}{3}\right)^{-16} = \left(\frac{5}{3}\right)^{8x}$

On comparing both sides, we get

$16 = 8x$

$\Rightarrow x = -2$

(ii) We have $(-2)^3 \times (-2)^{-6} = (-2)^{2x-1}$

Using law of exponents, $a^m \times a^n = (a)^{m+n}$ [$\because a$ is non-zero integer]

Then, $(-2)^3 \times (-2)^{-6} = (-2)^{2x-1}$

$\Rightarrow (-2)^{3-6} = (-2)^{2x-1}$

$\Rightarrow (-2)^{-3} = (-2)^{2x-1}$

On comparing both sides, we get

$3- = 2x - 1$

$\Rightarrow 2x = -2 \Rightarrow x = -1$

(iii) We have, $(2^{-1} + 4^{-1} + 6^{-1} + 8^{-1})^x = 1$

Using law of exponents, $a^{-m} = \frac{1}{a^m}$ [$\because a$ is non-zero integer]

Then, $\left(\frac{1}{2} + \frac{1}{4} + \frac{1}{6} + \frac{1}{8}\right)^x = 1$

$\Rightarrow \left(\frac{12+6+4+3}{24}\right)^x = 1$ [$\because$ LCM of 2, 4, 6 and 8 = 24]

$\Rightarrow \left(\frac{25}{24}\right)^x = 1$

This can be possible only if $x = 0$. Since, $a^0 = 1$. [law of exponents]

Q. 100 Divide 293 by 1000000 and express the result in standard form.

Sol. $\because 1000000 = 10^6$

$\because \frac{293}{10^6} = 293 \times 10^{-6}$ $\left[\because \frac{1}{a^m} = a^{-m}\right]$

$= 2.93 \times 10^{-6} \times 10^2 = 2.93 \times 10^{-4}$

Q. 101 Find the value of x^{-3}, if $x = (100)^{1-4} \div (100)^0$.

Sol. Given, $x = (100)^{1-4} \div (100)^0$

$\Rightarrow x = (100)^{-3} \div (100)^0$

$\Rightarrow x = (100)^{-3-0}$ [$\because a^m \div a^n = (a)^{m-n}$]

$\Rightarrow x = (100)^{-3}$

So, $x^{-3} = [(100)^{-3}]^{-3} = (100)^9$ [$\because (a^m)^n = (a)^{mn}$]

Q. 102 **By what number should we multiply $(-29)^0$, so that the product becomes $(+29)^0$.**

Sol. Let n be multiplied with $(-29)^0$ to get $(+29)^0$.

So, $x \times (-29)^0 = (29)^0$

$\Rightarrow$ $x \times 1 = 1$ $[\because a^0 = 1]$

$\Rightarrow$ $x = 1$

Q. 103 **By what number should $(-15)^{-1}$ be divided so that quotient may be equal to $(-15)^{-1}$?**

Sol. Let $(-15)^{-1}$ be divided by x to get quotient $(-15)^{-1}$.

So, $\dfrac{(-15)^{-1}}{x} = (-15)^{-1}$

$\Rightarrow$ $\dfrac{(-15)^{-1}}{(-15)^{-1}} = x$

$\Rightarrow$ $x = (-15)^{-1+1}$ $[\because a^m \div a^n = (a)^{m-n}]$

$\Rightarrow$ $x = (-15)^0 = 1$ $[\because a^0 = 1]$

Q. 104 **Find the multiplicative inverse of $(-7)^{-2} \div (90)^{-1}$.**

Sol. a is called multiplicative inverse of b, if $a \times b = 1$.

We have, $(-7)^{-2} \div (90)^{-1} = \dfrac{1}{(7)^2} \div \dfrac{1}{(90)^1} = \dfrac{1}{49} \div \dfrac{1}{90} = \dfrac{1}{49} \times \dfrac{90}{1} = \dfrac{90}{49}$

$\left[\because (-a)^m = a^m, \text{if } m \text{ is an even number and } a^{-m} = \dfrac{1}{a^m}\right]$

Put $b = \dfrac{90}{49}$

$\therefore$ $a \times \dfrac{90}{49} = 1$

$\Rightarrow$ $a = \dfrac{49}{90}$

Q. 105 **If $5^{3x-1} \div 25 = 125$, find the value of x.**

Sol. Given, $5^{3x-1} \div 25 = 125$

$\because$ $25 = 5 \times 5 = 5^2$

and $125 = 5 \times 5 \times 5 = 5^3$

$\therefore$ $5^{3x-1} \div (5)^2 = (5)^3$

$\Rightarrow$ $(5)^{3x-1-2} = 5^3$ $[\because a^m \div a^n = (a)^{m-n}]$

$\Rightarrow$ $5^{3x-3} = (5)^3$

On comparing both sides, we get

$3x - 3 = 3$

$\Rightarrow$ $3x = 6$

$\Rightarrow$ $x = 2$

Q. 106 Write 390000000 in the standard form.

Sol. For standard form $390000000 = 39 \times 10 \times 10 \times 10 \times 10 \times 10 \times 10 \times 10$

$= 39 \times 10^7 = 3.9 \times 10^7 \times 10^1$

$= 3.9 \times 10^8$ $\quad [\because a^m \times a^n = (a)^{m+n}]$

Q. 107 Write 0.000005678 in the standard form.

Sol. For standard form, $0.000005678 = 0.5678 \times 10^{-5} = 5.678 \times 10^{-5} \times 10^{-1} = 5.678 \times 10^{-6}$
Hence, 5.678×10^{-6} is the standard form of 0.000005678.

Q. 108 Express the product of 3.2×10^6 and 4.1×10^{-1} in the standard form.

Sol. Product of 3.2×10^6 and 4.1×10^{-1}

$= (3.2 \times 10^6)(4.1 \times 10^{-1})$

$= (3.2 \times 4.1) \times 10^6 \times 10^{-1}$

$= 13.12 \times 10^5 = 1.312 \times 10^5 \times 10^1$ $\quad [\because a^m \times a^n = a^{m+n}]$

$= 1.312 \times 10^6$

Q. 109 Express $\dfrac{1.5 \times 10^6}{2.5 \times 10^{-4}}$ in the standard form.

Sol. Given, $\dfrac{1.5 \times 10^6}{2.5 \times 10^{-4}} = \dfrac{15}{25} \times 10^{6+4}$ $\quad [\because a^m \div a^n = (a)^{m-n}]$

$= \dfrac{3}{5} \times 10^{10} = 0.6 \times 10^{10}$

$= 6 \times 10^{10} \times 10^{-1} = 6 \times 10^9$ $\quad [\because a^m \times a^n = a^{m+n}]$

Q. 110 Some migratory birds travel as much as 15000 km to escape the extreme climatic conditions at home. Write the distance in metres using scientific notation.

Sol. Total distance travelled by migratory bird = 15000 km

$= 15000 \times 1000$ m $\quad [\because 1\text{ km} = 1000\text{ m}]$

$= 15000000$ m

$= 15 \times 10^6$ m

Scientific notation of $15 \times 10^6 = 1.5 \times 10^7$ m

Q. 111 Pluto is 5913000000 m from the Sun. Express this in the standard form.

Sol. Distance between Pluto and Sun = 5913000000

Standard form of $5913000000 = 5913 \times 10^6$

$= 5.913 \times 10^6 \times 10^3$

$= 5.913 \times 10^9$ $\quad [\because a^m \times a^n = (a)^{m+n}]$

Q. 112 Special balances can weigh something as 0.00000001 gram. Express this number in the standard form.

Sol. Weight = 0.00000001 g

Standard form of 0.00000001 g = 0.1×10^{-7} g

$= 1 \times 10^{-7} \times 10^{-1}$ g

$= 1.0 \times 10^{-8}$ g $\quad [\because a^m \times a^n = (a)^{m+n}]$

Q. 113 A sugar factory has annual sales of 3 billion 720 million kilograms of sugar. Express this number in the standard form.

Sol. Annual sales of a sugar factory = 3 billion 720 million kilograms = 3720000 kg

Standard form of 3720000 = $372 \times 10 \times 10 \times 10 \times 10 = 372 \times 10^4$ kg

$= 3.72 \times 10^4 \times 10^2 = 3.72 \times 10^6$ kg $\quad [\because a^m \times a^n = (a)^{m+n}]$

Q. 114 The number of red blood cells per cubic millimetre of blood is approximately 5.5 million. If the average body contains 5 L of blood, what is the total number of red cells in the body? Write the standard form. ($1 \text{ L} = 100000 \text{ mm}^3$)

Sol. The average body contain 5 L of blood.

Also, the number of red blood cells per cubic millimetre of blood is approximately 5.5 million.

Blood contained by body = 5 L = $5 \times 100000 \text{ mm}^3$

Red blood cells = $5 \times 100000 \text{ mm}^3$

Blood = $5.5 \times 1000000 \times 5 \times 100000 = 55 \times 5 \times 10^{5+5}$

$= 275 \times 10^{10} = 2.75 \times 10^{10} \times 10^2 = 2.75 \times 10^{12}$

Q. 115 Express each of the following in standard form:

(a) The mass of a proton in gram is $\dfrac{1673}{1000000000000000000000000000}$

(b) A helium atom has a diameter of 0.000000022 cm.

(c) Mass of a molecule of hydrogen gas is about 0.00000000000000000000334 tonnes.

(d) Human body has 1 trillon of cells which vary in shapes and sizes.

(e) Express 56 km in m.

(f) Express 5 tonnes in g.

(g) Express 2 yr in seconds.

(h) Express 5 hectares in cm^2. ($1 \text{ hec} = 10000 \text{ m}^2$)

Sol. (a) Given, mass of a proton in gram = $\dfrac{1673}{1000000000000000000000000000}$

Standard form = $\dfrac{1673}{10^{27}} = 1673 \times 10^{-27}$ g $\quad \left[\because a^{-m} = \dfrac{1}{a^m}\right]$

$= 1.673 \times 10^{-27} \times 10^3$ g

$= 1.673 \times 10^{-27+3} = 1.673 \times 10^{-24}$ g $\quad [\because a^m \times a^n = (a)^{m+n}]$

(b) A helium atom has a diameter of 0.000000022 cm.

Standard form of 0.000000022 cm $= 0.22 \times 10^{-7} = 2.2 \times 10^{-7} \times 10^{-1}$

$= 2.2 \times 10^{-8}$ cm $[\because a^m \times a^n = (a)^{m+n}]$

(c) Mass of a molecule of hydrogen gas is about 0.00000000000000000000334 tonnes

Standard form $= 0.334 \times 10^{-20} = 3.34 \times 10^{-20} \times 10^{-1}$

$= 3.34 \times 10^{-21}$ $[\because a^m \times a^n = (a)^{m+n}]$

(d) Cells in human body = 1 trillon

$\because$ 1 trillon = 1000000000000

Standard form of 1000000000000

$= 10 \times 10 \times 10 \times 10 \times 10 \times 10 \times 10 \times 10 \times 10 \times 10 \times 10 \times 10 = 10^{12}$ $[\because a^m \times a^n = (a)^{m+n}]$

(e) Given, 56 km = 56 × 1000 m $[\because 1\text{ km} = 1000\text{ m}]$

= 56000 m

Standard form of 56000 m $= 56 \times 10^3 = 5.6 \times 10^3 \times 10^1 = 5.6 \times 10^4$ m

$[\because a^m \times a^n = (a)^{m+n}]$

(f) Given, 5 tonnes = 5 × 100 kg $[\because 1\text{ tonne} = 100\text{ kg}]$

= 5 × 100 × 1000 g $[\because 1\text{ kg} = 1000\text{ g}]$

= 500000 g

Standard form of 500000 $= 5 \times 10 \times 10 \times 10 \times 10 \times 10 = 5 \times 10^5$ $[\because a^m \times a^n = (a)^{m+n}]$

(g) Given, 2 yr = 2 × 365 days $[\because 1\text{ yr} = 365\text{ days approx.}]$

= 2 × 365 × 24 h $[\because 1\text{ day} = 24\text{ h}]$

= 2 × 365 × 24 × 60 min $[\because 1\text{ h} = 60\text{ min}]$

= 2 × 365 × 24 × 60 × 60 s $[\because 1\text{ min} = 60\text{ s}]$

= 63072000 s

Standard form of 63072000 $= 63072 \times 10 \times 10 \times 10 = 63072 \times 10^3$

$[\because a^m \times a^n = (a)^{m+n}]$

$= 6.3072 \times 10^3 \times 10^4 = 6.3072 \times 10^7$ s

(h) Given, 5 hec = 5 × 10000 m^2 $[\because 1\text{ hec} = 10000\text{ m}^2]$

= 5 × 10000 × 100 × 100 cm^2 $[\because 1\text{ m} = 100\text{ cm}]$

Standard form of 5 × 10000 × 100 × 100 cm^2

$= 5 \times 10 \times 10 \times 10 \times 10 \times 10 \times 10 \times 10 \times 10$

$= 5 \times 10^8$ cm^2 $[\because a^m \times a^n = (a)^{m+n}]$

Q. 116 Find x, so that $\left(\frac{2}{9}\right)^3 \times \left(\frac{2}{9}\right)^{-6} = \left(\frac{2}{9}\right)^{2x-1}$.

Sol. Given, $\left(\frac{2}{9}\right)^3 \times \left(\frac{2}{9}\right)^{-6} = \left(\frac{2}{9}\right)^{2x-1}$

Using law of exponents, $a^m \times a^n = (a)^{m+n}$ $[\because a \text{ is non-zero integer}]$

Then, $\left(\frac{2}{9}\right)^{3-6} = \left(\frac{2}{9}\right)^{2x-1}$

$\Rightarrow$ $\left(\frac{2}{9}\right)^{-3} = \left(\frac{2}{9}\right)^{2x-1}$

On comparing, we get

$$-3 = 2x - 1$$
$$\Rightarrow \quad -2 = 2x$$
$$\Rightarrow \quad x = -1$$

Q. 117 **By what number should $\left(\frac{-3}{2}\right)^{-3}$ be divided so that the quotient may be $\left(\frac{4}{27}\right)^{-2}$?**

Sol. Let $\left(\frac{-3}{2}\right)^{-3}$ be divided by x to get $\left(\frac{4}{27}\right)^{-2}$ as quotient.

Then, $$\left(\frac{-3}{2}\right)^{-3} \div x = \left(\frac{4}{27}\right)^{-2}$$

$$\Rightarrow \quad x = \left(\frac{-3}{2}\right)^{-3} \div \left(\frac{2^2}{3^3}\right)^{-2} = \left(\frac{-3}{2}\right)^{-3} \div \frac{(2)^{-4}}{(3)^{-6}}$$

$$= \left(\frac{-3}{2}\right)^{-3} \times \frac{(3)^{-6}}{(2)^{-4}}$$

$$= \frac{(-3)^{-3} \times (3)^{-6}}{2^{-3} \times 2^{-4}} = \frac{3^{-9}}{2^{-7}} \qquad [\because a^m \times a^n = a^{m+n}]$$

$$= \frac{2^7}{3^9} \qquad \left[\because a^{-m} = \frac{1}{a^m} \text{ and } (a^m)^n = (a)^{mn}\right]$$

In questions 118 and 119, find the value of n.

Q. 118 $\frac{6^n}{6^{-2}} = 6^3$

Sol. Given, $\frac{6^n}{6^{-2}} = 6^3$

Using law of exponents, $\frac{6^n}{6^{-2}} = 6^3$ [$\because a$ is non-zero integer]

$$\Rightarrow \quad 6^{n+2} = 6^3 \qquad [\because a^m \div a^n = a^{m-n}]$$

On comparing both sides,we get

$$n + 2 = 3 \Rightarrow n = 1$$

Q. 119 $\frac{2^n \times 2^6}{2^{-3}} = 2^{18}$

Sol. Given, $\frac{2^n \times 2^6}{2^{-3}} = 2^{18}$

Using law of exponents, $a^{-m} = \frac{1}{a^m}$ [$\because a$ is non-zero integer]

$$\Rightarrow \quad 2^n \times 2^6 \times 2^3 = 2^{18}$$

$$\Rightarrow \quad 2^{n+9} = 2^{18} \qquad [\because a^m \times a^n = a^{m+n}]$$

On comparing both sides , we get

$$n + 9 = 18 \Rightarrow n = 9 \qquad [\because a^m \div a^n = (a)^{m-n}]$$

Q. 120 $\dfrac{125 \times x^{-3}}{5^{-3} \times 25 \times x^{-6}}$

Sol. Using laws of exponents, $a^m \div a^n = (a)^{n-m}$ and $a^{-m} = \dfrac{1}{a^m}$ [$\because a$ is non-zero integer]

$$\therefore \quad \frac{125 \times x^{-3}}{5^{-3} \times 25 \times x^{-6}} = (5)^3 \times 5^3 \times 5^{-2} \times x^{-3} \times x^6 \qquad \left[\because 125 = 5 \times 5 \times 5 \text{ and } 25 = 5 \times 5\right]$$

$$= 5^4 \times x^3$$

$$= 5 \times 5 \times 5 \times 5 \times x^3$$

$$= 625\, x^3 \qquad [\because a^m \times a^n = a^{m+n}]$$

Q. 121 $\dfrac{16 \times 10^2 \times 64}{2^4 \times 4^2}$

Sol. Using laws of exponents, $a^m \div a^n = (a)^{m-n}$ and $a^m \times a^n = a^{m+n}$ [$\because a$ is non-zero integer]

$$\therefore \quad \frac{16 \times 10^2 \times 64}{2^4 \times 4^2} = (4)^2 \times 10^2 \times 2^{-4} \times (4)^3 \times 4^{-2} \qquad \left[\because 64 = 4 \times 4 \times 4 \text{ and } 16 = 4 \times 4\right]$$

$$= (4)^3 \times 10^2 \times 2^{-4}$$

$$= (2^2)^3 \times 10^2 \times 2^{-4}$$

$$= 2^6 \times 10^2 \times 2^{-4}$$

$$= 2^2 \times 10^2 = 4 \times 100 = 400 \qquad [\because 2^2 = 4]$$

Q. 122 If $\dfrac{5^m \times 5^3 \times 5^{-2}}{5^{-5}} = 5^{12}$, then find m.

Sol. Given, $\dfrac{5^m \times 5^3 \times 5^{-2}}{5^{-5}} = 5^{12}$

Using laws of exponents, $a^m \div a^n = (a)^{m-n}$ and $a^{-m} = \dfrac{1}{a^n}$ [$\because a$ is non-zero integer]

Then, $5^m \times 5^3 \times 5^{-2} \times 5^5 = 5^{12}$

$\Rightarrow \quad 5^m \times 5^8 \times 5^{-2} = 5^{12}$

$\Rightarrow \quad 5^m \times 5^6 = 5^{12}$

$\Rightarrow \quad 5^{m+6} = 5^{12}$ [$\because a^m \times a^n = a^{m+n}$]

On comparing both sides, we get

$m + 6 = 12$

$\Rightarrow \quad m = 6$

Q. 123 A new born bear weights 4 kg. How many kilograms might a five year old bear weight if its weight increases by the power of 2 in 5 yr?

Sol. Weight of new born bear = 4 kg

Weight increases by the power of 2 in 5 yr.

Weight of bear in 5 yr = $(4)^2 = 16$ kg

Q. 124 **The cell of a bacteria doubles in every 30 min. A scientist begins with a single cell. How many cells will be thereafter**

(a) 12 h **(b) 24 h ?**

Sol. The cell of a bacteria in every 30 min = 2 [∵ 1 + 1 = 2 in 30 min]

So, cell of a bacteria in 1 h = 2^2 [∵ 2 + 2 in 1 h]

(a) Cell of a bacteria in 12 h = $2^2 \times 2^2 \times 2^2 \times 2^2 \times 2^2 \times 2^2 \times 2^2 \times 2^2 \times 2^2 \times 2^2 \times 2^2 \times 2^2$

$= 2^{24}$ [$\because a^m \times a^n = a^{m+n}$]

(b) Similarly, bacteria in 24 h = $2^{24} \times 2^{24} = 2^{24+24} = 2^{48}$ [$\because a^m + a^n = a^{m+n}$]

Q. 125 **Planet *A* is at a distance of 9.35×10^6 km from Earth and planet *B* is 6.27×10^7 km from Earth. Which planet is nearer to Earth?**

Sol. Distance between planet *A* and Earth = 9.35×10^6 km

Distance between planet *B* and Earth = 6.27×10^7 km

For finding difference between above two distances, we have to change both in same exponent of 10, i.e. $9.35 \times 10^6 = 0.935 \times 10^7$, clearly 6.27×10^7 is greater.

So, planet *A* is nearer to Earth.

Q. 126 **The cells of a bacteria double itself every hour. How many cells will be there after 8 h, if initially we start with 1 cell. Express the answer in powers.**

Sol. The cell of a bacteria double itself every hour = $1 + 1 = 2 = 2^1$

Since, the process started with 1 cell.

∴ The total number of cell in 8 h = $2^1 \times 2^1 \times 2^1 \times 2^1 \times 2^1 \times 2^1 \times 2^1 \times 2^1$

$= 2^{1+1+1+1+1+1+1+1} = 2^8$ [$\because a^m \times a^n = (a)^{m+n}$]

Q. 127 **An insect is on the 0 point of a number line, hopping towards 1. She covers half the distance from her current location to 1 with each hop. So, she will be at $\frac{1}{2}$ after one hop, $\frac{3}{4}$ after two hops and so on.**

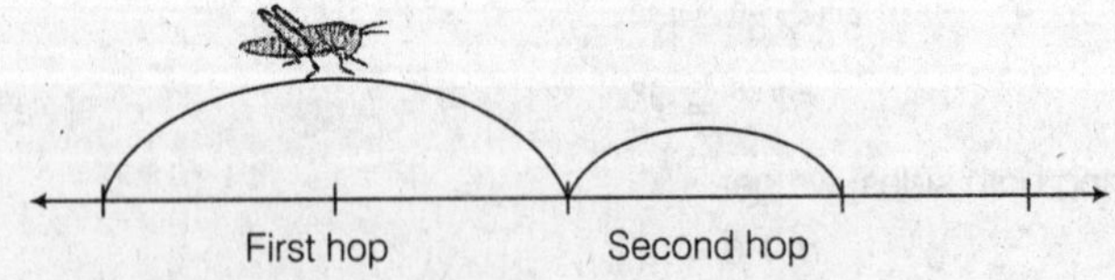

(a) Make a table showing the insect's location for the first 10 hops.

(b) Where will the insect be after *n* hops?

(c) Will the insect ever get to 1? Explain.

Sol. (a) On the basis of given information in the question, we can arrange the following table which shows the insect's location for the first 10 hops.

Number of hops	Distance Covered	Distance left	Distance covered
1.	$\frac{1}{2}$	$\frac{1}{2}$	$1-\frac{1}{2}$
2.	$\frac{1}{2}\left(\frac{1}{2}\right)+\frac{1}{2}$	$\frac{1}{4}$	$1-\frac{1}{4}$
3.	$\frac{1}{2}\left(\frac{1}{4}\right)+\frac{3}{4}$	$\frac{1}{8}$	$1-\frac{1}{8}$
4.	$\frac{1}{2}\left(\frac{1}{8}\right)+\frac{7}{8}$	$\frac{1}{16}$	$1-\frac{1}{16}$
5.	$\frac{1}{2}\left(\frac{1}{16}\right)+\frac{15}{16}$	$\frac{1}{32}$	$1-\frac{1}{32}$
6.	$\frac{1}{2}\left(\frac{1}{32}\right)+\frac{31}{32}$	$\frac{1}{64}$	$1-\frac{1}{64}$
7.	$\frac{1}{2}\left(\frac{1}{64}\right)+\frac{63}{64}$	$\frac{1}{128}$	$1-\frac{1}{128}$
8.	$\frac{1}{2}\left(\frac{1}{128}\right)+\frac{127}{128}$	$\frac{1}{256}$	$1-\frac{1}{256}$
9.	$\frac{1}{2}\left(\frac{1}{256}\right)+\frac{255}{256}$	$\frac{1}{512}$	$1-\frac{1}{512}$
10.	$\frac{1}{2}\left(\frac{1}{512}\right)+\frac{511}{512}$	$\frac{1}{1024}$	$1-\frac{1}{1024}$

(b) If we see the distance covered in each hops

Distance covered in 1st hop $= 1-\frac{1}{2}$

Distance covered in 2nd hops $= 1-\frac{1}{4}$

Distance covered in 3rd hops $= 1-\frac{1}{8}$

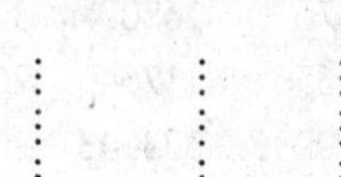

Distance covered in n hops $= 1-\left(\frac{1}{2}\right)^n$

(c) No, because for reaching 1, $\left(\frac{1}{2}\right)^n$ has to be zero for some finite n which is not possible.

Q. 128 Predicting the ones digit, copy and complete this table and answer the questions that follow.

Powers Table

x	1^x	2^x	3^x	4^x	5^x	6^x	7^x	8^x	9^x	10^x
1	1	2								
2	1	4								
3	1	8								
4	1	16								
5	1	32								
6	1	64								
7	1	128								
8	1	256								
Ones digits of the powers	1	2,4,6,8								

(a) Describe patterns you see in the ones digits of the powers.

(b) Predict the ones digit in the following.

(i) 4^{12} (ii) 9^{20}

(iii) 3^{17} (iv) 5^{100}

(v) 10^{500}

(c) Predict the ones digit in the following.

(i) 31^{10} (ii) 12^{10}

(iii) 17^{21} (iv) 29^{10}

Sol. (a) On the basis of given pattern in 1^x and 2^x, we can make more patterns for 3^x 4^x, 5^x, 6^x, 7^x, 8^x, 9^x, 10^x.

Thus, we have following table which shows all details about the patterns.

x	1^x	2^x	3^x	4^x	5^x	6^x	7^x	8^x	9^x	10^x
1	1	2	3	4	5	6	7	8	9	10
2	1	4	9	16	25	36	49	64	81	100
3	1	8	27	64	125	216	343	512	729	1000
4	1	16	81	256	625	1296	2401	4096	6561	10000
5	1	32	243	1024	3125	7776	16807	32768	59049	100000
6	1	64	729	4096	15625	46656	117649	262144	531441	1000000
7	1	128	2187	16384	78125	279936	823543	2097152	4782969	10000000
8	1	256	6561	65536	390625	1679616	5764801	16777216	43046721	100000000
Ones digits of the powers	1	2,4,8,6	3,9,7,1	4,6	5	6	7,9,3,1	8,4,2,6	9.1	0

(b) (i) ones digit in 4^{12} is 6. (ii) ones digit in 9^{20} is 1.

(iii) ones digit in 3^{17} is 3. (iv) ones digit in 5^{100} is 5.

(v) ones digit in 10^{500} is 0.

Note *Follow the above given table.*

(c) (i) ones digit in 31^{10} is 1. (ii) ones digit in 12^{10} is 4.

(iii) ones digit in 17^{21} is 7. (iv) ones digit in 29^{10} is 1.

Q. 129 Astronomy The table shows the mass of the planets, the Sun and the Moon in our solar system.

Celestial Body	Mass (kg)	Mass (kg) Standard Notation
Sun	1,990,000,000,000,000,000,000,000,000,000	1.99×10^{30}
Mercury	330,000,000,000,000,000,000,000	
Venus	4,870,000,000,000,000,000,000,000	
Earth	5,970,000,000,000,000,000,000,000	
Mars	642,000,000,000,000,000,000,000,000,000	
Jupiter	1,900,000,000,000,000,000,000,000,000	
Saturn	568,000,000,000,000,000,000,000,000	
Uranus	86,800,000,000,000,000,000,000,000	
Neptune	102,000,000,000,000,000,000,000,000	
Pluto	12,700,000,000,000,000,000,000	
Moon	79,500,000,000,000,000,000,000	

(a) Write the mass of each planet and the Moon in scientific notation.
(b) Order the planets and the Moon by mass, from least to greatest.
(c) Which planet has about the same mass as Earth?

Sol. (a) Mass of each planet and Moon in scientific notation is given below:

Using law ot exponents, $a^m \times a^n = a^{m+n}$

Sun $= 199 \times 10^{28} = 1.99 \times 10^{28} \times 10^2 = 1.99 \times 10^{30}$

Mercury $= 33 \times 10^{22} = 3.3 \times 10^{22} \times 10 = 3.3 \times 10^{23}$

Venus $= 487 \times 10^{22} = 4.87 \times 10^{22} \times 10^2 = 4.87 \times 10^{24}$

Earth $= 597 \times 10^{22} = 5.97 \times 10^{22} \times 10^2 = 5.97 \times 10^{24}$

Mars $= 642 \times 10^{27} = 6.42 \times 10^{27} \times 10^2 = 6.42 \times 10^{29}$

Jupiter $= 19 \times 10^{26} = 1.9 \times 10^{26} \times 10 = 1.9 \times 10^{27}$

Saturn $= 568 \times 10^{24} = 5.68 \times 10^{24} \times 10^2 = 5.68 \times 10^{26}$

Uranus $= 868 \times 10^{23} = 8.68 \times 10^{23} \times 10^2 = 8.68 \times 10^{25}$

Neptune $= 102 \times 10^{24} = 1.02 \times 10^{24} \times 10^2 = 1.02 \times 10^{26}$

Pluto $= 127 \times 10^{20} = 1.27 \times 10^{20} \times 10^2 = 1.27 \times 10^{22}$

Moon $= 795 \times 10^{20} = 7.95 \times 10^{20} \times 10^2 = 7.95 \times 10^{22}$

(b) Order of mass of all planets and Moon from least to greatest

Pluto < Moon < Mercury < Venus < Earth < Uranus < Neptune < Saturn < Jupiter < Mars

(c) Venus has about the same mass as Earth.

Q. 130 Investigating Solar System The table shows the average distance from each planet in our solar system to the Sun.

Planet	Distance from Sun (km)	Distance from Sun (km) Standard Notation
Earth	149,600,000	1.496×10^8
Jupiter	778,300,000	
Mars	227,900,000	
Mercury	57,900,000	
Neptune	4,497,000,000	
Pluto	5,900,000,000	
Saturn	1,427,000,000	
Uranus	2,870,000,000	
Venus	108,200,000	

(a) Complete the table by expressing the distance from each planet to the Sun in scientific notation.

(b) Order the planets from closest to the Sun to farthest from the Sun.

Sol. (a) Scientific notation of distance from Sun to

Earth $= 149600000 = 1496 \times 10^5 = 1.496 \times 10^8$

Jupiter $= 149600000 = 1496 \times 10^5 = 1.496 \times 10^8$

Mars $= 227900000 = 2279 \times 10^5 = 2.279 \times 10^8$

Mercury $= 57900000 = 579 \times 10^5 = 5.79 \times 10^7$

Neptune $= 4497000000 = 4497 \times 10^6 = 4.497 \times 10^9$

Pluto $= 5900000000 = 59 \times 10^8 = 5.9 \times 10^9$

Saturn $= 1427000000 = 1427 \times 10^6 = 1.427 \times 10^9$

Uranus $= 2870000000 = 287 \times 10^7 = 2.87 \times 10^9$

Venus $= 108200000 = 1082 \times 10^5 = 1.082 \times 10^8$

(b) Order of planet from closest to the Sun to farthest from the Sun is given by

Mercury $<$ Venus $<$ Earth $<$ Mars $<$ Jupiter $<$ Saturn $<$ Uranus $<$ Neptune $<$ Pluto

Q. 131 This table shows the mass of one atom for five chemical elements. Use it to answer the question given.

Elements	Mass of atom (kg)
Titanium	7.95×10^{-26}
Lead	3.44×10^{-25}
Silver	1.79×10^{-25}
Lithium	1.15×10^{-26}
Hydrogen	1.674×10^{-27}

(a) Which is the heaviest element?

(b) Which element is lighter, Silver or Titanium?

(c) List all the five elements in order from lightest to heaviest.

Sol. Arrangement of masses of atoms in same power of 10 is given by

Titanium $= 7.95 \times 10^{-26}$

Lead $= 34.4 \times 10^{-26}$

Silver $= 17.9 \times 10^{-26}$

Lithium $= 1.15 \times 10^{-26}$

Hydrogen $= 0.1674 \times 10^{-26}$

Thus, we have

$34.4 > 17.9 > 7.95 > 1.15 > 0.1674$

(a) Lead is the heaviest element.

(b) Silver $= 17.9 \times 10^{-26}$ and Titanium $= 7.95 \times 10^{-26}$, so titanium is lighter.

(c) Arrangement of elements in order from lightest to heaviest is given by
Hydrogen < Lithium < Titanium < Silver < Lead

Q. 132 The planet Uranus is approximately 2,896,819,200,000 metres away from the Sun. What is this distance in standard form?

Sol. Distance between the planet Uranus and the Sun is 2896819200000 m.

Standard form of $2896819200000 = 28968192 \times 10 \times 10 \times 10 \times 10 \times 10$

$= 28968192 \times 10^5 = 2.8968192 \times 10^{12}$ m

Q. 133 An inch is approximately equal to 0.02543 metres. Write this distance in standard form.

Sol. Standard form of 0.02543 m $= 0.2543 \times 10^{-1}$ m $= 2.543 \times 10^{-2}$ m

Hence, standard form of 0.02543 is 2.543×10^{-2} m.

Q. 134 The volume of the Earth is approximately 7.67×10^{-7} times the volume of the Sun. Express this figure in usual form.

Sol. Given, volume of the Earth is 7.67×10^{-7} times the volume of the Sun.

Usual form of $7.67 \times 10^{-7} = 0.000000767$

[$\because$ placing decimal 7 places towards the left of original position]

Q. 135 An electron's mass is approximately $9.1093826 \times 10^{-31}$ kilograms. What is its mass in grams?

Sol. Mass of electron $= 9.1093826 \times 10^{-31}$ kg

$= 9.1093826 \times 10^{-31} \times 1000$ g [$\because$ 1 kg = 1000 g]

$= 9.1093826 \times 10^{-31} \times 10^3 = 9.1093826 \times 10^{-28}$ g [$\because a^m \times a^n = (a)^{m+n}$]

Q. 136 At the end of the 20th century, the world population was approximately 6.1×10^9 people. Express this population in usual form. How would you say this number in words?

Sol. Given, at the end of the 20th century, the world population was 6.1×10^9 (approx).

People population in usual form = $6.1 \times 10^9 = 6100000000$

Hence, population in usual form was six thousand one hundred million.

Q. 137 While studying her family's history, Shikha discovers records of ancestors 12 generations back. She wonders how many ancestors she had in the past 12 generations. She starts to make a diagram to help her figure this out. The diagram soon becomes very complex.

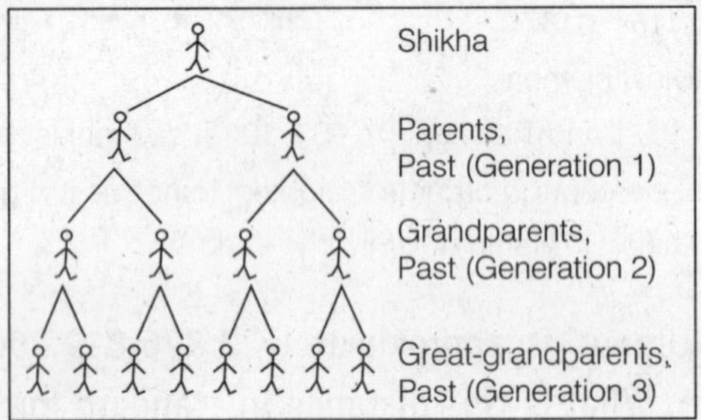

(a) Make a table and a graph showing the number of ancestors in each of the 12 generations.

(b) Write an equation for the number of ancestors in a given generation *n*.

Sol. (a) On the basis of given diagram, we can make a table that shows the number of ancestors in each of the 12 generations.

Generations	Ancestors
1st	2
2nd	2^2
3rd	2^3
⋮	⋮
12th	2^{12}

Hence, we can also make a graph that shows the relation between generation and ancestor.

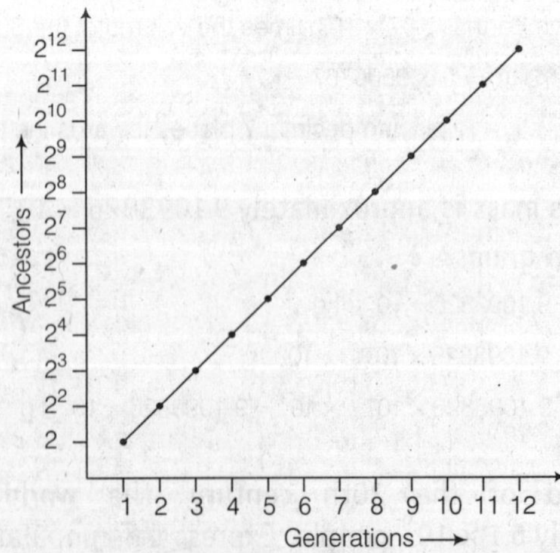

(b) On the basis of generation-ancestor graph, the number of ancestors in n generations will 2^n.

Q. 138 About 230 billion litres of water flows through a river each day, how many litres of water flows through that river in a week? How many litres of water flows through the river in an year? Write your answer in standard notation.

Sol. Water flows through a river in each day = 230000000000 or 230 billion

Water flows through the river in a week $= 7 \times 230000000000$ [$\because$ 1 week = 7 days]

$= 1610000000000$

$= 1610$ billion

$= 1.61 \times 10^{12}$ L

Water flows through the river in an year $= 230000000000 \times 365$ [$\because$ 1 yr = 365 days]

$= 83950000000000$

$= 8.395 \times 10^{13}$ L

Q. 139 A half-life is the amount of time that it takes for a radioactive substance to decay one-half of its original quantity.

Suppose radioactive decay causes 300 grams of a substance to decrease 300×2^{-3} grams after 3 half-lives. Evaluate 300×2^{-3} to determine how many grams of the substance is left.

Explain why the expression 300×2^{-n} can be used to find the amount of the substance that remains after n half-lives.

Sol. Since, 300 g of a substance is decrease to 300×2^{-3} g after 3 half-lives.

So, we have to evaluate $300 \times 2^{-3} = \frac{300}{8} = 37.5$ g [$\because 2^3 = 8$]

Q. 140 Consider a quantity of a radioactive substance. The fraction of this quantity that remains after t half-lives can be found by using the expression 3^{-t}.

(a) What fraction of the substance remains after 7 half-lives?

(b) After how many half-lives will the fraction be $\frac{1}{243}$ of the original?

Sol. (a) Since, 3^{-t} expression is used for finding the fraction of the quantity that remains after t half-lives.

Hence, the fraction of substance remains after 7 half-lives will be equal to 3^{-7}, i.e. $\frac{1}{3^7}$.

(b) Given, t half-lives $= 3^{-t}$

So, $\frac{1}{243} = 3^{-t}$

$\Rightarrow \frac{1}{3^5} = \frac{1}{3^t}$ $\left[\because 3 \times 3 \times 3 \times 3 \times 3 = 3^5 \text{ and } a^{-m} = \frac{1}{a^m}\right]$

On comparing both sides, we get $t = 5$ half-lives.

Q. 141 One fermi is equal to 10^{-15} metre. The radius of a proton is 1.3 fermi. Write the radius of a proton (in metres) in standard form.

Sol. The radius of a proton is 1.3 fermi.

One fermi is equal to 10^{-15} m.

So, the radius of the proton is 1.3×10^{-15} m.

Hence, standard form of radius of the proton is 1.3×10^{-15} m.

Q. 142 The paper clip below has the indicated length. What is the length in standard form.

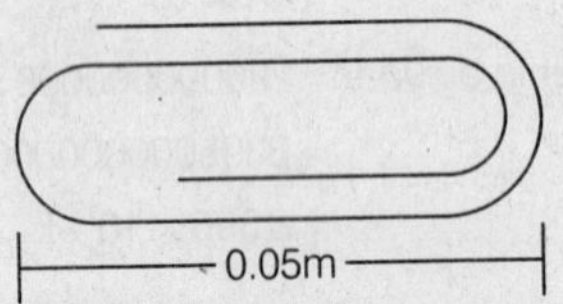

Sol. Length of the paper clip = 0.05 m

In standard form, $0.05\text{ m} = 0.5 \times 10^{-1} = 5.0 \times 10^{-2}$ m

Hence, the length of the paper clip in standard form is 5.0×10^{-2} m.

Q. 143 Use the properties of exponents to verify that each statement is true.

(a) $\frac{1}{4}(2^n) = 2^{n-2}$ (b) $4^{n-1} = \frac{1}{4}(4)^n$

(c) $25(5^{n-2}) = 5^n$

Sol. (a) $\frac{1}{4}(2^n) = 2^{n-2}$

$\text{RHS} = 2^{n-2} = 2^n \div 2^2$ $[\because a^m \div a^n = (a)^{m-n}]$

$= \frac{2^n}{4} = \text{LHS}$

(b) $4^{n-1} = \frac{1}{4}(4)^n$

$\text{LHS} = 4^{n-1} = 4^n \div 4^1$ $[\because a^m \div a^n = (a)^{m-n}]$

$= \frac{4^n}{4} = \text{RHS}$

(c) $25(5^{n-2}) = 5^n$

$\text{LHS} = 25(5^{n-2}) = 5^2(5^n \div 5^2)$

$= 5^2 \times 5^n \times \frac{1}{5^2} = 5^n = \text{RHS}$

Q. 144 Fill in the blanks.

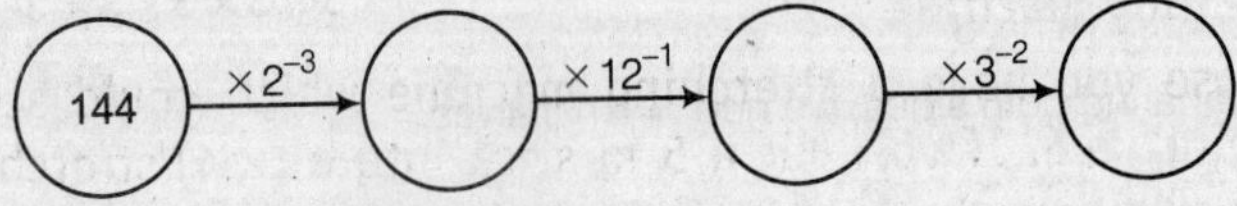

Sol. $144 \times 2^{-3} = 144 \times \frac{1}{8} = \mathbf{18}$

$18 \times 12^{-1} = 18 \times \frac{1}{12} = \mathbf{\frac{3}{2}}$

$\frac{3}{2} \times 3^{-2} = \frac{3}{2} \times \frac{1}{3^2} = \frac{1}{2 \times 3} = \mathbf{\frac{1}{6}}$

Q. 145 There are 86400 sec in a day. How many days long is a second? Express your answer in scientific notation.

Sol. Total seconds in a day = 86400

So, a second is long as $\frac{1}{86400} = 0.000011574$

Scientific notation of $0.000011574 = 1.1574 \times 10^{-5}$ days

Q. 146 The given table shows the crop production of a state in the year 2008 and 2009. Observe the table given below and answer the given questions.

Crop	**2008 Harvest** (Hectare)	**Increase/Decrease** (Hectare) **in 2009**
Bajra	1.4×10^3	-100
Jowar	1.7×10^6	-440000
Rice	3.7×10^3	-100
Wheat	5.1×10^5	$+ 190000$

(a) For which crop(s) did the production decrease?

(b) Write the production of all the crops in 2009 in their standard form.

(c) Assuming the same decrease in rice production each year as in 2009, how many acres will be harvested in 2015? Write in standard form.

Sol. (a) On the basis of given table, bajra, jowar and rice crops's production decreased.

(b) The production of all crop in 2009

$$\text{Bajra} = 1.4 \times 10^3 - 0.1 \times 10^3 = 1.3 \times 10^3$$

$$\text{Jowar} = 1.7 \times 10^6 - 44 \times 10^4$$

$$= 1.7 \times 10^6 - 0.44 \times 10^6 = 1.26 \times 10^6$$

$$\text{Rice} = 3.7 \times 10^3 - 0.1 \times 10^3 = 3.6 \times 10^3$$

$$\text{Wheat} = 5.1 \times 10^5 + 19 \times 10^4$$

$$= 5.1 \times 10^5 + 1.9 \times 10^5 = 7 \times 10^5$$

(c) Incomplete information

Q. 147 Stretching Machine

Suppose you have a stretching machine which could stretch almost anything. e.g. If you put a 5 m stick into a (× 4) stretching machine (as shown below), you get a 20 m stick.

Now, if you put 10 cm carrot into a (× 4) machine, how long will it be when it comes out?

Sol. According to the question, if we put a 5m stick into a (× 4) stretching machine, then machine produces 20 m stick.

Similarly, if we put 10 cm carrot into a (× 4) stretching machine, then machine produce $10 \times 4 = 40$ cm stick.

Q. 148 Two machines can be hooked together. When something is sent through this hook up, the output from the first machine becomes the input for the second.

(a) Which two machines hooked together do the same work a ($\times 10^2$) machine does? Is there more than one arrangement of two machines that will work?

(b) Which stretching machine does the same work as two (× 2) machines hooked together?

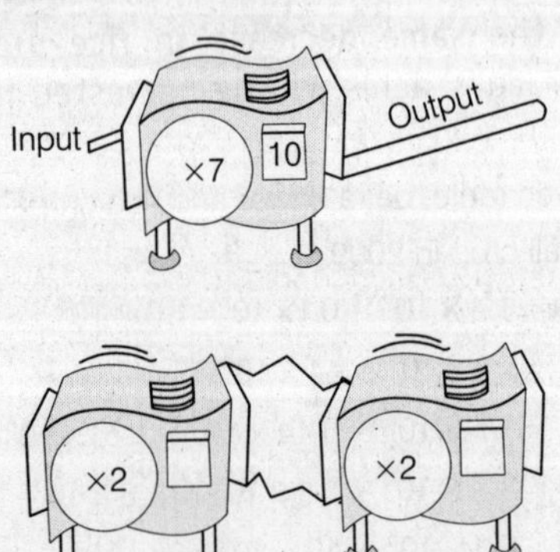

Sol. (a) For getting the same work a ($\times 10^2$) machine does, we have to ($\times 2^2$) and ($\times 5^2$) machines hooked together.

$\therefore \quad \times 10^2 = \times 100$

Similarly, $\times 2^2 \times 5^2 = \times 4 \times 25 = \times 100$

(b) If two machines (× 2) and (× 2) are hooked together to produce × 4, then a (× 4) single machine produce the same work.

Q. 149 Repeater Machine

Similarly, repeater machine is a hypothetical machine which automatically enlarges items several times. e.g. Sending a piece of wire through a ($\times 2^4$) machine is the same as putting it through a ($\times$ 2) machine four times.

So, if you send a 3 cm piece of wire thorugh a $(\times 2)^4$ machine, its length becomes $3 \times 2 \times 2 \times 2 \times 2 = 48$ cm. It can also be written that a base (2) machine is being applied 4 times.

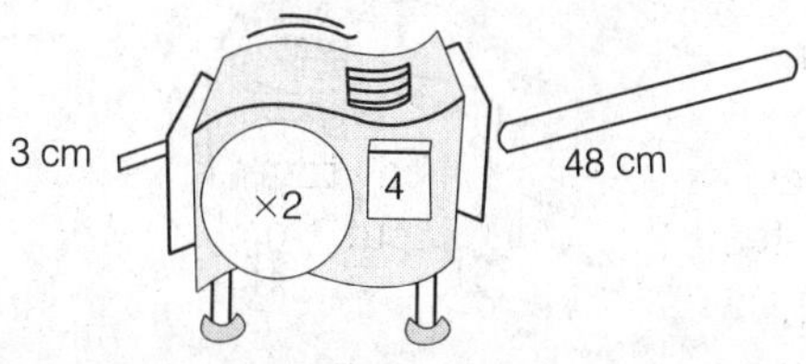

What will be the new length of a 4 cm strip inserted in the machine?

Sol. According to the question, if we put a 3 cm piece of wire through a ($\times 2^4$) machine, its length becomes $3 \times 2 \times 2 \times 2 \times 2 = 48$ cm.

Similarly, 4 cm long strip becomes $4 \times 2 \times 2 \times 2 \times 2 = 64$ cm.

Q. 150 For the following repeater machines, how many times the base machine is applied and how much the total stretch is?

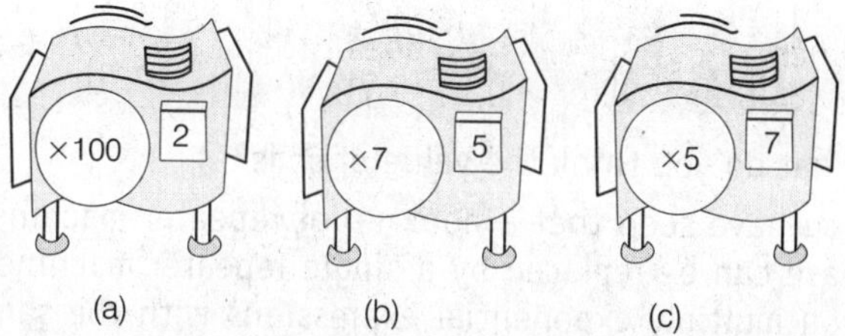

Sol. In machine (a), ($\times 100^2$) = 10000 stretch. Since, it is two times the base machine.

In machine (b), ($\times 7^5$) = 16807 stretch.

Since, it is fair times the base machine.

In machine (c), ($\times 5^7$) = 78125 stretch.

Since, it is 7 times the base machine.

Q. 151 Find three repeater machines that will do the same work as a ($\times$ 64) machine. Draw them, or describe them using exponents.

Sol. We know that, the possible factors of 64 are 2, 4, 8.

If $2^6 = 64$, $4^3 = 64$ and $8^2 = 64$

Hence, three repeater machines that would work as a (× 64) will be $(\times 2^6)$, $(\times 4^3)$ and $(\times 8^2)$. The diagram of $(\times 2^6)$, $(\times 4^3)$ and $(\times 8^2)$ is given below.

Q. 152 What will the following machine do to a 2 cm long piece of chalk?

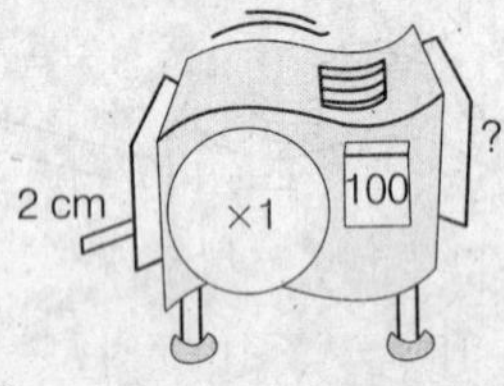

Sol. The machine produce $\times 1^{100} = 1$

So, if we insert 2 cm long piece of chalk in that machine, the piece of chalk remains same.

Q. 153 In a repeater machine with 0 as an exponent, the base machine is applied 0 times.

(a) What do these machines do to a piece of chalk?

(b) What do you think the value of 6^0 is?

You have seen that a hook up of repeater machines with the same base can be replaced by a single repeater machine. Similarly, when you multiply exponential expressions with the same base, you can replace them with a single expression.

Asif Raza thought about how he could rewrite the expression $2^{20} \times 2^5$.

Asif Raza's idea is one of the product laws of exponents, which can be expressed like this

Multiplying Expressions with the Same Base $a^b \times a^c = a^{b+c}$

Actually, this law can be used with more than two expressions. As long as the bases are the same, to find the product you can add the exponents and use the same base.

e.g. $3^2 \times 3^3 \times 3^{10} = 3^{2+3+10} = 3^{15}$

Sol. (a) Since, $3^0 = 1, 13^0 = 1, 29^0 = 1$

Using law of exponents, $a^0 = 1$ [$\because a$ is non-zero integer]

So, machine $(\times 3^0)$, $(\times 13^0)$ and $(\times 29^0)$ produce nothing on not change the piece 7 chalk.

(b) Using the law of exponent, $a^0 = 1$ [$\because a$ is non-zero integer]

Similarly, $(\times 6^0)$ machine does not change the piece.

Q. 154 Shrinking Machine In a shrinking machine, a piece of stick is compressed to reduce its length. If 9 cm long sandwich is put into the shrinking machine below, how long will it be when it emerges?

Sol. According to the question, in a shrinking machine, a piece of stick is compressed to reduce its length. If 9 cm long sandwich is put into the shrinking machine, then the length of sandwich will be $9 \times \frac{1}{3^{-1}} = 9 \times 3 = 27$ cm.

Q. 155 What happens when 1 cm worms are sent through these hook-ups?

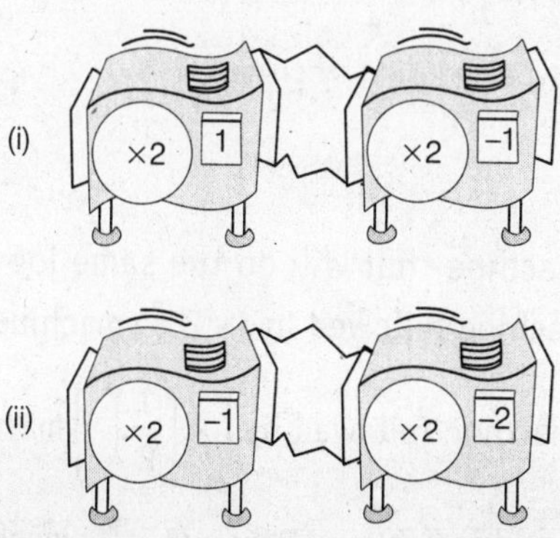

Sol. (i) If 1 cm worms are sent through $(\times 2^1)$ and $(\times 2^{-1})$ machine, then the result comes with $1 \times 2 \times \frac{1}{2} = 1\,\text{cm}$.

(ii) If 1 cm worms are sent through $(\times 2^{-1})$ and $(\times 2)^{-2}$ hooked machine, the result comes with $1 \times \frac{1}{2} \times \frac{1}{2 \times 2} = \frac{1}{2 \times 4} = \frac{1}{8}\,\text{cm} = 0.125\,\text{cm}$.

Q. 156 Sanchay put a 1 cm stick of gum through a (1×3^{-2}) machine. How long was the stick when it came out?

Sol. If sanchay put a 1 cm stick of gum through a (1×3^{-2}) machine.

Negation (–) sign in power shrews it is a shrinking machine. So, $1 \times \frac{1}{3^2} = 1 \times \frac{1}{9} = \frac{1}{9}$ cm

Hence, $\frac{1}{9}$ cm stick came out.

Q. 157 Ajay had a 1 cm piece of gum. He put it through repeater machine given below and it came out $\frac{1}{100000}$ cm long. What is the missing value?

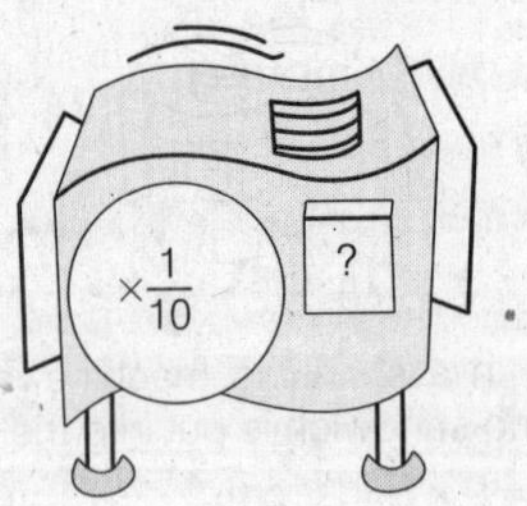

Sol. Since, Ajay put a 1 cm piece of gum and came out $\frac{1}{100000}$.

So, it is shrinking machine.

Hence, it is a $\left(\times \frac{1^1}{10}\right)^5$ type shrinking machine.

Thus, missing value is 5.

Q. 158 Find a single machine that will do the same job as the given hook-up.

(a) a$(\times 2^3)$ machine followed by $(\times 2^{-2})$ machine.

(b) a $(\times 2^4)$ machine followed by $\left(\times \left(\frac{1}{2}\right)^2\right)$ machine.

(c) a $(\times 5^{99})$ machine followed by a (5^{-100}) machine.

Maya multiplied $(4^2 \times 3^2)$ by thinking about stretching machines.

Use Maya's idea to multiply $5^3 \times 2^3$.

Maya's idea is another product law of exponents.

Multiplying Expressions with the Same Exponents

$$a^c \times b^c = (a \times b)^c$$

You can use this law with more than two expressions. If the exponents are the same, multiply the expressions by multiplying the bases and using the same exponent. e.g. $2^8 \times 3^8 \times 7^8 = (2 \times 3 \times 7)^8 = 42^8$.

Sol. (a) $(\times 2^3)$ machine followed by $(\times 2^{-2})$ machine. So, it produces $2 \times 2 \times 2 \times \frac{1}{2} \times \frac{1}{2} = 2^1$

Hence, $(\times 2^1)$ single machine can do the same job as the given hook-up.

(b) $(\times 2^4)$ machine followed by $\left(\times \left(\frac{1}{2}\right)^2\right)$ machine.

So, it produces $2 \times 2 \times 2 \times 2 \times \frac{1}{2} \times \frac{1}{2} = 4$

Hence, $(\times 2^2)$ single machine can do the same job as the given hook-up.

(c) $(\times 5^{99})$ machine followed by $(\times 5^{-100})$ machine. So, it produces $= 5^{99} \times \frac{1}{5^{100}} = \frac{1}{5}$

Hence, $\left(\times \frac{1}{5}\right)$ machine can do the same job as the given hook-up.

Q. 159 Find a single repeater machine that will do the same work as each hook-up.

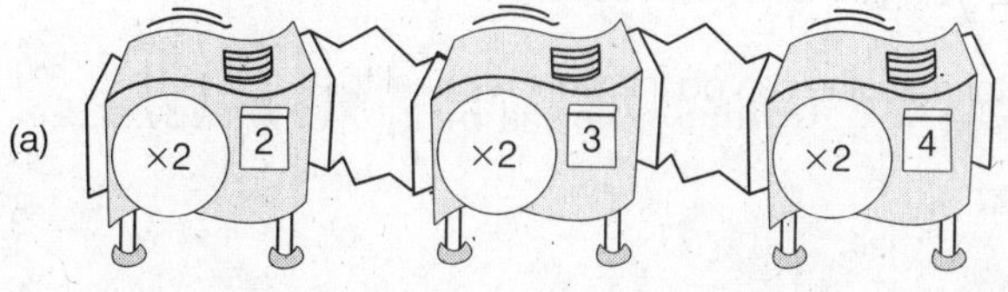

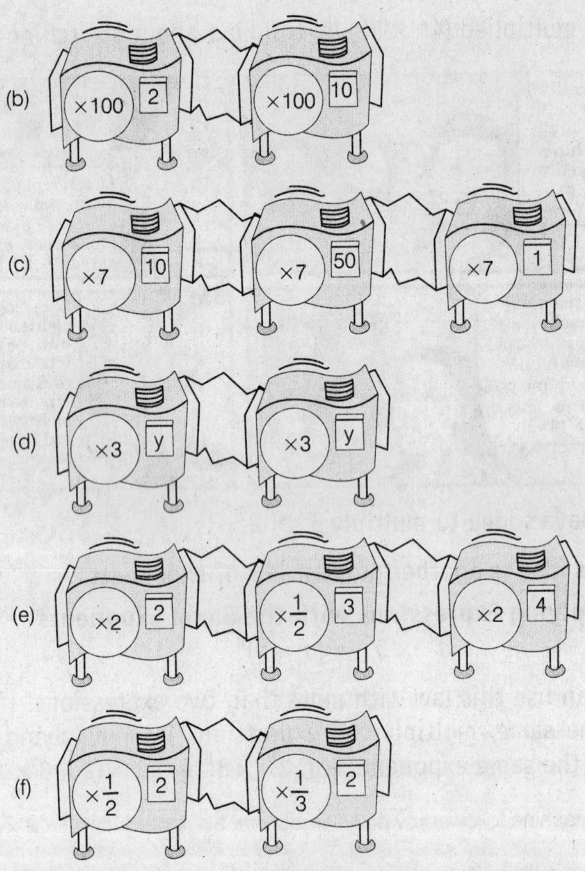

Sol. Using law of exponents, $(a^m \times a^n = a^{m+n})$ [$\because a$ is non-zero integer]

(a) Repeator machine can do the work is equal to $2^2 \times 2^3 \times 2^4 = 2^9$
So, $(\times 2^9)$ single machine can do the same work.

(b) Repeator machine can do the work is equal to $100^2 \times 100^{10}$.
So, $(\times 100^{12})$ single machine can do the same work.

(c) Repeator machine can do the work is equal to $7^{10} \times 7^{50} \times 7^1 = 7^{61}$
So, $(\times 7^{61})$ single machine can do the same work.

(d) Repeator machine can do the work is equal to $3^y \times 3^y = 3^{2y}$.
So $(\times 3^{2y})$ single machine can do the same work.

(e) Repeator machine can do the work is equal $2^2 \times \left(\frac{1}{2}\right)^3 \times 2^4 = 2^6 \times \frac{1}{2^3} = 2^3$

$$\left[\because \frac{a^m}{a^n} = a^{m-n}\right]$$

So, $(\times 2^3)$ single machine can do the same work.

(f) Repeator machine can do the work is equal to $\left(\frac{1}{2}\right)^2 \times \left(\frac{1}{3}\right)^2$

$$= \frac{1}{2} \times \frac{1}{2} \times \frac{1}{3} \times \frac{1}{3} = \frac{1}{2 \times 3 \times 2 \times 3} = \frac{1}{(6)^2}$$

So, $\left(\times \left(\frac{1}{6}\right)^2\right)$ single machine can do the same work.g47

Q. 160 For each hook-up, determine whether there is a single repeater machine that will do the same work. If so, describe or draw it.

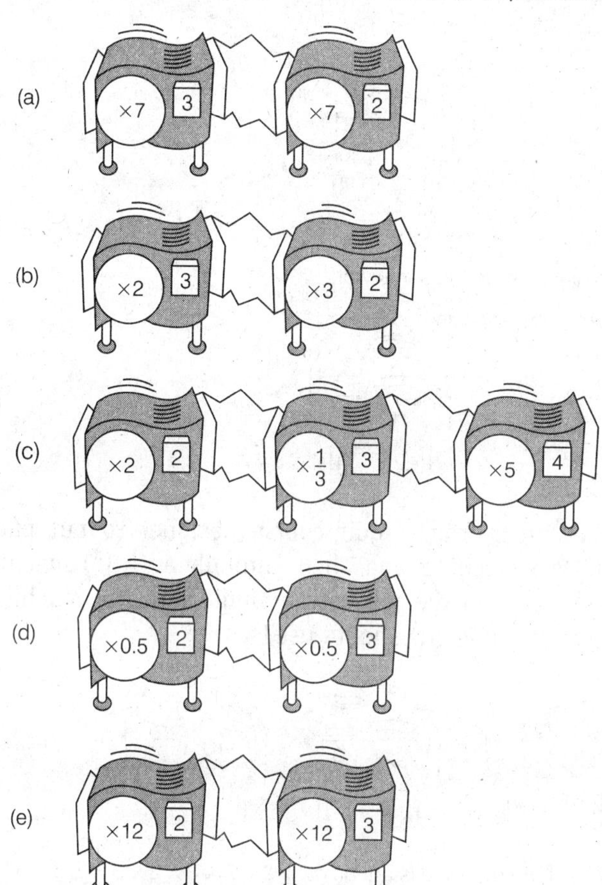

Sol. Using law of exponents, $a^m \times a^n = (a)^{m+n}$ [∵ a is non-zero integer]

(a) Hook-up machine can do the work $= 7^3 \times 7^2 = 7^5$

So, $(\times 7^5)$ single machine can do the same work.

Diagram of single $\times 7^5$ machine.

(b) Hook-up machine can do the work $= 2^3 \times 3^2 = 8 \times 9 = 72$

So, it is not possible for a single machine to do the same work.

Since, $(\times 8^2) = 64$ and $(\times 9^2) = 81$

(c) Hook-up machine can do the work $= 2^2 \times \left(\frac{1}{3}\right)^3 \times 5^4 = 4 \times \frac{1}{27} \times 625 = \frac{2500}{27} = 92.59$

So, it is not possible for a single machine to do the same work.

(d) Hook-up machine's work $= (0.5)^2 \times (0.5)^3 = (0.5)^5$ 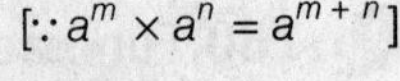 $[\because a^m \times a^n = a^{m+n}]$

So $(\times (0.5)^5)$ machine can for the same work.

Diagram of single $\times(0.5)^5$ machine.

(e) Hook-up machine can do the work $= 12^2 \times 12^3 = 12^5$ $[\because a^m \times a^n = (a)^{m+n}]$

So, $(\times 12^5)$ machine can do the same work.

Diagram of $\times 12^5$ single machine.

Q. 161 Shikha has an order from a golf course designer to put palm trees through a $(\times 2^3)$ machine and then through a $(\times 3^3)$ machine. She thinks that she can do the job with a single repeater machine. What single repeater machine she should use?

Sol. The work done by hook-up machine is equal to $2 \times 2 \times 2 \times 3 \times 3 \times 3 = 216 = 6^3$

So, she should use $(\times 6^3)$ single machine for the purpose.

Q. 162 Neha needs to stretch some sticks to 25^2 times of their original lengths, but her $(\times 25)$ machine is broken. Find a hook-up of two repeater machines that will do the same work as a $(\times 25^2)$ machine. To get started, think about the hook-up you could use to replace the $(\times 25)$ machine.

Sol. Work done by single machine $(\times 25^2) = 25 \times 25 = 625$ or $5 \times 5 \times 5 \times 5$ or $5^2 \times 5^2$

Hence, $(\times 5^2)$ and $(\times 5^2)$ hook-up machine can replace the $(\times 25)$ machine.

Q. 163 **Supply the missing information for each diagram.**

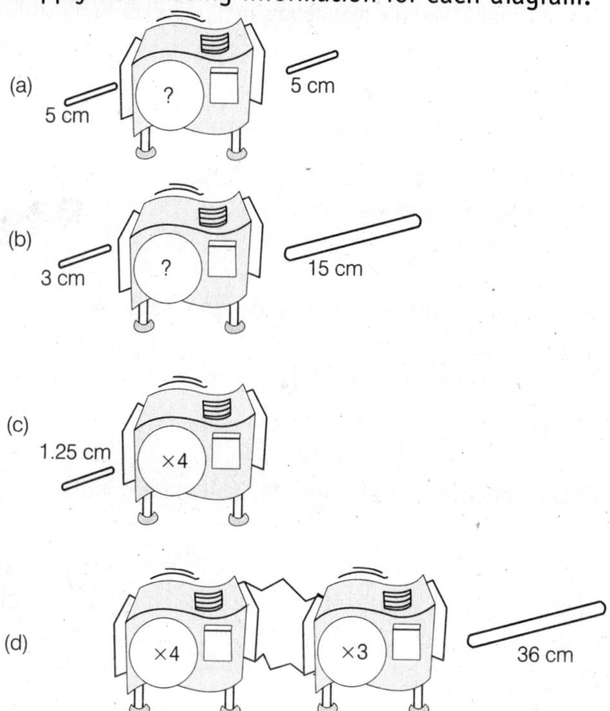

Sol. (a) If 5 cm long piece is inserted in single machine, then it produce same 5 cm long piece.

So, it is (× 1) repeated machine.

$\therefore \quad ? = 1$

(b) If 5 cm long piece inserted in single machine, then it produce 15 cm long piece.

So, it is (× 5) repeated machine.

$\therefore \quad ? = 5$

(c) If 1.25 cm long piece inserted in (× 4) repeated machine, then it will produce $1.25 \times 4 = 10$ cm long piece.

$\therefore \quad ? = 10$ cm

(d) If x cm long piece is inserted in (× 4) and (× 3) hooked machine, then it will produce 36 cm long piece.

So, $\quad x \times 4 \times 3 = 36 \Rightarrow x = 3$cm

Q. 164 **If possible, find a hook-up of prime base number machine that will do the same work as the given stretching machine. Do not use (× 1) machines.**

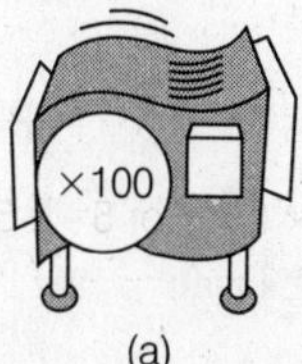

(a)

(b)

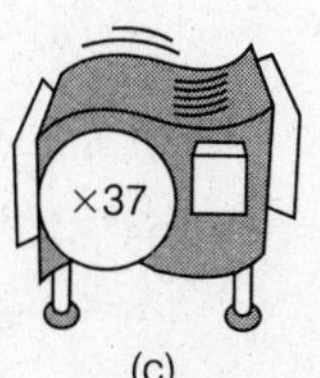

(c)

(d)

Sol. (a) Single machine work = 100

Hook-up machine of prime base number that do the same work down by × 100

$$= 2^2 \times 5^2$$

$$= 4 \times 25$$

$$= 100$$

(b) $\times\, 99 = 3^2 \times 11^1$ hook-up machine.

(c) × 37 machine cannot do the same work.

(d) $\times\, 1111 = 101 \times 11$ hook-up machine.

Q. 165 **Find two repeater machines that will do the same work as a (× 81) machine.**

Sol. Two repeater machines that do the same work as (× 81) are $(\times\, 3^4)$ and $(\times\, 9^2)$.

Since, factor of 81 are 3 and 9.

Q. 166 **Find a repeater machine that will do the same work as a $\left(\times \frac{1}{8}\right)$ machine.**

Sol. Since, $\frac{1}{8}$ are $\frac{1}{2}, \frac{1}{2}, \frac{1}{2}$.

So, $\frac{1}{8} = \frac{1}{2} \times \frac{1}{2} \times \frac{1}{2} = \left(\frac{1}{2}\right)^3$

Hence, $\left(\times \frac{1}{2^3}\right)$ repeater machine can do the same work as a $\left(\times \frac{1}{8}\right)$ machine.

Q. 167 **Find three machines that can be replaced with hook-up of (× 5) machines.**

Sol. Since, $5^2 = 25$, $5^3 = 125$, $5^4 = 625$

Hence, $(\times\, 5^2)$, $(\times\, 5^3)$ and $(\times\, 5^4)$ machine can replace (× 5) hook-up machine.

Q. 168 **The left column of the chart lists is the length of input pieces of ribbon. Stretching machines are listed across the top.**

The other entries are the outputs for sending the input ribbon from that row through the machine from that column. Copy and complete the chart.

Input length	Machine			
	× 2			
	1	5		
3				15
	14		7	

Sol. In the given table, the left column of chart list is the length of input piece of ribbon. Thus, the outputs for sending the input ribbon are given in the following table.

Input length	Machine		
	$\times 2$	$\times 10$	$\times 5$
5	1	5	**2.5**
3	**6**	**30**	15
7	14	**70**	**35**

Q. 169 The left column of the chart lists is the length of input chains of gold. Repeater machines are listed across the top. The other entries are the outputs you get when you send the input chain from that row through the repeater machine from that column. Copy and complete the chart.

Input length	Repeater machine		
	$\times 2^3$		
	40		125
2			
		162	

Sol. In the given table, the left column of the chart lists is the length of input chains of gold. Thus, the output we get when we send the input chain from the row through the repeater machine are detailed in the following table.

Input length	$\times 3$	$\times 12$	$\times 9$
13.3	40	**160**	125
2	**6**	**24**	**18**
13.5	**141**	162	**121**

Q. 170 Long back in ancient times, a farmer saved the life of a king's daughter. The king decided to reward the farmer with whatever he wished. The farmer, who was a chess champion, made an unusal request

"I would like you to place 1 rupee on the first square of my chessboard. 2 rupees on the second square, 4 on the third square, 8 on the fourth square and so on, until you have covered all 64 squares. Each square should have twice as many rupees as the previous square." The king thought this to be too less and asked the farmer to think of some better reward, but the farmer didn't agree.

How much money has the farmer earned?

[**Hint** The following table may help you. What is the first square on which the king will place atleast ₹ 10 lakh?]

Position of square on chessboard	Amount (in ₹)
1st square	1
2nd square	2
3rd square	4

Sol. Given, a 8×8 grid.

Now, find the sum of each row,

e.g. 1st row $= 2^0 + 2^1 + 2^2 + 2^3 + 2^4 + 2^5 + 2^6 + 2^7 = 255$

2nd row $= 2^8 + 2^9 + 2^{10} + 2^{11} + 2^{12} + 2^{13} + 2^{14} + 2^{15}$

$= 2^8 (2^0 + 2^1 + 2^2 + 2^3 + 2^4 + 2^5 + 2^6 + 2^7)$

$= 2^8 \times 255 = 255 \times 256 = 65280$

3rd row $= 2^{16} \times 255 = 16711680$

[$\because 2^8 = 256$ and $2^{16} = 2^8 \times 2^8 = 256 \times 256$ and so on]

Q. 171 The diameter of the Sun is 1.4×10^9 m and the diameter of the Earth is 1.2756×10^7 m. Compare their diameters by division.

Sol. Diameter of the Sun $= 1.4 \times 10^9$ m

Diameter of the Earth $= 1.2756 \times 10^7$ m

For comparison, we have to change both diameter in same powers of 10 i.e.
$1.2756 \times 10^7 = 0.012756 \times 10^9$

Hence, if we divide diameter of Sun by diameter of Earth, we get

$$\frac{1.4 \times 10^9}{0.012756 \times 10^9} = 110$$

So, diameter of Sun is 110 times the diameter of Earth.

Q. 172 Mass of Mars is 6.42×10^{29} kg and mass of the Sun is 1.99×10^{30} kg. What is the total mass?

Sol. Mass of Mars $= 6.42 \times 10^{29}$ kg

Mass of the Sun $= 1.99 \times 10^{30}$ kg

Total mass of Mars and Sun together $= 6.42 \times 10^{29} + 1.99 \times 10^{30}$

$= 6.42 \times 10^{29} + 19.9 \times 10^{29} = 26.32 \times 10^{29}$ kg

Q. 173 The distance between the Sun and the Earth is 1.496×10^8 km and distance between the Earth and the Moon is 3.84×10^8 m. During solar eclipse, the Moon comes in between the Earth and the Sun. What is the distance between the Moon and the Sun at that particular time?

Sol. The distance between the Sun and the Earth is 1.496×10^8 km

$= 1.496 \times 10^8 \times 10^3 \text{ m} = 1496 \times 10^8$ m

The distance between the Earth and the Moon is 3.84×10^8 m.

The distance between the Moon and the Sun at particular time (solar eclipse)

$$= (1496 \times 10^8 - 3.84 \times 10^8)\text{ m}$$
$$= 1492.16 \times 10^8 \text{ m}$$

Q. 174 A particular star is at a distance of about 8.1×10^{13} km from the Earth. Assuring that light travels at 3×10^8 m per second, find how long does light takes from that star to reach the Earth?

Sol. The distance between star and Earth $= 8.1 \times 10^{13}$ km $= 8.1 \times 10^{13} \times 10^3$ m

[$\because$ 1 km = 1000 m]

Since, light travels at 3×10^8 m per second.

So, time taken by light to reach the Earth

$$= \frac{8.1 \times 10^{13} \times 10^3}{3 \times 10^8} = \frac{8.1 \times 10^{16}}{3 \times 10^8} = \frac{8.1}{3} \times 10^8 = 2.7 \times 10^8 \text{ s}$$

Q. 175 By what number should $(-15)^{-1}$ be divided so that the quotient may be equal to $(-5)^{-1}$?

Sol. Let x be the number divide $(-15)^{-1}$ to get $(-5)^{-1}$ as a quotient.

So, $(-15)^{-1} \div x = (-5)^{-1}$

$\Rightarrow \frac{1}{-15} \times \frac{1}{x} = \frac{1}{5}$ $\left[\because a^{-m} = \frac{1}{a^m}\right]$

$\Rightarrow \frac{1}{x} = \frac{1}{5} \div \frac{1}{-15} \Rightarrow \frac{1}{x} = \frac{1}{5} \times \frac{-15}{1}$

$\Rightarrow x = 3$

Q. 176 By what number should $(-8)^{-3}$ be multiplied so that the product may be equal to $(-6)^{-3}$?

Sol. Let x be the number multiplied with $(-8)^{-3}$ to get the product equal to $(-6)^{-3}$.

$\Rightarrow x \times (-8)^{-3} = (-6)^{-3}$

$\Rightarrow x = \frac{(-6)^{-3}}{(-8)^{-3}} = \frac{(-8)^3}{(-6)^3} = \frac{512}{216} = \frac{64}{27}$

Q. 177 Find x.

(i) $\left(-\frac{1}{7}\right)^5 \div \left(-\frac{1}{7}\right)^{-7} = (-7)^x$ (ii) $\left(\frac{2}{5}\right)^{2x+6} \times \left(\frac{2}{5}\right)^3 = \left(\frac{2}{5}\right)^{x+2}$

(iii) $2^x + 2^x + 2^x = 192$ (iv) $\left(\frac{-6}{7}\right)^{x-7} = 1$

(v) $2^{3x} = 8^{2x+1}$ (vi) $5^x + 5^{x-1} = 750$

Sol. (i) $\left(-\frac{1}{7}\right)^{5} \div \left(-\frac{1}{7}\right)^{-7} = (-7)^{x}$

Using law of exponents, $a^m \div a^n = (a)^{m-n}$ [$\because a$ is non-zero integer]

Then, $\left(-\frac{1}{7}\right)^{-5+7} = (-7)^{x}$

$\Rightarrow \left(-\frac{1}{7}\right)^{2} = (-7)^{x}$

$\Rightarrow (-7)^{-2} = (-7)^{x}$

On comparing powers of (-7), we get $x = -2$

(ii) We have, $\left(\frac{2}{5}\right)^{2x+6} \times \left(\frac{2}{5}\right)^{3} = \left(\frac{2}{5}\right)^{x+2}$

Using law of exponents, $a^m \times a^n = (a)^{m+n}$ [$\because a$ is non-zero integer]

Then, $\left(\frac{2}{5}\right)^{2x+6+3} = \left(\frac{2}{5}\right)^{x+2}$

On comparing powers of $\left(\frac{2}{5}\right)$, we get

$$2x + 6 + 3 = x + 2$$

$$\Rightarrow 2x + 9 = x + 2$$

$$\Rightarrow x = -7$$

(iii) We have, $2^x + 2^x + 2^x = 192$

$$\Rightarrow 2^x\,(1+1+1) = 192$$

$$\Rightarrow 3 \times (2^x) = 192$$

$$\Rightarrow 2^x = \frac{192}{3} = 64$$

$$\Rightarrow 2^x = 2 \times 2 \times 2 \times 2 \times 2 \times 2$$

$$\Rightarrow 2^x = 2^6$$

On comparing the powers of 2, we get $x = 6$

(iv) We have, $\left(-\frac{6}{7}\right)^{x-7} = 1$

Using law of exponents, $x^0 = 1$ [$\because a$ is non-zero integer]

Then, $\left(-\frac{6}{7}\right)^{x-7} = 1$

It is possible only, if $x = 7$.

So, $\left(-\frac{6}{7}\right)^{7-7} = 1$

$\Rightarrow \left(-\frac{6}{7}\right)^{0} = 1$

Hence, $x = 7$ [$\because a^0 = 1$]

(v) We have, $2^{3x} = 8^{2x+1}$

$$\Rightarrow 2^{3x} = (2^3)^{2x+1}$$

$$\Rightarrow 2^{3x} = (2)^{6x+3} \quad [\because (a^m)^n = (a)^{m \times n}]$$

On comparing the powers of 2, we get

$$3x = 6x + 3 \Rightarrow x = -1$$

(vi) $5^x + 5^{x-1} = 750$

$\Rightarrow \quad 5^x + \frac{5^x}{5} = 750$ $\left[\because a^{-m} = \frac{1}{a^m}\right]$

$\Rightarrow \quad 5^x\left(1 + \frac{1}{5}\right) = 750$

$\Rightarrow \quad 5^x\left(\frac{6}{5}\right) = 750$

$\Rightarrow \quad 5^x = 750 \times \frac{5}{6}$

$\Rightarrow \quad 5^x = 125 \times 5$

$\Rightarrow \quad 5^x = 625$

$\Rightarrow \quad 5^x = 5^4$

On comparing the powers of 5, we get

$x = 4$

Q. 178 If $a = -1$, $b = 2$, then find the value of the following.

(i) $a^b + b^a$ (ii) $a^b - b^a$

(iii) $a^b \times b^a$ (iv) $a^b \div b^a$

Sol. (i) Given, $a^b + b^a$

If $a = -1$ and $b = 2$, then $(-1)^2 + (2)^{-1} = 1 + \frac{1}{2}$ $\left[\because a^{-m} = \frac{1}{a^m}\right]$

$= \frac{2+1}{2} = \frac{3}{2}$

(ii) Given, $a^b - b^a$

If $a = -1$ and $b = 2$, then $(-1)^2 - (2)^{-1} = 1 - \frac{1}{2^1}$ $\left[\because a^{-m} = \frac{1}{a^n}\right]$

$= \frac{2-1}{2} = \frac{1}{2}$

(iii) Given, $a^b \times b^a$

If $a = -1$, $b = 2$, then $(-1)^2 \times (2)^{-1} = 1 \times \frac{1}{2} = \frac{1}{2}$ $\left[\because a^{-m} = \frac{1}{a^m}\right]$

(iv) Given, $a^b \div b^a$

If $a = -1$ and $b = 2$, then $(-1)^2 \div (2)^{-1} = 1 \div \frac{1}{2^1} = 1 \times 2 = 2$ $\left[\because a^{-m} = \frac{1}{a^m}\right]$

Q. 179 Express each of the following in exponential form.

(i) $\frac{-1296}{14641}$ (ii) $\frac{-125}{343}$

(iii) $\frac{400}{3969}$ (iv) $\frac{-625}{10000}$

Sol. (i) Given, $\frac{-1296}{14641}$

Since, $(6) \times (6) \times (6) \times (6) = 1296 = (6)^4$ and $11 \times 11 \times 11 \times 11 = 14641 = (11)^4$

Exponential form of $\frac{-1296}{14641} = -\frac{(6)^4}{(11)^4} = -\left(\frac{6}{11}\right)^4$

(ii) Given, $\frac{-125}{343}$

Since, $(-5) \times (-5) \times (-5) = -125 = (-5)^3$ and $7 \times 7 \times 7 = 343 = (-7)^3$

Exponential form of $\frac{-125}{343} = \frac{(-5)^3}{(7)^3} = \left(\frac{-5}{7}\right)^3$

(iii) Given, $\frac{400}{3969}$

Since, $20 \times 20 = 400 = (20)^2$ and $63 \times 63 = 3969 = (63)^2$

Exponential form of $\frac{400}{3969} = \frac{(20)^2}{(63)^2} = \left(\frac{20}{63}\right)^2$

(iv) Given, $\frac{-625}{10000}$

Since, $5 \times 5 \times 5 \times 5 = 625 = (5)^4$ and $10 \times 10 \times 10 \times 10 = 1000 = (10)^4$

Exponential form of $\frac{-625}{10000} = \frac{-(5)^4}{(10)^4} = -\left(\frac{1}{2}\right)^4$

Q. 180 Simplify

(i) $\left[\left(\frac{1}{2}\right)^2 - \left(\frac{1}{4}\right)^3\right]^{-1} \times 2^{-3}$

(ii) $\left[\left(\frac{4}{3}\right)^{-2} - \left(\frac{3}{4}\right)^2\right]^{(-2)}$

(iii) $\left(\frac{4}{13}\right)^4 \times \left(\frac{13}{7}\right)^2 \times \left(\frac{7}{4}\right)^3$

(iv) $\left(\frac{1}{5}\right)^{45} \times \left(\frac{1}{5}\right)^{-60} - \left(\frac{1}{5}\right)^{28} \times \left(\frac{1}{5}\right)^{-43}$

(v) $\frac{(9)^3 \times 27 \times t^4}{(3)^{-2} \times (3)^4 \times t^2}$

(vi) $\frac{(3^{-2})^2 \times (5^2)^{-3} \times (t^{-3})^2}{(3^{-2})^5 \times (5^3)^{-2} \times (t^{-4})^3}$

Sol. (i) Given, $\left[\left(\frac{1}{2}\right)^2 - \left(\frac{1}{4}\right)^3\right]^{-1} \times 2^{-3} = \left(\frac{1}{4} - \frac{1}{64}\right)^{-1} \times 2^{-3}$

$$= \left(\frac{16-1}{64}\right)^{-1} \times 2^{-3}$$

$$= \left(\frac{15}{64}\right)^{-1} \times 2^{-3}$$

$$= \frac{64}{15} \times \frac{1}{8} \qquad \left[\because a^{-m} = \frac{1}{a^m}\right]$$

$$= \frac{8}{15}$$

(ii) $\left[\left(\frac{4}{3}\right)^{-2} - \left(\frac{3}{4}\right)^{2}\right]^{(-2)} = \left[\left(\frac{3}{4}\right)^{2} - \left(\frac{3}{4}\right)^{2}\right]^{-2} = [0]^{-2} = 0$

(iii) $\left(\frac{4}{13}\right)^{4} \times \left(\frac{13}{7}\right)^{2} \times \left(\frac{7}{4}\right)^{3} = \frac{(4)^4}{(13)^4} \times \frac{(13)^2}{(7)^2} \times \frac{(7)^3}{(4)^3}$

$= (4)^4 \times (4)^{-3} \times (13)^2 \times (13)^{-4} \times (7)^3 \times (7)^{-2}$ $\left[\because a^{-m} = \frac{1}{a^m}\right]$

$= (4)^{4-3} \times (13)^{2-4} \times (7)^{3-2}$ $[\because a^m \times a^n = a^{m-n}]$

$= (4)^1 \times (13)^{-2} \times (7)^1$

$= 4 \times \frac{1}{169} \times 7$ $\left[\because a^{-m} = \frac{1}{a^m}\right]$

$= \frac{28}{169}$

(iv) $\left(\frac{1}{5}\right)^{45} \times \left(\frac{1}{5}\right)^{-60} - \left(\frac{1}{5}\right)^{28} \times \left(\frac{1}{5}\right)^{-43} = \frac{1}{(5)^{45}} \times \frac{1}{(5)^{-60}} - \frac{1}{(5)^{28}} \times \frac{1}{(5)^{-43}}$

$= \frac{1}{(5)^{45-60}} - \frac{1}{(5)^{28-43}}$ $[\because a^m \times a^n = (a)^{m+n}]$

$= \frac{1}{(5)^{-15}} - \frac{1}{(5)^{-15}} = (5)^{15} - (5)^{15}$ $\left[\because a^{-m} = \frac{1}{a^m}\right]$

$= 0$

(v) $\frac{(9)^3 \times 27 \times t^4}{(3)^{-2} \times (3)^4 \times t^2} = \frac{(3^2)^3 \times (3)^3 \times t^4}{(3)^{-2} \times (3)^4 \times t^2}$ $[\because 3 \times 3 = 3^2 = 9]$

$= \frac{(3)^6 \times (3)^3 \times t^4}{(3)^{-2} \times (3)^4 \times t^2} = (3)^6 \times (3)^3 \times (3)^2 \times (3)^{-4} \times t^4 \times t^{-2}$ $\left[\because a^{-m} = \frac{1}{a^m}\right]$

$= (3)^{11-4} \times t^{4-2} = (3)^7 \times t^2$ $[\because a^m \times a^n = (a)^{m+n}]$

(vi) $\frac{(3^{-2})^2 \times (5^2)^{-3} \times (t^{-3})^2}{(3^{-2})^5 \times (5^3)^{-2} \times (t^{-4})^3} = \frac{(3)^{-4} \times (5)^{-6} \times (t)^{-6}}{(3)^{-10} \times (5)^{-6} \times (t)^{-12}}$ $[\because (a^m)^n = (a)^{mn}]$

$= (3)^{-4} \times (3)^{10} \times (5)^{-6} \times (5)^6 \times (t)^{-6} \times (t)^{12}$

$= (3)^{-4+10} \times (5)^{-6+6} \times (t)^{-6+12}$ $\left[\because a^{-m} = \frac{1}{a^m}\right]$

$= (3)^6 \times 5^0 \times (t)^6 = (3t)^6$ $[\because a^0 = 1]$

9

Comparing Quantities

Multiple Choice Questions (MCQs)

Q. 1 Suppose for the principal P, rate $R\%$ and time T, the simple interest is S and compound interest is C. Consider the possibilities

(i) $C > S$

(ii) $C = S$

(iii) $C < S$

Then,

(a) only (i) is correct (b) either (i) or (ii) is correct

(c) either (ii) or (iii) is correct (d) only (iii) is correct

Sol. *(a)* Let the principal (P) = ₹100

Rate of interest (R) = 100%

and time period (T) = 2 yr

Then, simple interest $= \frac{P \times R \times T}{100} = \frac{100 \times 10 \times 2}{100} =$ ₹20

We know that,

$$A = P\left(1 + \frac{R}{100}\right)^T = 100\left(1 + \frac{10}{100}\right)^2$$

$$= 100 \times \frac{11}{10} \times \frac{11}{10} = ₹121$$

$\therefore$ Compound interest, CI $= A - P =$ ₹121 − ₹100 = ₹21

So, $C > S$

Hence, option (a) is correct.

Q. 2 Suppose a certain sum doubles in 2 yr at $r\%$ rate of simple interest per annum and $R\%$ rate of interest per annum compounded annually. Then,

(a) $r < R$ (b) $R < r$

(c) $R = r$ (d) Cannot be determined

Sol. *(b)* If the total amount received after 2 yr is same for both simple interest and compound interest on same principal, then the rate of simple interest is greater than the rate of compound interest.

i.e. $R < r$

Hence, option (b) is correct.

Q. 3 **The compound interest on ₹ 50000 at 4% per annum for 2 yr compounded annually is**

(a) ₹ 4000 (b) ₹ 4080 (c) ₹ 4280 (d) ₹ 4050

Sol. *(b)* Given, principal (P) = ₹ 50000

Rate of interest (R%) = 4% per annum

Time period (T) = 2 yr

We know that,

$$A = P\left(1 + \frac{R}{100}\right)^T$$

$$\therefore \quad A = 50000\left(1 + \frac{4}{100}\right)^2$$

$$= 50000\left(1 + \frac{1}{25}\right)^2 = 50000 \times \frac{26}{25} \times \frac{26}{25} = 80 \times 26 \times 26 = ₹54080$$

$\therefore$ Compound interest, CI = $A - P$ = ₹54080 − ₹50000 = ₹ 4080

Hence, option (b) is correct.

Q. 4 **If marked price of an article is ₹ 1200 and the discount is 12%, then the selling price of the article is**

(a) ₹ 1056 (b) ₹ 1344 (c) ₹ 1212 (d) ₹ 1188

Sol. *(a)* Given, marked price of an article = ₹ 1200

Discount % = 12%

$\therefore$ Discount = Discount % on marked price

$$= \frac{12}{100} \times 1200 = 12 \times 12 = ₹144$$

$\because$ Selling price = Marked price − Discount

$\therefore$ Selling price = ₹1200 − ₹ 144 = ₹1056

Hence, option (a) is correct.

Q. 5 **If 90% of x is 315 km, then the value of x is**

(a) 325 km (b) 350 km (c) 350 m (d) 325 m

Sol. *(b)* We have, 90% of x = 315 km

$$\Rightarrow \quad \frac{90}{100} \times x = 315$$

$$\Rightarrow \quad x = \frac{315 \times 100}{90} = \frac{315 \times 10}{9} = 350$$

$$\Rightarrow \quad x = 350 \text{ km}$$

Hence, option (b) is correct.

Q. 6 To gain 25% after allowing a discount of 10%, the shopkeeper must mark the price of the article which cost him ₹ 360 as

(a) ₹ 500 (b) ₹ 450 (c) ₹ 460 (d) ₹ 486

Sol. *(a)* Let the marked price of the article be ₹x.

Cost price of the article = ₹ 360

According to the question,

$$x - x \times \frac{10}{100} - \frac{25 \times 360}{100} = 360$$

$$\Rightarrow \quad x - \frac{x}{10} - 90 = 360$$

[∵ discount is always calculated on marked price and profit is always calculated on cost price]

$$\Rightarrow \quad \frac{9x}{10} - 90 = 360$$

$$\Rightarrow \quad \frac{9x}{10} = 360 + 90$$

$$\Rightarrow \quad x = \frac{450 \times 10}{9}$$

$$\Rightarrow \quad \frac{9x}{10} = 450$$

$$\Rightarrow \quad x = ₹\,500$$

So, the marked price is ₹ 500.

Hence, option (a) is correct.

Q. 7 If a% is the discount per cent on marked price x, then discount is

(a) $\frac{x}{a} \times 100$ (b) $\frac{a}{x} \times 100$

(c) $x \times \frac{a}{100}$ (d) $\frac{100}{xa}$

Sol. *(c)* Since, discount can be calculated always on marked price, when discount percentage is given.

∴ Discount = Discount % on marked price = $\frac{a}{100} \times x$

Hence, option (c) is correct.

Q. 8 Ashima took a loan of ₹ 100000 at 12% per annum compounded half-yearly. She paid ₹ 112360. If $(1.06)^2$ is equal to 1.1236, then the period for which she took the loan is

(a) 2 yr (b) 1 yr

(c) 6 months (d) $1\frac{1}{2}$ yr

Sol. *(b)* Given, principal (P) = ₹ 100000

Rate of interest (R%) = 12% per annum compounded half-yearly

Let m be the time period.

∵ Amount paid = ₹ 112360

We know that,

Amount, when interest is compounded half-yearly

$$\text{i.e.} \quad A = P\left(1 + \frac{R}{200}\right)^{2n}, \text{ where } n = \text{time period}$$

$$\Rightarrow \quad 112360 = 100000\left(1 + \frac{12}{200}\right)^{2m}$$

$$\Rightarrow \quad \left(\frac{53}{50}\right)^{2m} = \frac{112360}{100000}$$

$$\Rightarrow \quad \left(\frac{53}{50}\right)^{2n} = \frac{2809}{2500}$$

$$\Rightarrow \quad \left(\frac{53}{50}\right)^{2} = \left(\frac{53}{50}\right)^{2n}$$

On comparing both sides, we get

$$2n = 2$$

$$\Rightarrow \quad n = 1$$

So, the time period is 1 yr.

Hence, option (b) is correct.

Q. 9 For calculation of interest compounded half-yearly, keeping the principal same, which one of the following is true?

(a) Double the given annual rate and half the given number of years
(b) Double the given annual rate as well as the given number of years
(c) Half the given annual rate as well as the given number of years
(d) Half the given annual rate and double the given number of years

Sol. ***(d)*** If interest is compounded half-yearly, then $R = \frac{R}{2}$ and $T = 2T = 2n$.

Now, the amount will be

$$A = P\left(1 + \frac{R}{200}\right)^{2n}$$

$$\therefore \quad C = A - P$$

So, half the given annual rate and double the given number of years.

Hence, option (d) is correct.

Q. 10 Shyama purchases a scooter costing ₹ 36450 and the rate of sales tax is 9%, then the total amount paid by her is

(a) ₹ 36490.50 (b) ₹ 39730.50
(c) ₹ 36454.50 (d) ₹ 33169.50

Sol. ***(b)*** Since, sales tax is charged on the sale of an item by the government and is added to the bill amount.

$\because$ Shyama purchase a scooter of costing = ₹ 36450

Sales tax paid = 9%

So, total amount paid by her

= ₹ 36450 of 9% + ₹ 36450

$= \frac{9}{100} \times 36450 + 36450$

$= 9 \times 364.5 + 36450$

$= 3280.5 + 36450$

$= ₹39730.5$

Hence, option (b) is correct.

Q. 11 The marked price of an article is ₹ 80 and it is sold at ₹ 76, then the discount rate is

(a) 5%
(b) 95%
(c) 10%
(d) approx 11%

Sol. *(a)* The marked price of an article = ₹ 80

Sold price of the article = ₹ 76

We know that,

Selling price = Marked price − Discount

∴ Discount = Marked price − Selling price

⇒ Discount = ₹ 80 − ₹ 76 = ₹ 4

$\therefore \text{Discount } \% = \frac{4}{80} \times 100 = \frac{40}{8} = 5\%$ $\left[\because \text{discount } \% = \frac{\text{discount}}{\text{marked price}} \times 100\right]$

Hence, option (a) is correct.

Q. 12 *A* bought a tape recorder for ₹ 8000 and sold it to *B*. *B* in turn sold it to *C*, each earning a profit of 20%. Which of the following is true?

(a) *A* and *B* earn the same profit
(b) *A* earns more profit than *B*
(c) *A* earns less profit than *B*
(d) Cannot be determined

Sol. *(c)* ∵ Cost price of tape recorder for *A* = ₹8000

∴ Cost price of tape recorder for *B* = 20% profit on cost price for *A*

$= \frac{20}{100} \times 8000 + 8000$

$= 20 \times 80 + 8000$

$= 1600 + 8000 = ₹9600$

Cost price of tape recorder for *C* = 20% profit on cost price for *B*

$= \frac{20}{100} \times 9600 + 9600$

$= 1920 + 9600 = ₹11520$

Here, profit for *A* = ₹1600

Profit for *B* = ₹1920

So, *A* earns less profit than *B*.

Hence, option (c) is correct.

Q. 13 Latika bought a teapot for ₹ 120 and a set of cups for ₹ 400. She sold teapot at a profit of 5% and cups at a loss of 5%. The amount received by her is

(a) ₹ 494 (b) ₹ 546
(c) ₹ 506 (d) ₹ 534

Sol. *(c)* Latika bought a teapot = ₹ 120

and a set of cups = ₹ 400

She sold teapot at a profit of 5%.

So, selling price of teapot $= \frac{5}{100} \times 120 + 120$

$= \frac{120}{20} + 120$

$= 6 + 120 =$ ₹126

Also, she sold cups at a loss of 5%.

So, selling price of cups $= 400 - \frac{5}{100} \times 400$

$= 400 - 20 =$ ₹380

Then, the total amount received by her = ₹126 + ₹380 = ₹506

Hence, option (c) is correct.

Q. 14 A jacket was sold for ₹ 1120 after allowing a discount of 20%. The marked price of the jacket is

(a) ₹ 1440 (b) ₹ 1400 (c) ₹ 960 (d) ₹ 866.66

Sol. *(b)* Let the marked price of the jacket be ₹ x.

Discount % on marked price = 20%

Selling price of jacket = ₹1120

Then, $1120 = x - x \times \frac{20}{100}$

$\Rightarrow \quad 1120 = x - \frac{x}{5}$

$\Rightarrow \quad 1120 = \frac{4x}{5}$

$\Rightarrow \quad x = \frac{1120 \times 5}{4} = 280 \times 5 =$ ₹1400

So, marked price of the jacket is ₹ 1400.

Hence, option (b) is correct.

Q. 15 A sum is taken for two years at 16% per annum. If interest is compounded after every three months, the number of times for which interest is charged in 2 yrs is

(a) 8 (b) 4 (c) 6 (d) 9

Sol. *(a)* Since, rate of interest is calculated after every three months. Similarly, the time period for amount in a year will 4 times.

If amount is taken for 2 yr, means $4 \times 2 = 8$ times charged in 2 yr.

Hence, option (a) is correct.

Q. 16 The original price of a washing machine which was bought for ₹ 13500 including of 8% VAT, is

(a) ₹ 12420 (b) ₹ 14580 (c) ₹ 12500 (d) ₹ 13492

Sol. *(a)* The price of the washing machine = ₹13500

VAT [Value Added Tax] is included in selling price, which is 8%.

∴ The original price of the washing machine including of 8% VAT

$$= 13500 - 13500 \times \frac{8}{100}$$

$$= 13500 - 135 \times 8$$

$$= 13500 - 1080 = ₹12420$$

Hence, option (a) is correct.

Q. 17 Avinash bought an electric iron for ₹ 900 and sold it at a gain of 10%. He sold another electric iron at 5% loss which was bought ₹ 1200. On the transaction, he has a

(a) profit of ₹ 75 (b) loss of ₹ 75 (c) profit of ₹ 30 (d) loss of ₹ 30

Sol. *(c)* Avinash bought an electric iron = ₹ 900

He sold it, at 10% profit.

So, selling price of the electric iron $= \frac{10}{100} \times 900 + 900$

$= 90 + 900 = ₹990$

He also sold another electric iron at 5% loss.

Cost price of another electric iron = ₹1200

So, selling price of the electric iron $= 1200 - \frac{5}{100} \times 1200$

$= 1200 - 60 = ₹1140$

Total amount paid by Avinash for purchasing electric irons = ₹ 900 + ₹1200 = ₹2100

Total received amount = ₹ 990 + ₹1140 = ₹ 2130

So, his profit = ₹2130 – ₹2100 = ₹ 30 in transaction.

Hence, option (c) is correct.

Q. 18 A TV set was bought for ₹ 26250 including 5% VAT. The original price of the TV set is

(a) ₹ 27562.50 (b) ₹ 25000 (c) ₹ 24937.50 (d) ₹ 26245

Sol. *(c)* Cost price of TV set = ₹ 26250.

VAT including = 5%

∴ Original price = Cost price of article including VAT $= 26250 - \frac{5}{100} \times 26250$

$= 26250 - \frac{26250}{20}$

$= 26250 - 1312.5 = ₹ 24937.5$

So, original price of the TV set = ₹ 24937.5

Hence, option (c) is correct.

Q. 19 40% of [100 – 20% of 300] is equal to

(a) 20 (b) 16 (c) 140 (d) 64

Sol. *(b)* 40% of [100 – 20% of 300]

$$= \frac{40}{100} \times \left[100 - \frac{20}{100} \times 300\right]$$

$$= \frac{40}{100}[100 - 60]$$

$$= \frac{40}{100} \times 40 = 4 \times 4 = 16$$

Hence, option (b) is correct.

Q. 20 Radhika bought a car for ₹ 250000. Next year, its price decreased by 10% and further next year, it decreased by 12%. In the two years, overall decrease per cent in the price of the car is

(a) 3.2% (b) 22% (c) 20.8% (d) 8%

Sol. *(c)* Radhika bought a car for ₹ 250000.

∴ Cost price of a car = ₹250000

Its price decreased next year for 10%.

So, price became $= 250000 - \frac{10}{100} \times 250000$

$= 250000 - 25000 = ₹225000$

Further next year, its price decreased by 12%, then price will be

$$= 225000 - 225000 \times \frac{12}{100}$$

$$= 225000 - 27000 = ₹198000$$

In two years, overall decrease per cent $= \frac{250000 - 198000}{250000} \times 100$

$$= \frac{52000}{250000} \times 100 = \frac{520}{25} = 20.8\%$$

Hence, option (c) is correct.

Fill in the Blanks

In questions 21 to 45, fill in the blanks to make the statements true.

Q. 21 _____ is a reduction on the marked price of the article.

Sol. **Discount** is a reduction on the marked price of the article.

Q. 22 Increase of a number from 150 to 162 is equal to increase of _____ per cent.

Sol. Initial number = 150

Final number = 162

Increased number = 162 – 150 = 12

∴ Per cent of increased number $= \frac{12}{150} \times 100 = \frac{120}{15} = $ **8%**

Q. 23 15% increase in price of an article, which is ₹ 1620, is the increase of ₹ ______.

Sol. Let the price of the article be ₹ x.

After 15% increased in price, price became ₹1620.

So, $$1620 = x + x \times \frac{15}{100}$$

$$\Rightarrow \quad 1620 = \frac{115x}{100}$$

$$\Rightarrow \quad 115x = 1620 \times 100$$

$$\Rightarrow \quad x = \frac{1620 \times 100}{115}$$

$$\Rightarrow \quad x = ₹\, 1408$$

Hence, increase in price = ₹1620 − ₹1408 = **₹212**

Q. 24 Discount = ____ − ____

Sol. Discount = **MP − SP**

Here, MP = Marked price, and SP = Selling price

Q. 25 Discount = Discount % of ____.

Sol. Discount = Discount % of **marked price**

[∵ discount is a reduction given on marked price]

Q. 26 ____ is charged on the sale of an item by the government and is added to the bill amount.

Sol. **Sales tax** is charged on the sale of an item by the government and is added to the bill amount.

∴ Sales tax = Tax % of bill amount

Q. 27 Amount when interest is compounded annually, is given by the formula ______.

Sol. Amount when interest is compounded annually, is given by the formula

$$A = P\left(1 + \frac{R}{100}\right)^T$$

where, P = principal, R = rate per annum and T = time

Q. 28 Sales tax = Tax% of ______

Sol. Sales tax = Tax % of **bill amount**

Q. 29 The time period after which the interest is added each time to form a new principal, is called the ______.

Sol. The time period after which the interest is added each time to form a new principal, is called the **conversion period**.

Q. 30 ____ expenses are the additional expenses incurred by a buyer for an item over and above its cost of purchase.

Sol. **Overhead** expenses are the additional expenses incurred by a buyer for an item over and above its cost of purchase.

Q. 31 The discount on an item for sale is calculated on the _____.

Sol. The discount on an item for sale is calculated on the **marked price**.

Q. 32 When principal P is compounded semi-annually at $r\%$ per annum for t years, then amount = _____.

Sol. When principal P is compounded semi-annually at $r\%$ per annum for t years.

i.e. Rate $= \frac{r}{2}$ and time $= 2 \times t$

Then, amount $= \text{Principal}\left(1+\frac{\text{Rate}}{200}\right)^{2\times \text{Time}}$

i.e. $A = P\left(1+\frac{r}{200}\right)^{2t}$

Q. 33 Percentages are ____ to fractions with ____ equal to 100.

Sol. Percentages are **equal** to fractions with **denominator** equal to 100.

e.g. 8% means $\frac{8}{100}$.

Q. 34 The marked price of an article when it is sold for ₹ 880 after a discount of 12%, is _____.

Sol. $\because$ Selling price of an article = ₹880

Discount % = 12%

We know that, discount is calculated on marked price.

Let the marked price be ₹ x.

So, $x - x \times \frac{12}{100} = 880$

$\Rightarrow \frac{88x}{100} = 880$

$\Rightarrow x = \frac{880}{88} \times 100 = ₹1000$

So, marked price = **₹ 1000**

Q. 35 The compound interest on ₹ 8000 for one year at 16% per annum compounded half-yearly is ____, given that $(1.08)^2 = 1.1664$.

Sol. Given, principal (P) = ₹8000

Time period (T) = 1 yr

Rate (R) = 16% per annum compounded half-yearly

We know that,
Amount, when interest is compounded half-yearly,

$$A = P\left(1 + \frac{R}{200}\right)^{2T}$$

$$\Rightarrow \quad A = 8000\left(1 + \frac{16}{200}\right)^{2 \times 1}$$

$$\Rightarrow \quad A = 8000 \times \frac{27}{25} \times \frac{27}{25} = 12.8 \times 27 \times 27$$

$\therefore$ Amount, $A = ₹\,9331.2$

$\because$ Compound interest. CI $= A - P$

$= ₹\,9331.2 - ₹\,8000 =$ **₹ 1331.2**

Note *In compound interest, if interest is compounded half-yearly, then time taken is doubled while rate of interest become halved.*

Q. 36 In the first year on an investment of ₹ 600000, the loss is 5% and in the second year, the gain is 10%, the net result is _____.

Sol. Investment amount = ₹600000

In Ist year, the loss in Ist year = 5%.

So, investment in Ist year $= 600000 - \frac{5}{100} \times 600000 = 600000 - 30000 = ₹\,570000$

In IInd year, the gain is 10%.

So, net investment $= 570000 + \frac{10}{100} \times 570000 = 570000 + 57000 =$ **₹627000**

Q. 37 If amount on the principal of ₹ 6000 is written as $6000\left(1 + \frac{5}{100}\right)^3$ and compound interest payable half-yearly, then rate of interest per annum is ____ and time (in years) is ____.

Sol. If amount on the principal of ₹ 6000 is written as $6000\left(1 + \frac{5}{100}\right)^3$ and compound interest payable half-yearly, then rate of interest per annum is **10**% and time (in years) is $\mathbf{1\frac{1}{2}}$ **yr**.

Q. 38 By selling an article for ₹ 112000, a girl gains 40%. The cost price of the article was _____.

Sol. Selling price of an article = ₹ 112000

Gain% = 40%

Let ₹ x be the cost price of the article.

$\because$ Cost price = Selling price – Profit% on cost price

$\therefore$ Selling price = Cost price + Profit% on cost price

So, $\quad 112000 = x + x \times \frac{40}{100}$

$$\Rightarrow \quad 112000 = \frac{7x}{5}$$

$$\Rightarrow \quad x = \frac{112000 \times 5}{7} = 16000 \times 5 = ₹\,\mathbf{80000}$$

Q. 39 The loss per cent on selling 140 geometry boxes at the loss of SP of 10 geometry boxes is equal to _____.

Sol. Let the selling price of 1 geometry box be ₹ 1.

So, the selling price for 140 geometry boxes = ₹1 × 140 = ₹140

Similarly, selling price of 10 geometry boxes = ₹1 × 10 = ₹10

$\because$ Loss = Selling price of 10 geometry boxes = ₹10

$\therefore$ Loss percentage $= \frac{\text{Loss}}{\text{CP}} \times 100 = \frac{10}{140+10} \times 100 = \frac{10}{150} \times 100 = \frac{20}{3}\% = \mathbf{6\frac{2}{3}\%}$

Q. 40 The cost price of 10 tables is equal to the sale price of 5 tables. The profit per cent in this transaction is _____.

Sol. Let the cost price of 1 table be ₹ 1.

The cost price of 10 tables = Sale price of 5 tables

Profit = Cost price of 5 tables = ₹5

$\therefore$ Profit percentage $= \frac{\text{Profit}}{\text{CP}} \times 100 = \frac{5}{5} \times 100 = \mathbf{100\%}$

Q. 41 Abida bought 100 pens at the rate of ₹ 3.50 per pen and pays a sales tax of 4%. The total amount paid by Abida is _____.

Sol. Number of pens bought by Abida = 100

Rate of per pen = ₹3.50

So, cost of 100 pens = 100 × 3.50 = ₹ 350

Abida also paid 4% sales tax on ₹ 350.

So, the total amount paid by Abida $= 350 \times \frac{4}{100} + 350 = 350 \times \frac{1}{25} + 350 = 14 + 350 =$ ₹ **364**

Q. 42 The cost of a tape recorder is ₹ 10800 inclusive of sales tax charged at 8%. The price of the tape recorder before sales tax was charged, is ___.

Sol. The cost of tape recorder, inclusive of 8% sales tax = ₹10800

Let the price of the tape recorder before sales tax be ₹ x.

So, $$x + x \times \frac{8}{100} = 10800$$

$\Rightarrow$ $$\frac{108x}{100} = 10800$$

$\Rightarrow$ $$x = \frac{10800}{108} \times 100 = 100 \times 100$$

$$x = ₹10000$$

Hence, the price of the tape recorder before sales tax charged, is ₹ **10000**.

Q. 43 2500 is greater than 500 by ____ %.

Sol. Difference between 2500 and 500 = 2500 − 500 = 2000

Hence, $\frac{2000}{500} \times 100 = \frac{2000}{5} = \mathbf{400\%}$

Q. 44 **Four times a number is a _____% increase in the number.**

Sol. Let x be the number.

So, four times of x is $4x$.

Hence, $4x$ is greater than x by $4x - x = 3x$

$\therefore$ Percentage increase in $x = \frac{3x}{x} \times 100 = \mathbf{300\%}$

Q. 45 **5% sales tax is charged on an article marked ₹ 200 after allowing a discount of 5%, then the amount payable is _____.**

Sol. The marked price of the article = ₹ 200

Discount = 5%

Selling price of the article $= 200 - \frac{5}{100} \times 200$

$= 200 - 10 =$ ₹190

Selling price including 5% sales tax $= 190 + \frac{5}{100} \times 190$

$= 190 + 9.5 =$ ₹199.5

$\therefore$ Payable amount = **₹ 199.50**

True/False

Inquestions 46 to 65, state whether the statements are True or False.

Q. 46 **To calculate the growth of a bacteria if the rate of growth is known, the formula for calculation of amount in compound interest can be used.**

Sol. ***True***

For calculating the growth of a bacteria if the rate of growth is known, then we can use the formula for calculation of amount in compound interest.

i.e., $A = P\left(1 + \frac{R}{100}\right)^n$

where, A = growth after n years, P = initial number of bacteria and R = rate of growth

Q. 47 **Additional expenses made after buying an article are included in the cost price and are known as Value Added Tax.**

Sol. ***False***

In the selling price (known as MRP) include the tax known as VAT (Value Added Tax). Hence, VAT is always included in selling price.

Q. 48 **Discount is a reduction given on cost price of an article.**

Sol. ***False***

Discount is a reduction given on marked price not on cost price.

Q. 49 Compound interest is the interest calculated on the previous year's amount.

Sol. ***True***

$\because$ Compound interest, $CI = A - P$

where, $$A = P\left(+ \frac{R}{100}\right)^n$$

Here, P = Principal on previous year's amount and A = Present year's amount

R = Rate of interest and n = Time

Q. 50 CP = MP – Discount

Sol. ***False***

The relation between marked price and discount is given by

Selling price = Marked price – Discount

Q. 51 A man purchased a bicycle for ₹ 1040 and sold it for ₹ 800. His loss per cent is 30%.

Sol. ***False***

Cost price of the bicycle = ₹ 1040

Selling price of the bicycle = ₹ 800

$\therefore$ Loss = Cost price – Selling price = ₹1040 – ₹ 800 = ₹240

Hence, loss % = $\frac{\text{Loss}}{\text{Cost price}} \times 100 = \frac{240}{1040} \times 100$

$$= \frac{2400}{104} = 23.07\%$$

Q. 52 Three times a number is 200% increase in the number, then one-third of the same number is 200% decrease in the number.

Sol. ***False***

Let x be the number.

So, three times of $x = 3x$

$\therefore$ Difference between $3x$ and $x = 3x - x = 2x$

$\therefore$ Percentage increase in $x = \frac{2x}{x} \times 100 = 200\%$

If one-third of $x = \frac{1}{3}x$

$\therefore$ Difference between x and $\frac{x}{3} = x - \frac{x}{3} = \frac{2x}{3}$

$\therefore$ Percentage decrease = $\frac{\frac{2x}{3}}{x} \times 100$

$$= \frac{2}{3} \times 100$$

$$= 66.66\%$$

Q. 53 Simple interest on a given amount is always less than or equal to the compound interest on the same amount for the same time period and at the same rate of interest per annum.

Sol. ***False***

For 1 yr, the simple interest and compound interest for same amount on same rate of interest are equal.

But for 2 yr, the simple interest is less than the compound interest for same amount on same rate of interest.

Q. 54 The cost of a sewing machine is ₹ 7000. Its value depreciates at 8% per annum. Then, the value of the machine after 2 yr is ₹ 5924.80.

Sol. ***True***

Principal = ₹7000

Rate of depreciation = 8% per annum

Time period = 2 yr

∴ Depreciated amount after 2 yr is given by

$$A = P\left(1 - \frac{R}{100}\right)^n = 7000\left(1 - \frac{8}{100}\right)^2$$

$$= 7000 \times \frac{23}{25} \times \frac{23}{25}$$

$$= 11.2 \times 23 \times 23 = ₹\,5924.8$$

Q. 55 If the discount of ₹ y is available on the marked price of ₹ x, then the discount per cent is $\frac{x}{y} \times 100\%$.

Sol. ***False***

Marked price = ₹x

Discount amount = ₹y

$$\therefore \text{Discount percentage} = \frac{\text{Discount}}{\text{Marked price}} \times 100\,\% = \frac{y}{x} \times 100\,\%$$

Q. 56 Number of students appearing for class X CBSE examination increases from 91422 in 1999-2000 to 116054 in 2008-09. Increase in the number of students appeared is approximately 27%.

Sol. ***True***

Number of students increase from 116054 in 2008-09 to 91422 in 1999-2000

$$= 116054 - 91422 = 24632$$

Percentage of increase in number of students

$$= \frac{\text{Number of students increase}}{\text{Number of students in previous year}} \times 100$$

$$= \frac{24632}{91422} \times 100 = 0.2694 \times 100 = 26.9 \approx 27\%$$

Q. 57 Selling price of 9 articles is equal to the cost price of 15 articles. In this transaction, there is profit of $66\frac{2}{3}\%$.

Sol. ***True***

Selling price of 9 articles = Cost price of 15 articles

It means, 15 articles – 9 articles = 6 articles

Cost price of 6 articles is the profit on transaction.

$\therefore$ Profit % $= \frac{6}{9} \times 100 = \frac{600}{9} = \frac{200}{3} = 66\frac{2}{3}\%$

Q. 58 The compound interest on a sum of ₹ P for T years at $R\%$ per annum compounded annually is given by the formula $P\left(1+\frac{R}{100}\right)$.

Sol. ***False***

The compound interest on a sum of ₹ P for T years at $R\%$ per annum compounded annually is given by the formula,

Compound interest $= A - P$

where, $A = P\left(1+\frac{R}{100}\right)^T$

Q. 59 In case of gain, $SP = \frac{(100+\text{gain}\%)\times CP}{100}$

Sol. ***True***

We know that,

$$\text{Gain} = \text{Selling price} - \text{Cost price}$$

$$\therefore \quad \text{Gain}\,\% = \frac{\text{Gain}}{\text{Cost price}} \times 100$$

$$\therefore \quad \text{Selling price} = \frac{100+\text{Gain}\%}{100} \times \text{Cost price}$$

Note *Gain or loss is always calculated on cost price.*

Q. 60 In case of loss, $CP = \frac{100 \times SP}{100 + \text{Loss}\%}$

Sol. ***False***

We know that,

$$\text{Loss} = \text{Cost price} - \text{Selling price}$$

$$\therefore \quad \text{Loss}\,\% = \frac{\text{Loss}}{\text{Cost price}} \times 100$$

$$\therefore \quad \text{Cost price} = \frac{100}{100-\text{Loss}\%} \times \text{Selling price}$$

Q. 61 The value of a car, bought for ₹ 440000 depreciates each year by 10% of its value at the beginning of that year. So, its value becomes ₹ 308000 after three years.

Sol. ***False***

The value of a car i.e. principal = ₹440000

Rate of depreciation ($R\%$) = 10% per annum

Time period (T) = 3 yr

The value of the car after depreciation in 3 yr is given by

$$A = P\left(1 - \frac{R}{100}\right)^T$$

$$= 440000\left(1 - \frac{10}{100}\right)^3$$

$$= 440000 \times \frac{9}{10} \times \frac{9}{10} \times \frac{9}{10}$$

$$= 440 \times 729 = ₹320760$$

Q. 62 **The cost of a book marked at ₹ 190 after paying a sales tax of 2% is ₹ 192.**

Sol. ***False***

Marked price of a book = ₹190

Sales tax = 2%

The cost price of the book after 2% sales tax $= 190 + \frac{2}{100} \times 190$

$$= 190 + \frac{190}{50} = 190 + 3.8 = ₹193.8$$

Q. 63 **The buying price of 5 kg of flour with the rate ₹ 20 per kg, when 5% sales tax is added on the purchase, is ₹ 21.**

Sol. ***True***

Total flour bought = 5 kg

Rate of one kg flour = ₹20

Cost of 5 kg flour with 5% sales tax $= 5 \times 20 + \frac{5}{100} \times (5 \times 20)$

$$= 100 + \frac{5}{100} \times 100 = 100 + 5 = ₹105$$

Per kg flour rate after 5% sales tax $= \frac{105}{5} = ₹21$

Q. 64 **The original price of a shampoo bottle bought for ₹ 324, if 8% VAT is included in the price, is ₹ 300.**

Sol. ***False***

The original price of a shampoo bottle = ₹300

Cost price of shampoo bottle after 8% VAT

$$= 300 + \frac{8}{100} \times 300$$

$$= 300 + 8 \times 3 = 300 + 24 = ₹324$$

Q. 65 **Sales tax is always calculated on the cost price of an item and is added to the value of the bill.**

Sol. ***False***

Sales tax is always calculated on the selling price of an item and is added to the value of the bill.

Q. 66 **In a factory, women are 35% of all the workers, the rest of the workers being men. The number of men exceeds that of women by 252. Find the total number of workers in the factory.**

Sol. Percentage of women in factory = 35%

Percentage of men in factory = 100 – 35 = 65%

Let the number of persons in the factory be x.

According to the question,

$$x \times \frac{65}{100} - x \times \frac{35}{100} = 252$$

$$\Rightarrow \quad \frac{65x - 35x}{100} = 252$$

$$\Rightarrow \quad \frac{30x}{100} = 252$$

$$\Rightarrow \quad x = \frac{2520}{3} = 840$$

Hence, total number of workers in the factory is 840.

Q. 67 **Three bags contain 64.2 kg of sugar. The second bag contains $\frac{4}{5}$ of the contents of the first and the third contains $45\frac{1}{2}$% of what there is in the second bag. How much sugar is there in each bag?**

Sol. The total weight of sugar in three bags = 64.2 kg

Let the first bag contains x kg sugar.

The second bag contains $= x \times \frac{4}{5}$ kg $= \frac{4x}{5}$ kg

Third bag contains $= x \times \frac{4}{5} \times \frac{91}{2}\% = x \times \frac{4}{5} \times \frac{\frac{91}{2}}{100} = \frac{91x}{250}$ kg

According to the question,

$$x + \frac{4x}{5} + \frac{91x}{250} = 64.2$$

$$\Rightarrow \quad \frac{250x + 200x + 91x}{250} = 64.2$$

$$\Rightarrow \quad 541x = 64.2 \times 250$$

$$541x = 16050$$

$$\Rightarrow \quad x = \frac{16050}{541} = 29.67 \text{ kg}$$

So, first bag contains the sugar = 23.73 kg

Second bag contains the sugar $= 29.67 \times \frac{4}{5} = 23.73$ kg

and third bag contains the sugar $= \frac{91}{250} \times 29.67 = 10.8$ kg

Q. 68 Find the SP, if

(a) MP = ₹5450 and discount = 5%

(b) MP = ₹1300 and discount = 1.5%

Sol. (a) Marked price = ₹ 5450

Discount % = 5%

$\therefore$ Selling price = Marked price $- \frac{\text{Discount \%}}{100} \times$ Marked price

$$= 5450 - \frac{5}{100} \times 5450$$

$$= 5450 - 272.5 = ₹\,5177.5$$

(b) Marked price (MP) = ₹1300

Discount % = 1.5%

Selling price = Marked price $- \frac{\text{Discount \%}}{100} \times$ MP

$$= 1300 - \frac{1.5}{100} \times 1300 = 1300 - 19.5 = ₹\,1280.5$$

Q. 69 Find the MP, if

(a) SP = ₹ 495 and discount = 1%

(b) SP = ₹9250 and discount = $7\frac{1}{2}$%

Sol. (a) Selling price (SP) = ₹495

Discount % = 1%

Let the marked price be ₹ x.

$\therefore$ Selling price = Marked price $- \frac{\text{Discount \%}}{100} \times$ MP

$\Rightarrow$ $495 = x - \frac{1}{100} \times x$

$\Rightarrow$ $495 = \frac{100x - x}{100}$

$\Rightarrow$ $495 = \frac{99x}{100}$ [by cross-multiplication]

$\Rightarrow$ $99x = 49500$

$\Rightarrow$ $x = 500$

Hence, the marked price = ₹ 500.

(b) Selling price (SP) = ₹9250

Discount % $= 7\frac{1}{2}\% = \frac{15}{2}\%$

Let marked price be ₹ x.

$\therefore$ Selling price = Marked price $-\dfrac{\text{Discount \%}}{100}\times$ MP

$$\Rightarrow \quad 9250 = x - \frac{15}{2\times 100}\times x$$

$$\Rightarrow \quad 9250 = \frac{200x - 15x}{200}$$

$$\Rightarrow \quad 9250 = \frac{185x}{200}$$

$$\Rightarrow \quad x = \frac{9250\times 200}{185} \qquad \text{[by cross-multiplication]}$$

$$\Rightarrow \quad x = \frac{1550000}{185} = ₹10000$$

Hence, the marked price = ₹ 10000.

Q. 70 Find discount in per cent when

(a) MP = ₹625 and SP = ₹562.50

(b) MP = ₹900 and SP = ₹873

Sol. (a) Marked price (MP) = ₹625

Selling price (SP) = ₹ 562.50

$\because$ Discount = Marked price – Selling price = ₹ 625 – ₹562.5 = ₹ 62.5

$$\therefore \text{Discount \%} = \frac{\text{Discount}}{\text{Marked price}}\times 100 = \frac{62.5}{625}\times 100 = \frac{6250}{625} = 10\%$$

(b) Marked price (MP) = ₹900

Selling price (SP) = ₹873

$\because$ Discount = Marked price – Selling price = ₹900 – ₹873 = ₹27

$$\therefore \text{Discount \%} = \frac{\text{Discount}}{\text{Marked price}}\times 100 = \frac{27}{900}\times 100 = \frac{27}{9} = 3\%$$

Q. 71 The marked price of an article is ₹ 500. The shopkeeper gives a discount of 5% and still makes a profit of 25%. Find the cost price of the article.

Sol. Given, marked price of an article = ₹500

Discount % = 5%

But it makes a profit of 25%.

Let the cost price of the article be ₹x.

Cost price after 5% discount $= 500 - \dfrac{5}{100}\times 500$

$= 500 - 25 = ₹ 475$

According to the question,

$$(100 + 25)\% \text{ of } x = 475$$

$$\Rightarrow \quad \frac{125}{100}\times x = 475$$

$$\Rightarrow \quad x = \frac{475\times 100}{125}$$

$$= 3.8\times 100 = ₹380$$

Hence, cost price of an article is ₹ 380.

Q. 72 In 2007-08, the number of students appeared for Class X examination was 105332 and in 2008-09 the number was 116054. If 88151 students pass the examination in 2007-08 and 103804 students in 2008-09. What is the increase or decrease in pass percentage in class X result?

Sol. Number of students appeared in 2007-08 = 105332

Number of students appeared in 2008-09 = 116054

Number of students passed in 2007-08 = 88151

Number of students passed in 2008-09 = 103804

Passed percentage of students in 2007-08

$$= \frac{\text{Number of students passed in 2007-08}}{\text{Number of students appeared in 2007-08}} \times 100$$

$$= \frac{88151}{105332} \times 100$$

$$= \frac{8815100}{105332} = 83.68\%$$

Passed percentage of students in 2008-09

$$= \frac{\text{Number of students passed in 2008-09}}{\text{Number of students apppeared in 2008-09}} \times 100$$

$$= \frac{103804}{116054} \times 100$$

$$= \frac{10380400}{116054} = 89.44\%$$

$\therefore$ Increase in percentage = 89.44 – 83.68 = 5.76%

Q. 73 A watch worth ₹ 5400 is offered for sale at ₹ 4500. What per cent discount is offered during the sale?

Sol. Marked price of a watch = ₹5400

Selling price = ₹4500

Discount = Marked price – Selling price = ₹5400 – ₹4500 = ₹900

$$\therefore \text{Discount\%} = \frac{\text{Discount}}{\text{Marked price}} \times 100$$

$$= \frac{900}{5400} \times 100$$

$$= \frac{900}{54} = \frac{450}{27} = \frac{150}{9} = \frac{50}{3}\%$$

Q. 74 In the year 2001, the number of malaria patients admitted in the hospitals of a state was 4375. Every year this number decreases by 8%. Find the number of patients in 2003.

Sol. The number of malaria patients admitted in a hospital in 2001 = 4375

Rate of decrement of malaria patients = 8%

Time period = 2 yr [$\because$ 2003-2001 = 2 yr]

Let the number of patients in 2003 be A.

By using formula, $A = P\left(1-\frac{R}{100}\right)^T$

$= 4375\left(1-\frac{8}{100}\right)^2$

$= 4375 \times \frac{23}{25} \times \frac{23}{25}$

$= 7 \times 23 \times 23 = 3703$

Hence, the number of patients in 2003 was 3703.

Q. 75 Jyotsana bought a product for ₹ 3155 including 4.5% sales tax. Find the price before tax was added.

Sol. A product bought by Jyotsana for ₹ 3155 including 4.5% sales tax.

Let the price of the product before sales tax be ₹ x.

So, $x + x \times \frac{4.5}{100} = 3155$

$\Rightarrow \quad x + \frac{x \times 45}{1000} = 3155$

$\Rightarrow \quad \frac{1045x}{1000} = 3155$ [∵ sales tax included in selling price]

$\Rightarrow \quad x = \frac{3155 \times 1000}{1045} = \frac{3155000}{1045} =$ ₹ 3019.1387

$\Rightarrow \quad x \approx$ ₹ 3019.14

Hence, the price of the product before sales tax is ₹ 3019.14.

Q. 76 An average Urban Indian uses about 150 L of water everyday.

Activity	Litres per person per day
Drinking	3
Cooking	4
Bathing	20
Sanitation	40
Washing clothes	40
Washing utensils	20
Gardening	23
Total	**150**

(a) What per cent of water is used for bathing and sanitation together per day?

(b) How much less per cent of water is used for cooking in comparison to that used for bathing?

(c) What per cent of water is used for drinking, cooking and gardening together?

Sol. (a) On the basis of given details, water used for bathing per day = 20 L

Water used for sanitation = 40 L

∴ Total water used per day = 150 L

Percentage of water is used for bathing and sanitation together per day

$$= \frac{20+40}{150} \times 100 = \frac{60}{150} \times 100$$

$$= \frac{600}{15} = 40\%$$

(b) Water used for cooking per day = 4 L

Water used for bathing per day = 20 L

Difference between water used for cooking and bathing = 20 – 4 = 16 L

= 16 L water less used for cooking in comparision of bathing

In percentage $= \frac{16}{150} \times 100 = \frac{160}{15} = \frac{32}{3}\%$

(c) Water used for drinking per day = 3 L

Water used for cooking per day = 4 L

Water used for gardening per day = 23 L

Water used for drinking, cooking and gardening together = 3 + 4 + 23 = 30 L

In percentage $= \frac{30}{150} \times 100 = \frac{100}{5} = 20\%$

Q. 77 In 1975, the consumption of water for human use was about 3850 cu km/yr. It increased to about 6000 cu km/yr in the year 2000. Find the per cent increase in the consumption of water from 1975 to 2000. Also, find the annual per cent increase in consumption (assuming water consumption increases uniformly).

Sol. The consumption of water for human in 1975 = 3850 cu km/yr

The consumption of water for human in 2000 = 6000 cu km/yr

Increase in consumption of water in 1975 to 2000 = 6000 – 3850 = 2150 cu km/yr

In percentage $= \frac{2150}{3850} \times 100 = 55.84\%$

In 25 yr total increase in water consumption = 2150 cu km/yr

$\therefore$ Annualy, i.e. per year water consumption $= \frac{2150}{25} = 86$ cu km/yr [$\because$ 2000 – 1975 = 25 yr]

$\therefore$ In percentage $= \frac{86}{3850} \times 100 = \frac{8600}{3850} = 2.23\%$

Q. 78 Harshna gave her car for service at service station on 27-05-2009 and was charged as follows

(a) 3.10 L engine oil @ ₹ 178.75 per litre and VAT @ 20%.

(b) ₹ 1105.12 for all other services and VAT @ 12.5%.

(c) ₹ 2095.80 as labour charges and service tax @ 10%.

(d) 3% cess on service tax.

Find the bill amount.

Sol. (a) The total litres of engine oil used = 3.10 L

Rate of engine oil per litres = ₹ 178.75

The cost of engine oil = 3.10 × 178.75 = ₹ 554.125

The cost of engine oil including 20% VAT $= 554.125 + 554.125 \times \frac{20}{100}$

$= 554.125 + \frac{554.125}{5}$

$= 554.125 + 110.825 =$ ₹ 664.95

(b) Amount paid for all services = ₹ 1105.12

Amount paid including 12.5% VAT $= 1105.12 + \frac{12.5}{100} \times 1105.12$

$= 1105.12 + 138.14 =$ ₹ 1243.26

(c) Labour charges = ₹ 2095.80

Service tax = 10%

Total labour charges including 10% sevice tax

$= 2095.80 + \frac{10}{100} \times 2095.8 = 2095.80 + 209.58 =$ ₹ 2305.38

(d) Cess on service tax @ 3% $= 209.58 \times \frac{3}{100} = 2.095 \times 3$

[∵ service tax = ₹ 209.58, get above]

= ₹6.285 ≈ ₹6.29

Thus, total bill amount = ₹ 664.95 + ₹ 1243.26 + ₹ 2305.38 + ₹ 6.29 = ₹ 4219.88

Q. 79 Given, the principal = ₹40000, rate of interest = 8% per annum compound annually. Find

(a) Interest if period is one year.

(b) Principal for IInd year.

(c) Interest for IInd year.

(d) Amount if period is two year.

Sol. Given, principal (P) = ₹40000

Rate of interest (R) = 8% per annum

(a) Compound interest for one year,

We know that,

$$A = P\left(1 + \frac{R}{100}\right)^n$$

$$= 40000\left(1 + \frac{8}{100}\right)^1 \qquad [\because n = 1\text{yr}]$$

$$= 40000 \times \frac{108}{100}$$

∴ Amount, $A = 400 \times 108 =$ ₹43200

∴ Compound interest, CI $= A - P =$ ₹43200 − ₹ 40000 = ₹ 3200

(b) Amount of Ist year = Principal of IInd year = ₹ 43200

(c) Now, for IInd year,

Principal = ₹ 43200

Rate of interest, R = 8% per annum

Time, n = 1yr

Amount for IInd year $= 43200\left(1+\frac{8}{100}\right)^1$

$$= 43200 \times \frac{108}{100} = 432 \times 108 = ₹\ 46656$$

Compound interest, CI $= A - P = ₹\ 46656 - ₹\ 43200 = ₹\ 3456$

(d) Now, if period i.e. time $(n) = 2$ yr

Principal = ₹ 40000 and rate = 8% per annum

$$\because \quad A = P\left(1+\frac{R}{100}\right)^n$$

$$\Rightarrow \quad A = 40000\left(1+\frac{8}{100}\right)^2 = 40000 \times \frac{108}{100} \times \frac{108}{100} = ₹\ 46656$$

$\therefore$ Amount, $A = ₹\ 46656$

Q. 80 **In Delhi University, in the year 2009-10, 49000 seats were available for admission to various courses at graduation level. Out of these 28200 seats were for the students of General Category while 7400 seats were reserved for SC and 3700 seats for ST. Find the percentage of seats available for**

(a) students of General Category.

(b) students of SC Category and ST Category taken together.

Sol. The total number of seats available for admission in 2009-10 = 49000

Seats reserved for General Category students = 28200

Seats reserved for SC Category students = 7400

Seats reserved for ST Category students = 3700

(a) Percentage of seats reserved for students of General Category

$$= \frac{28200}{49000} \times 100$$

$$= \frac{282 \times 100}{490} = \frac{28200}{490} = 57.55\%$$

(b) Percentage of seats reserved for students of SC and ST Category together

$$= \frac{3700 + 7400}{49000} \times 100$$

$$= \frac{11100}{49000} \times 100 = \frac{11100}{490} = 22.65\%$$

Q. 81 **Prachi bought medicines from a medical store as prescribed by her doctor for ₹ 36.40 including 4% VAT. Find the price of before VAT was added.**

Sol. The cost of medicine including 4% VAT = ₹ 36.40

The price of medicine before 4% VAT [$\because$ selling price = cost price + VAT]

$$= 36.40 - \frac{4}{100} \times 36.40$$

$$= 36.40 - 4 \times 0.364$$

$$= 36.40 - 1.456$$

$$= ₹\ 34.944 \approx ₹\ 35$$

Q. 82 **Kritika ordered one pizza and one garlic bread from a pizza store and paid ₹ 387 inclusive of taxes of ₹ 43. Find the tax%.**

Sol. The cost of one pizza and one garlic bread inclusive as tax = ₹ 43

∴ The cost of one pizza and one garlic bread without tax = ₹ 387 − ₹ 43 = ₹ 344

$\therefore$ Tax % = $\frac{43}{344} \times 100 = \frac{100}{8} = 12.5\%$

Q. 83 **Arunima bought household items whose marked price and discount % is as follows**

	Item	Quantity	Rate (in ₹)	Discount %
(i)	Atta	1 packet	200	16%
(ii)	Detergent	1 packet	371	22.10%
(iii)	Namkeen	1 packet	153	18.30%

Find the total amount of the bill she has to pay.

Sol. On the basis of given data in the above table,

Rate of one packet of atta = ₹200

Discount % = 16%

So, price = $200 - \frac{16}{100} \times 200 = 200 - 32 =$ ₹ 168

Rate of one packet of detergent = ₹ 371

Discount % = 22.10%

So, price = $371 - 371 \times \frac{22.10}{100} = 371 - 81.991 =$ ₹ 289.009

Rate of one packet of namkeen = 153

Discount% = 18.30%

So, price = $153 - 153 \times \frac{18.30}{100} = 153 - 1.53 \times 18.30 = 153 - 27.999 =$ ₹ 125.001

∴ Total bill amount = ₹ 168 + ₹ 289.009 + ₹ 125.001 = ₹ 582.01

Q. 84 **Devangi's phone subscription charges for the period 17-02-09 to 16-03-09 were as follows**

Period	Amount (in ₹)	Service tax %
17-02-09 to 23-02-09	199.75	12%
24-02-09 to 16-03-09	599.25	10%

Find the final bill amount, if 3% education cess was also charged on service tax.

Sol. On the basis of above given table,

Amount for period 17-02-09 to 23-02-09 = ₹ 199.75

∴ Amount with service tax 12% = $199.75 + \frac{12}{100} \times 199.75 = 199.75 + 23.97 =$ ₹ 223.72

Amount for period 24-02-09 to 16-03-09 = ₹599.25

Amount with service tax @ 10% $= 599.25 + 599.25 \times \frac{10}{100}$

$= 599.25 + 59.925 =$ ₹ 659.175

$\therefore$ Total bill amount = ₹ 223.72 + ₹ 659.175 = ₹ 882.895

Total bill amount including education cess of 3%

$= 882.895 + 3\%$ of 882.895

$= 882.895 + \frac{3}{100} \times 882.895$

$= 882.895 + 26.486$

= ₹ 909.39

Q. 85 If principal = ₹100000, rate of interest = 10% compounded half-yearly. Find

(a) Interest for 6 months. (b) Amount after 6 months.

(c) Interest for next 6 months. (d) Amount after one year.

Sol. Principal (P) = ₹100000

Rate of interest (R) = 10% compounded half-yearly

(a) Interest for 6 months,

We know that,

Compound interest, CI $= A - P$

where, $A = P\left(1 + \frac{R}{200}\right)^n$ [for 6 months]

$\therefore \quad A = P\left(1 + \frac{R}{200}\right)^n = 100000\left(1 + \frac{10}{200}\right)^1$ [$\because n = 1$ for 6 months]

$= 100000 \times \frac{21}{20} =$ ₹ 105000

$\therefore$ Compound interest, CI $= A - P =$ ₹105000 − ₹100000 = ₹ 5000

(b) Amount after 6 months = ₹ 105000

(c) Interest for next 6 months

Principal = Amount after 6 months

$\therefore$ Principal (P) = ₹ 105000

Rate of interest (R) = 10%

$\therefore \quad A = P\left(1 + \frac{R}{200}\right)^n$

$= 105000\left(1 + \frac{10}{200}\right)^1$ [$\because n = 1$ for 6 months]

$= 105000 \times \frac{21}{20}$

$= \frac{2205000}{20} =$ ₹ 110250

$\because$ Compound interest, CI $= A - P =$ ₹110250 − ₹105000 = ₹ 5250

(d) Amount after one year = ₹ 110250

Q. 86 **Babita bought 160 kg of mangoes at ₹ 48 per kg. She sold 70% of the mangoes at ₹ 70 per kg and the remaining mangoes at ₹ 40 per kg. Find Babita's gain or loss per cent on the whole dealing.**

Sol. Babita bought 160 kg of mangoes = ₹ 48 per kg

So, total amount she paid = ₹ 48 × 160 = ₹ 7680

She sold 70% of mangoes at ₹ 70 per kg.

$\because$ Cost of 70% mangoes $= 160 \times \frac{70}{100} \times 70 = 70 \times 16 \times 7 =$ ₹ 7840

Remaining mangoes = (100 − 70)% = 30%

Cost of remaining at ₹ 40 per kg $= 160 \times \frac{30}{100} \times 40 = 16 \times 3 \times 40 =$ ₹ 1920

Total amount received after selling mangoes = ₹7840 + ₹1920 = ₹ 9760

$\therefore$ SP > CP, so there is a gain.

$$\text{Gain} = \text{SP} - \text{CP} = ₹\,9760 - ₹\,7680 = ₹\,2080$$

$$\because \quad \text{Gain \%} = \frac{\text{Gain}}{\text{CP}} \times 100$$

$$\therefore \quad \text{Gain \%} = \frac{2080}{7680} \times 100 = 27.08\%$$

Q. 87 **A shopkeeper was selling all his items at 25% discount. During the off season, he offered 30% discount over and above the existing discount. If Pragya bought a skirt which was marked for ₹ 1200, how much did she pay for it?**

Sol. Marked price of the skirt = ₹1200

During normal season discount @ 25% $= \frac{25}{100} \times 1200 = 25 \times 12 =$ ₹ 300

Price of the skirt after discount = ₹1200 − ₹ 300 = ₹ 900

In off season, the shopkeeper also offer discount @ 30% $= \frac{30}{100} \times 900 =$ ₹ 270

Price of skirt after 30% discount = ₹ 900 − ₹270 = ₹ 630

So, ₹ 630 paid by Pragya for the skirt.

Q. 88 **Ayesha announced a festival discount of 25% on all the items in her mobile phone shop. Ramandeep bought a mobile phone for himself. He got a discount of ₹ 1960. What was the marked price of the mobile phone?**

Sol. Let the marked price of the mobile phone be ₹ x.

Festival discount on mobile phone = 25%

Ramandeep got total discount = ₹1960

According to the question,

$$1960 = x \times \frac{25}{100}$$

$$\Rightarrow \quad 1960 = \frac{x}{4}$$

$$\Rightarrow \quad \frac{x}{4} = 1960$$

$$\Rightarrow \quad x = 1960 \times 4 = ₹\,7840$$

Hence, marked price of mobile phone was ₹ 7840.

Q. 89 **Find the difference between compound interest and simple interest on ₹ 45000 at 12% per annum for 5 yr.**

Sol. Principal (P) = ₹45000

Rate of interest (R) = 12% per annum

Time period (T) = 5 yr

Simple interest, $SI = \frac{P \times R \times T}{100} = \frac{45000 \times 12 \times 5}{100}$

$$= 450 \times 60 = ₹\,27000$$

$\because$ Compound interest, $CI = A - P$

where, $A = P\left(1 + \frac{R}{100}\right)^T$

$$\therefore \quad A = 45000\left(1 + \frac{12}{100}\right)^5 = 45000\left(\frac{28}{25}\right)^5$$

$$= 45000 \times \frac{28}{25} \times \frac{28}{25} \times \frac{28}{25} \times \frac{28}{25} \times \frac{28}{25}$$

$$= \frac{45000 \times 17210368}{9765625}$$

$$= 45000 \times 1.76 = ₹\,79200$$

$\therefore$ Compound interest, CI = ₹79200 − ₹ 45000

= ₹ 34200

$\therefore$ Difference between SI and CI = ₹ 34200 − ₹27000 = ₹ 7200

Q. 90 **A new computer costs ₹ 100000. The depreciation of computers is very high as new models with better technological advantages are coming into the market. The depreciation is as high as 50% every year. How much will the cost of computer be after two years?**

Sol. The cost of the new computer = ₹ 100000

The depreciation rate = 50% per annum

Time period (T) = 2 yr

Let the cost of computer after 2 yr = ₹ A

$$\because \quad A = P\left(1 - \frac{R}{100}\right)^T$$

$$= 100000\left(1 - \frac{50}{100}\right)^2$$

$$\Rightarrow \quad A = 100000 \times \frac{1}{2} \times \frac{1}{2}$$

$$= 25000 \times 1$$

$$\therefore \quad A = ₹\,25000$$

Hence, the cost of computer after 2 yr is ₹ 25000.

Q. 91 The population of a town was decreasing every year due to migration, poverty and unemployment. The present population of the town is 631680. Last year the migration was 4% and the year before last, it was 6%. What was the population two years ago?

Sol. Let the population two years ago = P (Principal)

Present population of the town = A = 631680

Rate of migration in Ist year = 4%

Rate of migration in IInd year = 6%

By using the formula, $A = P\left(1-\frac{R}{100}\right)\left(1-\frac{R}{100}\right)$

$$\Rightarrow \quad 631680 = P\left(1-\frac{4}{100}\right)\left(1-\frac{6}{100}\right)$$

$$\Rightarrow \quad 631680 = P \times \frac{24}{25} \times \frac{47}{50}$$

$$\Rightarrow \quad P = \frac{631680 \times 25 \times 50}{24 \times 47}$$

$$\Rightarrow \quad = 560 \times 1250 = 700000$$

Hence, the population of town was 700000 two years ago.

Q. 92 Lemons were bought at ₹ 48 per dozen and sold at the rate of ₹ 40 per 10. Find the gain or loss per cent.

Sol. Cost of 12 lemons = ₹ 48 [∵ 1 dozen = 12 pieces]

∴ Cost of 1 lemon = ₹ $\frac{48}{12}$ = ₹ 4

Also, 10 lemons sold by = ₹ 40

∴ Selling price of 1 lemon = ₹ $\frac{40}{10}$ = ₹ 4

∴ Cost price of 1 lemon = Selling price of 1 lemon

∴ No profit and no loss.

Q. 93 If the price of petrol, diesel and LPG is slashed as follows

Fuel	Old price/litre (in ₹)	New price/litre (in ₹)	% Decrease
Petrol/L	45.62	40.62	---
Diesel/L	32.86	30.86	---
LPG/14.2 kg	304.70	279.70	---

Complete the above table.

Sol. For Petrol/L,

Old price = ₹ 45.62

New price = ₹ 40.62

Decrement in price = ₹ 45.62 – ₹ 40.62 = ₹ 5

∴ Decrease % = $\frac{5}{45.62} \times 100 = \frac{50000}{4562} = 10.96\%$

For Diesel/L,

Old price = ₹ 32.86

New price = ₹ 30.86

Decrement in price = ₹32.86 − ₹ 30.86 = ₹ 2

$\therefore$ Decrease % = $\frac{2}{32.86} \times 100 = \frac{200}{32.86} = 6.0869 \approx 6.09\%$

For LPG,

Old price = ₹ 304.70

New price = ₹ 279.70

Decrement in price = ₹ 304.70 − ₹279.70 = ₹ 25

$\therefore$ Decrease % = $\frac{25}{304.70} \times 100 = \frac{2500}{304.70} = 8.20\%$

Q. 94 What is the percentage increase or decrease in the number of seats won by A, B, C and D in the general elections of 2009 as compared to the results of 2004?

Political party	Number of seats won in 2004	Number of seats won in 2009
A	206	145
B	116	138
C	4	24
D	11	12

Sol. For Political party A,

Number of seats won in 2004 = 206

Number of seats won in 2009 = 145

Decrement in the number of seats won by party A = 206 − 145 = 61

$\therefore$ Decrease % = $\frac{61}{206} \times 100 = 29.61\%$

For Political party B,

Number of seats won in 2004 = 116

Number of seats won in 2009 = 138

Increment in the number of seats won by party B = 138 − 116 = 22

$\therefore$ Increase % = $\frac{22}{116} \times 100 = 18.96\%$

For Political party C,

Number of seats won in 2004 = 4

Number of seats won in 2009 = 24

Increment in the number of seats won by party C = 24 − 4 = 20

$\therefore$ Increase % = $\frac{20}{4} \times 100 = 500\%$

For Political party D,

Number of seats won in 2004 = 11

Number of seats won in 2009 = 12

Increment in the number of seat won by party D = 12 − 11 = 1

$\therefore$ Increase % = $\frac{1}{11} \times 100 = 9.09\%$

Q. 95 **How much more per cent seats were won by X as compared to Y in assembly election in the state based on the data given below?**

Party	**Won** (out of 294)
X	158
Y	105
Z	18
W	13

Sol. On the basis of above give table

The total number of seats won by party $X = 158$

The total number of seats won by party $Y = 105$

$\therefore$ Total number of seats in election $= 294$

$\therefore$ Percentage of seats won by party $X = \frac{158}{294} \times 100 = 53.74\%$

$\therefore$ Percentage of seats won by party $Y = \frac{105}{294} \times 100 = 35.71\%$

So, difference of percentage $= (53.74 - 35.71)\% = 18.03\%$

Hence, party X won 18.03% compared to party Y.

Q. 96 **Ashima sold two coolers for ₹ 3990 each. On selling one cooler she gained 5% and on selling the other she suffered a loss of 5%. Find her overall gain or loss % in whole transaction.**

Sol. Selling price of each cooler = ₹ 3990

Let ₹ x be the cost price of both coolers for Ashima.

If Ashima gets 5% gain on transaction of first cooler.

Then, $$3990 = x + x \times \frac{5}{100} \quad [\because \text{profit} = \text{SP} - \text{CP}]$$

$$\Rightarrow \quad 3990 = \frac{21x}{20}$$

$$\Rightarrow \quad x = \frac{3990 \times 20}{21}$$

$$= 190 \times 20 = ₹\ 3800$$

Also, on the another transaction of other cooler she has a loss of 5%.

Then, $$3990 = x - \frac{x \times 5}{100} \quad [\because \text{loss} = \text{CP} - \text{SP}]$$

$$\Rightarrow \quad 3990 = \frac{19x}{20}$$

$$\Rightarrow \quad x = \frac{3990 \times 20}{19} = 210 \times 20 = ₹\ 4200$$

So, the total cost price for Ashima = ₹ 3800 + ₹ 4200 = ₹ 8000

Ashima sold both coolers = ₹ 3990 × 2 = ₹ 7980

Here, CP>SP. So, Ashima has loss on overall transaction.

$\because$ Loss = ₹ 8000 − ₹ 7980 = ₹ 20

$\therefore$ Loss % $= \frac{20}{8000} \times 100 = \frac{2000}{8000} = \frac{1}{4}\% = 0.25\%$

Q. 97 **A lady buys some pencils for ₹ 3 and an equal number for ₹ 6. She sells them for ₹ 7. Find her gain or loss%.**

Sol. Let the Lady buys x number of pencils for ₹ 3.

Cost price for one pencil, $CP_1 = ₹\,\frac{3}{x}$

Also, she buys same number of pencils for ₹ 6.

$\therefore$ Cost price for one pencil, $CP_2 = ₹\,\frac{6}{x}$

Now, total pencils $= x + x = 2x$

$\because$ She sells, $2x$ pencils = ₹7

$\therefore$ Selling price of 1 pencil $= ₹\,\frac{7}{2x}$

Case I We know that,

Gain = SP – CP

$\therefore$ Gain $= ₹\left(\frac{7}{2x} - \frac{3}{x}\right) = ₹\left(\frac{7-6}{2x}\right) = ₹\,\frac{1}{2x}$

$$\therefore \qquad \text{Gain\%} = \frac{\text{Gain}}{\text{CP}} \times 100 = \frac{\frac{1}{2x}}{\frac{3}{x}} \times 100 = \frac{100}{2 \times 3} = \frac{50}{3}\%$$

Case II

Also, we know that,

Loss = CP – SP

$\text{Loss} = \frac{6}{x} - \frac{7}{2x} = \frac{6 \times 2 - 7}{2x} = ₹\,\frac{5}{2x}$

$$\therefore \qquad \text{Loss \%} = \frac{\text{Loss}}{\text{CP}} \times 100 = \frac{\frac{5}{2x}}{\frac{6}{x}} \times 100 = \frac{250}{6} = \frac{125}{3}\%$$

$$\therefore \qquad \text{Net gain \%} = \frac{125}{3} - \frac{50}{3} = \frac{75}{3} = 25\%$$

Q. 98 **On selling a chair of ₹ 736, a shopkeeper suffers a loss of 8%. At what price should he sell it, so as to gain 8%?**

Sol. Let the cost price of a chair = ₹ x

Selling price of a chair = ₹736

At selling a shopkeeper suffers 8% loss.

According to the question,

$$x - x \times \frac{8}{100} = 736$$

$$\Rightarrow \qquad \frac{92x}{100} = 736$$

$$\Rightarrow \qquad x = \frac{73600}{92} = ₹\,800$$

To gain 8% profit the price should be $= 800 + \frac{8}{100} \times 800 = 800 + 64 = ₹\,864$

Q. 99 **A dining table is purchased for ₹ 3200 and sold at a gain of 6%. If a customer pays sales tax at the rate of 5%. How much does the customer pay in all for the table?**

Sol. The cost price of the dining table = ₹3200

∴ The dining table sold at a gain of 6%.

So, selling price of the dining table = $3200 + \frac{6}{100} \times 3200 = 3200 + 192 =$ ₹ 3392

Also, customer pay sale tax = 5%

Selling price with sales tax = $3392 + 3392 \times \frac{5}{100} = 3392 + 169.6 =$ ₹ 3561.60

Q. 100 **Achal bought a second hand car for ₹ 225000 and spend ₹ 25000 for repairing. If she sold it for ₹ 325000, what is his profit per cent?**

Sol. The cost price of second hand car = ₹225000

Also, Achal spends for repairing = ₹ 25000

So, actual cost for car = ₹225000 + ₹25000 = ₹250000

She sold the car = ₹ 325000

Profit = ₹ 325000 − ₹ 250000

= ₹ 75000

$\therefore \text{Profit } \% = \frac{\text{Profit}}{\text{CP}} \times 100 = \frac{75000}{250000} \times 100 = \frac{7500}{250} = 30\%$

Q. 101 **A lady bought an air-conditioner for ₹ 15200 and spent ₹ 300 and ₹ 500 on its transportation and repair, respectively. At what price should she sell it to make a gain of 15%?**

Sol. The cost price of air conditioner = ₹ 15200

Also, spent amount on transportation = ₹300

Spent amount on repair = ₹ 500

Actual cost price of air conditioner with transportation charge and repair charges

= ₹15200 + ₹ 300 + ₹ 500 = ₹15500 + ₹ 500 = ₹ 16000

For gain 15% she should sell it for = $16000 + 16000 \times \frac{15}{100}$

$= 16000 + 160 \times 15 = 16000 + 2400 =$ ₹ 18400

Q. 102 **What price should a shopkeeper mark on a article that costs him ₹600 to gain 20%, after allowing a discount of 10%?**

Sol. The cost price of the article = ₹ 600

Gain% = 20%

∴ Gain = $\frac{600 \times 20}{100}$ = ₹120

∵ SP = Gain + CP = ₹600 + ₹120 = ₹720

Let marked price be ₹ x.

Since, he allow a discount of 10%.

According to the question,

$$x - 10\% \text{ of } x = ₹720$$

$$\Rightarrow \quad x - \frac{10 \times x}{100} = 720$$

$$\Rightarrow \quad \frac{100x - 10x}{100} = 720$$

$$\Rightarrow \quad \frac{90x}{100} = 720$$

$$\Rightarrow \quad x = \frac{720 \times 100}{90}$$

$$\Rightarrow \quad x = ₹800$$

Hence, required marked price is ₹ 800.

Q. 103 Brinda purchased 18 coats at the rate of ₹ 1500 each and sold them at a profit of 6%. If customer is to pay sales tax at the rate of 4%, how much will one coat cost to the customer and what will be the total profit earned by Brinda after selling all coats?

Sol. The cost of each coat = ₹ 1500

The total number of coat = 18

The total cost of 18 coat = ₹1500 × 18 = ₹ 27000

If Brinda sold them at profit = 6%

The amount received by Brinda $= 27000 + 27000 \times \frac{6}{100}$

$= 27000 + 270 \times 6 = 27000 + 1620 = ₹\ 28620$

If customer pay sale tax = 4%

So, cost price with sale tax $= 28620 + \frac{4}{100} \times 28620 = 28620 + 1144.8 = ₹\ 29764.80$

Cost price of one coat for customer $= \frac{29764.8}{18} = ₹\ 1653.60$

Profit earned by Brinda = ₹28620 − ₹27000 = ₹ 1620

Q. 104 Film borrowed ₹ 1024000 from a bank for one year. If the bank charges interest of 5% per annum, compounded half-yearly, what amount will he have to pay after the given time period. Also, find the interest paid by him.

Sol. Borrowed amount by Rahim (P) = ₹1024000

Time period (T) = 1 yr

Interest rate (R) = 5% per annum compounded half-yearly

Let amount = A

For compounded half-yearly, $A = P\left(1 + \frac{R}{200}\right)^{2T} = 1024000\left(1 + \frac{5}{200}\right)^2$

$\left[\because \text{in half-yearly, } R = \frac{R}{2} \text{ and } T = 2T\right]$

$= 1024000 \times \frac{41}{40} \times \frac{41}{40} = 640 \times 41 \times 41 = ₹\ 1075840$

$\therefore$ Compound Interest, CI $= A - P =$ ₹1075840 − ₹1024000 = ₹ 51840

Q. 105 The following items are purchased from showroom
T-Shirt worth ₹ 1200
Jeans worth ₹ 1000
2 skirts worth ₹ 1350 each.
What will these items cost to Shikha if the sales tax is 7%?

Sol. On the basis of given information in the question,

Cost of T-shirt = ₹1200

Cost of Jeans = ₹1000

Cost of 2 skirts = ₹1350

Total cost = ₹1200 + ₹1000 + ₹1350 = ₹3550

Shikha have to pay sale tax = 7%

So, the total amount to be paid = $3550 + \frac{7}{100} \times 3550 = 3550 + 248.5 =$ ₹ 3798.5

Q. 106 The food labels given below information about 2 types of soup cream of tomato and sweet corn. Use these labels to answer the given questions. (all the servings are based on a 2000 calories diet.)

Sweet corn		**Cream of tomato**	
Nutrition facts		**Nutrition facts**	
Serving size 1 cup (240 mL)		Serving size 1 cup (240 mL)	
About 2 serving per container		About 2 serving per container	
Amount per serving		Amount per serving	
Calories 90	**Calories from fat 9**	**Calories 100**	**Calories from fat 20**
	% Daily value		% Daily value
Total fat 2 g	2%	Total fat 2 g	3%
Saturated Fat-0 g	0%	Saturated fat-1.5 g	6%
Cholesterol 0 mg	0%	Cholesterol 10 mg	3%
Sodium 540 mg	22%	Sodium 690 mg	29%
Sweet corn		**Cream of tomato**	
Total carbohydrate 17g	6%	Total carbohydrate 17g	6%
Dietary fibre 3 g	14%	Dietary fibre 4 g	18%
Sugar 5g		Sugar 11g	
Protein 3 g		**Protein 2 g**	
Vitamin A 30%	Vitamin C 10%	Vitamin A 20%	Vitamin C 20%
Calcium 2%	Iron 6%	Calcium 0%	Iron 8%
Per cent daily values are based on a 2000 calories diet.		Per cent daily values are based on a 2000 calories diet.	

(a) Which can be measured more accurately the total amount of fat in cream of tomato soup or the total amount of fat in sweet corn soup? Explain.

(b) On serving of cream of tomato soup contains 29% of the recommended daily value of sodium for a 2000 calories diet. What is the recommended daily value of sodium in milligrams? Express the answer upto 2 decimal places.

(c) Find the increase per cent of sugar consumed, if cream of tomato soup is chosen over sweet corn soup.

(d) Calculate ratio of calories from fat in sweet corn soup to the calories from fat in cream of tomato soup.

Sol. (a) Serving size of 1 cup of sweet corn = 240 mL

Total fat = 2g on 2%

2% of fat in sweet corn of 1 cup (with 2 serving per container)

$$= \frac{2}{100} \times 240$$

$$= \frac{48}{10} = 4.8 \text{ g}$$

For one serving $= \frac{4.8}{2} = 2.4 \text{ g}$

Serving size of 1 cup of cream of tomato = 240 mL

Total fat = 2 g on 3%

3% of fat in cream tomato of 1 cup

$$= \frac{3}{100} \times 240$$

$$= \frac{72}{10} = 7.2 \text{ g}$$

For one serving $= \frac{7.2}{2} = 3.6 \text{ g}$

Hence, 2.4g is nearest to 2g in comparision of 3.6 g to 3 g.

(b) On the basis of given information in the question, the cream of tomato soup contains 29% of the recommended daily value of sodium for a 2000 calories diet.

where, 29% of 2000 calories = 690 mg

(c) If cream of tomato soup is chosen over sweet corn soup, the increase in sugar consumed = 11g − 5g = 6g

[∵ sugar in sweet corn soup = 5 g and sugar in cream of tomato soup = 11 g]

Increase % $= \frac{6}{5} \times 100 = \frac{600}{5} = 120\%$

(d) Fat in sweet corn soup in calories = 9

Fat in cream tomato soup in calories = 20

$\because$ Ratio $= \frac{9}{20} = \frac{9}{21} = \frac{3}{7} = 3:7$

Q. 107 Music CD originally priced at ₹ 120 is on sale for 25% off. What is the SP?

Sonia and Rahul have different ways of calculating the sale price for the items they bought.

As you work on the next problem, try both of these methods to see which your refer.

Sol. Original price of music CD = ₹120

25% discount on ₹120, if sale is applicable $= 120 \times \frac{25}{100} = \frac{120}{4} =$ ₹ 30

Discount = ₹ 30

Selling price after discount = ₹120 − ₹ 30 = ₹ 90

Q. 108 Store *A* and store *B* both charge ₹ 750 for a video game. This week the video game is on sale ₹ 600 at store *B* and for 25% off at store *A*. At which store is the game less expensive?

Sol. Video game available in store *A* and store *B* at rate = ₹750

Store *B* sells video game on sale offer = ₹ 600

Store *A* sells video game at discount = 25%

So, the price of video game at store $B = 750 - \frac{25}{100} \times 750 = 750 - 187.5 =$ ₹ 562.5

Hence, at store *A* the video game is less expensive.

Q. 109 At a toy shop price of all the toys is reduced to 66% of the original price.

(a) What is the sale price of a toy that originally costs ₹ 90?

(b) How much money would you save on a toy costing ₹ 90?

Sol. (a) Original cost of the toy = ₹90

If price, reduce to 66% of the original price, then price became

$$= 90 - \frac{66}{100} \times 90 = 90 - 59.4 = ₹\ 30.6$$

(b) We have discounted amount = 66% of 90 $= \frac{66}{100} \times 90 =$ ₹ 59.4

Q. 110 A store is having a 25% discount sale. Sheela has a ₹ 50 gift voucher and wants to use it to buy a board game marked for ₹ 320. She is not sure how to calculate the concession she will get. The sales clerk has suggested two ways to calculate the amount payable.

Method 1 Subtract ₹ 50 from the price and take 25% off the resulting price.

Method 2 Take 25% off the original price and then subtract ₹ 50.

(a) Do you think both the methods will give the same result? If not, predict which method will be beneficial for her.

(b) For each method, calculate the amount Sheela would have to pay. Show your work.

(c) Which method do you think stores actually use? Why?

Sol. (a) Marked price of board game = ₹320

Discount in store = 25%

Sheela have a gift voucher value = ₹ 50

In method 1 ₹320 – ₹50 = ₹270

Now, 25% discount on ₹ 270 $= 270 - \frac{25}{100} \times 270$

$= 270 - 67.5 =$ ₹ 202.5

In method 2 25% off on ₹ 320, then subtract ₹ 50

$= 320 - \frac{25}{100} \times 320 - 50 = 320 - 80 - 50 =$ ₹190

Hence, method 2 will be beneficial for her.

(b) **In method 1** Amount paid = ₹ 202.5

In method 2 Amount paid = ₹ 190

(c) Method 1 will be used by stores because in this method actual discount is loss.

Q. 111 Living on your own Sanjay is looking for one bedroom appartment on rent. At Neelgiri appartments, rent for the first two months is 20% off. The one bedroom rate at Neelgiri is ₹ 6000 per month. At Savana appartments, the first month is 50% off. The one bedroom rate at Savana appartments is ₹ 7000 per month. Which appartment will be cheaper for the first two months? By how much?

Sol. The one bedroom rate at Neelgiri = ₹ 6000 per month

Also, 20% off for first two months,

∵ Rent for first 2 months $= 2 \times \left(6000 - \frac{20}{100} \times 6000\right) = 2 \times 4800 =$ ₹ 9600

In comparison of Savana appartments, it offers 50% off for first month, where the rent for bedroom is ₹ 7000 per month $= 7000 - \frac{50}{100} \times 7000$

$= 7000 - 3500 =$ ₹ 3500

But rent for two months in Savana appartment = ₹ 3500 + ₹7000 = ₹10500

Hence, Neelgiri appartment will be cheaper by = ₹ 10500 – ₹ 9600 = ₹ 900

Q. 112 For an amount, explain why, a 20% increase followed by a 20% decrease is less than the original amount.

Sol. Let the original amount = ₹100

20% increase in ₹ 100 will be $= 100 + \frac{20}{100} \times 100$

$= 100 + 20 =$ ₹120

Now, 20% decrease in ₹ 120 $= 120 - \frac{20}{100} \times 120 = 120 - 24 =$ ₹ 96

Hence, decreased price is less than the original amount.

Q. 113 Sunscreens block harmful ultraviolet (UV) rays produced by the sun. Each sunscreen has a Sun Protection Factor (SPF) that tells you how many minutes you can stay in the sun before you receive one minute of burning UV rays. e.g. If you apply sunscreen with SPF 15, you get one minute of UV rays for every 15 minutes you stay in the sun.

(i) A sunscreen with SPF 15 allows only $\frac{1}{15}$ of the sun's UV rays. What per cent of UV rays does the sunscreen abort?

(ii) Suppose, a sunscreen allows 25% of the sun's UV rays.

(a) What fraction of UV rays does this sunscreen block? Give your answer in lowest terms.

(b) Use your answer from part (a) calculate this sunscreen's SPF. Explain how you found your answer?

(iii) A label on a sunscreen with SPF 30 claims that the sunscreen blocks about 97% of harmful UV rays. Assuming the SPF factor is accurate, is this claim true. Explain.

Sol. (i) A sunscreen with spf 15 allows only $\frac{1}{15}$ of the sun's UV rays.

It means $= 1 - \frac{1}{15} = \frac{14}{15}$ of the sun's UV rays abort by sunscreen.

In percentage $= \frac{\frac{14}{15}}{1} \times 100 = \frac{1400}{15} = 93.333\%$

(ii) (a) Sunscreen allows 25% of the sun's UV rays.

$\therefore$ It blocks UV rays $= 100 - 25 = 75\% = \frac{75}{100} = \frac{3}{4}$

(b) Suncreen allows 25% on $\frac{3}{4}$ of UV rays. It means, it protect $= 1 - \frac{3}{4} = \frac{1}{4}$ of UV rays.

Hence, it's a SPF 4.

(iii) False,

According to the claim, for $\frac{3}{100}$ affect of UV rays

1 minute $= 33\frac{1}{3}$ SPF

Affect ≠ 30 SPF claim

Q. 114 **A real estate agent receives ₹ 50000 as commission, which is 4% of the selling price. At what price does the agent sell the property?**

Sol. Let price of the property = ₹ x

Commission received = ₹ 50000

Commission percentage = 4%

According to the question,

$$x \times \frac{4}{100} = 50000$$

$$\Rightarrow \quad x = \frac{50000 \times 100}{4} = 50000 \times 25 = ₹\,1250000$$

Q. 115 **With the decrease in prices of tea by 15%, Tonu, the chaiwallah, was able to buy 2 kg more of tea with the same ₹ 45 that he spent each month on buying tea leaves for his chai shop. What was the reduced price of tea? What was the original price of tea?**

Sol. Let chaiwallah purchase y kg tea.

Let price of tea per kg = ₹x

Discount 15% per kg = $x - \frac{15}{100} \times x = \frac{85x}{100}$

Chaiwallah can buy 2 kg extra with 15% discount.

But without discount,

$$xy = 45 \quad \ldots \text{(i)}$$

and

$$\left(x - \frac{15x}{100}\right)\left(\frac{85x}{100}\right)(x + 2) = 45 \quad \ldots \text{(ii)}$$

After solving Eqs. (i) and (ii),

$$\frac{85}{100}(45) + \frac{85 \times 2x}{100} = 45$$

$$45\left[1 - \frac{85}{100}\right] = \frac{85 \times 2x}{100}$$

$$\frac{45 \times 15}{100} = \frac{85 \times 2x}{100}$$

$$x = \frac{45 \times 15}{2 \times 85} = \frac{135}{34} \text{ per kg} = 3.97 \text{ per kg}$$

$$\therefore \text{Reduced price} = \frac{85}{100} \times 3.97 = \frac{337.45}{100} = 3.3748 \approx 3.38 \text{ per kg}$$

Q. 116 **Below is the report card of Vidit Atrey. Vidit's teacher left the last column blank. Vidit is not able to make out, in which subject he performed better and in which he needs improvement. Complete the table to help Vidit know his comparative performance.**

Assessment report for- 2009-2010

	Class 9B		**Name : Vidit Atrey**		**Date : 31 March 2010**
	Subject	**Internal Assessment**	**Examination**	**Total**	**Final %**
1.	English literature	20/25	82/100	102/125	
2.	English language	22/25	91/100	113/125	
3.	Hindi literature	18/25	67/75	85/100	
4.	Hindi language	16/25	68/75	84/100	
5.	Mathematics	42/50	88/100	130/150	
6.	Sanskrit	14/20	75/100	89/120	
7.	Physics	45/50	90/100	135/150	
8.	Chemistry	41/50	82/100	123/150	
9.	Biology	43/50	87/100	130/150	
10.	History and Civics	19/25	68/75	87/100	
11.	Geography	17/20	71.5/80	88.5/100	

Sol. On the basis of the given data in above table, we can calculate final percentage of each subjects.

1. English literature $= \frac{102}{125} \times 100 = \frac{102}{5} \times 4 = \frac{408}{5} = 81.6\%$
2. English language $= \frac{113}{125} \times 100 = \frac{113 \times 4}{5} = \frac{452}{5} = 90.4\%$
3. Hindi literature $= \frac{85}{100} \times 100 = 85\%$
4. Hindi language $= \frac{84}{100} \times 100 = 84\%$
5. Mathematics $= \frac{130}{150} \times 100 = \frac{1300}{15} = 86.67\%$
6. Sanskrit $= \frac{89}{120} \times 100 = \frac{890}{12} = 74.16\%$
7. Physics $= \frac{135}{150} \times 100 = \frac{1350}{15} = 90\%$
8. Chemistry$= \frac{123}{150} \times 100 = \frac{1230}{15} = 82\%$
9. Biology $= \frac{130}{150} \times 100 = \frac{1300}{15} = 86.66\%$
10. History and Civics $= \frac{87}{100} \times 100 = 87\%$
11. Geography $= \frac{88.5}{100} \times 100 = 88.5\%$

Q. 117 **Sita is practicing basket ball. She has managed to score 32 baskets in 35 attempts. What is her success rate in percentage?**

Sol. Sita managed to score 32 baskets in 35 attempts.

Her success rate $= \frac{32}{35} \times 100 = \frac{3200}{35} = 91.428\% = 91.43\%$

Q. 118 **During school hours, Neha finished 73% of her homework and Minakshi completed $\frac{5}{8}$ of her homework. Who must finish a greater per cent of homework?**

Sol. Neha finished her homework in percentage $= 73\% = \frac{73}{100}$

Where Minakshi completed $= \frac{5}{8}$ of her home work

Home work left for Minakshi $= 1 - \frac{5}{8} = \frac{3}{8}$

In percentage $= \frac{3}{8} \times 100 = 37.5\%$

Home work left for Neha $= (100 - 73) = 27\% = \frac{27}{100}$

Hence, Minakshi finished a greater percentage of homework.

Q. 119 **Rain forests are home to 90000 of the 250000 identified plant species in the world. What per cent of the world's identified plant species are found in rain forests?**

Sol. 90000 of the 250000 identified plant species in the world are specified as rain forest.

In percentage $= \frac{90000}{250000} \times 100 = \frac{900}{25} = 36\%$

Q. 120 **Madhu's room measures 6m × 3m. Her carpet covers 8 m^2. What per cent of floor is covered by the carpet?**

Sol. Madhu's room measures = 6 m × 3 m

Area of the room $= 6 \times 3 = 18 m^2$ [∵ area of rectangle = length × breadth]

Her carpet covers $= 8 m^2$

Area covered by the carpet in percentage $= \frac{8}{18} \times 100 = \frac{800}{18} = 44.44\%$

Q. 121 The human body is made up mostly of water. In fact about 67% of a person total body weight is water. If Jyoti weights 56 kg, how much of her weight is water?

Sol. Jyoti's weight = 56 kg

Where 67% of a person is total body weight is water.

Water in Jyoti body = $\frac{67}{100} \times 56 = \frac{3752}{100} = 37.52$ kg

Q. 122 The per cent of pure gold in 14 carat gold is about 58.3%. A 14 carat gold ring weights 7.6 grams. How many grams of pure gold are in the ring?

Sol. The percentage of gold in 14 carat gold = 58.3%

Weight of 14 carat gold = 7.6 g

Pure gold in 14 carat gold of 7.6 g = $7.6 \times \frac{58.3}{100} = \frac{443.08}{100} = 4.431$ g

Hence, pure gold in 7.6 g of 14 carat gold is equal to 4.431 g.

Q. 123 A student used the proportion $\frac{n}{100} = \frac{5}{32}$ to find 5% of 32. What did the student do wrong?

Sol. 5% of 32 will be calculated as = $\frac{5}{100} \times 32 = \frac{32}{20} = 1.6$

But student finding per cent is 5 of 32.

Q. 124 The table shows the cost of sunscreen of two brands with and without sales tax. Which brand has a greater sales tax rate? Give the sales tax rate of each brand?

		Cost (in ₹)	**Cost + Tax** (in ₹)
1.	*X* (100 g)	70	75
2.	*Y* (100 g)	62	65

Sol. Brand *X* sunscreen cost = ₹ 70

With sales tax = ₹ 75

Sales tax paid = ₹ 75 – ₹ 70 = ₹ 5

Brand *Y* sunscreen cost = ₹ 62

With sales tax = ₹ 65

Sales tax = ₹ 65 – ₹ 62 = ₹ 3

Hence, brand *X* has greater sales tax rate.

Sales tax for brand $X = \frac{5}{70} \times 100 = \frac{50}{7} = 7.14\%$

Sales tax for brand $Y = \frac{3}{62} \times 100 = \frac{300}{62} = 4.838 \approx 4.84\%$

10

Direct and Inverse Proportion

Multiple Choice Questions (MCQs)

Q. 1 Both u and v vary directly with each other. When u is 10, v is 15, which of the following is not a possible pair of corresponding values of u and v?

(a) 2 and 3 (b) 8 and 12 (c) 15 and 20 (d) 25 and 37.5

Sol. *(c)* Since, u and v vary directly, i.e. $u / v = k$ (constant)

If $u = 10$ and $v = 15$, then, $\frac{u}{v} = \frac{10}{15} = \frac{2}{3}$

In option (b), $\frac{8}{12} = \frac{2}{3}$

In option (c), $\frac{15}{20} = \frac{3}{4}$

In option (d), $\frac{25}{37.5} = \frac{2}{3}$

So, option (c) is not a possible pair of corresponding values of u and v.

Hence, option (c) is correct.

Q. 2 Both x and y vary inversely with each other. When x is 10, y is 6, which of the following is not a possible pair of corresponding values of x and y?

(a) 12 and 5 (b) 15 and 4 (c) 25 and 2.4 (d) 45 and 1.3

Sol. *(d)* Since, x and y vary inversely, i.e. $x \times y = k$ (constant)

If $x = 10$ and $y = 6$

$\therefore$ $xy = 10 \times 6 = 60$

In option (a), $12 \times 5 = 60$

In option (b), $15 \times 4 = 60$

In option (c), $25 \times 2.4 = 60$

But in option (d), $45 \times 1.3 = 58.3$

Hence, option (d) is correct.

Q. 3 Assuming land to be uniformly fertile, the area of land and the yield on it vary

(a) directly with each other

(b) inversely with each other

(c) neither directly nor inversely with each other

(d) sometimes directly and sometimes inversely with each other

Sol. *(a)* If land to be uniformly fertile, then the area of land and the yield on it vary directly with each other.

Hence, option (a) is correct.

Note *Two quantities x and y are said to be in direct proportion, if they increase or decrease together in such a manner that the ratio of their corresponding values remains constant.*

Q. 4 The number of teeth and the age of a person vary

(a) directly with each other

(b) inversely with each other

(c) neither directly nor inversely with each other

(d) sometimes directly and sometimes inversely with each other

Sol. *(d)* The number of teeth and the age of a person vary sometimes directly and sometimes inversely with each other, we cannot predict about the number of teeth with exactly the age of a person. It change with person-to-person.

Hence, option (d) is correct.

Q. 5 A truck needs 54 litres of diesel for covering a distance of 297 km. The diesel required by the truck to cover a distance of 550 km is

(a) 100 litres (b) 50 litres (c) 25.16 litres (d) 25 litres

Sol. *(a)* A truck need 54 L of diesel for covering a distance = 297 km

$\therefore$ In 1 L, the truck can cover the distance $= \frac{297}{54} = 5.5$ km

Thus, for 550 km, the required diesel of truck $= \frac{550}{5.5} = 100$ L

Hence, option (a) is correct.

Q. 6 By travelling at a speed of 48 km/h, a car can finish a certain journey in 10 hours. To cover the same distance in 8 hours, the speed of the car should be

(a) 60 km/h (b) 80 km/h (c) 30 km/h (d) 40 km/h

Sol. *(a)* $\because$ Speed of the car = 48 km/h

and time taken by car = 10 h

$\therefore$ Distance = Speed × Time = 48 × 10 = 480 km

If car need to cover 480 km in 8 h, then

Required speed $= \frac{480}{8} = 60$ km/h $\left[\because \text{speed} = \frac{\text{distance}}{\text{time}}\right]$

Hence, option (a) is correct.

Q. 7 In which of the following cases, do the quantities vary directly with each other?

(a)

x	0.5	2	8	32
y	2	8	32	128

(b)

p	1^2	2^2	3^2	4^2
q	1^3	2^3	3^3	4^3

(c)

r	2	5	10	25	50
s	25	10	5	2	0.5

(d)

u	2	4	6	9	12
v	18	9	6	4	3

Sol. *(a)* In option (a),

$$x = 0.5, 2, 8, 32 \text{ and } y = 2, 8, 32, 128$$

If we multiply x with 4, we get the directly required result as same as shown in corresponding y. In this case, as the value of x increases, the value of y also increases. Hence, option (a) is correct.

Q. 8 Which quantities in the previous question vary inversely with each other?

(a) x and y (b) p and q (c) r and s (d) u and v

Sol. *(d)* In option (b),

p	1^2	2^2	3^2	4^2
q	1^3	2^3	3^3	4^3

If we multiply p and q with 1, 2, 3 and 4, we get the given result. But it is not given inversely.

In option (c),

r	2	5	10	25	50
s	25	10	5	2	0.5

If we multiply r with 2.5 and s with 2.5, we will get the given result.

In option (d),

u	2	4	6	9	12
v	18	9	6	4	3

If $u = 2$, then $v = 18$

If $u = 4$, then $v = 9$

If $u = 6$, then $v = 6$

If $u = 9$, then $v = 4$

and if $u = 12$, then $v = 3$

It show, when u increases, then v decreases.

Hence, it is inversely with each other.

Q. 9 Which of the following vary inversely with each other?

(a) Speed and distance covered (b) Distance covered and taxi fare
(c) Distance travelled and time taken (d) Speed and time taken

Sol. *(d)* We know that, when we increases the speed, then the time taken by vehicle decreases.

Hence, speed and time taken vary inversely with each other.

So, option (d) is correct.

Q. 10 Both x and y are in direct proportion, then $\frac{1}{x}$ and $\frac{1}{y}$ are

(a) in indirect proportion
(b) in inverse proportion
(c) neither in direct nor in inverse proportion
(d) sometimes in direct and sometimes in inverse proportion

Sol. *(b)* If both x and y are in directly proportion, then $\frac{1}{x}$ and $\frac{1}{y}$ are in inverse proportion.

Hence, option (b) is correct.

Note *Two quantities x and y are said to be in inverse proportion, if an increase in x cause a proportional decrease in y and vice-versa.*

Q. 11 Meenakshee cycles to her school at an average speed of 12 km/h and takes 20 minutes to reach her school. If she wants to reach her school in 12 minutes, her average speed should be

(a) $\frac{20}{3}$ km/h (b) 16 km/h (c) 20 km/h (d) 15 km/h

Sol. *(c)* Given, speed of cycle = 12 km/h

Time taken by Meenakshee through cycle = 20 min

Then, total distance cover $= \frac{12 \times 20}{60} = 4$ km [$\because$ distance = time × speed]

If Meenakshee want to reach her school in 12 min, then her cycle speed should be

$\frac{4}{\frac{12}{60}}$ i.e. 20 km/h. $\left[\because \text{speed} = \frac{\text{distance}}{\text{time}}\right]$

Hence, option (c) is correct.

Q. 12 100 persons had food provision for 24 days. If 20 persons left the place, the provision will last for

(a) 30 days (b) $\frac{96}{5}$ days (c) 120 days (d) 40 days

Sol. *(a)* $\because$ 100 persons had food provision for 24 days.

$\therefore$ 1 person had food provision for 24×100 i.e. 2400 days.

If 20 persons left the place, then remaining persons $= (100 - 20) = 80$

$\therefore$ 80 persons had food provision for $\frac{2400}{80}$ i.e. 30days.

Hence, option (a) is correct.

Q. 13 If two quantities x and y vary directly with each other, then

(a) $\frac{x}{y}$ remains constant (b) $x - y$ remains constant

(c) $x + y$ remains constant (d) $x \times y$ remains constant

Sol. *(a)* If two quantities x and y vary directly with each other, then $\frac{x}{y} = k =$ constant.

Since, in direct proportion, both x and y increases or decreases together such a manner that the ratio of their corresponding value remains constant.

Hence, option (a) is correct.

Q. 14 If two quantities p and q vary inversely with each other, then

(a) $\frac{p}{q}$ remains constant (b) $p + q$ remains constant

(c) $p \times q$ remains constant (d) $p - q$ remains constant

Sol. *(c)* If two quantities p and q vary inversely with each other, then $p \times q$ remains constant.

Since, in inverse proportion, an increase in p cause a proportional decrease in q and *vice-versa*.

Hence, option (c) is correct.

Q. 15 If the distance travelled by a rickshaw in one hour is 10 km, then the distance travelled by the same rickshaw with the same speed in one minute is

(a) $\frac{250}{9}$ m (b) $\frac{500}{9}$ m

(c) 1000 m (d) $\frac{500}{3}$ m

Sol. *(d)* The distance travelled by a rickshaw in 1h = 10 km

In 1 min, rickshaw covered the distance

$$= \frac{10}{60} \text{ km} = \frac{10 \times 1000}{60} \text{ m} \quad [\because 1\text{h} = 60 \text{ min and } 1\text{km} = 1000\text{m}]$$

$$= \frac{1000}{6} = \frac{500}{3} \text{ m}$$

Hence, option (d) is correct.

Q. 16 Both x and y vary directly with each other and when x is 10, y is 14, which of the following is not a possible pair of corresponding values of x and y?

(a) 25 and 35 (b) 35 and 25

(c) 35 and 49 (d) 15 and 21

Sol. *(b)* Both x and y vary directly with each other.

i.e. $x \propto y$

If $x = 10$ and $y = 14$

So, $10 \propto 14$ or $5 \propto 7$

This proportion is not follow in option (b) pairs.

Hence, option (b) is correct.

Fill in the Blanks

In questions 17 to 42, fill in the blanks to make the statements true.

Q. 17 If $x = 5y$, then x and y vary ________ with each other.

Sol. Given, $x = 5y$

Then, $\frac{x}{y} = \frac{5}{1} = k = \text{constant}$

$\therefore$ x and y vary **directly** with each other.

Q. 18 If $xy = 10$, then x and y vary ________ with each other.

Sol. Given, $xy = 10$

$\therefore$ $x = \frac{10}{y}$

Hence, x and y vary **inversly** with each other.

Note *Since, in case, if y_1, y_2 are the values of y corresponding to the values x_1, x_2 of x, respectively, then*

$$x_1 y_1 = x_2 y_2 \quad or \quad \frac{x_1}{x_2} = \frac{y_1}{y_2}$$

Q. 19 When two quantities x and y are in ________ proportion or vary ________, they are written as $x \propto y$..

Sol. When two quantities x and y are in **direct** proportion or vary **directly**, they are written as $x \propto y$. [see definition of direct proportion]

Q. 20 When two quantities x and y are in ________ proportion or vary ________, they are written as $x \propto \frac{1}{y}$.

Sol. When two quantities x and y are in **inverse** proportion or vary **inversely**, they are written as $x \propto \frac{1}{y}$. [see definition of inverse proportion]

Q. 21 Both x and y are said to vary ________ with each other, if for some positive number k, $xy = k$.

Sol. Both x and y are said to vary **inversely** with each other, if for some positive number k, $xy = k$. [see condition of inverse proportion]

Q. 22 x and y are said to vary directly with each other, if for some positive number k, ________ $= k$.

Sol. x and y are said to vary directly with other, if for some positive number k, $\frac{x}{y} = k$.

Q. 23 Two quantities are said to vary _______ with each other, if they increase (decrease) together in such a manner that the ratio of their corresponding values remains constant.

Sol. Two quantities are said to vary **directly** with each other, if they increase (decrease) together in such a manner that the ratio of their corresponding values remains constant.

Q. 24 Two quantities are said to vary _______ with each other, if an increase in one causes a decrease in the other in such a manner that the product of their corresponding values remains constant.

Sol. Two quantities are said to vary **inversely** with each other, if increase in one cause a decrease in the other in such a manner that the product of their corresponding values remains constant.

Q. 25 If 12 pumps can empty a reservoir in 20 hours, then time required by 45 such pumps to empty the same reservoir in _______ hours.

Sol. $\because$ 12 pumps can empty a reservoir in 20 h.

$\therefore$ 1 pump can empty in 20×12 i.e. 240 h.

Then, 45 pumps can empty the same reservoir in

$$\frac{240}{45}\text{h} = \frac{240 \times 60}{45}\text{min} \quad [\because 1\text{ h} = 60\text{ min}]$$

$$= \frac{14400}{45} = 320\text{ min}$$

$$= 5 \times 60 + 20$$

$$= \mathbf{5h\ 20\ min}$$

Q. 26 If x varies inversely as y, then

x	–	60
y	2	10

Sol. If x varies inversely as y, then

$$xy = k \text{ (constant)} \quad \ldots\text{(i)}$$

If $x = 60$ and $y = 10$

$\therefore$ $xy = 60 \times 10 = 600$

$\Rightarrow$ $k = 600$

When $y = 2$, then from Eq. (i),

$$x \times 2 = k$$

$\Rightarrow$ $2x = 600$ [putting the value of k]

$\Rightarrow$ $x = \mathbf{300}$

Q. 27 If x varies directly as y, then

x	12	6
y	48	–

Sol. If x varies directly as y, then

$$\frac{x}{y} = k \text{ (constant)} \quad \ldots\text{(i)}$$

If $x = 12$ and $y = 48$, then

$$\frac{x}{y} = \frac{12}{48} = \frac{1}{4}$$

$$\Rightarrow \quad k = \frac{1}{4}$$

When $x = 6$, then from Eq. (i),

$$\frac{6}{y} = k$$

$$\Rightarrow \quad \frac{6}{y} = \frac{1}{4} \quad \text{[putting the value of } k\text{]}$$

$$\Rightarrow \quad 6 \times 4 = y \times 1 \quad \text{[by cross-muliplication]}$$

$$\Rightarrow \quad \mathbf{y = 24}$$

Q. 28 When the speed remains constant, the distance travelled is ________ proportional to the time.

Sol. When the speed remains constant, the distance travelled is **directly** proportional to the time.

e.g. If 10 km cover in 10 min with uniform speed, then 20 km cover in 20 min with same speed.

Q. 29 On increasing *a*, *b* increases in such a manner that $\frac{a}{b}$ remains ________ and positive, then *a* and *b* are said to vary directly with each other.

Sol. On increasing *a*, *b* increases in such a manner that $\frac{a}{b}$ remains **constant** and positive, then *a* and *b* are said to vary directly with each other.

Q. 30 If on increasing *a*, *b* decreases in such a manner that ________ remains ________ and positive, then *a* and *b* are said to vary inversely with each other.

Sol. If on increasing *a*, *b* decreases in such a manner that ***ab*** remains **constant** and positive, then *a* and *b* are said to vary inversely with each other.

[see definition of inverse proportion]

Q. 31 If two quantities *x* and *y* vary directly with each other, then ________ of their corresponding values remains constant.

Sol. If two quantities x and y vary directly with each other, then **ratio** of their corresponding values remains constant. [see definition of direct proportion]

Q. 32 If two quantities *p* and *q* vary inversely with each other, then ________ of their corresponding values remains constant.

Sol. If two quantities *p* and *q* vary inversely with each other, then **product** of their corresponding values remains constant.

Q. 33 The perimeter of a circle and its diameter vary _______ with each other.

Sol. The perimeter of a circle and its diameter vary **directly** with each other.

Perimeter of a circle $= 2\pi r$

Diameter of a circle $= 2 \times r$

$\Rightarrow$ Perimeter $= \pi \times$ Diameter [$\because \pi =$ constant]

Q. 34 A car is travelling 48 km in one hour. The distance travelled by the car in 12 minutes is _______.

Sol. A car travelling in 1h = 48 km

So, car travelled in 1 min $= \frac{48}{60}$ km [$\because$ 1 h = 60 min]

Similarly, car travelled in 12 min $= \frac{48}{60} \times 12 = \frac{48}{5} =$ **9.6 km**

Q. 35 An auto rickshaw takes 3 hours to cover a distance of 36 km. If its speed is increased by 4 km/h, the time taken by it to cover the same distance is _______ .

Sol. An auto rickshaw takes 3 h to cover a distance of 36 km.

Then, its speed $= \frac{36}{3} = 12$ km/h $\left[\because \text{speed} = \frac{\text{distance}}{\text{time}}\right]$

If its speed increases 4 km/h, then

New speed = 12 + 4 = 16 km/h

Now, time taken by auto rickshaw to cover 36 km in $\frac{36}{16}$ h $= \frac{36 \times 60}{16} = 135$ min

[$\because$ 1h = 60 min]

$= 2 \times 60 + 15 =$ **2 h 15 min**

Q. 36 If the thickness of a pile of 12 cardboard sheets is 45 mm, then the thickness of a pile of 240 sheets is _______ cm.

Sol. The thickness of a pile of 12 cardboard sheets = 45 mm

$\therefore$ The thickness of a pile of 1 cardboard sheet $= \frac{45}{12}$ mm

So, the thickness of a pile of 240 cardboard sheets $= \frac{45}{12} \times 240$ mm $= 45 \times 20 = 900$ mm

$= \frac{900}{10}$ cm = **90** cm $\left[\because 1 \text{ mm} = \frac{1}{10} \text{cm}\right]$

Q. 37 If x varies inversely as y and $x = 4$ when $y = 6$, when $x = 3$, then value of y is _______ .

Sol. x varies inversely as y.

In inverse proportion, $xy = k$ (constant)

If $x = 4$ and $y = 6$, then $k = 4 \times 6 = 24$

Now, when $x = 3$, then $y = \frac{k}{x}$

$\Rightarrow$ $y = \frac{24}{3} =$ **8**

Q. 38 In direct proportion, $\frac{a_1}{b_1}$ ________ $\frac{a_2}{b_2}$.

Sol. In direct proportion,

$$\frac{a_1}{b_1} = \frac{a_2}{b_2}$$

where, $\frac{a_1}{a_2} = k$ (constant)

Q. 39 In case of inverse proportion, $\frac{a_2}{\_} = \frac{b_2}{\_}$.

Sol. In inverse proportion,

$$\frac{a_2}{a_1} = \frac{b_2}{b_1}$$

$\Rightarrow$ $a_2 b_1 = a_1 b_2$

Q. 40 If the area occupied by 15 postal stamps is 60 cm^2, then the area occupied by 120 such postal stamps will be ________.

Sol. $\because$ The area occupied by 15 postal stamps = 60 cm^2.

$\therefore$ The area occupied by 1 postal stamp $= \frac{60}{15} = 4$ cm^2

Similarly, the area occupied by 120 such postal stamps = 4×120 = **480 cm^2**

Q. 41 If 45 persons can complete a work in 20 days, then the time taken by 75 persons will be ________ hours.

Sol. $\because$ 45 persons can complete a work in 20 days.

$\therefore$ 1 person can complete a work in 45×20 i.e. 900 days.

Similarly, 75 persons can complete the same work in $\frac{900}{75} = 12$ days

$= 12 \times 24 =$ **288** h [$\because$ 1 day = 24 h]

Q. 42 Devangi travels 50 m distance in 75 steps, then the distance travelled in 375 steps is ________ km.

Sol. $\because$ Devangi covers the distance in 75 steps = 50 m

So, she cover the distance in 1 step $= \frac{50}{75}$ m

In 375 steps, she will cover

$$= \frac{50}{75} \times 375$$

$$= \frac{18750}{75} = 250\text{m}$$

$$= \frac{250}{1000} \text{ km} \quad [\because 1 \text{ km} = 1000\text{m}]$$

$= \mathbf{0.25}$ km

True/False

In questions from 43 to 59, state whether the statements are True or False.

Q. 43 Two quantities x and y are said to vary directly with each other, if for some rational number k, $xy = k$.

Sol. ***False***

Two quantities x and y are said to vary directly with each other, if $\frac{x}{y} = k$ (constant)

Q. 44 When the speed is kept fixed, time and distance vary inversely with each other.

Sol. ***False***

When the speed is kept fixed, time and distance vary directly with each other.

Q. 45 When the distance is kept fixed, speed and time vary directly with each other.

Sol. ***False***

When the distance is kept fixed, speed and time vary indirectly/inversely with each other. Since, if we increase speed, then taken time will less and *vice-versa*.

Q. 46 Length of a side of a square and its area vary directly with each other.

Sol. ***False***

Length of a side of a square and its area does not vary directly with each other.

e.g. Let a be length of each side of a square.

So, area of the square = $(\text{Side})^2 = (a)^2$

So, if we increase the length of the side of a square, then their area increases but not directly.

Q. 47 Length of a side of an equilateral triangle and its perimeter vary inversely with each other.

Sol. ***False***

Length of a side of an equilateral triangle and its perimeter vary directly with each other.

e.g. Let a be the side of an equilateral triangle. So, perimeter = $3 \times (\text{Side}) = 3 \times a = 3a$

So, if we increase the length of side of the equilateral triangle, then their perimeter will also increases.

Q. 48 If d varies directly as t^2, then we can write $dt^2 = k$, where k is some constant.

Sol. ***False***

If d varies inversely as t^2, then we can write $dt^2 = k$, where k is some constant.

Since, two quantities x and y are said to be in inverse proportion, if an increases in x cause a proportional decreases in y and *vice-versa*, in such a manner that the product of their corresponding values remains constant.

Q. 49 **If a tree 24 m high casts a shadow of 15 m, then the height of a pole that casts a shadow of 6 m under similar conditions is 9.6 m.**

Sol. ***True***

$\because$ Height of a tree = 24 m

Then, its shadow = 15 m

With the similar condition, if a pole has a shadow of length = 6 m

Let the height of pole = x m

Since, length and shadow vary directly.

Then, $\frac{24}{15} = \frac{x}{6}$

$15 \times x = 24 \times 6$ [by cross-multiplication]

$\Rightarrow x = \frac{24 \times 6}{15}$

$\Rightarrow x = 9.6$ m [$\because$ height and shadow ratio are same]

Q. 50 **If x and y are in direct proportion, then $(x - 1)$ and $(y - 1)$ are also in direct proportion.**

Sol. ***False***

If x and y are in direct proportion, then,

$\frac{x}{y} = k$ (constant)

e.g. Let $x = 4$ and $y = 6$

$\therefore \frac{x}{y} = \frac{4}{6} = \frac{2}{3}$

Now, $x - 1 = 4 - 1 = 3$ and $y - 1 = 6 - 1 = 5$

$\therefore \frac{x-1}{y-1} = \frac{3}{5}$ [not in direct proportion]

Q. 51 **If x and y are in inverse proportion, then $(x + 1)$ and $(y + 1)$ are also in inverse proportion.**

Sol. ***False***

If x and y are in inverse proportion, then $xy = k$ (constant)

e.g. Let $x = 2$ and $y = 3$

$\therefore xy = 2 \times 3 = 6$. Now, $x + 1 = 2 + 1 = 3$ and $y + 1 = 3 + 1 = 4$

Then, $(x + 1)(y + 1) = 3 \times 4 = 12$ [not in inverse proportion]

Hence, $(x + 1)$ and $(y + 1)$ cannot be in inverse proportion.

Q. 52 **If p and q are in inverse proportion, i.e. $pq = k$ (constant), then $(p + 2)$ and $(q - 2)$ are also in inverse proportion.**

Sol. ***False***

If p and q are in inverse proportion, then

$xy = k$ (constant)

e.g. Let $p = 3$ and $q = 4$

Then, $pq = 3 \times 4 = 12$

Now, $p + 2 = 3 + 2 = 5$ and $q - 2 = 4 - 2 = 2$

$\therefore (p+2)(q-2) = 5 \times 2 = 10$ [not in inverse proportion]

Henc, $(p+2)$ and $(q-2)$ cannot be in inverse proportion.

Q. 53 If one angle of a triangle is kept fixed, then the measure of the remaining two angles vary inversely with each other.

Sol. ***False***

If one angle of a triangle is kept fixed, then the measure of the remaining two angles can't vary inversely with each other.

e.g. In ΔABC, $\angle A + \angle B + \angle C = 180°$ [$\because$ sum of all angles of a triangle is $180°$]

If $\angle A = 50°$, then $\angle B + \angle C = 180° - 50° = 130°$

So, it is not depend on any proportion by applying angle sum properties of a triangle.

Q. 54 When two quantities are related in such a manner that, if one increases, the other also increases, then they always vary directly.

Sol. ***True***

When two quantities are related in such a manner that if, one increases the other also increases, then they always vary directly.

Above statement is correct for direct proportion. It is a basic properties of direct proportion.

Q. 55 When two quantities are related in such a manner that if one increases and the other decreases, then they always vary inversely.

Sol. ***True***

When two quantities are related in such a manner that if one increases and the other decreases, then they always vary inversely. Above statement is correct for inverse proportion. It is a basic properties of inverse proportion.

Q. 56 If x varies inversely as y and when $x = 6$, $y = 8$, then for $x = 8$, the value of y is 10.

Sol. ***False***

If x varies inversely as y, i.e. $xy = k$ (constant)

If $x = 6$ and $y = 8$

$\therefore$ $xy = 6 \times 8 = 48$

But if $x = 8$ and $y = 10$

$\therefore$ $xy = 8 \times 10 = 80$

Here, $48 \neq 80$

Hence, the value of y is not 10.

Q. 57 The number of workers and the time to complete a job is a case of direct proportion.

Sol. ***False***

The number of workers and the time to complete a job is a case of indirect proportion.

e.g. If 60 workers can complete a work in 10 days.

Then, 120 workers can complete the same work in 5 days.

Q. 58 For fixed time period and rate of interest, the simple interest is directly proportional to the principal.

Sol. ***True***

For fixed time period (T) and rate of interest (R), the simple interest is directly proportional to the principal.

We know that, $\text{SI} = \frac{P \times R \times T}{100}$

$\Rightarrow \frac{\text{SI}}{P} = \frac{R \times T}{100} = \text{constant}$ (as R and T are constants)

$\therefore$ Simple interest is directly proportional to the principal.

Q. 59 The area of cultivated land and the crop harvested is a case of direct proportion.

Sol. ***True***

The area of cultivated land and the crop harvested is a case of direct proportion.

Since, the quantities of crop harvested is depend upon area of cultivated land.

In questions 60 to 62, which of the following vary directly and which vary inversely with each other and which are neither of the two?

Q. 60 (i) The time taken by a train to cover a fixed distance and the speed of the train.

(ii) The distance travelled by CNG bus and the amount of CNG used.

(iii) The number of people working and the time to complete a given work.

(iv) Income tax and the income.

(v) Distance travelled by an auto-rickshaw and time taken.

Sol. (i) The time taken by a train to cover a fixed distance and the speed of the train are inversely proportional.

e.g. Let a train cover 100 km in 1 h with speed 100 km/h.

Then, the same train cover 100 km in 30 min with speed 200 km/h.

(ii) The distance travelled by CNG bus and the amount of CNG used are directly proportional.

e.g. Let a CNG bus can travelled 10 km in 1 kg of CNG.

Then, the same CNG bus travelled 20 km in $2 \times 1 = 2$ kg of CNG.

(iii) The number of people working and the time to complete a given work are inversely proportional to each other.

e.g. Let 20 workers can complete a work in 1day.

Then, 10 workers can complete the same work in 2 days.

(iv) Income tax and the income are directly proportional to each other.

e.g. Let Mr X have 4.5 lakh annual income.

Then, he pay 10% income tax on his income.

But if Mr X have 5.5 lakh annual income, then he has to pay 30% income tax on his salary/income.

(v) Distance travelled by an auto rickshaw and time taken are directly proportional to each other.

e.g. Let an auto rickshaw takes 2 h to travel 10 km.

Then, it will take 4 h to travel 20 km.

Q. 61 (i) Number of students in a hostel and consumption of food.

(ii) Area of the walls of a room and the cost of white washing the walls.

(iii) The number of people working and the quantity of work.

(iv) Simple interest on a given sum and the rate of interest.

(v) Compound interest on a given sum and the sum invested.

Sol. (i) Number of students in a hostel and consumption of food are directly proportional to each other.

e.g. Let 200 students in a hostel can consume 100 kg of rice in a month.

Then, 400 students in a hostel can consume 200 kg of rice in a month.

(ii) Area of the walls of a room and the cost of white washing the walls are directly proportional to each other.

e.g. Let ₹ 1000 required for white washing a room with (12×8) m size.

Then, ₹ 2000 required for white washing a room with (12×16) m size.

(iii) The number of people working and the quantity of work are directly proportional to each other.

e.g. Let 20 workers can complete 20% of a work. Then, 40 workers can complete 40% of the same work.

(iv) Simple interest on a given sum and the rate of interest are directly proportional to each other.

e.g. Let $P =$ ₹ 1000, $R = 10\%$ and $T = 1$ yr

$$\therefore \quad \text{SI} = \frac{P \times R \times T}{100} = \frac{1000 \times 10 \times 1}{100} = ₹\ 100$$

But if $P = 1000$, $R = 20\%$ and $T = 1$ yr

$$\therefore \quad \text{SI} = \frac{P \times R \times T}{100} = \frac{1000 \times 20 \times 1}{100} = ₹\ 200$$

(v) Compound interest on a given sum and the sum invested are neither depend directly nor inversely.

Q. 62 (i) The quantity of rice and its cost.

(ii) The height of a tree and the number of years.

(iii) Increase in cost and number of shirts that can be purchased, if the budget remains the same.

(iv) Area of land and its cost.

(v) Sales tax and the amount of the bill.

Sol. (i) The quantity of rice and its cost are directly proportional to each other.

e.g. Let 1 kg of rice price = ₹ 40

Then, 2 kg of rice price = ₹ 2 × 40 = ₹ 80

(ii) The height of a tree and the number of years are neither directly nor inversely proportional to each other.

(iii) Increase in cost and number of shirts that can be purchased, if the budget remains the same are inversely proportional to each other.

e.g. Let 2 shirts price = ₹ 800

After increasing in price of each shirt,

1 shirt price became ₹ 800

where budget = ₹ 800

(iv) Area of land and its cost are directly proportional to each other.

e.g. Let 200 m^2 land cost = ₹ 5000

Then, 400 m^2 land cost = ₹ 10000

(v) Sales tax and the amount of the bill are directly proportional to each other.

e.g. Let bill amount = ₹ 1000

Sales tax = 10%

Then, sales tax $= \frac{10}{100} \times 1000 =$ ₹ 100

But if, bill amount = 2000

Sales tax = 10%

Then, sales tax $= \frac{10}{100} \times 2000 = 10 \times 20 =$ ₹ 200

Q. 63 If x varies inversely as y and $x = 20$ when $y = 600$, find y when $x = 400$.

Sol. If x varies inversely as y.

$\therefore \quad xy = k$ (constant) ...(i)

If $\quad x = 20$ and $y = 600$

$\therefore \quad xy = 20 \times 600 = 12000$

$\Rightarrow \quad k = 12000$

When $x = 400$, then from Eq. (i),

$y \times 400 = k$

$\Rightarrow \quad y \times 400 = 12000$ [putting the value of k]

$\Rightarrow \quad y = \frac{12000}{400} = 30$

Q. 64 The variable x varies directly as y and $x = 80$ when y is 160. What is y when x is 64?

Sol. If x varies directly as y.

$\therefore \quad x / y = k$ (constant) ...(i)

If $\quad x = 80$ and $y = 160$

$\therefore \quad \frac{x}{y} = \frac{80}{160} = \frac{1}{2} \Rightarrow k = \frac{1}{2}$

When $x = 64$, then from Eq. (i),

$\frac{64}{y} = \frac{1}{2}$ [putting the value of k]

$\Rightarrow \quad y = 64 \times 2 = 128$

Q. 65 l varies directly as m and $l = 5$, when $m = \frac{2}{3}$. Find l when $m = \frac{16}{3}$.

Sol. If l varies directly as m.

$\therefore \quad l / m = k =$ (constant) ...(i)

If $\quad l = 5$ and $m = \frac{2}{3}$

$\therefore \quad \frac{l}{m} = \frac{5}{2/3}$

$= \frac{5}{1} \times \frac{3}{2} = \frac{15}{2}$

$\Rightarrow \quad k = \frac{15}{2}$

When $m = \frac{16}{3}$, then from Eq. (i),

$\frac{l}{16/3} = \frac{15}{2}$ [putting the value of k]

$\Rightarrow \quad l = \frac{15}{2} \times \frac{16}{3} = 40$

Q. 66 If x varies inversely as y and $y = 60$ when $x = 1.5$. Find x, when $y = 4.5$.

Sol. If x varies inversely as y.

$\therefore \quad xy = k$ (constant) ...(i)

If $\quad x = 1.5$ and $y = 60$

$\therefore \quad xy = 1.5 \times 60 = 90$

$\Rightarrow \quad k = 90$

When $y = 4.5$, then from Eq. (i),

$4.5 \times y = k$

$\Rightarrow \quad 4.5 \times y = 90$ [putting the value of k]

$\Rightarrow \quad y = \frac{90}{4.5} = 20$

Q. 67 In a camp, there is enough flour for 300 persons for 42 days. How long will the flour last, if 20 more persons join the camp?

Sol. $\because$ For 300 persons flour is enough for 42 days.

$\therefore$ For 1 person flour enough $= 300 \times 42 = 12600$ days

Now, 20 more persons join the camp.

So, total persons $= 300 + 20 = 320$

$\therefore$ For 320 persons flour enough $= \frac{12600}{320} = \frac{3}{8}$ days

Q. 68 A contractor undertook a contract to complete a part of a stadium in 9 months with a team of 560 persons. Later on, it was required to complete the job in 5 months. How many extra persons should he employ to complete the work?

Sol. $\because$ In 9 months, a part of stadium can complete by 560 persons.

$\therefore$ In 1 month, the work can be complete by $9 \times 560 = 5040$ persons

$\because$ In 5 months, the work can be complete by $\frac{5040}{5} = 1008$ persons

Now, number of extra persons required to complete the work in 5 months

$= 1008 - 560 = 448$

Q. 69 **Sobi types 108 words in 6 minutes. How many words would she type in half an hour?**

Sol. Sobi can types 108 words in 6 min.

In 1 min, she can type $= \frac{108}{6} = 18$ words

Thus, in 30 min, she can type $= 18 \times 30 = 540$ words

Q. 70 **A car covers a distance in 40 minutes with an average speed of 60 km/h. What should be the average speed to cover the same distance in 25 minutes?**

Sol. A car covers a distance in 40 min with an average speed $= 60$ km/h $= \frac{60 \times 1000}{60}$ m/min

In 1 min, the same distance can be cover with speed $= \frac{60 \times 1000 \times 40}{60} = 40000$ m/min

In 25 min, the same distance can be cover with speed $= \frac{40000}{25} = 1600$ m/min

$$= \frac{1600}{1000} \times 60 = 16 \times 6 = 96 \text{ km/h} \qquad \left[\because 1\text{m} = \frac{1}{1000} \text{ km and } 1\text{min} = \frac{1}{60} \text{ h}\right]$$

Q. 71 **It is given that l varies directly as m.**

(a) Write an equation which relates l and m.

(b) Find the constant of proportion (k), when l is 6, then m is 18.

(c) Find l, when m is 33.

(d) Find m, when l is 8.

Sol. Since, l varies directly as m.

(a) Equation related to l and m is $\frac{l}{m} = k$ (constant)

(b) If $l = 6$ and $m = 18$, then $k = \frac{6}{18} = \frac{1}{3}$

(c) If $m = 33$, then

$$\frac{l}{m} = \frac{1}{3}$$

$$\Rightarrow \quad \frac{l}{33} = \frac{1}{3} \Rightarrow l = \frac{33}{3} = 11$$

(d) If $l = 8$

$$\therefore \quad \frac{l}{m} = k \Rightarrow \frac{8}{m} = \frac{1}{3} \qquad \left[\because k = \frac{1}{3}\right]$$

$$\Rightarrow \quad m = 8 \times 3 = 24$$

Q. 72 **If a deposit of ₹ 2000 earns an interest of ₹ 500 in 3 years, how much interest would a deposit of ₹ 36000 earn in 3 years with the same rate of simple interest?**

Sol. If deposit of ₹ 2000 earns in 3 yr with an interest = ₹ 500

Then, a deposit of ₹1000 earns in 3 yr with an interest $= \frac{500}{2} =$ ₹250

Similarly, deposit of ₹ 3600 i.e. ₹36×1000 earns in 3 yr with an interest $= 250 \times 36 =$ ₹ 9000

Q. 73 **The mass of an aluminium rod varies directly with its length. If a 16 cm long rod has a mass of 192 g, find the length of the rod whose mass is 105 g.**

Sol. According to the question, the mass (m) of an aluminium rod varies directly with its length (l). Here, we use the direct proportion.

In direct proportion, $\frac{m}{l} = k$ (constant)

$\therefore \quad \frac{m}{l} = \frac{192}{16} = 12$

$\Rightarrow \quad k = 12$

If mass of the rod $= 105$ g

Then, $\quad \frac{m}{l} = k$

$\Rightarrow \quad \frac{105}{l} = 12$

$\Rightarrow \quad l = \frac{105}{12} = 8.75$ cm

Q. 74 **Find the values of x and y, if a and b are in inverse proportion.**

(a) 12 x 8 (b) 305 y

Sol. In an inverse proportion,

When we multiply the first quantity by any constant k, then the another quantity is divided by the same constant k.

Given,

a	12	x	8
b	30	5	y

Here, we see that in part, (b) when we divide 30 by 6, we will get 5.

So in part (a), we will get the value of x,

i.e. $\quad x = 12 \times 6 = 72$

Similarly, in part (a), when we divide x i.e. 72 by 9, we will get 8.

So in part (b), we will get the value of y.

i.e. $\quad y = 5 \times 9 = 45$

Q. 75 **If Naresh walks 250 steps to cover a distance of 200 metres, find the distance travelled in 350 steps.**

Sol. $\because$ Naresh walks 250 steps to cover distance $= 200$ m

$\therefore$ In 1 step, he covers the distance $= \frac{200}{250}$ m

$\because$ In 350 steps, he covers $= \frac{200}{250} \times 350 = \frac{20 \times 350}{25}$

$= \frac{7000}{25} = 280$ m

Q. 76 A car travels a distance of 225 km in 25 litres of petrol. How many litres of petrol will be required to cover a distance of 540 kilometres by this car?

Sol. A car travels 225 km distance in 25 L of petrol.

$\because$ For 1 km, petrol required $= \frac{25}{225}$ L

$\therefore$ For 540 km, the petrol required $= \frac{25}{225} \times 540 = 60$ L

Q. 77 From the following table, determine if x and y are in direct proportion or not.

(a)

x	3	6	15	20	30
y	12	24	45	60	120

(b)

x	4	7	10	16
y	24	42	60	96

(c)

x	1	4	9	20
y	1.5	6	13.5	30

Sol. In direct proportion, $\frac{x}{y} = k$ (constant)

For table (a),

x	3	6	15	20	30
y	12	24	45	60	120

$\Rightarrow \quad \frac{x}{y} = \frac{3}{12}, \frac{6}{24}, \frac{15}{45}, \frac{20}{60}, \frac{30}{120}$

i.e. $\quad \frac{1}{4}, \frac{1}{4}, \frac{1}{3}, \frac{1}{3}, \frac{1}{4}$

So, (a) is not in direct proportion.

For table (b),

x	4	7	10	16
y	24	42	60	96

$\Rightarrow \quad \frac{x}{y} = \frac{4}{24}, \frac{7}{42}, \frac{10}{60}, \frac{16}{96}$

i.e. $\quad \frac{1}{6}, \frac{1}{6}, \frac{1}{6}, \frac{1}{6}$

So, (b) is in direct proportion.

For table (c),

x	1	4	9	20
y	1.5	6	13.5	30

$\Rightarrow \quad \frac{x}{y} = \frac{1}{1.5}, \frac{4}{6}, \frac{9}{13.5}, \frac{20}{30}$

i.e. $\quad \frac{1}{1.5}, \frac{1}{1.5}, \frac{1}{1.5}, \frac{1}{1.5}$

So, (c) is in direct proportion.

Q. 78 If a and b vary inversely to each other, then find the values of p, q, r; x, y, z and l, m, n.

(a)

a	6	8	q	25
b	18	p	39	r

(b)

a	2	y	6	10
b	x	12.5	15	z

(c)

a	l	9	n	6
b	5	m	25	10

Sol. It a and b are vary inversely to each other.

i.e. $ab = k$ (constant)

For table (a),

a	6	8	q	25
b	18	p	39	r

If $a = 6$ and $b = 18$

Then, $a \times b = 6 \times 18 = 108$

$\Rightarrow k = 108$

When $a = 8$ and $b = p$, then

$ab = k$

$\Rightarrow 8 \times p = 108$ [putting the value of k]

$\Rightarrow p = \frac{27}{2}$

When $a = q$ and $b = 39$, then

$ab = k$

$\therefore q \times 39 = 108$ [putting the value of k]

$\Rightarrow q = \frac{108}{39} = \frac{36}{13}$

When $a = 25$ and $b = r$, then

$ab = k$

$\Rightarrow 25 \times r = 108$ [putting the value of k]

$\Rightarrow r = \frac{108}{25}$

For table (b),

a	2	y	6	10
b	x	12.5	15	z

If $a = 6$ and $b = 15$, then

$a \times b = 6 \times 15 = 90$

$\Rightarrow k = 90$

When $a = 2$ and $b = x$, then

$ab = k$

$\Rightarrow \quad 2 \times x = 90$ [putting the value of k]

$\Rightarrow \quad x = 45$

When $a = y$ and $b = 12.5$, then

$$ab = k$$

$\Rightarrow \quad y \times 12.5 = 90$ [putting the value of x]

$\Rightarrow \quad y = \frac{90}{12.5} = 7.2$

When $a = 10$ and $y = z$, then

$$ab = k$$

$\Rightarrow \quad 10 \times z = 90$ [putting the value of x]

$\Rightarrow \quad z = 9$

For table (c),

a	l	9	n	6
b	5	m	25	10

If $a = 6$ and $b = 10$, then

$$ab = 6 \times 10 = 60$$

$\Rightarrow \quad k = 60$

When $a = l$ and $b = 5$, then

$$ab = k$$

$\Rightarrow \quad l \times 5 = 60$ [putting the value of k]

$\Rightarrow \quad l = 12$

When $a = 9$ and $b = m$, then

$$ab = k$$

$\Rightarrow \quad 9 \times m = 60$ [putting the value of k]

$\Rightarrow \quad m = \frac{20}{3}$

When $a = n$ and $b = 25$, then

$$ab = k$$

$\Rightarrow \quad n \times 25 = 60$ [putting the value of k]

$\Rightarrow \quad n = \frac{60}{25}$

$\Rightarrow \quad n = \frac{12}{5}$

Q. 79 If 25 metres of cloth costs ₹ 337.50, then

(a) what will be the cost of 40 metres of the same type of cloth?

(b) what will be the length of the cloth bought for ₹ 810?

Sol. According to the question,

$\because$ 25 m of cloth cost = ₹ 337.50

$\therefore$ 1 m of cloth cost = ₹ $\frac{337.50}{25}$

(a) Cost of 40 m of the same type of cloth $= \frac{337.50}{25} \times 40 = \frac{13500}{25} = ₹\ 540$

(b) The length of cloth bought for ₹ 810 $= \frac{810 \times 25}{337.50} = \frac{20250}{337.50} = 60$ cm

Q. 80 A swimming pool can be filled in 4 hours by 8 pumps of the same type. How many such pumps are required, if the pool is to be filled in $2\frac{2}{3}$ hours?

Sol. A swimming pool can be filled in 4 hours by 8 pumps.

If we want to fill the swimming pool in 1 h, we required $4 \times 8 = 32$ pumps

In $2\frac{2}{3}$ i.e. $\frac{8}{3}$ h, the number of pumps required $= 32 \div \frac{8}{3} = \frac{32 \times 3}{8} = 4 \times 3 = 12$ pumps

Q. 81 The cost of 27 kg of iron is ₹ 1080, what will be the cost of 120 kg of iron of the same quality?

Sol. $\because$ The cost of 27 kg of iron = ₹ 1080

$\therefore$ Cost of 1 kg of iron $= \frac{1080}{27} = ₹40$

$\therefore$ The cost of 120 kg $= 40 \times 120 = ₹\ 4800$

Hence, the cost of 120 kg of iron is ₹ 4800.

Q. 82 At a particular time, the length of the shadow of Qutub Minar whose height is 72 m is 80 m. What will be the height of an electric pole, the length of whose shadow at the same time is 1000 cm?

Sol. $\because$ Length of Qutub Minar = 72 m

and its shadow at particular time = 80 m

Length of shadow of electric pole = 1000 cm = 10m $\left[\because 1 \text{ cm} = \frac{1}{100} \text{ m}\right]$

$\therefore$ Length of electric pole $= \frac{72}{80} \times 10 = 9$ m

Q. 83 In a hostel of 50 girls, there are food provisions for 40 days. If 30 more girls join the hostel, how long will these provisions last?

Sol. In a hostel of 50 girls, food are available = 40 days

For 1 girl, food provisions $= 50 \times 40 = 2000$ days

Now, for (50 + 30) girls i.e 80 girls, the food provision $= \frac{2000}{80} = \frac{200}{8} = 25$ days

Q. 84 Campus and Welfare Committee of school is planning to develop a blue shade for painting the entire school building. For this purpose, various shades are tried by mixing containers of blue paint and white paint. In each of the following mixtures, decide which is a lighter shade of blue and also find the lightest blue shade among all of them.

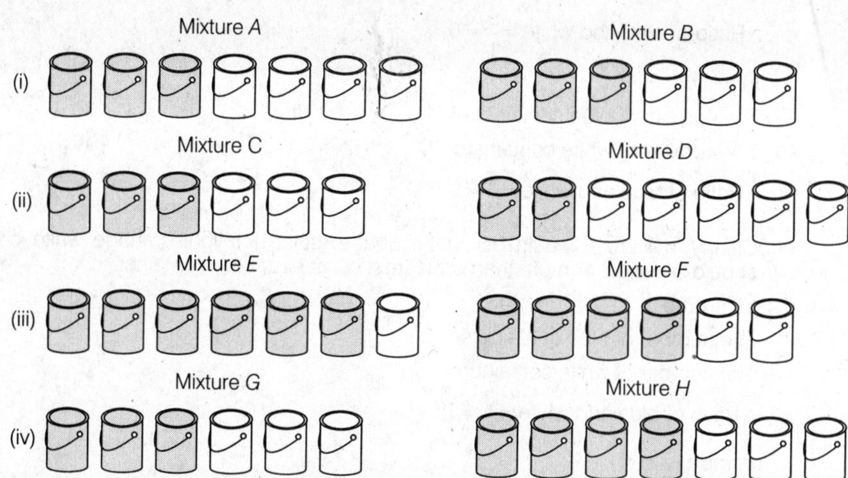

If one container has one litre paint and the building requires 105 litres for painting, how many container of each type is required to paint the building by lightest blue shade?

Sol. (i) In mixture A,

The number of blue containers = 3

The number of white containers = 4

$\therefore$ Ratio of blue and white $= \frac{3}{4} = 0.75$

In mixture B,

The number of blue containers = 3

The number of white containers = 3

$\therefore$ Ratio of blue and white $= \frac{3}{3} = 1$

Clearly, mixture A would be lighter shade.

(ii) In mixture C,

The number of blue containers = 3

The number of white containers = 3

$\therefore$ Ratio of blue and white $= \frac{3}{3} = 1$

In mixture D,

The number of blue containers = 2

The number of white containers = 5

$\therefore$ Ratio of blue and white $= \frac{2}{5} = 0.4$

Clearly, mixture D would be lighter shade, since for lighter shade white container should be more than blue container.

(iii) In mixture E,

The number of blue containers = 6

The number of white containers = 1

$\therefore$ Ratio of blue and white $= \frac{6}{1} = 6$

In mixture *F*,

The number of blue containers = 4

The number of white containers 2

$\therefore$ Ratio of blue and white $= \frac{4}{2} = 2$

Clearly, mixture *F* would be lighter shade, since for lighter shade white container should be equal or more than or nearest number of blue container.

(iv) In mixture *G*,

The number of blue containers = 3

The number of white containers = 3

$\therefore$ Ratio of blue and white $= \frac{3}{3} = 1$

In mixture *H*,

The number of blue containers = 4

The number of white containers = 3

$\therefore$ Ratio of blue and white $= \frac{4}{3} = 1.33$

Clearly, mixture *G* would be lighter shade, since for lighter shade white container should be more than blue container.

From the above all mixtures, mixture *D* is lightest among them.

$\therefore$ The total number of containers required for painting = 105

$\therefore$ Number of blue containers required for painting $= \frac{2}{7} \times 105 = 2 \times 15 = 30$

$\therefore$ Number of white containers required for painting $= \frac{5}{7} \times 105 = 5 \times 15 = 75$

Q. 85 Posing a Question Work with a partner to write atleast five ratio statement about this quilt, which has white, blue and purple squares.

How many squares of each colour will be there in 12 such quilts?

Sol. On the basis of given figure in which white, blue and purple squaes are given.

$\therefore$ Purple = 12, Blue = 20 and White = 16

Total squares = 12 + 20 + 16 = 48

Statement I Purple : Total = 12 : 48 = 1 : 4

Statement II Blue : Total = 20 : 48 = 5 : 12

Statement III White : Total = 16 : 48 = 1 : 3

Statement IV Purple : Blue = 12 : 20 = 3 : 5

Statement V Purple : White = 12 : 16 = 3 : 4

Q. 86 A packet of sweets was distributed among 10 children and each of them received 4 sweets. If it is distributed among 8 children, how many sweets will each child get?

Sol. The total number of children = 10

If each children received 4 sweets, then

The total number of sweets = $10 \times 4 = 40$ sweets

If 40 sweets distributed between 8 children, then each get $\frac{40}{8}$ i.e. 5 sweets.

Q. 87 44 cows can graze a field in 9 days. How many less/more cows will graze the same field in 12 days?

Sol. 44 cows can graze a field = 9 days

The number of cows that can graze the same field in 1 day = 44×9 cows

In 12 days, the number of cows required $= \frac{44 \times 9}{12} = \frac{44 \times 3}{4} = 11 \times 3 = 33$ cows

Hence, (44 – 33) i.e. 11 cows less required for graze the same field in 12 days.

Q. 88 30 persons can reap a field in 17 days. How many more persons should be engaged to reap the same field in 10 days?

Sol. $\because$ 30 persons can reap a field in 17 days.

1 person can reap the same field in 30×17 i.e. 510 days.

In 10 days, the number of persons required = $\frac{510}{10} = 51$ persons

Q. 89 Shabnam takes 20 minutes to reach her school, if she goes at a speed of 6 km/h. If she wants to reach school in 24 minutes, what should be her speed?

Sol. Shabnam's speed = 6 km/h = $\frac{6 \times 1000}{60}$ m/min

$\therefore$ Total distance covered by Shabnam in 20 min = $\frac{6 \times 1000}{60} \times 20$

[$\because$ distance = speed $\times$ time]

$$= \frac{1000}{10} \times 20 = 100 \times 20$$

$$= 2000 \text{ m}$$

If she want to reach the school in 24 min, then she should maintain the speed $= \dfrac{2000}{24}$

$$= \frac{1000}{12} = \frac{500}{6} \text{ m/min}$$

$$= \frac{500 \times 60}{1000 \times 6} = 5 \text{km/h} \qquad \left[\because 1\text{km} \frac{1}{1000} \text{ and } 1 \text{ h} = 60 \text{ min}\right]$$

Q. 90 **Ravi starts for his school at 8 : 20 am on his bicycle. If he travels at a speed of 10 km/h, then he reaches his school late by 8 minutes but on travelling at 16 km/h, he reaches the school 10 minutes early. At what time does the school start?**

Sol. Let the total distance = x km

Let the time taken by Ravi to reach the school at sharp time = t min

If the speed of the bicycle is 10 km/h, then he reach his school late by 8 min.

$$\therefore \quad \frac{x}{10} = t + \frac{8}{60} \qquad \left[\because 1 \text{min} = \frac{1}{60} \text{h}\right] \ldots \text{(i)}$$

$$\Rightarrow \quad \frac{x}{10} = t + \frac{2}{15}$$

If the speed of the bicycle is 16 km/h, then he reach his school 10 min early.

$$\therefore \quad \frac{x}{16} = t - \frac{10}{60}$$

$$\Rightarrow \quad \frac{x}{16} = t - \frac{1}{6} \qquad \ldots \text{(ii)}$$

On solving Eqs. (i) and (ii), we get

$$\frac{x}{10} - \frac{x}{16} = \frac{2}{15} + \frac{1}{6}$$

$$\Rightarrow \quad \frac{8x - 5x}{80} = \frac{4 + 5}{30}$$

$$\Rightarrow \quad \frac{3x}{80} = \frac{9}{30}$$

$$\Rightarrow \quad x = \frac{9 \times 80}{30 \times 3} = 8 \text{km} \qquad \text{[by cross-multiplication]}$$

Now, put $x = 8$ in Eq. (i), we get

$$\frac{8}{10} = t + \frac{2}{15}$$

$$\Rightarrow \quad t = \frac{8}{10} - \frac{2}{15} = \frac{24 - 4}{30}$$

$$\Rightarrow \quad t = \frac{20}{30} = \frac{2}{3} \text{h}$$

$$= \frac{2}{3} \times 60 = 40 \text{min} \qquad [\because 1\text{h} = 60 \text{ min}]$$

Hence, starting time of school is 8 : 20 + 40 min i.e. 9 : 00 am.

Q. 91 Match each of the entries in Column I with the appropriate entry in Column II.

	Column I		Column II
1.	x and y vary inversely to each other	A.	$\frac{x}{y}=$ constant
2.	Mathematical representation of inverse variation of quantities p and q	B.	y will increase in proportion
3.	Mathematical representation of direct variation of quantities m and n	C.	$xy=$ constant
4.	When $x=5$, $y=2.5$ and when $y=5$, $x=10$	D.	$p\propto\frac{1}{q}$
5.	When $x=10$, $y=5$ and when $x=20$, $y=2.5$	E.	y will decrease in proportion
6.	x and y vary directly with each other	F.	x and y are directly proportional
7.	If x and y vary inversely, then on decreasing x	G.	$m\propto n$
8.	If x and y vary directly, then on decreasing x	H.	x and y vary inversely
		I.	$p\propto q$
		J.	$m\propto\frac{1}{n}$

Sol.

Column I	Column II
x and y vary inversely to each other	$xy=$ constant
Mathematical representation of inverse variation of quantities p and q	$p\propto\frac{1}{q}$
Mathematical representation of direct variation of quantities m and n	$m\propto n$
When $x=5$, $y=2.5$ and when $y=5$, $x=10$	x and y are directly proportional $\left[\because \frac{5}{2.5}=2 \text{ and } \frac{10}{5}=2\right]$
When $x=10$, $y=5$ and when $x=20$, $y=2.5$	x and y vary inversely $[\because 10\times5=50 \text{ and } 20\times2.5=50]$
x and y vary directly with each other	$\frac{x}{y}=$ constant
If x and y vary inversely, then on decreasing x	y will increase in proportion
If x and y vary directly, then on decreasing x	y will decrease in proportion

Q. 92 There are 20 grams of protein in 75 grams of sauted fish. How many grams of protein is in 225 grams of that fish?

Sol. In 20 g of sauted fish, protein is 75g

$\therefore$ In 1 g of souted fish, protein is $\frac{20}{75}$g

In 225 g of sauted fish, protein $=\frac{20}{75}\times225=20\times3=60$ g

Q. 93 **Ms Anita has to drive from Jhareda to Ganwari. She measures a distance of 3.5 cm between these village on the map. What is the actual distance between the villages, if the map scale is 1 cm = 10 km?**

Sol. The distance between Jhareda to Ganwari in the map = 3.5 cm

Given scale, 1 cm = 10 km

So, actual distance between the villages = $3.5 \times 10 = 35$ km

Q. 94 **A water tank casts a shadow 21 m long. A tree of height 9.5 m casts a shadow 8 m long at the same time. The length of the shadows are directly proportional to their heights. Find the height of the tank.**

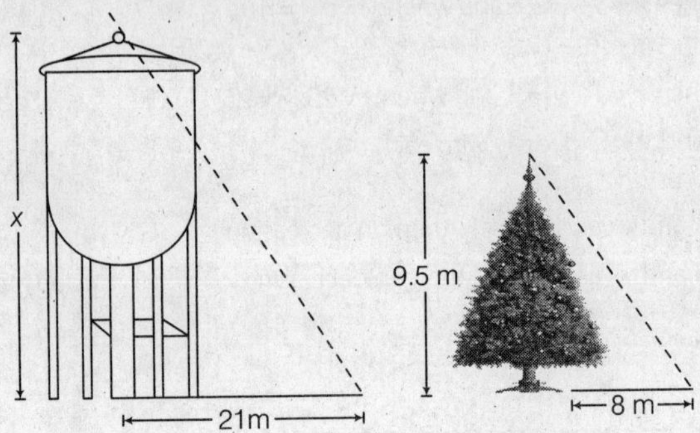

Sol. The height of the tree = 9.5 m

The shadow of the tree = 8 m

According to the given condition in the question, the lenghts of the shadows are in direct proportion.

$$\therefore \quad \frac{8}{9.5} = \frac{21}{x}$$

$$\Rightarrow \quad x = \frac{21 \times 9.5}{8} = \frac{199.5}{8} = 24.9375 \approx 24.9 \text{ m}$$

Hence, height of the water tank is 24.9 m.

Q. 95 **The table shows the time four elevators take to travel various distances. Find, which elevator is fastest and which is slowest.**

	Distance (in m)	**Time** (in s)
Elevator *A*	435	29
Elevator *B*	448	28
Elevator *C*	130	10
Elevator *D*	85	5

How much distance will be travelled elevators *B* and *C* seperately in 140 sec? Who travelled more and by how much?

Sol. On the basis of given table,

Elevator *A* takes 29 s to cover 435 m.

$\therefore$ Distance covered by elevator *A* in 1s $= \frac{435}{29} = 15$ m

Elevator *B* takes 28 s to cover 448 m.

$\therefore$ Distance covered by elevator B in 1s $= \frac{448}{28} = 16\text{ m}$

Elevator C takes 10 s to cover 130 m.

$\therefore$ Distance covered by elevator C in 1s $= \frac{130}{10} = 13\text{ m}$

Elevator D takes 5 s to cover 85 m.

$\therefore$ Distance covered by elevator D in 1 s $= \frac{85}{5} = 17\text{ m}$

Hence, in 1s, elevator D covers more distance as compare to elevators A, B and C. So, elevator D is fastest, while elevator C covers least. Hence, elevator C is slowest.

Now, elevator B covers distance in 140 s $= 140 \times 16 = 2240\text{ m}$ [$\because$ distance = speed × time]

Elevator C covers distance in 140s $= 140 \times 13 = 1820$ m

$\therefore$ Elevator B covers more distance than $C = 2240 - 1820$

$= 420\text{ m}$

Q. 96 **A volleyball court is in a rectangular shape and its dimensions are directly proportional to the dimensions of the swimming pool given below. Find the width of the pool.**

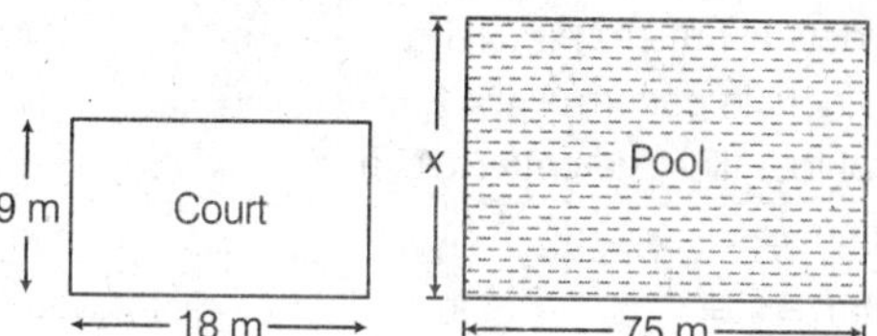

Sol. From the given figures,

Length of volleyball court = 18 m

Breadth of volleyball court = 9 m

Length of pool = 75 m

Let the width of swimming pool = x m

According to the question, the size of volleyball court and swimming pool are in direct proportion to each other.

$$\therefore \quad \frac{9}{18} = \frac{x}{75}$$

$$\Rightarrow \quad x = \frac{75 \times 9}{18} = \frac{75}{2} = 37.5\text{ m} \quad \text{[by cross-multiplication]}$$

Hence, the width of the swimming pool is 37.5 m.

Q. 97 **A recipe for a particular type of muffins requires 1 cup of milk and 1.5 cups of chocolates. Riya has 7.5 cups of chocolates. If she is using the recipe as a guide, how many cups of milk will she need to prepare muffins?**

Sol. A particular type of muffins requires 1 cup of milk and 1.5 cups of chocolates.

Riya has 7.5 cups of chocolates.

The number of cups of milk required for 7.5 cups of chocolates $= \frac{7.5}{1.5} = 5$ cups

[since, number of cups of milk and chocolates are indirect proportion]

Q. 98 Pattern *B* consists of four tiles like pattern *A*. Write a proportion involving blue dots and total dots in patterns *A* and *B*. Are they in direct proportion? If yes, write the constant of proportion.

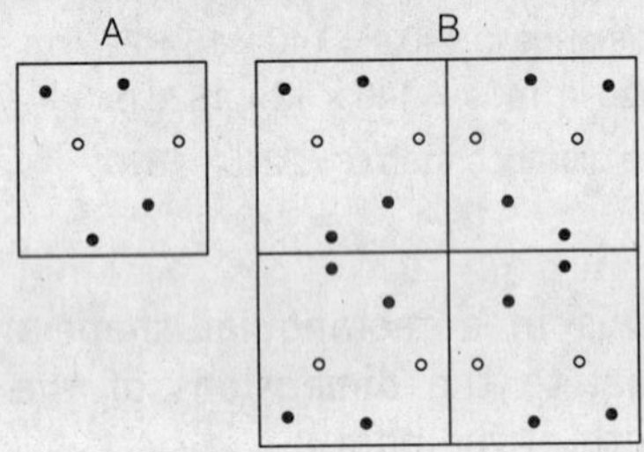

Sol. The number of red dots in pattern $A(\bullet) = 4$

The number of blue dots in pattern $A(\circ) = 2$

Pattern *B* consists of four tiles like pattern *A* i.e.

Pattern $A \times 4 =$ Pattern *B*

$\therefore$ Proportion in pattern $= \frac{2}{6} = \frac{1}{3}$ [$\because$ total number of dots $= 4 + 2 = 6$]

Now, proportion of blue dots and red dots in pattern $B = \frac{8}{32} = \frac{1}{4}$

Q. 99 A bowler throws a cricket ball at a speed of 120 km/h. How long does this ball take to travel a distance of 20 m to each the batsman?

Sol. The speed of the cricket ball = 120 km/h

$$= \frac{120 \times 1000}{60} \text{ m/min} \quad [\because 1 \text{ km} = 1000 \text{ m and } 1 \text{ h} = 60 \text{ min}]$$

$$= 2 \times 1000$$

$$= 2000 \text{ m/min}$$

Now, speed in m/s $= \frac{2000}{60} = \frac{200}{6} = \frac{100}{3}$ m/s [$\because$ 1 min = 60 s]

So, 20 m can be cover in $\frac{20}{\frac{100}{3}} = \frac{60}{100} = 0.6$ s $\left[\because \text{time} = \frac{\text{distance}}{\text{speed}}\right]$

Q. 100 The variable *x* is inversely proportional to *y*. If *x* increases by *p*%, then by what per cent will *y* decrease?

Sol. The variable x is inversely proportionls to y.

$\therefore \quad xy = k$ (constant)

Since, we know that two quantities x and y are said to be in inverse proportion, if an increase in x cause a proportional decrease in y and *vice-versa*.

So, we can say y decrease by p%.

Q. 101 Here is a keyboard of a harmonium.

(a) Find the ratio of white keys to black keys on the keyboard.

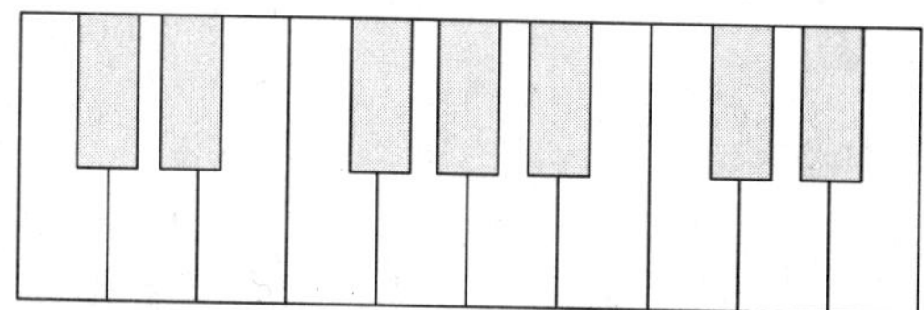

(b) What is the ratio of black keys to all keys on the given keyboard?

(c) This pattern of keys is repeated on larger keyboard. How many black keys would you expect to find on a keyboard with 14 such patterns?

Sol. According to the given figure,

(a) The total number of black keys = 7

The total number of white keys = 10

Hence, the ratio of white keys to black keys on the keyboard = $\frac{10}{7}$

(b) The total number of all keys = 10 + 7 = 17

The ratio of black keys to all keys on the given keyboard = $\frac{7}{17}$

(c) Black keys in 1 keyboard = 7

Black keys in 14 such keyboards = $14 \times 7 = 98$ keys

Q. 102 The following table shows the distance travelled by one of the new eco-friendly energy-efficient car travelled on gas.

Litres of gas	1	0.5	2	2.5	3	5
Distance (in km)	15	7.5	30	37.5	45	75

Which type of properties are indicated by the table? How much distance will be covered by the car in 8 litres of gas?

Sol. On the basis of given table, the distance travelled by one of the new eco-friendly energy-efficient earns travelled on gas.

The car travelled 15 km in 1 L of gas.

The car travelled 7.5 km in 0.5 L of gas.

The car travelled 30 km in 2 L of gas.

This rate shows direct proportion between litres of gas and the distance cover.

The car can cover the distance in 8 L of gas = $8 \times 15 = 120$ km

Q. 103 Kritika is following this recipe for bread. She realises her sister used most of sugar syrup for her breakfast. Kritika has only $\frac{1}{6}$ cup of syrup, so she decides to make a small size of bread. How much of each ingredient shall she use?

Bread recipe

1 cup quick cooking oats

2 cups bread flour

$\frac{1}{3}$ cup sugar syrup **1 tablespoon cooking oil**

$1\frac{1}{3}$ cups water **3 tablespoons yeast**

1 tablespoon salt

Sol. After used of most of sugar syrup for her breakfast, the remaining sugar is $\frac{1}{6}$ cup of sugar syrup. Thus, its means $1-\frac{1}{6}=\frac{5}{6}$ has been used. She need $\frac{1}{3}$ cup of sugar syrup for one piece of bread. So, new quantity of ingredient will be in proportion of $\frac{1}{2}$.

Now, the bread recipe will be look like

$\frac{1}{2}$ cup quick cooking oats 1 cup bread flour

$\frac{1}{6}$ cup sugar syrup $\frac{1}{2}$ tablespoon cooking oil

$\frac{2}{3}$ cup water $\frac{3}{2}$ tablespoons yeast

$\frac{1}{2}$ tablespoon salt

Q. 104 **Many schools have a recommended students-teachers ratio as 35:1. Next year, school expects an increase in enrollment by 280 students. How many new teachers will they to appoint to maintain the students-teachers ratio?**

Sol. Students-teachers ratio = 35 : 1

It show every 35 students-one teacher should available in the school.

In the school, number of students increases = 280 students

The number of teachers required for 280 students $=\frac{280}{35}=8$ teachers

Q. 105 **Kusum always forgets how to convert miles to kilometres and back again. However, she remembers that her car's speedometer shows both miles and kilometres. She knows that travelling 50 miles per hour is same as travelling 80 kilometres per hour. To cover a distance of 200 km, how many miles Kusum would have to go?**

Sol. 50 miles per hour is same as travelling 80 km per hour.

So, 1 km covers distance in 1 h to $\frac{50}{80}$ miles.

To cover a distance of 200 km $=\frac{50}{80}\times 200=\frac{5\times 200}{8}=125$ miles

Hence, 125 miles Kusum has to go for 200 km.

Q. 106 The student of Anju's class sold posters to raise money. Anju wanted to create a ratio for finding the amount of money, her class would make for different numbers of posters sold. She knew, they could raise ₹ 250 for every 60 posters sold.

(a) How much money would Anju's class make for selling 102 posters?

(b) Could Anju's class raise exactly ₹ 2000? If so, how many posters would they need to sell? If not, why?

Sol. (a) Every 60 posters, Anju's class students raise = ₹ 250

So, from 1 poster, Anju's class students raise

$$= \frac{250}{60} = ₹\frac{25}{6}$$

If Anju's sell 102 posters, then they raise

$$= \frac{25}{6} \times 102$$

$$= 17 \times 25$$

$$= ₹\ 425$$

Hence, Anju's class make ₹ 425 for selling of 102 posters.

(b) Since, by selling 1 poster, Anju's class raise = ₹ $\frac{25}{6}$

For raise exactly ₹ 2000, they needs to sell

$$= 2000 \div \frac{25}{6}$$

$$= 2000 \times \frac{6}{25}$$

$$= 480 \text{ posters}$$

11

Mensuration

Multiple Choice Questions (MCQs)

Q. 1 A cube of side 5 cm is painted on all its faces. If it is sliced into 1 cubic centimetre cubes, then how many 1 cubic centimetre cubes will have exactly one of their faces painted?

(a) 27 (b) 42 (c) 54 (d) 142

Sol. *(c)* Given, a cube of side 5 cm is painted on all its faces and is sliced into 1 cm^3 cubes.

Then, from figure, it is clear that there are 9 cubes available on face.

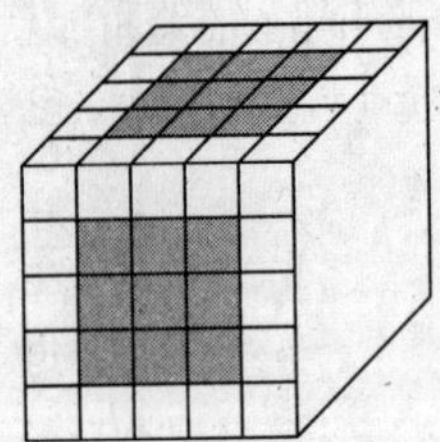

Since, there are six faces available.

Hence, total number of smaller cubes $= 6 \times 9 = 54$

Q. 2 A cube of side 4 cm is cut into 1 cm cubes. What is the ratio of the surface areas of the original cube and cut-out cubes?

(a) 1 : 2 (b) 1 : 3 (c) 1 : 4 (d) 1 : 6

Sol. *(c)* Volume of the original cube having side of length 4 cm $= (4)^3 = 64\ cm^3$

[$\because$ volume of cube with side $a = a^3$]

Volume of the cut-out cubes with side of length 1 cm $= 1\ cm^3$

$\therefore$ Number of cut-out cubes $= \dfrac{\text{Volume of the original cube}}{\text{Volume of a smaller cube}} = \dfrac{64}{1} = 64$

Now, surface area of cut-out cubes $= 64 \times 6 \times (1)^2\ cm^2$

[$\because$ surface area of cube with side $a = 6a^2$]

and surface area of the original cube $= 6 \times 4^2\ cm^2$

$\therefore$ The required ratio of surface areas of the original cube and cut-out cubes

$$= \frac{6 \times 4^2}{64 \times 6} = 1:4$$

Q. 3 A circle of maximum possible size is cut from a square sheet of board. Subsequently, a square of maximum possible size is cut from the resultant circle. What will be the area of the final square?

(a) $\frac{3}{4}$ of original square (b) $\frac{1}{2}$ of original square

(c) $\frac{1}{4}$ of original square (d) $\frac{2}{3}$ of original square

Sol. ***(b)*** Let a be the side of a square sheet.

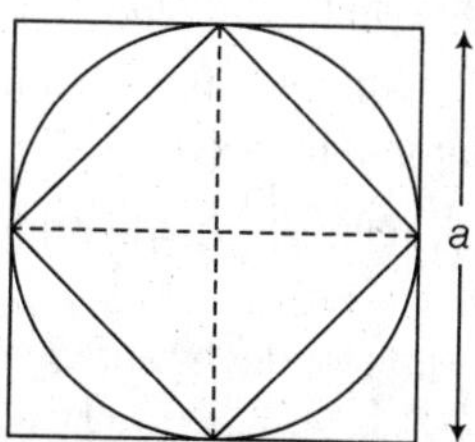

Then, area of bigger square sheet $= a^2$ ...(i)

Now, we make the circle of maximum possible size from it.

Then, the radius of circle $= \frac{a}{2}$ ...(ii)

So, its diameter $(d) = 2 \cdot \frac{a}{2} = a$

Now, any square in a circle of maximum size will have the length of diagonal equal to the diameter of circle.

i.e. diagonal of square made inside the circle $= a$

So, the side of this square $= \frac{a}{\sqrt{2}}$ [$\because$ diagonal = side $\sqrt{2}$]

$\therefore$ Area of this square $= a^2/2$ ...(iii)

From Eqs. (i) and (iii),

Area of final square is $\frac{1}{2}$ of original square.

Q. 4 What is the area (in sq units) of the largest triangle, that can be fitted into a rectangle of length l units and width w units?

(a) $\frac{lw}{2}$ (b) $\frac{lw}{3}$ (c) $\frac{lw}{6}$ (d) $\frac{lw}{4}$

Sol. ***(a)***

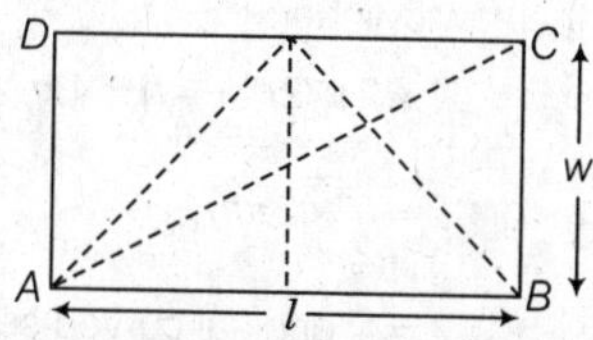

Let $ABCD$ be the rectangle of length l and width w.

Now, we construct a triangle of maximum area inside it in all possible ways.

$\because$ We know that,

Area of triangle $= \frac{1}{2} \times$ Base $\times$ Height

So, for maximum area, base and height of maximum, length is needed.
Here, maximum base length = l
and maximum height = w

$\therefore$ Area (maximum) of triangle = $\frac{1}{2} \times l \times w = \frac{l \times w}{2}$ sq units

Q. 5 **If the height of a cylinder becomes $\frac{1}{4}$ of the original height and the radius is doubled, then which of the following will be true?**

(a) Volume of the cylinder will be doubled
(b) Volume of the cylinder will remain unchanged
(c) Volume of the cylinder will be halved
(d) Volume of the cylinder will be $\frac{1}{4}$ of the original volume

Sol. ***(b)*** We know that, the volume of a cylinder having base radius r and height h is $V = \pi r^2 h$

Now, if new height is $\frac{1}{4}$th of the original height and the radius is doubled, i.e.

$h' = \frac{1}{4}h$ and $r' = 2r$, then

New volume, $V' = \pi(2r)^2 \times \frac{1}{4}h = 4\pi r^2 \times \frac{1}{4}h$

$= \pi r^2 h = V$

Hence, the new volume of cylinder is same as the original volume.

Q. 6 **If the height of a cylinder becomes $\frac{1}{4}$ of the original height and the radius is doubled, then which of the following will be true?**

(a) Curved surface area of the cylinder will be doubled
(b) Curved surface area of the cylinder will remain unchanged
(c) Curved surface area of the cylinder will be halved
(d) Curved surface area will be $\frac{1}{4}$ of the original curved surface

Sol. ***(c)*** Let the new height and radius be $\frac{h}{4}$ and $2r$ respectively, where r and h are original radius and original height respectively of the cylinder.

We know that, curved surface area of cylinder = $2\pi rh$

Then, curved surface of the new cylinder

$= 2\pi(2r) \times \frac{1}{4}h = 4\pi r \times \frac{1}{4}h = \pi rh$

$= \frac{1}{2} \times 2\pi rh$ [multiplying and dividing by 2]

$= \frac{1}{2}$ original curved surface area

Hence, the curved surface area of the cylinder will be halved.

Q. 7 If the height of a cylinder becomes $\frac{1}{4}$ of the original height and the radius is doubled, then which of the following will be true?

(a) Total surface area of the cylinder will be doubled
(b) Total surface area of the cylinder will remain unchanged
(c) Total surface area of the cylinder will be halved
(d) None of the above

Sol. (d) We know that,

Total surface area of cylinder having radius r and height $h = 2\pi r (h + r)$

Total surface area of the cylinder with new height $\left(\frac{h}{u}\right)$ and radius $2r$

$$= 2\pi(2r)\left(2r + \frac{1}{4}h\right)$$

$$= 4\pi r(8r + h) \times \frac{1}{4}$$

$$= \pi r (8r + h)$$

Q. 8 The surface area of the three coterminus faces of a cuboid are 6, 15 and 10 cm^2, respectively. The volume of the cuboid is

(a) 30 cm^3 (b) 40 cm^3 (c) 20 cm^3 (d) 35 cm^3

Sol. (a) If l, b and h are the dimensions of the cuboid. Then,

Volume of the cuboid $= l \times b \times h$

Here, $6 = l \times b$

$15 = l \times h$

$10 = b \times h$

$\therefore$ $6 \times 15 \times 10 = l^2 b^2 h^2$

$\therefore$ Volume $= l \times b \times h$

$= \sqrt{6 \times 15 \times 10} = 30 \text{cm}^3$

Q. 9 A regular hexagon is inscribed in a circle of radius r. The perimeter of the regular hexagon is

(a) $3r$ (b) $6r$ (c) $9r$ (d) $12r$

Sol. (b) A regular hexagon comprises 6 equilateral triangles, each of them having one of their vertices at the centre of the hexagon.

The sides of the equilateral triangle are equal to the radius of the smallest circle inscribing the hexagon.

Hence, each side of the hexagon is equal to the radius of the hexagon and the perimeter of the hexagon is $6r$.

Q. 10 The dimensions of a godown are 40 m, 25 m and 10 m. If it is filled with cuboidal boxes each of dimensions 2 m $\times$ 1.25 m $\times$ 1 m, then the number of boxes will be

(a) 1800 (b) 2000 (c) 4000 (d) 8000

Sol. (c) Given, dimensions of a godown are 40 m, 25 m and 10 m.

$\therefore$ Volume of godown $= 40 \times 25 \times 10$

$= 10000 \text{ m}^3$

Now, volume of each cuboidal box $= 2 \times 1.25 \times 1$

$= 2.5 \text{ m}^3$

$\therefore$ The number of boxes, that can be filled in the godown $= \dfrac{\text{Volume of godown}}{\text{Volume of each cuboidal box}}$

$= \dfrac{10000}{2.5} = 4000$

Q. 11 The volume of a cube is 64 cm^3. Its surface area is

(a) 16 cm^2 (b) 64 cm^2

(c) 96 cm^2 (d) 128 cm^2

Sol. ***(c)*** Let the side of the cube be a. Then,

Volume of cube $= a^3 = 64$ [given]

$\Rightarrow \quad a = 4$

Now, surface area of the cube $= 6a^2 = 6 \times 4^2 = 96 \text{ cm}^2$

Q. 12 If the radius of a cylinder is tripled but its curved surface area is unchanged, then its height will be

(a) tripled (b) constant

(c) one-sixth (d) one-third

Sol. ***(d)*** Let h' be the new height.

Curved surface area of a cylinder with radius r and height h

$= 2\pi rh$

Now, according to the question, radius is tripled. Then,

Curved surface area $= 2\pi \times 3r \times h' = 2\pi rh$ [given]

$\Rightarrow \quad 6\pi r \times h' = 2\pi rh$

$\Rightarrow \quad h' = \dfrac{2\pi rh}{6\pi r}$

$\therefore \quad h' = \dfrac{1}{3}h$

Hence, the new height will be $\dfrac{1}{3}$ of the original height.

Q. 13 How many small cubes with edge of 20 cm each can be just accommodated in a cubical box of 2 m edge?

(a) 10 (b) 100 (c) 1000 (d) 10000

Sol. ***(c)*** Volume of cube $= (\text{Side})^3$

Volume of each small cube $= 20^3 = 8000 \text{ cm}^3$

$= 0.008 \text{ m}^3$

Now, volume of the cubical box $= 2^3 = 8 \text{ m}^3$

$\therefore$ Number of small cubes, that can just be accommodated in the cubical box

$= \dfrac{\text{Volume of cubical box}}{\text{Volume of small cube}} = \dfrac{8}{0.008}$

$= 1000$

Q. 14 The volume of a cylinder whose radius r is equal to its height, is

(a) $\frac{1}{4}\pi r^3$ (b) $\frac{\pi r^3}{32}$ (c) πr^3 (d) $\frac{\pi r^3}{8}$

Sol. *(c)* Given, $r = h$

Then, volume of cylinder $= \pi r^2 h = \pi r^2 r = \pi r^3$

Q. 15 The volume of a cube whose edge is $3x$, is

(a) $27x^3$ (b) $9x^3$ (c) $6x^3$ (d) $3x^3$

Sol. *(a)* We know that, the volume of a cube = (Side)^3

$= a^3$

$= (3x)^3$ $[\because a = 3x, \text{ given}]$

$= 27x^3$

Q. 16 The figure *ABCD* is a quadrilateral, in which $AB = CD$ and $BC = AD$. Its area is

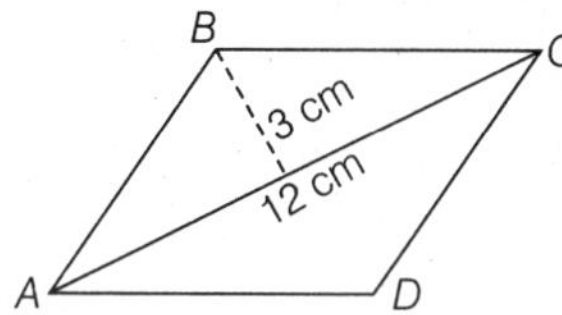

(a) 72 cm^2 (b) 36 cm^2 (c) 24 cm^2 (d) 18 cm^2

Sol. *(b)* It is clear from the figure that, quadrilateral *ABCD* is a parallelogram. The diagonal *AC* of the given parallelogram *ABCD* divides it into two triangles of equal areas.

Area of the $\Delta ABC = \frac{1}{2} \times \text{Base} \times \text{Height}$

$= \frac{1}{2} \times 12 \times 3 = 18 \text{ cm}^2$

$\therefore$ Area of the parallelogram $ABCD = 2 \times$ Area of ΔABC

$= 2 \times 18$

$= 36 \text{ cm}^2$

Q. 17 What is the area of the rhombus *ABCD* below, if $AC = 6$ cm and $BE = 4$ cm?

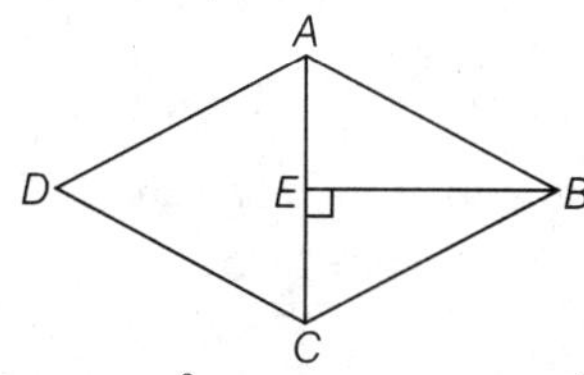

(a) 36 cm^2 (b) 16 cm^2 (c) 24 cm^2 (d) 13 cm^2

Sol. *(c)* The diagonal *AC* of the rhombus *ABCD* divides it into two triangles of equal areas.

Now, area of $\Delta ABC = \frac{1}{2} \times \text{Base} \times \text{Height} = \frac{1}{2} \times 4 \times 6 = 12 \text{ cm}^2$

$\therefore$ Area of the rhombus $ABCD = 2 \times$ Area of ΔABC

$= 2 \times 12 = 24 \text{ cm}^2$

Q. 18 **The area of a parallelogram is 60 cm^2 and one of its altitude is 5 cm. The length of its corresponding side is**

(a) 12 cm (b) 6 cm (c) 4 cm (d) 2 cm

Sol. ***(a)*** We know that,

Area of a parallelogram = Side × Altitude

$\Rightarrow \quad a \times h = 60$

$\Rightarrow \quad a \times 5 = 60$

$\Rightarrow \quad a = \frac{60}{5}$

$\therefore \quad a = 12$ cm

Q. 19 **The perimeter of a trapezium is 52 cm and its each non-parallel side is equal to 10 cm with its height 8 cm. Its area is**

(a) 124 cm^2 (b) 118 cm^2 (c) 128 cm^2 (d) 112 cm^2

Sol. ***(c)*** Given, perimeter of a trapezium is 52 cm and each non-parallel side is of 10 cm.

Then, sum of its parallel sides

$= 52 - (10 + 10) = 52 - 20 = 32$ cm

$\therefore$ Area of the trapezium $= \frac{1}{2}(a + b) \times h$

$= \frac{1}{2} \times 32 \times 8$ [$\because h = 8$ cm and $a + b = 32$ cm]

$= 128 \text{ cm}^2$

Q. 20 **Area of a quadrilateral *ABCD* is 20 cm^2 and perpendiculars on *BD* from opposite vertices are 1 cm and 1.5 cm. The length of *BD* is**

(a) 4 cm (b) 15 cm (c) 16 cm (d) 18 cm

Sol. ***(c)*** Area of the given quadrilateral $= \frac{1}{2}$ (Sum of altitudes) × Corresponding diagonal

$\Rightarrow \quad 20 = \frac{1}{2}(1 + 1.5) \times BD$ [given]

$\Rightarrow \quad \frac{1}{2} \times 2.5 \times BD = 20 \text{ cm}^2$

$\Rightarrow \quad BD = 20 \times \frac{2}{2.5} = \frac{40}{2.5} = 16$ cm

Q. 21 **A metal sheet 27 cm long, 8 cm broad and 1 cm thick is melted into a cube. The side of the cube is**

(a) 6 cm (b) 8 cm (c) 12 cm (d) 24 cm

Sol. ***(a)*** Given, a metal sheet 27 cm long, 8 cm broad and 1 cm thick.

Then, volume of the sheet (cubiodal) $= l \times b \times h$

$= 27 \times 8 \times 1 = 216 \text{ cm}^3$

Now, since this sheet is melted to form a cube of edge length a (say).

Then, volume of the cube = Volume of the metal sheet

$\Rightarrow \quad a^3 = 216 \text{ cm}^3$

$\Rightarrow \quad a = 6$ cm

Hence, the side of the cube is 6 cm.

Q. 22 Three cubes of metal whose edges are 6 cm, 8 cm and 10 cm respectively, are melted to form a single cube. The edge of the new cube is

(a) 12 cm (b) 24 cm
(c) 18 cm (d) 20 cm

Sol. *(a)* The edges of three cubes are 6 cm, 8 cm and 10 cm, respectively.

$\therefore$ Sum of volumes of the three metal cubes

$$= 6^3 + 8^3 + 10^3 \quad [\because \text{volume of cube} = (\text{edge})^3]$$
$$= 216 + 512 + 1000$$
$$= 1728 \text{ cm}^3$$

Since, a new cube is formed by melting these three cubes.

Let *a* be the side of new cube. Then,

Volume of the new cube = Sum of volumes of three metal cubes

$\Rightarrow \quad a^3 = 1728$

$\therefore \quad a = 12 \text{ cm}$

Hence, the edge of the new cube is 12 cm.

Q. 23 A covered wooden box has the inner measures as 115 cm, 75 cm and 35 cm and thickness of wood as 2.5 cm. The volume of the wood is

(a) 85000 cm^3 (b) 80000 cm^3
(c) 82125 cm^3 (d) 84000 cm^3

Sol. *(c)* Given, inner measures of a wooden box as 115 cm, 75 cm and 35 cm.

Since, thickness of the box is 2.5 cm, then outer measures will be 115 + 5, 75 + 5 and 35 + 5, i.e. 120 cm, 80 cm and 40 cm.

$\therefore$ The outer volume $= 120 \times 80 \times 40 = 384000 \text{ cm}^3$

and the inner volume $= 115 \times 75 \times 35 = 301875 \text{ cm}^3$ $\quad [\because \text{volume of cuboid} = l \times b \times h]$

$\therefore$ Volume of the wood = Outer volume – Inner volume

$$= 384000 - 301875 = 82125 \text{ cm}^3$$

Q. 24 The ratio of radii of two cylinders is 1 : 2 and heights are in the ratio 2 : 3. The ratio of their volumes is

(a) 1 : 6 (b) 1 : 9 (c) 1 : 3 (d) 2 : 9

Sol. *(a)* Let r_1, r_2 be radii of two cylinders and h_1, h_2 be their heights.

Then, $\frac{r_1}{r_2} = \frac{1}{2}$ and $\frac{h_1}{h_2} = \frac{2}{3}$

Now,
$$\frac{V_1}{V_2} = \frac{\pi r_1^2 h_1}{\pi r_2^2 h_2} = \left(\frac{r_1}{r_2}\right)^2 \times \frac{h_1}{h_2} = \left(\frac{1}{2}\right)^2 \times \frac{2}{3}$$
$$= \frac{1}{4} \times \frac{2}{3} = \frac{1}{6} = 1 : 6$$

Hence, $V_1 : V_2 = 1 : 6$

Q. 25 **Two cubes have volumes in the ratio 1 : 64. The ratio of the areas of a face of first cube to that of the other is**

(a) 1 : 4 (b) 1 : 8
(c) 1 : 16 (d) 1 : 32

Sol. *(c)* Let a and b be the edges of the two cubes, respectively.

Then, according to the question,

$$a^3 : b^3 = 1 : 64 \quad [\because \text{volume of cube} = (\text{edge})^3]$$

$$\Rightarrow \frac{a^3}{b^3} = \frac{1}{64}$$

$$\Rightarrow \left(\frac{a}{b}\right)^3 = \left(\frac{1}{4}\right)^3$$

$$\Rightarrow \frac{a}{b} = \frac{1}{4} \quad \text{[taking cube roots on both sides]}$$

Now, ratio of areas, $\left(\frac{a}{b}\right)^2 = \left(\frac{1}{4}\right)^2$ $[\because \text{surface area of cube} = 6 \times (\text{edge})^2]$

$$\Rightarrow \frac{a^2}{b^2} = \frac{1}{16}$$

$$\therefore a^2 : b^2 = 1 : 16$$

Q. 26 **The surface areas of the six faces of a rectangular solid are 16, 16, 32, 32, 72 and 72 sq cm. The volume of the solid (in cu cm) is**

(a) 192 (b) 384
(c) 480 (d) 2592

Sol. *(a)* Since, the solid has rectangular faces.

So, we have $l \times b = 16$ ...(i)

$b \times h = 32$ ...(ii)

$l \times h = 72$ ...(iii)

where l, b and h are the length, breadth and height respectively, of the solid.

On multiplying Eqs. (i), (ii) and (iii), we get

$$l \times b \times b \times h \times l \times h = 16 \times 32 \times 72$$

$$\Rightarrow l^2 \times b^2 \times h^2 = 36864$$

$$\Rightarrow (lbh)^2 = 36864$$

$$\therefore lbh = 192$$

Hence, the volume of the solid is 192 cu cm.

Q. 27 **Ramesh has three containers.**

(i) Cylindrical container A having radius r and height h.

(ii) Cylindrical container B having radius $2r$ and height $\frac{1}{2}h$.

(iii) Cuboidal container C having dimensions $r \times r \times h$.

The arrangement of the containers in the increasing order of their volumes is

(a) A, B, C (b) B, C, A
(c) C, A, B (d) Cannot be arranged

Sol. ***(c)*** (i) The volume of the cylindrical container having radius r and height h

$$= \pi r^2 h$$

(ii) The volume of the cylindrical container with radius $2\,r$ and height $\frac{1}{2}h$

$$= \pi\,(2r)^2 \times \frac{1}{2}h = \pi \times 4r^2 \times \frac{1}{2}h$$

$$= 2\pi r^2 h$$

(iii) The volume of the cuboidal container having dimensions $r \times r \times h$

$$= r^2 h$$

From parts (i), (ii) and (iii), we have the following order C, A, B.

Q. 28 **If R is the radius of the base of the hat, then the total outer surface area of the hat is**

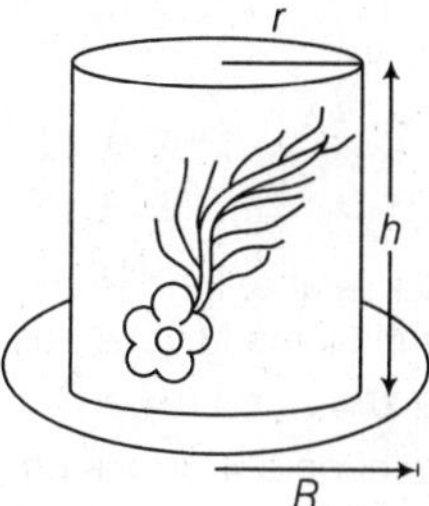

(a) $\pi r\,(2h + R)$ (b) $2\pi r\,(h + R)$ (c) $2\pi rh + \pi R^2$ (d) None of these

Sol. ***(c)***. Given, a cylindrical hat with base radius R and r is radius of the top surface.

Now, total surface area of hat = Curved surface area + Top surface area + Base surface area

$$= 2\pi rh + \pi r^2 + \pi(R^2 - r^2)$$

$$= 2\pi rh + \pi r^2 + \pi R^2 - \pi r^2$$

$$= 2\pi rh + \pi R^2$$

Fill in the Blanks

In questions 29 to 52, fill in the blanks to make the statements are true.

Q. 29 **A cube of side 4 cm is painted on all its sides. If it is sliced in 1 cu cm cubes, then number of such cubes that will have exactly two of their faces painted, is ______**

Sol. **24**

The volume of a cube of side 4 cm = $4 \times 4 \times 4 = 64\ \text{cm}^3$

When it is sliced into $1\ \text{cm}^3$ cubes, we will get 64 small cubes.

In each side of the larger cube, the smaller cubes in the edges will have more than one face painted.

The cubes which are situated at the corners of the big cube, have three faces painted.

So, to each edge two small cubes are left which have two faces painted. As, the total number of edges in a cube are 12.

Hence, the number of small cubes with two faces painted = $12 \times 2 = 24$

Q. 30 A cube of side 5 cm is cut into 1 cm cubes. The percentage increase in volume after such cutting is ______.

Sol. none

Given, a cube of side 5 cm is cut into 1 cm cubes.

The volume of big cube $= 5 \times 5 \times 5$

$= 125 \text{ cm}^3$

Now, the big cube is cut into 1 cm cubes.

$\therefore$ The number of small cubes $= \dfrac{125}{\text{Volume of 1 small cube}} = \dfrac{125}{1}$

Thus, the volume of big cube = The volume of 125 cubes having an edge 1 cm

Hence, there is no change in the volume.

Q. 31 The surface area of a cuboid formed by joining two cubes of side a face-to-face, is ______.

Sol. $10a^2$

We have, two cubes of side a.

These two cubes are joined face-to-face, then the resultant solid figure is a cuboid which has same breadth and height as the joined cubes has length twice of the length of a cube.

i.e. $l = 2a,\ b = a$ and $h = a$

Thus, the total surface area of the cuboid $= 2(lb + bh + hl)$

$= 2(2a \times a + a \times a + a \times 2a)$

$= 2(2a^2 + a^2 + 2a^2) = 2 \times 5a^2$

$= 10a^2$

Q. 32 If the diagonals of a rhombus get doubled, then the area of the rhombus becomes ______ its original area.

Sol. 4 times

We know that,

Area of a rhombus $= \dfrac{1}{2} \times d_1 \times d_2$

where, d_1 and d_2 are diagonals of the rhombus.

If diagonals get doubled, then the area $= \dfrac{1}{2} 2d_1 \times 2d_2 = 4\left(\dfrac{1}{2} \times d_1 \times d_2\right)$

Hence, the new area becomes 4 times its original area.

Q. 33 If a cube fits exactly in a cylinder with height h, then the volume of the cube is ______ and surface area of the cube is ______.

Sol. $h^3, 6h^2$

Since, the cube fits exactly in the cylinder with height h, therefore each side of the cube $= h$

Now, volume of the cube $= (\text{Side})^3 = h^3$

and surface area of the cube $= 6 \times (\text{Side})^2$

$= 6 \times h^2$

Q. 34 The volume of a cylinder becomes ______ the original volume, if its radius becomes half of the original radius.

Sol. $\frac{1}{4}$

The volume of a cylinder with radius r and height $h = \pi r^2 h$

If radius is halved, then new volume $= \pi\left(\frac{r}{2}\right)^2 h = \frac{1}{4}\pi r^2 h$

Hence, the new volume is $\frac{1}{4}$th of the original volume.

Q. 35 The curved surface area of a cylinder is reduced by ______ per cent, if the height is half of the original height.

Sol. 50%

The curved surface area of a cylinder with radius r and height $h = 2\pi rh$

If the height is halved, then new curved surface area of cylinder

$$= 2\pi r\frac{h}{2} = \pi rh$$

$\therefore$ Percentage reduction in curved surface area $= \frac{2\pi rh - \pi rh}{2\pi rh} \times 100$

$$= \frac{\pi rh}{2\pi rh} \times 100$$

$$= 50\%$$

Q. 36 The volume of a cylinder which exactly fits in a cube of side a, is ______.

Sol. $\frac{\pi a^3}{4}$

Since, the cylinder that exactly fits in cube of side a, has its height equal to the edge of the cube and radius equal to half the edge of the cube.

$\therefore$ Height $= a$ and radius $= \frac{a}{2}$

Now, volume of the cylinder $= \pi r^2 h = \pi\left(\frac{a}{2}\right)^2 a$

$$= \frac{1}{4}\pi a^3$$

Q. 37 The curved surface area of a cylinder which exactly fits in a cube of side b, is ______.

Sol. πb^2

Since, the cylinder that exactly fits in a cube of side b, has its height equal to the edge of the cube and radius equal to half the edge of the cube.

$\therefore$ Height $= b$ and radius $= \frac{b}{2}$

Now, curved surface area of the cylinder $= 2\pi rh = 2\pi \times \frac{b}{2} \times b$

$$= \pi b^2$$

Q. 38 If the diagonal d of a quadrilateral is doubled and the heights h_1 and h_2 falling on d are halved, then the area of quadrilateral is ______.

Sol. $\frac{1}{2}(h_1 + h_2)d$

Let $ABCD$ be a quadrilateral, where h_1 and h_2 are altitudes on the diagonal $BD = d$.

Then, area of quadrilateral $ABCD = \frac{1}{2}(h_1 + h_2) \times BD$

If altitudes are halved and the diagonal is doubled, then

$$\text{Area of quadrilateral } ABCD = \frac{1}{2}\left(\frac{h_1}{2} + \frac{h_2}{2}\right) \times 2d = \frac{1}{2}\left(\frac{h_1 + h_2}{2}\right) \times 2d$$

$$= \frac{1}{2}(h_1 + h_2) \times d$$

Q. 39 The perimeter of a rectangle becomes ______ times its original perimeter, if its length and breadth are doubled.

Sol. 2 times

Perimeter of a rectangle with length l and breadth $b = 2(l + b)$

If the length and the breadth are doubled, then the new perimeter

$$= 2(2l + 2b)$$
$$= 2[2(l + b)]$$

Hence, the perimeter becomes 2 times of original perimeter.

Q. 40 A trapezium with 3 equal sides and one side double the equal side, can be divided into ______ equilateral triangles of ______ area.

Sol. 3, equal

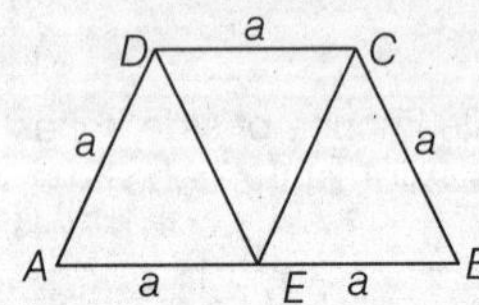

Let $ABCD$ be a trapezium, in which

$$AD = DC = BC = a \text{ (say)}$$

and $AB = 2a$ [given]

Draw medians through the vertices D and C on the side AB.

$\therefore$ $AE = EB = a$

Now, in parallelogram $ADCE$, we have

$AD = EC = a$ and $AE = CD = a$ [$\because$ opposite sides in a parallelogram are equal]

In ΔADE and ΔDEC, $AD = EC$

$AE = CD$

and $DE = DE$ [common]

By SSS, $\Delta ADE \cong \Delta DEC$

By triangle rule, $\Delta ADE \cong \Delta DEC$

Thus, ΔADE and ΔDEC are equilateral triangles having equal sides.

Similarly, in parallelogram $DEBC$, we can show that $\Delta DEC \cong \Delta ECB$.

Hence, the trapezium can be divided into 3 equilateral triangles of equal area.

Q. 41 All six faces of a cuboid are ______ in shape and of ______ area.

Sol. **rectangular, different**

We know that, a cuboid is made of 6 rectangular plane regions, i.e. 6 rectangular faces, which have different lengths and breadths. Therefore, the area of the rectangular faces are different.

Q. 42 Opposite faces of a cuboid are ______ in area.

Sol. **equal**

We know that, a cuboid has 6 rectangular faces, of which opposite faces have the same length and breadth. Therefore, area of the opposite faces are equal.

Q. 43 Curved surface area of a cylinder of radius h and height r is ______.

Sol. $2\pi hr$ **or** $2\pi rh$

We know that, the curved surface area of a cylinder of radius h and height r

$$= 2\pi \times \text{Radius} \times \text{Height}$$
$$= 2\pi \times h \times r = 2\pi hr$$
$$= 2\pi rh$$

Q. 44 Total surface area of a cylinder of radius h and height r is ______.

Sol. $2\pi h(r + h)$

Given, radius of cylinder $= h$ and height of cylinder $= r$

$\therefore$ Total surface area of a cylinder = Curved surface area + Area of top surface + Area of base

$$= 2 \times \pi \times \text{Radius} \times \text{Height} + \pi\ (\text{Radius})^2 + \pi\ (\text{Radius})^2$$
$$= 2\pi hr + \pi h^2 + \pi h^2$$
$$= 2\pi rh + 2\pi h^2$$
$$= 2\pi h(r + h)$$

Q. 45 Volume of a cylinder with radius h and height r is ______.

Sol. $\pi h^2 r$

Given, radius of cylinder $= h$ and height of cylinder $= r$.

Now, volume of a cylinder

$$= \pi \times (\text{Radius})^2 \times \text{Height} = \pi \times h^2 \times r = \pi h^2 r$$

Q. 46 Area of a rhombus $= \frac{1}{2}$ product of ______.

Sol. **diagonals**

We know that, the area of a rhombus = Half of the product of its diagonals

$$= \frac{1}{2}\ [\text{Product of diagonals}]$$

Q. 47 Two cylinders A and B are formed by folding a rectangular sheet of dimensions 20 cm $\times$ 10 cm along its length and also along its breadth, respectively. Then, volume of A is ______ of volume of B.

Sol. **twice**

We have, a rectangular sheet of dimensions 20 cm × 10 cm.

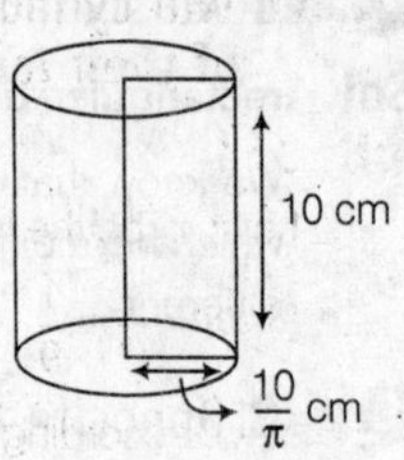

If we fold it along its length, which is 20 cm, then the resultant figure is a cylinder with height, $h = 10$ cm and base circumference, $2\pi r = 20$ cm

$$\Rightarrow \qquad r = \frac{20}{2\pi} = \frac{10}{\pi} \text{ cm}$$

∴ The volume of the cylinder, so formed $= \pi r^2 h$

$$= \pi \times \frac{10}{\pi} \times \frac{10}{\pi} \times 10$$

$$= \frac{1000}{\pi} \text{ cm}^3$$

$$= V_1 \text{(say)} \qquad \ldots\text{(i)}$$

Again, if we fold the rectangular sheet along its breadth, which is 10 cm, the figure so obtained is a cylinder with height, $h = 20$ cm and the base circumference $2\pi r = 10$ cm

20 cm

$\frac{5}{\pi}$ cm

$$\Rightarrow \qquad r = \frac{10}{2\pi} = \frac{5}{\pi} \text{ cm}$$

∴ Volume of the cylinder $= \pi r^2 h = \pi \times \frac{5}{\pi} \times \frac{5}{\pi} \times 20$

$$= \frac{500}{\pi} \text{ cm}^3 = V_2 \text{ (say)} \qquad \ldots\text{(ii)}$$

i.e. $\qquad V_2 = 2V_1$

From Eqs. (i) and (ii), we see that the volume of A is twice the volume of B.

Q. 48 In the above question, curved surface area of *A* is ______ surface area of *B*.

Sol. **equal**

For cylinder A, $\qquad h = 10$ cm and $r = \frac{10}{\pi}$ cm

∴ Curved surface area of $A = 2\pi rh = 2\pi \times \frac{10}{\pi} \times 10 = 200 \text{ cm}^2$

Again, for cylinder B, $\qquad r = \frac{5}{\pi}$ cm and $h = 20$ cm

∴ Curved surface area of $B = 2\pi rh = 2\pi \times \frac{5}{\pi} \times 20 = 200 \text{ cm}^2$

Hence, the curved surface area of both the cylinders are same.

Q. 49 ______ of a solid is the measurement of the space occupied by it.

Sol. **Volume**

We know that, a solid always occupies some space and magnitude of this space region is known as the volume of the solid.

Q. 50 ______ surface area of room = Area of 4 walls.

Sol. **Lateral**

We know that, a room is in the shape of a cuboid. Its 4 walls are treated as lateral faces of the cuboid.

∴ Lateral surface area of room = Area of 4 walls

Q. 51 Two cylinders of equal volume have heights in the ratio 1 : 9. The ratio of their radii is ______.

Sol. **3 : 1**

Let r_1, r_2 be the radii and h_1, h_2 be the heights of two cylinders.

Given, $\frac{h_1}{h_2} = \frac{1}{9}$

Now, according to the question,

$$\pi r_1^2 h_1 = \pi r_2^2 h_2 \quad [\because \text{volume of cylinder} = \pi r^2 h]$$

$$\Rightarrow \frac{r_1^2}{r_2^2} = \frac{h_2}{h_1}$$

$$\Rightarrow \left(\frac{r_1}{r_2}\right)^2 = \frac{9}{1}$$

$$\Rightarrow \frac{r_1}{r_2} = \frac{\sqrt{9}}{1}$$

$$\Rightarrow \frac{r_1}{r_2} = \frac{3}{1}$$

Hence, $r_1 : r_2 = 3 : 1$

Q. 52 Two cylinders of same volume have their radii in the ratio 1 : 6. Then, ratio of their heights is ______.

Sol. **36 : 1**

Let r_1, r_2 be the radii and h_1, h_2 be the heights of two cylinders.

Given, $\frac{r_1}{r_2} = \frac{1}{6}$

Now, according to the question,

$$\pi r_1^2 h_1 = \pi r_2^2 h_2 \quad [\because \text{volume of cylinder} = \pi r^2 h]$$

$$\Rightarrow \frac{r_1^2}{r_2^2} = \frac{h_2}{h_1}$$

$$\Rightarrow \left(\frac{r_1}{r_2}\right)^2 = \frac{h_2}{h_1}$$

$$\Rightarrow \left(\frac{1}{6}\right)^2 = \frac{h_2}{h_1}$$

$$\Rightarrow \frac{1}{36} = \frac{h_2}{h_1}$$

or $$\frac{h_1}{h_2} = \frac{36}{1}$$

or $$h_1 : h_2 = 36 : 1$$

True/False

In questions 53 to 61, state whether the statements are True or False.

Q. 53 The areas of any two faces of a cube are equal.

Sol. ***True***

Since, all the faces of a cube are squares of same side length, therefore the areas of any two faces of a cube are equal.

Q. 54 The areas of any two faces of a cuboid are equal.

Sol. ***False***

A cuboid has rectangular faces with different lengths and breadths. Only opposite faces of cuboid have the same length and breadth.
Therefore, areas of only opposite faces of a cuboid are equal.

Q. 55 The surface area of a cuboid formed by joining face-to-face 3 cubes of side x is 3 times the surface area of a cube of side x.

Sol. ***False***

Three cubes having side x are joined face-to-face, then the cuboid so formed has the same height and breadth as the cubes but its length will be thrice that of the cubes.
Hence, the length, breadth and height of the cuboid so formed are $3x$, x and x, respectively.
Then, its surface area $= 2\,(lb + bh + hl)$

$$= 2(3x \times x + x \times x + x \times 3x) = 2(3x^2 + x^2 + 3x^2)$$
$$= 2 \times 7x^2 = 14x^2$$

Now, the surface area of the cube of side $x = 6\,(\text{Side})^2 = 6x^2$

Hence, the statement is false.

Q. 56 Two cuboids with equal volume will always have equal surface area.

Sol. ***False***

We discard the statement by a counter example.

Let the dimensions of two cuboids be 1 cm × 1 cm × 2 cm and 1 cm × $\frac{1}{2}$ cm × 4 cm, respectively.

Then, volume of first cuboid $= l \times b \times h = 1 \times 1 \times 2 = 2\text{ cm}^3$

and volume of second cuboid $= l \times b \times h = 1 \times \frac{1}{2} \times 4 = 2\text{ cm}^3$

Now, the surface area of first cuboid $= 2\,(lb + bh + hl)$

$$= 2\,(1 \times 1 + 1 \times 2 + 2 \times 1)$$
$$= 2\,(1 + 2 + 2) = 10\text{ cm}^2$$

and surface area of the second cuboid $= 2(lb + bh + hl)$

$$= 2\left(1 \times \frac{1}{2} + \frac{1}{2} \times 4 + 1 \times 4\right) = 2\left(\frac{1}{2} + \frac{4}{2} + 4\right)$$
$$= 2\left(\frac{5}{2} + 4\right) = 2\left(\frac{13}{2}\right) = 13\text{ cm}^2$$

which are not equal.
So, the statement is false.

Q. 57 The area of a trapezium becomes 4 times, if its height gets doubled.

Sol. ***False***

We know that,

Area of a trapezium $= \frac{1}{2}(a+b)\times h$

where, a and b are the lengths of parallel sides and h is the altitude (height).

Now, if the height gets doubled, then

Area of trapezium $= \frac{1}{2}(a+b)\times 2h = 2\left[\frac{1}{2}(a+b)\times h\right]$

Hence, the area is doubled.

So, the statement is false.

Q. 58 A cube of side 3 cm painted on all its faces, when sliced into 1 cu cm cubes, will have exactly 1 cube with none of its faces painted.

Sol. ***True***

Given, a cube of side 3 cm is painted on all its faces. Now, it is sliced into 1 cu cm cubes. Then, there will be 8 corner cubes that have 3 sides painted, 6 centre cubes with only one side painted and only 1 cube in the middle that has no side painted.

Q. 59 Two cylinders with equal volume will always have equal surface area.

Sol. ***False***

Consider two cylinders with the following measures

e.g. $r_1 = 2$ cm, $h = 9$ cm and $r = 3$ cm, $h = 4$ cm

For the first cylinder,

$$\text{Volume} = \pi r^2 h = \pi \times 2^2 \times 9 = 36\,\pi\ \text{cm}^3$$

Again, for the second cylinder,

$$\text{Volume} = \pi r^2 h = \pi \times 3^2 \times 4 = 36\,\pi\ \text{cm}^3$$

$\therefore$ The volumes are equal.

Now, surface area of first cylinder $= 2\pi rh = 2\pi \times 2 \times 9 = 36\,\pi\ \text{cm}^2$

and surface area of second cylinder $= 2\pi rh = 2\pi \times 3 \times 4 = 24\,\pi\ \text{cm}^2$

which are not equal.

So, the statement is false.

Q. 60 The surface area of a cube formed by cutting a cuboid of dimensions $2\times1\times1$ in 2 equal parts, is 2 sq units.

Sol. ***False***

The dimensions of the given cuboid are $2\times1\times1$. It is sliced into two equal parts, which are cubes.

Then, the dimensions of the cube, so formed are $1\times1\times1$.

$\therefore$ The surface area of the cube so formed $= 6\,(\text{Side})^2 = 6\times(1)^2 = 6$ sq units

Hence, the surface area of the sliced cube is 6 sq units.

Q. 61 **Ratio of area of a circle to the area of a square whose side equals radius of circle, is 1 : π.**

Sol. ***False***

Given, side of a square equals radius of a circle.

Then, area of the square $= r^2$

and area of the circle $= \pi r^2$

where r is a radius of the circle.

Now, the ratio of area of the circle to area of the square $= \pi r^2 : r^2 = \pi : 1.$

Q. 62 **The area of a rectangular field is 48 m² and one of its sides is 6m. How long will a lady take to cross the field diagonally at the rate of 20 m/min?**

Sol. Given, the area of a rectangular field is 48 m^2 and one side of the rectangle is $= 6$ m.

$\therefore$ Area of a rectangle = Length × Breadth

$\Rightarrow \quad 48 = 6 \times \text{Breadth}$

$\Rightarrow \quad \text{Breadth} = 8 \text{ m}$

In ΔACD, $\angle D = 90°$ [$\because$ in a rectangle, all angles are of 90°]

So, it is a right-angled triangle.

By using Pythagoras theorem, we have

$$(AC)^2 = (AD)^2 + (DC)^2$$

$$\Rightarrow \quad (AC)^2 = (6)^2 + (8)^2$$

$$\Rightarrow \quad (AC)^2 = 36 + 64$$

$$\Rightarrow \quad AC = \sqrt{100}$$

$$\therefore \quad AC = 10 \text{ m}$$

Time taken by lady to cross the field diagonally at rate of 20 m/min $= \dfrac{\text{Distance}}{\text{Speed}}$

$$= \frac{10}{20} = \frac{1}{2} \text{ min or } 30 \text{ s}$$

Q. 63 **The circumference of the front wheel of a cart is 3 m long and that of the back wheel is 4 m long. What is the distance travelled by the cart, when the front wheel makes five more revolutions than the rear wheel?**

Sol. Given, circumference of front wheel = 3 m

Now, distance covered by front wheel of the cart in 1 revolution

= Circumference of front wheel

$\therefore$ Distance covered by front wheel in 5 revolutions $= 3 \times 5 = 15$ m

Hence, the distance covered by the cart is 15 m.

Q. 64 **Four horses are tethered with equal ropes at 4 corners of a square field of side 70 m, so that they just can reach one-another. Find the area left ungrazed by the horses.**

Sol. Given, side of a square = 70 m

Also, four horses are tethered with equal ropes at 4 corners of the square field. Hence, each horse can graze upto 35 m of distance along the side.

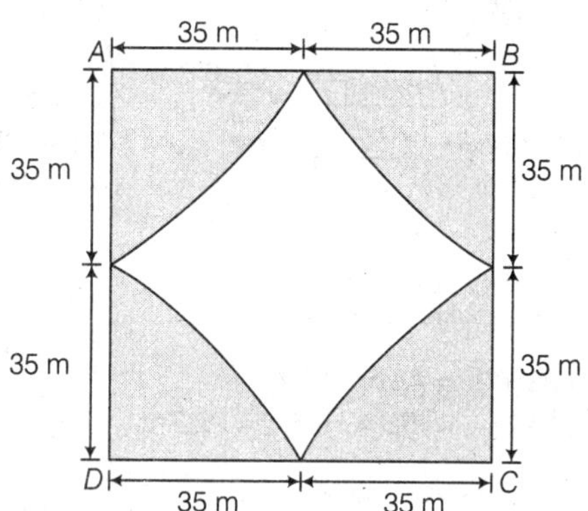

$\therefore$ Area of the square field = Side × Side

$= 70 \times 70$

$= 4900\ m^2$

The grazed area is making a complete circle by taking all the four grazed parts.

So, area of grazed part = πr^2

$= \frac{22}{7} \times 35 \times 35$ $\quad [\because r = 35\ m]$

$= 22 \times 5 \times 35$

$= 3850\ m^2$

Area left ungrazed by the horses = Area of square field – Area of grazed part

$= 4900 - 3850$

$= 1050\ m^2$

Q. 65 **The walls and ceiling of a room are to be plastered. The length, breadth and height of the room are 4.5 m, 3 m and 350 cm, respectively. Find the cost of plastering at the rate of ₹ 8 per m^2.**

Sol. Given, length of the room (l) = 4.5 m

Breadth of the room (b) = 3 m

Height of the room (h) = 350 cm = 3.5 m $\quad [\because 100\ cm = 1\ m]$

and the cost of plastering = ₹ 8 per m^2

$\therefore$ Area of the walls = $2h\,(l + b)$

$= 2 \times 3.5\,(4.5 + 3)$

$= 7 \times (7.5) = 52.5\ m^2$

Area of the ceiling = $lb = 4.5 \times 3 = 13.5\ m^2$

Area of the room = $52.5 + 13.5 = 66\ m^2$

Hence, the cost of plastering = 66×8 = ₹ 528

Q. 66 **Most of the sailboats have two sails, the jib and the mainsail. Assume that the sails are triangles. Find the total area of each sail of the sailboats to the nearest tenth.**

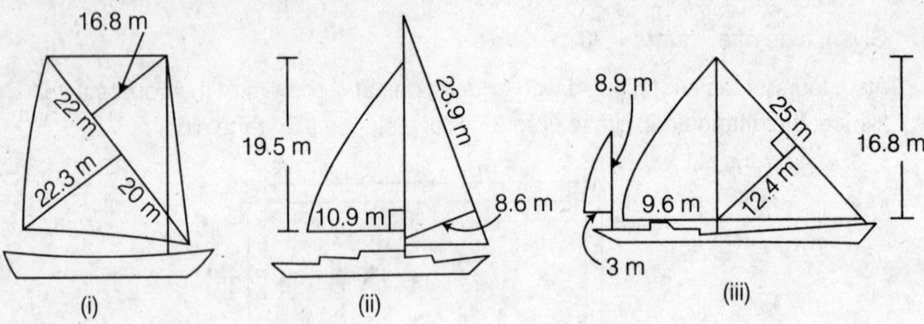

Sol. In the sailboat (i),

Area of a triangle $= \frac{1}{2} \times \text{Base} \times \text{Height}$

In ΔABC, AC = Base = 22 + 20 = 42 m

BD = Height = 22.3 m

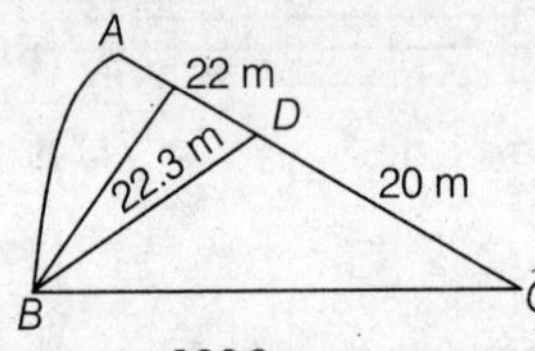

$\therefore$ Area of $\Delta ABC = \frac{1}{2} \times 42 \times 22.3 = \frac{936.6}{2} = 468.3 \text{ m}^2$

In another triangular part,

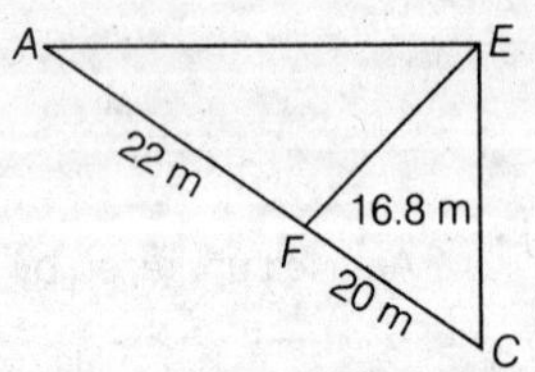

In ΔACE, EF = Height = 16.8 m

AC = Base = 22 + 20 = 42 m

$\therefore$ Area of $\Delta ACE = \frac{1}{2} \times 42 \times 16.8$

$= \frac{705.6}{2} = 352.8 \text{ m}^2$

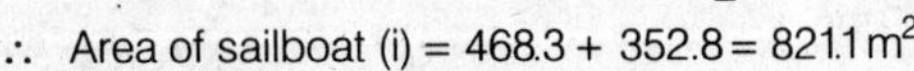

$\therefore$ Area of sailboat (i) $= 468.3 + 352.8 = 821.1 \text{ m}^2$

In sailboat (ii),

Area of a triangle $= \frac{1}{2} \times \text{Base} \times \text{Height}$

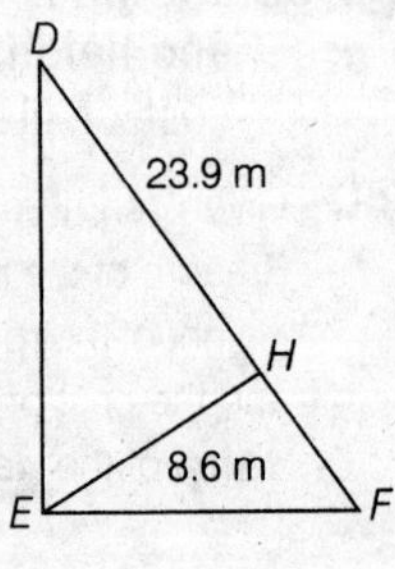

In ΔABC, $\angle B = 90°$, base (BC) = 10.9 m and height (AB) = 19.5 m

Area of $\Delta ABC = \frac{1}{2} \times 10.9 \times 19.5 = \frac{212.55}{2} = 106.275 \text{ m}^2$

In another triangular part,

Area of $\Delta DEF = \frac{1}{2} \times DF \times EH$

$= \frac{1}{2} \times 23.9 \times 8.6$

$= \frac{205.54}{2} = 102.77 \text{ m}^2$

Area of sailboat (ii) $= 106.275 + 102.77 = 209.045 \text{ m}^2$

In sailboat (iii),

Area of triangle $= \frac{1}{2} \times \text{Base} \times \text{Height}$

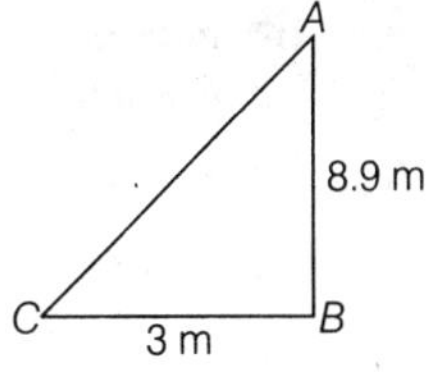

In ΔABC, $AB = 8.9$ m and $BC = 3$ m.

Area of $\Delta ABC = \frac{1}{2} \times BC \times AB$

$$= \frac{1}{2} \times 8.9 \times 3$$

$$= \frac{26.7}{2} = 13.35 \text{ m}^2$$

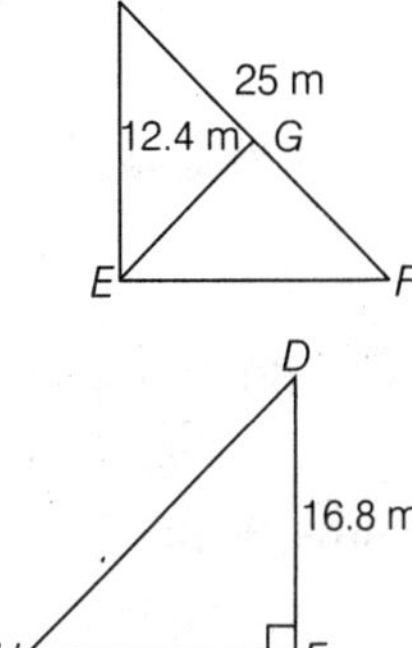

In another triangular part,

Area of $\Delta DEF = \frac{1}{2} \times DF \times EG$

$$= \frac{1}{2} \times 25 \times 12.4$$

$$= 155 \text{ m}^2$$

In another triangular part,

Area of $\Delta DEH = \frac{1}{2} \times DE \times EH$

$$= \frac{1}{2} \times 9.6 \times 16.8$$

$$= 80.64 \text{ m}^2$$

$\therefore$ Area of sailboat (iii) $= 155 + 80.64$

$$= 235.64 \text{ m}^2$$

Q. 67 The area of a trapezium with equal non-parallel sides is 168 m^2. If the lengths of the parallel sides are 36 m and 20 m, then find the length of the non-parallel sides.

Sol. Length of the parallel sides are 36 m and 20 m.

Area of a trapezium $= 168 \text{ m}^2$

$\because$ Area of a trapezium $= \frac{1}{2} \times$ [Sum of parallel sides] $\times$ Height

$\therefore \quad 168 = \frac{1}{2} \times [36 + 20] \times \text{Height}$

$\Rightarrow \quad \text{Height} = \frac{168 \times 2}{56} = \frac{336}{56} = 6 \text{ m}$

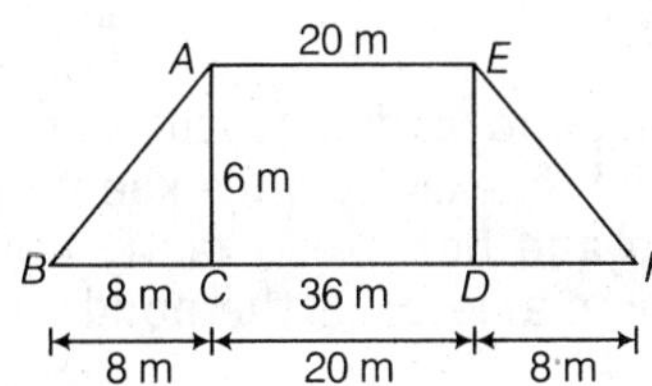

In ΔACB, using Pythagoras theorem,

$$(AB)^2 = (BC)^2 + (AC)^2$$

$\Rightarrow \quad (AB)^2 = (8)^2 + (6)^2$

$\Rightarrow \quad (AB)^2 = 64 + 36$

$\Rightarrow \quad (AB)^2 = 100$

$\therefore \quad AB = \sqrt{100} = 10 \text{ m}$

Hence, length of the non-parallel side is 10 m.

Q. 68 Mukesh walks around a circular track of radius 14 m with a speed of 4 km/h. If he takes 20 rounds of the track, for how long does he walk?

Sol. Radius of the circular track = 14 m

Circumference of the circular track $= 2\pi r = 2 \times \frac{22}{7} \times 14$

$= 44 \times 2 = 88$ m

Total distance cover in 20 rounds $= 88 \times 20 = 1760$ m

Speed of Mukesh on the circular track = 4 km/h

$= \frac{4 \times 1000}{60} = \frac{2 \times 100}{3} = \frac{200}{3}$ m/min

Time taken by Mukesh $= \frac{1760}{200/3} = \frac{1760 \times 3}{200} = \frac{176 \times 3}{20} = 26.4$ min

26.4 min = 26 min and 24 s

Q. 69 The areas of two circles are in the ratio 49 : 64. Find the ratio of their circumferences.

Sol. Given, the area of two circles are in the ratio 49 : 64.

Area of a circle $= \pi r^2$

Let area of the first circle $= \pi r_1^2$

and area of the second circle $= \pi r_2^2$

According to the question, $\frac{49}{64} = \frac{\pi r_1^2}{\pi r_2^2}$

$\Rightarrow \frac{49}{64} = \frac{r_1^2}{r_2^2}$

$\Rightarrow \frac{(7)^2}{(8)^2} = \frac{r_1^2}{r_2^2} \Rightarrow \left(\frac{7}{8}\right)^2 = \left(\frac{r_1}{r_2}\right)^2$

$\therefore$ $r_1 = 7$ and $r_2 = 8$

The ratio of circumferences of these two circles

$= \frac{2\pi r_1}{2\pi r_2} = \frac{r_1}{r_2} = \frac{7}{8}$ [$\because$ circumference of circle $= 2\pi r$]

Hence, required ratio is 7 : 8.

Q. 70 There is a circular pond and a footpath runs along its boundary. A person walks around it, exactly once keeping close to the edge. If his step is 66 cm long and he takes exactly 400 steps to go around the pond, then find the diameter of the pond.

Sol. Let the radius of the pond be r. Then, diameter of the pond, $d = 2 \times r$

[$\because$ diameter = 2 × radius]

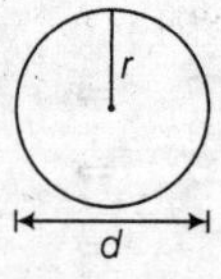

Since, a person takes exactly 400 steps with 66 cm long each step to go round the pond.

Hence, the circumference of the pond $= 66 \times 400$

$= 26400$ cm

$= \frac{26400}{100}$ m $= 264$ m [$\because$ 100 cm = 1 m]

We know that, circumference of a circle is $2\pi r$.

$\therefore \quad 2\pi r = 264$

$\Rightarrow \quad r = \frac{264}{2} \times \frac{7}{22} = \frac{264 \times 7}{44} = 42$ m

Hence, radius of the pond = 42 m

So, diameter of the pond $= 2 \times 42 = 84$ m

Q. 71 A running track has 2 semi-circular ends of radius 63 m and two straight lengths. The perimeter of the track is 1000 m. Find each straight length.

Sol. Radius of semi-circular track = 63 m

Perimeter of 2 semi-circles = Perimeter of 1 circle

Perimeter of a circular track = $2\pi r$

Perimeter of circular track $= 2 \times \frac{22}{7} \times 63$

$= 2 \times 22 \times 9$

$= 44 \times 9$

$= 396$ m

$\because$ The perimeter of the total track is 1000 m.

$\therefore$ Length of two straight lengths track

$= 1000 - 396$

$= 604$ m

Length of 1 straight length track $= \frac{604}{2} = 302$ m

Q. 72 Find the perimeter of the given figure.

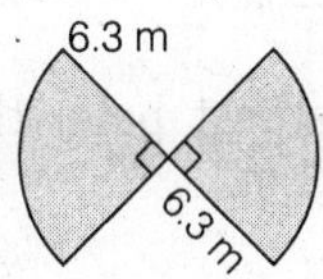

Sol. Radius of the given figure = 6.3 m

Two sections in figure form a semi-circle.

Perimeter of semi-circular figure $= \frac{2\pi r}{2} + 2r = \pi r + 2r$

$= \frac{22}{7} \times 6.3 + 2 \times 6.3$

$= 22 \times 0.9 + 2 \times 6.3$

$= 19.8 + 12.6 = 32.4$ m

Q. 73 A bicycle wheel makes 500 revolutions in moving 1 km. Find the diameter of the wheel.

Sol. A bicycle wheel makes 500 revolutions in moving 1 km.

In 1 revolution, the bicycle wheel covers

$= \frac{1}{500}$ km $= \frac{1000}{500}$ m $= 2$ m [$\because$ 1 km = 1000 m]

1 revolution distance = Circumference/Perimeter of the wheel

$\Rightarrow \quad 2\pi r = 2$

$\Rightarrow \quad 2 \times \frac{22}{7} \times r = 2$

$\Rightarrow \quad r = \frac{2 \times 7}{2 \times 22} = \frac{7}{22}$ [$\because$ circumference of a circle $= 2\pi r$]

$\therefore$ Diameter $(d) = 2r = \frac{7}{22} \times 2 = \frac{7}{11} = 0 \cdot 636$ m

Q. 74 **A boy is cycling such that the wheels of the cycle are making 140 revolutions per hour. If the diameter of the wheel is 60 cm, then calculate the speed (in km/h) with which the boy is cycling.**

Sol. The cycle makes 140 revolutions per hour.

Diameter of the wheel = 60 cm

Radius of the wheel = 30 cm

Circumference of a circle $= 2\pi r$

$= 2 \times \frac{22}{7} \times 30$

$= \frac{44 \times 30}{7}$

$= 188.57$ cm

Distance cover in 140 revolutions

$= 140 \times 188.57$

$= 26400$ cm

$\therefore$ Speed $= \frac{26400}{100000}$ km/h

$= 0.264$ km/h [$\because$ 1 km = 100000 cm]

Q. 75 **Find the length of the largest pole, that can be placed in a room of dimensions 12 m× 4 m× 3 m.**

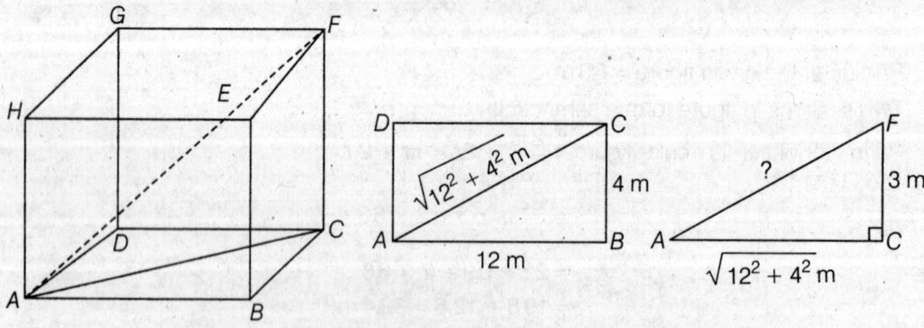

Sol. We have, ΔACF, in which $\angle C = 90°$, $CF = 3$ m and $AC = \sqrt{(12)^2 + (4)^2}$ m

The length of the largest pole = Length of diagonal of cuboid (in shape of room)

$\Rightarrow \quad (AF)^2 = (AC)^2 + (CF)^2$

$\Rightarrow \quad (AF)^2 = (12)^2 + (4)^2 + (3)^2$

$\Rightarrow \quad AF = \sqrt{144 + 16 + 9}$

$= \sqrt{169}$

$= 13$ m

Q. 76 Find the area of the following fields. All dimensions are in metres.

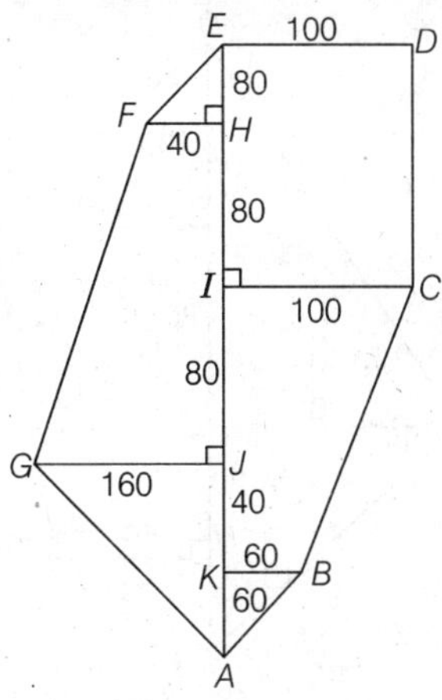

Sol. Area of the given figure

= Area of ΔEFH + Area of rectangle $EDCI$ + Area of trapezium $FHJG$ + Area of trapezium $ICBK$ + Area of ΔGJA + Area of ΔKBA

Area of $\Delta EFH = \frac{1}{2} \times \text{Base} \times \text{Height}$

$= \frac{1}{2} \times 40 \times 80 = 40 \times 40 = 1600 \text{ m}^2$

Area of rectangle $EDCI$ = Length × Breadth = $100 \times 160 = 16000 \text{ m}^2$

Area of trapezium $FHJG = \frac{1}{2} \times [\text{Sum of parallel sides}] \times \text{Height}$

$= \frac{1}{2} \times [40 + 160] \times 160$

$= \frac{200}{2} \times 160 = 100 \times 160$

$= 16000 \text{ m}^2$

Area of trapezium $ICBK = \frac{1}{2} \times [\text{Sum of parallel sides}] \times \text{Height}$

$= \frac{1}{2} \times [60 + 100] \times 120$

$= \frac{1}{2} \times 160 \times 120$

$= 80 \times 120 = 9600 \text{ m}^2$

Area of $\Delta AJG = \frac{1}{2} \times \text{Base} \times \text{Height} = \frac{1}{2} \times 160 \times 100$

$= 80 \times 100 = 8000 \text{ m}^2$

Area of $\Delta KBA = \frac{1}{2} \times \text{Base} \times \text{Height}$

$= \frac{1}{2} \times 60 \times 60 = 60 \times 30 = 1800 \text{ m}^2$

Thus, the area of the complete figure

$= 1600 + 16000 + 16000 + 9600 + 8000 + 1800$

$= 53000 \text{ m}^2$

Q. 77 Find the area of the following fields. All dimensions are in metres.

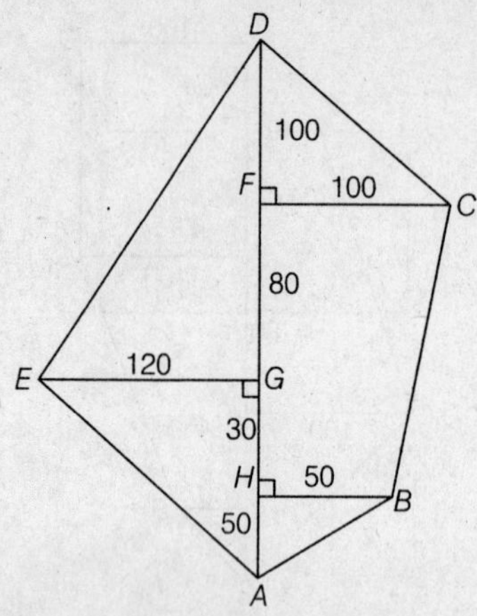

Sol. Area of the given figure = Area of ΔDCF + Area of ΔEGD + Area of trapezium $FCBH$ + Area of ΔEGA + Area of ΔAHB

$\therefore$ Area of $\Delta DCF = \frac{1}{2} \times \text{Base} \times \text{Height}$

$= \frac{1}{2} \times 100 \times 100$

$= \frac{10000}{2} = 5000 \text{ m}^2$

Area of $\Delta EGD = \frac{1}{2} \times \text{Base} \times \text{Height}$

$= \frac{1}{2} \times 120 \times 180$

$= 60 \times 180 = 10800 \text{ m}^2$

Area of trapezium $= \frac{1}{2} \times [\text{Sum of parallel sides}] \times \text{Height}$

$= \frac{1}{2} \times [100 + 50] \times 110 = \frac{1}{2} \times 150 \times 110$

$= 75 \times 110 = 8250 \text{ m}^2$

Area of $\Delta EGA = \frac{1}{2} \times \text{Base} \times \text{Height}$

$= \frac{1}{2} \times 120 \times 80$

$= 60 \times 80 = 4800 \text{ m}^2$

Area of $\Delta AHB = \frac{1}{2} \times \text{Base} \times \text{Height}$

$= \frac{1}{2} \times 50 \times 50$

$= 25 \times 50$

$= 1250 \text{ m}^2$

Thus, the area of the complete figure $= 5000 + 10800 + 8250 + 4800 + 1250$

$= 30100 \text{ m}^2$

In questions from 78 to 85, find the area of the shaded portion in the following figures.

Q. 78

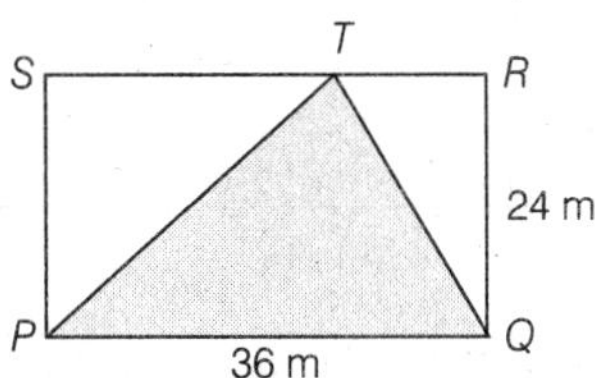

Sol. Area of the shaded portion = Area of ΔPTQ

$\because$ Area of a triangle $= \frac{1}{2} \times \text{Base} \times \text{Height}$

So, in ΔPTQ, RQ = Height

$\therefore$ Area of $\Delta PTQ = \frac{1}{2} \times 36 \times 24$

$= 18 \times 24 = 432 \text{ m}^2$

Q. 79

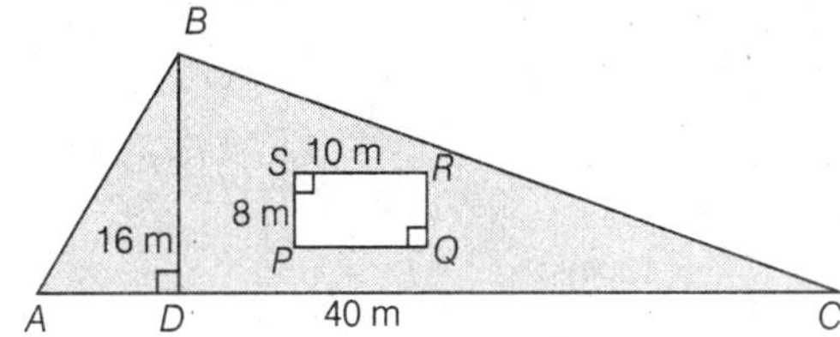

Sol. Area of shaded region = Area of ΔABC – Area of rectangle $PQRS$

$\therefore$ Area of a triangle $= \frac{1}{2} \times \text{Base} \times \text{Height}$

$\therefore$ Area of $\Delta ABC = \frac{1}{2} \times AC \times BD = \frac{1}{2} \times 40 \times 16 \text{ m}^2$

$= 20 \times 16 = 320 \text{ m}^2$

$\because$ Area of a rectangle = Length $\times$ Breadth

$\therefore$ Area of the rectangle $= 10 \times 8 = 80 \text{ m}^2$

Area of shaded region $= 320 - 80 = 240 \text{ m}^2$

Q. 80

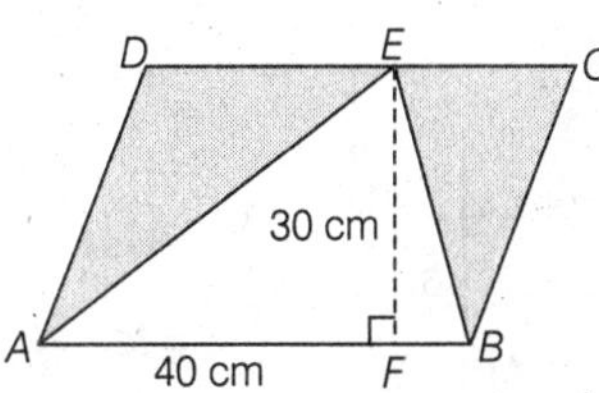

Sol. Area of shaded region = Area of the parallelogram $ABCD$ – Area of ΔABE

$\because$ Area of a parallelogram = Side $\times$ Height

$\therefore$ Area of a parallelogram $ABCD = 40 \times 30 = 1200 \text{ cm}^2$

Area of $\Delta AEB = \frac{1}{2} \times AB \times EF = \frac{1}{2} \times 40 \times 30 = 600 \text{ cm}^2$

$\therefore$ Area of shaded region $= 1200 - 600 = 600 \text{ cm}^2$

Q. 81

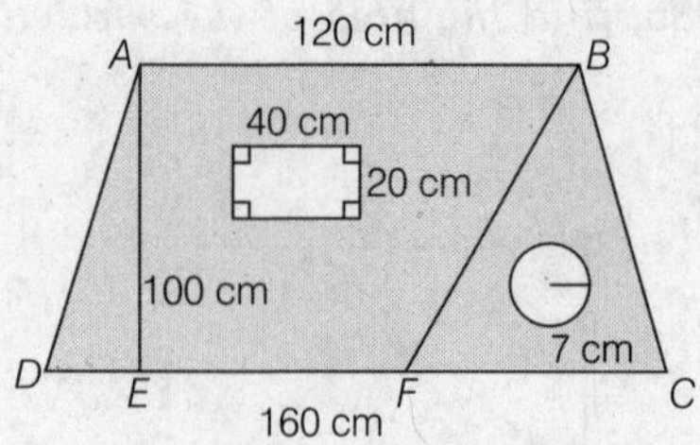

Sol. Area of shaded portion = Area of trapezium – Area of rectangle – Area of circle

Area of trapezium $= \frac{1}{2} \times$ [Sum of parallel sides] $\times$ Height

$= \frac{1}{2} \times (120 + 160) \times 100$

$= \frac{1}{2} \times 280 \times 100$

$= \frac{28000}{2} = 14000 \text{ cm}^2$

Area of rectangle = Length $\times$ Breadth $= 40 \times 20 = 800 \text{ cm}^2$

Area of circle $= \pi r^2 = \frac{22}{7} \times 7 \times 7$

$= 154 \text{ cm}^2$

$\therefore$ Area of shaded portion $= 14000 - 800 - 154$

$= 13046 \text{ cm}^2$

Q. 82

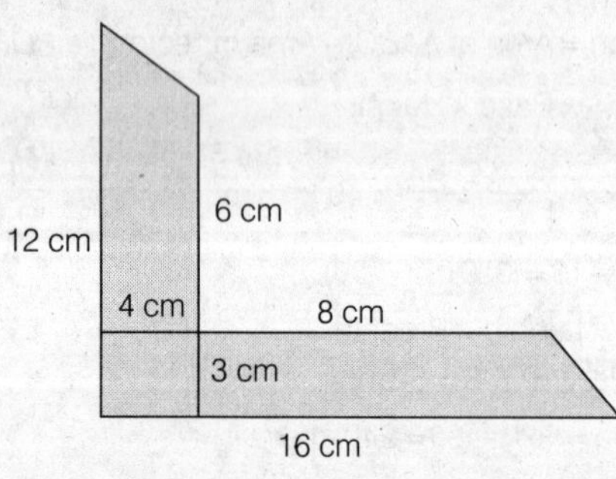

Sol.

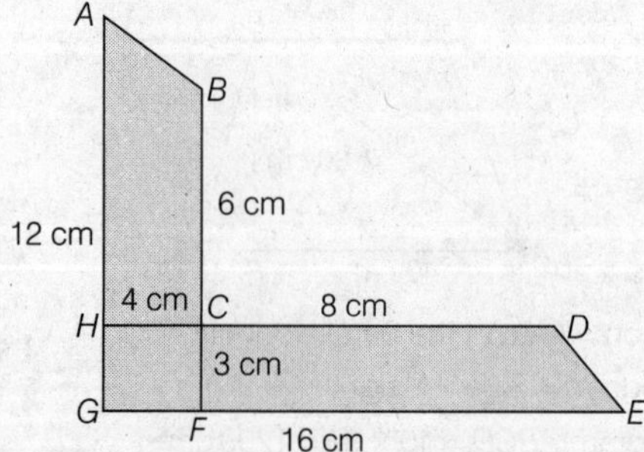

Area of shaded portion = Area of trapezium *ABCH* + Area of trapezium *CDEF*

Area of trapezium $= \frac{1}{2} \times$ (Sum of parallel sides) $\times$ (Height)

$\therefore$ Area of trapezium $ABCH$

$$= \frac{1}{2} \times (12 + 6) \times 4 = \frac{1}{2} \times 18 \times 4 = 18 \times 2 = 36 \text{ cm}^2$$

$\therefore$ Area of trapezium $CDEF = \frac{1}{2} \times (8 + 16) \times 3$

$$= \frac{24 \times 3}{2} = 36 \text{ cm}^2$$

Area of shaded portion $= 36 + 36 = 72 \text{ cm}^2$

Q. 83

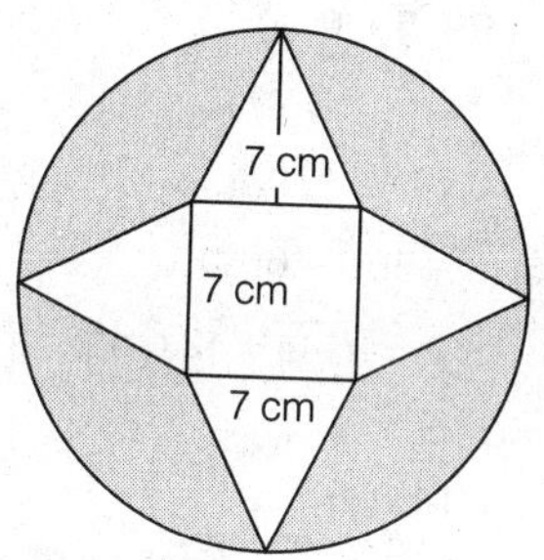

Sol. Area of shaded region = Area of the circle – Area of four triangles – Area of a square

Area of four triangles $= 4 \times \frac{1}{2} \times$ Base $\times$ Height

$$= 4 \times \frac{1}{2} \times 7 \times 7 = \frac{4 \times 49}{2} = 2 \times 49 = 98 \text{ cm}^2$$

Area of a square $= (\text{Side})^2 = (7)^2 = 49 \text{ cm}^2$

Area of the circle $= \pi r^2 = \frac{22}{7} \times \frac{21}{2} \times \frac{21}{2} = \frac{11 \times 3 \times 21}{2} = \frac{693}{2}$

$$= 346.5 \text{ cm}^2$$

Area of shaded region $= (346.5 - 98 - 49)$

$$= 199.5 \text{ cm}^2$$

Q. 84

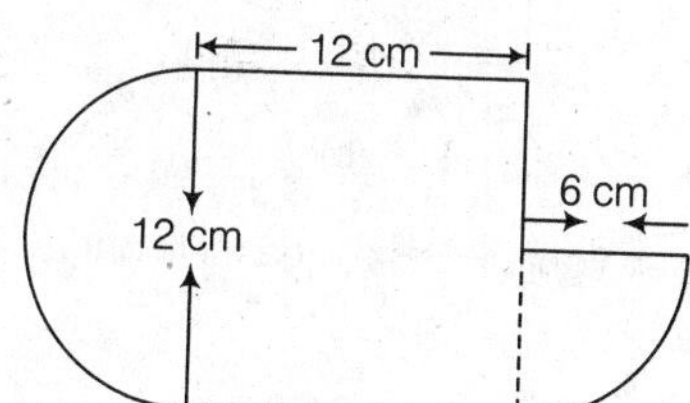

Sol. Area of the given figure = Area of section with 6 cm + Area of square with side measure 12 cm + Area of semi-circle with radius 6 cm

$$= \frac{22 \times 6 \times 6}{7 \times 4} + (12)^2 + \frac{22 \times 6 \times 6}{7 \times 2} = \frac{11 \times 18}{7} + 144 + \frac{11 \times 36}{7}$$

$$= \frac{198}{7} + 144 + \frac{396}{7}$$

$$= \frac{198 + 1008 + 396}{7} = \frac{1602}{7} = 228.85 \text{ cm}^2$$

Hence, area of the given figure is 225.85 cm^2.

Q. 85

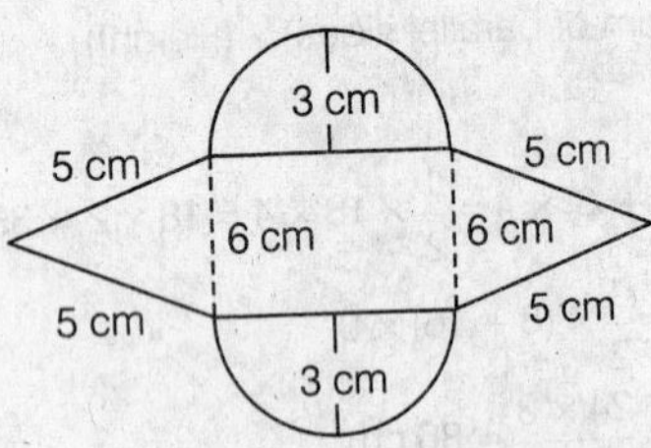

Sol. Area of the given figure = Area of two semi-circles + Area of two triangles + Area of a square

$\therefore$ Area of triangle $= \sqrt{s(s-a)(s-b)(s-c)}$ $[\because a = 5\text{ cm}, b = 5\text{ cm and } c = 6\text{ cm, given}]$

where, $s = \frac{a+b+c}{2} = \frac{5+5+6}{2}$

$= \frac{16}{2} = 8\text{ cm}$

$\therefore$ Area of a triangle $= \sqrt{8(8-5)(8-5)(8-6)}$

$= \sqrt{8 \times 3 \times 3 \times 2} = \sqrt{144} = 12\text{ cm}^2$

$\therefore$ Area of 2 triangles $= 2 \times 12 = 24\text{ cm}^2$

$\therefore$ Area of 2 semi-circles = Area of 1 circle

Area of a circle $= \pi r^2 = \frac{22}{7} \times 3 \times 3 = \frac{9 \times 22}{7} = \frac{198}{7} = 28.28\text{ cm}^2$

$\therefore$ Area of a square $= 6 \times 6 = 36\text{ cm}^2$

Area of the given figure $= (24 + 28.28 + 36) = 88.28\text{ cm}^2$

Q. 86 Find the volume of each of the given figure, if Volume = Base area × Height.

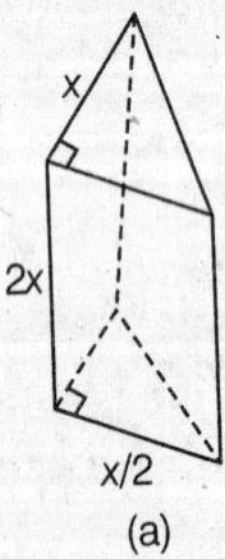

(a)

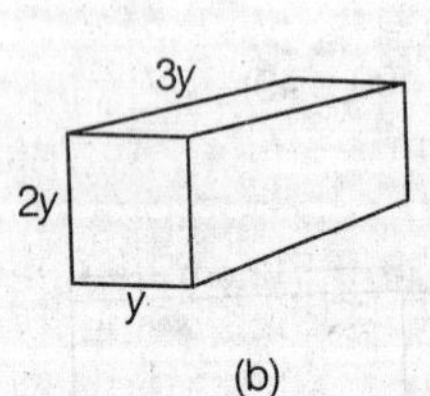

(b)

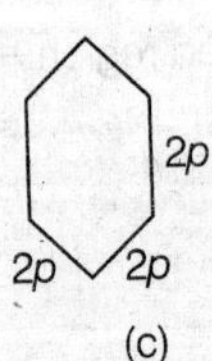

(c)

Sol. $\because$ Volume of each of the given figure = Base area × Height

In Fig. (a), base is rectangle.

So, area of rectangle $= 2x \times \frac{x}{2} = x^2$

$\therefore$ Height $= \frac{x}{2}$

$\therefore$ Volume of the figure $= x^2 \times \frac{x}{2} = \frac{x^3}{2}$

In Fig. (b), base is rectangle.

So, area of rectangle $= y \times 3y = 3y^2$

Height $= 2y$

$\therefore$ Volume of the figure $= 3y^2 \times 2y = 6y^3$

In Fig. (c), base is rectangle.

So, area of rectangle $= 2p \times 2p = 4p^2$

Height $= 2p$

Volume of the figure $= 4p^2 \times 2p = 8p^3$

Q. 87 A cube of side 5 cm is cut into as many 1 cm cubes as possible. What is the ratio of the surface areas of the original cube to that of the sum of the surface areas of the smaller cubes?

Sol. Surface area of a cube $= 6a^2$, where a is side of a cube.

$\therefore$ Side of cube $= 5$ cm

$\therefore$ Surface area of the cube $= 6 \times (5)^2 = 6 \times 25$

$= 150 \text{ cm}^2$

Now, surface area of the cube with side 1 cm $= 6 \times (1)^2 = 6 \text{ cm}^2$

$\therefore$ Surface area of 5 cubes with side 1 cm $= 5 \times 6 = 30 \text{ cm}^2$

Ratio of the surface area of the original cube to that of the sum of the surface area of the smaller cubes

$$= \frac{30}{150} = \frac{3}{15} = 1:5$$

Q. 88 A square sheet of paper is converted into a cylinder by rolling it along its side. What is the ratio of the base radius to the side of the square?

Sol. Let the sides of a square paper be a.

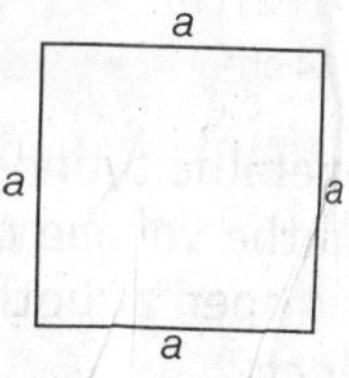

A cylinder is formed by rolling the paper along its side.

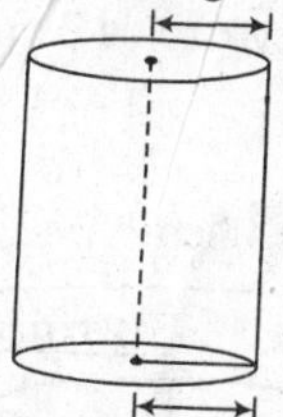

$\therefore$ Base of the cylinder is circle, so the circumference of the circle is equal to the length of each side of the square sheet.

$$\Rightarrow \quad 2\pi r = a \quad [\because \text{circumference of circle} = 2\pi r]$$

$$\therefore \quad r = \frac{a}{2\pi}$$

$\therefore$ Ratio $= \frac{a}{2\pi} : a = \frac{1}{2\pi} : 1 = 1 : 2\pi$

Hence, the ratio of the base radius to the side of the square is $1 : 2\pi$.

Q. 89 **How many cubic metres of Earth must be dug to construct a well 7 m deep and of diameter 2.8 m?**

Sol. A well is in the form of cylinderical form.

Earth must be dug to construct a well 7 m deep and diameter 2.8 m is equal to the volume of a cylinder with 7 m height and diameter 2.8 m.

Volume of a cylinder = $\pi r^2 h$

$$= \frac{22}{7} \times \frac{2.8}{2} \times \frac{2.8}{2} \times 7 = 11 \times 2.8 \times 1.4 = 43.12 \text{ m}^3$$

Q. 90 **The radius and height of a cylinder are in the ratio 3 : 2 and its volume is 19404 cm^3. Find its radius and height.**

Sol. The radius and height of a cylinder are in the ratio 3 : 2.

Let the radius be $3x$ and height be $2x$. Then,

Volume of cylinder = 19404 cm^3 [given]

$\because$ Volume of a cylinder = $\pi r^2 h$

$$\therefore \quad 19404 = \frac{22}{7} \times (3x)^2 \times (2x)$$

$$\Rightarrow \quad 19404 = \frac{22}{7} \times 9x^2 \times 2x = \frac{22 \times 18x^3}{7}$$

$$\Rightarrow \quad 19404 = \frac{396x^3}{7}$$

$$\Rightarrow \quad x^3 = 343 \Rightarrow x^3 = (7)^3$$

$$\therefore \quad x = 7 \text{ cm}$$

Hence, radius of the cylinder = $3 \times 7 = 21$ cm

and height of the cylinder = $2 \times 7 = 14$ cm

Q. 91 **The thickness of a hollow metallic cylinder is 2 cm. It is 70 cm long with outer radius of 14 cm. Find the volume of the metal used in making the cylinder, assuming that it is open at both the ends. Also, find its weight if the metal weighs 8 g per cm^3.**

Sol. The thickness of the hollow metallic cylinder is 2 cm.

Height of the cylinder = 70 cm

Outer radius of the cylinder = 14 cm

Inner radius of the cylinder = 14 − 2 = 12 cm

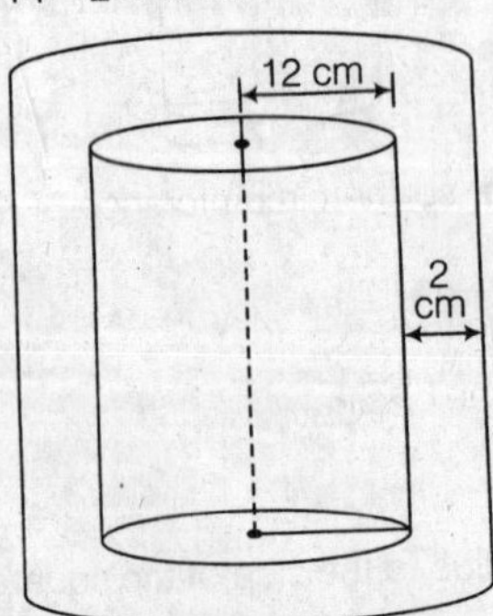

Volume of the metal used in making the cylinder = Volume of the hollow cylinder

$$= \pi(R^2 - r^2) \times h$$

$$= \frac{22}{7} \times [(14)^2 - (12)^2] \times 70$$
$$= 22 \times [196 - 144] \times 10$$
$$= 22 \times 52 \times 10 = 11440 \text{ cm}^3$$

Weight of 11440 cm^3, if metal is 8 g per cm^3

$$= 11440 \times 8 = 91520 \text{ g}$$

Q. 92 Radius of a cylinder is r and the height is h. Find the change in the volume if the

(i) height is doubled.

(ii) height is doubled and the radius is halved.

(iii) height remains same and the radius is halved.

Sol. $\because$ Volume of a cylinder $= \pi r^2 h$

where, h is height and r is radius of base of the cylinder.

(i) If height is double i.e. $h = 2 \times h = 2h$

Then, its volume $= \pi r^2 \times 2h$

$$= 2\pi r^2 h$$

Hence, volume became double of original volume.

(ii) If height is doubled and the radius is halved,

i.e. $h = 2h$ and $r = \frac{r}{2}$

$$\therefore \text{Volume} = \pi \times \left(\frac{r}{2}\right) \times \left(\frac{r}{2}\right) \times 2h$$
$$= \pi \times \frac{r^2}{4} \times 2h = \frac{\pi r^2 h}{2}$$

Hence, volume became half of the original volume.

(iii) If height remains same and radius is halved,

i.e. $h = h$ and $r = \frac{r}{2}$

$$\therefore \text{Volume} = \pi \times \frac{r}{2} \times \frac{r}{2} \times h = \pi \times \frac{r^2}{4} \times h$$

Hence, volume became $\frac{1}{4}$th of the original volume.

Q. 93 If the length of each edge of a cube is tripled, what will be the change in its volume?

Sol. Let the edge of a cube be a.

If edge of the cube became tripled i.e. $a = 3 \times a = 3a$

$\because$ Volume of the cube $= a^3$

$\therefore$ Volume of the cube with edge tripled $= (3a)^3 = 27a^3$

Hence, volume is 27 times of the original volume.

Q. 94 **A carpenter makes a box which has a volume of 13400 cm^3. The base has an area of 670 cm^2. What is the height of the box?**

Sol. Let the height of the box be h.

Volume of the box = 13400 cm^2

Area of base of the box = 670 cm^2

$\because$ Volume of a box = Area of base × Height

$\therefore \quad 13400 = 670 \times h$

$\Rightarrow \quad h = \dfrac{13400}{670}$

$\Rightarrow \quad h = \dfrac{1340}{67} = 20$ cm

Hence, the height of the box is 20 cm.

Q. 95 **A cuboidal tin box opened at the top has dimensions 20 cm × 16 cm × 14 cm. What is the total area of metal sheet required to make 10 such boxes?**

Sol. Dimensions of cuboidal tin box are 20 cm × 16 cm × 14 cm.

$\therefore$ Area of metal sheet for 1 box = Surface area of cuboid

$= 2(lb + bh + hl)$

$= 2(20 \times 16 + 16 \times 14 + 14 \times 20)$

$= 2(320 + 224 + 280)$

$= 2(824)$

$= 1648 \text{ cm}^2$

$\therefore$ Area of metal sheet required to make 10 such boxes = $10 \times 1648 = 16480 \text{ cm}^2$

Q. 96 **Find the capacity of water tank, in litres, whose dimensions are 4.2 m, 3 m and 1.8 m?**

Sol. Dimensions of the water tank are 4.2 m, 3 m and 1.8 m.

Capacity of water tank = Length × Breadth × Height

$= 4 \cdot 2 \times 3 \times 1.8$

$= 22 \cdot 68 \text{ m}^3$

$\therefore$ Capacity of the water tank in litres = $22.68 \times 1000 = 22680$ L [$\because 1 \text{ m}^3 = 1000$ L]

Q. 97 **How many cubes each of side 0.5 cm are required to build a cube of volume 8 cm^3?**

Sol. Volume of a cube = (Side)^3

$\because$ Side of cube = 0.5 cm

$\therefore$ Volume of the cube = $(0.5)^3 = 0.125 \text{ cm}^3$

The number of cubes required to make volume of 8 cm^3 cube

$= \dfrac{8}{0.125}$

$= \dfrac{8000}{125} = 64$ cubes

Q. 98 A wooden box (including the lid) has external dimensions $40 \text{ cm} \times 34 \text{ cm} \times 30 \text{ cm}$. If the wood is 1 cm thick, how many cm^3 of wood is used in it?

Sol. External dimensions of wooden box are $40 \text{ cm} \times 34 \text{ cm} \times 30 \text{ cm}$.

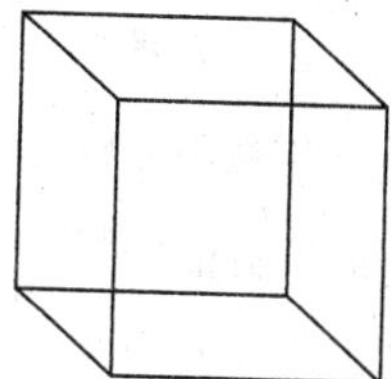

Since, the wood is 1 cm thick, it means the internal dimensions will be $(40-2) \text{ cm} \times (34-2) \text{ cm} \times (30-2) \text{ cm} = 38 \text{ cm} \times 32 \text{ cm} \times 28 \text{ cm}$

$\therefore$ Wood used for the box

= Volume of the wooden box with external dimensions

− Volume of the wooden box with internal dimensions

$= 40 \times 34 \times 30 - 38 \times 32 \times 28$

$= 40800 - 34048$

$= 6752 \text{ cm}^3$

Q. 99 A river 2 m deep and 45 m wide is flowing at the rate of 3 km per hour. Find the amount of water in cubic metres that runs into the sea per minute.

Sol. Depth of the river = 2 m

Width of the river = 45 m

Flowing rate of the water = 3 km/h

$$= 3 \times \frac{1000}{60} = \frac{3000}{60} \qquad [\because 1 \text{ km} = 1000 \text{ m and } 1 \text{ h} = 60 \text{ min}]$$

$$= \frac{300}{6} = 50 \text{ m/min}$$

The amount of water into sea per minute

= Depth × Width × Length of water of 1 min

$= 2 \times 45 \times 50$

$= 4500 \text{ m}^3/\text{min}$

Q. 100 Find the area to be painted in the following block with a cylindrical hole. Given that, length is 15cm, width 12cm, height 20cm and radius of the hole 2.8 cm.

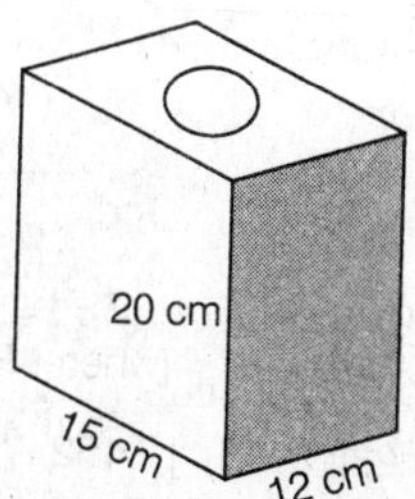

Sol. Lenght of the given figure = 15 cm

Width of the given figure = 12 cm

Height of the given figure = 20 cm

Radius of the hole = 2.8 cm

$\therefore$ The area to be painted = Surface area of the figure − 2 × Area of the circular hole

$$= 2\,(lb + bh + lh) - 2\pi r^2$$

$$= 2\,(15 \times 12 + 12 \times 20 + 15 \times 20) - 2 \times \frac{22}{7} \times 2.8 \times 2.8$$

$$= 2(180 + 240 + 300) - \frac{44 \times 2.8 \times 2.8}{7}$$

$$= 2 \times 720 - 49.28$$

$$= 1440 - 49.28$$

$$= 1390.72 \text{ cm}^2$$

Q. 101 A truck carrying 7.8 m^3 concrete arrives at a job site. A platform of width 5 m and height 2 m is being constructed at the site. Find the length of the platform, constructed from the amount of concrete on the truck?

Sol. Total volume of concrete = 7.8 m^3

Width of the platform= 5 m

Height of the platform = 2 m

Let the length of the platform = x m

According to the question,

Volume of concrete = Volume used to make platform

$\therefore \quad 7.8 = 5 \times 2 \times x$

$\Rightarrow \quad 7.8 = 10x$ [$\because$ volume = length × breadth × height]

$\Rightarrow \quad 10x = 7.8$

$\Rightarrow \quad x = 0.78$ m

Hence, the length of the platform is 0.78 m.

Q. 102 A hollow garden roller of 42 cm diameter and length 152 cm is made of cast iron 2 cm thick. Find the volume of iron used in the roller.

Sol. Diameter of the hollow garden roller = 42 cm

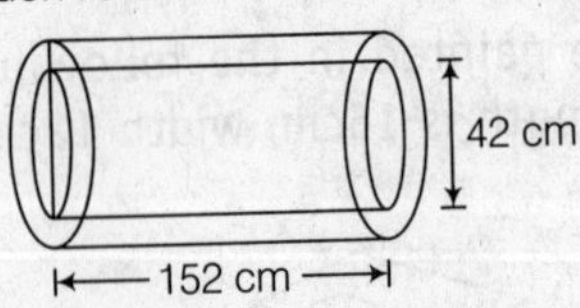

$\therefore$ Inner radius $= \frac{42}{2} = 21$ cm $\left[\because \text{radius} = \frac{\text{diameter}}{2}\right]$

$\because$ Thickness of cast iron = 2 cm

$\therefore$ Outer radius = 21 + 2 = 23 cm

Volume of hollow cylinder = $\pi\,(R^2 - r^2) \times h$ [where, R is outer-radius and r is inner-radius]

$$= \frac{22}{7} \times [(23)^2 - (21)^2] \times 152$$

$$= \frac{22}{7} \times (529 - 441) \times 152$$

$$= \frac{22}{7} \times 88 \times 152 = \frac{22 \times 88 \times 152}{7} = \frac{294272}{7}$$

$$= 42038.85 \text{ cm}^3$$

Q. 103 Three cubes each of side 10 cm are joined end to end. Find the surface area of the resultant figure.

Sol. If three cubes each of side 10 cm are joined, then a cuboid will be formed of dimensions 30 cm × 10 cm × 10 cm.

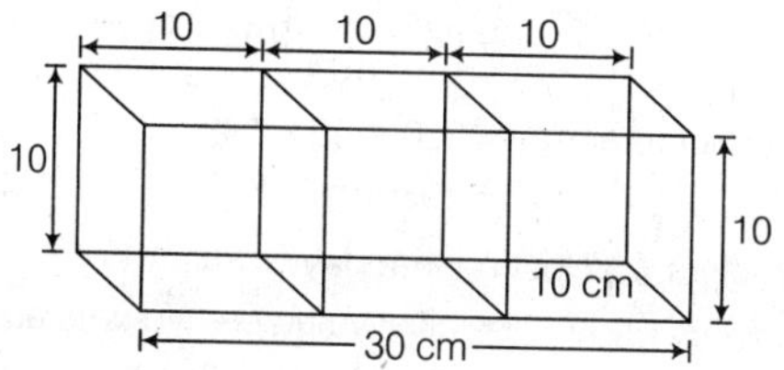

$\therefore$ Surface area of the cuboid $= 2[lb + bh + hl]$

$$= 2[30 \times 10 + 10 \times 10 + 30 \times 10]$$

$$= 2[300 + 100 + 300] = 2[700] = 1400 \text{ cm}^2$$

Q. 104 Below are the drawings of cross sections of two different pipes used to fill swimming pools. Figure A is a combination of 2 pipes each having a radius of 8 cm. Figure B is a pipe having a radius of 15 cm. If the force of the flow of water coming out of the pipes is the same in both the cases, which will fill the swimming pool faster?

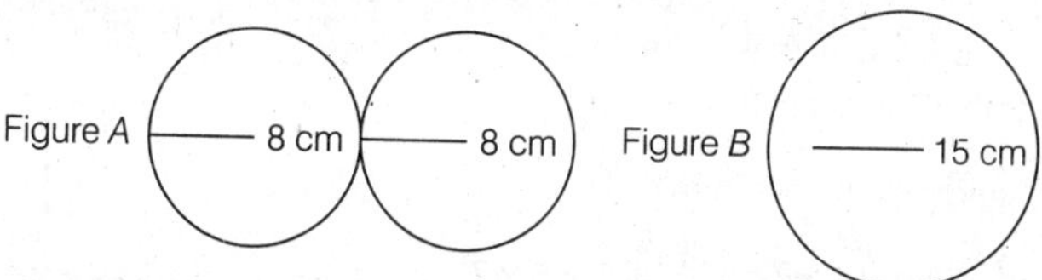

Sol. In figure A, 2 pipes each having a radius of 8 cm.

$\because$ Area of a circle $= \pi r^2$

$\therefore$ Area of one pipe $= \frac{22}{7} \times 8 \times 8$

$$= \frac{22 \times 8 \times 8}{7} = \frac{22 \times 64}{7} \text{ cm}^2$$

Area of 2 pipes $= \frac{2 \times 1408}{7} = \frac{2816}{7} \text{ cm}^2 = 402.28 \text{ cm}^2$

In figure B, a pipe having radius of 15 cm.

$\therefore$ Area of the pipe $= \pi r^2$

$$= \frac{22}{7} \times 15 \times 15 = \frac{22}{7} \times 225$$

$$= \frac{4950}{7} = 707.14 \text{ cm}^2$$

Clearly, the surface area of pipe B is greater. So, pipe B fill the swimming pool faster.

Q. 105 **A swimming pool is 200 m × 50 m and has an average depth of 2 m. By the end of a summer day, the water level drops by 2 cm. How many cubic metres of water is lost on the day?**

Sol. Dimensions of swimming pool are 200 m × 50 m.

Average depth of the swimming pool = 2 m

At the end of summer day the water level drops by 2 cm.

∴ Volume of water in swimming pool = Length × Breadth × Depth

$= 200 \times 50 \times 2 = 20000 \text{ m}^3$

If water level drops by 2 cm, it means new level of water

$= \left(2 - \frac{2}{100}\right) \text{m} = 1.98 \text{ m}$ $\left[\because 1 \text{ cm} = \frac{1}{100} \text{m}\right]$

Volume of water after summer day $= 200 \times 50 \times 1.98$

$= 19800 \text{ m}^3$

So, water in cubic metres was lost on that day

= Initial volume − Volume after summer day

$= 20000 - 19800 = 200 \text{ m}^3$

Q. 106 **A housing society consisting of 5500 peoples needs 100 L of water per person per day. The cylindrical supply tank is 7 m high and has a diameter 10 m. For how many days will the water in the tank last for the society?**

Sol. Total number of peoples = 5500

Water required per person per day = 100 L

Total requirement of water by 5500 peoples

$= 100 \times 5500 = 550000 \text{ L}$

Height of the cylindrical tank = 7m

Diameter of the cylindrical tank = 10 m

∴ Radius = 5 m $\left[\because \frac{\text{diameter}}{2} = \text{radius}\right]$

∴ Volume of cylinder $= \pi r^2 h = \frac{22}{7} \times 5 \times 5 \times 7$

$= 22 \times 25 = 550 \text{ m}^3$

$= 550 \times 1000 = 550000 \text{ L}$ $[\because 1 \text{ m}^3 = 1000 \text{ L}]$

Hence, for 1 day the water in the tank lost for the society and in one day society needs 550000 L of water.

Q. 107 **Metallic discs of radius 0.75 cm and thickness 0.2 cm are melted to obtain 508.68 cm³ of metal. Find the number of disc melted. (Use π = 3.14)**

Sol. Radius of metallic disc = 0.75 cm

Thickness of disc = 0.2 cm

Total volume of material which will be used in forming/melting of disc = 508.68 cm³

∴ Material required for one disc = Volume of cylinder

$= \pi r^2 h = \frac{22}{7} \times 0.75 \times 0.75 \times 0.2$ [$\because$ shape of a disc is a cylinder]

$= 3.14 \times 0.75 \times 0.75 \times 0.2$

$= 0.35325 \text{ cm}^3$

Number of discs can be melted $= \frac{\text{Total volume of metal obtained after melting}}{\text{Volume of one disc}}$

$= \frac{508.68}{0.35325} = 1440$ discs

Q. 108 The ratio of the radius and height of a cylinder is 2 : 3. If its volume is 12936 cm^3, find the the total surface area of the cylinder.

Sol. The ratio of the radius and height of a cylinder = 2 : 3

Let the radius of the cylinder be $2x$ and the height of the cylinder be $3x$.

Volume of the cylinder = 12936 cm^3

$\because$ Volume of a cylinder = $\pi r^2 h$

$\therefore \quad 12936 = \frac{22}{7} \times (2x)^2 \times 3x$

$\Rightarrow \quad 12936 = \frac{22}{7} \times 4x^2 \times 3x$

$\Rightarrow \quad 12936 = \frac{264}{7} x^3$

$\Rightarrow \quad x^3 = \frac{12936 \times 7}{264} = 49 \times 7$

$\Rightarrow \quad x^3 = 7 \times 7 \times 7 = (7)^3$

$\Rightarrow \quad x^3 = (7)^3$

$\therefore \quad x = 7$

So, radius = $2x = 2 \times 7 = 14$ cm and height = $3x = 3 \times 7 = 21$ cm

The total surface area of the cylinder = $2\pi r(r + h)$

$= 2 \times \frac{22}{7} \times 14\,(14 + 21)$

$= \frac{44 \times 14}{7} \times 35 = 44 \times 14 \times 5 = 3080 \text{ cm}^2$

Q. 109 External dimensions of a closed wooden box are in the ratio 5 : 4 : 3. If the cost of painting its outer surface at the rate of ₹ 5 per dm^2 is ₹ 11750, find the dimensions of the box.

Sol. External dimensions of a closed wooden box are in the ratio 5 : 4 : 3.

Let the external dimensions of the closed wooden box be $5x$, $4x$ and $3x$.

The cost of painting = ₹ 5 per dm^2

Total cost of painting = ₹ 11750

$\therefore$ Total surface area = $\frac{\text{Total cost of painting}}{\text{Cost of painting per dm}^2} = \frac{11750}{5}$

$= 2350 \text{ dm}^2$

Total surface area of a cuboid

$= 2(lb + bh + hl)$

$$= 2(5x \times 4x + 4x \times 3x + 3x \times 5x)$$
$$= 2(20x^2 + 12x^2 + 15x^2)$$
$$= 2 \times 47x^2 = 94x^2$$

Since, total surface area = 2350 dm^2

$\Rightarrow \quad 94x^2 = 2350$

$\Rightarrow \quad x^2 = \frac{2350}{94} = 25$

$\therefore \quad x = 5$

Hence, dimensions of the box are $5x \times 5 = 25$ dm, $4x \times 5 = 20$ dm and $3x \times 5 = 15$ dm.

Q. 110 **The capacity of a closed cylindrical vessel of height 1 m is 15.4 L. How many square metres of metal sheet would be needed to make it?**

Sol. Height of cylindrical vessel = 1 m

Capacity of the cylindrical vessel = 15.4 L

In metre cube = $\frac{15.4}{1000} = .0154$ m^3 [$\because$ 1 m^3 = 1000 L]

Volume of a cylinder = $\pi r^2 h$

$\Rightarrow \quad \frac{22}{7} \times r^2 \times 1 = 0.0154$

$\Rightarrow \quad r^2 = \frac{0.0154}{3.14} = 0.0049$

$\Rightarrow \quad r = \sqrt{0.0049} = 0.07$ m

$\therefore$ Metal of sheet required $= 2\pi rh = 2 \times \frac{22}{7} \times 0.07 \times 1 = 0.4396 = 0.44$ m^2

Q. 111 **What will happen to the volume of the cube, if its edge**

(a) tripled **(b) reduced to one-fourth?**

Sol. Let each side of the cube be a, then its volume = a^3 [$\because$ volume of a cube = (side)^3]

(a) If side became triple, then volume will be = $(3a)^3 = 27a^3$

Hence, new volume of the cube will 27 times of original volume of the cube.

(b) If side reduced to one fourth = $a \times \frac{1}{4} = \frac{a}{4}$

Now, its volume = $\left(\frac{a}{4}\right)^3 = \frac{a^3}{64}$

Hence, new volume $\frac{1}{64}$ times of original volume.

Q. 112 **A rectangular sheet of dimensions 25 cm × 7 cm is rotated about its longer side. Find the volume and the whole surface area of the solid thus generated.**

Sol. A rectangular sheet of demensions 25 cm × 7 cm is rotated about its longer side which makes a cylinder with base 25 cm /and height 7 cm.

7 cm

25 cm

Surface area of a base $= 2\pi r$

$\therefore \quad 2\pi r = 25 \text{ cm}$

$\Rightarrow \quad r = \frac{25 \times 7}{2 \times 22} = \frac{175}{44} \text{ cm}$

7 cm

2.5 cm

Volume of a cylinder $= \pi r^2 h$

$$= \frac{22}{7} \times \frac{175}{44} \times \frac{175}{44} \times 7$$

$$= \frac{175 \times 175}{2 \times 44} = \frac{30625}{88}$$

$$= 348.011 \text{ cm}^3$$

Surface area $= 2\pi rh = 2 \times \frac{22}{7} \times \frac{175}{44} \times 7$

$$= \frac{44}{44} \times 175$$

$$= 175 \text{ cm}^2$$

Q. 113 **From a pipe of inner radius 0.75 cm, water flows at the rate of 7 m per second. Find the volume in litres of water delivered by the pipe in 1 h.**

Sol. Radius of pipe $= 0.75 \text{ cm} = 0.0075 \text{ m}$ $\left[\because 1 \text{ cm} = \frac{1}{100} \text{m}\right]$

The rate of water flow $= 7$ m/s

$\therefore$ Length of water in 1 sec $= 7$ m

$\therefore$ Volume of water flow in 1 hour $= 60 \times 60 \times \frac{22}{7} \times 0.0075 \times 0.0075 \times 7$

$$= 3600 \times 3.14 \times 0.00005625 \times 7$$

$$= 11304 \times 7 \times 0.00005625$$

$$= 79128 \times 0.00005625$$

$$= 4.45095 \text{ m}^3$$

$$\simeq 4.45000 \text{ m}^3$$

$$\simeq 4450000 \text{ cm}^3 \simeq 4450 \text{ L}$$ $[\because 1000 \text{ cm}^3 = 1 \text{ L}]$

Q. 114 **Four times the area of the curved surface of a cylinder is equal to 6 times the sum of the areas of its bases. If its height is 12 cm, find its curved surface area.**

Sol. Let the radius and height of the cylinder be r and h, respectively.

Curved surface area of cylinder $= 2\pi rh$

Area of base $= \pi r^2$

Sum of areas of bases $= 2\pi r^2$

According to the question,

4 × Curved surface area = 6 × Sum of areas of bases

$$4 \times 2\pi rh = 6 \times 2\pi r^2$$

$$\Rightarrow \quad 8\pi rh = 12\pi r^2$$

$$\Rightarrow \quad 2h = 3r$$

$$\Rightarrow \quad r = \frac{2}{3}h$$

$$\therefore \quad r = \frac{2}{3} \times 12 = 8\,\text{cm} \quad [\because h = 12\text{ cm, given}]$$

$\therefore$ Curved surface area of the cylinder $= 2\pi rh$

$$= 2 \times \frac{22}{7} \times 8 \times 12 = \frac{44 \times 8 \times 12}{7}$$

$$= 603.428\,\text{cm}^2$$

Q. 115 **A cylindrical tank has a radius of 154 cm. It is filled with water to a height of 3 m. If water to a height of 4.5 m is poured into it, what will be the increase in the volume of water in kL?**

Sol. Radius of cylindrical tank = 154 cm

Initial height of water tank = 3 m = 3 × 100 cm [$\because$ 1 m = 100 cm]

$$\therefore \text{Volume of water} = \pi r^2 h = \frac{22}{7} \times 154 \times 154 \times 3 \times 100$$

$$= 22360800\,\text{cm}^3$$

If height of water 4.5 m is poured into it, then volume of water

$$= \frac{22}{7} \times 154 \times 154 \times 4.5 \times 100$$

$$= 33541200\,\text{cm}^3$$

Increase in volume = 33541200 − 22360800

$$= 11180400\,\text{cm}^3$$

$$= 11180.4\,\text{L} \quad [1000\,\text{cm}^3 = 1\,\text{L}]$$

$$= 11.1804\,\text{kL} \quad [1\,\text{kL} = 1000\,\text{L}]$$

Q. 116 **The length, breadth and height of a cuboidal reservoir is 7 m, 6 m and 15 m respectively. 8400 L of water is pumped out from the reservoir. Find the fall in the water level in the reservoir.**

Sol. Length of a cuboidal reservoir = 7 m

Breadth of a cuboidal reservoir = 6 m

Height of a cuboidal reservoir = 15 m

Capacity of cuboidal reservoir $= l \times b \times h = 7 \times 6 \times 15 = 630\,\text{m}^3$

If 8400 L of water is pumped out.

$$\text{In meter cubic} = \frac{8400}{1000} = 8.4\,\text{m}^3$$

Fall in water level $= 630 - 8.4 = 621.6\,\text{m}^3$

$$= 621.6 \times 1000 \quad [\because 1\,\text{m}^3 = 1000\,\text{L}]$$

$$= 621600\,\text{L}$$

Q. 117 How many bricks of size 22 cm × 10 cm × 7 cm are required to construct a wall 11 m long, 3.5 m high and 40 cm thick, if the cement and sand used in the construction occupy (1/10)th part of the wall?

Sol. Volume of each brick $= 22\text{ cm} \times 10\text{ cm} \times 7\text{ cm}$

$$= 1540\text{ cm}^3 = 0.00154\text{ m}^3$$

Volume of wall $= l \times b \times h = 11\text{ m} \times 3.5\text{ m} \times \frac{40}{100}\text{ m}$ $[\because 1\text{ m} = 100\text{ cm}]$

$$= 11 \times 3.5 \times 0.4 = 15.4\text{ m}^3$$

If 1/10th part of the wall used in cement and sand, then part of wall used by cement and sand remaining $= \frac{15.4}{10}\text{m}^3 = 1.54\text{ m}^3$

Remaining part $= 15.4 - 1.54 = 13.86\text{ m}^3$

Number of bricks $= \frac{\text{Volume of wall to be construct}}{\text{Volume of each brick}} = \frac{13.86}{0.00154} = 9000$

Q. 118 A rectangular examination hall having seats for 500 candidates has to be built so, as to allow 4 cubic metres of air and 0.5 square metres of floor area per candidate. If the length of hall be 25 m, find the height and breadth of the hall.

Sol. Total number of seats in rectangular examination hall = 500

Length of the hall = 25 m

Cubic metres of air for per candidates $= 4\text{ m}^3$

Square metres of floor area for per candidate $= 0.5\text{ m}^2$

$\therefore$ Height of the hall $= \frac{\text{Volume of air per candidate}}{\text{Square metre of floor area for one candidate}} = \frac{4}{0.5} = \frac{40}{5} = 8\text{ m}$

Total capacity of the hall $= 500 \times 4 = 2000\text{m}^3$

$\therefore$ Breadth of the hall $= \frac{2000}{25 \times 8} = \frac{80}{8} = 10\text{ m}$

Q. 119 The ratio between the curved surface area and the total surface area of a right circular cylinder is 1 : 2. Find the ratio between the height and radius of the cylinder.

Sol. Curved surface area of a cylinder $= 2\pi rh$

Total surface area of a cylinder $= 2\pi r(r + h)$

The ratio between the curved surface area and the total surface area of a cylinder is 1 : 2.

$$\therefore \quad \frac{1}{2} = \frac{2\pi rh}{2\pi r(r + h)}$$

$$\Rightarrow \quad \frac{1}{2} = \frac{h}{(r + h)}$$

$$\Rightarrow \quad 2h = (r + h)$$

$$\Rightarrow \quad 2h - h = r \Rightarrow h = r$$

$\therefore$ Ratio of height and radius = 1 : 1.

Q. 120 A birthday cake has two tiers as shown in the figure below. Find the volume of the cake.

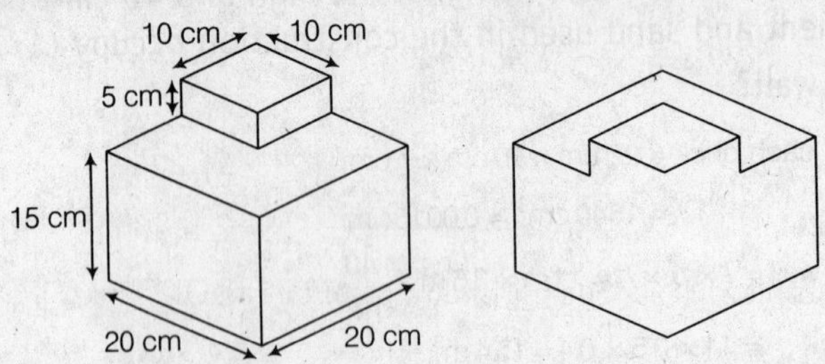

Sol. Volume of the cake = Volume of lower cuboid + Volume of upper cuboid

$= 20 \times 20 \times 15 + 10 \times 10 \times 5$ [$\because$ volume of cuboid $= l \times b \times h$]

$= 6000 + 500 = 6500 \text{ cm}^3$

Work out the surface area of following shapes in questions 121 to 124 (Use $\pi = 3.14$).

Q. 121

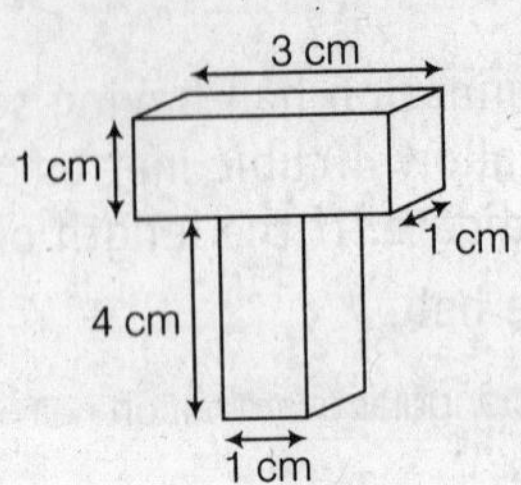

Sol. Surface area of the figure

$= 2[3 \times 1 + 1 \times 1 + 3 \times 1] + 2[4 \times 1 + 1 \times 1 + 4 \times 1] - [1 \times 1 + 1 \times 1]$

$= 2[3 + 1 + 3] + 2[4 + 1 + 4] - [1 + 1]$

$= 2[7] + 2[9] - [2] = 14 + 18 - 2$

$= 32 - 2$

$= 30 \text{ cm}^2$

Q. 122

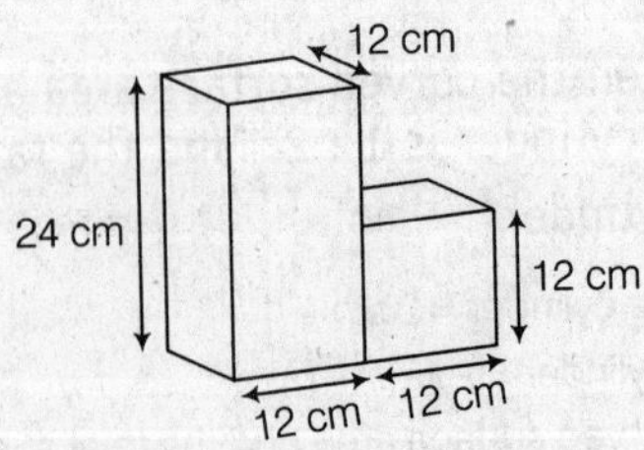

Sol. In the given figure, there are two cuboides are joined.

$\therefore$ Total surface area of the given solid

$= 2(24 \times 12 + 12 \times 12 + 12 \times 24) + 2(12 \times 12 + 12 \times 12 + 12 \times 12) - 2(12 \times 12)$

$= 1440 + 864 - 288$

$= 2016 \text{ cm}^2$

Q. 123

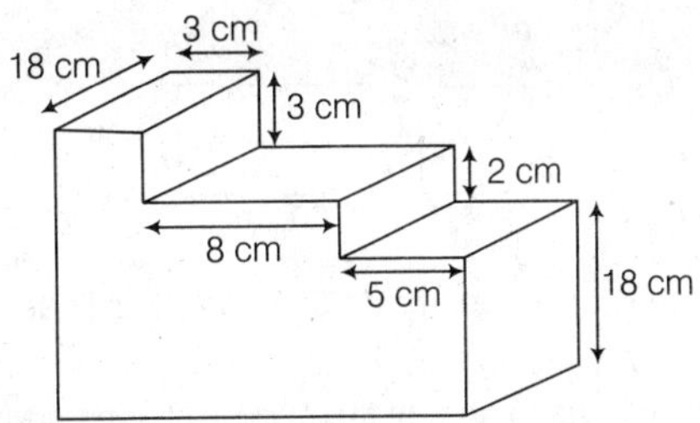

Sol. To find the total surface area, we draw the figure as given below.

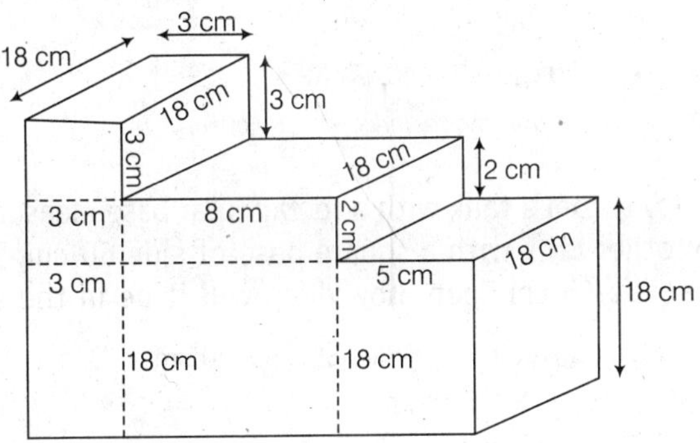

$\therefore$ Upper surface area

$$= 18 \times 3 + 8 \times 18 + 5 \times 18$$
$$= 54 + 144 + 90$$
$$= 288 \text{ cm}^2$$

$\therefore$ Lower surface area $= 288 \text{ cm}^2$

$\therefore$ Surface area of thosse faces which are flat from right

$$= 18 \times 18 + 2 \times 18 + 3 \times 18$$
$$= 324 + 36 + 54$$
$$= 414 \text{ cm}^2$$

Also, surface area of that face which are flat from left

$$= 414 \text{ cm}^2$$

Surface area of from face

$$= 18 \times 5 + 2 \times 8 + 8 \times 18 + 3 \times 2 + 3 \times 18 + 3 \times 3$$
$$= 90 + 16 + 144 + 6 + 54 + 9$$
$$= 319 \text{ cm}^2$$

Surface area of the back face $= 319 \text{ cm}^2$

$\therefore$ Total surface area

$$= 288 + 288 + 414 + 414 + 319 + 319$$
$$= 288 + 1754$$
$$= 2042 \text{ cm}^2$$

Q. 124

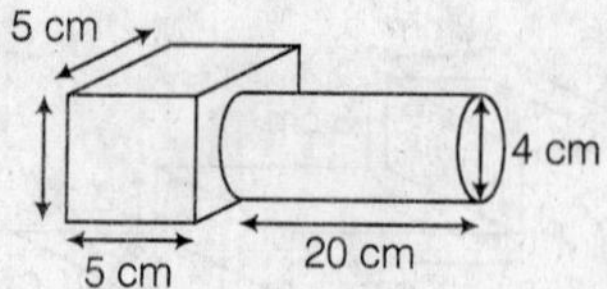

Sol. In the given figure, there is a cube of side 5 cm and a cylinder of hight 20 cm and radius is 2 cm.

So, total surface area = Surface area of the cube + Curved surface area of cylinder

$$= 6(5)^2 + 2\pi(2) \times 20 \qquad \left[\begin{array}{l}\because \text{surface area of cube} = 6a^2 \\ \therefore \text{surface area of cylinder} = 2\pi rh\end{array}\right]$$

$$= 150 + 80\pi$$

Total surface area = 150 + 251.2 = 401.2 cm^2

Note *In this question assume that cylinder is at end open.*

Q. 125 Water flows from a tank with a rectangular base measuring 80 cm × 70 cm into another tank with a square base of side 60 cm. If the water in the first tank is 45 cm deep, how deep will it be in the second tank?

Sol. Dimensions of rectangular base tank are 80 cm × 70 cm.

Height of rectangle base tank = 45 cm

Each side of square base tank = 60 cm

Let h be the height of square base tank.

Volume of rectangular tank = Volume of square tank

$$\Rightarrow \quad 80 \times 70 \times 45 = 60 \times 60 \times h \qquad [\because \text{volume of cuboidal} = l \times b \times h]$$

$$\Rightarrow \quad \frac{80 \times 70 \times 45}{60 \times 60} = h$$

$$\therefore \quad h = 70 \text{ cm}$$

Hence, water in second tank will be 70 cm deep.

Q. 126 A rectangular sheet of paper is rolled in two different ways to form two different cylinders. Find the volume of cylinders in each case if the sheet measures 44 cm × 33 cm.

Sol.

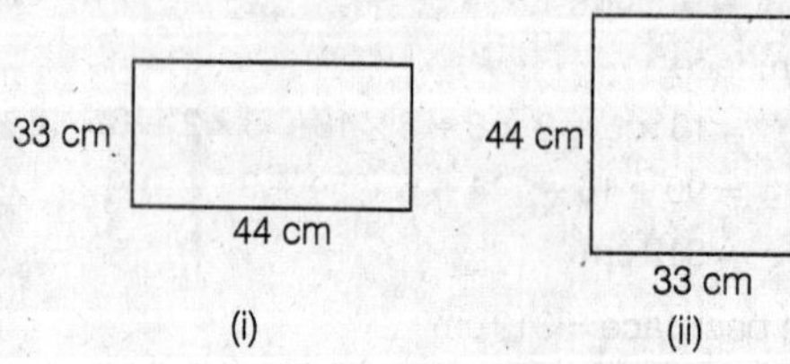

In Ist case,

If sheet rolled along 44 cm

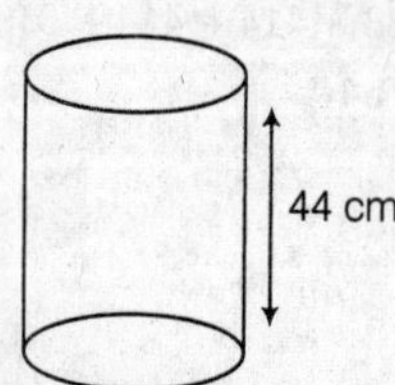

$\Rightarrow \quad 2\pi r = 44 \text{ cm}$

$\therefore \quad r = \frac{44}{2\pi} = \frac{44}{2} \times \frac{7}{22} = 7 \text{ cm}$

In IInd case,

It sheet rolled along 33 cm.

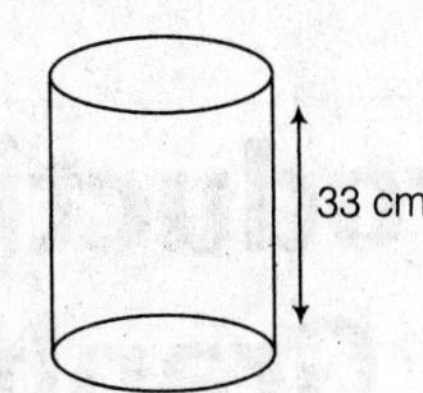

$\Rightarrow \quad 2\pi r = 33$

$\therefore \quad r = \frac{33}{2\pi} = \frac{33 \times 7}{2 \times 22}$

$= \frac{3 \times 7}{2 \times 2} = \frac{21}{4} \text{ cm}$

Volume in Ist case,

Volume of cylinder $= \pi \times r^2 \times h = \frac{22}{7} \times 7 \times 7 \times 33$ $\quad [\because r = 7 \text{ cm and } h = 33 \text{ cm}]$

$= 22 \times 33 \times 7$

$= 5082 \text{ cm}^3$

Volume in IInd case,

Volume of cylinder $= \pi r^2 h = \frac{22}{7} \times \frac{21}{4} \times \frac{21}{4} \times 44$ $\quad \left[\because r = \frac{21}{4} \text{ cm and } h = 44 \text{cm}\right]$

$= \frac{22 \times 3 \times 21 \times 11}{4}$

$= 3811.5 \text{ cm}^3$

12

Introduction to Graphs

Multiple Choice Questions (MCQs)

Q. 1 Comparison of parts of a whole may be done by a

(a) bar graph
(b) pie chart
(c) linear graph
(c) line graph

Sol. *(b)* There are various ways to represent and compare the data. One of them is pie chart. Pie chart is a pictorial representation of the data in which the whole is represented by a circle and the parts, by non-intersecting adjacent sectors.

Hence, comparison of parts of a whole may be done by a pie chart.

Q. 2 A graph that displays data that changes continuously over periods of time is

(a) bar graph
(b) pie chart
(c) histogram
(d) line graph

Sol. *(d)* Line graph is an important way to represent and compare the data which varies continuously.

A line graph displays the relation between two varying quantities.

In a line graph, we connect all the points by a line segment while in bar graph and histogram, we use rectangles of uniform width.

Q. 3 In the given graph the coordinates of point P are

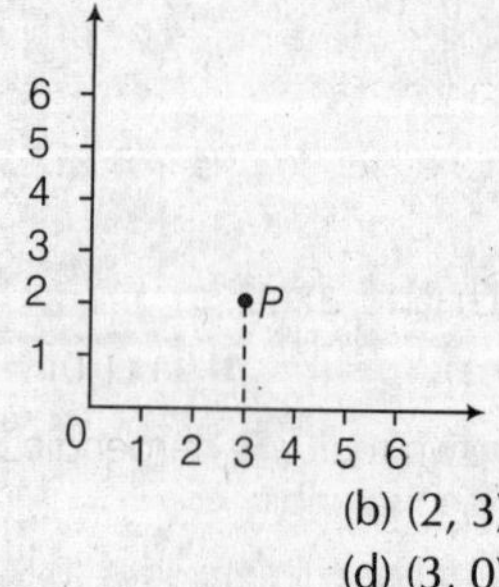

(a) (0, 2)
(b) (2, 3)
(c) (3, 2)
(d) (3, 0)

Sol. ***(c)*** The foot of the perpendicular drawn from the indicated point on X-axis is at a distance of 3 units from the origin.

$\therefore$ The x-coordinate of the point is 3.

Again, the perpendicular drawn from the given point on Y-axis meets the Y-axis at a point which is at a distance of 2 units from origin.

$\therefore$ The y-coordinate of the point is 2.

Hence, the coordinates of the point are (3,2).

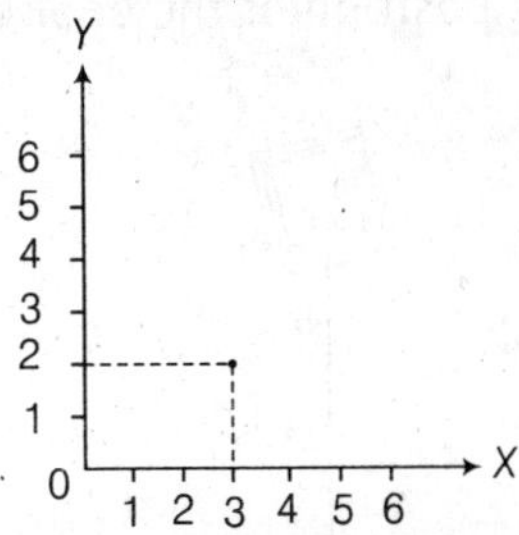

Q. 4 In the given graph the letter that indicates the point (0,3) is

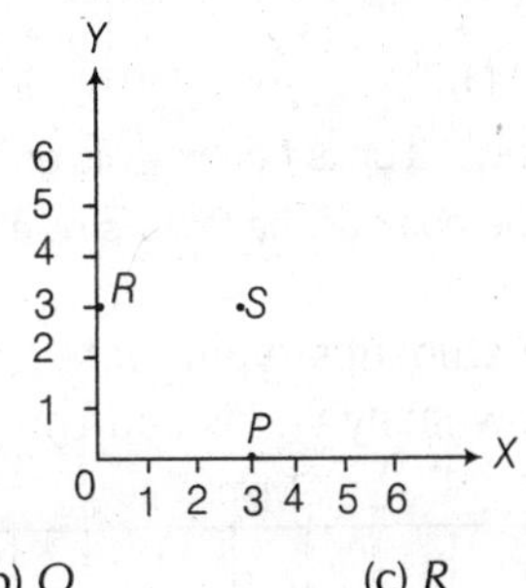

(a) P (b) Q (c) R (d) S

Sol. ***(c)*** The letter that indicates the point (0,3) is R as it lies on the Y-axis at a distance of 3 units from the origin.

The coordinates of the point P and S are (3,0) and (3,3), respectively.

Q. 5 The point (3,4) is at a distance of

(a) 3 from both the axes
(b) 4 from both the axes
(c) 4 from the X-axis and 3 from Y-axis
(d) 3 from X-axis and from Y-axis

Sol. ***(c)*** We know that, the x-coordinate is the distance of the point from Y-axis and that of y-coordinate is the distance from X–axis.

Hence, the point (3,4) is at a distance of 4 from the X-axis and 3 from Y-axis.

Q. 6 A point which lies on both the axes is

(a) (0,0) (b) (0,1) (c) (1,0) (d) (1,1)

Sol. ***(a)*** We know that, the axes are two mutually perpendicular lines intersecting each other at the point (0,0) also known as the origin.

Hence, the point which lies on both the axes is (0,0).

Q. 7 **The coordinates of a point at a distance of 3 units from the *X*-axis and 6 units from the *Y*-axis are**

(a) (0,3) (b) (6,0) (c) (3,6) (d) (6,3)

Sol. ***(d)*** We know that, the x-coordinate is the distance of the point from *Y*-axis and the *y*-coordinate is the distance of the point from *X*-axis.
Hence, the coordinates of the required point are (6,3).

Q. 8 **In the given figure, the position of the book on the table may be given by**

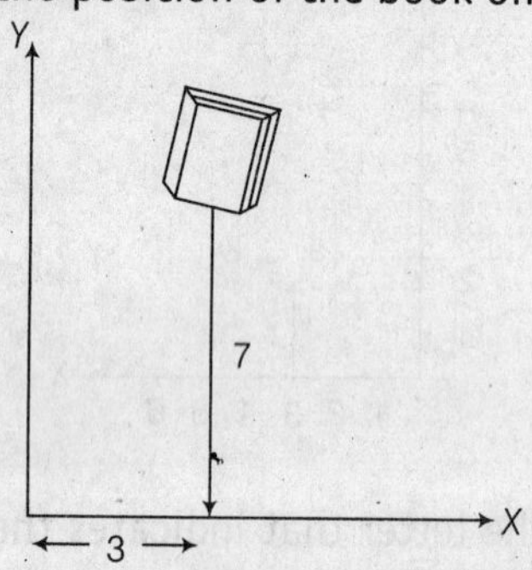

(a) (7,3) (b) (3,7) (c) (3,3) (d) (7,7)

Sol. ***(b)*** The book is at a distance of 3 units from *Y*–axis and 7 units from *X*-axis.
Hence, the position of the book on the table is given by (3,7).

Q. 9 **Data was collected on a student's typing rate and graph was drawn as shown below. Approximately how many words had this student typed in 30 s?**

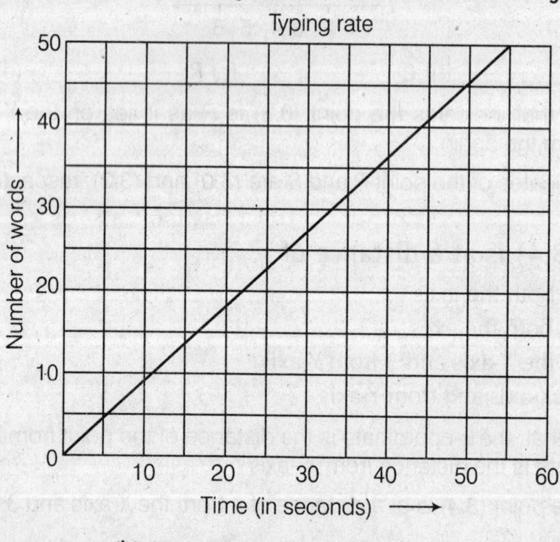

(a) 20 (b) 24 (c) 28 (d) 34

Sol. ***(c)*** Observing the graph, we see that the graph intersects the line $x = 30$ just below the point (30,30), which is the intersection of the lines $x = 30$ and $y = 30$.
Since, the *X*-axis represents the time (in seconds) and the *Y*-axis represents the number of words typed, therefore we conclude that the students had typed approximately 28 words in 30 s.

Q. 10 Which graph of the following represents the table below?

Length of side of a square	1	2	3	4	5
Perimeter	4	8	12	16	20

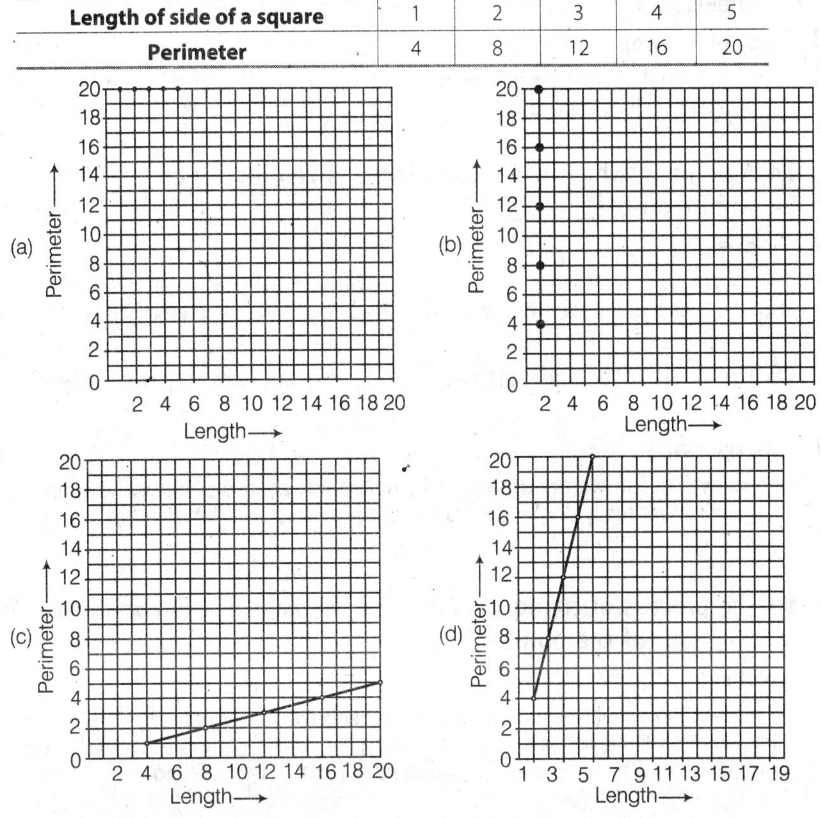

Sol. *(d)* Here, the lengths of sides of squares are represented on X-axis and their perimeters are represented on Y-axis.

∴ The points are (1,4),(2,8),(3,12),(4,16) and(5,20).

Now, observing all the 4 graphs carefully we see that these points lie on the graph(d).

Fill in the Blanks

In questions 11 to 25, fill in the blanks to make the statements true.

Q. 11 ________ displays data that changes continuously over periods of time.

Sol. **Line graph**

We have already discussed in the previous question that a line graph displays data that changes continuously over periods of time.

Q. 12 The relation between dependent and independent variables is shown through a________.

Sol. **graph**

Various types of graph depicts the relation between two variables, one of them is independent and the other is dependent.

A graph shows how a change in the independent variable changes the dependent variable.

Q. 13 We need ______ coordinates for representing a point on the graph sheet.

Sol. **pair of (or two)**

To represent the position of a point on the graph sheet we require two measures namely x-coordinate and y-coordinate.

Q. 14 A point in which the x-coordinate is zero and y-coordinate is non- zero will lie on the______.

Sol. ***Y*-axis**

Since, the x-coordinate is zero, i.e. the distance of the point from Y-axis is 0, the point lies on the Y-axis at a certain distance from the origin, which is given by y-coordinate.

Q. 15 The horizontal and vertical lines in a graph are usually called _____ and _____ .

Sol. ***X*-axis, *Y*-axis**

To draw a graph we need pairs of points known as coordinates and to plot a point we require two mutually perpendicular axes, also known as the X-axis (horizontal line) and the Y-axis (vertical line).

Q. 16 The process of fixing a point with the help of the coordinates is known as _____ of the point.

Sol. **plotting**

To locate the exact position of a point we need two coordinates *viz*, the x-coordinate and the y-coordinate and this process of finding the position or representing the numbers on a graph sheet with the help of the coordinates is known as plotting of the point.

Q. 17 The distance of any point from the Y-axis is the ______ coordinate.

Sol. ***x***

x-coordinate of a point is the distance of any point from the Y-axis.

Q. 18 All points with y-coordinate as zero lie on the_____ .

Sol. ***X*-axis**

Since, y-coordinate is zero, i.e. the distance of the point from X-axis is zero.
Hence, the points lies on the X-axis.

Q. 19 For the point (5,2), the distance from the X-axis is ____ units.

Sol. **2**

We know that, the y-coordinate represents the distance of the point from the X-axis.
Hence, the point (5,2) is at a distance of 2 units from the X-axis.

Q. 20 The x-coordinate of any point lying on the Y-axis will be______.

Sol. **zero**

Since, the x-coordinate represents the distance of the point from Y-axis is zero, therefore the points lying on the Y-axis have x-coordinate as zero.

Q. 21 The y-coordinate of the point (2,4) is______.

Sol. **4**

In the ordered pair (2,4), i.e. coordinates of a point, the second number is called as the y-coordinate of the point.

Hence, the y-coordinate of (2,4) is 4.

Q. 22 In the point (4,7), 4 denotes the ______.

Sol. **x-coordinate (abscissa)**

First number (coordinate) of the ordered pair is called as the x-coordinate or abscissa.

Hence, in the point (4,7),4 denotes the x-coordinate.

Q. 23 A point has 5 as its x-coordinate and 4 as its y-coordinate. Then, the coordinates of the point are given by______.

Sol. **(5,4)**

To denote a point in 2-D, we use two numbers *viz.* the x-coordinate, the y-coordinate.

In the ordered pair, the x-coordinate is written in the first slot and the y-coordinate in the second slot separated by comma. Hence, the required point is (5,4).

Q. 24 In the coordinates of a point, the second number denotes the ________ .

Sol. **y-coordinate / ordinate**

As we have discussed in the above question, that the second number denotes the y–coordinate, also known as the ordinate.

Q. 25 The point where the two axes intersect is called the ________ .

Sol. **origin**

The X-axis and Y-axis intersect each other at the point representing the origin. Coordinates of origin are (0,0).

True/False

In questions 26 to 34, state whether the statements are True or False.

Q. 26 For fixing a point on the graph sheet we need two coordinates.

Sol. ***True***

To plot a point on the graph sheet we require two numbers, known as coordinates *viz.* the x-coordinate and the y-coordinate.

Q. 27 A line graph can also be a whole unbroken line.

Sol. ***True***

A line graph, which represents the variation of a quantity with respect to the other, may be an unbroken line.

Q. 28 The distance of any point from the X-axis is called the x-coordinate.

Sol. ***False***

The distance of any point from the X-axis is called the y-coordinate.

Q. 29 The distance of the point (3,5) from the Y-axis is 5.

Sol. ***False***

We know that the x-coordinate of a point represents the distance of the point from Y-axis.

Here x-coordinate is 3, so the distance of the point (3,5) from the Y-axis is 3.

Q. 30 The ordinate of a point is its distance from the Y-axis.

Sol. ***False***

The ordinate of a point is nothing but y-coordinate of the point and the y-coordinate denotes the distance of a point from X-axis.

Q. 31 In the point (2,3), 3 denotes the y-coordinate.

Sol. ***True***

In the ordered pair (2,3), the second number is called the y-coordinate or ordinate of the number.

Hence, 3 denotes the y-coordinate of the point (2,3).

Q. 32 The coordinates of the origin are (0,0).

Sol. ***True***

Origin is the point, where two axes meet and its coordinates are (0,0).

Q. 33 The points (3,5) and (5,3) represent the same point.

Sol. ***False***

Two ordered pairs are equal, if they have same numbers at corresponding slot, i.e. x-coordinates are equal and y-coordinates are equal. Hence, (3,5) and (5,3) are different points.

Q. 34 The y-coordinate of any point lying on the X-axis will be zero.

Sol. ***True***

The distance of the points which lie on X-axis, will be zero from the X-axis, i.e. y-coordinate is zero for the points lying on X-axis.

Q. 35 Match the coordinates given in Column A with the items mentioned in Column B.

	Column A		Column B
a.	(0,5)	(i)	y-coordinate is $2 \times x$-coordinate + 1.
b.	(2,3)	(ii)	Coordinates of origin.
c.	(4,8)	(iii)	Only y-coordinate is zero.
d.	(3,7)	(iv)	The distance from X-axis is 5.
e.	(0,0)	(v)	y-coordinate is double of x-coordinate
f.	(5,0)	(vi)	The distance from Y-axis is 2.

Sol. (a) In the pair (0,5), the second number also known as ordinate represents the distance from *X*-axis, i.e. 5.

(b) In the pair (2,3), 2 the first number, also known as abscissa represents the distance from *Y*-axis that is 2.

(c) We have the coordinates (4,8). Clearly, *y*-coordinate is double of *x*-coordinate.

(d) We have the coordinate (3,7), where *x*-coordinate = 3 and *y*-coordinate = 7
Evidently, *y*-coordinate = 2 × *x*-coordinate + 1

(e) (0,0) are the coordinates of origin.

(f) In the point (5,0), the *y*-coordinate is zero.

Hence, (a) → iv, (b) → vi, (c) → v, (d) → i, (e) → ii, (f) → iii.

Q. 36 Match the ordinates of the points given in Column A with the items mentioned in Column B.

	Column A		Column B
a.	(7,0)	(i)	The ordinate is double the abscissa.
b.	(11,11)	(ii)	The ordinate is zero.
c.	(4,8)	(iii)	The ordinate is equal to the abscissa.
d.	(6,2)	(iv)	The abscissa is double the ordinate.
e.	(0,9)	(v)	The abscissa is triple the ordinate.
f.	(6,3)	(vi)	The abscissa is zero.

Sol. (a) Clearly, the ordinate of the point (7,0) is zero.

(b) In the point (11,11), the ordinate is equal to the abscissa.

(c) In the point (4,8), the ordinate is double of the abscissa.

(d) In the point (6,2), the abscissa, i.e. *x*-coordinate is triple of the ordinate, i.e. *y*-coordinate.

(e) The abscissa of the point (0,9) is zero.

(f) Clearly,the abscissa is double of the ordinate.

Hence, (a) → ii, (b) → iii, (c) → i, (d) → v, (e) → vi, (f) → iv.

Q. 37 From the given graph, choose the letters that indicate the location of the points given below.

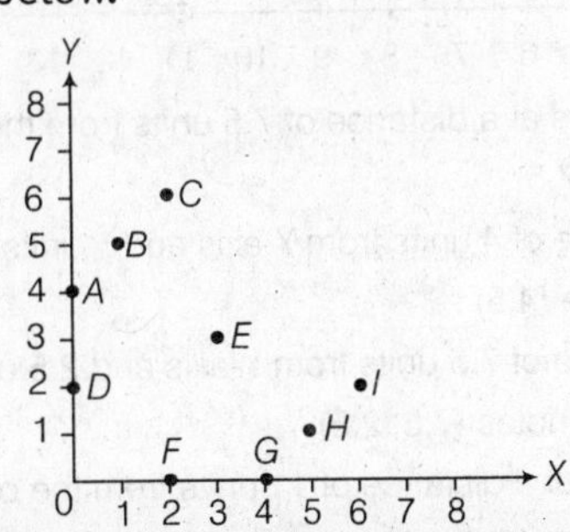

Sol. On observing the graph, we see that the point *F* is on *X*-axis, so its *Y*-coordinate will be zero.

Also, it is at a distance of 2 units from origin.

∴ The coordinates of *F* are (2,0), similarly the coordinates of *G* are (4,0).
H is at a distance of 5 units from *Y*-axis and 1 unit from *X*-axis.

∴ The coordinates of *H* are (5,1).

I is at a distance of 6 units from *Y*-axis and 2 units from *X*-axis.

∴ The coordinates of *I* are (6,2).

The point *D* and *A* are on *Y*-axis at distances of 2 units and 4 units respectively from the origin.

Hence, the coordinates of *D* and *A* are (0,2) and (0,4), respectively.

B is at a distance of 1 unit from *Y*-axis and 5 units from *X*-axis.

∴ The coordinates of *B* are (1,5).

C is at a distance of 2 units from *Y*-axis and 6 units from *X*-axis.

∴ The coordinates of *C* are (2,6).

E is at a distance of 3 units from *Y*-axis and *X*-axis both.

∴ The coordinates of *E* are (3,3).

Q. 38 Find the coordinates of all letters in the graph given below.

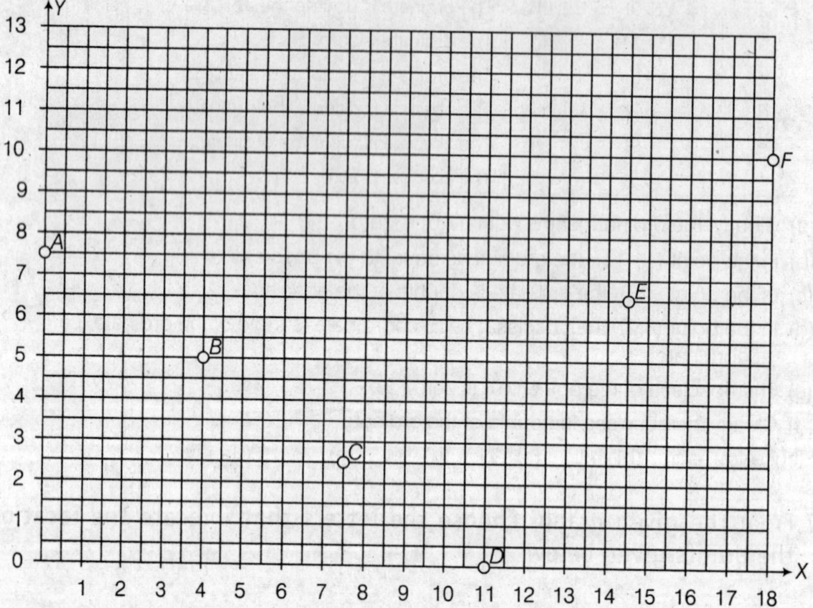

Sol. The point *A* is on the *Y*-axis at a distance of 7.5 units from the origin.

∴ The coordinates are (0,7.5).

The point *B* is at a distance of 4 units from *Y*-axis and 5 units from *X*-axis.

∴ The coordinates of *B* are (4,5) .

The point *C* is at a distance of 7.5 units from *Y*-axis and 2.5 units from *X*-axis .

∴ The coordinates of *C* denotes (7.5, 2.5).

The point *D* lies on *X*-axis at a distance of 11 units from the origin.

∴ The coordinates of *D* are (11,0).

The point *E* is at a distance of 14.5 units from *Y*-axis and 6.5 units from *X*-axis.

∴ The coordinates of *E* are (14.5, 6.5).

The point *F* is at a distance of 18 units from *Y*-axis and 9.5 units from *X*-axis.

∴ The coordinates of *F are* (18,9.5).

Q. 39 Plot the given points on a graph sheet.

(a) (5,4) (b) (2,0) (c) (3,1) (d) (0,4) (e) (4,5)

Sol.

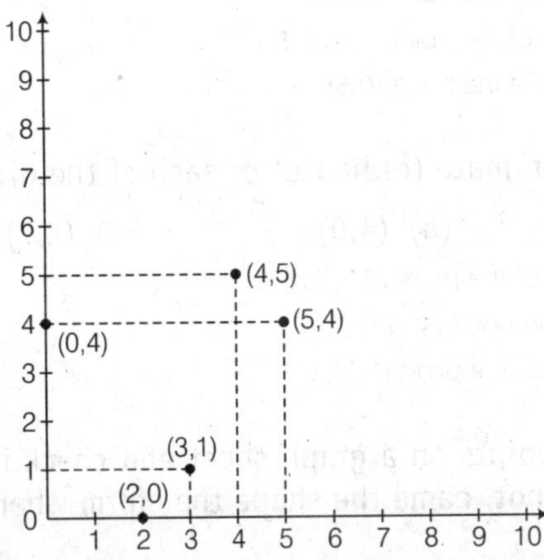

Q. 40 Study the given map of a zoo and answer the following questions.

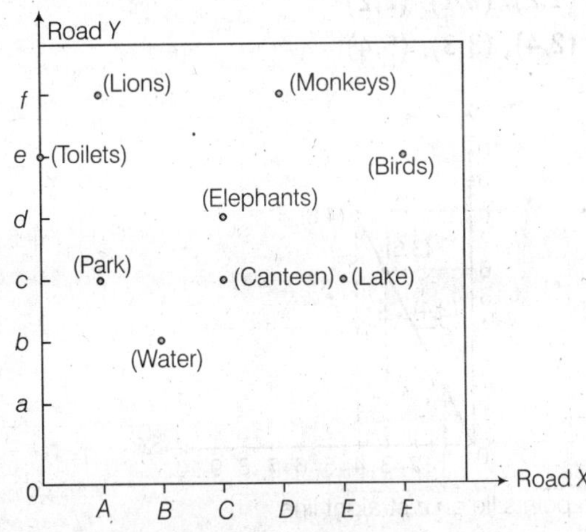

(a) Give the location of lions in the zoo.

(b) (D, f) and (C, d) represent locations of which animals in the zoo?

(c) Where are the toilets located?

(d) Give the location of canteen?

Sol. (a) Lions are at a distance of A units from road Y and f units from road X.

$\therefore$ The location of lions is represented by the point (A, f).

(b) Observing the map carefully, we see that (D, f) denotes the location of monkeys and (C, d) denotes the location of elephants.

(c) Toilets are located on the road Y at a distance of e units from the origin. Hence, the location of toilets is $(0, e)$.

(d) Canteen is located at a distance of C units from road Y and c units from road X.

Hence, the location of the canteen is (C, c).

Q. 41 Write the x-coordinate (abscissa) of each of the given points.

(a) (7,3) (b) (5,7) (c) (0,5)

Sol. (a) The x-coordinate of the point (7,3) is 7

(b) The x-coordinate of the point (5,7) is 5.

(c) The x-coordinate of the point (0,5) is 0.

Q. 42 Write the y-coordinate (ordinate) of each of the given points.

(a) (3,5) (b) (4,0) (c) (2,7)

Sol. (a) The y-coordinate of the point (3,5) is 5.

(b) y-coordinate of the point (4,0) is 0.

(c) The y-coordinate of the point (2,7) is 7.

Q. 43 Plot the given points on a graph sheet and check if the points lie on a straight line. If not, name the shape they form when joined in the given order.

(a) (1,2), (2,4), (3,6), (4,8)
(b) (1,1), (1,2), (2,1), (2,2)
(c) (4,2), (2,4), (3,3), (5,4)

Sol. (a)

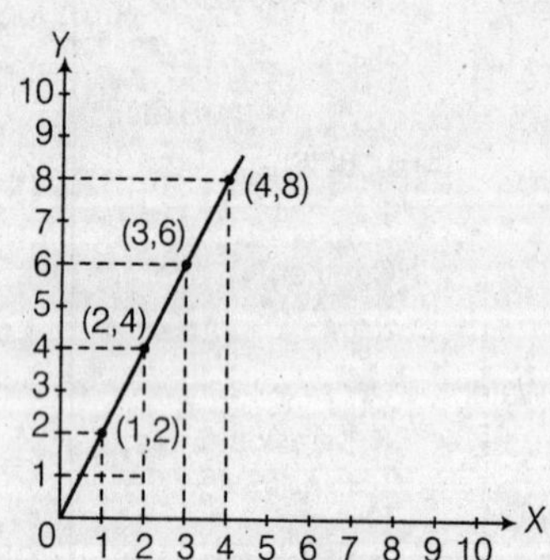

Yes, the given points lie on a straight line.

(b)

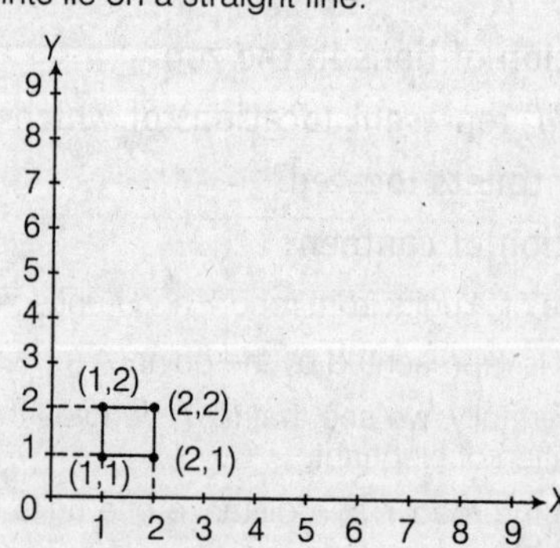

No, the points do not form a straight line, they form a square.

(c)

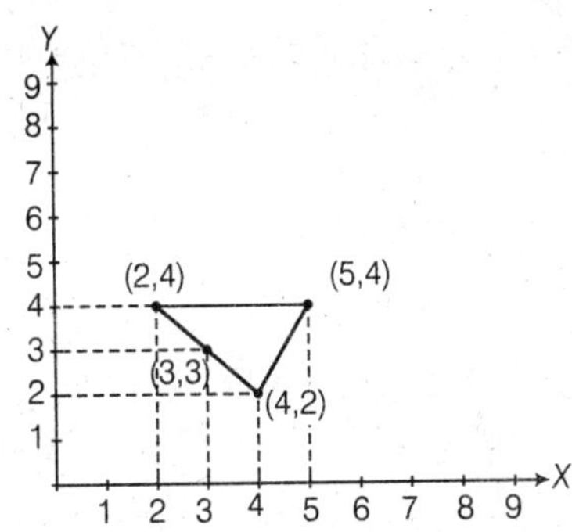

No, the points do not form a straight line, they form a triangle.

Q. 44 If y-coordinate is 3 times x-coordinate, form a table for it and draw a graph.

Sol. Since, the ordinate is 3 times the abscissa, we get the following values.

x	1	2	3	4
y	3	6	9	12

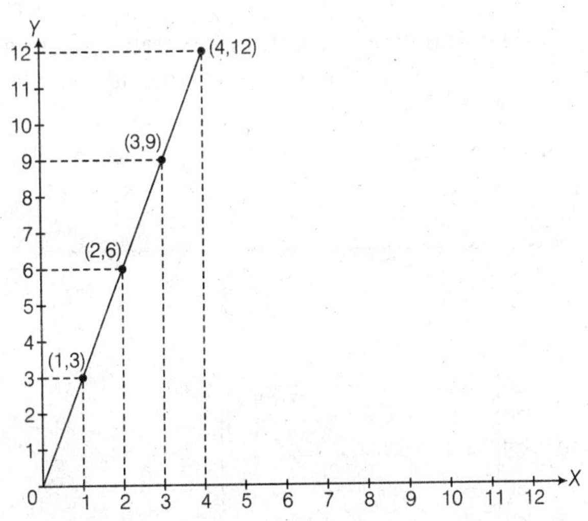

Q. 45 Make a line graph for the area of a square as per the given table.

Side (in cm)	1	2	3	4
Area (in cm^2)	1	4	9	16

It is a linear graph?

Sol.

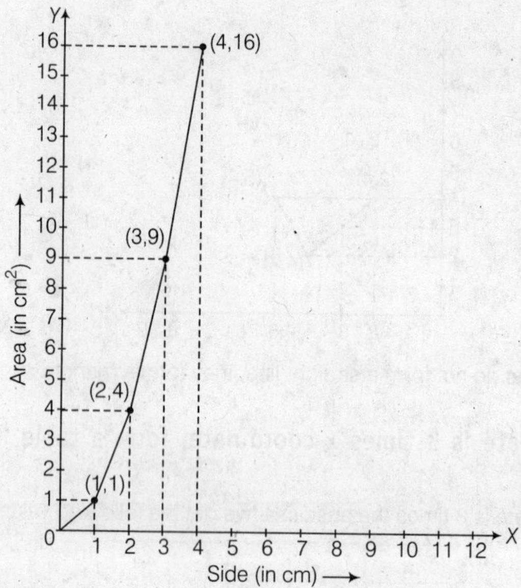

Yes, it is a linear graph.

Q. 46 The cost of a notebook is ₹10. Draw a graph after making a table showing cost of 2,3,4... notebooks. Use it to find

(a) the cost of 7 notebooks.

(b) the number of notebooks that can be purchased with ₹ 50.

Sol. Let x : number of notebooks

y : cost of a notebook

x	1	2	3	4	5	6	7	8
y	10	20	30	40	50	60	70	80

Y
X
0
1 2 3 4 5 6 7 8 9 10 11
10 20 30 40 50 60 70 80
(1,10) (2,20) (3,30) (4,40) (5,50) (6,60) (7,70) (8,80)
Cost of notebooks (in ₹) ⟶
Number of notebooks ⟶

(a) The cost of 7 notebooks is equal to the ordinate of the point (7,70), i.e. cost of 7 notebooks = ₹ 70

(b) The number of notebooks that can be purchased with ₹ 50 is equal to the abscissa of the point (5,50).

Hence, 5 notebooks can be purchased with ₹ 50.

Q. 47 Explain the situations represented by the following distance-time graphs.

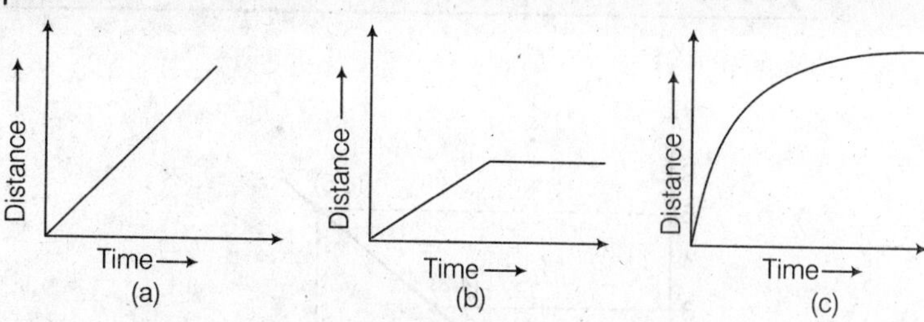

Sol. Here X-axis represents time and Y-axis represents distance.

(a) In the first graph, we observe that when time changes, distance also varies at the same rate.

When we move along time axis away from the origin, then the graph is strictly increasing.

Hence, the object is moving at a uniform speed.

(b) In the graph (b), we observe that initially graph increases steadily i.e. at uniform speed and after a certain period of time, it comes to rest position i.e. constant.

(c) In the graph (c), we see that the graph increases strictly with non-uniform speed and then slowly comes to the rest position.

Q. 48 Complete the given tables and draw a graph for each.

(a)

x	0	1	2	3
$y = 3x + 1$	1	4	—	—

(b)

x	1	2	4	6
$y = x - 1$	0	—	—	—

Sol.

(a)

x	0	1	2	3
$y = 3x + 1$	1	4	7	10

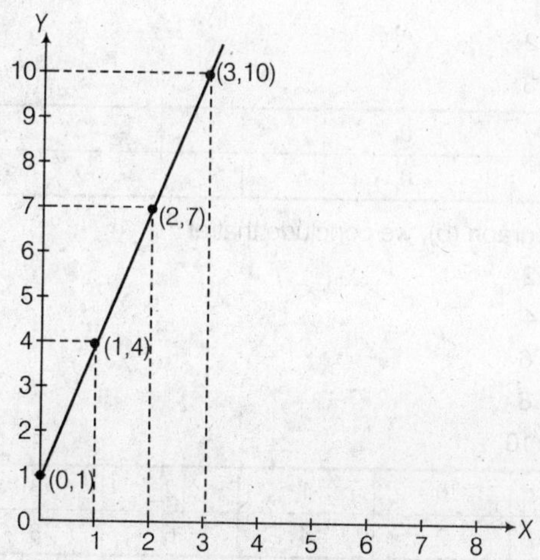

(b)

x	1	2	4	6
$y = x - 1$	0	1	3	5

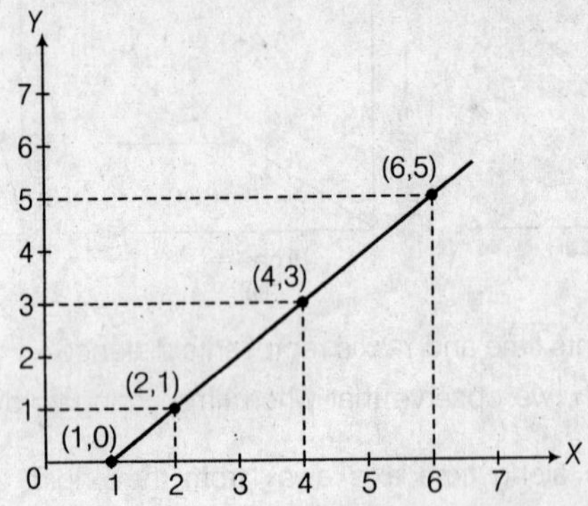

Q. 49 Study the given graphs (a) and (b) and complete the corresponding tables below.

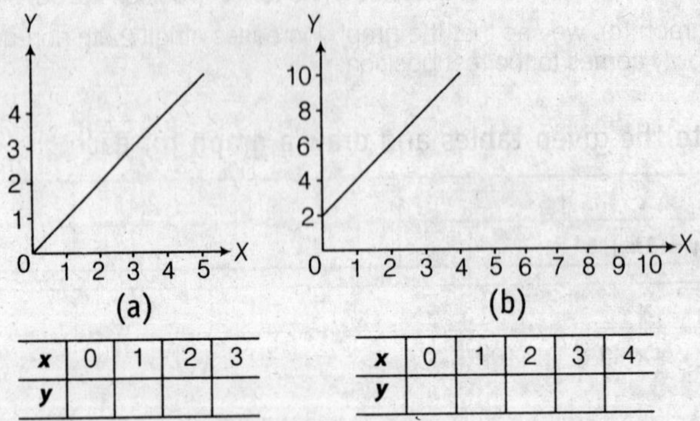

(a)

(b)

x	0	1	2	3
y				

x	0	1	2	3	4
y					

Sol. (a) Observing the graph (a), we conclude that at

$x = 0, y = 0$

$x = 1, y = 1$

$x = 2, y = 2$

$x = 3, y = 3$

x	0	1	2	3
y	0	1	2	3

(b) Observing the graph (b), we conclude that at

$x = 0, y = 2$

$x = 1, y = 4$

$x = 2, y = 6$

$x = 3, y = 8$

$x = 4, y = 10$

x	0	1	2	3	4
y	2	4	6	8	10

Q. 50 Draw a graph for the radius and circumference of circle using a suitable scale.

[Hint Take radius = 7,14,21 units and so on.]

Form the graph,

(a) find the circumference of the circle when radius is 42 units.

(b) at what radius will the circumference of the circle be 220 units?

Sol. If radius is 7 units, then circumference of the circle $= 2 \times \pi \times 7$

$$= 2 \times \frac{22}{7} \times 7 = 2 \times 22 = 44 \text{ units}$$

[$\because$ circumference of a circle $= 2\pi r$]

If radius is 14 units, then circumference $= 2 \times \pi \times 14 = 28 \times \frac{22}{7} = 88$ units units

If radius is 21 units, then circumference $= 2 \times \pi \times 21 = 42 \times \frac{22}{7} = 132$ units

If radius is 28 units, then circumference $= 2 \times \pi \times 28 = 56 \times \frac{22}{7} = 176$ units

If radius is 35 units, then circumference $= 2 \times \pi \times 35 = 70 \times \frac{22}{7} = 220$ units

If radius is 42 units, then circumference $= 2 \times \pi \times 42 = 84 \times \frac{22}{7} = 264$ units

Table for the graph,

Radius of the circle	7	14	21	28	35	42
Circumference of the circle	44	88	132	176	220	264

Graph from the above data

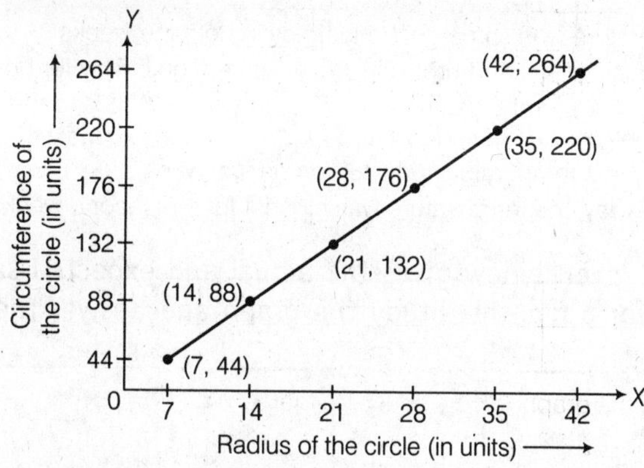

(a) The circumference of the circle will be 264 units when radius is 42 units.

(b) The radius of the circle will be 35 units, when the circumference of the circle equals 220 units.

Q. 51 The graph shows the maximum temperatures recorded for two consecutive weeks of a town. Study the graph and answer the questions that follow.

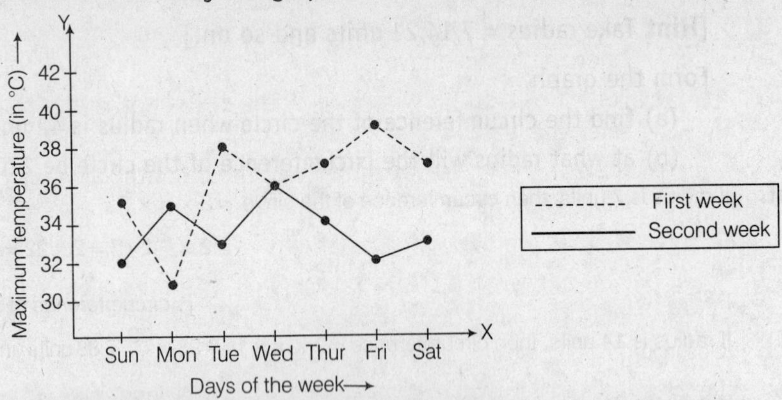

(a) What information is given by the two axes?

(b) In which week was the temperature higher on most of the days?

(c) On which day was the temperature same in both the weeks?

(d) On which day was the difference in temperatures the maximum for both the weeks?

(e) What were the temperatures for both the weeks on Thursday?

(f) On which day was the temperature 35°C for the first week?

(g) On which day was the temperature highest for the second week?

Sol. (a) The X-axis represents days of a particular week and the Y-axis represents the maximum temperature (in °C) recorded.

(b) Observing the graph, we see that in the first week temperature was higher on most of the days.

(c) The temperature was same on Wednesday in both the weeks.

(d) The difference in temperatures was the maximum on Friday for both the weeks.

(e) The temperature for the first week on Thursday was 37°C and the temperature for the second week on the same day was 34°C.

(f) On Sunday, the temperature was 35° for the first week.

(g) On Wednesday, the temperature was highest for the second week.

Q. 52 The graph given below gives the actual and expected sales of cars of a company for 6 months. Study the graph and answer the questions that follow.

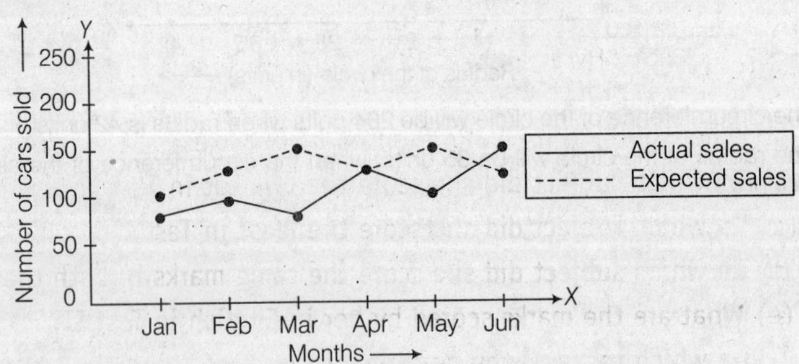

(a) In which month was the actual sales same as the expected sales?

(b) For which month(s) was (were) the difference in actual and expected sales the maximum?

(c) For which month(s) was (were) the difference in actual and expected sales the least?

(d) What was the total sales of cars in the months-January, February and March?

(e) What is the average sales of cars in the last three months?

(f) Find the ratio of sales in the first three months to the last three months.

Sol. Observing the graph carefully, we conclude that

(a) In April, the actual sales was same as the expected sales.

(b) In March, the difference in actual and expected sales was the maximum.

(c) In April, the difference in actual and expected sales was the least.

(d) The total sales of cars in the months January, February and March was $(75+100+75)$ i.e. 250.

(e) The average sales of cars in the last three months is 125 i.e. $\frac{125+100+150}{3} = 125.$

(f) The number of sales of car in the first three months = 250 and the number of sales of car in the last three months = 375

$\therefore$ The required ratio is $250 : 375$ i.e. $2 : 3$.

Q. 53 The graph given below shows the marks obtained out of 10 by Sonia in two different tests. Study the graph and answer the questions that follow.

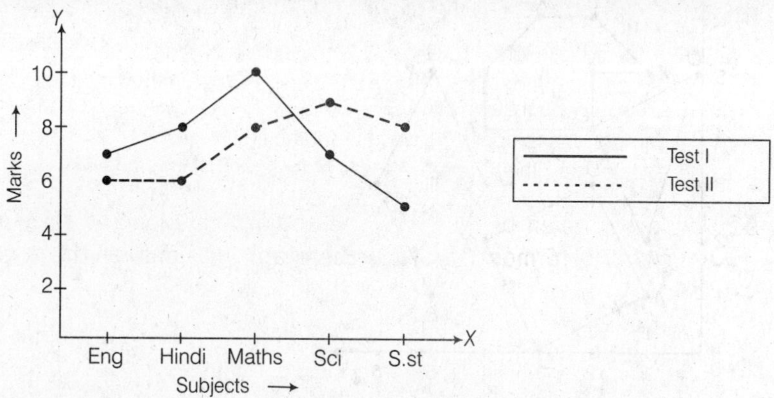

(a) What information is represented by the axes?

(b) In which subject did she score the highest in Test I?

(c) In which subject did she score the least in Test II?

(d) In which subject did she score the same marks in both the Tests?

(e) What are the marks scored by her in English in Test II?

(f) In which test was the performance better?

(g) In which subject and which test did she score full marks?

Sol. Observing the graph carefully, we conclude that

(a) The X-axis represents subjects and the Y-axis represents the marks obtained by Sonia.

(b) In Maths, she scored the highest in Test I.

(c) In English and Hindi, she scored the least in Test II.

(d) In Hindi and Maths, she scored the same marks in both tests.

(e) She scored 6 marks in English in Test II.

(f) Same performance in both tests.

(g) Test I in Maths, she scored full marks i.e. 10 marks.

Q. 54 Find the coordinates of the vertices of the given figures.

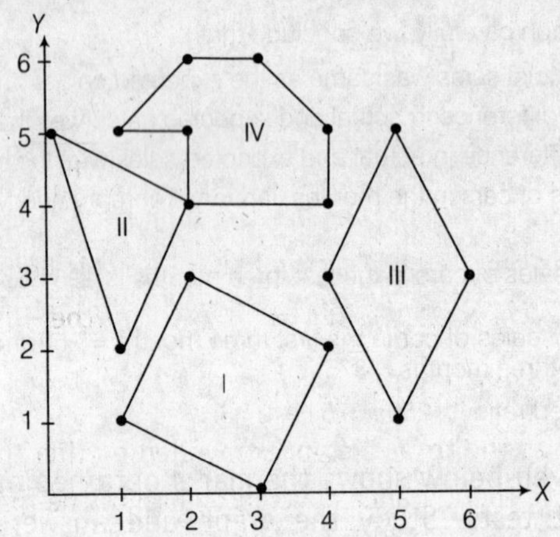

Sol.

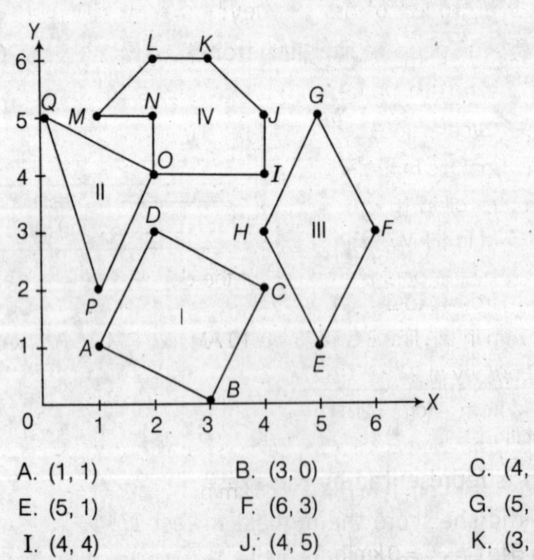

A. (1, 1)	B. (3, 0)	C. (4, 2)	D. (2, 3)
E. (5, 1)	F. (6, 3)	G. (5, 5)	H. (4, 3)
I. (4, 4)	J. (4, 5)	K. (3, 6)	L. (2, 6)
M. (1, 5)	N. (2, 5)	O. (2, 4)	
P. (1, 2)	Q. (0, 5)		

Q. 55 Study the graph given below of a person who started from his home and returned at the end of the day. Answer the questions that follow.

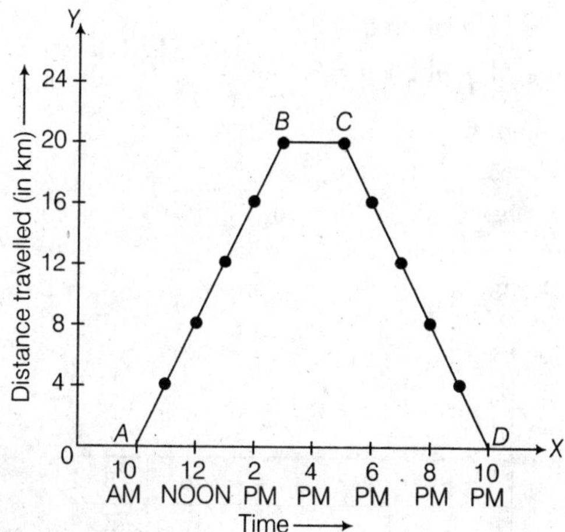

(a) At what time did the person start from his home?

(b) How much distance did he travel in the first four hours of his journey?

(c) What was he doing from 3 PM to 5 PM?

(d) What was the total distance travelled by him throughout the day?

(e) Calculate the distance covered by him in the first 8 h of his journey.

(f) At what did he cover 16 km of his journey?

(g) Calculate the average speed of the man from *A* to *B* and *B* to *C*.

(h) At what time did he return home?

Sol. Observing the graph carefully, we conclude that

(a) At 10 AM, the person start from his home.

(b) In first 4 h (i.e. till 2PM), he travelled 16 km.

(c) He was taking rest from 3 PM to 5 PM.

(d) The total distance covered by the person throughout the day was 40 km, i.e. 20 km from *A* to *B* and then 20 km from *C* to *D*.

(e) The distance covered by him in the first 8 h i.e. from 10 AM to 6 PM was 24 km.

(f) He covered 16 km of his journey at 2 PM.

(g) The total distance covered from *A* to *B* = 20 km

and the time taken to travel from *A* to *B* = 5 h

$\therefore$ Average speed of the man from *A* to *B* $= \frac{20}{5} = 4$ km/h

and average speed from *B* to *C* $= \frac{0}{2} = 0$ km/h

(h) He returned home at 10 PM.

Q. 56 Plot a line graph for the variables p and q, where p is two times q i.e. the equation is $p = 2q$. Then, find

(a) the value of p when $q = 3$.

(b) the value of q when $p = 8$.

Sol. Given, equation is $p = 2q$

If $p = 2$, then $q = \frac{p}{2} = \frac{2}{2} = 1$

If $p = 4$, then $q = \frac{p}{2} = \frac{4}{2} = 2$

If $p = 6$, then $q = \frac{p}{2} = \frac{6}{2} = 3$

If $p = 8$, then $q = \frac{p}{2} = \frac{8}{2} = 4$

Hence, table for the graph

p	2	4	6	8
q	1	2	3	4

(a) When $q = 3$, the value of p is 6.

(b) When $p = 8$, the value of q is 4.

Q. 57 Study the graph and answer the questions that follow.

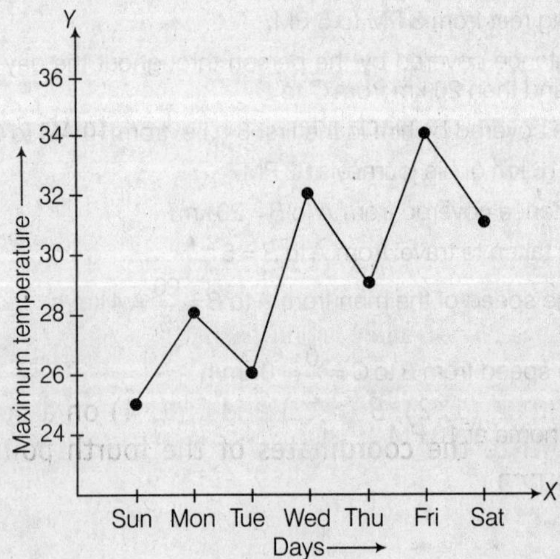

(a) What information does the graph give?
(b) On which day was the temperature the least?
(c) On which day was the temperature 31°C?
(d) Which was the hottest day?

Sol. (a) The information obtained from the given graph is that the maximum temperature is 34°C and minimum temperature is 25°C in a week.
(b) On Sunday, the temperature was 25°C. So, it is least temperature in the week.
(c) On Saturday, the temperature was 31°C.
(d) On Friday, the temperature was maximum i.e. 34°C. Hence, it is the hottest day of the week.

Q. 58 Study the distance-time graph given below for a car to travel to certain places and answer the questions that follow.

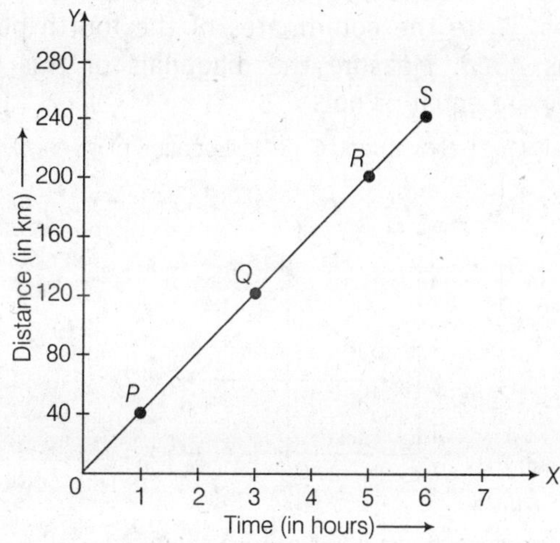

(a) How far does the car travel in 2 h?
(b) How much time does the car take to reach *R*?
(c) How long does the car take to cover 80 km?
(d) How far is *Q* from the starting point?
(e) When does the car reach the place *S* after starting?

Sol. (a) From the given graph, the car travels 80 km in 2h.
(b) 5 h taken by car to reach *R*.
(c) 2 h taken by car to cover 80 km.
(d) *Q* is 120 km far from the starting point.
(e) The car reaches the place *S* after starting in 6 h.

Q. 59 Locate the points *A* (1, 2), *B* (4, 2) and *C* (1, 4) on a graph sheet taking suitable axes. Write the coordinates of the fourth point *D* to complete the rectangle *ABCD*.

Sol. Given, points are A (1, 2), B (4, 2) and C (1, 4). Location of given points on the graph given below.

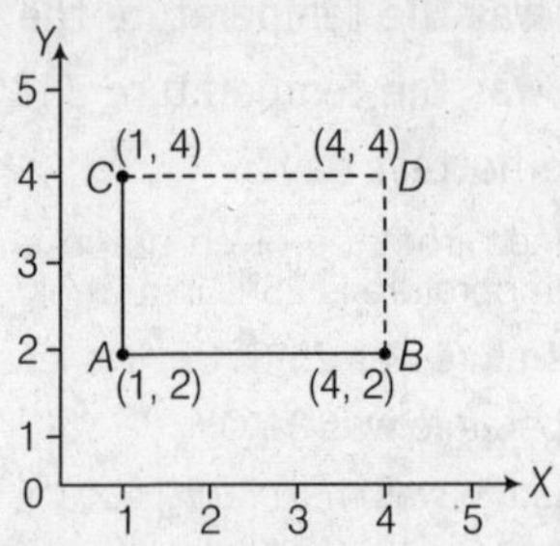

To complete the rectangle $ABCD$, the coordinates of the fourth point D will be (4, 4), i.e. D (4,4).

Q. 60 **Locate the points A (1, 2), B (3, 4) and C (5, 2) on a graph sheet taking suitable axes. Write the coordinates of the fourth point D to complete the rhombus $ABCD$. Measure the diagonals of this rhombus and find whether they are equal or not.**

Sol. Given points are A (1, 2), B (3, 4) and C (5, 2). Location of given points on the graph given below.

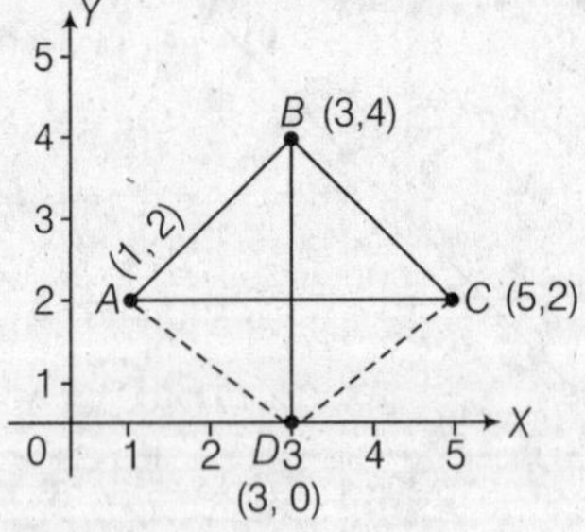

To complete the rhombus the fourth point will be (3,0).

$\therefore$ The Length of the diagonals, $AC = BD = 4$ units and they are equal.

Q. 61 **Locate the points P (3,4), Q (1,0), R (0,4), S (4,1) on a graph sheet and write the coordinates of the point of intersection of line segments PQ and RS.**

Sol.

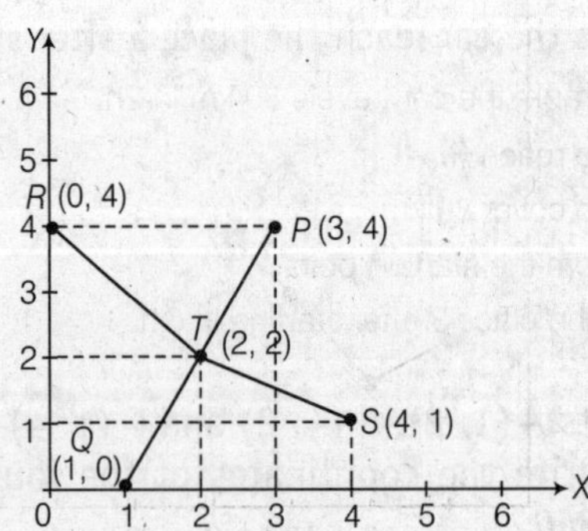

Observing the graph, we see that the line segments PQ and RS intersect at the point T (2, 2).

Q. 62 The graph given below compares the sales of ice-creams of two vendors for a week.

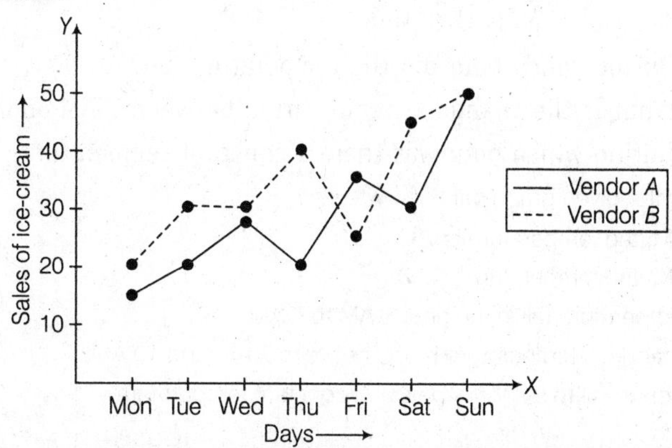

Observe the graph and answer the following questions.

(a) Which vezndor has sold more ice-creams on Friday?

(b) For which day was the sales same for both the vendors?

(c) On which day did the sale of vendor A increase the most as compared to the previous day?

(d) On which day was the difference in sales the maximum?

(e) On which two days was the sales same for vendor B?

Sol. Observing the graph carefully, we conclude that

(a) Vendor A has sold more ice-creams on Friday.

(b) On Sunday , the sales was the same for both the vendors.

(c) On Sunday, the sale of vendor A increased the most as compared to Saturday.

(d) The difference in sales was the maximum on Thursday.

(e) On Tuesday and Wednesday, the sales was the same for vendor B.

Q. 63 The table given below shows the temperatures recorded on a day at different times.

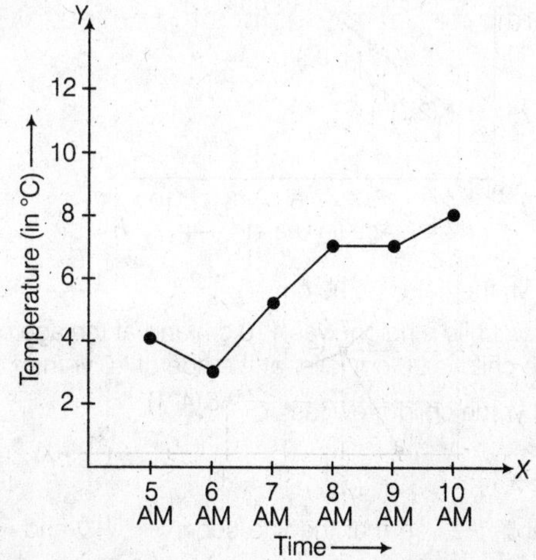

Observe the graph and answer the following questions.

(a) What is the temperature at 8 AM?

(b) At what time is the temperature 3°C?

(c) During which hour did the temperature fall?

(d) What is the change in temperature between 7 AM and 10 AM?

(e) During which hour was there a constant temperature?

Sol. Observing the given graph carefully, we have

(a) At 8 AM, the temperature is 7°C.

(b) At 6 AM, the temperature is 3°C.

(c) The temperature fall in the hour 5 AM to 6 AM.

(d) The change in temperature is 3°C between 7 AM and 10 AM.

(e) Between 8 AM to 9 AM, there was a constant temperature.

Q. 64 The following table gives the growth chart of a child.

Height (in cm)	75	90	110	120	130
Age (in years)	2	4	6	8	10

Draw a line graph for the table and answer the questions that follow.

(a) What is the height at the age 4 yr?

(b) How much taller was the child at the age of 10 yr than at the age of 6 yr?

(c) Between which two consecutive periods did the child grow more faster?

Sol.

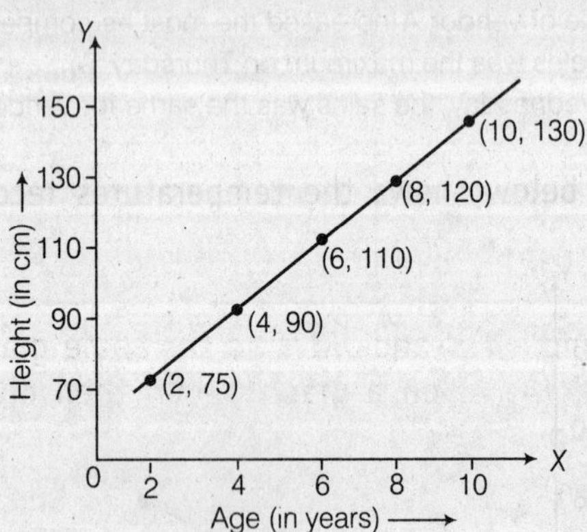

(a) At the age of 4 yr, the height is 90 cm.

(b) At the age of 6 yr, child's height was 110 cm and at the age of 10 yr child's height was 130 cm. So, the child is 20 cm taller at the age of 10 yr than at the age of 6 yr.

(c) Between 4 to 6 yr the child grow faster.

Q. 65 The following is the time-distance graph of Sneha's walking.

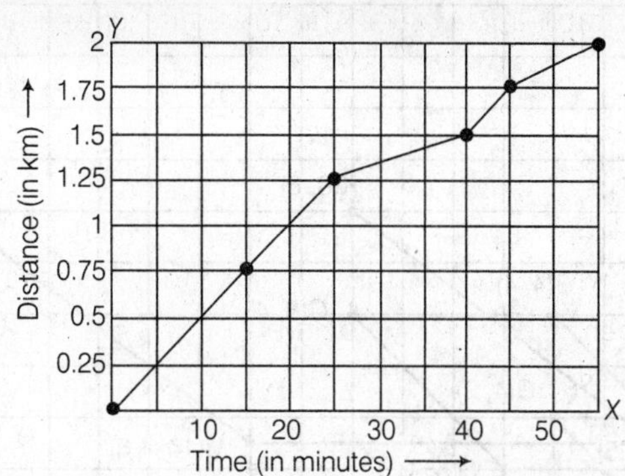

(a) When does Sneha make the least progress ? Explain your reasoning.

(b) Find her average speed in km/h.

Sol. (a) Sneha made least progress between 25 min to 40 min.
Observing the graph carefully, we see that initially, she is travelling approximately 0.5 km in 10 min, 0.25 km in 5 min, till the first 25 min. But after 25 min, her speed decreased as she travelled 0.25 km in 15 min (between 25 min to 40 min).

(b) Average speed $= \dfrac{\text{Total distance travelled}}{\text{Time}}$

$$= \frac{2}{55/60} = \frac{2}{55} \times 60 = 2.18 \text{ km/h}$$

Q. 66 Draw a parallelogram *ABCD* on a graph paper with the coordinates given in Table I. Use this table to complete Tables II and III to get the coordinates of *E*, *F*, *G*, *H* and *J*, *K*, *L*, *M*.

Table I

Point	(x, y)
A	(1, 1)
B	(4, 4)
C	(8, 4)
D	(5, 1)

Table II

Point	(0.5x, 0.5y)
E	(0.5, 0.5)
F	(2,2)
G	(4,2)
H	(2.5, 0.5)

Table III

Point	(2x, 1.5y)
J	(2, 1.5)
K	(8, 6)
L	(16, 6)
M	(10,1.5)

Draw parallelograms *EFGH* and *JKLM* on the same graph paper. Plot the points (2, 4) and (4, 2) on a graph paper, then draw a line segment joining these two points.

Sol. Complete table is shown below

Points	(0.5x, 0.5y)	Points	(2x, 1.5y)
E	(0.5, 0.5)	J	(2,1.5)
F	(2,2)	K	(8, 6)
G	(4,2)	L	(16, 6)
H	(2.5, 0.5)	M	(10,1.5)

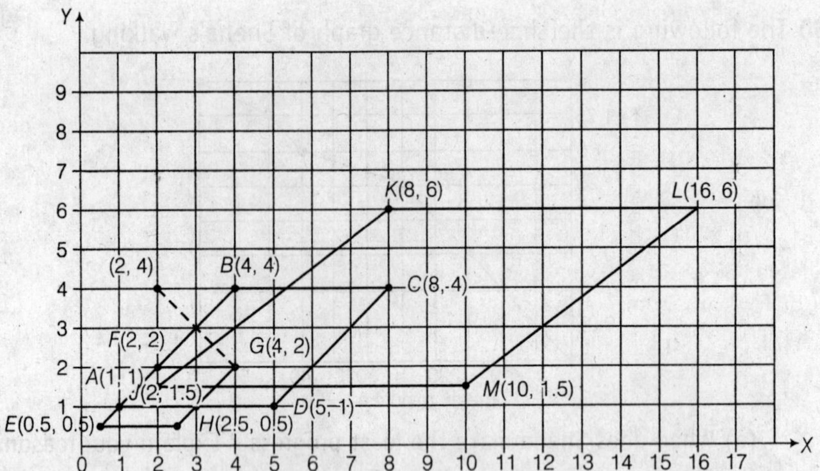

Q. 67 **Extend the line segment on both sides to meet the coordinate axes. What are the coordinate of the points, where this line meets the X-axis and the Y-axis?**

Sol. Let *PQ* is a line segment which is extened from both ends to meet the axes.

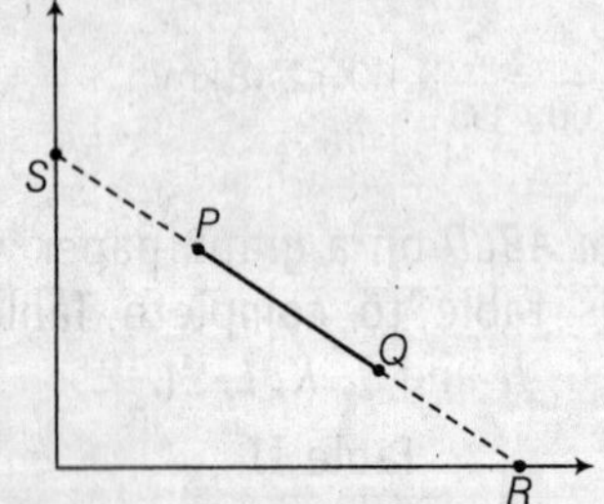

The coordinates of the point on *Y*-axis, where the line segment meet will be of form (0, *y*) whereas the coordinates of the point of interaction on *X*-axis will be of type (*x*, 0).

Q. 68 **The following graph shows the change in temperature of a block of ice when heated. Use the graph to answer the following questions.**

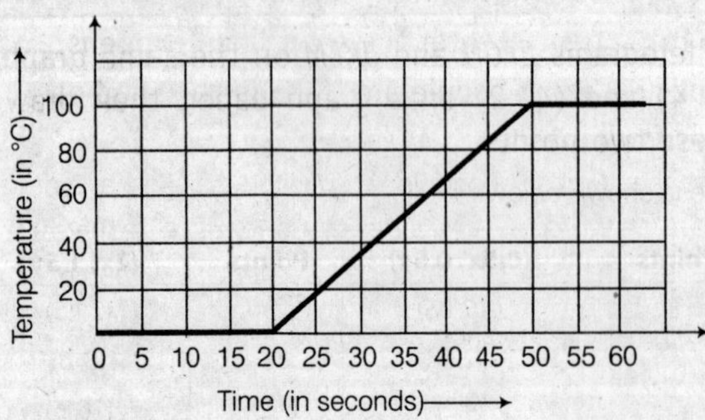

(a) For how many seconds did the ice block have no change in temperature?

(b) For how long was there a change in temperature?

(c) After how many seconds of heating did the temperature become constant at 100°C?

(d) What was the temperature after 25 s?

(e) What will be the temperature after 1.5 min? Justify your answer.

Sol. (a) In the first 20 s, the ice block have no change in temperature.

(b) There was a change in temperature from 20 s to 50 s, i.e. $50-20=30$s.

(c) Observing the graph, we see that after 50 s of heating the temperature became constant.

(d) 20°C was the temperature after 25 s.

(e) Since, the temperature became constant at 100°C after 50 s heating, so the temperature will be 100°C even after 1.5 min.

Q. 69 The following graph shows the number of people present at a certain shop at different times. Observe the graph and answer the following questions.

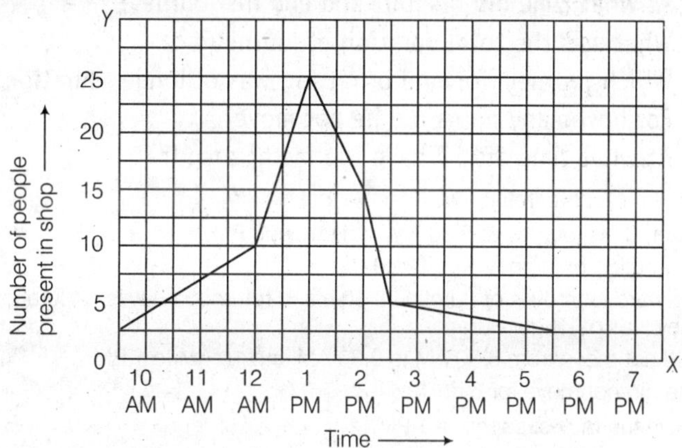

(a) What types of a graph is this?

(b) What information does the graph give?

(c) What is the busiest time of day at the shop?

(d) How many people enter the shop when it opens?

(e) About how many people are there in the shop at 1:30 PM?

Sol. (a) This is a line graph.

(b) It represents the number of people, who visited the store at a particular time.

(c) The busiest time of day is 1 PM at a shop, as at this time maximum number of people i.e. 25 visited the shop.

(d) When it opens less than 5 people enter the shop.

(e) There are 20 people in the shop at 1:30 PM.

Q. 70 A man started his journey on his car from location *A* and came back. The given graph shows his position at different times during the whole journey.

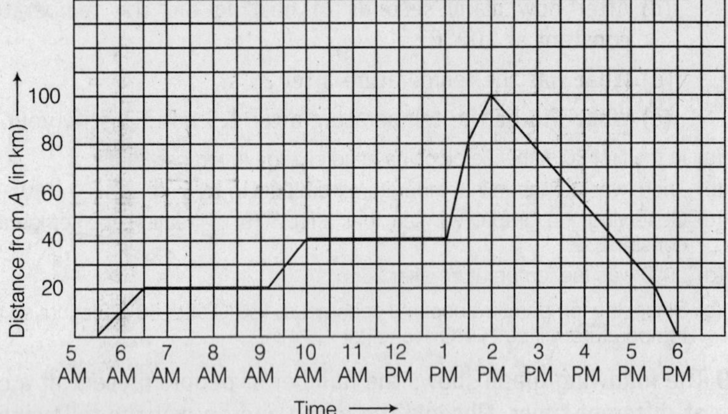

(a) At what time did he start and end his journey?

(b) What was the total duration of journey?

(c) Which journey, forward or return, was of longer duration?

(d) For how many hours did he not move?

(e) At what time did he have the faster speed?

Sol. Analysing the graph carefully, we observe that

(a) He started his journey at 5:30 AM and end at 6 PM.

(b) Total duration of journey was 12:30 h.

(c) His forward journey is of duration 8:30 h and return journey is of duration 4 h. Forward journey was of longer duration.

(d) He did not move from 6:30 AM to 9:30 AM and 10 AM to 1 PM.

So, he did not move for 6 h.

(e) He have the fastest speed at 1 PM.

Q. 71 The following graph shows the journey made by two cyclists, one from town *A* to *B* and the other from town *B* to *A*.

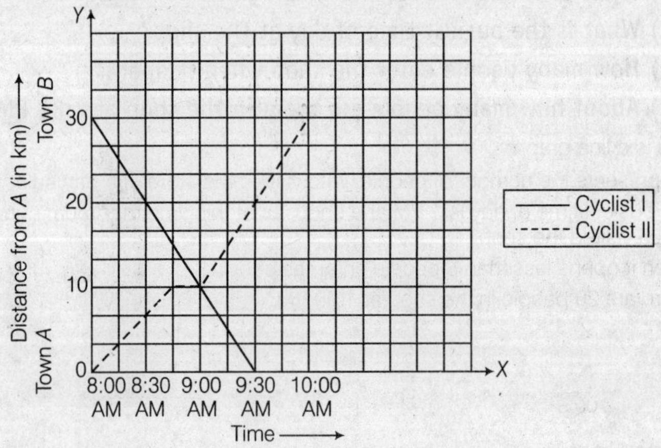

(a) At what time did cyclist II rest? How long did the cyclist rest?
(b) Was cyclist II cycling faster or slower after the rest?
(c) At what time did the two cyclists meet?
(d) How far had cyclist II travelled when he met cyclist I?
(e) When cyclist II reached town *A*, how far was cyclist I from town *B*?

Sol. (a) On the basis of given graph, the cyclist II rest at 8 : 45 AM for 15 min.
(b) Cyclist II is cycling faster after rest as he has covered a distance of 20 km in 1 h.
(c) Both cyclists meet at 9:00 AM.
(d) The cyclist II had travelled 20 km, when he met cyclist I.
(e) When cyclist II reached town *A*, the cyclist I was 10 km for from town *B*.

Q. 72 **Ajita starts off from home at 07.00 h with her father on a scooter that goes at a uniform speed of 30 km/h and drops her at her school after half an hour. She stays in the school till 13.30 h and takes an auto rickshaw to return home. The rickshaw has a uniform speed of 10 km/h. Draw the graph for the above situation and also determine the distance of Ajita's school from her house.**

Sol. Uniform speed of Ajita's father on scooter = 30 km/h

Time take by her father to drop Ajita to her school = $\frac{1}{2}$ h on 30 min

$\therefore$ Distance between Ajita's school and her home = $30 \times \frac{1}{2} = 15$ km

[$\because$ distance = speed × time]

Distance cover in 1 min = $\frac{15}{30} = \frac{1}{2}$ km = 500 m

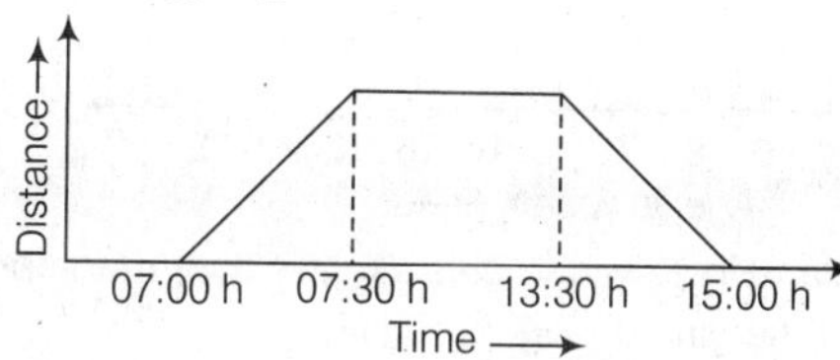

Q. 73 **Draw the line graph using suitable scale to show the annual gross profit of a company for a period of five years.**

Years	1st	2nd	3rd	4th	5th
Gross profit (in ₹)	1700000	1550000	1140000	1210000	1490000

Sol. We have taken years on *X*-axis and gross profit on *Y*-axis. The line graph of an annual gross profit of a company for a period of five years are given below.

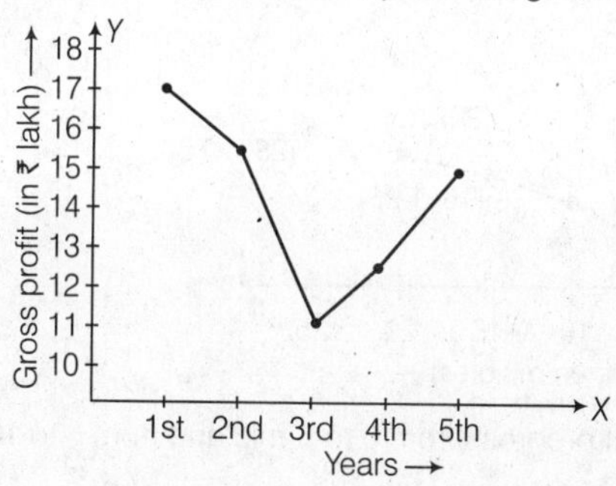

Q. 74 **The following chart gives the growth in height in terms of percentage of full height of boys and girls with their respective ages.**

Age (in years)	8	9	10	11	12	13	14	15	16	17	18
Boys	72%	75%	78%	81%	84%	88%	92%	95%	98%	99%	100%
Girls	77%	81%	84%	88%	91%	95%	98%	99%	99.5%	100%	100%

Draw the line graph of above data on the same sheet and answer the following questions.

(a) In which year both the boys and the girls achieve their maximum height?

(b) Who grows faster at puberty (14 yr to 16 yr of age)?

Sol.

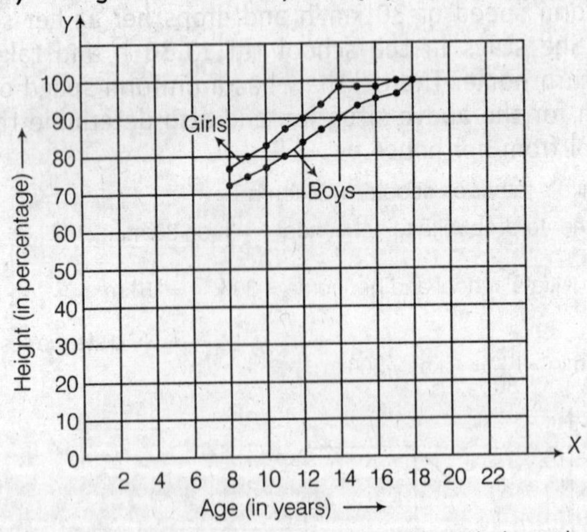

(a) In 18 yr, the boys and in 17 yr, the girls achieve their maximum height.

(b) Boys grows faster the girls during puberty.

Q. 75 **The table shows the data collected for Dhruv's walking on a road.**

Time (in minutes)	0	5	10	15	20	25
Distance (in km)	0	0.5	1	1.25	1.5	1.75

(a) Plot a line graph for the given data using a suitable scale.

(b) In what time periods did Dhruv make the most progress?

Sol. (a)

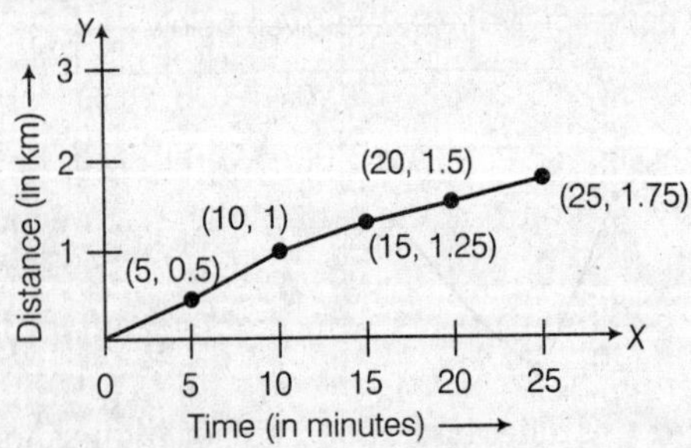

(b) Dhruv made most progress from 0 to 5 min and from 5 to 10 min.

Q. 76 Observe the given graph carefully and complete the table given below.

x	1	2	3	4	5
y					

Sol. Watching the graph carefully, we see that at

$x = 1, y = 2.5$

$x = 2, y = 5$

$x = 3, y = 10$

$x = 4, y = 15$

$x = 5, y = 20$

$\therefore$ We have the following table,

x	1	2	3	4	5
y	2.5	5	10	15	20

Q. 77 This graph shows the per cent of students who dropped out of school after completing high school. The point labelled *A* shown that, in 1996, about 4.7% of students dropped out.

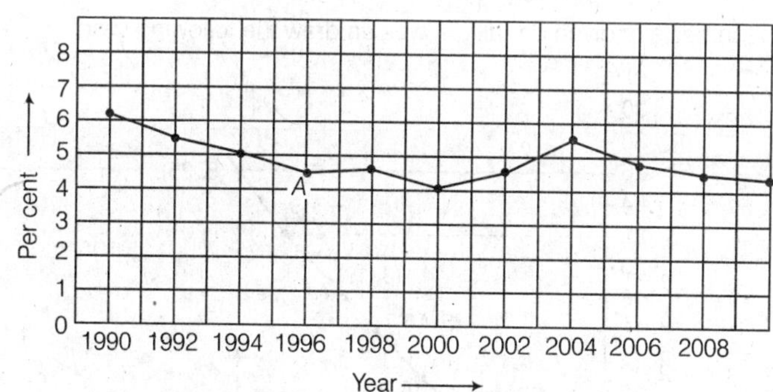

(a) In which year was the drop out the rate highest? In which year was it the lowest?

(b) When did the per cent of students who dropped out of high school first fall below 5%?

(c) About what per cent of students dropped out of high school in 2007? About what per cent of students stayed in high school in 2008?

Sol. Observing the graph carefully, we have

(a) The drop out rate was the highest in the year 1990 and the least in 2000.

(b) In the year 1996, the per cent of students dropped out of high school first fall below 5%.

(c) About 4.7% students dropped out of high school in 2007.

Q. 78 Observe the toothpick pattern given below

Pattern 1 Pattern 2 Pattern 3 Pattern 4

(a) Imagine that this pattern continues. Complete the table to show the number of toothpicks in the first six terms.

Pattern	1	2	3	4	5	6
Toothpicks	4			13		

(b) Make a graph by taking the pattern numbers on the horizontal axis and the number of toothpicks on the vertical axis. Make the horizontal axis from 0 to 10 and the vertical axis from 0 to 30.

(c) Use your graph to predict the number of toothpicks in patterns 7 and 8. Check your answers by actually drawing them.

(d) Would it make sense to join the points on this graph? Explain.

Sol. (a) On the basis of given patterns, we can arrange the following table which show the number of toothpicks in the first six terms.

Pattern	1	2	3	4	5	6
Toothpicks	4	7	10	13	16	19

Pattern and toothpicks shows the following relation as

$$1 \rightarrow 4,\ 2 \rightarrow 4 + 3 = 7$$
$$3 \rightarrow 7 + 3 = 10,\ 4 \rightarrow 10 + 3 = 13$$
$$5 \rightarrow 13 + 3 = 16,\ 6 \rightarrow 16 + 3 = 19$$

(b) On the basis of given condition, we can draw the following graph

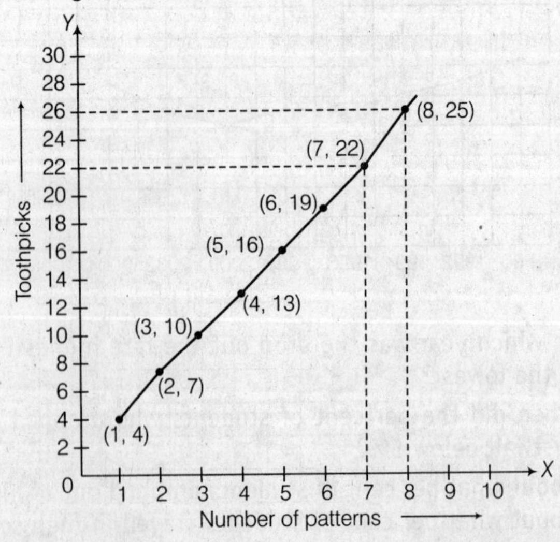

(c) The graph follows the $y = 3x + 1$ pattern. If $x = 7$, then $y = 3 \times 7 + 1 = 21 + 1 = 22$ and if $x = 8$, then $y = 3 \times 8 + 1 = 24 + 1 = 25$.

x	7	8
y	22	25

(d) Yes, it shows the relation between x and y follows the given pattern $y = 3x + 1$.

Q. 79 Consider this input/output table.

Input	1	2	4	5	7
Output	2	5	11	14	20

(a) Graph the values from the table by taking input along horizontal axis from 0 to 8 and output along vertical along vertical axis from 0 to 24.

(b) Use your graph to predict the outputs for inputs of 3 and 8.

Sol. (a) On the basis of given input/output table, we can draw the following table.

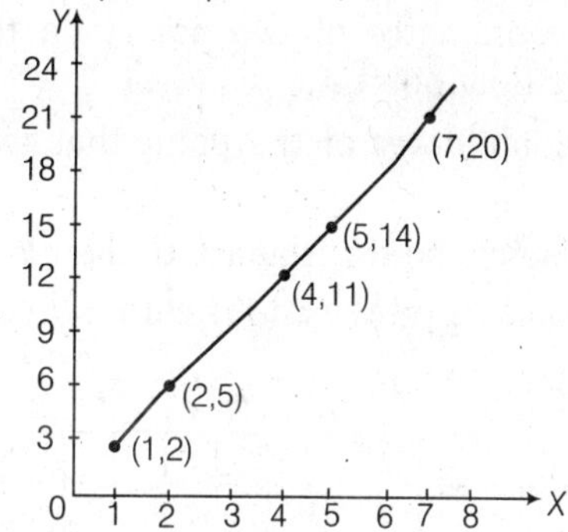

The graph shows $y = 3x - 1$ pattern.

(b) $\therefore$ Pattern is $y = 3x - 1$

If $x = 3$, then $y = 3 \times 3 - 1 = 9 - 1 = 8$

If $x = 8$, then $y = 3 \times 8 - 1 = 24 - 1 = 23$

Q. 80 This graph shows a map of an island just off the coast of a continent. The point labelled B represents a major city on the coast. The distance between grid lines represents 1 km.

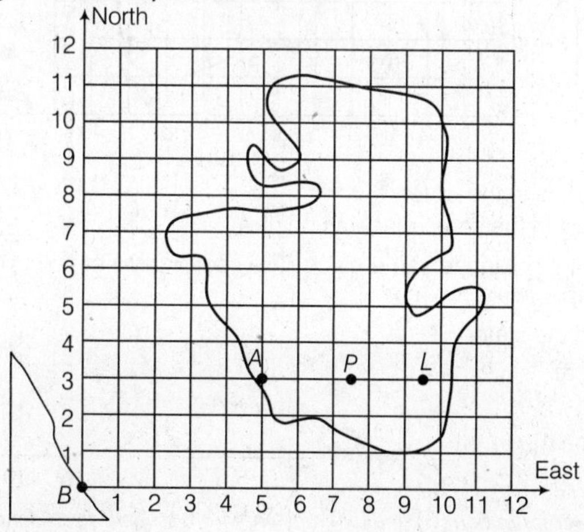

Point A represents a resorts that is located 5 km East and 3 km North of point B. The values 5 and 3 are the coordinates of point A. The coordinates can be given as the ordered pair (5,3), where 5 is the horizontal coordinate and 3 is the vertical coordinate.

(i) On a copy of the map, mark the point that is 3 km East and 5 km North of point and lebel it S. Is point S in the water or on the island? Is point S in the same place as point A?

(ii) Mark the point that is 7 km east and 5 km north of point B and label it C. Then, mark the point that is 5 km east and 7 km north of point B and label it D. Are points C and D in the same place? Give the coordinates of points C and D.

(iii) Which points is in the water (2, 7) or (7, 2)? Mark the point which is in water on your map and label it E.

(iv) Give the coordinates of two points on the island that are exactly 2 km apart from point A.

(v) Give the coordinates of the point that is halfway between points L and P.

(vi) List three points on the island with their x-coordinates greater than 8.

(vii) List three points on the island with a y-coordinate less than 4.

Sol.

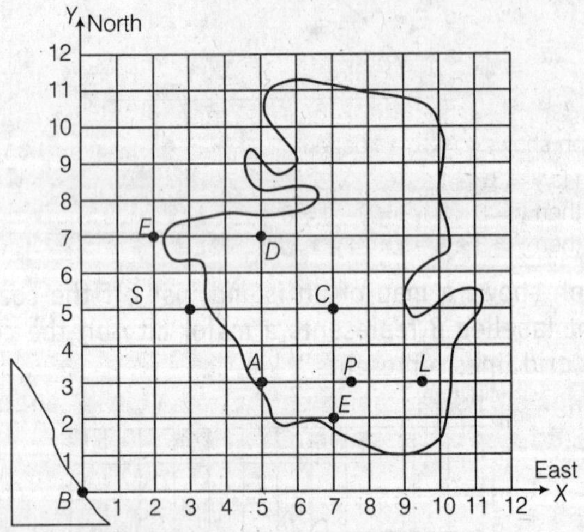

(i) The point S is in the water.
No, it is not in the same place as point A.

(ii) No, they are not in the same place. The coordinates of points C and D are (7, 5) and (5, 7), respectively.

(iii) (2, 7) is in the water.

(iv) (7, 3), (5, 5)

(v) (8.5, 3)

(vi) (9, 4), (10, 4), (11, 5)

(vii) (5, 3), (6, 2), (7, 2)

Note *Answer for option (vi) and (vii) may vary from student to student.*

Q. 81 As part of his science project, Prithvi was supposed to record the temperature every hour one Saturday from 6 AM to midnight. At noon, he was taking lunch and forgot to record the temperature. At 8:00 PM, his favourite show came on and so forgot again. He recorded the data. So, collected on a graph sheet as shown below.

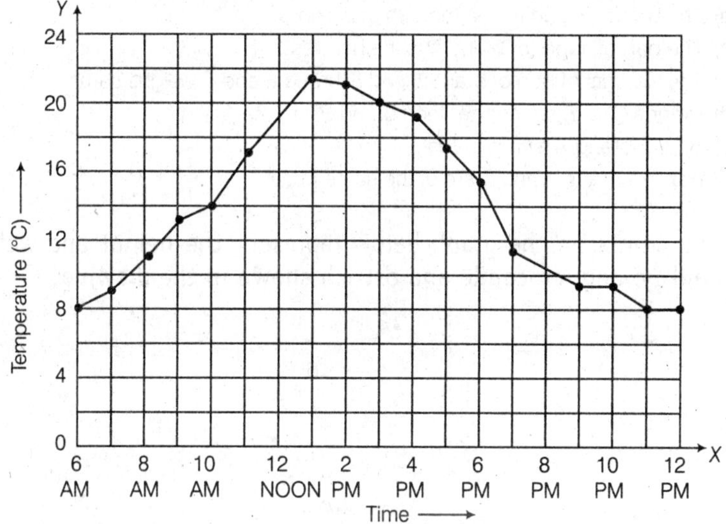

(a) Why does it make sense to connect the points in the situation?

(b) Describe the overall trend, or pattern, in the way the temperature changes over the time period shown on the graph.

(c) Estimate the temperature at noon and 8 PM.

Sol. (a) By connecting the points, it is easier to understand a change in the temperature.

(b) Initially the temperature was 8°C at 6 AM and started increasing strictly till 1 PM and after that it decreased to 8°C till 12 PM.

(c) At 12 PM 19°C and at 8 PM 10°C.

Q. 82 The graph given below compares the price (in ₹) and weight of 6 bags (in kg) of sugar of different brands *A*, *B*, *C*, *D*, *E*, *F*.

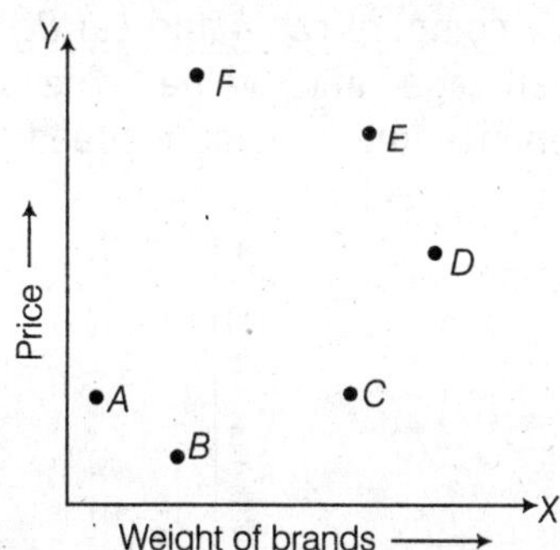

(a) Which brand(s) cost/costs more than brand *D*?

(b) Bag of which brand of sugar is the heaviest?

(c) Which brands weigh the same?
(d) Which brands are heavier than brand *B*?
(e) Which bag is the lightest?
(f) Which bags are of the same price?

Sol. On observing the graph carefully, we note that

(a) The brands *E* and *F* cost more than brand *D*.
(b) The bag of sugar of brand *D* is the heaviest.
(c) The weights of bag of brand *B* and *F*; brand *E* and *C* weighs same.
(d) Brands *C*, *D*, *E* are heavier than brand *B*.
(e) Bag of brand *A* is the lightest.
(f) Bags of brand *A* and *C* are of the same price.

Q. 83 The points on the graph below represent the height and weight of the donkey, dog, crocodile and ostrich shown in the drawing.

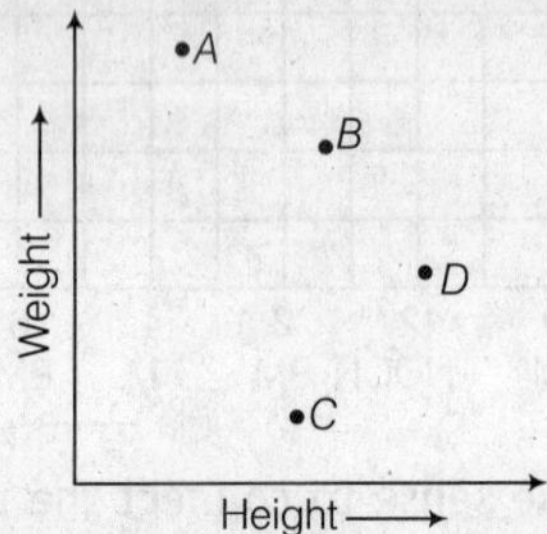

(a) What are the two variables represented in the graph?
(b) Which point represents each animals? Explain.

Sol. (a) Height and weight are the two variables in the graph.

(b) In the graph,we observe that the points *A* represents a crocodile as it has least height and greatest weight among all animals.

A – Crocodile [least height, greatest weight]
B – Donkey [height and weight more than dog]
C – Dog
D – Ostrich [greatest height]

Q. 84 The two graph below compare car *A* and car *B*. The left graph shows the relationship between age and value. The right graph shows the relationship between size and maximum speed.

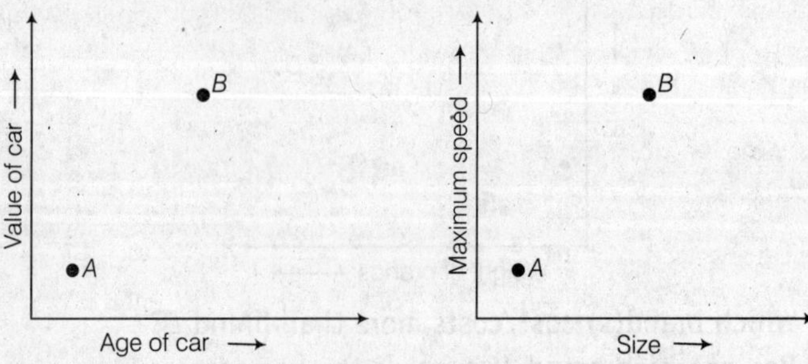

Use the graphs to determine whether each statement is true or false and explain your answer.

(a) The older car is less valuable.

(b) The faster car is larger.

(c) The larger car is older.

(d) The faster car is older.

(e) The more valuable car is slower.

Sol. (a) False, the older car is *B* i.e. *B* valuable more than car *A*.

(b) True, in the second graph *B* is larger car having greater speed.

(c) True, larger car is *B* which is older than *A*.

(d) True, as *B* is faster as well as older than *A*.

(e) False, as *B* is more valuable but not slower.

Q. 85 Sonal and Anmol made a sequence of the designs from square white tiles surrounding one square purple tile. The purple tiles come in many sizes. Three of the designs are shown below.

(a) Copy and complete the table

Side length of purple	1	2	3	4	5	10	100
Number of white tiles in border							

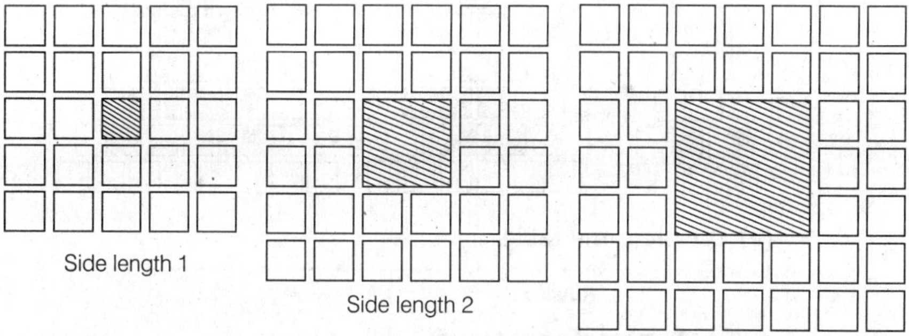

Side length 1

Side length 2

Side length 3

(b) Draw a graph using the first five pairs of numbers in your table.

(c) Do the points lie on a line?

Sol. (a) In side length 1 the number of white tile surrounding purple tile is 4.

Similarly, in side length 2 the number of white tiles surrounding purple tile is 8.

Thus, we can arrange the following table which shows side length of purple corresponding to the number of white tiles in border.

Side length of purple	1	2	3	4	5	10	100
Number of white tiles in border	4	8	12	16	20	40	400

Hence, the table shows $y = 8x + 16$.

(b) On the basis of table given in sol. (a) part, we draw the following graph

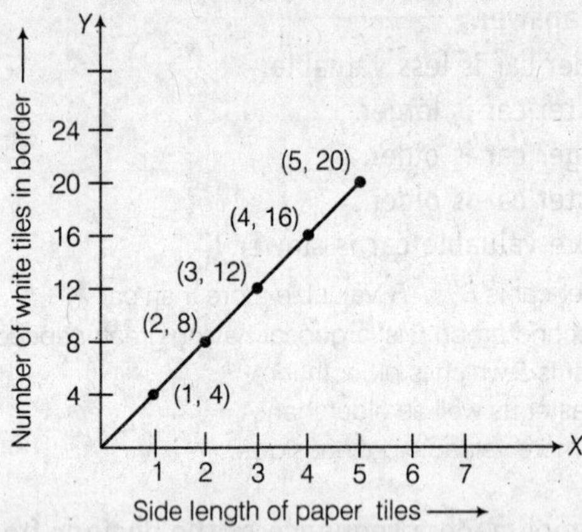

(c) If we join all points in above graph, we get a straight line. This shows, that all points lies on a line.

Q. 86 Sonal and Anmol then made another sequence of the designs. Three of the designs are shown below.

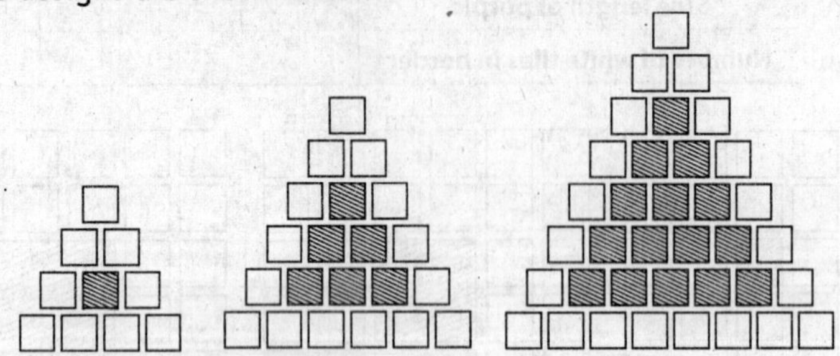

(a) Complete the table.

Rows, *r*	4	6	8
Number of white tiles, *w*	9		
Number of purple tiles, *p*	1		

(b) Draw a graph of rows and number of white tiles. Draw another graph of the number of rows and the number of purple tiles. Put the number of rows on the horizontal axis.

(c) Which graph is linear?

Sol. (a) The complete table is shown below

Rows, *r*	4	6	8
Number of white tiles, *w*	9	15	21
Number of purple tiles, *p*	1	6	15

(b) Graph between rows and number of white tiles is shown below

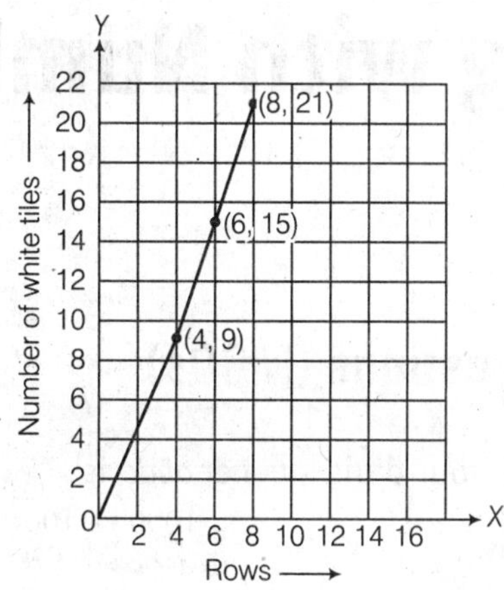

Graph between rows and number of purple tiles is shown below

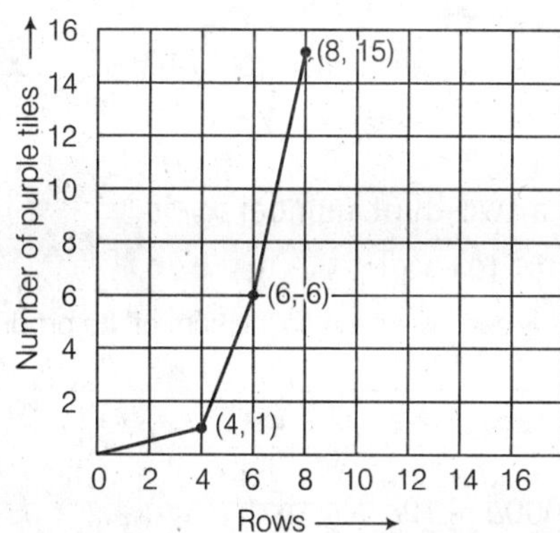

(c) No graph is linear.

13

Playing with Numbers

Multiple Choice Questions (MCQs)

Q. 1 Generalised form of a four-digit number *abdc* is

(a) $1000a + 100b + 10c + d$ (b) $1000a + 100c + 10b + d$
(c) $1000a + 100b + 10d + c$ (d) $a \times b \times c \times d$

Sol. *(c)* In generalised form, we express a number as the sum of the products of its digits with their respective place values.

$\therefore$ *abdc* is written in generalised form as $1000a + 100b + 10d + c$.

i.e. $$abdc = 1000a + 100b + 10d + c$$

Q. 2 Generalised form of a two-digit number *xy* is

(a) $x + y$ (b) $10x + y$ (c) $10x - y$ (d) $10y + x$

Sol. *(b)* In generalised form, *xy* can be written as the sum of the products of its digits with their respective place values.

i.e. $$xy = 10x + y$$

Q. 3 The usual form of $1000a + 10b + c$ is

(a) *abc* (b) *abc*0 (c) *a*0*bc* (d) *ab*0*c*

Sol. *(c)* Given expanded (or generalised) form of a number is $1000a + 10b + c$. Then, we have to find its usual form.

We can write it as $1000 \times a + 100 \times 0 + 10 \times b + c$

i.e. *a*0*bc*, which is the usual form.

Q. 4 Let *abc* be a three-digit number. Then, *abc* − *cba* is not divisible by

(a) 9 (b) 11 (c) 18 (d) 33

Sol. *(c)* Given, *abc* is a three-digit number.

Then, $abc = 100a + 10b + c$

and $cba = 100c + 10b + a$

$\therefore$ $$abc - cba = (100a + 10b + c) - (100c + 10b + a)$$

$= 100a - a + 10b - 10b + c - 100c$
$= 99a - 99c = 99(a - c)$

$\Rightarrow$ $abc - cba$ is divisible by 99.

$\Rightarrow$ $abc - cba$ is divisible by 9, 11, 33, but it is not divisible by 18.

Q. 5 The sum of all the numbers formed by the digits x, y and z of the number xyz is divisible by

(a) 11 (b) 33 (c) 37 (d) 74

Sol. *(c)* We have, $xyz + yzx + zxy$

$$= (100x + 10y + z) + (100y + 10z + x) + (100z + 10x + y) \quad \text{...(i)}$$
$$= 100x + 10x + x + 10y + 100y + y + z + 100z + 10Z$$
$$= 111x + 111y + 111z = 111(x + y + z)$$
$$= 3 \times 37 \times (x + y + z)$$

Hence, Eq. (i) is divisible by 37, but not divisible by 11, 33 and 74.

Q. 6 A four-digit number $aabb$ is divisible by 55. Then, possible value(s) of b is/are

(a) 0 and 2 (b) 2 and 5 (c) 0 and 5 (d) 7

Sol. *(c)* It is given that, $aabb$ is divisible by 55. Then, it is also divisible by 5.
Now, if a number is divisible by 5, then its unit digit is either 0 or 5.
Hence, the possible values of b are 0 and 5.

Q. 7 Let abc be a three-digit number. Then, $abc + bca + cab$ is not divisible by

(a) $a + b + c$ (b) 3 (c) 37 (d) 9

Sol. *(d)* We know that, the sum of three-digit numbers taken in cyclic order can be written as $111(a + b + c)$.

i.e. $abc + bca + cab = 3 \times 37 \times (a + b + c)$

Hence, the sum is divisible by 3, 37 and $(a + b + c)$ but not divisible by 9.

Q. 8 A four-digit number $4ab5$ is divisible by 55. Then, the value of $b - a$ is

(a) 0 (b) 1 (c) 4 (d) 5

Sol. *(b)* Given, a four-digit number $4ab5$ is divisible by 55. Then, it is also divisible by 11.
The difference of sum of its digits in odd places and sum of its digits in even places is either 0 or multiple of 11.
i.e. $(4 + b) - (a + 5)$ is 0 or a multiple of 11, if $4 + b - a - 5 = 0$

$\Rightarrow$ $b - a = 1$

Q. 9 If abc is a three-digit number, then number $abc - a - b - c$ is divisible by

(a) 9 (b) 90 (c) 10 (d) 11

Sol. *(a)* We have, $abc = 100a + 10b + c$

$\therefore$ $abc - a - b - c = (100a + 10b + c) - a - b - c$
$= 100a - a + 10b - b$
$= 99a + 9b = 9(11a + b)$

Hence, the given number $abc - a - b - c$ is divisible by 9.

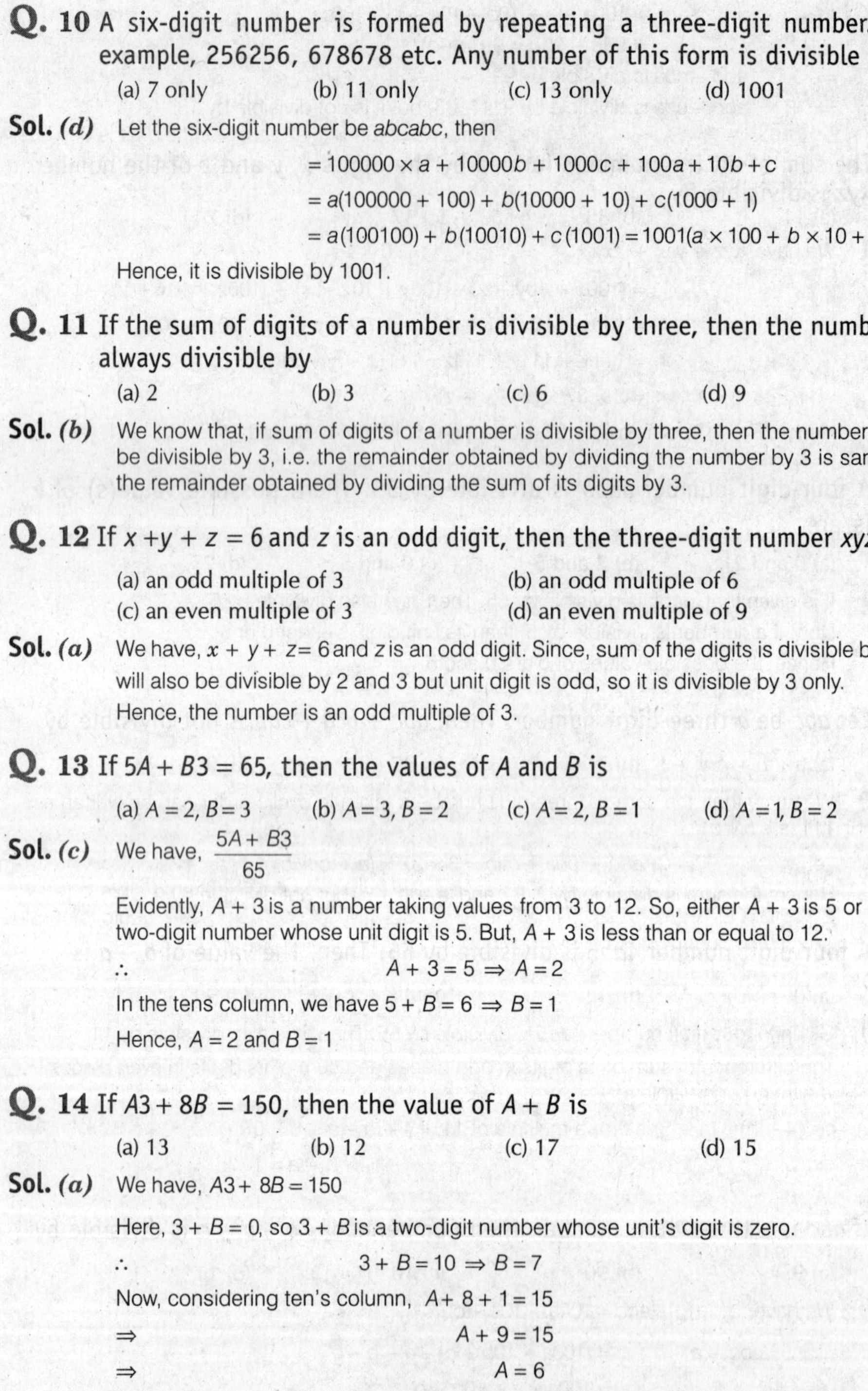

Q. 10 **A six-digit number is formed by repeating a three-digit number. For example, 256256, 678678 etc. Any number of this form is divisible by**

(a) 7 only (b) 11 only (c) 13 only (d) 1001

Sol. *(d)* Let the six-digit number be *abcabc*, then

$$= 100000 \times a + 10000b + 1000c + 100a + 10b + c$$
$$= a(100000 + 100) + b(10000 + 10) + c(1000 + 1)$$
$$= a(100100) + b(10010) + c(1001) = 1001(a \times 100 + b \times 10 + c)$$

Hence, it is divisible by 1001.

Q. 11 **If the sum of digits of a number is divisible by three, then the number is always divisible by**

(a) 2 (b) 3 (c) 6 (d) 9

Sol. *(b)* We know that, if sum of digits of a number is divisible by three, then the number must be divisible by 3, i.e. the remainder obtained by dividing the number by 3 is same as the remainder obtained by dividing the sum of its digits by 3.

Q. 12 **If $x + y + z = 6$ and z is an odd digit, then the three-digit number xyz is**

(a) an odd multiple of 3 (b) an odd multiple of 6

(c) an even multiple of 3 (d) an even multiple of 9

Sol. *(a)* We have, $x + y + z = 6$ and z is an odd digit. Since, sum of the digits is divisible by 3, it will also be divisible by 2 and 3 but unit digit is odd, so it is divisible by 3 only.

Hence, the number is an odd multiple of 3.

Q. 13 **If $5A + B3 = 65$, then the values of A and B is**

(a) $A = 2, B = 3$ (b) $A = 3, B = 2$ (c) $A = 2, B = 1$ (d) $A = 1, B = 2$

Sol. *(c)* We have, $\begin{array}{r} 5A + B3 \\ \hline 65 \end{array}$

Evidently, $A + 3$ is a number taking values from 3 to 12. So, either $A + 3$ is 5 or it is a two-digit number whose unit digit is 5. But, $A + 3$ is less than or equal to 12.

$\therefore$ $$A + 3 = 5 \Rightarrow A = 2$$

In the tens column, we have $5 + B = 6 \Rightarrow B = 1$

Hence, $A = 2$ and $B = 1$

Q. 14 **If $A3 + 8B = 150$, then the value of $A + B$ is**

(a) 13 (b) 12 (c) 17 (d) 15

Sol. *(a)* We have, $A3 + 8B = 150$

Here, $3 + B = 0$, so $3 + B$ is a two-digit number whose unit's digit is zero.

$\therefore$ $$3 + B = 10 \Rightarrow B = 7$$

Now, considering ten's column, $A + 8 + 1 = 15$

$\Rightarrow$ $$A + 9 = 15$$

$\Rightarrow$ $$A = 6$$

Hence, $$A + B = 6 + 7 = 13$$

Q. 15 If $5A \times A = 399$, then the value of A is

(a) 3 (b) 6 (c) 7 (d) 9

Sol. *(c)* We have, $5A \times A = 399$

Here, $A \times A = 9$ i.e. $A \times A$ is the number 9 or a number whose unit's digit is 9. Thus, the number whose product with itself produces a two-digit number having its unit's digit as 9 is 7.

i.e. $A \times A = 49 \Rightarrow A = 7$

Now, $5 \times A + 4 = 39$

$\Rightarrow$ $5 \times 7 + 4 = 39$

$39 = 39$

So, A satisfies the product.

Hence, the value of A is 7.

Q. 16 If $6A \times B = A8B$, then the value of $A - B$ is

(a) −2 (b) 2 (c) −3 (d) 3

Sol. *(c)* Given, $6A \times B = A8B$

Let us assume, $A = 1$ and $B = 3$

Then, LHS $= 61 \times 3 = 183$

and RHS $= 183$

Thus, our assumption is true.

$\therefore$ $A - B = 1 - 3 = -2$

Q. 17 Which of the following numbers is divisible by 99?

(a) 913462 (b) 114345 (c) 135792 (d) 3572406

Sol. *(b)* Given a number is divisible by 99.

Now, going through the options, we observe that the number (b) is divisible by 9 and 11 both as the sum of digits of the number is divisible by 9 and sum of digits at odd places = sum of digits at even places.

Fill in the Blanks

In questions 18 to 33, fill in the blanks to make the statements true.

Q. 18 3134673 is divisible by 3 and ________

Sol. 9

3134673 is divisible by 3 and 9 as sum of the digits, $3 + 1 + 3 + 4 + 6 + 7 + 3 = 27$ is divisible by both 3 and 9.

Q. 19 $20x3$ is a multiple of 3, if the digit x is ________ or ________ or ________.

Sol. 1, 4, 7

We know that, if a number is a multiple of 3, then the sum of its digits is again a multiple of 3, i.e. $2 + 0 + x + 3$ is a multiple of 3.

$\Rightarrow \quad x + 5 = 0, 3, 6, 9, 12, 15$

But, x is a digit of the number $20x3$.

$\therefore$ x can take values 0, 1, 2, 3, ..., 9.

$\Rightarrow \quad x + 5 = 6$ or 9 or 12

Hence, $\quad x = 1$ or 4 or 7

Q. 20 3x5 is divisible by 9, if the digit x is ________

Sol. 1

Since, the number $3x5$ is divisible by 9, then the sum of its digits is also divisible by 9.

i.e. $3 + x + 5$ is divisible by 9.

$\Rightarrow x + 8$ can take values 9, 18, 27, ...

But x is a digit of the number $3x5$, so $x = 1$.

Q. 21 The sum of a two-digit number and the number obtained by reversing the digits is always divisible by ________ .

Sol. 11

Let ab be any two-digit number, then the number obtained by reversing its digits is ba.

Now, $\quad ab + ba = (10a + b) + (10b + a)$

$= 11a + 11b$

$= 11(a + b)$

Hence, $ab + ba$ is always divisible by 11 and $(a + b)$.

Q. 22 The difference of two-digit number and the number obtained by reversing its digits is always divisible by ________ .

Sol. 9

Let ab be any two-digit number, then we have

$ab - ba = (10a + b) - (10b + a)$

$= 9a - 9b$

$= 9(a - b)$

Hence, $ab - ba$ is always divisible by 9 and $(a - b)$.

Q. 23 The difference of three-digit number and the number obtained by putting the digits in reverse order is always divisible by 9 and ________.

Sol. 11

Let abc be a three-digit number, then we have

$abc - cba = (100a + 10b + c) - (100c + 10b + a)$

$= (100a - a) + (c - 100c)$

$= 99a - 99c$

$= 99(a - c)$

$= 9 \times 11 \times (a - c)$

Hence, $abc - cba$ is always divisible by 9, 11 and $(a - c)$.

Q. 24 If $\begin{array}{r} 2\ B \\ +A\ B \\ \hline 8\ A \end{array}$, then $A =$ ________ and $B =$ ________ .

Sol. 6, 3

We have, $\begin{array}{r} 2\ B \\ +A\ B \\ \hline 8\ A \end{array}$

Here, B can take values from 0 to 9.

For $B = 0$, $A = 0$, which does not fit in tens column

For $B = 1$, $A = 2$, which does not fit in tens column

For $B = 3$, $A = 6$, which satisfies the tens column.

Hence, $A = 6$ and $B = 3$

Q. 25 If $\begin{array}{r} A\ B \\ \times\ B \\ \hline 9\ 6 \\ \hline \end{array}$, then $A =$ ________ and $B =$ ________ .

Sol. 2, 4

We have, $\begin{array}{r} A\ B \\ \times\ B \\ \hline 9\ 6 \\ \hline \end{array}$

Here $B \times B = 6$, therefore B can take values either 4 or 6.

For $B = 4$, $A \times B + 1 = 9$

$\Rightarrow A \times 4 + 1 = 9 \Rightarrow A = 2$

Hence, $A = 2, B = 4$

Q. 26 If $\begin{array}{r} B\ 1 \\ \times\ B \\ \hline 4\ 9B \\ \hline \end{array}$, then $B =$ ________ .

Sol. 7

We have, $\begin{array}{r} B\ 1 \\ \times\ B \\ \hline 4\ 9B \\ \hline \end{array}$

Here, B can take values from 0 to 9. But for $B = 0$ to 6, the second multiplication i.e. $B \times B = 49$ is not satisfied.

Hence, $B = 7$

Q. 27 $1x35$ is divisible by 9, if $x =$ ________ .

Sol. 0

If $1x35$ is divisible by 9, then the sum of its digits is also divisible by 9.

i.e. $1 + x + 3 + 5$ is divisible by 9.

$\Rightarrow 9 + x$ can take values 0, 9, 18, 27, ...

$\Rightarrow 9 + x = 9$ or 18 [$\because x$ is a digit]

$\Rightarrow x = 0$ or 9

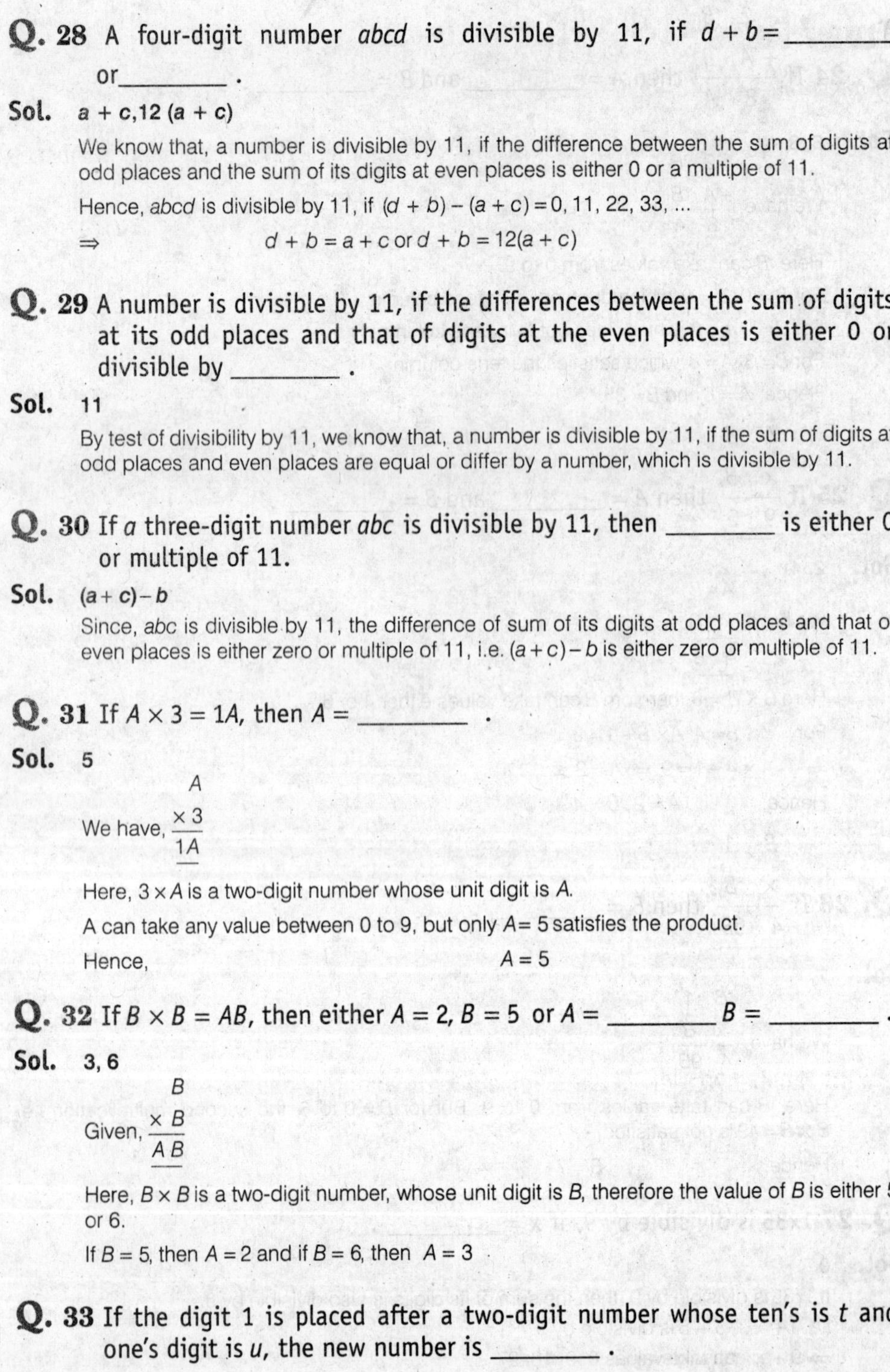

Q. 28 A four-digit number *abcd* is divisible by 11, if $d + b =$ ________ or ________ .

Sol. $a + c, 12(a + c)$

We know that, a number is divisible by 11, if the difference between the sum of digits at odd places and the sum of its digits at even places is either 0 or a multiple of 11.

Hence, *abcd* is divisible by 11, if $(d + b) - (a + c) = 0, 11, 22, 33, \ldots$

$$\Rightarrow \quad d + b = a + c \text{ or } d + b = 12(a + c)$$

Q. 29 A number is divisible by 11, if the differences between the sum of digits at its odd places and that of digits at the even places is either 0 or divisible by ________ .

Sol. 11

By test of divisibility by 11, we know that, a number is divisible by 11, if the sum of digits at odd places and even places are equal or differ by a number, which is divisible by 11.

Q. 30 If *a* three-digit number *abc* is divisible by 11, then ________ is either 0 or multiple of 11.

Sol. $(a + c) - b$

Since, *abc* is divisible by 11, the difference of sum of its digits at odd places and that of even places is either zero or multiple of 11, i.e. $(a + c) - b$ is either zero or multiple of 11.

Q. 31 If $A \times 3 = 1A$, then $A =$ ________ .

Sol. 5

We have, $\begin{array}{r} A \\ \times 3 \\ \hline 1A \\ \hline \end{array}$

Here, $3 \times A$ is a two-digit number whose unit digit is A.

A can take any value between 0 to 9, but only $A = 5$ satisfies the product.

Hence, $\quad A = 5$

Q. 32 If $B \times B = AB$, then either $A = 2, B = 5$ or $A =$ ________ $B =$ ________ .

Sol. 3, 6

Given, $\begin{array}{r} B \\ \times B \\ \hline A\,B \\ \hline \end{array}$

Here, $B \times B$ is a two-digit number, whose unit digit is B, therefore the value of B is either 5 or 6.

If $B = 5$, then $A = 2$ and if $B = 6$, then $A = 3$

Q. 33 If the digit 1 is placed after a two-digit number whose ten's is t and one's digit is u, the new number is ________ .

Sol. $tu1$

Given, a two-digit number whose ones digit is u in and tens digit is t. If the digit 1 is placed after this number, then the next number will be $tu1$.

True / False

In questions 34 to 44, state whether the given statements are True or False.

Q. 34 A two-digit number *ab* is always divisible by 2, if *b* is an even number.

Sol. ***True***

By the test of divisibility by 2, we know that a number is divisible by 2, if its unit's digit is even.

Q. 35 A three-digit number *abc* is divisible by 5, if *c* is an even number.

Sol. ***False***

By the test of divisibility by 5, we know that if a number is divisible by 5, then its one's digit will be either 0 or 5, i.e. the numbers ending with the digits 0 or 5 are divisible by 5.

Q. 36 A four-digit number *abcd* is divisible by 4, if *ab* is divisible by 4.

Sol. ***False***

As we know that, if a number is divisible by 4, then the number formed by its digits in unit's and ten's place is divisible by 4.

Q. 37 A three-digit number *abc* is divisible by 6, if *c* is an even number and $a+b+c$ is a multiple of 3.

Sol. ***True***

If a number is divisible by 6, then it is divisible by both 2 and 3. Since, *abc* is divisible by 6, it is also divisible by 2 and 3. Therefore, c is an even number and the sum of digits is divisible by 3, i.e. multiple of 3.

Q. 38 Number of the form $3N+2$ will leave remainder 2 when divided by 3.

Sol. ***True***

Let $x = 3N + 2$. Then, it can be written as

$x =$ (a multiple of 3) + 2

i.e. x is a number which is 2 more than a multiple of 3

i.e. x is a number, which when divided by 3, leaves the remainder 2.

Q. 39 Number $7N+1$ will leave remainder 1 when divided by 7.

Sol. ***True***

Given, a number of the form $7N + 1 = x$ (say)

Here, we observe that x is a number which is one more than a multiple of 7.

i.e. when x is divided by 7, it leaves the remainder 1.

Q. 40 If a number *a* is divisible by *b*, then it must be divisible by each factor of *b*.

Sol. ***True***

Given, *a* is divisible by *b*.

Let $b = p_1 \cdot p_2$, where p_1 and p_2 are primes.

Since, *a* is divisible by *b*, *a* is a multiple of *b*

i.e. $a = mb$

$\Rightarrow$ $a = m \cdot p_1 \cdot p_2$

or $a = cp_2 = dp_1$, where $c = mp_1, d = mp_2$

$\Rightarrow a$ is a multiple of p_1 as well as p_2.

Hence, a is divisible by each factor b.

Q. 41 If $AB \times 4 = 192$, then $A + B = 7$.

Sol. ***False***

We have, $\begin{array}{r} A\ B \\ \times\ \ 4 \\ \hline 192 \end{array}$

Here, $B \times 4$ is a two-digit number whose unit's digit is 2.

Therefore, the value of B is either 3 or 8.

But $B = 3$ is not possible as $A \times 4 + 1 \neq 19$ for any value of A between 0 to 9

$\therefore$ $B = 8$ and then $A = 4$

Hence, $A + B = 12$

Q. 42 If $AB + 7C = 102$, where $B \neq 0$, $C \neq 0$, then $A + B + C = 14$.

Sol. ***True***

We have, $\begin{array}{r} A\ B \\ +\ 7\ C \\ \hline 102 \end{array}$

Here, $B + C$ is either 2 or a two-digit number whose one's digit is 2.

If $B = C = 1$, $A = 3$ but $A + B + C \neq 14$

If $B = 5$, $C = 7$, $A = 2$ and $A + B + C = 2 + 5 + 7 = 14$

Q. 43 If $213x\,27$ is divisible by 9, then the value of x is 0.

Sol. ***False***

Given, $213x\,27$ is divisible by 9, so sum of its digits is also divisible by 9.

i.e. $2 + 1 + 3 + x + 2 + 7 = 0, 9, 18, 27, 36, \ldots$

$\Rightarrow$ $x + 15 = 0, 9, 18, 27, 36, \ldots$

$\Rightarrow$ $x + 15 = 18$ [$\because x$ is a digit of a number]

$\Rightarrow$ $x = 3$

Q. 44 In $N \div 5$ leaves remainder 3 and $N \div 2$ leaves remainder 0, then $N \div 10$ leaves remainder 4.

Sol. ***False***

$\because N \div 5$ leaves remainder 3.

$\Rightarrow N = 5n + 3$, where $n = 0, 1, 2, 3, \ldots$

Now, it is also given, $N \div 2$ leaves remainder 0.

So, N must be an even number.

But $N = 5n + 3$ i.e. sum of two terms whose second term is odd.

So, for N should be even it is necessary that $5n$ must be odd.

which is possible, when $n = 1, 3, 5, ...$

So, in this case value of N should be

$$N = 8, 18, 28, 38, ...$$

i.e. $$N = 10n + 8, n = 0, 1, 2, 3, ...$$

When $N \div 10$ leaves remainder 8 always.

Q. 45 Find the least value that must be given to number a, so that the number $91876a2$ is divisible by 8.

Sol. Given, $91876a2$ is divisible by 8.

Since, we know that, if a number is divisible by 8, then the number formed by last 3 digits is divisible by 8.

So, $6a2$ is divisible by 8.

Here, a can take values from 0 to 9.

For $a = 0$, 602 is not divisible by 8.

For $a = 1$, 612, which is not divisible by 8.

For $a = 3$, 632 is divisible by 8.

Hence, the minimum value of a is 3 to make $91876a2$ divisible by 8.

Q. 46 If $\begin{array}{r} 1\ P \\ \times\ P \\ \hline Q\ 6 \\ \hline \end{array}$, where $Q - P = 3$, then find the values of P and Q.

Sol. We have, $\begin{array}{r} 1\ P \\ \times\ P \\ \hline Q\ 6 \\ \hline \end{array}$ and $Q - P = 3$

Here, $P \times P$ is 6, so the value of P is either 4 or 6.

But if $P = 4$, $Q = 5$, which does not satisfy the relation $Q - P = 3$.

Hence, $P = 6$ and then $Q = 9$.

Q. 47 If $1AB + CCA = 697$ and there is no carry-over in addition, find the value of $A + B + C$.

Sol. We have, $\begin{array}{r} 1\ A\ B \\ +\ C\ C\ A \\ \hline 6\ 9\ 7 \\ \hline \end{array}$

Since, there is no carry-over in addition,

$$1 + C = 6$$

$\Rightarrow$ $$C = 5$$

$$A + C = 9$$

$\Rightarrow$ $$A + 5 = 9$$

$\Rightarrow$ $$A = 4$$

and $$B + A = 7$$

$\Rightarrow \quad B + 4 = 7$

$\Rightarrow \quad B = 3$

Hence, $\quad A + B + C = 4 + 3 + 5 = 12$

Q. 48 A five-digit number *AABAA* is divisible by 33. Write all the numbers of this form.

Sol. Given, a number of the form *AABAA* is divisible by 33. Then, it is also divisible by 3 and 11, as if a number *a* is divisible by *b*, then it is also divisible by each factor of *b*.

Since, *AABAA* is divisible by 3, sum its digits is also divisible by 3.

i.e. $\quad A + A + B + A + A = 0, 3, 6, 9 \ldots$

or $\quad 4A + B = 0, 3, 6, 9, \ldots \qquad \ldots(i)$

Further, the given number is also divisible by 11, therefore $(2A + B) - 2A = 0, 11, 22, \ldots$

$\Rightarrow \quad B = 0, 11, 22, \ldots$

$\Rightarrow \quad B = 0 \qquad [\because B$ is a digit of the given number$]$

From Eq. (i), we have

$4A = 12$ or 24 or 36

$\Rightarrow \quad A = 3, 6, 9$

Hence, the required numbers are 33033, 66066 and 99099.

In questions 49 to 60, find the value of the letters in each of the following questions.

Q. 49
$$\begin{array}{r} A\ A \\ +A\ A \\ \hline XA\ Z \\ \hline \end{array}$$

Sol. We have, $\begin{array}{r} A\ A \\ +A\ A \\ \hline XA\ Z \\ \hline \end{array}$

Here $A + A = Z$, therefore A can take any value between 0 to 9.

Since, the sum in second column is a two-digit number, the possible values of A are 5 to 9.

The values $A = 5$ to 8 are not fitted in second column.

Hence, $A = 9 \Rightarrow Z = 8$ and $X = 1$

Q. 50
$$\begin{array}{r} 8\ 5 \\ +4\ A \\ \hline B\ C\ 3 \\ \hline \end{array}$$

Sol. We have, $\begin{array}{r} 8\ 5 \\ +4\ A \\ \hline B\ C\ 3 \\ \hline \end{array}$

Here, $5 + A = 3 \Rightarrow 5 + A$ can be a single-digit number.

So, $5 + A$ is a two-digit number whose one's digit is 3.

$\therefore \quad A = 8$

$\Rightarrow \quad B = 1, C = 3 \qquad [\because BC = 8 + 4 + 1 \Rightarrow 10B + C = 13 = 10 \times 1 + 3 \Rightarrow B = 1, C = 3]$

Q. 51
$$\begin{array}{r} B\ 6 \\ +8\ A \\ \hline C\ A\ 2 \\ \hline \end{array}$$

Sol. We have,
$$\begin{array}{r} B\ 6 \\ +8\ A \\ \hline C\ A\ 2 \\ \hline \end{array}$$

Here, $6+A=2$, therefore the possible value of A is 6.

Now, $CA = B + 8 + 1$

$\Rightarrow$ $C6 = B + 9$

i.e. $B+9$ is a number whose one's digit is 6.

Therefore, $B=7$ and $C=1$

Q. 52
$$\begin{array}{r} 1\ B\ A \\ +A\ B\ A \\ \hline 8\ B\ 2 \\ \hline \end{array}$$

Sol. We have,
$$\begin{array}{r} 1\ B\ A \\ +A\ B\ A \\ \hline 8\ B\ 2 \\ \hline \end{array}$$

Here, $A+A$ is a number whose one's digit is 2, therefore $A=6$.

Now, $B+B+1=B$

So, the possible value of B is 9.

Again, in third column,

$$A+1+1=8$$

$\Rightarrow$ $A=6$, which is true.

Hence, $A=6$ and $B=9$

Q. 53
$$\begin{array}{r} C\ B\ A \\ +C\ B\ A \\ \hline 1A\ 3\ 0 \\ \hline \end{array}$$

Sol. We have,
$$\begin{array}{r} C\ B\ A \\ +C\ B\ A \\ \hline 1A\ 3\ 0 \\ \hline \end{array}$$

In first column, $A+A=0$

$\Rightarrow$ $A=0$ or 5

For $A=0$, the second and third column, sums are not satisfied.

So, $A=5$

Now, in second column,

$$B+B+1=3$$

For $B=1$, third column sum is not satisfied.

So, $B=6$

Again, in third column, $C + C + 1 = 1A$

$\Rightarrow \quad C + C = 15 - 1 \Rightarrow 2C = 14$

$\Rightarrow \quad C = 7$

Hence, $A = 5$, $B = 6$ and $C = 7$

Q. 54
$$\begin{array}{r} B\ A\ A \\ +\ B\ A\ A \\ \hline 3\ A\ 8 \\ \hline \end{array}$$

Sol. We have, $\begin{array}{r} B\ A\ A \\ +\ B\ A\ A \\ \hline 3\ A\ 8 \\ \hline \end{array}$

Here, $A + A = 8$

$\Rightarrow \quad A = 9$ [$\because$ rejecting $A = 4$ as $A + A$ can not be a single digit number]

Now, in third column, we have $B + B + 1 = 3$

$\Rightarrow \quad 2B = 2 \Rightarrow B = 1$

Hence, $A = 9$ and $B = 1$

Q. 55
$$\begin{array}{r} A\ 0\ 1\ B \\ +\ 1\ 0\ A\ B \\ \hline B\ 1\ 0\ 8 \\ \hline \end{array}$$

Sol. We have, $\begin{array}{r} A\ 0\ 1\ B \\ +\ 1\ 0\ A\ B \\ \hline B\ 1\ 0\ 8 \\ \hline \end{array}$

In first column, $B + B = 8$

$\Rightarrow \quad B = 9$ [$\because B = 4$ does not fit in fourth column]

In second column, we have

$A + 1 + 1 = 0$

So, A should be 8.

Third column is true for these values.

Also, the fourth column is satisfied.

Hence, $A = 8$ and $B = 9$

Q. 56
$$\begin{array}{r} A\ B \\ \times\ \ 6 \\ \hline C\ 6\ 8 \\ \hline \end{array}$$

Sol. We have, $\begin{array}{r} A\ B \\ \times\ \ 6 \\ \hline C\ 6\ 8 \\ \hline \end{array}$ and $B - A = 1$

Here, $6 \times B$ is a number, whose unit's digit is 8. Therefore, the possible values of B are 3 and 8.

If $B = 3$, then $A \times 6 + 1 = C6$ which is not possible for any value of A between 0 to 9.

$\therefore B = 8$ and then $A = 7$

The values of A and B also satisfies the given condition i.e 8–7=1.

If $A = 7$, then $7 \times 6 + 4 = C6$

$$46 = C6$$

$$\therefore \quad C = 4$$

Hence, $A = 7, B = 8$ and $C = 4$

Q. 57
$$\begin{array}{r} A\ B \\ \times A\ B \\ \hline 6\ A\ B \\ \hline \end{array}$$

Sol. Given,
$$\begin{array}{r} A\ B \\ \times A\ B \\ \hline 6\ A\ B \\ \hline \end{array}$$

i.e. $AB \times AB = 6AB$ ...(i)

Here, $B \times B$ is a number whose unit's digit is B. Therefore, $B = 1$ or 5

[$\because B \neq 0$, else $AB \times A + \neq 6A$]

Again, $AB \times AB = 6AB$

$\Rightarrow$ The square of a two-digit number is a three-digit number.

So, A can take values 1, 2 and 3.

For $A = 1, 2, 3$ and $B = 1$, Eq. (i) is not satisfied.

Now, for $A = 1$, $B = 5$, Eq. (i) is not satisfied.

We find that $A = 2$, $B = 5$ satisfies the Eq. (i).

Hence, $A = 2, B = 5$

Q. 58
$$\begin{array}{r} A\ A \\ \times\ \ A \\ \hline C\ A\ B \\ \hline \end{array}$$
and $B - A = 1$

Sol. Given,
$$\begin{array}{r} A\ A \\ \times\ \ A \\ \hline C\ A\ B \\ \hline \end{array}$$

Here, $AA \times A$ is a three-digit number, whose unit's digit is B, therefore A can take values from 4 to 9 as $A = 0, 1, 2, 3$ give a single digit or a two-digit number. Further, since ten's digit of the product is A itself. So, A cannot take values 4, 5, 6, 7 and 8.

Hence, $A = 9$ and then $B = 1, C = 8$.

Q. 59
$$\begin{array}{r} A\ B \\ -B\ 7 \\ \hline 4\ 5 \\ \hline \end{array}$$

Sol. Given,
$$\begin{array}{r} A\ B \\ -B\ 7 \\ \hline 4\ 5 \\ \hline \end{array}$$

In the ones column,

$$B - 7 = 5$$

Clearly, $12 - 7 = 5$ so $B = 2$

Now, in ten's column, we have

$$A - (B + 1) = 4$$

$$\Rightarrow \quad A - B = 5$$

$$\Rightarrow \quad A - 2 = 5$$

$$\Rightarrow \quad A = 7$$

Hence, $A = 7$ and $B = 2$

Q. 60

$$\begin{array}{r} 8\ A\ B\ C \\ -\ A\ B\ C\ 5 \\ \hline D\ 4\ 8\ 8 \\ \hline \end{array}$$

Sol. Given, $\begin{array}{r} 8\ A\ B\ C \\ -\ A\ B\ C\ 5 \\ \hline D\ 4\ 8\ 8 \\ \hline \end{array}$

In the ones column, $C - 5 = 8$

Obviously, $13 - 5 = 8$, so $C = 3$

In the ten's column, $B - (C + 1) = 8$

$$\Rightarrow \quad B = 8 + C + 1$$

$$\Rightarrow \quad B = 8 + 3 + 1$$

$$\Rightarrow \quad B = 12 \text{ i.e. } B = 2$$

In the hundred's column, $A - (B + 1) = 4$

$$\Rightarrow \quad A = 4 + B + 1$$

$$\Rightarrow \quad A = 4 + 2 + 1 = 7$$

In the thousand's column, $8 - A = D$

$$\Rightarrow \quad 8 - 7 = D$$

$$\Rightarrow \quad D = 1$$

Hence, $A = 7$, $B = 2$, $C = 3$ and $D = 1$

Q. 61 If $2A7 \div A = 33$, then find the value of A.

Sol. We observe that, $A \times 3$ can never be a single digit number 2, so $A \times 3$ must be a two-digit number, whose ten's digit is 2 and unit's digit is the number less than or equal to A. Therefore, the value of A can be 9, as the values of A from 1 to 8 do not fit.

Q. 62 $212x5$ is a multiple of 3 and 11. Find the value of x.

Sol. Since, $212x5$ is a multiple of 3,

$$2 + 1 + 2 + x + 5 = 0, 3, 6, 9, 12, 15, 18,$$

$$\Rightarrow \quad 10 + x = 0, 3, 6, \ldots$$

$$\Rightarrow \quad x = 2, 5, 8 \quad \ldots\text{(i)}$$

Again, $212x5$ is a multiple of 11, $(2 + 2 + 5) - (1 + x) = 0, 11, 22, 33$

$$\Rightarrow \quad 8 - x = 0, 11, 22, \ldots$$

$$\Rightarrow \quad x = 8 \quad \ldots\text{(ii)}$$

From Eqs. (i) and (ii), we have

$$x = 8$$

Q. 63 Find the value of k, where $31k2$ is divisible by 6.

Sol. Given, $31k2$ is divisible by 6. Then, it is also divisible by 2 and 3 both.

Now, $31k2$ is divisible by 3, sum of its digits is a multiple of 3.

i.e. $$3 + 1 + k + 2 = 0, 3, 6, 9, 12, \ldots$$

$\Rightarrow$ $$k + 6 = 0, 3, 6, 9, 12$$

$\Rightarrow$ $$k = 0 \text{ or } 3, 6, 9$$

Q. 64 $1y3y6$ is divisible by 11. Find the value of y.

Sol. It is given that, $1y3y6$ is divisible by 11.

Then, we have $(1 + 3 + 6) - (y + y) = 0, 11, 22, \ldots$

$\Rightarrow$ $$10 - 2y = 0, 11, 22, \ldots$$

$\Rightarrow$ $$10 - 2y = 0$$ [other values give a negative number]

$\Rightarrow$ $$2y = 10$$

$\Rightarrow$ $$y = 5$$

Q. 65 $756x$ is a multiple of 11, find the value of x.

Sol. We are given that, $756x$ is a multiple of 11. Then, we have to find the value of x.

Since, $756x$ is divisible by 11, then $(7 + 6) - (5 + x)$ is a multiple of 11,

i.e. $$8 - x = 0, 11, 22, \ldots$$

$\Rightarrow$ $$8 - x = 0$$

$\Rightarrow$ $$x = 8$$

Q. 66 A three-digits number $2a3$ is added to the number 326 to give a three-digits number $5b9$ which is divisible by 9. Find the value of $b - a$.

Sol. Given, $$\begin{array}{r} 2\ a\ 3 \\ +\,3\ 2\ 6 \\ \hline 5\ b\ 9 \\ \hline \end{array}$$

We see that,

In one's column, $3 + 6 = 9$ (true)

In third column, $2 + 3 = 5$ (true)

$\therefore$ $a + 2$ is a single digit number b as there is no carry-over in the addition.

Thus, $$a + 2 = b \Rightarrow b - a = 2$$

Q. 67 Let $E = 3$, $B = 7$ and $A = 4$. Find the other digits in the sum

$$\begin{array}{r} B\ A\ S\ E \\ +\ B\ A\ L\ L \\ \hline G\ A\ M\ E\ S \\ \hline \end{array}$$

Sol. Given, $$\begin{array}{r} B\ A\ S\ E \\ +\ B\ A\ L\ L \\ \hline G\ A\ M\ E\ S \\ \hline \end{array}$$, $E = 3$, $B = 7$ and $A = 4$

$$\text{Now,}\quad \begin{array}{r} 7\;4\;S\;3 \\ +\;7\;4\;L\;L \\ \hline G\;4\;M\;3\;S \\ \hline \end{array}$$

In one's column, we have $3 + L = S$ or $S - L = 3$ ...(i)

In ten's column, we have $S + L = 3$ ...(ii)

On solving Eqs. (i) and (ii), we get.

$$S = 3 \text{ and } L = O$$

In hundred's column, we have

$$4 + 4 = M$$

$$\therefore \quad M = 8$$

and in thousand's column, we have

$$7 + 7 = G4$$

$$14 = G4$$

$$\therefore \quad G = 1$$

Hence $L = O, S = 3, M = 8$ and $G = 1$

Q. 68 Let $D = 3$, $L = 7$ and $A = 8$. Find the other digits in the sum

$$\begin{array}{r} M\;A\;D \\ +\;A\;S \\ +\;A \\ \hline B\;U\;L\;L \\ \hline \end{array}$$

Sol. In the first column, we have

$3 + S + 8$, which is definitely a two digits number whose unit's digit is 7.

$\therefore$ S must be 6.

Now, in second column, $2A + 1 = 16 + 1 = 7$ [1 is carry forward]

In third column, $M + 1$ is a 2 digit number, therefore M must be 9.

Then, $M + 1 = 9 + 1 = 10$

$\therefore$ $B = 1, U = 0$

Hence, $S = 6$, $M = 9$, $B = 1$ and $U = 0$

Q. 69 If from a two-digit number, we subtract the number formed by reversing its digits then the result so obtained is a perfect cube. How many such numbers are possible? Write all of them.

Sol. Let ab be any two-digit number. Then, the digit formed by reversing it digits is ba.

Now,
$$ab - ba = (10a + b) - (10b + a)$$
$$= (10a - a) + (b - 10b)$$
$$= 9a - 9b$$
$$= 9(a - b)$$

Further, since $ab - ba$ is a perfect cube and is a multiple of 9.

$\therefore$ The possible value of $a - b$ is 3.

i.e. $a = b + 3$

Here, b can take value from 0 to 6.
Hence, possible numbers are as follow.

For $b = 0$, $a = 3$, i.e. 30

For $b = 1$, $a = 4$, i.e. 41

For $b = 2$, $a = 5$, i.e. 52

For $b = 3$, $a = 6$, i.e. 63

For $b = 4$, $a = 7$, i.e. 74

For $b = 5$, $a = 8$, i.e. 85

For $b = 6$, $a = 9$, i.e. 96

Q. 70 Work out the following multiplication.

$$\begin{array}{r} 12345679 \\ \times \quad\quad 9 \\ \hline \\ \hline \end{array}$$

Use the result to answer the following questions.

(a) What will be 12345679×45?

(b) What will be 12345679×63?

(c) By what number should 12345679 be multiplied to get 888888888?

(d) By what number should 12345679 be multiplied to get 999999999?

Sol. We have, $\begin{array}{r} 12345679 \\ \times \quad\quad 9 \\ \hline 111111111 \end{array}$

Here, we observe that in the product all the digits are same i.e. 1, which is actually the unit digit of the product 9×9. Also, total of digits in the multiplier is 90°.

(a) We have to compute, $\begin{array}{r} 12345679 \\ \times \quad\quad 45 \\ \hline \\ \hline \end{array}$

Here, multiplier is 45 whose sum of digits is 9.
Thus, by conjecture we conclude that the product consists of digits 5 only as unit's digit of 9×5 is 5

$$\therefore \quad \begin{array}{r} 12345679 \\ \times \quad\quad 45 \\ \hline 555555555 \end{array}$$

(b) We have to compute the value of 12345679×63.
Here, sum of the digits of the multiplier is 9 and unit's digit of the product is 9 and unit's digit of the products of 3×9 is 7.

$$\therefore \quad 12345679 \times 63 = 777777777$$

(c) We have to obtain the number 8 in the product, we should multiply the given number 12345679 by 72 as sum of its digits is 9 and 2×9 has only digit as 8.

(d) To get the number 9 in the product we have to find out a two-digit number whose sum of digits is 9 and the product of its unit's digit with the unit's digit of the given number is 9, such number is 81..

Q. 71 Find the value of the letters in each of the following.

(i) $\begin{array}{r} P\ Q \\ \times\ 6 \\ \hline Q\ Q\ Q \\ \hline \end{array}$ (ii) $\begin{array}{r} 2\ L\ M \\ L\ M\ 1 \\ \hline M\ 1\ 8 \\ \hline \end{array}$

Sol.

(i) We have, $\begin{array}{r} P\ Q \\ \times\ 6 \\ \hline Q\ Q\ Q \\ \hline \end{array}$

Here, in first column, we see that $6 \times QP = Q$. Therefore, the possible values of Q are 2, 4, 6 and 8

For $Q = 2$, $6 \times P + 1$ can not be equal to 22 for any value of P.

So, $Q = 2$ is not possible.

$\therefore$ $Q = 4$

$\Rightarrow$ $6 \times P + 2 = 44$

$\Rightarrow$ $6P = 42$

$\Rightarrow$ $P = 7$

Hence, $P = 7$ and $Q = 4$

(ii) We have, $+\begin{array}{r} 2\ L\ M \\ L\ M\ 1 \\ \hline M\ 1\ 8 \\ \hline \end{array}$

In first column, $M + 1 = 8$

Clearly, $M = 7$

In second column, $L + M = 1$

$\Rightarrow$ $L + 7 = 1$

$\therefore$ The value of L can be 4.

In third column, $2 + L + 1 = M$

$\Rightarrow$ $2 + 4 + 1 = 7$.

$\Rightarrow 7 = 7$, so the third column is satisfied for $L = 4$, $M = 7$.

Hence, $L = 4$ and $M = 7$

Q. 72 If 148101*B*095 is divisible by 33, find the value of *B*.

Sol. Given that the number 148101*B*095 is divisible by 33, therefore it is also divisible by 3 and 11 both.

Now, the number is divisible by 3; its sum of digits is a multiple of 3.

i.e. $1 + 4 + 8 + 1 + 0 + 1 + B + 0 + 9 + 5$ is a multiple of 3.

$$29 + B = 0, 3, 6, 9, \ldots$$

$\Rightarrow$ $B = 1, 4, 7$ ...(i)

Also, given number is divisible by 11, therefore

$$(1 + 8 + 0 + B + 9) - (4 + 1 + 1 + 0 + 5) = 0, 11, 22, \ldots$$

$\Rightarrow$ $(18 + B) - 11 = 0, 11, 22$

$B + 7 = 0, 11, 22$

$\Rightarrow$ $B + 7 = 11 \Rightarrow B = 4$ ...(ii)

From Eqs. (i) and (ii), we have $B = 4$

Q. 73 If 123123A4 is divisible by 11, find the value of A.

Sol. Given, 123123A4 is divisible by 11, then we have $(1+3+2+A)-(2+1+3+4)$ is a multiple of 11.

i.e. $$(6+A)-10=0, 11, 22, \ldots$$

$$\Rightarrow \quad A-4=0, 11, 22, \ldots$$

$$\Rightarrow \quad A-4=0 \quad [\because A \text{ is a digit of the given number}]$$

$$\Rightarrow \quad A=4$$

Q. 74 If 56x32y is divisible by 18, find the least value of y.

Sol. It is given that, the number 56x32y is divisible by 18. Then, it is also divisible by each factor of 18.

Thus, it is divisible by 2 as well as 3.

Now, the number is divisible by 2, its unit's digit must be an even number that is 0, 2, 4, 6, ...

Therefore, the least value of y is 0.

Again, the number is divisible by 3 also, sum of its digits is a multiple of 3.

i.e. $5+6+x+3+2+y$ is a multiple of 3

$$\Rightarrow \quad 16+x+y=0, 3, 6, 9, \ldots$$

$$\Rightarrow \quad 16+x=18$$

$\Rightarrow x=2$, which is the least value of x.